DANNY

GOODMAN'S MACINTOSH

HANDBOOK FEATURING SYSTEM 7

with Richard Saul Wurman

foreword by John Sculley

BANTAM BOOKS
NEW YORK • TORONTO • LONDON • SYDNEY • AUCKLAND

DANNY GOODMAN'S MACINTOSH HANDBOOK
A Bantam Book/March 1992

Produced by Nathan Shedroff

For information address: Bantam Books

ISBN 0-553-35485-X

Published simultaneously in the
United States and Canada

Bantam Books are published by Bantam Books, a division of Bantam Doubleday Dell Publishing Group, Inc. Its trademark, consisting of the words "Bantam Books" and the portrayal of a rooster, is Registered in the U.S. Patent and Trademark Office and in other countries. Marca Registrada, Bantam Books, 666 FIfth Avenue, New York, New York, 10103

PRINTED IN THE UNITED STATES OF AMERICA

0 9 8 6 4 3 2 1

Hardware

Table of Contents cont.

Software

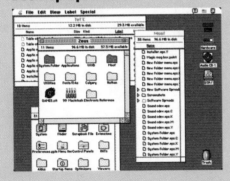

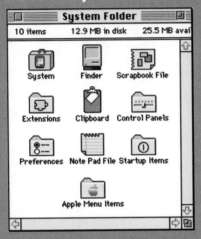

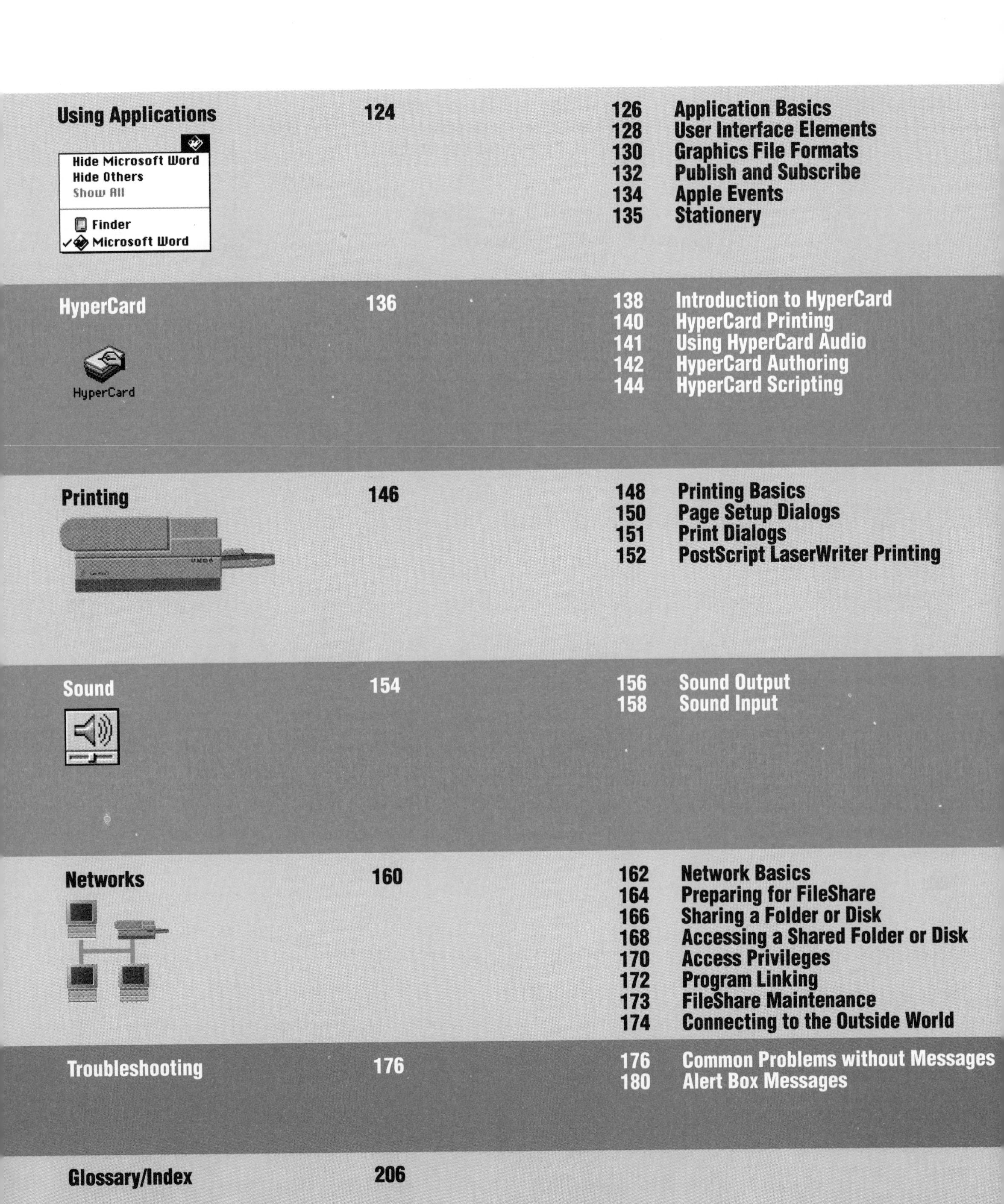
Hide Microsoft Word
Hide Others
Show All
Finder
Microsoft Word
HyperCard

Most chapters are two-page spreads like this one.

You can see all related information at a glance.

Mac-like menubar shows you which chapter and section you are in.

Each section and chapter starts with a contents spread that explains the information within that section or chapter.

The information in the top level is for beginners.

Special symbols alert you to warnings or other special information.

The warning symbol alerts you to problems or dangerous activities that could do you or your Macintosh harm.

The System 7 symbol alerts you to information specific to System 7.

Hypertext-like jumps point-out other pages within this book that contain more information on a particular topic.

Highlighted words alert you to key concepts and help you find your way around a page quickly.

Balloons may appear on the page from time to time to explain fun facts, tips and trivia.

Introduction Hardware Software Troubleshooting Glossary/Index
Connecting Components

Connectors at the ends of most Macintosh cables supplied by Apple are marked with symbols representing their counterparts on the computer itself.

Many of the connectors—especially the small diameter round ones—look alike. Even though their sizes are identical, the pins on the connectors are in a different layout to prevent you from accidentally plugging a cable into the wrong connector.

A connector on the Macintosh is frequently called a port, as if it were part of an electronic harbor. Not all Macintosh models have all the ports described below.

Electric Power
All desktop Macintosh models have a three-pronged power connector to which the electrical power cord is connected. The connector on the Macintosh is a recessed male connector. Many modular Macintosh models also have a female power connector that allows you to power the video monitor via the Macintosh. This reduces competition for power outlets, and also allows you to control the monitor and Macintosh with the same power-on/power-off sequence 10. The video monitor will likely have its own power switch, but if you connect the power via the Macintosh system unit, you can leave the monitor switch in the On position all the time—power to this external connection is cut when the Macintosh is turned off.

Important Warning
Completely turn off your Macintosh and any external peripherals before connecting or disconnecting the cables described here. On connectors with lots of pins (like the SCSI connector), not all of the pins may make contact at the same instant—a significant hazard. Since some pins carry electrical current (at levels usually safe to humans in case of accidental contact), power may be applied to the circuitry in the Mac or peripheral device (like the keyboard or external hard disk) before other important pins have made contact as you wiggle the connector on or off. Such abuse can render the port or device completely unusable.

Audio Input
A 1/8" phono jack on some Macintosh models (like the Macintosh LC and IIsi) allow direct connection of a monophonic (i.e., not two-channel stereo) microphone or other sound input. A Macintosh with an audio input port comes with a small microphone, with which you can record system sounds 152 or use sound recording in software programs that allow voice annotation (e.g., voice content to an electronic mail message). Using the line level output from other sound sources (e.g., radio or VCR), you can record other sounds with the help of the Sound control panel device 80. If the sound source is in stereo, you will need a cable converter that has a female stereo input and a male monophonic output (e.g., Radio Shack model #274-368).

SCSI
The Small Computer Standard Interface is a standard among Macintosh peripherals. There is a slightly different and incompatible SCSI standard for other computers, so make sure that a SCSI device you intend to connect to the Macintosh is designed for the Mac. Actually, the 25-pin SCSI port on the Macintosh (and the rectangular PowerBook SCSI connector) is non-standard even among Macintosh SCSI devices. The hefty 50-pin connector on most external SCSI devices (including Apple-brand devices like hard disks, CD-ROM players, and scanners) is the more recognized standard. The 50-pin connector pair have two metal spring clips on either edge of the connector. When attaching one of these connectors, always squeeze the clips into the locked position. Connecting a chain of SCSI devices can be a headache. See page 58 for details about the mysteries of SCSI devices and cabling.

100/240V ~ 3A

On/Off Switch

Disk Drive
Those Macintoshes that allow connection of an external floppy disk drive have a 19-pin disk drive port. The floppy disk icon indicates that this port is not for attaching a hard disk (although before the advent of the Macintosh SCSI port, the earliest Macintosh hard disks did so).

Ethernet Port
Available on the Quadra models (and surely more to come), the Ethernet port offers effortless connection to an ethernet network 162. Data can flow twn times faster via ethernet than via LocalTalk built into all Macintoshes.

Telephone Jack
The Macintosh Portable and PowerBooks has a space for an optional telephone modem board, including a hole in the rear of the cabinet for a telephone jack. The jack is the same RJ-11 style modular phone jack found in most homes and on consumer telephone eqipment. This connector requires a simple telephone cable with RJ-11 plugs on both ends—one for the Macintosh, one for the wall telephone jack.

Video
Some Macintosh models have video driving circui built into the main circuit board (called on-boa video) and a video port to which you can conne the video cable of a monitor. This 15-pin connector contains only the video signals, and n the AC power required for the monitor. Be sure the monitor you are using is compatible with t on-board video characteristics of your Macint 30. For more sophisticated monitors (e.g. two-page displays and high-quality color mo you may need an additional video board (i Macintosh can accommodate one).

More and more business traveler hotel rooms have phones with similar RJ-11 jacks ("dataports"). Don't forget your phone cable!

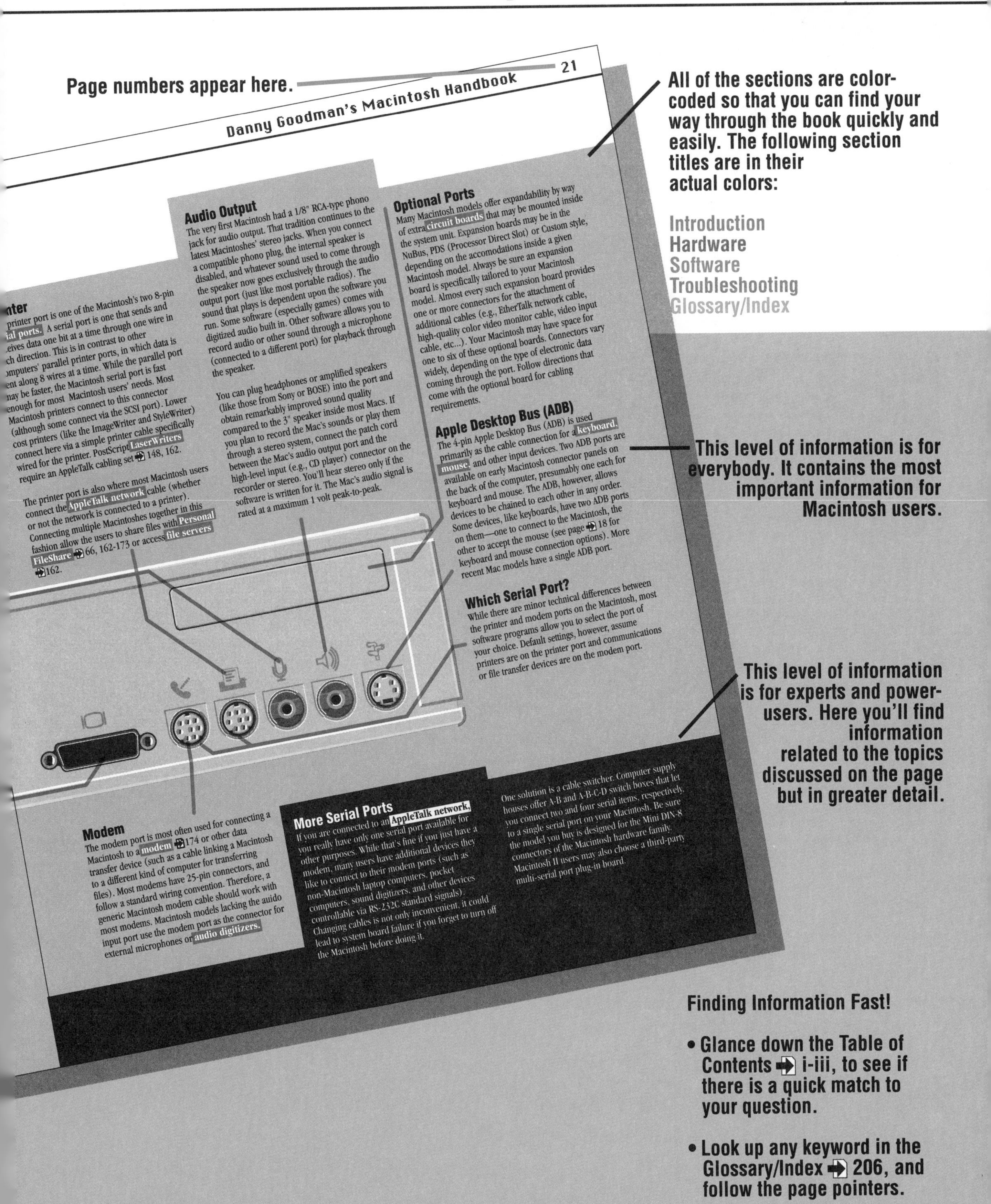

Page numbers appear here.

21

Danny Goodman's Macintosh Handbook

nter

printer port is one of the Macintosh's two 8-pin ial ports. A serial port is one that sends and eives data one bit at a time through one wire in ch direction. This is in contrast to other omputers' parallel printer ports, in which data is ent along 8 wires at a time. While the parallel port nay be faster, the Macintosh serial port is fast enough for most Macintosh users' needs. Most Macintosh printers connect to this connector (although some connect via the SCSI port). Lower cost printers (like the ImageWriter and StyleWriter) connect here via a simple printer cable specifically wired for the printer. PostScript LaserWriters require an AppleTalk cabling set ➔ 148, 162.

The printer port is also where most Macintosh users connect the AppleTalk network cable (whether or not the network is connected to a printer). Connecting multiple Macintoshes together in this fashion allow the users to share files with Personal FileShare ➔ 66, 162-173 or access file servers ➔ 162.

Audio Output

The very first Macintosh had a 1/8" RCA-type phono jack for audio output. That tradition continues to the latest Macintoshes' stereo jacks. When you connect a compatible phono plug, the internal speaker is disabled, and whatever sound used to come through the speaker now goes exclusively through the audio output port (just like most portable radios). The sound that plays is dependent upon the software you run. Some software (especially games) comes with digitized audio built in. Other software allows you to record audio or other sound through a microphone (connected to a different port) for playback through the speaker.

You can plug headphones or amplified speakers (like those from Sony or BOSE) into the port and obtain remarkably improved sound quality compared to the 3" speaker inside most Macs. If you plan to record the Mac's sounds or play them through a stereo system, connect the patch cord between the Mac's audio output port and the high-level input (e.g., CD player) connector on the recorder or stereo. You'll hear stereo only if the software is written for it. The Mac's audio signal is rated at a maximum 1 volt peak-to-peak.

Optional Ports

Many Macintosh models offer expandability by way of extra circuit boards that may be mounted inside the system unit. Expansion boards may be in the NuBus, PDS (Processor Direct Slot) or Custom style, depending on the accomodations inside a given Macintosh model. Always be sure an expansion board is specifically tailored to your Macintosh model. Almost every such expansion board provides one or more connectors for the attachment of additional cables (e.g., EtherTalk network cable, high-quality color video monitor cable, video input cable, etc...). Your Macintosh may have space for one to six of these optional boards. Connectors vary widely, depending on the type of electronic data coming through the port. Follow directions that come with the optional board for cabling requirements.

Apple Desktop Bus (ADB)

The 4-pin Apple Desktop Bus (ADB) is used primarily as the cable connection for a keyboard, mouse, and other input devices. Two ADB ports are available on early Macintosh connector panels on the back of the computer, presumably one each for keyboard and mouse. The ADB, however, allows devices to be chained to each other in any order. Some devices, like keyboards, have two ADB ports on them—one to connect to the Macintosh, the other to accept the mouse (see page ➔ 18 for keyboard and mouse connection options). More recent Mac models have a single ADB port.

Which Serial Port?

While there are minor technical differences between the printer and modem ports on the Macintosh, most software programs allow you to select the port of your choice. Default settings, however, assume printers are on the printer port and communications or file transfer devices are on the modem port.

Modem

The modem port is most often used for connecting a Macintosh to a modem ➔ 174 or other data transfer device (such as a cable linking a Macintosh to a different kind of computer for transferring files). Most modems have 25-pin connectors, and follow a standard wiring convention. Therefore, a generic Macintosh modem cable should work with most modems. Macintosh models lacking the auido input port use the modem port as the connector for external microphones or audio digitizers.

More Serial Ports

If you are connected to an AppleTalk network, you really have only one serial port available for other purposes. While that's fine if you just have a modem, many users have additional devices they like to connect to their modem ports (such as non-Macintosh laptop computers, pocket computers, sound digitizers, and other devices controllable via RS-232C standard signals). Changing cables is not only inconvenient, it could lead to system board failure if you forget to turn off the Macintosh before doing it.

One solution is a cable switcher. Computer supply houses offer A-B and A-B-C-D switch boxes that let you connect two and four serial items, respectively, to a single serial port on your Macintosh. Be sure the model you buy is designed for the Mini DIN-8 connectors of the Macintosh hardware family. Macintosh II users may also choose a third-party multi-serial port plug-in board.

All of the sections are color-coded so that you can find your way through the book quickly and easily. The following section titles are in their actual colors:

Introduction
Hardware
Software
Troubleshooting
Glossary/Index

This level of information is for everybody. It contains the most important information for Macintosh users.

This level of information is for experts and power-users. Here you'll find information related to the topics discussed on the page but in greater detail.

Finding Information Fast!

- Glance down the Table of Contents ➔ i-iii, to see if there is a quick match to your question.
- Look up any keyword in the Glossary/Index ➔ 206, and follow the page pointers.

Inventing the Future

John Sculley

With the advent of personal computing technology, the world witnessed a major transition from one economic order to another—a fundamental shift that has set in motion one of the most exciting periods in human history.

For most of this century, the industrialized countries succeeded by taking natural resources out of the ground—oil, wheat, coal—adding manufacturing know-how to those resources and turning them into products. Then, they developed services around these new products.

In a very short time we have seen a dramatic change in that economic system. Today we are no longer in the Industrial Age. We are in an **information-intensive, global economy.**

The resources are no longer just those that come out of the ground. The resources today come out of our minds. They are ideas and information.

Through the years there's never been a shortage of great ideas. The great challenge has always been to capture those ideas whenever and wherever they happen. That was one of the basic ideas behind the original **personal computer**. But by and large, those systems have been confined to individual desktops. People have needed devices that take them beyond the traditional desktop computer—personal communications devices—that give them the **freedom** to work whenever and wherever they choose.

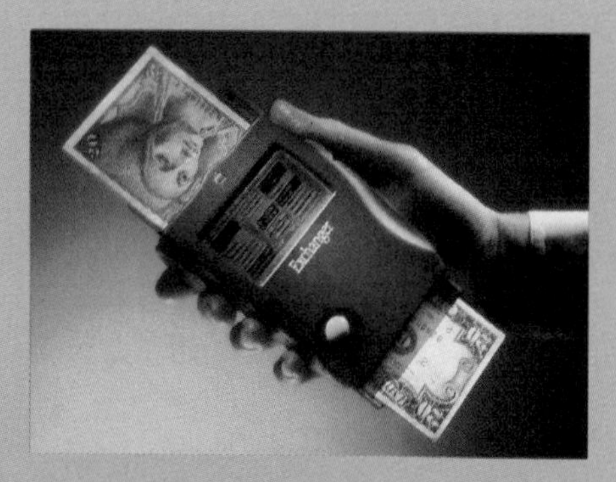

In fact, at the most basic level, the **Macintosh PowerBook** family represents the first step toward what we are calling **"Pervasive Computing"**—the idea that personal computing shouldn't be confined to a desktop or a server, but should be with you everywhere you go. All of the PowerBooks have been designed to help people focus on their ideas and not exclusively while sitting at their desktops.

Even beyond this trend toward more miniature and mobile technology, I'm personally interested in doing whatever it takes to give individuals and institutions a platform upon which to take full advantage of the convergence of industries: **communications**, **content** and **computing**. This is based on the view that the technology landscape of the future will depend not just on text, graphics and simple animation, but on sound input, full motion video and innovative on-line services. These media forms are quickly becoming a regular and indispensable part of the grammar of our times.

But at the end of the day, all of the information in the world is useless if people do not have the **enabling technologies** that allow them to access that information in the most personal and intuitive way possible.

To that end, I believe we must make personal computers even more personal—a goal we can achieve through careful implementation of new ideas and technologies, such as alternative input devices that respond to **speech recognition** and **human gestures**.

Since 1984, the Macintosh has provided a fertile seedbed for people to implement new ideas. Established ways of doing things are often left behind as new ways prove to be more intuitive and productive. The Macintosh empowers people who aren't computer engineers to use sophisticated technology to contribute to everyday knowledge and **understanding**.

In that spirit, it is refreshing to find a book like *Danny Goodman's Macintosh Handbook*. This book blends the distinguished talents of two of my friends: **Danny Goodman**, a writer well-known for translating technology into everyday language; and **Richard Saul Wurman**, a world-class information architect who cares deeply about clear presentation of instructions and information. Together they've created a seminal work that illuminates Macintosh system software and hardware in a highly accessible way. They simply tossed aside what they knew about computer books and started with a fresh slate, beginning with figuring out how to get information to a Macintosh user in the most efficient and enlightening way.

Perhaps the most impressive aspect of the book is its construction—similar to the design of the Macintosh itself. Depending on the level of interest, users are at liberty to drill down into the document as deeply as they'd like in order to gain a more in-depth understanding of the material. Also like the Macintosh, the Handbook is just plain fun to use! Instead of the static, linear format that people customarily associate with "computer manuals," Danny and Richard have broken the rules, and the result is a book that's both engaging and dynamic.

If there is one lesson that stands out for me in the time that I've been involved in the industry, it's that the success of a product can always be measured in terms of how people begin using it in ways that the original innovators never anticipated. That's why at Apple we often say, **"The best way to predict the future is to invent it."** I predict that the deeper people delve into *Danny Goodman's Macintosh Handbook*, the more likely they will be to invent their own future.

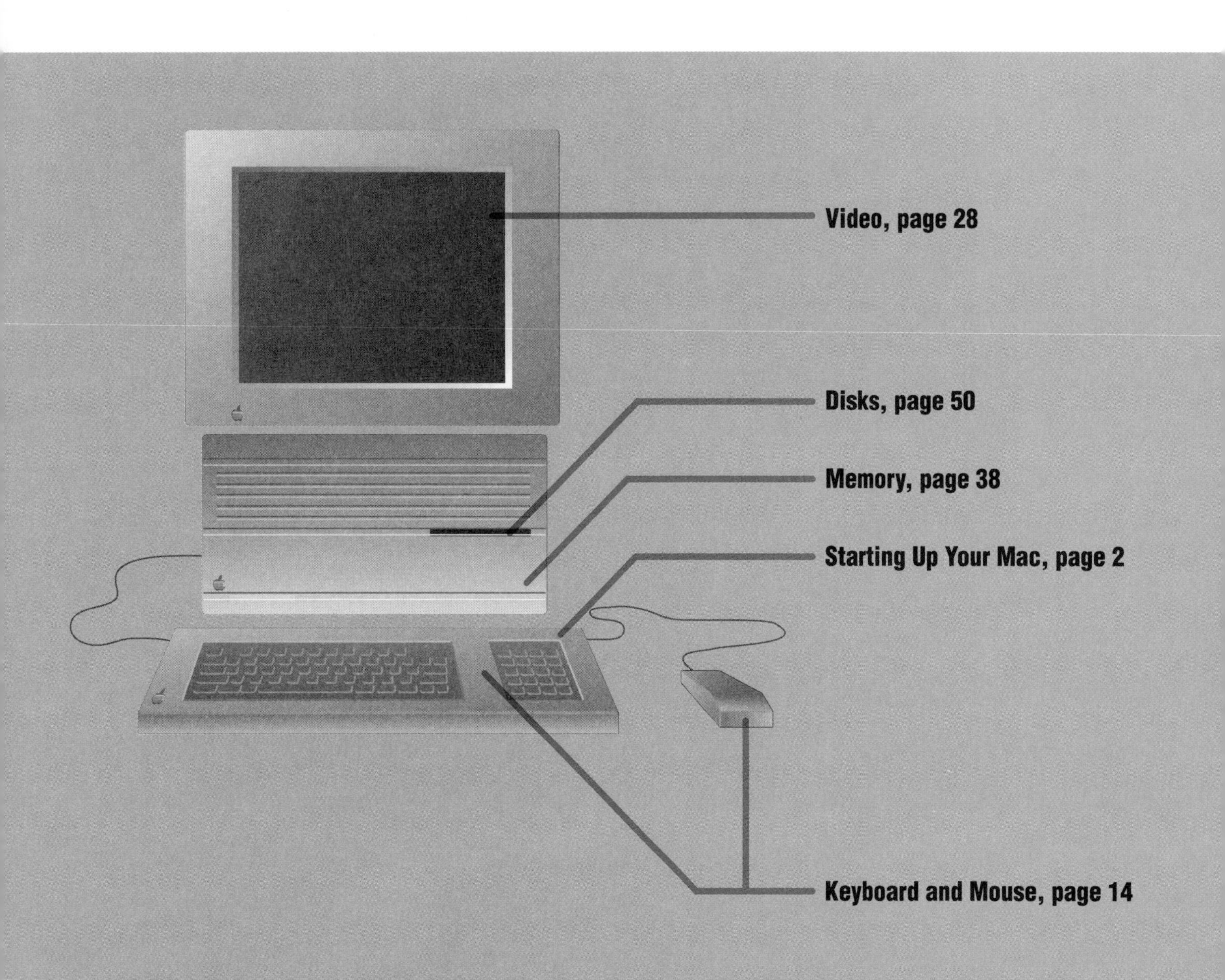

Video, page 28
Disks, page 50
Memory, page 38
Starting Up Your Mac, page 2
Keyboard and Mouse, page 14

Introduction Hardware Software Troubleshooting Glossary/Index

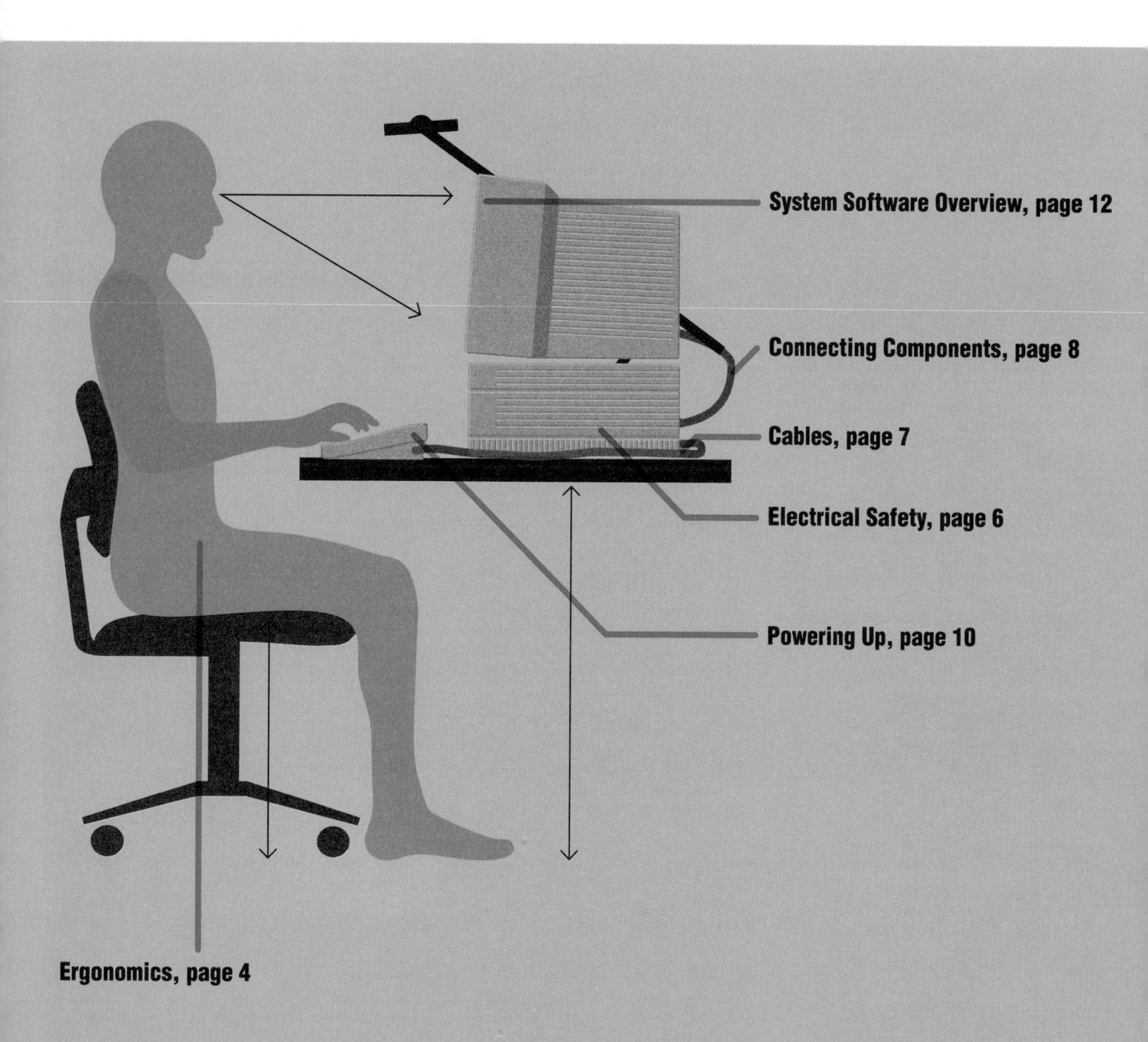
System Software Overview, page 12
Connecting Components, page 8
Cables, page 7
Electrical Safety, page 6
Powering Up, page 10
Ergonomics, page 4

Too many personal computer owners overlook the importance of a comfortable work area for their machines and themselves.

Ergonomics, the study of human interaction with work, should play a key role in setting up your work environment. Ignoring these issues can lead to muscular and skeletal health problems if you frequently spend many hours in front of a computer.

In particular, you should pay close attention to the height of the **keyboard** from the floor and the angle between your eyes and the **video monitor.** If typing at the keyboard is a major part of your work, then also investigate wrist supports to reduce the likelihood of contracting a **repetitive strain injury.**

Viewing Angle

Establishing the proper angle between your eyes and the **video monitor** can make the difference between headaches and painless computing. To impose the least stress on your eyes, the monitor should not be straight ahead (although this is difficult to avoid with 19" and 21" monitors). An angle of 5° to 15° from your eyes down to the center of the screen is considered comfortable for most computer users, especially if you must move your eyes constantly from copy source to keyboard to screen. Try to avoid frequent **focus adjustments** (i.e., the distance between your eyes and what you're looking at) by adding a document holder (a device that lets you set papers adjacent to the monitor).

If you are using a separate video monitor, a tilting swivel **monitor stand** is highly recommended. It allows for myriad adjustments to suit your mood or fatigue level, as well as allowing you to adjust the monitor for reduced **glare.** For more about video monitor safety, see page ➔ 37.

A compact Macintosh (like today's Classic model) takes up so little space on the desk that it is often convenient to place one or more peripherals (external hard disks, CD-ROM players, etc.) underneath the machine. The problem with this tower arrangement, however, is that the **viewing angle** may get uncomfortably high with too many items stacked below.

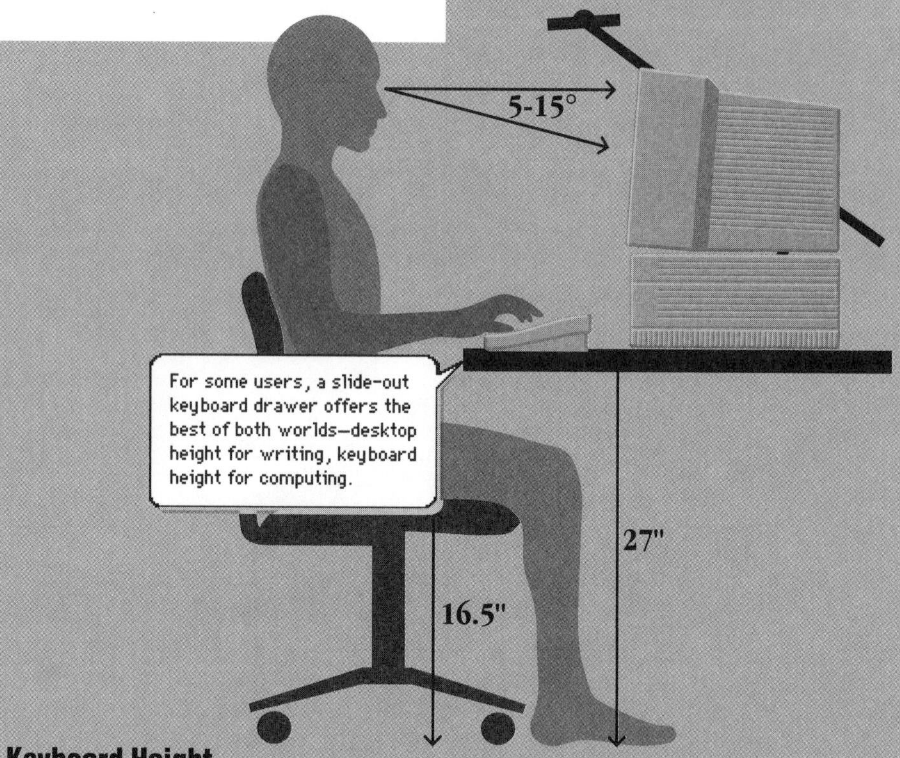
5-15°
For some users, a slide-out keyboard drawer offers the best of both worlds—desktop height for writing, keyboard height for computing.
27"
16.5"

Keyboard Height

Don't confuse **keyboard height** with able height. In both homes and offices (other than at secretarial stations), the tendency is to put the Macintosh and keyboard on the main desk surface. In the United States, a standard office desk surface is 29" from the floor. But for most people, a keyboard at that height is uncomfortable, and may be dangerous during extensive use. If you must use a standard, fixed-height table for your Macintosh, make sure the keyboard is either in a recessed keyboard tray or on a typewriter height desk (typically 27" high).

While the exact height of the keyboard is dependent on your height and the height of the chair seat, the angle of your forearms (from elbow to keys) should be about parallel with the floor. The chair should offer good lower back support, be very mobile, and allow your feet to touch the floor fully.

Repetitive Strain Injury

Only within the past few years have the potential health dangers of excessive computer keyboard typing been observed and studied. While not everything is understood at this point, it is clear that repetitive hand, wrist, and upper body motions—especially when some level of force is applied—can lead to painful injuries. This affects virtually every occupation that requires repetitive motions, from store clerks to assembly line workers. A common cause is straining tendons that can lead to inflammation and swelling, which starts squeezing on nerves.

Among the most common injuries are tendinitus, tenosynovitis, and carpal tunnel syndrome (CTS). As a group, these are called repetitive strain injuries (RSIs) or cumulative trauma disorders (CTDs).

No exact measure exists about how much keyboarding is too much, so be aware of these symptoms: pain, numbness, or tingling anywhere from your neck down to your fingers; inability to grasp objects; swelling. If you suspect a problem caused by intensive computing work, consult a physician experienced in RSIs.

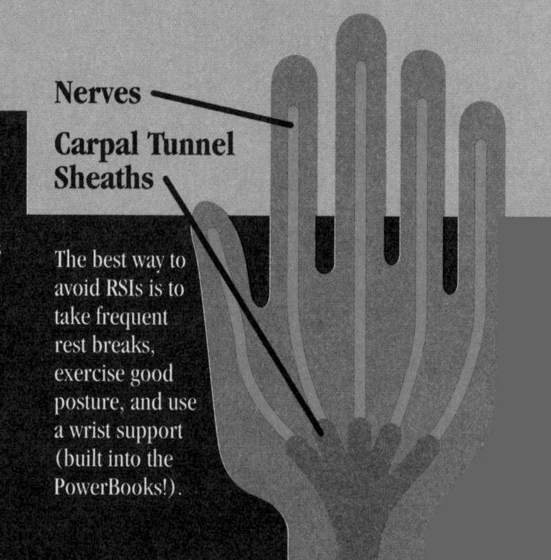
Nerves
Carpal Tunnel Sheaths

The best way to avoid RSIs is to take frequent rest breaks, exercise good posture, and use a wrist support (built into the PowerBooks!).

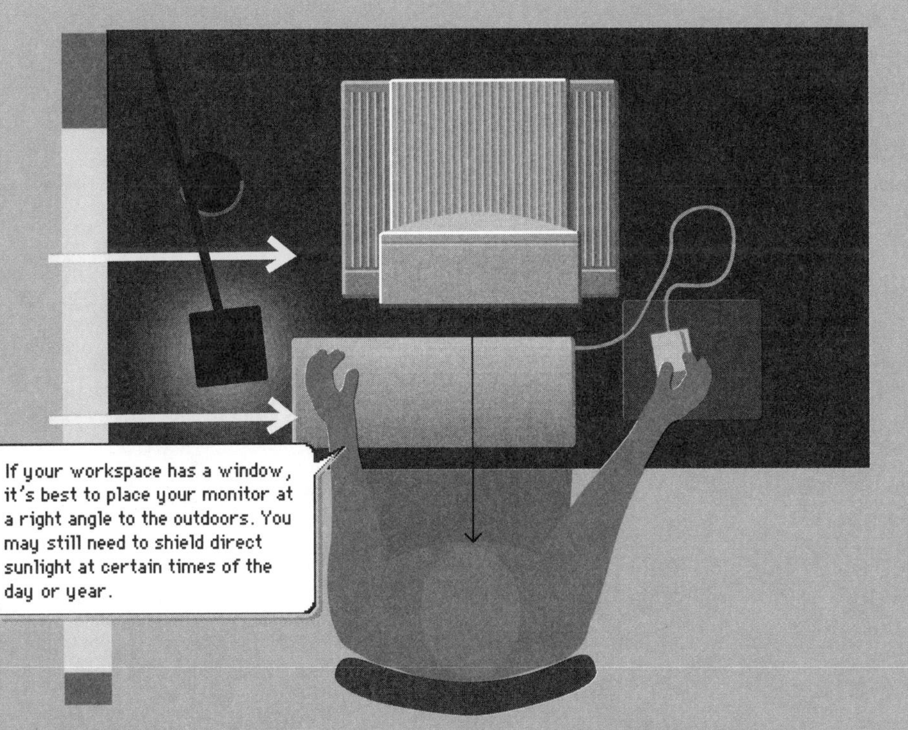

If your workspace has a window, it's best to place your monitor at a right angle to the outdoors. You may still need to shield direct sunlight at certain times of the day or year.

Keep it Moving

Ergonomic studies of workers who spend their entire workdays at computer keyboards have discovered that it is important to allow for frequent adjustment of all the surfaces surrounding your workspace. That includes **chair height, chair angle, keyboard height,** and **viewing angles.** Office and computer supply companies offer self-contained carts that provide almost infinite adjustment of virtually every part of your workstation. In concert with a highly adjustable chair, these carts give each individual the most flexibility in creating a comfortable environment.

Mouse Pads

The **mouse** is an important element of the Macintosh, but few commercial computer desks take them into account (after all, a mouse is still optional on most IBM-style personal computers). The undersides of Macintosh mice have become more durable over time, but running them around a hard desk surface can wear them down after a couple of years. Moreover, many desk surfaces don't give the mouse ball good traction.

A **mouse pad** is a slice of rubber measuring about 6" by 8". Pads have various surfaces, such as plain rubber, cloth, and a slightly mottled plastic. Few mouse pads are available that don't have some advertising printed on them. That's actually good in a way, because it is often possible to get mouse pads for free from hardware and software manufacturers at Macintosh trade shows (you may have to sit through a formal demo of the product to qualify) or as a bonus when you buy goods at computer stores.

Importantly, a mouse pad reserves space on your desk for the mouse. If you leave too little space on your desk for the mouse, you may find the mouse rather inconvenient, since you'll constantly run out of surface to move the pointer where you need it (and then have to pick up the mouse and shift to the other side of the space to continue moving the pointer). Even if you don't use a mouse pad, try to reserve a 10 by 8-inch space for the mouse next to your keyboard (either on the right or left, depending on your mouse hand of preference).

Lighting

In many circumstances lighting conditions are out of your control, especially in an office. Most overhead lighting **glare** (light reflecting off the screen, looking like hot spots) can be reduced with the help of a tilting monitor stand. Light from windows can be especially troublesome because the quantity and direction changes during the day. **Direct sunlight** on most video screens renders them useless, because the monitors can't deliver enough brightness to overcome the sun's light. If you are near a **window,** it is best to keep the window to one of your sides. This reduces glare (when the monitor faces the window) and the strong contrast between outside light and the monitor (when the monitor's back faces the window). Depending on your window's exposure and the time of year, you may still need to shield the monitor from the sun's rays during parts of the day.

Also, be sure to adjust the **monitor brightness** to fit the surrounding light ➔31, 35. During the day, the brightness may need to be turned up full blast. At night, in a darkened room, turn the brightness down to reduce the sharp contrast between surrounding darkness and the illuminated screen.

Breathing Room

No, not for you. For the Macintosh. As a piece of electronic equipment, all Macintoshes heat up while in use. The power supply generates **heat.** Some microchips on the circuit boards get hot. The hard disk motor gets warm.

Heat is a personal computer's worst natural enemy. The Macintosh's designers know that, and have devised various systems to prevent the Macintosh's innards from overheating. Key to those systems are **ventilation** holes, most of which you can't see because they're disguised by aesthetic cabinet designs. Most of the holes are located along the outside bottoms of the cabinets (to allow cool air to come in) and on the top (to allow the heated air to flow out). This kind of convection cooling is a critical part of your Macintosh's hardware. Keep at least a one-inch breathing zone around your Macintosh's sides. And if you see vents along the top of the machine or monitor, don't block them with other equipment, a notebook, or papers.

Some modular Macintosh system units (the Macintosh IIci for example) may be set on their sides while maintaining proper cooling—but use the special feet included. The Quadra 700 even encourages a vertical orientation. The largest Macintosh II models (e.g., Macintosh II, IIx, IIfx) should be placed on end only if they are used in cool environments and with stands designed to allow a free flow of air from the side nearest the floor.

Earthquake Proofing

You probably won't think about this until after you've lost a Macintosh or monitor to a tremor, but it's important for Macintosh owners in many parts of the world to prepare for an earthquake. In the experience of the October 1989 Loma Prieta earthquake (which rocked San Francisco, Silicon Valley, and Santa Cruz areas), many Macintosh users had their system units or monitors creep off the table as the buildings shook from side to side.

A couple of low-cost electrical add-ons can prevent damage to your Macintosh by numerous anomalies in the electrical power delivered to your power outlet.

You should not take the quality of that power—at home or at work—for granted. Fortunately, some offices have specially marked power outlets that should do a better job of protecting your machine from the vagaries of the electric utility company.

A pioneering sage in the personal computer industry once prophesized, "I have seen the future—and it is power strips."

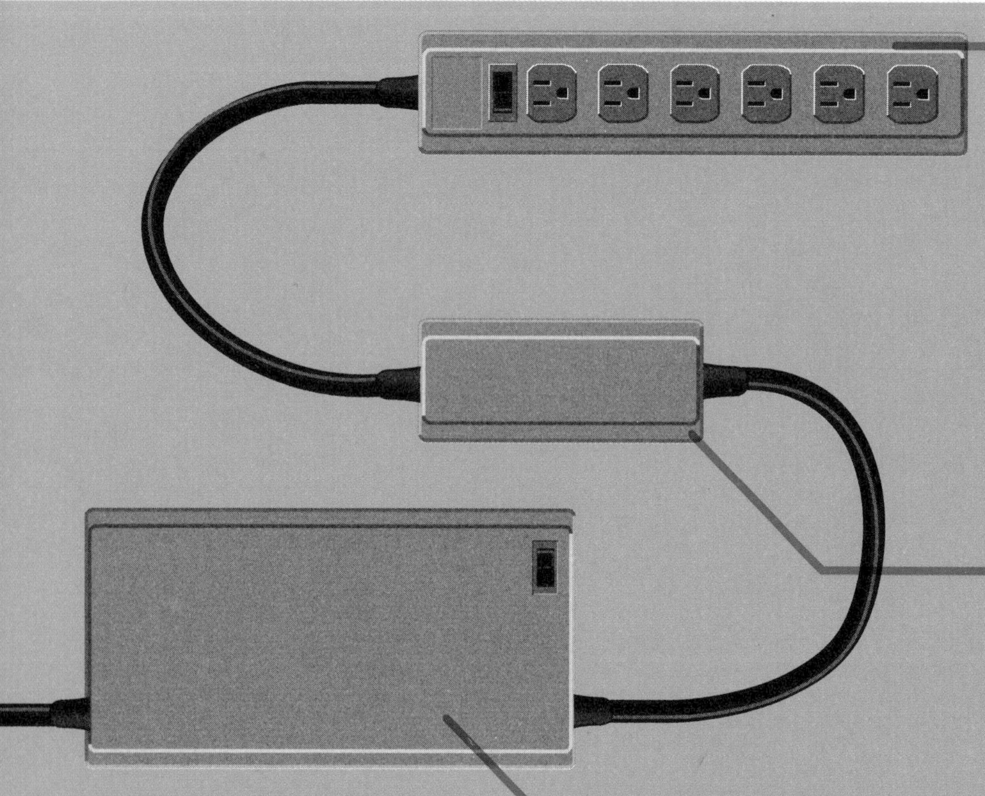

Power Strips

Most homes and offices were not wired for the computer age. While a Macintosh, by itself, doesn't impose that great a threat to the electrical wall socket, additional peripherals begin to occupy outlets at an alarming rate, especially when one of those items has a bulky black transformer that plugs into the outlet.

To prevent overloading any circuit into which you plug your computer equipment, a fused power strip is a good addition. Such strips have 4 to 8 electrical outlets, often with a master on-off switch that lets you control the whole collection with a single switch. The advantage of a fuse in the power strip is that it should blow its fuse before the main fuse or circuit breaker controlling many other outlets. Some power strips also have surge protectors built in, but the protection may wear out over time.

Surge Protector

Electricity can be hazardous even to electronic equipment when the power fluctuates wildly. Macintosh power supplies (except for some early Macintosh models) are capable of adapting to normal fluctuations in power. But any number of electrical utility companies and systems sporadically send out very strong (and very short) pulses of varying types (called surges and spikes). These are what can literally fry an electrical device, sometimes even if the item is turned off (usually one side of the electrical wire is still connected while switched off).

A **surge protector** is a device that attempts to absorb these power anomalies. Surge protectors come in varying quality ranges. Key ratings to demand are a response time of 10 nanoseconds (or faster) and a clamping voltage in the 350-400 volt range.

Lightning Storms

If you live or work in an area prone to electrical storms, take special precautions. Overhead power lines can absorb and transmit the strong currents generated by near-hit lightning static discharges. The best precaution is unplugging all electronic gear during such storms. Surge protectors may offer some level of protection, but may fry in a direct hit to the power lines nearby.

Standby Power Supplies

When the power goes out, you could find yourself in big trouble, especially if you haven't saved your work in awhile. If power outages are common—or you can't bear to think of your Macintosh or file server unexpectedly shutting down—then consider adding a standby power supply, more often called an **uninterruptible power supply** (UPS). A standby power supply goes in-line between the power outlet and your equipment. It contains a battery that is continually charged while the AC power flows normally. When the power quits, the power supply instantaneously puts its charged batteries to work, usually sounding an audible alert to warn you that you are on emergency power. The purpose of a standby power supply is to give you enough warning and power to save what you're working on and shut down safely. They're excellent ideas for network servers, because others on the network may not have their Macintoshes affected by a power outage at the server, and you'll want to give remote users a few minutes' warning that the server will be shutting down.

Static Electricity

When their outer cases are closed up, Macintosh computers are well insulated from potential damage caused by casual static electricity—the kind that zaps you in dry weather. If the case is open, and you're installing boards, chips, or disk drives, static electricity can do significant damage to the Mac's circuits. Before touching anything on a board, always (even in humid weather) touch the metal power supply box or some other metal frame part to discharge any residual static electricity that has built up on you. Even shuffling your feet a couple steps or rolling your chair can build up a charge again, so continually discharge yourself. Also try to ground yourself before touching any rear panel connector. Better safe than $orry.

Although inanimate, connectors have genders—male and female. If you look head-on into the end of a connector and see free-standing metal pins (even if the pins are shielded by a metal housing), then that cable is a male connector or plug.

A connector consisting strictly of holes (into which the pins go) is a female connector (jack or outlet). Cabling is a strictly heterosexual affair—requiring one male and one female to make a coupling.

When connecting a cable, make sure it is securely fastened to its connector. Push small round male connectors until they are firmly seated against female connectors. A connector with screw posts should be screwed to its counterpart to prevent the pair from accidentally coming loose or being kicked apart.

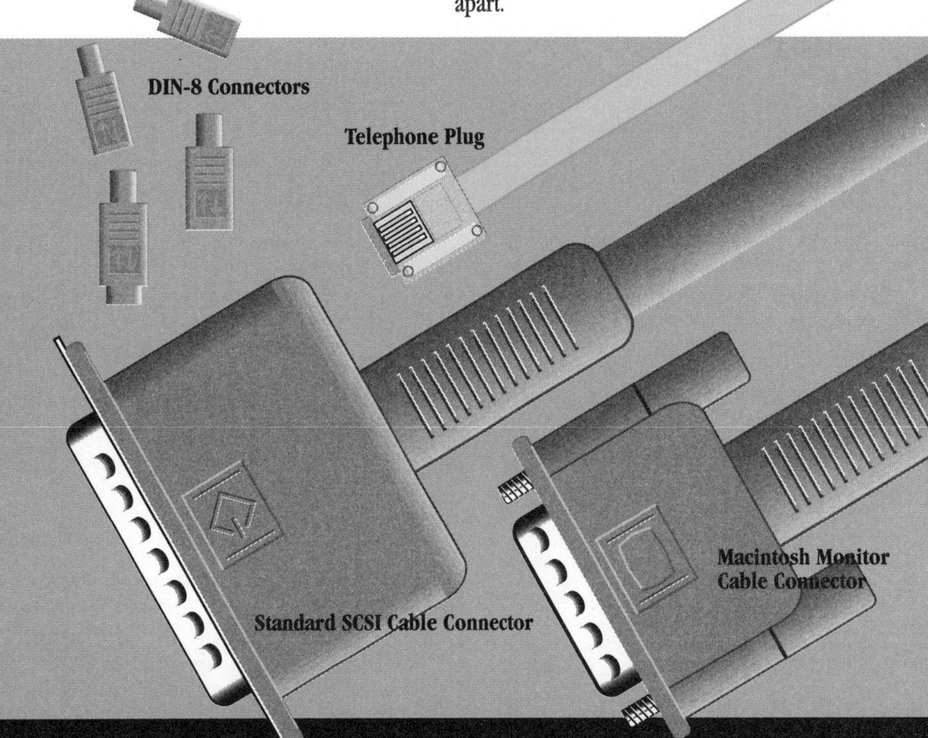

Unmarked (or almost) Cables

While cables that come with Apple equipment have appropriate symbols molded into the connectors, many third-party cables do not. This usually doesn't cause problems except in the case of the small, round Mini DIN-8 connectors, which tend to look alike. To make sure you don't exert improper force on such a connector, look for either an arrow on the molded housing or for a dimple in the metal shielding near the end of the connector. Both the arrow and dimple are to be matched to the top of the female connector on the hardware device—the side with the symbol on the hardware cabinet.

Connector Types

For most ports on a Macintosh, there are two families of connectors. The larger connectors are known in the trade by the letters **"DB"** and the number of pins in the connector. For example, a **25-pin jack** on the back of the Macintosh is a female **DB-25.** The original Macintosh modem and printer ports were female **DB-9** connectors. DB-style connectors can couple only when the same size male and female connectors are used together and both are oriented the same way.

With the Macintosh Plus, Apple started using the small round connector called a **Mini DIN-8. DIN** is a primarily European standard of electrical connections found frequently in audio equipment. Regular DIN connectors are about 1/2" in diameter. The miniature variety on the Macintosh are about 3/8" in diameter, and have different pinouts and plastic "keys" depending on which port you're working with. The keys prevent a connector that uses only 4 pins from accidentally being inserted into a jack that requires 8 pins (and might do damage to something if the four pins were inserted into their spots in the 8-pin jack).

Audio jacks (both input and output) are a well-known standard, called the **RCA phono jack.** Macintosh phono jacks are 1/8-inch in diameter, a common size these days for Walkman-compatible headphones. A full range of adapters are available at places such as Radio Shack for conversion between the 1/8-inch stereo jacks on most Macintoshes to other plug styles on other audio cables.

Cable Extensions

Setting up a modular Macintosh workstation in which the system unit is not on the desktop requires extension cables for the keyboard, video, and video monitor power. Major computer supply houses offer such cabling kits designed specifically for the Macintosh. The longer you make the ADB and video cables, however, the more likely these cables can generate interference to radio and television signals in your home. The Macintosh is rated for **Class B usage** (in-home) with the cables Apple provides. Anything beyond that may not be as electronically "clean."

You may also wish to set up **SCSI** hardware, such as a scanner, at some distance from your system unit. Typical SCSI cables supplied with hardware are notoriously short. Longer cables are available through computer supply houses, but they may affect the installation of multiple SCSI devices 58.

Making Your Own Cables

Those who are handy with a soldering iron can make cables when a pre-fabricated kind is either unavailable or ridiculously expensive (the latter being a common occurrence). Components for wiring DB-style and phono plugs are readily available at Radio Shack stores. Mini DIN-8 plugs are extremely difficult to find, even at well-equipped electronics supply houses.

Choosing the proper cable is very important. Due to the nature of signals being passed in many Macintosh peripheral cables, you should use **shielded cable** wherever possible, and make sure the shield is connected to a pin that connects to the Macintosh's ground. Failure to use shielded cable, especially in a home installation, may cause radio and television interference, even on a neighbor's set. Also, check your work very carefully before attaching the connector to the Mac. Look for possible solder bridges and shorts between pins. Use a continuity checker to make sure no two pins are wired together (unless they're supposed to be) and that you have good solder joints at both ends of the cable.

Pinouts for various cables can be found in ***Guide to the Macintosh Family Hardware***, published by Addison-Wesley.

This is an excellent source for deep secrets about your

Connectors at the ends of most Macintosh cables supplied by Apple are marked with symbols representing their counterparts on the computer itself.

Many of the connectors—especially the small diameter round ones—look alike. Even though their sizes are identical, the pins on the connectors are in a different layout to prevent you from accidentally plugging a cable into the wrong connector.

A connector on the Macintosh is frequently called a port, as if it were part of an electronic harbor. Not all Macintosh models have all the ports described below.

Electric Power

All desktop Macintosh models have a three-pronged power connector to which the electrical power cord is connected. The connector on the Macintosh is a recessed male connector. Many modular Macintosh models also have a female power connector that allows you to power the video monitor via the Macintosh. This reduces competition for power outlets, and also allows you to control the monitor and Macintosh with the same power-on/power-off sequence ➜10. The video monitor will likely have its own power switch, but if you connect the power via the Macintosh system unit, you can leave the monitor switch in the On position all the time—power to this external connection is cut when the Macintosh is turned off.

Important Warning

Completely turn off your Macintosh and any external peripherals before connecting or disconnecting the cables described here. On connectors with lots of pins (like the SCSI connector), not all of the pins may make contact at the same instant—a significant hazard. Since some pins carry electrical current (at levels usually safe to humans in case of accidental contact), power may be applied to the circuitry in the Mac or peripheral device (like the keyboard or external hard disk) before other important pins have made contact as you wiggle the connector on or off. Such abuse can render the port or device completely unusable.

Audio Input

A 1/8" phono jack on some Macintosh models (like the Macintosh LC and IIsi) allow direct connection of a monophonic (i.e., not two-channel stereo) microphone or other sound input. A Macintosh with an audio input port comes with a small microphone, with which you can record system sounds ➜152 or use sound recording in software programs that allow voice annotation (e.g., voice content to an electronic mail message). Using the line level output from other sound sources (e.g., radio or VCR), you can record other sounds with the help of the Sound control panel device ➜80. If the sound source is in stereo, you will need a cable converter that has a female stereo input and a male monophonic output (e.g., Radio Shack model #274-368).

SCSI

The **Small Computer Standard Interface** is a standard among Macintosh peripherals. There is a slightly different and incompatible SCSI standard for other computers, so make sure that a SCSI device you intend to connect to the Macintosh is designed for the Mac. Actually, the 25-pin SCSI port on the Macintosh (and the rectangular PowerBook SCSI connector) is non-standard even among Macintosh SCSI devices. The hefty 50-pin connector on most external SCSI devices (including Apple-brand devices like hard disks, CD-ROM players, and scanners) is the more recognized standard. The 50-pin connector pair have two metal spring clips on either edge of the connector. When attaching one of these connectors, always squeeze the clips into the locked position. Connecting a chain of SCSI devices can be a headache. See page ➜58 for details about the mysteries of SCSI devices and cabling.

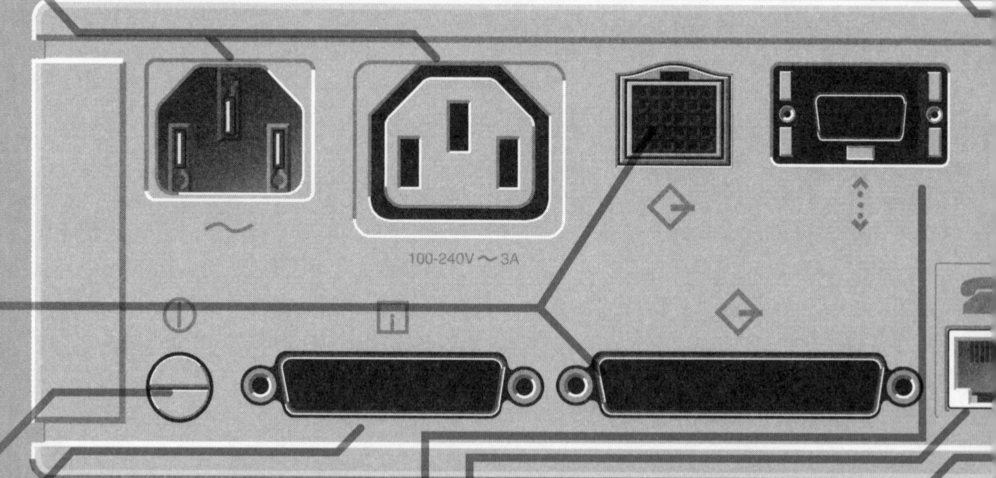

On/Off Switch

Disk Drive

Those Macintoshes that allow connection of an external floppy disk drive have a 19-pin disk drive port. The floppy disk icon indicates that this port is not for attaching a hard disk (although before the advent of the Macintosh SCSI port (except the PowerBook 100's 20-pin outlet), the earliest Macintosh hard disks did so).

More and more business traveler hotel rooms have phones with similar RJ-11 jacks ("dataports"). Don't forget your phone cable!

Ethernet Port

Available on the Quadra models (and surely more to come), the Ethernet port offers a ready connection to an ethernet network ➜162. Data can flow ten times faster via ethernet than via LocalTalk built into all Macintoshes.

Telephone Jack

The Macintosh Portable and PowerBooks have a space for an optional telephone modem board, including a hole in the rear of the cabinet for a telephone jack. The jack is the same RJ-11 style modular phone jack found in most homes and on consumer telephone equipment. This connector requires a simple telephone cable with RJ-11 plugs on both ends—one for the Macintosh, one for the wall telephone jack.

Video

Some Macintosh models have video driving circuitry built into the main motherboard (called on-board video) and a video port to which you can connect the video cable of a monitor. This 15-pin connector contains only the video signals, and not the AC power required for the monitor. Be sure that the monitor you are using is compatible with the on-board video characteristics of your Macintosh ➜30. For more sophisticated monitors (e.g., two-page displays and high-quality color monitors), you may need an additional video board (if your Macintosh can accommodate one).

Printer

The printer port is one of the Macintosh's two 8-pin **serial ports.** A serial port is one that sends and receives data one bit at a time through one wire in each direction. This is in contrast to other computers' parallel printer ports, in which data is sent along 8 wires at a time. While the parallel port may be faster, the Macintosh serial port is fast enough for most Macintosh users' needs. Most Macintosh printers connect to this connector (although some connect via the SCSI port). Lower cost printers (like the ImageWriter and StyleWriter) connect here via a simple printer cable specifically wired for the printer. PostScript **LaserWriters** require an AppleTalk cabling set ➜ 148, 162.

The printer port is also where most Macintosh users connect the **AppleTalk network** cable (whether or not the network is connected to a printer). Connecting multiple Macintoshes together in this fashion allows users to share files with **Personal FileShare** ➜66, 162-173 or access **file servers** ➜162.

Audio Output

The very first Macintosh had a 1/8" RCA-type phono jack for audio output. That tradition continues to the latest Macintoshes' stereo jacks. When you connect a compatible phono plug, the internal speaker is disabled, and whatever sound used to come through the speaker now goes exclusively through the audio output port (just like most portable radios). The sound that plays is dependent upon the software you run. Some software (especially games) comes with digitized audio built in. Other software allows you to record audio or other sound through a microphone (connected to a different port) for playback through the speaker.

You can plug headphones or amplified speakers (like those from Sony or BOSE) into the port and obtain remarkably improved sound quality compared to the 3" speaker inside most Macs. If you plan to record the Mac's sounds or play them through a stereo system, connect the patch cord between the Mac's audio output port and the high-level input (e.g., CD player) connector on the recorder or stereo. You'll hear stereo only if the software is written for it. The Mac's audio signal is rated at a maximum 1 volt peak-to-peak.

Optional Ports

Many Macintosh models offer expandability by way of extra **circuit boards** that may be mounted inside the system unit. Expansion boards may be in the NuBus, PDS (Processor Direct Slot) or Custom style, depending on the accomodations inside a given Macintosh model. Always be sure an expansion board is specifically tailored to your Macintosh model. Almost every such expansion board provides one or more connectors for the attachment of additional cables (e.g., EtherTalk network cable, high-quality color video monitor cable, video input cable, etc...). Your Macintosh may have space for one to six of these optional boards. External connectors vary widely, depending on the type of electronic data coming through the port. Follow directions that come with the optional board for cabling requirements.

Apple Desktop Bus (ADB)

The 4-pin Apple Desktop Bus (ADB) is used primarily as the cable connection for a **keyboard, mouse,** and other input devices. Two ADB ports are available on early Macintosh connector panels on the back of the computer, presumably one each for keyboard and mouse. The ADB, however, allows devices to be chained to each other in any order. Some devices, like keyboards, have two ADB ports on them—one to connect to the Macintosh, the other to accept the mouse (see page ➜ 18 for keyboard and mouse connection options). More recent Mac models have a single ADB port.

Which Serial Port?

While there are minor technical differences between the printer and modem ports on the Macintosh, most software programs allow you to select the port of your choice. Default settings, however, assume printers are on the printer port and communications or file transfer devices are on the modem port.

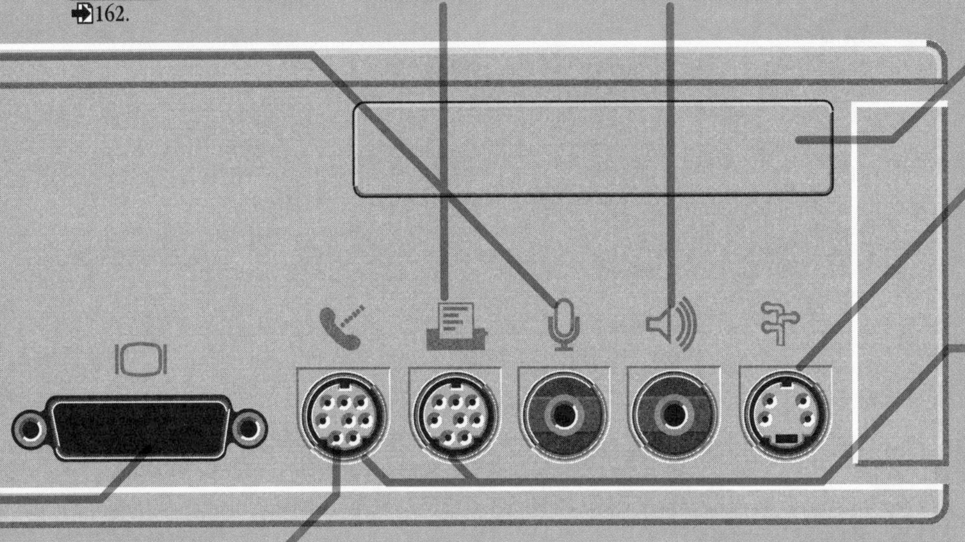

Modem

The modem port is most often used for connecting a Macintosh to a **modem** ➜174 or other data transfer device (such as a cable linking a Macintosh to a different kind of computer for transferring files). Most modems have 25-pin connectors, and follow a standard wiring convention. Therefore, a generic Macintosh modem cable should work with most modems. Macintosh models lacking the auido input port use the modem port as the connector for external microphones or **audio digitizers.**

More Serial Ports

If you are connected to an **AppleTalk network,** you really have only one serial port available for other purposes. While that's fine if you just have a modem, many users have additional devices they like to connect to their modem ports (such as non-Macintosh laptop computers, pocket computers, sound digitizers, and other devices controllable via RS-232C standard signals). Changing cables is not only inconvenient, it could

One solution is a cable switcher. Computer supply houses offer A-B and A-B-C-D switch boxes that let you connect two and four serial items, respectively, to a single serial port on your Macintosh. Be sure the model you buy is designed for the Mini DIN-8 connectors of the Macintosh hardware family. Macintosh II users may also choose a third-party multi-serial port plug-in board.

Also called booting or starting the computer, turing on the power is the strongest electrical shock to your Mac hardware short of a power company voltage spike.

Some Macintosh models have an on-off power switch, others have a power switch on the keyboard, and still others power up when you press any keyboard character key.

Shutting down the Macintosh is accomplished differently on different Macintosh models. Most respond to the **Shut Down** menu item in the Finder's **Special** menu. Others require flipping a mechanical switch on the back of the Macintosh cabinet. Battery-operated Macintoshes may be put to sleep, instead of being shut down entirely. This keeps all documents and applications in suspended animation until you wake up the machine later to pick up where you left off.

What Happens At Power On

Turning on the Macintosh brings the computer to life with the help of instructions preprogrammed into the Macintosh's ROM ➔ 42. Instructions include checking out the system board and RAM chips, emitting a startup tone or sound, displaying a startup alert box ("**Welcome...**"), and locating a diskette or hard disk containing a System file. If no System is found, a small Macintosh icon with a flashing question mark in its screen appears on your video monitor. If you believe your Macintosh should find a system disk (floppy or hard), but it thinks otherwise, consult troubleshooting page ➔177. Worse yet, if you are greeted with a frowning Macintosh icon (the "sad Mac") or an immediate **series** of chimes, see page ➔178.

Power On: Compact Macintosh

Starting a compact Macintosh couldn't be simpler. On the rear panel of the machine is a big rocker-style switch. A circle and line on facing sides of the switch are international symbols for on and off, but few people remember which is which.

1. Press the top side of the switch (the one with the line). It may take a deliberate push to flip the switch into the on position.

Power On: Modular Macintosh

Modular Macintoshes feature an On switch as one of the keys on the keyboard. The key is labeled with a left-pointing triangle.

On the Standard Keyboard, the On key is a large rectangular key just above the number 5 and 6 keys. On the Extended keyboard, the On key is a small key at the upper right corner of the keyboard.

1. Press the On key once to turn on the computer. Pressing the key again after the computer is on has no effect.

If no keyboard is connected to the Mac, you may also press the Power button at the rear panel of most Macintosh II models. This button toggles between power on and off.

Special
Clean Up Window
Empty Trash...
Eject Disk ⌘E
Erase Disk...
Restart
Shut Down

Shutting Down

Powering off (shutting down) the Macintosh is also a shock to the hardware. More importantly, you should use the prescribed methods of shutting down (the Shut Down menu item) instead of the brute force (e.g., pull the plug) method to make sure all document files have been saved and closed, all applications have quit naturally, any diskettes are ejected, and the Desktop file ➔94 has been updated with changes to your window layouts.

Brute force powering down (including a power failure) has been known to corrupt files and lose data. Protect yourself and your information: shut down gently.

Power On: Portable Macintoshes

Macintosh Portable and PowerBook 100 units turn on when you press any character key on the keyboard. This is also true of the PowerBook 140 and 170 only when the units are in Sleep mode. To turn on a PowerBook 140 or 170 that had been completely shut down, press the Power button inside the trap door on the rear panel of the unit.

Modular and Portable Macintosh Shut Down

Shutting down a modular or Portable Macintosh is done entirely with software.

1. Choose **Shut Down** from the **Special** menu.

The System software does the rest, including powering down the hardware.

If, on the other hand, you want to shut down but your Macintosh is frozen — you can't pull down the menus—you should try resetting your Macintosh (explained below) and shut down via the **Special** menu. But if you can't even reset the machine, then use the Power button on the back panel: the Off Switch of Last Resort. Pressing the button once (it may delay a few seconds before acting) removes all power from the Mac. This is not a safe way to power down on a daily basis, but if your Macintosh has hung up, you have nothing to lose anyway. Press it, and cross your fingers that your open files come back alive when you next power on the machine.

Compact Macintosh Shut Down

Don't be lured by that big switch on the back. There's some software shutting down to do first:

1. Choose **Shut Down** from the **Special** menu. This action does all the gentle closure for files and disks before showing this dialog box:

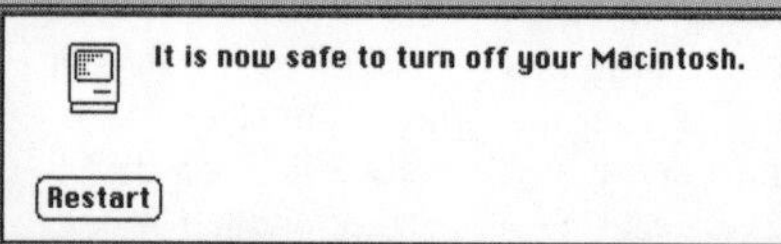

It is now safe to turn off your Macintosh.
Restart

2. Now, you can flip the big switch on the back to the Off (circle) position.

Occasionally it is necessary to restart, or reboot, the Macintosh (e.g., for a new **system extension** ➔ 83, to take effect) by choosing the **Restart** item in the Finder's **Special** menu. Restarting the Macintosh is much less traumatic to the internal circuits than turning the computer off and back on.

Restarting Your Macintosh

Frequently, after installing new software that affects the System Folder (or folders nested inside), you are instructed to restart the Macintosh. Restarting (re-booting) the Macintosh is the safest way to allow the System software to recognize new **extensions** and other accessories required by the addition of new hardware add-ons or software.

The safest way to restart is to choose **Restart** from the Finder's **Special** menu. This action properly closes files, ejects and unmounts disks, and shuts down all software before restarting. The restart, however, is performed without powering the machine down and up again—saving wear and tear on the hardware. Also, if your Macintosh model provides a **RAM disk** ➔ 43, its contents are not lost on restart.

Restart with the Reset's Switch (right) only when a frozen system prevents you from pulling down the Special menu in the Finder.

Install the Reset (Programmer's) Switch

Some of the Macintosh hardware manuals tell you to ignore the **Programmer's Switch** unless you plan to do serious programming. Poppycock! While it's true that an inadvertent press of either of the two keys can cause unsaved data to disappear, the Reset button is both a convenient and electrically safer way to restart a frozen Mac. It prevents the shock of a full power down and power up. On newer Macs, the switch is built into the case.

The **Reset button** (the one with the left pointing triangle) is the one to get out of a frozen Macintosh situation. Press it once, and in most cases the startup procedure will ensue. If nothing happens, then you'll have to resort to the Power switch on the rear panel—there's no other hope.

Unless you are, indeed, a programmer or knowledgeable about debuggers, the **Interrupt button** of the Programmer's Switch won't help you much. If you press it by mistake, just press the Restart button to re-boot the computer.

The most recent Macintosh models have their Programmer's Switches already installed. On the desktop machines, the switches on the front panel are protected against bumping by the keyboard by plastic ridges. On the Portable, a slide switch under the left side of the keyboard usually prevents accidental pressing of either switch when lifting the unit—provided the locking switch is in the proper position, and hasn't been pushed by normal jostling.

PowerBook Power

Macintosh PowerBooks use two different kinds of battery packs. The PowerBook 100's battery is a lead-acid type, while the 140 and 170 are powered by a nickel-cadmium (NiCad, pronounced NYE-kad) battery pack. You can expect 3-4 hours of use per charge on a PowerBook 100 and 2-3 hours on a 140 or 170. If your applications use the hard disk a lot (such as programs that auto save, e.g. HyperCard) you may get less operational time between charges. Using an internal modem also gobbles battery juice.

You may receive three warnings about low battery charge. The first dims yourbacklit screen as a way to conserve power. You may still have10-20 minutes of operationsleft, depending on your hard disk usage and overall battery condition. The last two warnings generally come pretty close together, with the final one giving you ten seconds before the machine goes to sleep. It is safe to plug in the charger when the machine is running when any of these power warnings appear.

While asleep, PowerBooks drain small amounts of current from the battery pack. A complete **Shut Down** stops that drain. If you remove the battery pack while the machine is asleep, all RAM contents will be lost. Remove the battery pack only after you have **Shut Down**.

Special
Clean Up Desktop
Empty Trash
Eject Disk ⌘E
Erase Disk...
Restart
Shut Down
Sleep

Parameter RAM (PRAM)

When your Macintosh comes to life, it "knows" certain things about the operating environment: things like the current time and date, all the **General control panel** settings, whether **AppleTalk** is turned on for the printer port, and so on. This information is stored in a special memory called **Parameter RAM** or **PRAM** (pronounced PEE-ram). A battery keeps the information intact when the power is off. On most Macs after the Macintosh Plus, the battery is on the motherboard.

One possible reason a Macintosh won't startup is that PRAM has been corrupted. Another symptom

To Sleep, Perchance to Dream

A feature of battery operated Macintoshes is the ability to put the system (and, separately, the hard disk) to **sleep** without shutting down the whole thing. In System Sleep, the screen blanks, all disk activity stops, and all processing comes to a halt. The contents of RAM remain intact (drawing minimal power), such that all your open applications and documents stay that way until you wake up the Macintosh later (provided the battery hasn't gone dead). A press of any character key brings you back to the exact spot you were working when the machine put its chewing gum on the

When Changing Cables...

Prudence calls for completely powering down the Macintosh before connecting or disconnecting any **cables** to the system unit. Typically, if any damage were to occur by changing a cable with the Macintosh still turned one, the problem would be local to the circuitry controlling that particular connector port. But the repair shop will replace the whole **motherboard** — a very costly proposition if

All the microchips, circuit boards, and wires inside your Macintosh would be of no value to you whatsoever without some intelligence showing the way to make those pieces work together.

Fortunately, the Macintosh contains pre-programmed instructions (stored on **ROM** chips, ➔42) to make the circuits work together. This software is called the **operating system.**

But when you start up your Macintosh, the machine also needs additional software to put the power of those circuits into your hands. That is the system software's job.

System Folder

You may see many folders in windows on the Macintosh, but only one may be the System Folder. Its icon features a small Macintosh on it, indicating its special status. In day-to-day operation of your Macintosh programs, you will rarely have to open this folder. If you do, you will notice that it contains not only the System and Finder files, but many other files and folders, such as: **Preferences** ➔89, **Extensions** ➔83, **Apple Menu Items** ➔76, **Control Panels** ➔80, **Startup Items** ➔91. Each of these has a special system software purpose.

Frequently, when you install a new application program on your hard disk, part of the installation process is to drag one or more files to the **System Folder.** The system software examines the nature of each of the files and asks you whether the files should go into their special purpose folders. It's generally advisable to let the Macintosh go ahead and figure out what goes where. For an in-depth discussion of the System Folder, see page ➔74.

System File

The **System File** contains many pieces that you can't truly grab hold of. It is, however, the first file that the operating system looks for when you start your Macintosh. What you can grab from the System File are **fonts,** sounds, and keyboard and other script resources ➔74, 84. Resources installed into the System File are available to any application you run on your Macintosh.

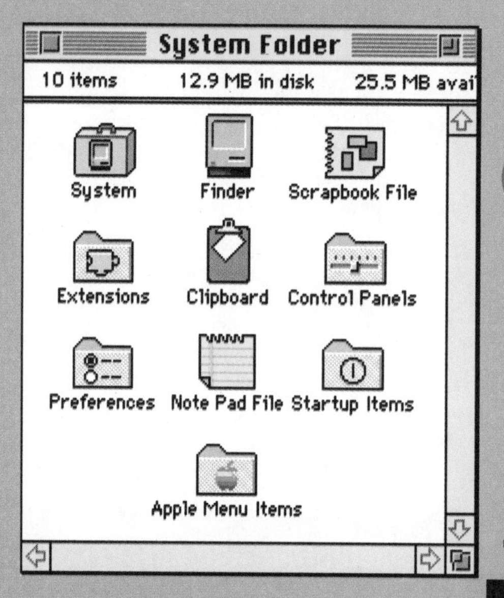

Finder

The **Finder** is responsible for the **graphical user interface** that appears on the screen and interacts with application programs. For example, while the internal mechanism that copies a file from one disk to another is a complex one, the Finder makes the process a simple click and drag exercise with the mouse and on-screen icons. The Finder also manages the display of files and folders we see on the screen. More information about the display (the Desktop) can be found on ➔94-95.

In System 7, the Finder continually runs in a mode that in earlier versions of the System software was known as **MultiFinder.** The System 7 Finder lets you open more than one application at a time (memory permitting). Switching between programs is as easy as clicking in the desired program's window or choosing the program from the **Application** menu (at the far right of the menu bar) ➔101.

The Finder also helps you locate ("find") a file that may be nested deeply inside several layers of folders ➔122.

System Numbering Conventions

Every generation of Macintosh system software is identified by a number. Even individual elements of the System software have version numbers. Until System 7, **version numbers** of each of the elements were not necessarily the same. Even the System and Finder pair (which are always updated and released at the same time) didn't have the same numbers. For example, the most recent System software prior to System 7 had the System File at version 6.0.7, and the Finder File at version 6.1.7. Printer drivers had their own numbering system that didn't even approach version 6. As a result this tended to be confusing.

In any case the System File had the number that most Macintosh owners referred to. Therefore, when someone says System 6.0.7 (spoken as either "six point oh point seven" or just "six oh seven"), the reference is to the entire set of system files that were released with the System File version 6.0.7.

The numbering system with the two decimals may seem a bit strange, but each number reveals something about the era of software you're working with. The first number signifies the **generation** of the software. This number changes only when significant changes have been made to the features and functionality of the software. The jump from 6 to 7 was larger than any previous generational leap

The number between the decimals indicates an interim **feature upgrade.** The changes aren't usually monumental, but significant enough to make you want to upgrade.

The last number usually indicates a **maintenance upgrade.** These come about for two reasons: 1) to fix software **bugs** that caused problems for a lot of users in the previous version; or 2) to update the system software to accommodate new Macintosh hardware. For example, System 7 evolved into version 7.0.1 when the Classic II, Quadras, and PowerBooks were introduced. These machines required some additional system software pieces, so a new maintenance release came with them. System 7 will likely go through similar upgrades as new Macintosh models flow from the company

Macintosh **system software** consists of several disk files stored in a special place called the **System Folder.** System software files, such as **System** and **Finder,** are responsible for the Macintosh's on-screen personality. Other files in the System Folder allow you to print on various Apple printers or share your files with other Macintosh users across a **network.**

Disk-based system software is often pre-installed when you buy a Macintosh. If it is not, or if you acquire a new hard disk, you may have to run an **installer program** to put the requisite system files on your hard disk.

Quick Installation

Installer

Your Macintosh comes with a set of **system diskettes** (or you may have acquired a set of disks as a System 7 upgrade package). The number of disks varies, depending on whether the disks are formatted as 800 kilobyte disks (for older Macintoshes) or 1.4 megabyte high density disks (all Macintoshes from the Macintosh IIcx and later).

If you are using a System 7 upgrade kit, be sure you have System 7-compatible **system extensions** (drivers) for any non-Apple hard disks and monitors connected to your Macintosh. Don't install System 7 until you are sure about these extensions' compatibility.

Before using any of these disks, you should protect them from **accidental erasure** or **virus infection.**

1. Turn the disk over so you can see the round metal piece in the center of the disk. Notice the indentation and black tab at the corner opposite the diagonal corner.
2. With your fingernail or pencil, slide the black tab toward the top of the disk. Push it all the way until it clicks into place, revealing a square hole you can see through.

Unprotected

Write-protected

The disk is now **locked**. Do the same for all system disks in the set.

On the first disk is a program called **Installer,** along with some other files (and the disk's own System File). If you are new to the Macintosh, see pages 66-69 for detailed instructions on installing System 7 software onto your hard disk. But if you are already familiar with Macintosh operation, here are the quick steps:

1. Start your Macintosh with the **Install 1** diskette in the floppy disk drive. The Installer opens automatically.
2. When the Installer finishes inspecting your system, click OK.
3. In the Installer window, click on Install.
4. Keep the system disks handy, because the Installer will prompt you to insert various disks during the installation process, which may take several minutes.
5. When the Installer has finished, **Quit** the Installer program.
6. Restart your Macintosh for the new system s software to take effect.

Always keep your system disks in a safe place. There may be need in the future to re-install some or part of the system software. You may also want to copy some other files from those disks to your hard disk, as described on page 160.

System Software vs. DOS and Windows

If you have come to the Macintosh after using an IBM Personal Computer or compatible, you may wonder what the difference is between **DOS** (Disk Operating System) and the Macintosh's system software (sometimes referred to as MacOS, for Macintosh Operating System—not precisely accurate).

A DOS computer has its core operating system in **ROM,** just like the Macintosh does. On the DOS side, that ROM software is called the **ROM BIOS** (Basic Input/Output System). The DOS `command.com` file is analogous to the Mac's System File and a small part of the Finder, although certainly not up to the same level of ease of use (for most people, a `C>` prompt doesn't compare favorably to the Macintosh desktop).

Microsoft Windows, on the other hand, is an additional layer on top of DOS. Windows is analogous to the Finder. The underlying difference between Windows and the Finder is that the Macintosh system software (and hardware, for that matter) was designed for the **graphical user interface** from the very beginning. Windows, on the other hand, is a graphical façade in front of a difficult-to-use disk operating system.

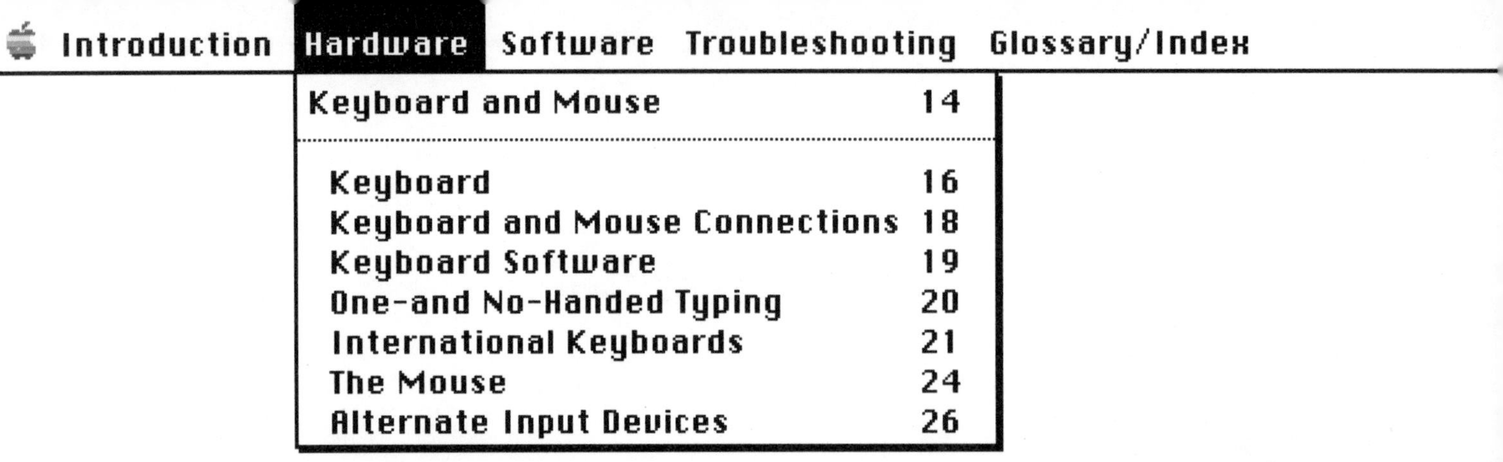
Introduction
Hardware
Software
Troubleshooting
Glossary/Index
Keyboard and Mouse 14
Keyboard 16
Keyboard and Mouse Connections 18
Keyboard Software 19
One-and No-Handed Typing 20
International Keyboards 21
The Mouse 24
Alternate Input Devices 26

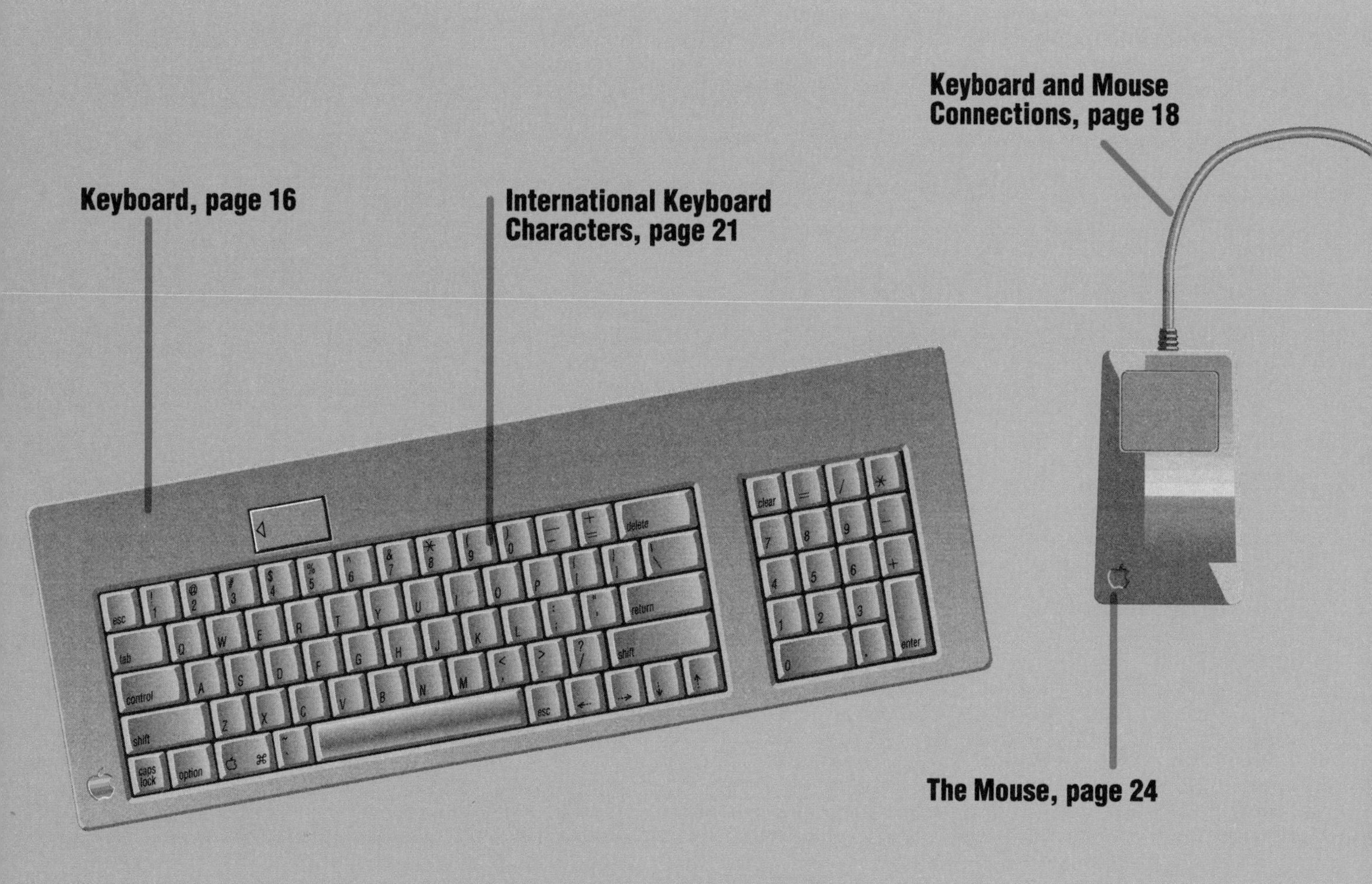
Keyboard and Mouse
Connections, page 18
Keyboard, page 16
International Keyboard
Characters, page 21
The Mouse, page 24

Apple offers Macintosh users two styles of keyboard: the Apple Keyboard or the Apple Extended Keyboard.

The Macintosh Classic and LC computers come with their own versions of the Apple Keyboard (just a few special key locations are different), and all Macintosh portable computers have built in keyboards with even fewer keys.

In addition to standard typewriter-like keys, all keyboards have special purpose keys (e.g., *escape* and *control*), which are often needed for accessing other computers and on-line services via a telephone **modem** ➔174. Other keys, like *option* and *command,* help you access menu commands and other choices from the keyboard.

Apple Keyboard

The Apple Keyboard features a standard alphanumeric character, typewriter-style layout for the language of the country in which the Macintosh was purchased. Additional keys include four **cursor keys** at the lower right of the main bank of keys and a **numeric keypad,** which makes rapid entry of numeric information (in spreadsheets, for example) more like working with a calculator keyboard.

The keyboard supplied with the Macintosh Classic and LC models has a different layout for several special function keys more closely resembling those of corresponding keys on the **Apple Extended Keyboard.** This is scheduled to become the standard Apple keyboard.

Tab

While this key is used often to align columns in tables and letters, the *tab* key also jumps between editable fields from top-left to bottom-right in save and open dialog boxes. Pressing *shift-tab* jumps to editable fields in the reverse direction.

Option

As a second modifier key (in addition to the *command* key), the *option* key on the Macintosh keyboard is used primarily to type additional characters beyond the letters, numbers, and punctuation characters you see on the typewriter keyboard. Foreign language letters and some symbols are available by holding down the *option* key while pressing one of the typewriter keys. The **Key Caps desk accessory** ➔76 shows you what *option* key combinations create the various symbols in each font. The *option* key is sometimes represented by the symbol

Cursor Keys

While the mouse is the device that controls the freewheeling pointer on the screen, the **cursor keys** often control a text insertion pointer ➔97 which shows you where the next character you type appears on the screen. In a spreadsheet program, the cursor keys usually control the movement of the active cell marker. Not all programs respond to the cursor keys, nor is their action consistent across all applications (e.g., some programs allow you to press the *command* key along with a left arrow key to shift the text cursor to the left in word increments).

Apple Extended Keyboard

Taking up much more room on the physical desktop, the Extended Keyboard is designed around the keyboards used in IBM Personal Computers and compatibles—the so-called **AT-style keyboard**, named after the IBM PC AT model. In addition to the typewriter and numeric keypads, the Extended Keyboard features fifteen **function keys,** a series of six **navigation keys,** and four cursor keys in an inverted "T" arrangement. Not all software programs utilize these extra keys, but for those that do, the keys often present a multitude of keyboard shortcuts for **pull-down menu** items and document navigation.

Caps Lock

This push-on/push-off key puts all letter keys into all **capital letters.** Numbers and punctuation symbols are not changed to their shifted equivalents, however. Therefore, you can type letters in all capital letters, but still have the period key produce a period, instead of its shifted character, ">". The regular *shift* key is often represented in print or menus with the symbol ⇧.

Control

The *control* key also had its start on telecommunications keyboards. While on-line, you press *control* and another character as a means of sending a command (instead of sending the character). On communications terminal screens, the *control* character appears as a caret symbol, as in ^C for *control-C.* IBM PC programs make frequent use of the *control* key, but few Macintosh programs do.

Command (⌘)

The two symbols on this key (and ⌘) differ only in the computer for which they are intended. The **Apple symbol** (technically, an "Open Apple," because the figure is not filled in black) applies when these keyboards are used with an Apple IIGS (which accepts an ADB keyboard). The curlicue symbol is the Macintosh equivalent. The most common application for this key is in concert with another key to issue a **pull-down menu** command. When a menu item has this symbol and another character at the right, it means that you can invoke this menu command by pressing the *command* key and that other key. Therefore, *command-P* (⌘-P) is the keyboard way of printing a document in most programs. The *command, option,* and *Shift* keys are called **modifier keys.**

Escape

Some telecommunications services require that the user press an *escape* key, a throwback to the old teletype machines. IBM PC software frequently uses the *escape* key as the equivalent of a **Cancel** command.

Macintosh Keyboard Evolution

You may wonder why there are so many keys, especially on the Extended Keyboard, that aren't used by Macintosh software, yet there are some keys, like *option* and *command*, that do the same things *alt* and *control* do on the PC keyboard. Two factors play a role in this mystery:

1. the Macintosh was designed to be something completely different than a PC; and
2. to be accepted by large companies and government, the Macintosh had to look more like a PC.

Function Keys

Labeled *F1* through *F15*, the **function keys** sometimes provide one-key alternatives to menu commands. This depends primarily on the software, but menu commands that virtually every program have in common—*undo*, *cut*, *copy*, and *paste*—are represented by function keys *F1* through *F4*. **Macro utility programs** (e.g., Tempo and QuickKeys) also allow you to assign these function keys (or *command*-key combinations) to an otherwise long series of mouse clicks and keystrokes ➔27.

Insert/Help

The need for an insert key is practically nil in Macintosh software, but it was necessary in early PC software (when inserting text required going into the insert mode). On the Macintosh this key also has the Help legend on it. Most applications programs navigate to on-line help when you press this key.

Print Screen and Pause

Also holdovers from the PC keyboard, these keys are rarely programmed into Macintosh software. They were used to print the current screen and pause any operating system operation (including printing the screen). Macintosh system software has different facilities for capturing screens ➔35.

Power On

A push-once key with the left-facing triangle is the power key (Macintosh II and Quadra models only). It appears in different locations and in different sizes on each keyboard. Pressing the key again once the computer is on does not turn off the computer— it has no effect.

Indicator Lights

Each of the three indicator lights of the Extended Keyboard is supposed to alert you to the status of the keyboard with respect to the software that is running. The **Caps Lock** light, which goes on when you push the *caps lock key* , is independent of any application program. *num lock* is a carryover from the PC-style keyboard, because the keys on the numeric keypad also acted as cursor keys—*num lock* set the keys to work as a numeric keypad only. On the Macintosh keyboard, however, *num lock* and *scroll lock* rely entirely on the program, but their conditions may be misleading. Starting up Microsoft Excel, for example, turns on the *num lock* light automatically. But if you switch to a program like Microsoft Word running at the same time, the light stays on, even though Word does not believe that *num lock* is on.

Home, End, Page Up, Page Down

The behavior of these four **document navigation keys** depends entirely on how the program's designers envisioned them (if the keys were programmed at all). Sometimes *home* takes you to the beginning of the document, or it just moves the cursor to the beginning of the first line visible on the screen. **Paging** also means different things to different programmers, but most often it corresponds to the action of clicking the cursor in the grey portion of a vertical scroll bar ➔102. Programs that fully support these navigation keys usually include multiple possibilities with the help of modifier keys like *option* or *command*. Consult your software manuals for how the programs react to these keys.

Delete vs. del

The *delete* key on all Macintosh keyboards typically deletes a character to the left of the text insertion pointer (or erases an entire selection), as the pointer shifts to the left (this action used to be called *backspace-delete*). The *del* key, however, is another holdover from the old PC days, but one you may use in some programs. This version of delete erases characters to the right of the stationary text insertion pointer. Most word processing programs have instructed the *del* key to work this way.

Enter

At the far right of the numeric keypad is the *enter* key. In most programs, the *enter* key differs from the *return* key in that the *enter* key does not move the text pointer or spreadsheet cell pointer to the next field or cell. In some **database programs**, the Enter key is the action key that stores the current screenful of information to the database file on the disk, while the *return* key inserts carriage returns (new lines) into a scrolling field on the screen. Since the response to this key is not consistent across applications, check with each program's manual for details on its precise operation.

The keyboard that shipped with the original Macintosh was spartan, to say the least. Even a numeric keypad was an option. The keyboard had the typewriter keys, plus an *option* and *command* key. That was it. Only after many complaints and wish lists from early Macintosh owners (who had migrated from the PC world) did cursor keys make it onto the Macintosh Plus keyboard two years later.

Real problems came, however, when Apple sought acceptance in the business and government world, where the IBM PC was the dominant machine. Specifications for computer purchases were usually couched in terms that applied strictly to PCs and their clones. Keyboards needed not only cursor keys, but also a *control* key to work when linked to other computers. IBM PC AT-style keyboards were the norm, with their function keys (especially when tied to mainframe computers that expected function keys on the terminal keyboard), navigation keys, and the *control-alt-delete* key sequence to restart the machine. With the Extended Keyboard, Apple

All Macintosh models since the Macintosh SE connect both the keyboard and mouse through the Apple Desktop Bus (ADB) connector on the rear panel.

Some Macintoshes have two ADB connectors while others have just one. Macintosh keyboards have two ADB connectors, allowing you to plug the mouse into the keyboard, and then the keyboard into the Macintosh. How you connect the keyboard and mouse cables depends a lot upon the physical setup of your Macintosh, and whether you are right- or left-handed.

Right-Handed Setup

Arrange the keyboard cable so that it plugs into the ADB port on the Macintosh rear panel (either one if your machine has two), and connects to the left port on the keyboard. Plug the mouse into the right port on the keyboard. Stow the excess mouse cable behind the keyboard.

Two-Port Strategy

If your Macintosh is set up close to your keyboard and mouse, and the machine has two ADB ports, you can plug the keyboard into one port and the mouse into the other.

Left-Handed Setup

Arrange the keyboard cable so that it plugs into the ADB port on the Macintosh rear panel (either one if your machine has two), and connects to the right port on the keyboard. Plug the mouse into the left port on the keyboard. Stow the excess mouse cable behind the keyboard.

Connector Warning

Although some of Apple's hardware manuals indicate that plugging and unplugging the keyboard and mouse on the ADB while the Macintosh is on does no harm, prudence should lead you the other way. Avoid connecting or disconnecting ADB (or any port's) cables while the power is on.

Cross-Port Strategy

To prevent the mouse cable from flopping about the desk, some users connect the mouse to the keyboard port opposite the location of the mouse—the left keyboard port for right-handed people. This works well, unless you occasionally sit back in your chair and pull the keyboard to your lap. In that situation, you want as much play in the mouse cable as possible.

It Spilled!

Spilling liquids on the keyboard is a serious problem. If it happens to you, avoid using the keyboard at all, and immediately shut down the Macintosh. Disconnect the keyboard, turn it upside down, and shake vigorously to get as much liquid out of the keyboard as possible. Sticky liquids, including syrupy carbonated drinks and fruit juices, may cause substantial problems that require cleaning by a service technician. Water, however, should just be allowed to air dry for about 12 hours before you try using the keyboard.

Apple Desktop Bus

A "bus" in computer lingo is like an electronic highway. A connection to the bus is like a highway interchange: it can be anywhere along the highway. Most ADB devices, like the Macintosh keyboards, have two ADB connectors on them, which allows other ADB devices to be connected to the Macintosh through the device. The mouse, however, has a single ADB connector.

The ADB was designed for low-speed input devices, such as **keyboards**, **mice**, **graphics tablets**, **light pens**, and **touch screens**. While the intelligence behind the ADB can accommodate up to 16 devices, Apple recommends a maximum of three in a single string of connected devices. This means a maximum of six devices on Macintoshes with two ADB ports.

Not many peripherals have been designed for the ADB. Recently, however, some hardware designers have been finding other uses for the ADB, including powering telephone **modems** and even output devices.

ADB Extensions

If you're having trouble locating an extension cable for your ADB keyboard or other device, check a well-stocked video store. New generations of VCRs and televisions have an additional connector for what is called S-Video, a high quality video signal. **S-Video** cables have the same connectors and wiring as ADB extension cables. Just remember that the maximum allowable length of an ADB chain is

When the Keyboard and Mouse Freeze

Keyboard cables on actively used Macintosh systems can become fragile. In some instances, you may encounter what appears to be a frozen Macintosh—neither the keyboard nor mouse seems alive. If this is the case even after restarting the computer, it is likely that the keyboard and/or mouse connection has gone flakey. Turn off the Macintosh, jiggle the cables and connectors at the keyboard, and turn on the Macintosh again. If that fixes the problem, and it occurs frequently, you

Two user-accessible pieces of Macintosh system software apply directly to the keyboard.

The **Keyboard control panel** lets you select which keyboard version (i.e., the country and language) to use as well as items that appear to reflect the physical response of the keyboard: the key **repeat rate** and the **delay** until a key repeats.

Key Caps is a desk accessory that shows you the character or symbol that you get when pressing all key combinations, including those in concert with **modifier keys.** You can use Key Caps as an on-screen reference to find the keyboard combination for an infrequently-used symbol.

Keyboard

To access the **Keyboard** control panel, choose **Control Panels** from the menu. This action opens a window showing the contents of the **Control Panels** folder (which is nested inside the System Folder). Double-click the icon or file named Keyboard. The **Keyboard** control panel is divided into three sections.

Key Repeat Rate

Controls how fast a character key you hold down types the character. Of the five possible radio button settings, the one just before the fastest is a time-tested favorite.

Delay Until Repeat

This controls how long it takes for the character key you press to begin repeating at whatever speed you indicated in the **Key Repeat Rate** section. Setting the **delay** too short causes slow typists to produce double and triple characters. You may turn off the repeat feature entirely by clicking the **Off** selection in this part of the control panel.

Multiple Keyboards

Chances are, your Macintosh System software comes with a single keyboard resource ➜ 84 tailored for the country in which the Macintosh is sold. But if you have installed **multiple keyboard resources** ➜ 100, you may need to select the resource to match the keyboard and language of choice.

All Keyboard control panel settings are preserved in **Parameter RAM** ➜41 so they are remembered when you turn off your Macintosh.

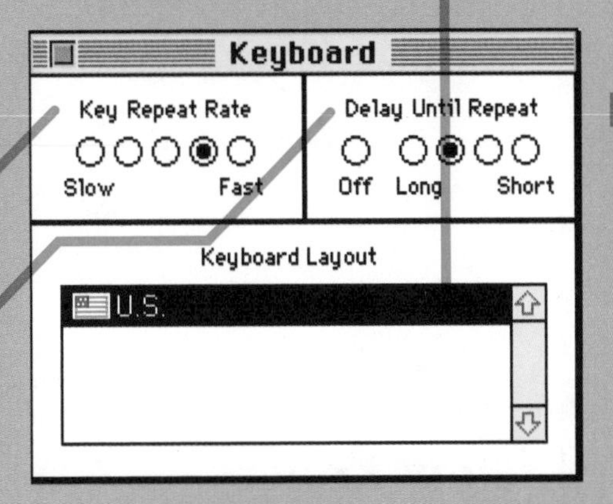

Key Caps

Choosing **Key Caps** from the menu starts this desk accessory, recognizable by the keyboard diagram in the resulting window and the **Key Caps** menu in the menubar.

As you press any key, it highlights on the keyboard diagram, and the character appears in the accessory's one-line window. If you hold down one or more **modifier keys,** such as the *shift* or *option* keys (or both), you see the other character and symbol possibilities (see U.S. character table on page ➜22). When vowels need accent marks, they usually require pressing two keys, called a **dead-key** and a **completer** (below).

Not all fonts have all the same characters. Some fonts include only graphic symbols. Key Caps offers a map to any **font,** but you must select the desired font from the **Key Caps** menu.

To capture symbols, you can type them (and any other characters) into the Key Caps field, select the text, and copy it to the clipboard ➜79, 108. Then open your document and paste the results. Importantly, you do not need Key Caps to type special characters—the same key sequences you use in Key Caps work when typing into a text field or document (try the *option-8* bullet).

Dead Keys and Completers

When you hold down the *option* key while viewing the Key Caps window, in most fonts you see several keys highlighted with a grey outline. These are called dead-keys, because by themselves they produce no character. They require the press of another character key to generate the accent or other vowel mark indicated on the key cap. If you type (or click) a **dead-key** in Key Caps, the display changes once more, with heavy black outlines surrounding the characters to which the dead-key applies. These keys are called **completers,** because they complete the two-key sequence. You even see

The Easy Access control panel offers two utilities that enable physically challenged people to use the Macintosh keyboard (and mouse with the help of Mouse Keys, **➔25****): Sticky Keys and Slow Keys.**

To display Easy Access, choose **Control Panels** from the menu, and then double-click the Easy Access icon or file listing.

On/Off Audio

Each item in Easy Access may be turned on by various keyboard combinations instead of requiring the control panel window. With this top checkbox checked, you hear a whistle to signify whether a feature is turned on (whistle pitch goes up) or off (whistle pitch goes down).

Slow Keys

Designed for those users who may type with an unsteady touch or by way of a stylus, the Slow Keys control lets you set how long you hold down a key before it actually registers as a pressed key. Therefore, if you aim for one key and accidentally touch an adjacent key momentarily, only the key you hold down for a second or two (depending on the **Acceptance Delay** setting in the control panel) registers as a typed key. Check the **Beep** checkbox if you like audio feedback each time a key registers.

Sticky Keys

You can type two-key combinations without two hands when Sticky Keys is on. Turn on Sticky Keys either via the Easy Access control panel or by pressing the *shift* key **five** times in a row (at no particular speed or interval, but without moving the mouse at all). A small icon appears at the far right of the menubar.

When you press a modifier key *(option, command, shift, control)*, an arrow appears in the icon, indicating that a modifier key is pending. Press the second key in the sequence to effect the two-key combination.

By pressing a modifier key twice, the icon fills with black, indicating that the modifier key is locked down, so you can do a series of modified key combinations by just typing the second keys. This latter operation can get confusing if you press more than one modifier key. If you keep the **Key Caps** desk accessory running, however, you can see by the key's highlight which ones are locked.

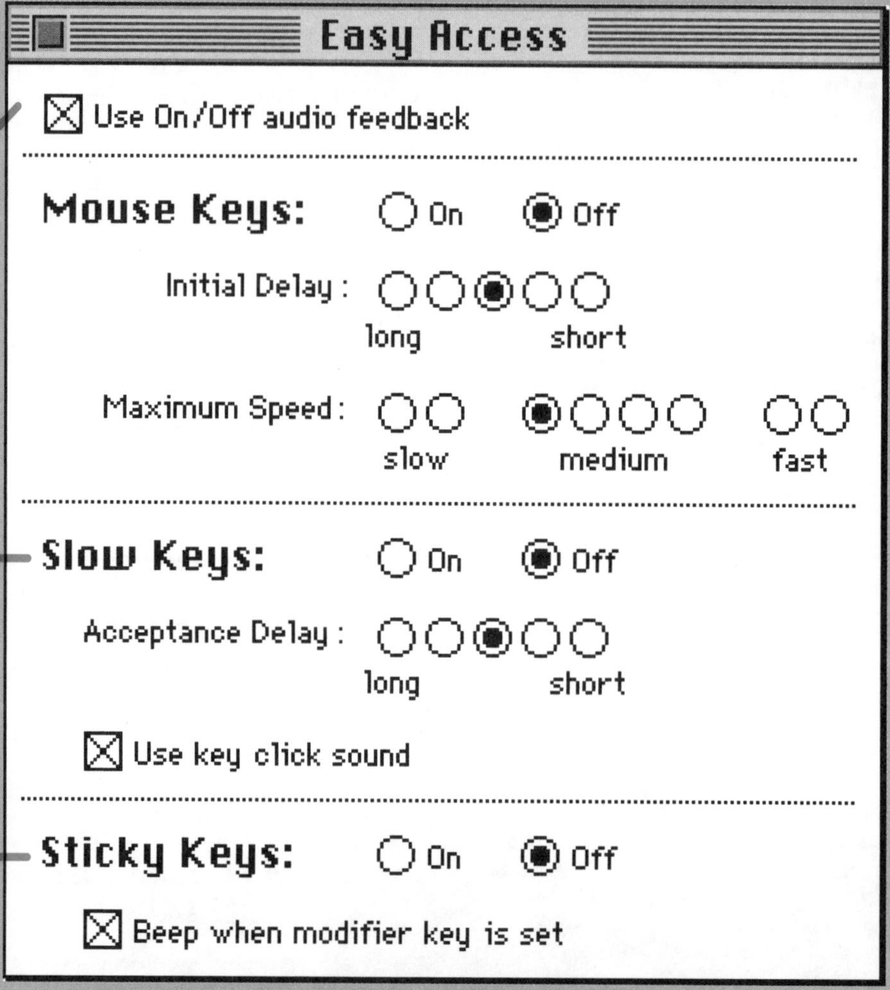

Easy Access

☒ Use On/Off audio feedback

Mouse Keys: ○ On ◉ Off

Initial Delay: ○ ○ ◉ ○ ○ long short

Maximum Speed: ○ ○ ◉ ○ ○ ○ ○ ○ slow medium fast

Slow Keys: ○ On ◉ Off

Acceptance Delay: ○ ○ ◉ ○ ○ long short

☒ Use key click sound

Sticky Keys: ○ On ◉ Off

☒ Beep when modifier key is set

Sticky Keys on

Modifier Key Pending

Modifier Key Locked

International Keyboards and Characters

Multilingual Macintosh users may purchase keyboards in dozens of languages. Even within the Roman languages, key layouts vary widely from language to language.

In addition to the physical keyboard, the Macintosh also needs one or two pieces of **system software** to recognize and utilize that new keyboard. All keyboards must have a **keyboard resource** (which is contained in the System File). And if the language of the additional keyboard is in a different language type than the machine's native language (Arabic instead of Roman, for example), then an installer program copies the required script resource to the System.

Most Roman language symbols can be created with a U.S. keyboard. You may use the **Key Caps desk accessory** to locate a symbol, or look up the keyboard combination in the table on the following two pages.

Installing an Alternate Keyboard

Physically, there is no difference in the connection of a foreign language keyboard. All Macintosh keyboards are ADB devices, and should be connected according to the way you work best ➔18. Moreover, if you need to switch frequently between keyboards, you might consider leaving multiple keyboards in the ADB chain, instead of disconnecting and reconnecting keyboards all the time.

The keyboard should be accompanied by a disk containing an **installer**. Use it to move all appropriate files (some of which you won't ever see, but are required for using the foreign keyboard) to your **System Folder.**

Changing Keyboards

With multiple keyboard resources in your **System File**, an additional menu appears between the **Help** and **Application** menu symbols at the right edge of the menubar. The **Keyboard** menu displays an icon that represents the currently selected keyboard. Pull down the menu to see all keyboards recognized by the system software. The menu listing is just like the list that appears in the **Keyboard control panel device** ➔19, but gives you quicker access to changing keyboards or character sets. Choose any item in the **Keyboard** menu to change to that keyboard, or change keyboards via the Keyboard control panel.

Of Scripts and Keyboards

The graphical nature of the Macintosh lends itself very well to being programmed to work with characters of non-Roman alphabets. As the Macintosh has matured, its international language abilities have improved so that dozens of languages now have their own Macintosh system software.

One of the internal mechanisms that makes alternate alphabets work on the Macintosh is called the **Script Manager.** In Macintosh programming parlance, a script is a writing system, each with its own alphabet and text direction. The Roman script, for example, is the one used for the English language. It includes a set of less than 256 characters and a text direction of left to right, top to bottom. The Cyrillic (Russian) script has a different set of characters but the same text direction. An ideographic script, like Japanese Kanji, can have thousands of characters, and requires more keystrokes and computer code to represent a single character. Some languages allow writing to go in two directions (one for the main language, like Hebrew's right-to-left, but accommodations for the insertion of foreign words from left-to-right languages). Still others, like Arabic and other Eastern languages, have characters whose shapes change depending on the adjacent characters (this is called a contextual script system).

As early as 1992, System 7 still didn't exist for non-Roman system versions.

Fortunately, most of the hard work has already been done by the Apple system software wizards. They have empowered the Macintosh to let you switch between a simple Roman and contextual Bengali script environment by switching keyboards and choosing a menu item. This is a breakthrough in personal computing that goes little noticed in the Roman script world.

Non-U.S. Roman Characters

If you have a U.S. Macintosh, the typewriter keys are those of the alphabet, numbers, and common punctuation. The character sets of most fonts, however, also include characters from other Roman languages, plus a few useful symbols. To type those characters, use the key combinations listed in the table, below.

Special fonts, such as the Symbol font that comes with the System software or the Zapf Dingbats font that comes with some LaserWriter printers, can provide letters from other languages and a variety of symbols not in the basic Macintosh character set.

Character	Keyboard Sequence	Note
Ä	*option-U; A*	
Å	*option-shift-A*	Usually tallest letter in a font
Ç	*option-shift-C*	
É	*option-E; E*	
Ñ	*option-N; N*	
Ö	*option-U; O*	
Ü	*option-U; U*	
á	*option-E; A*	
à	*option-~; A*	
â	*option-I; A*	
ä	*option-U; A*	
ã	*option-N; A*	
å	*option-A*	
ç	*option-C*	
é	*option-E; E*	
è	*option-~; E*	
ê	*option-I; E*	
ë	*option-u; E*	
í	*option-E; I*	
ì	*option-~; I*	
î	*option-I; I*	
ï	*option-U; I*	
ñ	*option-M; N*	

Character	Keyboard Sequence	Note
ó	*option-E; O*	
ò	*option-~; O*	
ô	*option-I; o*	
ö	*option-U; O*	
õ	*option-N; O*	
ú	*option-E; u*	
ù	*option-~; U*	
û	*option-I; U*	
ü	*option-U; U*	
†	*option-T*	
°	*option-shift-8*	Degree symbol
¢	*option-4*	
£	*option-3*	British Pound Sterling
§	*option-6*	
•	*option-8*	Bullet
¶	*option-7*	
ß	*option-S*	
®	*option-R*	Registered Trademark
©	*option-G*	Copyright
™	*option-2*	Trademark
´	*option-shift-E*	
¨	*option-shift-U*	
≠	*option-=*	Not Equals

Character	Keyboard Sequence	Note
Æ	*option-shift-'*	(Apostrophe key)
Ø	*option-shift-O*	(Letter "O" key)
∞	*option-5*	
±	*option-shift-=*	Plus or Minus
≤	*option-,*	(Comma key)
≥	*option-.*	(Period key)
¥	*option-Y*	Japanese Yen
µ	*option-M*	
∂	*option-D*	
∑	*option-W*	
∏	*option-shift-P*	
π	*option-P*	
∫	*option-B*	
ª	*option-G*	
º	*option-0*	(Zero key)
Ω	*option-Z*	
æ	*option-'*	(Apostrophe key)
ø	*option-shift-/*	
¿	*option-1*	
¡	*option-L*	Letter "l" key)
¬	*option-V*	
√	*option-F*	
ƒ	*option-X*	

A few common Macintosh symbols are also available in the TrueType Chicago font with the following keyboard sequences:

Character	Keyboard Sequence	Note
⌘	*control-Q*	
✓	*control-R*	
◆	*control-S*	
	control-T	
	control-P	
⌥	*option-control-shift-A*	(not 12 point)
⇧	*option-control-shift-D*	(not 12 point)

Character	Keyboard Sequence	Note
∆	*option-J*	
«	*option-*	(Backslash key)
»	*option-shift-*	
…	*option-;*	(Semicolon key)
	option-spacebar	Hard space
À	*option-~; A*	
Ã	*option-N; A*	
Õ	*option-N; O*	(Letter "O" key)
Œ	*option-shift-Q*	
œ	*option-Q*	
–	*option--*	En dash (Hyphen key)
—	*option-shift--*	Em dash (Hyphen key)
"	*option-[*	Left curly quote
"	*option-shift-[*	Right curly quote
'	*option-]*	Left curly apostrophe
'	*option-shift-]*	Right curly apostrophe
÷	*option-/*	
◊	*option-shift-V*	
ÿ	*option-U; Y*	
Ÿ	*option-shift; Y*	
¤	*option-shift-2*	
‹	*option-shift-3*	
›	*option-shift-4*	

Character	Keyboard Sequence	Note
ﬁ	*option-shift-5*	
ﬂ	*option-shift-6*	
‡	*option-shift-7*	
·	*option-H*	
‚	*option-shift-0*	(Number zero key)
„	*option-shift-W*	
‰	*option-shift-R*	
Â	*option-shift-M*	
Ê	*option-I; E*	
Á	*option-shift-Y*	
Ë	*option-U; E*	
È	*option-~; E*	
Í	*option-shift-S*	
Î	*option-shift-D*	
Ï	*option-shift-F*	
Ì	*option-~; I*	
Ó	*option-shift-H*	
Ô	*option-shift-J*	
	option-shift-K	
Ò	*option-shift-L*	
Ú	*option-shift-;*	(Semicolon key)
Û	*option-I; U*	
Ù	*option-E; U*	

Character	Keyboard Sequence	Note
ı	*option-shift-1*	
ˆ	*option-shift-I*	
˜	*option-shift-N*	
¯	*option-shift-,*	(Comma key)
˘	*option-shift-.*	(Period key)
˙	*option-H*	
˚	*option-J*	
¸	*option-shift-Z*	
˝	*option-shift-G*	
˛	*option-shift-X*	
ˇ	*option-shift-T*	

All desktop Macintosh computers come with a one-button mouse. You roll (drag) the mouse around the table to control the on-screen pointer.

Pressing (clicking) the mouse button indicates a deliberate action on your part. It may activate an icon or let you pull down a menu while you both hold down the button and move the mouse. Portable Macintoshes provide built-in trackballs, which operate on the same principles, except that your hand moves the ball.

With the mouse connected to the ADB port ➔ 9, the system software gets in the act. The **Mouse control panel** lets you adjust how the Macintosh responds to your physical action with the mouse.

Inside the Mouse

Although very lightweight, the mouse is more complex inside than it may seem. Since you need to access part of the mouse's insides for cleaning, you can remove the mouse ball to get a peek at the internal mechanism. As the mouse ball rotates, it drives two metal rollers (a single plastic roller is also there to stabilize the ball). Those rollers are connected to two small wheels that have slits in them. As the wheels spin in response to mouse ball motion, optical detectors measure the speed at which light from a tiny lamp flashes through the slits. By calculating those speeds from both wheels at once, the mouse and Macintosh can figure out exactly in what free flowing direction and at what speed you are moving the mouse along the table.

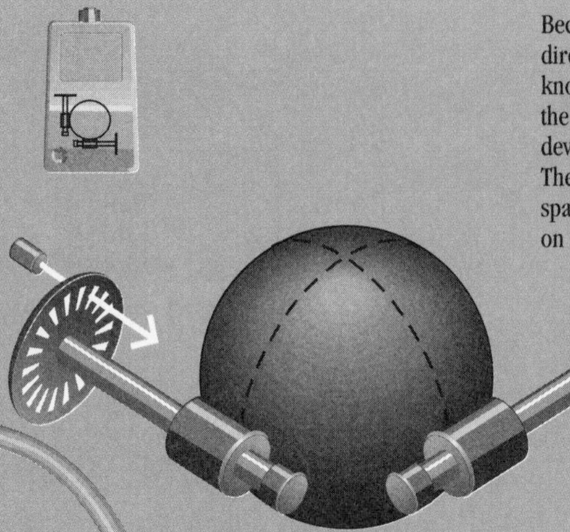

Because the mouse tells the Macintosh only which direction and how fast it's going, the mouse doesn't know anything about the location of the pointer on the screen. It is said to be a **relative-motion** device, independent of the physical screen space. Therefore, you may occasionally run out of desk space before the cursor has reached its destination on the screen. If so, you can pick up the mouse and position it elsewhere on your work table to give you enough space to continue the cursor's journey.

If the mouse rolls as if it has a flat tire, it needs cleaning.

Opening the Mouse

1. Turn the mouse over so that the ball is facing you, and the cable runs up and away from you.
2. Notice the plastic ring around the ball. Older style rings have a flat tab-like feature pointed at about the 2 o'clock position. Just beyond this ring is a plastic rim molded into the mouse case. The two letters debossed into the rim stand for Open and Lock. In normal use, the ring tab should point to the Lock position. Newer style rings do not rotate, as described in the next two steps. Instead, the ring slides out (away from the mouse cable).
3. Hold the mouse with both hands so that your humbs are on the ring, on either side of the ball.
4. Maneuver the ring counter-clockwise until the tab is beneath the Open mark.
5. With one hand under the mouse, turn the mouse over and catch the ring and ball.

To replace the ball later:

1. Drop the ball into the hole.
2. If your mouse ring is the rotating type, position it so that the tab is facing the Open mark.
3. Use the two-handed method to rotate the ring clockwise until the tab is at the Lock position. For newer rings, push the ring into its socket toward the mouse cable until it snaps into place.

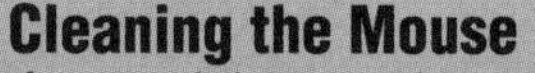

Cleaning the Mouse

If you're a daily Macintosh user, it's a good idea to clean the mouse every few months. In particular should make sure the rollers are clean and free to roll.

Once you've opened the mouse, examine the two metal rollers. If they aren't shiny, dip the end of a cotton swab into isopropyl alcohol (or drip some cassette tape cleaning fluid on an end) until the swab is moist (not dripping). Wipe the metal rollers with the swab until the rollers are clean. Use a dry swab to wipe up any leftover liquid.

If dogs or cats share your workspace, it is very important to look for hair that has wrapped itself around the axles of the wheels. If there is some there, use tweezers to pick it off until it is all removed. Left unchecked, the hair can lock up the rollers.

Before reinserting the ball (which you should wipe with a dry, lint-free cloth), make sure your mouth is dry, close your eyes, and blow strongly into the opening for the mouse ball a couple times. This will help dislodge dust that accumulates in the mouse case.

As an important input device, the mouse should be kept in good condition. Regular cleaning is highly recommended.

Mouse Control Panel

System software gives you the control over how the Macintosh responds to your mouse motions. Choose **Control Panel** from the menu, and double click the **Mouse control panel** icon. In the Mouse control panel are two settings: Mouse Tracking and Double-Click Speed.

Mouse Tracking controls how the pointer responds to fast mouse movement. The Very Slow setting, shown beneath the graphic tablet icon, offers linear response. The speed of the pointer is directly proportional to the speed you move the mouse around the table. When you choose any of the other settings, the pointer will move faster in response to a faster mouse movement. The faster the setting, the greater the distance the pointer travels as you whisk the mouse around the table. Either of the middle two settings is recommended, although if you have a very large video monitor, you may prefer the fastest setting. Whichever setting you choose, you still have precise **pixel**-by-pixel control ➔ 30 when moving the mouse slowly.

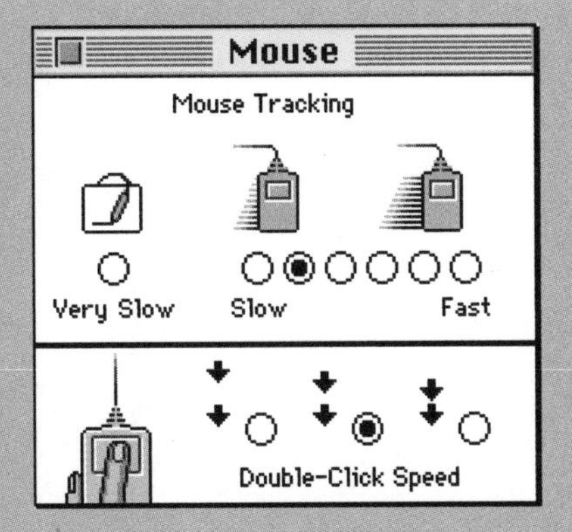

Double-Click Speed controls the time between clicks that the Macintosh recognizes as a double click ➔ 126 of the mouse button. Unless you have a physical disability that prevents rapid double clicking of the mouse button, the fastest double click speed (the one with the arrows closest together) is desirable. When the double click speed is set too slow, you can easily click once on a file icon and then click again to drag it—but the Macintosh interprets those two clicks as a double-click motion to open the document.

If You Can't Use a Mouse

Macintosh System software includes a control panel called **Easy Access,** which includes settings for those Macintosh users who cannot use a mouse due to a physical disability (or perhaps your mouse is broken or missing and you must access the machine). The Easy Access utility called **Mouse Keys** lets you work the on-screen pointer by way of the numeric keypad.

You can turn on **Mouse Keys** either via the **Easy Access** control panel (although you need the mouse for that) or by typing *command-shift-clear.* The *clear* key is the upper left corner of the numeric keypad. If the control panel is set to its default mode, you hear a rising whistle when Mouse Keys goes on. The same keyboard sequence turns off Mouse Keys, and the whistle sound starts high and

MouseKeys is great if you need precision dragging of graphics but your mouse hand isn't too steady.

The control panel settings allow you to adjust how quickly the pointer should start moving after you press one of the numeric keys and how fast the pointer should go the longer you hold down the key. As you become more familiar with the Macintosh operation, you will probably want to set the delay shorter and the speed faster.

Refer to the figure to see which way the pointer moves on the screen when you press the numeric keys. The **middle key (5)** is the Mouse Keys substitute for the mouse button. You may press it once or twice for single or double clicks. If you need to make a selection (either along a line of text or a group of icons), you need to click and drag. To replicate this action, move the pointer to the starting position and press the zero key. That plants the mouse button while you move the pointer with the numeric keys. A press of the period key (next to the zero), releases the mouse button, leaving the selection intact for your next action.

It's easiest to use menus by positioning the pointer atop the menu and then pressing the *0* (zero) key to hold the menu open. Hold down the *2* key to move the pointer to the desired menu item, then press the **Period key** to select it.

The **graphical user interface,** which at first glance, could be an impediment to handicapped usage, can be overcome with clever software design.

The keyboard is not the only way to put information into the Macintosh, nor the mouse the only way to control the cursor.

Existing printed graphics, including color, can be copied to a Macintosh file by way of a **scanner.** The same scanner, with the help of **optical character recognition** (OCR) software, can convert printed text into characters you can edit in word processing or page layout documents.

The most common mouse alternative is the trackball—standard equipment on portable Macintoshes. When drawing graphics is the task, a **digitizing pad** lets you use an electronic pencil, called a **stylus,** as a more natural way to control the cursor on the screen.

Scanners

A scanner is actually one half of a photocopy machine—the part that bounces light off a document and converts the image to a series of very fine dots. Scanners that are intended for use with personal computers put these dots into a format that can be saved as a graphics file. With a graphics program, you can then open the file and either edit the dots or copy the image (or any section of it) to another document, perhaps to have some text wrap around it on a newsletter page.

The most common style of scanner is the **flat-bed scanner,** like the Apple OneScanner (although handheld scanners, which cannot scan full pages easily, are attractive for their comparatively low cost). When you lift the hinged lid, you see a glass plate, just like in a photocopy machine. Place the printed material face down on the glass, and then instruct the scanner software on the Macintosh to scan the page. Software that comes with the scanner gives you many options as to scanning **resolution** (how many dots per inch you want the file to be saved as), **contrast** between light and dark areas, and other settings. Trial and error is the primary way to master the software, but you can usually save settings for a particular kind of source material, and reuse those settings later for similar material.

Scanners connect to the Macintosh via the **SCSI port** ➔ 8, 58. They also require a driver file (for the Extensions folder) that is compatible with the system software version running on your Macintosh.

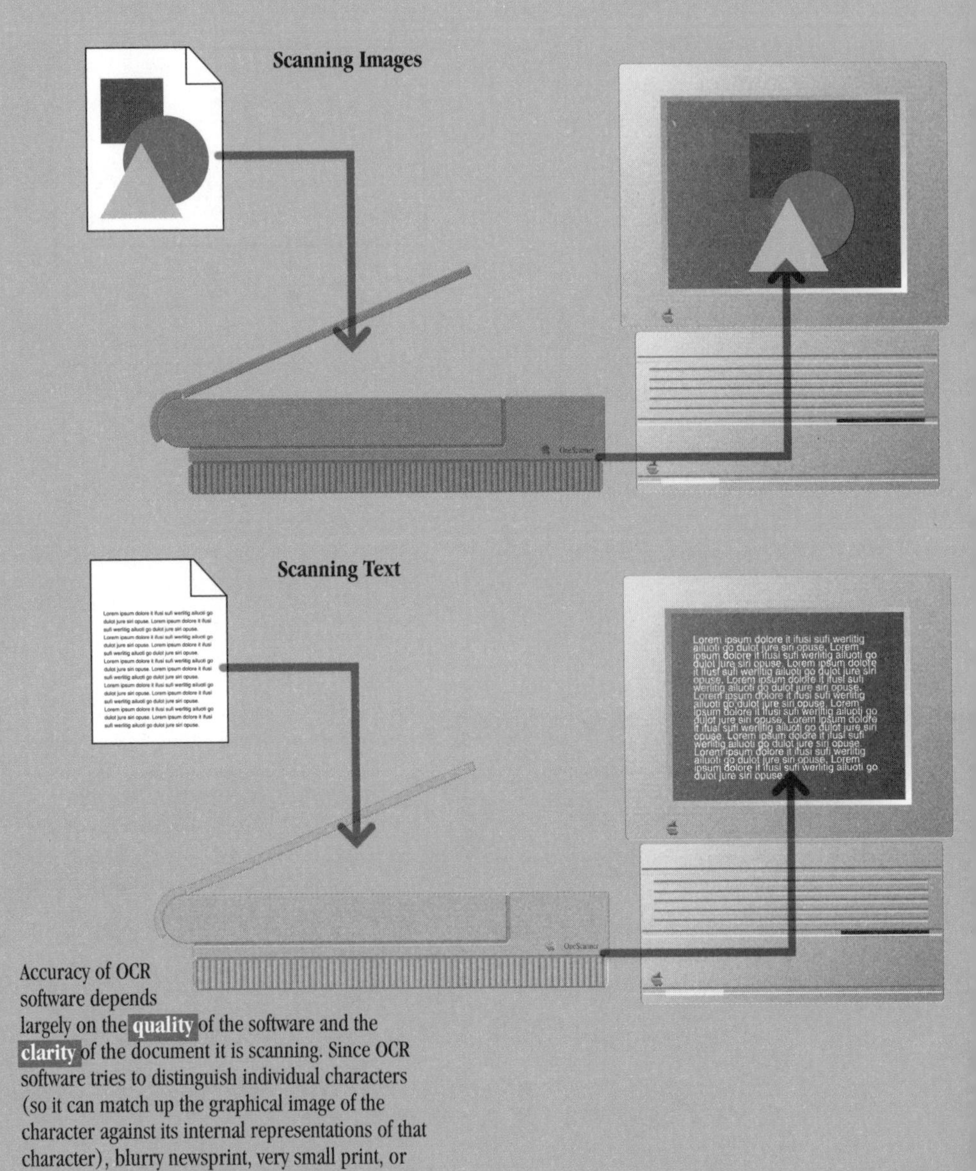

OCR

In combination with a scanner, **optical character recognition** (OCR) software is a practical alternative to retyping existing printed text into the Macintosh. To scan a document, lay it face down on the scanner glass, and then instruct the OCR software to scan the page. Each OCR software program treats the next steps differently, but the basic procedure is to select from a miniature representation of the page area(s) you wish the software to convert to text characters. When the conversion is complete, you see the text in a text editing window, which you can save to a disk file (often in a word processing program format).

Accuracy of OCR software depends largely on the **quality** of the software and the **clarity** of the document it is scanning. Since OCR software tries to distinguish individual characters (so it can match up the graphical image of the character against its internal representations of that character), blurry newsprint, very small print, or very light print may be difficult to decipher. Once in the editing window, however, you can touch up the text manually before saving it to a disk file. With crisp source material (e.g., a laser printed business letter), accuracy approaches 100 percent.

Mouse Alternatives

The mouse is not for everyone or for every situation. Users of some graphics programs, for example, prefer a **trackball** to the mouse. A trackball is like an inverted mouse, where the ball faces up. As you roll your hand around the ball, both it and the screen pointer move. Most trackballs come with either a single button below the ball, a button on either side of the ball, or a button above and below the ball. All of these arrangements allow left- and right-handed people to use the trackball with equal ease.

Another mouse substitute found on some portable versions of the Macintosh is called the **IsoPoint™.** This device is a horizontal roller installed on the keyboard just below the space bar. The roller has both vertical and horizontal movement, giving you free space control over the pointer. To activate the equivalent of a mouse button, you press down on the entire roller. It may take getting used to, but it is very space efficient in cramped working quarters.

Touch pads can also take the place of mechanical devices. A touch pad responds to your finger, dragging the screen pointer around with the movement of your finger on the pad. To replicate the click of the mouse button, you press firmly on the pad at any location.

Some users in the computer-aided design (CAD) and graphic arts fields prefer to use a **graphics tablet** (also called a digitizing tablet or just digitizer) to a mouse—or in conjunction with a mouse. For many artists, it is more natural to draw with a pen or **stylus** than with a mouse. A digitizer consists of a large drawing area similar to a mouse pad with electronic sensors underneath. A stylus, connected by wire to the tablet, controls the cursor on screen as it comes into contact with, and is dragged around, the tablet. A button on the stylus replicates the mouse button for clicking actions. As an ADB device, a digitizer may be kept in line with the mouse so the user can switch between input devices as the task requires.

Keyboard Macros

A few third-party software products allow you to combine dozens of keystrokes and mouse actions into a single keystroke or combination. These programs (Tempo and QuickKeys are the most popular) record the series of steps you take for automated playback at a later time. Such keystroke and mouse reductions are called **macros**. You can even teach a macro to make rudimentary decisions that cause a process to take a particular path if certain conditions are met. Typical applications of macros automate frequent and tedious processes, such as switching printers in the Chooser or typing the closing lines of a business letter.

Additional macro programming power is available in software systems such as Frontier. A full **scripting language** allows proficient Macintosh users to write and edit macros that link applications together and perform Finder operations.

FKeys

Macintosh System software reserves a series of special key sequences for **function key** resources. The name does not refer to the function keys of the Extended Keyboard, but just to a way of typing a command as a shortcut. Key combinations for these functions require the *command* key, the *shift* key, and any of the numerals across the top row of keys.

The resource for the programming code that performs the function key action is known by its four-letter name, **FKEY**. Consequently, utility programs that are triggered by these *command-shift*-<Number> commands are commonly called FKeys (EFF-keys). The most popular FKey built into the Macintosh is *command-shift-3,* which takes a snapshot of the current screen, and saves the image to a graphic image file. 35

Earlier in Macintosh history, many programmers developed FKeys, and distributed them widely via user groups and bulletin board systems. Today, while **desk accessories** and small standalone applications tend to be the norm, a few FKeys are still around, such as enhancements to the built-in snapshot function or one that toggles between two user-controlled color monitor settings (so the user doesn't have to go through the **Monitors** control

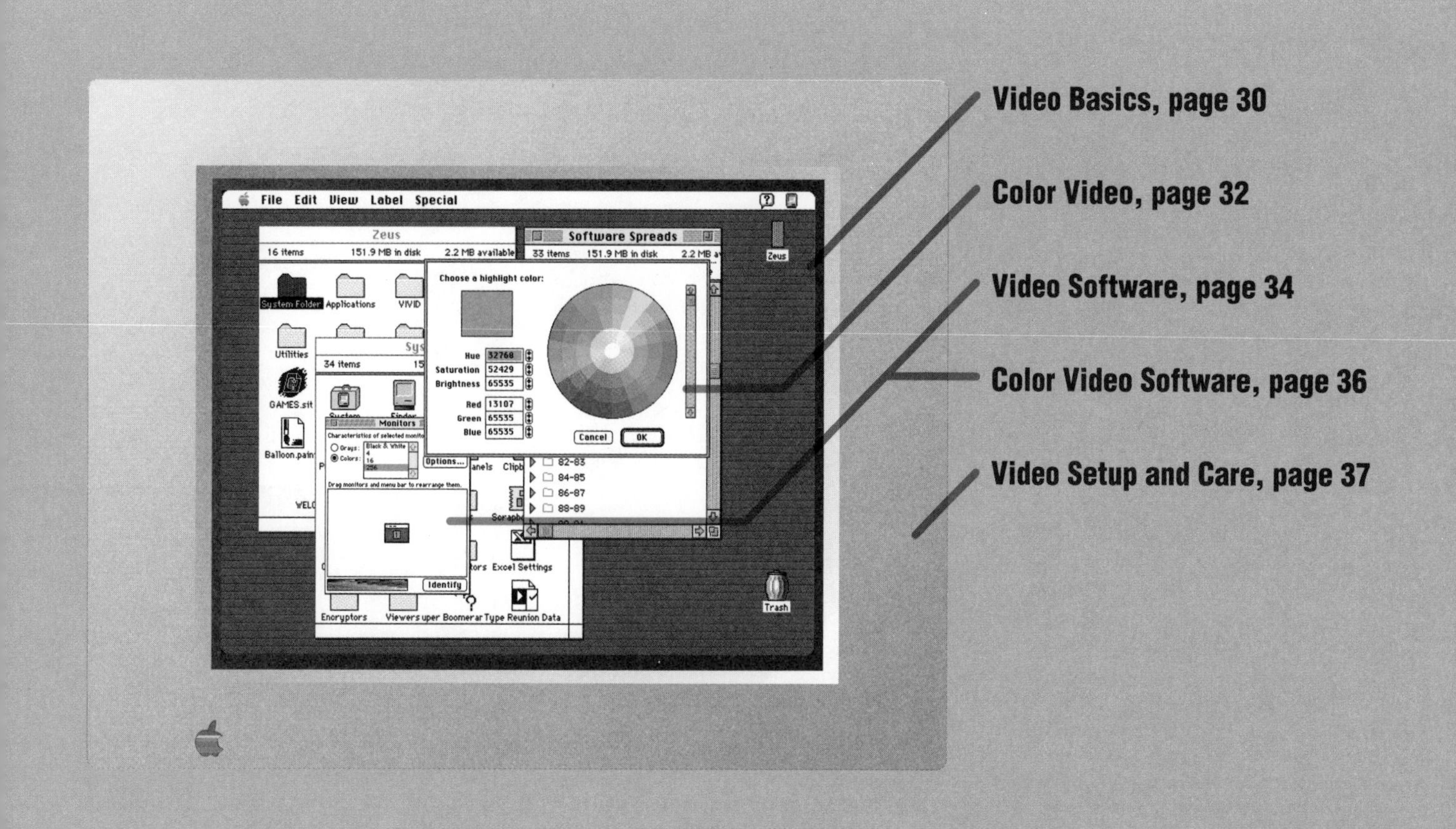
Video Basics, page 30
Color Video, page 32
Video Software, page 34
Color Video Software, page 36
Video Setup and Care, page 37
File Edit View Label Special
Zeus
Software Spreads
Choose a highlight color:
Hue
Saturation
Brightness
Red
Green
Blue
Cancel
OK
Monitors
Identify
Trash

Anything you see on a video monitor is the result of a combination of black, white, gray, or color spots on the screen.

Each spot is called a picture element, or pixel for short. The Macintosh display's inherent crispness is largely due to the square pixels it presents to the screen. Unlike rounded pixels of other computer monitors (pre-VGA on IBM PC-style computers, for example), square pixels fully abut each other, producing clean lines between black and white.

Choosing a video monitor presents many choices, which are couched in a flurry of jargon. Understanding the terminology is more than half the battle. The rest is up to your own personal taste about the quality of a display.

Video Support

Some Macintosh models include the built-in electronics necessary to drive separate video monitors—up to a point. Even the powerful Quadra models provide only 256 colors (instead of millions) for 21" monitors ➔41. When video is "built-in," a video port is provided for plugging the video cable from the monitor directly into the back panel of the computer ➔8-9. Connecting a monitor beyond the capabilities of internal video support, however, requires an optional video circuit board which has been engineered specifically for your Macintosh model or model family (e.g., all six-slot Macintosh II computers, such as the Macintosh IIfx). Macintoshes without built-in video absolutely require a plug-in video board before you may connect any video monitor.

Resolution

Often misused, resolution simply denotes the density of pixels on the screen. The common measure among Macintosh screens is dots per inch (dpi), with one dot representing one square pixel. The Macintosh standard is 72 dpi—that's 5184 pixels in a square inch—to correspond to the typesetting convention of 72 points per inch (a point is a printer's measure of 1/72 inch). The size and proportion of what you see on the screen is very close to what prints on paper.

Monitors that offer higher resolution actually shrink familiar elements on the screen. For example, the Macintosh generates a menubar that is 20 pixels tall. At 72 dpi, that comes to about 0.28 inches tall; at 80 dpi, the menubar is only 0.25 inches tall. At 80 dpi, menu wording and icons may be difficult to read at viewing distances considered comfortable for large monitors. Such monitors sometimes come with extra software that enlarges the menubar, but not other elements, such as document text and Finder icons.

Video Tube Size

Macintosh monitors come in many different video (cathode ray) tube sizes. Compact Macs have a 9" **diagonal measure**. Apple also produces monitors at 12", 13", 19", and 21" horizontally oriented (landscape) screens, plus a vertically oriented monitor called a portrait display. Third-party producers offer monitors in these and other sizes. But because the resolution (pixel density) varies from model to model, the size of the tube is not directly proportional to the number of pixels you can see on the screen.

Pixel Grid

The number of screen pixels, measured as the number of pixels horizontally by the number of pixels vertically, is an important consideration when matching a monitor to the type of work you do on the Macintosh. The smallest grid is the internal compact Macintosh screen, which displays 512-by-342 pixels. As we went to press, the largest available pixel grid was 1664-by-1200 on a monitor that allows software adjustment to view 120 dots per inch (the menubar in that mode is a mere 0.167 inches tall).

Portrait displays typically show one full page of U.S. letter size documents, with a grid of 640-by-870. Monitors claiming to be two-page monitors (in the 1152-by-870 pixel range) usually allow you to see most (but not all) of a two-page spread of, say, a newsletter in a desktop publishing program. The larger your monitor's pixel grid, the easier will be your navigating through large spreadsheets, desktop publishing documents, and multiple windows from different programs open at the same time.

Display	Pixel Grid
Classic	512 x 342
12" Color	512 x 384
PowerBook	640 x 400
12" Monochrome	640 x 480
13" Color	640 x 480
Portrait	640 x 870
16" Color	832 x 624
21" Color	1152 x 870

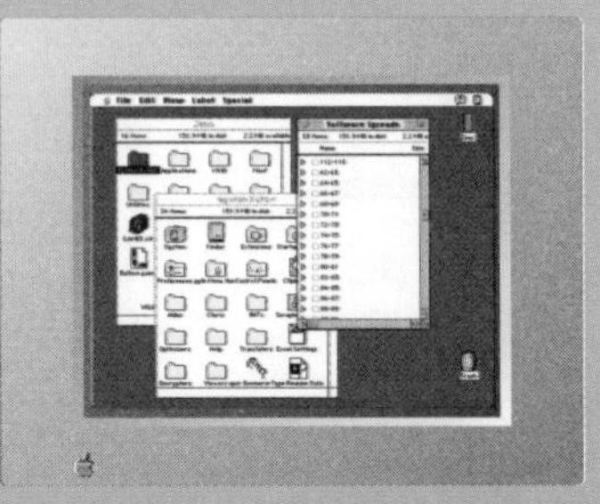

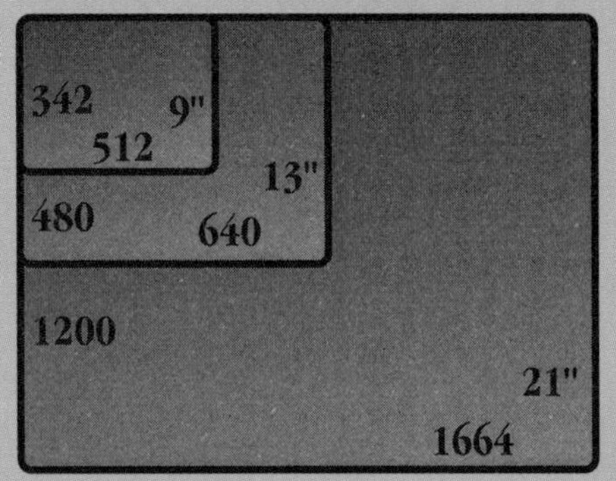

Refresh Rate

Video screens are painted (refreshed) by an electron beam dozens of times each second. The faster the refresh rate, the less likely your eye will be able to detect the constant refreshing and decay, which makes it look like the screen flickers. You must also be sure that on larger monitors, the screen's refresh rate is faster than surrounding fluorescent lighting, which flickers at 60 times per second (60 hertz). The two refresh rates may interfere with each other, causing significant screen flicker. Flicker is often subtle, but can become mentally tiring and a cause of eye strain and headaches. Refresh rates of 70 hertz or more on two-page monitors have proven to be adequate.

Persistence

Related to flicker is the **persistence** of the phosphor coating inside the video tube. Persistence refers to the length of time it takes for the phosphor to turn from its activated white state to its quiet black state. The longer the persistence, the less likely you will see flicker, because a pixel doesn't have enough time to dim before it is again refreshed in the next pass.

The downside to high persistence is that moving objects exhibit what are called **ghosts.** A black cursor, for example, appears to leave a momentary trail as you drag it across the screen.

Contrast

A comparison between the blackest black and the whitest white is how **contrast** of a monitor is measured. Higher contrast makes images stand out much better. As with brightness, no absolute standards of measurement are available in monitor specifications.

Focus

The larger the tube size, the more difficult it is for the monitor's internal circuitry to maintain good **focus** across the entire screen. On a monochrome monitor, single-pixel width black lines should be sharp and crisp no matter where you draw them on the screen. Watch out especially for out-of-focus **corners** and edges. If the entire screen is equally out of focus, this can be adjusted internally by a technician. Color monitors ➔ 32-33 tend to be a bit fuzzier because of the way they display pixels.

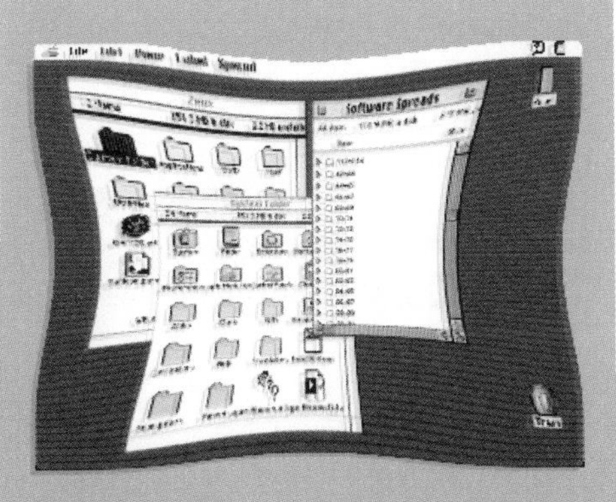

Distortion

Look carefully at the overall rectangle of the active area of the screen. Signs of **distortion** include a left-to-right narrowing of the rectangle in the middle of the screen (called **pincushioning**). Beware of one or more corners that bow out. The larger the monitor, the more difficult it is to eradicate distortion along the edges. If the entire rectangle is tilted slightly with respect to the plastic bezel of the monitor, it means that the yoke on the neck of the tube is out of adjustment, and can be easily repaired by a technician.

WARNING! There are extremely high voltages and currents running around the back of a video tube, even long after the monitor has been unplugged. Don't poke around there unless you know exactly what you're doing.

Glare

Primarily a function of ambient lighting and the texture of the video tube's front face, **glare** can be a headache- and fatigue-inducing byproduct of working with a video monitor for long stretches. Many monitors have an etched face plate, which helps reduce harsh reflections of light sources behind you. The more etching on the tube, however, the fuzzier will be the picture, since the etching also diffuses the light going from the tube to your eye. A slightly etched monitor and an **adjustable monitor stand** ➔4 can avoid most glare.

Getting a dealer to agree to this won't be easy.

Brightness

A monitor's **brightness** is a measure of how much light it emits when turned up full blast. The brighter your working environment (e.g., lots of windows or overhead lights), the brighter you'll want your monitor to be. Although this factor is rarely listed in a monitor's specifications, it is important to try to test out a monitor in your working environment before committing to it.

Jumpiness

If you see a monitor's picture rapidly jumping vertically or exhibiting a swaying motion, look for a source of electromagnetic radiation coming from a nearby device. The most common source of problems are the black **power transformers** you plug into a power strip near the monitor. The Macintosh's fan, a second video monitor, or other peripherals adjacent to the monitor can electrically interfere with the electron beam on its way to the tube's face plate (after all, magnetic fields in the coils around the tube's neck direct the beam in the first place). Try moving the potential source of magnetic field interference further from the affected monitor (six inches of more). In severe cases with large monitors, the solution requires that the monitor be plugged into a separate power outlet from the rest of the computer gear.

Phosphor Color

An issue with large monochrome displays is the tint of the phosphor on the inside of the video tube. Which color to choose is a matter of personal taste, but the range can be from nearly white to an inoffensive light blue (common to the Apple-brand and built-in displays) to an almost cream color.

Color Specifications

For color monitors, an additional set of criteria play roles in choosing a monitor. See page ➔32 for details.

Monochrome vs. Grayscale

There is a significant distinction between a **monochrome** (i.e., single color—white against the normal black) and **grayscale** monitor, which at first glance also appears to be black-and-white. In a monochrome monitor, a **pixel** is either on or off, white or black. In a grayscale monitor, a pixel is completely off, completely on, or a number of intermediate brightnesses in between—the shades of gray between black and white. In a sense, they are both monochrome, because they produce only one color—white. The grayscale monitor, however, can produce varying intensities of white to each pixel.

The number of shades of gray depends on the amount of memory associated with the video driving circuitry. You'll rarely encounter a grayscale monitor that offers fewer than 16 shades of gray. With a full complement of **video RAM** ➔ 41, however, 256 shades is easily attainable on most Macintoshes with an external grayscale monitor (color monitors can also double as grayscale monitors by turning off the color on the **Monitors** control panel, ➔ 34, 81). At 256 shades of gray, your graphics software can portray photo-realistic images.

Please don't write to tell me that white isn't a color.

Color adds life to Macintosh video. Even in the Finder, you can color code folders and other icons according to your muse.

In documents, application of color may range from **spot color** (like a red bar on a chart) to display of a photographic image converted to its electronic equivalent. Moreover, a color Macintosh can even display **motion video** images from a disk file thanks to the **QuickTime** system software extension 33.

While some Macintosh models include built-in circuitry to support a small color monitor for run-of-the-mill color (you simply attach the monitor to the Macintosh's rear panel, 8-9, you will need an extra accelerated **video circuit board** to use achieve photo-realistic color on video monitors.

Bits vs. Colors

Two fundamental (and often confused) terms in the color video world are **bits** and colors. A bit is also computer terminology for the smallest piece of information that a computer handles. A bit is either on or off, one or zero, black or white, or any other method you choose to denote two distinctly different states. The more bits you string together into a unit, the more combinations of ones and zeros can occur within that unit. For example, two bits together offer four possible combinations (00, 01, 10, and 11). If you let each combination of bits in a group represent a color value, then the more bits you bundle together, the greater the number of colors a bundle can represent.

Here's a table showing the number of bits and colors possible in Macintosh systems:

Bits	Colors	Comment
1	2	Basic monochrome display (e.g., built in 9-inch compact Macintosh or portable LCD).
2	4	Not often used, but possible on all color and grayscale Macintosh monitors.
4	16	Fine for spot color; uses very little video RAM.
8	256	Most common Macintosh II color mode; With color turned off, produces photorealistic black-and-white images.
16	65,536	Often available as faster. less RAM-hungry choice for 24 bit color monitors.
24	16,777,216	True color, viewable on the Apple High Resolution Color monitor and dozens of larger third-party monitors, requires special plug-in video board on most Macintoshes.

There's quite a jump to 24-bit color in both what you get and what you have to pay (except for Quadras, which can display millions of colors on the 13" RGB monitor by filling out its on-board video RAM 41). Twenty-four bit video boards capable of driving two-page monitors are available primarily for the Macintosh II family, and can cost almost as much as a large monitor (a couple thousand dollars).

A color screen also takes longer to refresh. For each pixel on the screen, more bits of information need to course through the Mac's veins and arteries. Two-page true color screen refreshing taxes even the fastest Macintosh.

Then What's 32-bit QuickDraw?

Even though the highest quality image is in the 24-bit color range, you may be confused by the term **32-bit QuickDraw.** QuickDraw is a large set of behind-the-scenes programs (most in the Macintosh ROM, 42) that directs how images are displayed on any Macintosh screen. For high quality color images, QuickDraw handles information in 32-bit bundles. Of those 32 bits, up to 24 can be used for color information. The remaining 8 go either unused or may include extra data about the color that only a particular software program stores. As far as the number of colors is concerned, 24-bit color and 32-bit color both produce the same photo-realistic 16,777,216 colors. System 7 includes 32-bit QuickDraw, so you don't actually know it's there until you plug in a 24-bit color video board.

Macintosh and Television

Strong interest in linking the Macintosh to television pictures has helped produce a wide variety of add-on products. They fall into three categories of things you might wish to do with video, with some of the add-in boards capable of more than one of these tasks.

First is **capturing** a frozen video picture, like taking a snapshot of a broadcast so you can store it on your hard disk and display it later (perhaps to work it into a slide-show type presentation). Devices that do this are called **frame grabbers** or **video digitizers,** and may be either standalone boxes (connecting to the SCSI port 8) or plug-in boards (nuBus) for Macintosh II style computers. New **electronic still cameras** (which store their pictures on small floppy disks) may also be used to capture a shot for conversion into a color graphical file.

Second is the ability to display live motion video on the Macintosh screen. Apple has established a multimedia standard called **QuickTime** which allows video and animation material to be compressed on disk and played back through any color Macintosh without expensive hardware

Finally is the desire to send what you see on the Macintosh screen on a television monitor. Perhaps the monitor is a projection television so you can let a roomful of people see your screen. Or perhaps you just want the video output to go directly to a VCR to capture your screen actions in a software training video. Solutions to the former may mean the addition of a plug-in board, while the latter often requires nothing more than a cable (prepared by a video-knowledgable technician with access to the ***Guide to the Macintosh Family Hardware,***

If you try to aim a **video camera** at a Macintosh monitor for the purpose of recording the screen images, beware of two items. First, the quality will not be good. The fine images of the Macintosh display will be fuzzy on the resulting recording. Secondly, the differences in refresh rates between your Macintosh monitor and the broadcast video standard will cause the recorded screen to have a recurring line rolling from bottom to top, even though the image is clean when you look at it live. Solving this visual interference requires a video board capable of **genlocking** The board synchronizes the refresh rates of the Macintosh and recording camera video signals.

In this rapidly moving corner of the Macintosh market, it is strongly advisable to keep a regular watch on developments via magazines

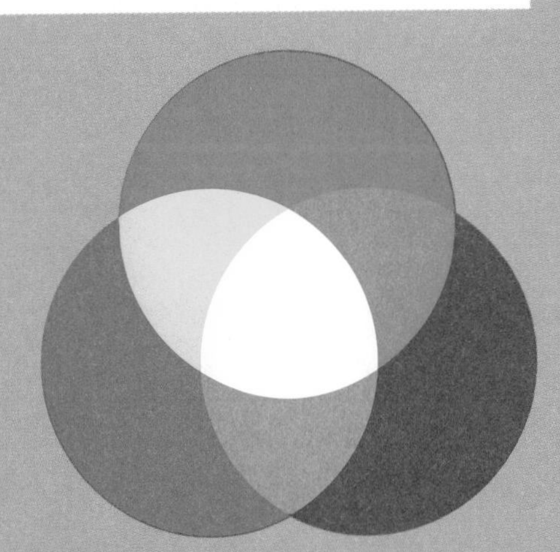

How Color Works

Color displays are more expensive than monochrome displays because they are much more complex devices.

It helps to know that each **pixel** on the screen is comprised of a mixture of three colors—***red, green,*** and ***blue***. In a color picture tube, a colorless **electron beam** representing each of those colors is directed to the phosphor inside the face where three colored phosphor spots are at each pixel location. The electron beam representing the red color is aimed precisely at the red phosphor spot at each pixel location while the green and blue beams reach their respective phosphor spots. Our eyes, in turn, see the blending of three color intensities at that spot as a particular color. The **Color Wheel** dialog box in the **Color** control panel ➜36, 80 allows you to choose from all available colors at your current color setting (in the **Monitors** control panel, ➜34, 81) by adjusting the intensity of the red, green, and blue beams.

Convergence

In addition to the specifications that apply to all Macintosh video monitors ➜ 30-31, one of the most obvious factors of a quality color video monitor is **convergence** — how well the three electron beams converge on a single spot. When convergence is perfect, a grid of single-pixel-wide white lines across the entire monitor is, indeed, all white, even upon very close inspection. On larger monitors, good convergence is difficult to achieve, especially at the edges of the screen. Poor convergence results in a distinct colored line appearing on one side of the white line.

Color Monitor Adjustments

Most large color monitors offer user access to a number of controls that allow you to correct misalignments that may occur when a monitor is jostled. Before making any adjustments, however, write down the settings of the various controls. That way, in case you get everything completely out of whack, you can return to the original settings and start over.

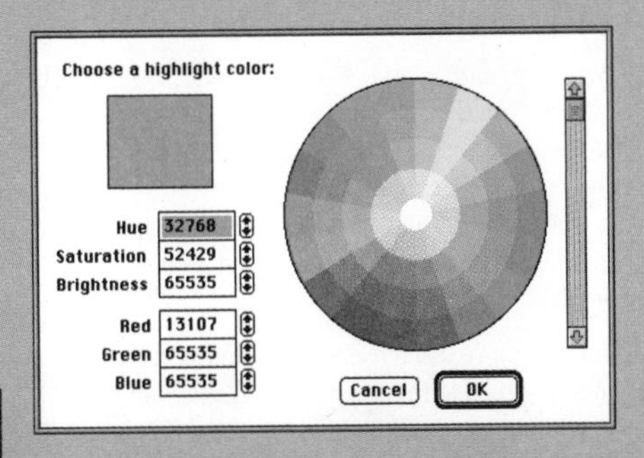

Faster Color

The high cost of a 24-bit large color monitor and video board will be wasted without a QuickDraw **accelerator**, circuitry that is optimized for refreshing 24-bit color screens without weighing down the Macintosh's own computing circuitry. Some 24-bit color boards come with an accelerator built in (or as a plug-in option). An unaccelerated 24-bit board may be sufficient for a 13-inch color monitor, but it's definitely too slow on big screen displays (on which it can take a full minute to refresh without acceleration).

If your current hardware setup is too slow when displaying color images, you can speed up the process by choosing a lower color level from the **Monitors** control panel ➜34, 81. In the tradeoff, however, you lose picture quality. For spot color, you may hardly notice the difference. Also be sure you have System 7-compatible extension software for your color video board and accelerator.

Color Calibration

If you work calls for close color matching to a printed result, you should investigate a **color calibration system.** Radius, RasterOps, and Tektronix, for example, offer different systems that perform software adjustments to the colors that appear on the screen. Work is underway to help desktop publishing programs display **Pantone colors** on screen that come close to the actual printed output. A perfect match, however, may be very difficult to achieve.

CAD Accelerators

Computer Aided Design (CAD) programs have special requirements of their own when it comes to displaying objects (color or not) on a large screen. These programs tend to store information about objects as long lists of vectors—lines containing various properties. A QuickDraw accelerator is of little value to this kind of drawing. Instead, some **CAD** software companies offer special accelerator boards tailored to their software products.

What About VGA Monitors?

A common standard among IBM PC-compatible computers is the **VGA display.** While significantly improved over earlier graphics standards on PCs (the CGA and EGA standards), the VGA is still inferior to the Macintosh quality. Cables are available, however, that let you connect Apple-brand **video cards** and built-in video connectors to various VGA monitors. Be sure, however, that you have the correct cable specific for your video card or built-in video system (e.g., the original Macintosh II High-Resolution Display Video Card has different

Macintosh system software comes with several video related modules.

These control the number of colors or shades of gray we view on a monitor, what the highlight color is, and how multiple monitors connected at the same time should behave.

Not so obvious is the software that lets you grab a snapshot of the current screen. And for those who have a hard time seeing the Macintosh screen, a special control panel enlarges images on the screen.

Monitors Control Panel

Any Macintosh that is connected to an external video monitor has access to the **Monitors** control panel. With a single external monitor capable of displaying colors or grayscale 31, the Monitors control panel allows you to adjust the number of colors or gray levels to be displayed on the monitor. The choices available to you depend on the video circuitry and video memory in your Macintosh 41. To change the level, or to change between monochrome and color (a color monitor can display both color and grayscale), simply click once on the button or color/gray number in the list. The screen characteristics change instantly. Notice, particularly, the rectangular area at the bottom center of the control panel. This area displays the colors or shades of gray available at the current setting. The difference between 256 and millions of colors (if you have a 24-bit color video setup 32) is subtle—the visible dividing lines between shades disappear.

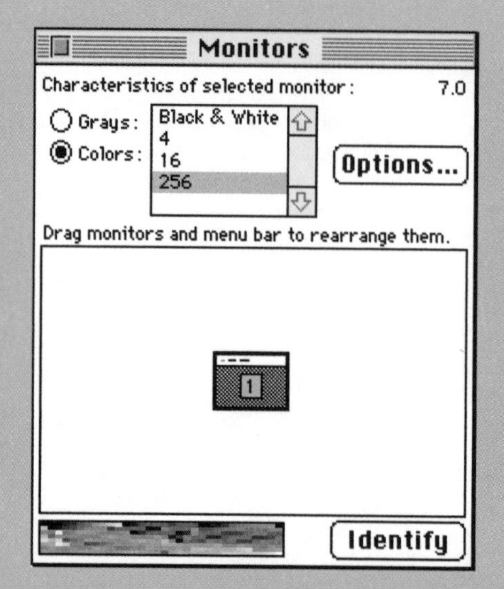

Nerd fun! Click and hold the "7.0" to see the control panel's authors. Then press the option key. Press the key 10 more times and watch the Blue Meanies (System 7 engineers) invade with each successive press.

Controlling Multiple Monitors

The Monitors control panel is also the panel that controls the behavior of multiple monitors connected to a Macintosh. If two monitors are connected, the control panel displays the two screens and their proportionate sizes. The numbers (1, 2, etc.) are simply for identification purposes, and do not indicate that one is the "main" monitor (the number order is determined by the location of video circuitry for each monitor).

The locations of the mini screens represent how the monitors view the one huge virtual screen space of the Macintosh. For example, if the two mini-monitors are shown next to each other with the small screen centered on the left and the large screen centered on the right, as you drag the cursor on the small screen to the right along the center of the actual screen, the cursor reappears at the left center of the right-hand screen. Although not essential, it is advisable to arrange the mini screens in the same orientation as the physical screens in your workspace. This does not mean that the

Before organizing your monitors, think about which monitor you'd like to be the "main" monitor—the one that has the menubar, trash, and disk icons at startup. Color or grayscale icons are more pleasant to view, so you may wish to designate a monitor that is not a strictly monochrome display as the main monitor.

In case you're using two monitors of the same size, you may need to identify which physical monitor is which mini screen in the control panel. Click and hold Identify in the control panel. The identification number from the miniscreens show as large block numbers on the physical screens. Drag the miniscreens (by their middles) to adjust locations relative each other. They automatically snap to the side of a nearby monitor—thus your cursor won't wind up in an invisible valley between two screen spaces.

To make a monitor the main monitor, drag the tiny menubar to the desired mini screen. This change won't take affect until the next time you restart your Macintosh.

Options... in the **Monitors** control panel leads to another dialog box, which varies widely with the type of video card and monitor you are using. Some monitors and video cards allow for allocating video RAM, adjusting gamma correction, screen saving delay times and other adjustments. Simple video cards display just their circuitry identification in this **Monitor Options** dialog, with no user adjustments.

Speaking of restarting, you may also adjust which monitor is to display the startup screen. With the Monitors control panel on the screen, hold down the *option* key. A small Macintosh smiley face icon appears in one of the mini screens. With the *option* key held down, you may drag the icon to the monitor in which you want the startup screen to appear. For example, if you have a colorful startup screen, you can have it appear in a color monitor, while the menubar and disk icons appear in a two-page monochrome display.

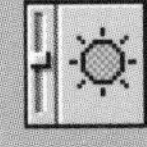

Brightness Control Panel

The built-in monochrome screens of the Macintosh Classics have no brightness control knobs, like the other compact Macintoshes before them. Brightness is controlled entirely by software—the **Brightness control panel.** A simple slider-type control lets you adjust brightness electronically. With the control panel showing, click and drag on the slider control to the left and right to see immediate changes to the monitor's brightness. Release the mouse button when brightness is set to the desired level.

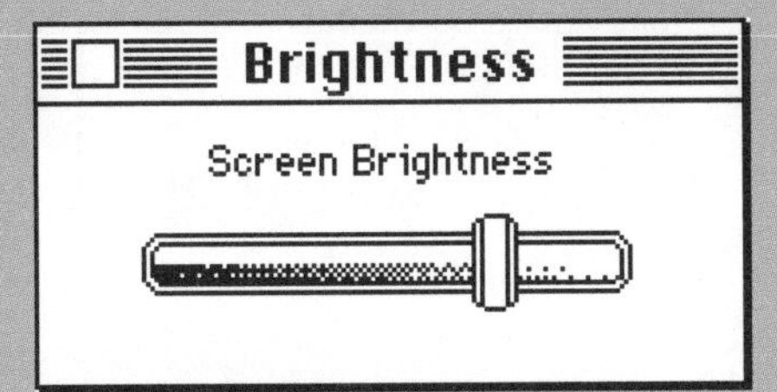

Losing the Cursor

When using multiple monitors, it is easy to temporarily lose sight of the **cursor** as it shifts between monitors. The cursor won't disappear entirely—it is always visible in one of the monitors. The smaller the shared border between mini screens, the less chance of the cursor slipping into the other monitor (it just "bumps" into the edge of the screen if there is no other monitor to go to). Therefore, you can adjust the mini screens so that only a small corner space offers a passageway between screens.

Capturing (Dumping) Screens

You may take a **snapshot** of any Macintosh monochrome or color screen at rest (i.e., when no **modal dialogs** ➜104, or **pull-down menus** ➜101, are showing). To do so, type *command-shift-3*. You hear the digitized sound of a camera shutter click. This action saves a file to the disk named "Picture" followed by a number. Numbering starts at 1, and continues until you run out of disk space.

These picture files are of the **PICT** type ➜130-131, and may be opened in most graphics, word processing, and desktop publishing programs for editing or inclusion into documents. Double clicking on a Picture file lets you launch **TeachText** and load the picture so you can view it (even in color), but not edit it.

To capture screens that the built-in screen dump facility cannot, such as **dialog boxes** and **pulled-down menus,** you will need the help of third-party utilities that do a more thorough job. A shareware product ➜138 called **Flash-It**, is highly regarded among enthusiasts.

Printing Screens

System 7 removes the previous ability to print the current screen or window to an **ImageWriter** . In its place is only the ability to print any **Finder** window to any printer. The **Print Window** command in the Finder's **File** menu prints either the iconic or text listings of a window's contents as shown on the screen at that instant. Thus, you can print a list organized anyway you can set the **View** menu and **Views** control panel ➜112.

If you wish to print the contents of the full screen or an application's window, you can capture the entire screen (*command-shift-3*), and then print it from TeachText. You may also use your favorite graphics program to crop and print the picture file.

Enlarging the View

For some Macintosh users, text and icons are occasionally too small to see comfortably. The **CloseView** control panel is a built-in utility that lets anyone magnify the screen from 2 to 16 times, and easily switch between regular size for some operations and the magnified view for others. Be sure the CloseView file is in the **Control Panels** folder of the **System Folder**, and restart your Macintosh.

You may control CloseView's basic operations from the keyboard. Typing *option-command-O* (the letter O—not a zero) toggles CloseView on and off. You'll know when it's on because a black rectangle surrounds the **cursor** on the screen, no matter where you move the cursor. This rectangle shows you the area that will be magnified when you turn magnification on. The size and thickness of the rectangle changes as the magnification changes.

Typing *option-command-X* turns **magnification** on and off. With magnification on, as you drag the cursor around the screen, the magnified area shifts with it. While magnification is on, typing *option-command-up arrow* increases the magnification up to a maximum of 16 times; *option-command-down arrow* reduces magnification in steps down to 2.

In the CloseView control panel are two other choices. One lets you **invert** the black and white pixels on the screen, in case it is easier for you to view white letters on a black background (the very white screens are hard for some users to work with). The other lets you turn off CloseView's keyboard shortcuts in case there is a conflict with a macro key combination you've set up.

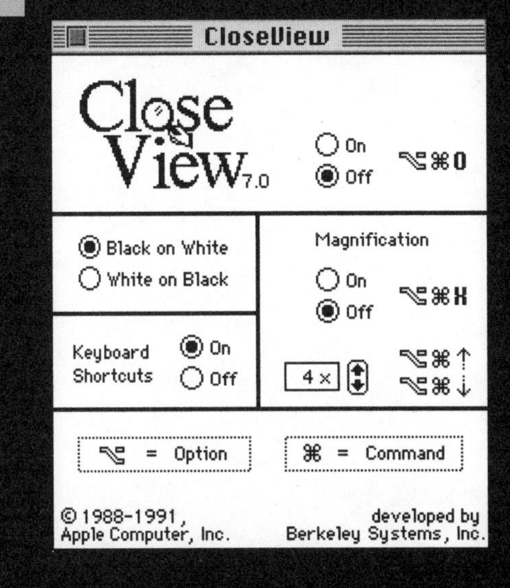

For color monitors, system software provides a modicum of support for setting a couple color parameters: highlighted text and window colors.

These items are in the **Color** control panel. Both let you choose from a menu of standard colors or any color available in the **Color Wheel**. The Color Wheel is also used in graphics programs as a standard way to define a color.

Text Highlight Color

Highlight color is the color that you see when you select text in a list or in word processing text. Other programs highlight objects in a variety of ways, including using the highlight color. The factory highlight setting is black, but if you open the **Color** control panel, you'll see a pop-up menu next to the **Highlight Color** label. Click and hold anywhere in the pop-up menu bar. A list of standard colors appears, plus a choice called Other. If you have at least 16 colors/grays selected in the **Monitors** control panel, you also see small samples of the colors or shades in the pop-up menu.

The **Other** menu choice leads you to the **Color Wheel**. This dialog appears in many software products that allow you to choose a color. There are several ways to use the Color Wheel. The simplest is to drag the pointer around the color circle, watching the top half of the color rectangle to the left. The lower half shows the setting right before you opened the Color Wheel; the upper half shows you what the change will be when you click OK (Cancel returns you to the lower color). To choose other tones of the colors in the wheel, drag the **Brightness** slider control between total brightness (top) to total black (bottom).

Window Color

If your video card and monitor can display at least 256 colors, then you may let the **Color** control panel modify subtle color highlighting of windows and window elements. Fine lines in the title bar and various controls in the window and scroll bars can be highlighted with a bit of color. The settings are anything but garish, but they were intended to be subtle so as not to draw the eye's attention from the window's contents. In the **Color** control panel, click and hold the **Window Color** pop-up menu to view the available colors. The standard color is almost purple, and most of the other colors have an iridescence to them that show nicely on color screens. Whatever setting you make applies to all windows, and is in no way linked to the **Label** menu settings for an application or document ➔100, 111.

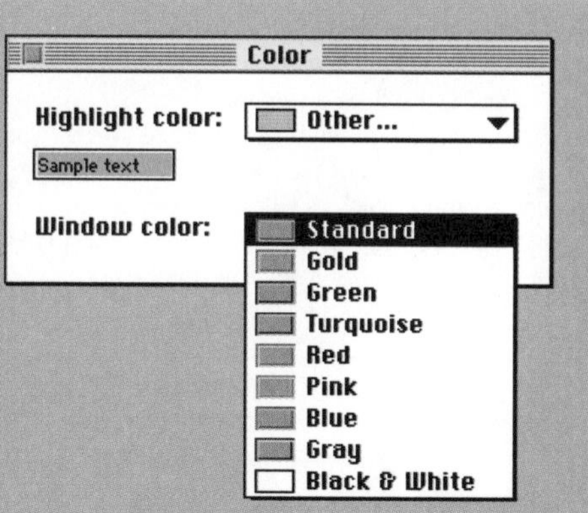

More About the Color Wheel

In addition to dragging the cursor around the color wheel, you may also enter values for hue, saturation, and brightness. Hue is a value between 0 and 65535 that represents the color. Pure red is 0; pure green is 21,845; pure blue is 43,690. Click and hold the up or down arrows next to the Hue field, and watch the colors and values change as the pointer rotates around the color wheel.

Saturation is a value that designates how saturated (i.e., absence of white) a particular color is. At zero saturation, the color is all white; at 65535 saturation, there is no white, and the color is fully saturated. Brightness, on the other hand, determines level of black in a color. Zero brightness is all black, while 65535 brightness has no black in the color. This HLS (hue, lightness, saturation) or HSV (hue, saturation, value) model of color representation is an alternate model to the RGB (red, green, blue) model, which determines the intensity of each of those three components in a color. The Color Wheel actually presents both models, displaying simultaneous values in both systems.

Occasionally you will open the Color Wheel only to discover a fully black circle. The brightness scrollbar is set to the bottom (zero). Drag it up to see color reappear.

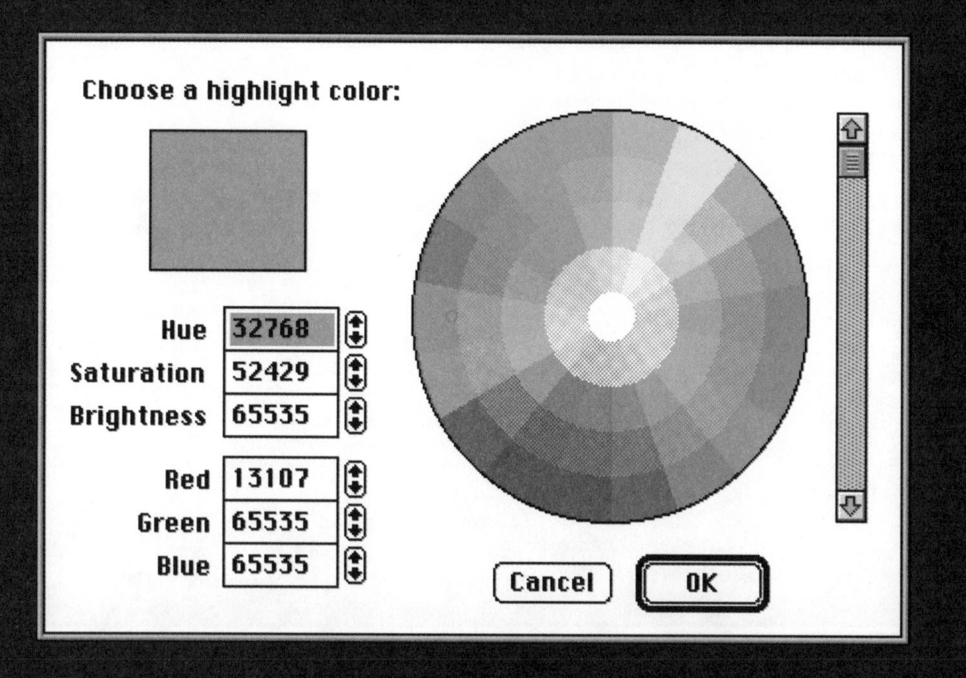

In addition to ergonomic ➔ 4-5 and cabling considerations ➔ 6, setting up a video monitor also means knowing about safety.

Video monitors are highly charged electronic devices and emit **electromagnetic force (EMF) fields.** Research on potential hazards to EMF continues and is controversial. Setting up your monitors correctly, however, can reduce exposure to these fields.

Part of the setup procedure should also be learning about controlling the brightness level of your monitor. In some cases, the control is done by software, not a knob.

Monitor Distances

Based on testing performed by various laboratories, a safe distance between your head or body and the monitor is around 30 inches. With **two-page monitors,** this is sometimes difficult because the monitors are extremely deep, and take up lots of desk space. If this is the case, put the monitor off to the side so that it angles toward you from about an arm's **length away.** More emissions, however, come from the rear of the monitor, where all the magnetic coils that aim the electron beams are. A distance of about **four feet** from the rear and sides of the cabinet to the nearest person should be adequate. The good news is that monitor makers are more aware of EMF, and are working on lower radiation-emitting monitors with each new generation.

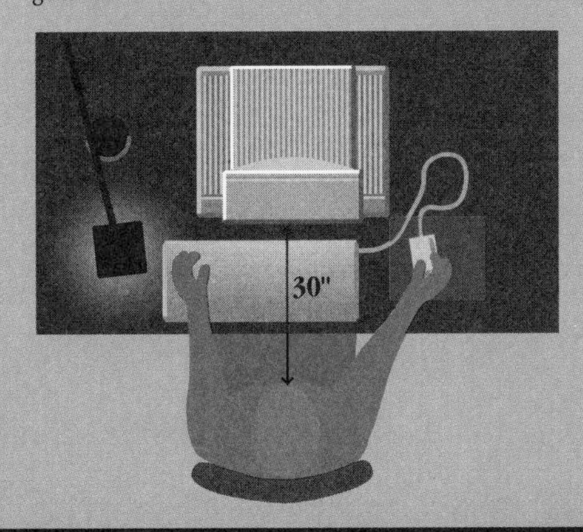

Preventing Burn-in

The high power electron beam in the video tube can eventually discolor the phosphor inside the tube. If an area of the screen, such as the menubar, is constantly illuminated, you may be able to see the area **"burned into"** the screen when the Macintosh is turned off. While the phosphor degradation is inevitable, it won't be noticed if the screen degrades evenly. When you plan to be away from your Macintosh for a half-hour or more while the machine is on, turn the brightness down all the way. Or, you may prefer the convenience of a screen-saver program. A **screen-saver** blanks the screen after a period of no mouse or keyboard activity (you set how long), and displays graphics in random patterns to even the wear. Any movement of the mouse restores the screen.

Surrounding Space

External monitors need breathing room around them. Cooling of the video tube is accomplished by convection cooling: cool air comes in from the bottom, warm air escapes through the top. Keep this air flow clear. An overheated monitor may automatically shut down as a safeguard against further damage.

External Monitors for Compact Macs

Owners of compact Macintoshes don't have to settle for the internal 9-inch monochrome screen. Virtually every Macintosh model from the Macintosh Plus to the Classic has optional video boards and **external monitors** available for a larger viewing area. The SE/30 is well supported with a number of color video boards that work with the Apple High Resolution Color Monitor and some with larger screens. Large monochrome monitors and boards can be found for all compact Macintosh models, usually allowing both the Mac's internal and external monitors to be used simultaneously.

LCDs

Macintosh Portables feature a **liquid crystal display** (LCD) instead of a picture tube. LCDs have much lower power requirements and don't emit any radiation. Despite the high quality of LCD panel used in Apple's portable computers, a backlight is very important for viewing under a variety of realworld working environments. A **backlight** insures sufficient contrast between the light and dark areas on the screen, but at the cost of slightly higher power drain.

In the future, **color LCD panels** will be within the reach of Macintosh owners, giving us virtually desktop computing on the go. In the meantime, several third-party SCSI peripherals allow you to connect a PowerBook to a desktop monitor—even a color one with the PowerBook 140 and 170.

Avoid temperature extremes and quick temperature changes for LCDs. Let them come to near room temperature before use.

Memory 38

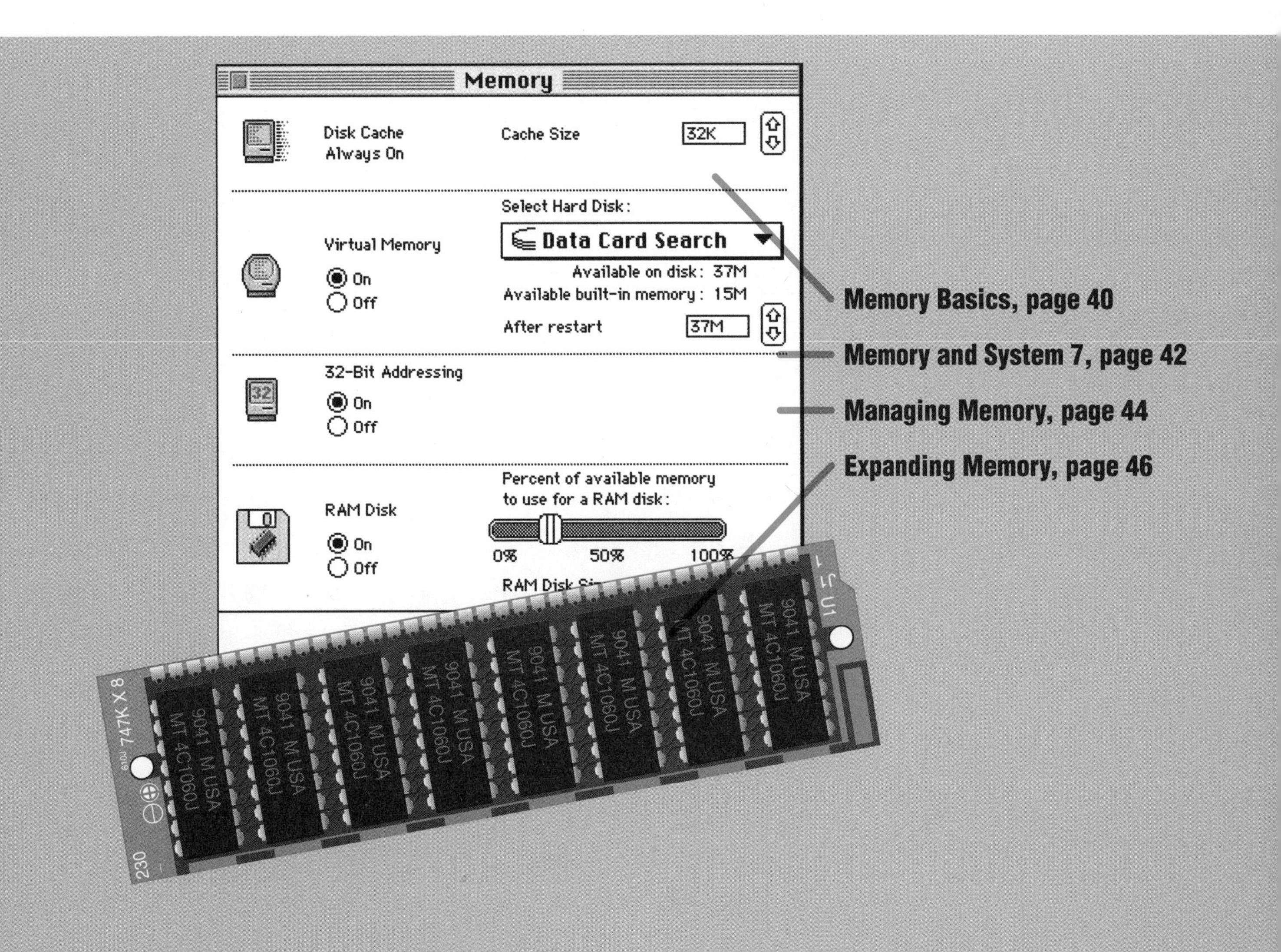
Memory
Disk Cache
Always On
Cache Size
32K
Select Hard Disk:
Virtual Memory
Data Card Search
Available on disk: 37M
Available built-in memory: 15M
On
Off
After restart
37M
32-Bit Addressing
On
Off
Percent of available memory
to use for a RAM disk:
RAM Disk
On
Off
0%
50%
100%
9041 M USA
MT 4C1060J
747K X 8
230
U1

Macintosh memory consists of three types: ROM (read-only memory), RAM (random access memory), and disk storage.

ROM contains software such as the **operating system** and other items preprogrammed at the factory. It cannot be changed or erased without exchanging the chip(s). **RAM,** on the other hand, is the temporary storage where applications and documents "live" while you use them. The contents of RAM change literally keystroke by keystroke. On all Macintoshes except portable models, RAM is completely erased when you turn off the computer.

In contrast, **Disk storage** is a safe place to store documents, because disks maintain their storage even when the power is turned off. Disk storage is also much larger than RAM, being able to hold hundreds or thousands of documents for retrieval and modification. See pages ➔ 52-57 for details on disk storage.

Bit, Byte, Kilobyte, Megabyte,...

Memory discussions focus around two primary terms: bit and byte. A **bit** is the smallest amount of information a computer knows about. It is like a switch, either on or off, one or zero, white or black. Memory chips consist of large amounts of electron-microscopic, non-mechanical switches that are either in the "on" or "off" position, each switch counting as one bit.

Since human information is more complex than that, it takes groups of bits bundled together to store information we can use. A convention of grouping 8 bits together into a **byte** gives us a possible combination of 256 arrangements of the ones and zeros in the group (00000001, 00000010, 00000011, etc.). That's enough to assign one combination to each letter and punctuation mark of most Roman languages, like English. Generally speaking, then, one byte equals one Roman language character.

Being a wordy species, we work with thousands and millions of characters at a time, especially in a computer, where the developers of applications programs need to temporarily load perhaps hundreds of thousands of characters (bytes) into memory for us to use the program. A thousand characters is known as a kilobyte, abbreviated KB or just K (because the quantity is calculated in base-2, a kilobyte is actually 2 to the tenth power (2^{10}), or 1024 characters). The kilobyte is the denomination for things like the sizes of files and memory segments used for specific purposes.

Macintosh computers since the Plus all have at least one megabyte (one million, or more accurately 2^{20}, or 1,048,576 bytes) of RAM. Most Macintoshes today have space on their circuit boards for 8 or more megabytes (MB) of RAM.

RAM Speed: the Nanosecond Factor

Individual RAM chips (and by extension their SIMMs) are rated not only by size but by speed. The speed, measured in **nanoseconds** (ns)—that's millionths of a second—represents the speed at which the Macintosh circuitry reads and writes bits to the chip. The faster the Macintosh main chip (the central processing unit, or **CPU**), the faster the RAM (the lower the ns rating) required to run inside the machine.

Since the access rate is determined by the CPU, adding faster RAM to a slower machine doesn't speed up the RAM access time in any way. But, there is no penalty (except perhaps a premium price) to install faster RAM than needed for your Macintosh, and you may later be able to transfer that fast RAM to a new, faster Macintosh.

Macintosh Model	SIMM Banks	SIMMs per Bank	Base RAM	1MB SIMMs	4MB SIMMs	16MB SIMMs	Virtual Memory	Min. Speed
Plus	2	2	1MB	4MB	-[1]	-	no[1]	150ns
SE	2	2	1MB	4MB	-[1]	-	no[1]	150ns
Classic	1[2]	2[2]	1MB	4MB	-[1]	-	no[1]	150ns
Classic II	1	2	2MB	4MB	10MB	-	yes	120ns
SE/30	2	4	1MB	8MB	32MB[6]	- 128MB[6]	yes	120ns
LC	1	2	2-3MB	4MB	10MB	-	no[1]	100ns
II	2	4	1MB	8MB	20MB[3,6]	128MB[4,6]	yes[5]	120ns
IIx	2	4	1MB	8MB	32MB[6,7]	128MB[6,7]	yes	120ns
IIcx	2	4	1MB	8MB	32MB[6,7]	128MB[6,7]	yes	120ns
IIci	2	4	1MB	8MB	32MB[8]	128MB[8]	yes	80ns
IIfx	2	4	4MB	8MB	32MB	128MB	yes	80ns[9]
IIsi	1	4	2MB	5MB	17MB	65MB	yes	100ns
Quadra 700	1	4	4MB	8MB	20MB	68MB	yes	80ns
Quadra 900	4	4	4MB	16MB	64MB	256MB	yes	80ns
Portable	-	-	1MB	5MB	-	-	no	-[10]
PowerBook 100	-	-	2MB	8MB[10]	-	-	no	-[10]
PowerBook 140	-	-	2MB	8MB[10]	-	-	yes	-[10]
PowerBook 170	-	-	4MB	8MB[10]	-	-	yes	-[10]
Expandable LaserWriters								
IINTX	3	4	2MB	≤12MB[11]	-	-	-	100ns[9]
IIf	2	4	2MB	8MB	32MB	-	-	80ns
IIg	2	4	5MB	8MB	32MB	-	-	80ns

Notes:

[1] Possible only with third-party 68030/68040 accelerator and additional software.

[2] SIMM sockets on optional RAM expansion card.

[3] Requires special PAL (Programmable Array Logic) 4MB SIMMs for Bank B; Bank A limited to 1MB SIMMs.

[4] Requires upgrade to IIx ROMS (in SuperDrive upgrade kit).

[5] Requires Motorola MC68851RC16A PMMU (Paged Memory Management Unit) chip, which plugs into socket on Macintosh II logic board.

[6] Requires MODE32 System 7 extension (free from most user groups and dealers) to use more than 8 MB.

[7] Requires PAL SIMMs.

[8] If using RAM for built-in video, 1MB SIMMs recommended for Bank A, limiting expansion to 20MB (4MB SIMMs) or 52MB (16MB SIMMs).

[9] Requires special 64-pin SIMMs.

[10] Requires specially constructed memory boards, which contain chips of proper size and speed for the machine.

[11] With three banks of 256K SIMMs, total reaches 3MB; with varying combinations of 256K and 1MB SIMMs, you can configure for 5, 8, 9, or 12MB, the last with all 1MB SIMMs.

In typical parlance, the amount of memory in your Macintosh is the amount of RAM installed in your machine. To upgrade your Macintosh to run **System 7,** you may need to install more memory than your Macintosh originally came with. Then, depending on the Macintosh model, you may take advantage of **Virtual Memory,** which expands the apparent RAM available to your applications, and **32-bit addressing,** which allows installation of comparatively huge amounts of RAM.

System 7's appetite for RAM often shocks users of previous system versions.

SIMM Memory

Macintosh RAM is commonly packaged in plug-in circuit modules called one megabyte **SIMMs** (Single In-Line Memory Modules). A SIMM consists of 8 (and sometimes 9) memory chips. A 1MB ("one-meg") SIMM not much larger than your index finger is exactly one megabyte of RAM. Newer SIMMs capable of holding 2, 4 and 16 megabytes each are also available, but not all Macintoshes can use them.

SIMMs are much more convenient to work with than individual chips when it comes to installing additional memory ➡46-49, 67. Their construction also allows more memory per square centimeter of space.

SIMMs plug into special sockets on the Macintosh system board. These sockets are not particularly easy to work with for the first time but you'll have to work with them if you plan to increase your RAM capability. Macintosh magazines are full of advertisements for mail order discount prices on SIMMs so it's often best to buy a Macintosh with the least possible RAM, and then add inexpensive SIMMs. Also, depending on the amount of memory you install into your Macintosh and what combination of 256K,1MB, or 4MB SIMMs you use, the layout of the SIMMs in the sockets is critical to proper operation ➡46-49. PostScript LaserWriter printers, too, use RAM to process print jobs. Some models accept higher capacity SIMMs to boost their font handling performance.

Video RAM

When a Macintosh has **internal video support** ➡30 (such as on a Macintosh IIci), part of the system RAM is often devoted to **video RAM**—memory that contains a copy of what you see on the screen at all times. When running a 13" color display at 256 colors ➡32), for example, 320K of your total memory is devoted entirely to video RAM, and is not available to your applications. The more total memory you add to your Macintosh, the smaller the impact of this memory grab.

System memory is not used for video RAM when you use a plug-in video board. These boards provide their own RAM (they still need memory to store the current screen), and can often be expanded to accommodate great amounts of memory-hungry color). Video RAM is similar to SIMMs, but you may still encounter boards that require plugging in individual RAM chips for upgrading. Quadras require special video RAM **SIMMs** for their separate video RAM sockets.

Parameter RAM (PRAM)

Separate from the SIMM memory in your Macintosh is another tiny section of 256 bytes (128 bytes in the Macintosh Portable) called **parameter RAM,** or better known as PRAM (pronounced PEE-ram). **PRAM** is actually part of the Mac's internal clock, but numerous control panel settings other than date and time are stored there. PRAM stays current due to an on-board battery. If you find your clock or other settings returning to their default settings, it's time to have the battery replaced—which may be a costly proposition for soldered batteries. You can reset PRAM to default settings (except the clock) by restarting your Mac while holding down the *control* (not *command*), *option*, *P*, and *R* keys.

How the Macintosh Uses Memory

Before you turn on your Macintosh (except portable Macintoshes that may be in Sleep mode), all RAM other than **PRAM** (Parameter RAM) is empty—without power, Mac RAM can't store a thing. When you turn on the machine, the CPU, following instructions in **ROM,** performs a number of system tests and then loads additional system software (including some system extensions ➡83 and control panels ➡80-82 that need loading) into RAM. System 7 software, itself, requires one megabyte or more of RAM. Whatever is left may be used for applications programs and desk accessories.

Each time you open an application, some or all of the program's code is copied from the hard disk into RAM. The RAM copy is what runs when you use an application. The amount of memory used by an application is adjustable before you start the application ➡126, but remains fixed once the program has started. This amount includes not only space for the program, but also for any documents you have open. Therefore, a small program that uses big documents (e.g., 24-bit color graphics or 100-page word processing documents) may still require a good amount of memory. See page ➡44 about methods of managing Macintosh memory.

Parity RAM

At the dawn of high power personal computing, IBM designed its original PC memory with a feature called **parity checking.** Parity is an error detection scheme that uses math to double check (although not in a foolproof way) the cumulative value of data in a byte of RAM and detect possible copying errors. Parity checking requires one extra bit of RAM for every byte, bringing the total number of RAM chips in a byte-wide bank of memory to 9 instead of 8. Because the IBM PC became so entrenched in government work, specifications such as parity RAM became standard requirements for any personal computers considered for purchase. Apple responded by offering some models with a parity RAM option. You can buy specially equipped Macintosh IIci and IIfx models that have the 9-chip SIMMs and parity checking circuits, but there is no evidence that non-parity Macintoshes are any less reliable than parity Macintoshes.

System 7 places increased memory requirements on the Macintosh.

At the same time, System 7 opens up memory powers such as **virtual memory** and **32-bit addressing** for more recent Macintosh models. Your Mac's **RAM** capabilities are largely dependent on the version of **ROM** in your machine.

Macintosh ROM

While ROM is permanent, the Macintosh operating system was designed so that when an application program requires something from ROM, it may actually get an updated version of that service coming from the System File on the disk. Unfortunately, there is only so much "patching" that the System File can do to ROM. It does not, for instance, impart **virtual memory** or **32-bit addressing** abilities to older ROMs, although a system extension, called **MODE32** can help for some Macintosh models ➔ 40, 46.

Each new generation of ROM in Macintosh computers incorporates more of the latest operating system software, reducing the necessity of patching the ROM with System File stuff. While each ROM has a version number, it is most common to refer to a Macintosh as having 64K, 128K, or 256K or larger ROMs. The size of the ROM indicates that more operating system software is imbedded in the chip, although not all the space is used (e.g., there is no need for color video ROM instructions in a Macintosh SE/30). This table shows the progression of ROM sizes in the course of Macintosh model history:

Macintosh	ROM Size
128K	64K
512K	64K
512K (Enhanced)	128K
Plus	128K
SE	256K
SE/30	256K
Classic	512K
Classic II	512K
LC	512K
II	256K
IIx	256K
IIcx	256K
IIci	512K
IIfx	512K
IIsi	512K
Quadra 700	1MB
Quadra 900	1MB
Portable	256K
PowerBook 100	512K
PowerBook 140	1MB
PowerBook 170	1MB

Although some Macs have expandable ROM capacity in the form of chip or SIMM sockets, as of this writing no ROM supplements have been available.

How Much RAM Do I Have?

To check how much memory you have or have available to load additional programs, you need the help of the menu in the Finder ➔ 100. To make sure you are viewing the Finder, pull down the **Application** menu at the far right of the menubar, and choose Finder. Then pull down the menu at the far left, and choose **About This Macintosh**.

You can tell a lot about your Macintosh from this dialog box. First, the **Total Memory** value shows you how many kilobytes of memory are installed. A value of 2048 kilobytes means 2 megabytes. Divide the Total Memory value by 1024 to determine the number of megabytes of RAM installed in your Macintosh. If the value is different from what you expect, then the installation of additional memory may be incorrect. See pages ➔ 46-47 for SIMM installation instructions.

The **Largest Unused Block** value represents approximately how much memory is available for applications. If you have opened and closed a lot of applications in the current session, the largest block may be much less than the total memory less the amounts currently being used in the list in this dialog box (see pages ➔ 44-45 about fragmented RAM).

Items in this dialog box's list are the open applications and system software element that are using RAM. System software for System 7 is rarely less than one megabyte (if you install a minimum system, page ➔ 68), but can grow to 2 megabytes or more if you have a lot of extensions and control panels that load into memory upon startup. The entire rectangle in each programs block indicates the total amount of memory allocated to that application. The dark area shows you how much of that allocation is currently in use. See page ➔ 126 about allocating application memory.

RAM Requirements

While System 7 requires 2 megabytes of RAM, that may be just a bare minimum for using a single application, especially if your Macintosh uses system memory for video RAM (up to 320 KB for a 640-by-480 256-color display) or you use a large program, such as HyperCard (which runs best run in at least one megabyte). The comparatively low cost of 1 MB SIMMs makes upgrading to 4 or more megabytes a cost effective way to improve productivity. You will be able to open two or three applications at a time, making it a simple click of the mouse button to switch instantly between programs.

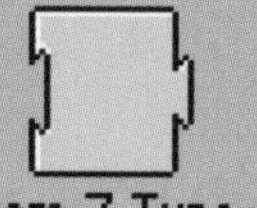

System 7 Tune-Up

System 7 Tune-Up

Acknowledging that some users were having difficulty with System 7 and low amounts of RAM, Apple in early 1992 released a software tune-up kit for existing System 7 users. Available free from most user groups and bulletin boards, **System 7 Tune-Up** consists of an extension and updates to the **Chooser**, **File Sharing Extension**, and **printer drivers** for the LaserWriter and StyleWriter.

If not part of a recently purchased Mac or System 7 Upgrade Kit, you should get this and install it.

Virtual Memory

When RAM isn't enough memory for a particular operation, your Macintosh may be capable of assigning an unused portion of your **hard disk** as temporary RAM of significant size. This function is called virtual memory, because the disk acts just like RAM, albeit at significantly slower transfer rates than RAM chips. Only Macintoshes with a **68030** microprocessor or a **68020** microprocessor plus a paged memory management unit (PMMU) chip can access virtual memory. The Macintosh SE/30, IIx, IIcx, IIci, IIsi, IIfx have the requisite 68030 chip. The Macintosh II, which has a 68020 chip also has a memory management unit chip that can be replaced by a **Motorola MC68851 PMMU** to enable the computer to work with virtual memory. See page 45 for using virtual memory to manage your memory.

32-Bit Addressing

Each byte of RAM has a unique address number, much like a street address for a house. Until higher power CPU chips were put into the Macintosh, it was customary to use a 24-digit binary number as a memory location address. While this gave a possible 16,777,216 addresses (equivalent to 16MB of memory), half of these addresses were reserved for the Macintosh hardware. That left a maximum of 8MB available for applications. To overcome this limit, a few years ago programmers were encouraged to use 32-digit numbers for addresses —a scheme, called **32-bit clean**, supported by ROMs in newer Macintosh models. A 32-bit address offers over 4 billion combinations, but because of addresses reserved for hardware, that leaves us with 1 gigabyte of addressible memory.

You need **32-bit addressing** to access RAM greater than 8MB. This is possible only on newer Macintoshes with 32-bit clean ROMs, although some models as old as the original Macintosh II can use 32-bit addressing with the help of **MODE32**, a system extension available free from most user groups and Apple dealers. Turn 32-bit addressing on from the **Memory** control panel. Some older programs, however, may not be compatible with 32-bit addressing.

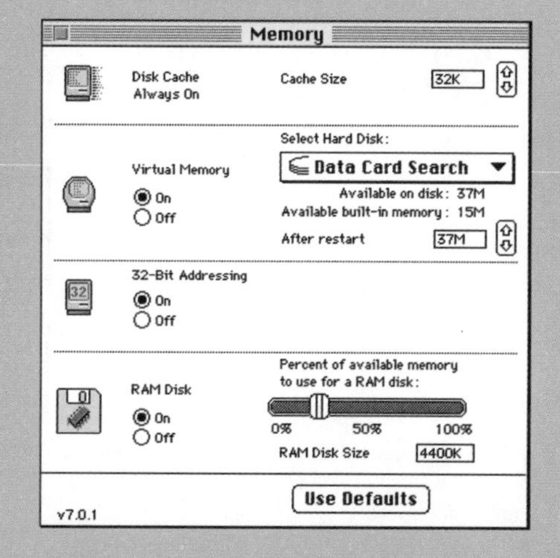

RAM Disk

When you have lots of RAM, you may consider assigning part of it to behave like another disk volume on the desktop 94. The advantage of this feature, called a **RAM Disk**, is that access to that volume is virtually instantaneous, because there is no physical access required, as with a floppy or hard disk.

On desktop Macintoshes, a RAM disk is not all that helpful these days. Hard disks tend to be quite fast, so they rarely slow you down unless you are accessing a huge file. Secondly, the memory you assign to a RAM disk is not available to your programs and documents. It is typically more valuable to have RAM available for multiple applications. Also, if you copy a program to the RAM disk, the program must still load into the application RAM area for you to use it—the program is then on the hard disk, in the RAM disk, and, when running, in your application RAM as well. Most dangerously, when you turn off your Macintosh (except the PowerBook 100 and other portables in Sleep mode), anything stored on the RAM disk is immediately erased. If you haven't save edited documents to a real disk, they'll be gone, probably without notice.

The RAM Disk option is built into Quadra and PowerBook Memory control panels.

A RAM disk can make sense, however, on a portable Macintosh, provided there is sufficient RAM installed. By keeping frequently used programs and documents on the RAM disk, you lower the need for the computer to access the battery-hungry hard disk. Moreover, putting a portable to sleep 10-11 doesn't erase the RAM—although it's a good idea to back up your documents to the hard disk before putting the machine to sleep, just in case you can't wake up the Mac again after a very long, battery-draining nap.

You can let the Macintosh manage the memory inside your machine, just like you can let a service station attendant fill up your gas tank, check your oil, and do tune ups.

But Macintosh owners, like car owners, should know something about what's happening under the hood when unexpected things occur. If you want to learn even more, you may be able to help the Macintosh do a better job of managing memory for more efficient day-to-day operation.

Applications and Memory

Each time you start an application program, the Macintosh loads some or all of that program into RAM. That's the copy you use. To use memory efficiently, however, most programs load only portions of themselves when they start. As other portions are needed (e.g., dialog box displays, code that carries out infrequently used menu commands, etc.) the program brings those items into RAM, perhaps flushing other expendable items at the same time. The less space that a program needs to operate, the more programs you can open at the same time for instant switching among them—a real productivity boost. The downside is that the program may need to fetch parts of itself from your hard disk, which may cause noticeable time delays.

Application Memory Sizes

You can adjust the amount of memory that a program occupies. Before System 7, when MultiFinder ➜12 was a user option, the segment of RAM associated with a program was called its MultiFinder partition. Since MultiFinder is always on in System 7, we call a program's memory requirements its application memory size.

There are actually up to three values that an application knows for its application memory size. One is the absolute minimum RAM required to run the program, as designated by the program's author. The only time you'll see this value is if you try to open the program when there is more than the minimum but less than the desired RAM available. An alert box warns you that there is enough memory to open the application, but less than optimum. If there isn't even the minimum RAM available, the alert box tells you that you can't open the program at all. Running a program at its barest minimum RAM usually results in slow operation (program segments have to be retrieved from disk more often) and often limits the size or number of documents you can open.

Every application program reserves a portion of RAM for its use. That segment is not only for the program, but also for any documents you open. To work with large documents, some programs even bring only portions of the document file into RAM, while the others remain in temporary files on the disk. When you save the document, the program recombines the temporary files and the RAM segment into the saved file.

HyperCard Info

HyperCard
HyperCard 2.1

Kind: application program
Size: 703K on disk (717,794 bytes used)

Where: Zeus: Applications: HyperCard:

Created: Wed, Apr 24, 1991, 5:00 PM
Modified: Fri, Jan 3, 1992, 9:12 PM
Version: HyperCard 2.1
©1987-91 Apple Computer, Inc.
Comments:

Locked

Memory
Suggested size: 1,000 K
Current size: 1500 K

The second value is the amount of RAM that the program's designer recommends as a practical minimum. From the Finder, click once on any application program icon (for a program not currently running), and choose **Get Info** from the **File** menu. At the bottom of the **Info dialog box** is a number showing the suggested memory in kilobytes.

The third value is the amount of RAM that you want the program to occupy. You may change that value in the Info dialog box by changing the Current size field in the Memory box at the bottom. You may enter values between the program's minimum RAM size and 99,999 K. Whatever RAM you assign to an application becomes reserved entirely for that application when it is loaded. Even if not all of it is used, no other application trespasses in that territory.

In most situations, the current and suggested sizes should be the same. You would enter less only if you are running into memory constraints with a combination of programs you like to run all the time. On the other hand, some programs that use lots of RAM for documents can be increased substantially. For example, while HyperCard ➜138-139 runs acceptably at the suggested 875K size, setting the current size to 1200K or 2000K allows many more windows open at the same time, color pictures, as well as the addition of several authoring tools.

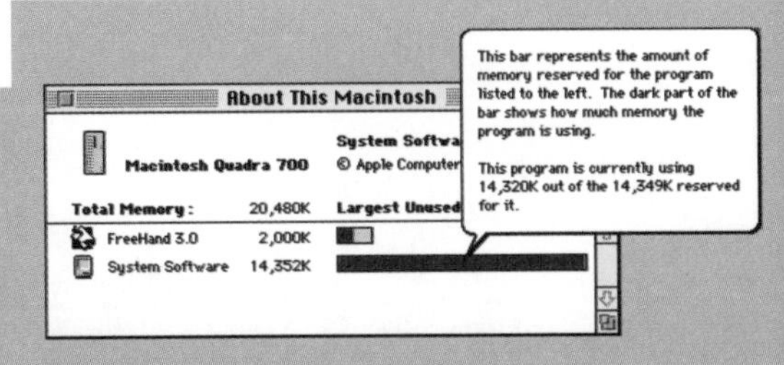

Memory Usage: the Global Picture

Open one or more applications, and then switch to the Finder by choosing **Finder** from the **Application** menu (far right of the menubar). Choose **About This Macintosh** from the menu to see how your machine's memory is being used. Each open application (listed in alphabetical order) has a rectangle that represents the application memory size. The black or gray space is the amount of that partition currently filled by the program and documents. If you see a lot of white space after opening a typical set of documents, then you can probably reduce the application memory size (you'll have to do it after quitting the program) to free up space for other applications. But if the dark bar almost fills the space, then it's probably time to increase the size. Try increasing the value in 100K increments over a period of time and see how that helps performance.

The amount of memory assigned to the System software varies according to its needs. The dark bar usually comes close to filling the space, but the Macintosh handles all memory management for the System. You can watch System Software vary its memory requirements. With the **About This Macintosh** window showing, choose **Show Balloons** from the **Help** menu (the question mark icon at the right of the menubar). Move the cursor around the screen to let Balloon Help show instructions about various parts of the screen. As Balloon Help loads and unloads the text, you see the System Software requirements change dynamically. When finished, choose **Hide Balloons** from the **Help** menu.

While the Largest Unused Block value is supposed to display the amount of RAM available to the next application you try to open, in practice the value is not always accurate. It is best to try to open an application. If there is insufficient memory, then let the alert box tell you more precisely what the situation is.

Virtual Memory is inherently slow even with the fastest hard disks. You'll probably be happier with a RAM upgrade.

When Memory Is Tight

You will notice that you may not have enough RAM when you frequently see the Not enough memory alert while trying to open needed applications. But before you run out to buy more SIMMs, there are some remedies to try.

First, it's possible that your RAM has become fragmented by opening and closing a lot of applications. While this happens less than it used to, consider this a possibility. Organize the loading of applications into memory in a last-in, first-out basis. In other words, first load applications that you plan to have running all the time. Then add the more transient programs. The more you can keep the launching and quitting of applications in the same memory space, the less likely RAM will fragment.

Another culprit is the disk cache (right). If you have it set high, it's occupying valuable applications space. Try throttling it back to just 32K or 64K to open up a bit more space for an application.

Next, check the silent thieves of RAM: system extensions (of the INIT variety) and control panels that load upon startup. A **networking extension,** for instance, can occupy 100K of RAM. A graphical desktop picture provided by some third-party extensions can eat 200-300K without you knowing it. As proof of these programs' memory appetite, compare the System software memory usage (in the **About This Macintosh** dialog box) after starting normally and after starting with the Shift key down to turn off all extensions. Then try removing a suspicious extension from the Extensions folder and restart the Macintosh.

RAM Disk

PowerBooks and Quadras include features of the Memory control panel that allow you to turn a portion of total RAM into a disk volume that appears on the Desktop. The speed of opening and saving files to a RAM disk is significantly faster than on your hard disk. The downside is that a RAM disk is not forever: its contents are lost when you shut down the computer (except with the PowerBook 100). Use a RAM disk only as a temporary disk, and copy files to the hard disk before shutting down.

More RAM on Disk: Virtual Memory

System 7 (and some third-party software for System 6) opens the way for more powerful Macintosh models to temporarily use a portion of the hard disk as additional RAM—a function called virtual memory. The system treats this disk space just like RAM (but more slowly). That disk space is occupied by an invisible file (called VM Storage), so you cannot use that space for saving items to disk. See the the RAM table on page ➜ 40 to see if your Macintosh qualifies.

Adjust virtual memory in the **Memory** control panel ➜ 43. The control panel lets you select which hard disk is to act as virtual memory, and shows you how much space is available on the disk for this purpose. With virtual memory off, the total memory value is that of internal RAM chips; with virtual memory on, the value reflects the total of chip and disk RAM. With virtual memory turned on, click the up or down arrows to adjust the total memory.

Unless your Macintosh is capable of 32-bit addressing (the **Memory** control panel features on-off buttons for it), you won't be able to assign more than 14 MB of disk space (and probably less if you have NuBus expansion cards installed) to virtual memory. Turning on 32-bit addressing, however, sets the limit to 1 gigabyte (1000 megabytes).

Importantly, virtual memory extends your RAM as a separate segment of memory—it's not **contiguous** with your SIMM RAM. For example, if you set up a 4MB virtual memory in addition to 4MB of SIMM RAM, you don't get a **contiguous** block of memory larger than 4MB (choose **About This Macintosh** from the menu to see how the System assigned programs to RAM and virtual memory). Since programs require contiguous blocks to load themselves and their documents, you might still have be careful about managing applications and memory, even with a large virtual memory.

Experienced virtual memory users recommend keeping virtual memory to between 1 and 2 times the internal RAM to prevent excessive disk access. You may still find virtual memory intolerably slow for some applications.

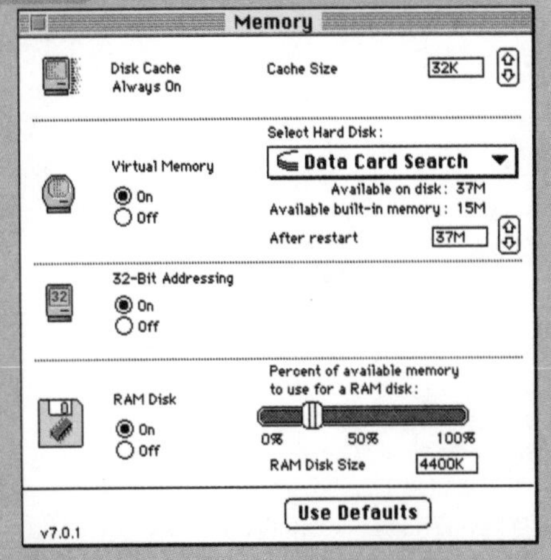

Disk Cache

System 7 sets aside a portion of RAM for the disk cache (pronounced kash). The disk cache silently stores a copy of information most recently read from and written to a disk (or at least as much as it can hold). Behind this concept is the idea that the Macintosh is very likely to need to re-read information that has recently passed to or from the disk. For example, if you open a large document, and only part of the document is in memory while the rest is in a temporary file, as you scroll through the file it is much faster to swap in data from the cache memory than from the comparatively slower hard disk file.

To adjust the size of your disk cache, open the **Memory** control panel. The default disk cache size is 32 KB per megabyte of RAM you have installed in your Mac, but if you prefer, you can scrunch the cache all the way down to 32K (or less in some memory configurations), no matter how much RAM you have. The maximum allowed is 128K per megabyte of RAM. Therefore, with 8 megabytes of RAM, you can allot a full megabyte to the disk cache. Unless you work with large color graphics documents, the default size or smaller should give you good all around performance.

Most Macintosh models have provision for expanding memory. While such expansion entails opening the system unit and dealing with circuit boards, the process is within the grasp of most users.

A typical installation requires the addition or reorientation of SIMMs ➔ 48 on the motherboard. SIMM sockets on older require care so as not to break the plastic tabs that hold the SIMMs securely in place.

Each Macintosh family has its own organization of SIMMs on the motherboard for the various memory configurations. It is vital that SIMMs be installed in their correct sockets, especially if you are mixing SIMMs of different sizes.

SIMM Basics

Single In-Line Memory Modules (SIMMs) each contain 8 (or 9 for parity RAM ➔ 40) chips on a small circuit board. One long edge of the circuit board has shiny metallic squares—the connecting points between the SIMM and the SIMM socket on the system board. When you buy SIMMs, be sure to tell the seller which Macintosh model you have —different Macintosh models require different SIMMs ➔ 41. SIMMs come packaged in special static shielding plastic envelopes or bags. Do not remove the SIMMs from this container until you have opened your Macintosh cabinet and are ready for installation.

CAUTION

SIMMs are extremely sensitive to static electricity. Always try to hold the SIMM like a precious photograph by its short edges, which have no connections. Before you come near a SIMM, ground yourself by touching something metal, like the power supply cabinet or rigid frame of your opened Macintosh. Electrostatic discharge wrist straps are available, but they don't offer much more protection than frequently touching the grounded metal points of your Macintosh while holding a SIMM. Even rolling your chair around the floor or sitting down can build up a static charge on your body. Discharge your static frequently during SIMM installation.

SIMM Sockets

All but the newest sockets for SIMMs can be difficult to work with. Look closely at how SIMMs already on the system board are fitted into the socket (if your Macintosh has SIMMs installed). A small, somewhat flexible plastic arm on each side holds the SIMM firmly in place, such that plastic tabs fit through the small round holes on each edge. The plastic arms are the most difficult parts to work with when removing a SIMM. You must take great care not to break any of these arms. If you break both of them on a socket, the SIMM will probably not set correctly in the socket, perhaps disabling your Macintosh. Worse yet, sockets are not replaceable—you'll have to replace the entire (extremely expensive) system board.

It almost looks as though you could use your thumbs to gently pry the arms back to free a SIMM. Their small size and tight fit, however, make it painful or impossible. One way to safely remove a SIMM is to use a small screwdriver to ***gently*** pry one arm away in stages from the SIMM, and then the other. You may have to repeat the operation a couple times, but eventually the arms will be clear enough that you can pull the SIMM forward and free it from the arms' clutches.

Newer sockets have spring metal clips, which are a pleasure to work with by comparison.

Plugging a SIMM into a socket is much easier. Insert the connector edge of the SIMM into the SIMM socket, and press down on the SIMM to insure a solid seat in the connector. The chips on the SIMM should face away from the arms and tabs of that socket (facing up on sockets that are slanted). Then press slowly but firmly on both edges of the SIMM toward the arms and tabs until the arms click securely in front of the SIMM.

4 and 16 Megabyte SIMMs

Only the latest high-power Macintoshes (Classic II, IIci, IIfx, IIsi, LC and Quadras) can accept 4 MB SIMMs without additional third-party software. All of these but the Classic II and LC can accept 16MB SIMMs. The original Macintosh II cannot accommodate even composite SIMMs (made from thirty-two 1-megabit chips instead of eight 4-megabit chips) without a ROM upgrade (the same upgrade you get if you upgrade the disk drive to a 1.4 high-density floppy). But even then, you'll still need the MODE32 System 7 extension to access RAM above 8 megabytes. Other models that require MODE32 are the SE/30, IIx, and IIcx. These machines have ROMs that are incapable of 32-bit addressing ➔ 43 which is necessary for managing memory above 8MB.

Before jumping to 16MB SIMMS, be aware that today's early versions are high-profile SIMMs, which are taller than most 1 MB and 4MB SIMMs. The Quadra 700, for example, has clearance inside the cabinet for low-profile SIMMs only. The Quadra 900, on the other hand, accepts high-profile SIMMs in only three of its four SIMM banks. Low-profile SIMMs fit all Macintoshes.

Macintosh IIci Cache Card

An optional plug-in board for the Macintosh IIci can improve performance by up to 50 percent. Called a RAM cache (pronounced KASH), the board consists of a small amount of very high speed RAM chips. Just as a disk cache stores recently read and written hard disk items in handy RAM, the IIci RAM cache stores items recently read and written RAM items in super fast RAM. It is independent of regular SIMM RAM.

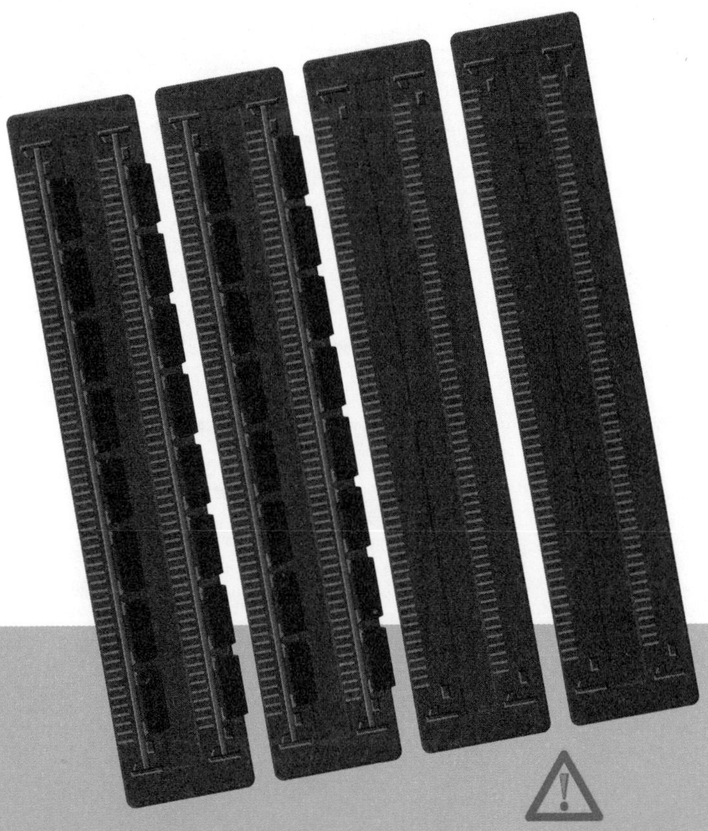

Your First Memory Test

Once the SIMMs are installed, close the Macintosh cabinet and start up the Macintosh. If the Macintosh does not start up properly see page 10. But if everything looks OK, check that your system memory is what you think it is. From the **Finder**, pull down the menu and choose **About This Macintosh**. The **Total Memory** value should show the new RAM amount. If not, go back into the Macintosh system unit and inspect the SIMM installation and orientation against the charts on the next two pages.

Opening Compact Macintoshes

Cabinets on the compact Macintoshes (Plus, SE, SE/30, Classic and Classic II) require special tools to open and pretty good hands to extract the main circuit board. You can buy third-party Macintosh cabinet crackers (consisting of a special screwdriver, cabinet prying tool, and instructions) from some RAM merchants. It's best to have watched an experienced compact Macintosh cabinet opener perform the operation before trying it yourself. The task can be dangerous, since you must poke your hands through narrow openings surrounded by high voltage components (some of which store their charges for an hour or more after turning off the Macintosh) to remove three cables from the main board. Opening a compact Macintosh yourself voids the warranty, so if you are still covered, have an authorized service technician perform memory upgrades, even if you buy the RAM elsewhere and have to pay the technician a labor charge.

Money in the Bank(s)

OSIMM sockets are usually on the motherboard in sets of two or four. Each group is called a **bank.**

Whenever you add RAM, you must have enough SIMMs to fill a complete bank. Moreover, a bank must contain SIMMs of the same size. See pages 40-41 for the bank configuration of your Macintosh.

Macintosh Plus and SE RAM Resistors

If you are doing the RAM upgrade yourself on a Macintosh Plus or SE (older models), two **resistors** on the logic circuit board help the system recognize various amounts of RAM installed in the four SIMM sockets. These resistors are marked on the circuit board with a border labeled **RAM SIZE.** The two 150-ohm resistors (**R8** and **R9** on the Plus, **R35** and **R36** on the SE) are individually labeled **256KB** and **1 ROW.** For 2MB RAM totals, there needs to be a resistor only in the 1 ROW position, and no resistor in the 256KB position. For 2.5 or 4 MB RAM, there should be no resistors in either location.

Macintosh Plus Upgrade

SIMM sockets on the Macintosh Plus are labeled 1 through 4. Mixing 256KB and 1MB SIMMs must be done only in the prescribed orientations. For System 7, possible memory configurations are:

Total Memory	SIMMs
2MB	(2) 1MB
2.5MB	(2) 256KB, (2) 1MB
4MB	(4) 1MB

Macintosh SE Jumper

On later models of the Macintosh SE, the RAM resistors were replaced by a simpler **circuit jumper.** This is a three-pin prong sticking out of the logic circuit board just above the SIMM sockets. A plastic jumper is installed on two of the pins if you are upgrading memory from one megabyte. Labeling on the circuit board may be misleading. The jumper should be in the **2/4M** position only for a 2MB total RAM. For 2.5 or 4 MB, the jumper should be removed entirely.

Macintosh SE

SIMM sockets on the Macintosh SE are labeled SIMM 1 through SIMM 4. Mixing 256KB and 1MB SIMMs must be done only in the prescribed orientations. The orientation of SIMMs for the 2 and 2.5 MB RAM are different for logic boards with resistors and jumper. Use only the orientation suitable for your logic board. For System 7, possible memory configurations are:

Total Memory	SIMMs
2MB	(2) 1MB
2.5MB	(2) 256KB, (2) 1MB
4MB	(4) 1MB

SE with Jumper

not filled	not filled
filled	filled

filled	filled
filled	filled

SE with Resistors

not filled	not filled
filled	filled

filled	filled
filled	filled

Macintosh Classic

The Macintosh Classic has 1MB of memory soldered to the logic board, and a connector for an optional RAM expansion board. That expansion board has 1MB of soldered RAM (bringing the total to 2MB). There are also two SIMM sockets for installation of two SIMMs. If you install SIMMs, you must install two at a time of the same size, either 256 KB (for a total of 2.5MB) or 1MB (for a total of 4 MB). In addition, the RAM expansion board has a jumper that has two settings. From the factory, the plastic jumper is over the SIMM NOT INSTALLED pins. If you plug SIMMs into this expansion board, you must pull off the jumper and place it over the "SIMM INSTALLED" pins.

Total Memory	SIMMs
2MB	Expansion Board
2.5MB	(2) 256KB and Board
4MB	(2) 1MB and Board

Macintosh Classic II

The Macintosh Classic II has 2MB of memory soldered to the logic board and two SIMM connectors for RAM expansion. Both SIMMs must be of the same capacity. With 2MB standard, you may run System 7 without expansion. In practice, however, 4MB is the minimum for running multiple applications. You may expand memory to the following amounts:

Total Memory	SIMMs
2MB	Soldered On
4MB	(2) 1MB
10MB	(2) 4MB

Macintosh LC

The Macintosh LC comes with 2 MB of RAM soldered to the system board. To expand RAM, you must plug SIMMs into the two RAM expansion SIMMs two at a time of the same size. RAM expansion sockets are close to the special video RAM SIMM. You may expand memory to the following amounts:

Total Memory	SIMMs
4MB	(2) 1MB
10MB	(2) 10MB

Macintosh SE/30, II, IIx, and IIcx

These models have two banks of four SIMM sockets—8 total. SIMMs must be added four at a time (one bank at a time), with all four in a bank being the same size. If you mix SIMM sizes, the larger SIMMs must be in Bank A. While the the SIMM sockets are in different locations on these circuit boards (the II and IIx are the same), the rule of thumb is that if you view the SIMMs so that the chips are on the right side of the SIMM modules, Bank A is on the right, Bank B on the left. For System 7, possible memory configurations are:

Total Memory	SIMMs
2MB	(8) 256KB
4MB	(4) 1MB
5MB	(4) 256KB, (4) 1MB
8MB	(8) 1MB
Macintosh SE/30, IIcx, and IIci only:	
16MB	(4) 4MB
17MB	(4) 256KB, (4) 4MB
20MB	(4) 1MB, (4) 4MB
32MB	(8)4MB
64MB	(4) 16MB
65MB	(4) 256KB,(4)16MB
68MB	(4) 1MB, (4) 16MB
80MB	(4) 4MB, (4) 16 MB
128MB	(8) 16MB

Macintosh IIci

Because of the on-board video RAM, the IIci SIMM arrangement is slightly different from the other II family members. While there are still two banks of SIMM sockets, Bank A is where the Macintosh looks for video RAM. You are free to put large or small SIMMs in any bank, as long as each bank has four SIMMs of the same size. If you use the built-in video circuitry, then you must have RAM in Bank A. Using an external video card, Bank A can be empty. Recommended memory configurations for System 7 are the same for the Macintosh SE/30 and IIcx above.

Macintosh IIsi

The Macintosh IIsi comes with 1MB of RAM soldered to the system board but only 4 SIMM sockets. SIMMs must be added four at a time, and all four must be the same size. Adding SIMMs brings the total memory up to sizes indicated in this table:

Total Memory	SIMMs
2 MB	(4) 256 KB
5 MB	(4) 1 MB
17 MB	(4) 4 MB
65 MB	(4) 16 MB

Macintosh IIfx

SIMM sockets in the Macintosh IIfx have a different connector setup, requiring 64-pin SIMMs especially for the IIfx. The IIfx works only with 1MB or larger SIMMs in its two four-socket banks. If you mix 1MB and 4MB SIMMs, the larger 4MB SIMMs must be in Bank A. Possible memory configurations are:

Total Memory	SIMMs
4MB	(4) 1MB
5MB	(4) 1MB, (4) 256KB
8MB	(8) 1MB
16MB	(4) 4MB
17MB	(4) 4MB, (4) 256KB
20MB	(4) 4MB, (4) 1MB
32MB	(8) 4MB
64MB	(4) 16MB
65MB	(4) 16MB, (4) 256KB
68MB	(4) 16MB, (4) 1MB
80MB	(4) 16MB, (4) 4MB
128MB	(8) 16MB

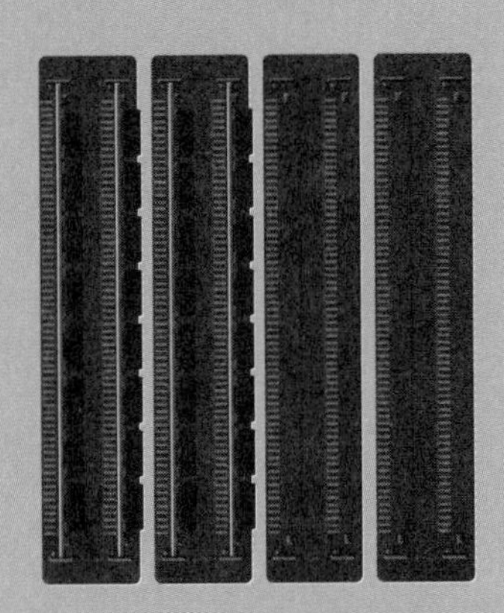

Quadra 700

The Quadra 700 comes with 4MB of RAM soldered to the logic board, plus one four-SIMM bank for memory expansion. Neither Quadra model accepts 256KB or 2MN SIMMs. All SIMMs in the bank must be of the same capacity, and should be no less than 1MB SIMMs. With 4MB of RAM, the Quadra 700 runs System 7 as-is.

Total Memory	SIMMs
8MB	(4) 1MB
20MB	(4) 4MB
68MB	(4) 16MB

Quadra 900

With 4MB of RAM soldered to the logic board, the Quadra 900 is ready to run System 7 immediately. Intended for heavy use, this model also has the most capacious RAM expansion to date. Four banks of four SIMM sockets allow theoretical expansion to 260MB with 16 MB SIMMs. Each bank must contain SIMMs of the same size, with larger capacity SIMMs filling out the lowest bank numbers first.

Total Memory	SIMMs
4MB	4MB Soldered On
8MB	(4) 1MB
12MB	(8) 1MB
16MB	(12) 1MB
20MB	(16) 1MBs
20MB	(4) 4MB
36MB	(8) 4MB
52MB	(12) 4MB
66MB	(16) 4MBs
66MB	(4) 16MB
132MB	(8) 16MB
196MB	(12) 16MB
260MB	(16) 16MBs

Macintosh Portable

There are two versions of the Macintosh Portable (the original and the backlit models), and each requires its own RAM expansion card. The original Portable uses very low power (and expensive) **static RAM** (SRAM), while the **backlit Portable** uses low power (and not so expensive) **pseudo-static RAM.** With one megabyte of RAM permanently installed on the system board, the RAM expansion card is the primary way to add memory (some developers may add memory via another connector, the **Processor Direct Slot**). Due to technical reasons beyond your control, it is unlikely that you will be able to expand the Portable's memory beyond 5MB.

In any case, make sure the RAM board you purchase for your Portable is for the particular model you have—they are not interchangeable. Follow the memory expansion installation instructions in the Macintosh Portable owner's manual for details on opening the Portable case and inserting the board. As always, exercise extreme care in handling any circuit board.

Macintosh PowerBooks

All PowerBooks require special RAM expansion modules designed to fit the confined space inside the unit. Only RAM modules specifically designed for the PowerBook model of your choice should be used.

Total Memory	Memory Boards
4MB	2MB Board
6MB	4MB Board
8MB	6MB Board

Expandable LaserWriters

A few PostScript LaserWriters are expandable in the RAM department. The LaserWriter IINTX may be increased from its basic 2MB to as much as 12MB by filling its 12 SIMM sockets (3 banks of four sockets) with 1MB SIMMs. The IINTX requires special 64-pin SIMMs. While these can be the same as the Macintosh IIfx, the LaserWriter IINTX requires only 100ns SIMMs, while the IIfx requires 80ns. You may use IIfx SIMMs in the IINTX without any problem.

The newer IIf and IIg LaserWriters each have 2 banks of four SIMM sockets. Both printers use the same 80ns SIMMs as the Macintosh IIci, and can accept 4MB SIMMs to bring total RAM to 32MB. A minimum of 5MB of RAM is required on either printer to use the higher resolution PhotoGrade printing for high-quality grayscale printing.

Total Memory	SIMMs
4MB	(4) 1MB
8MB	(8) 1MB
12MB (NTX only)	(12) 1MB
16MB	(4) 4MB
32MB	(8) 4MB
48MB (NTX only)	(12) 4MB

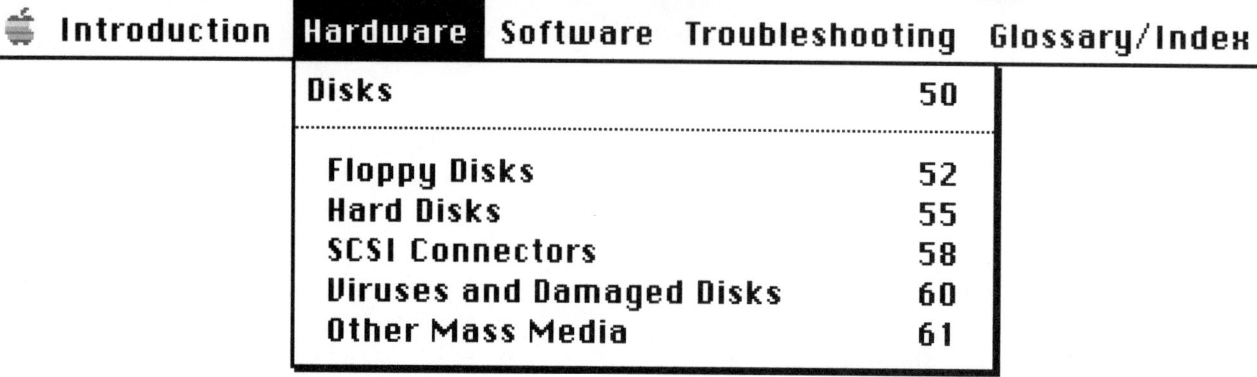

Introduction
Hardware
Software
Troubleshooting
Glossary/Index

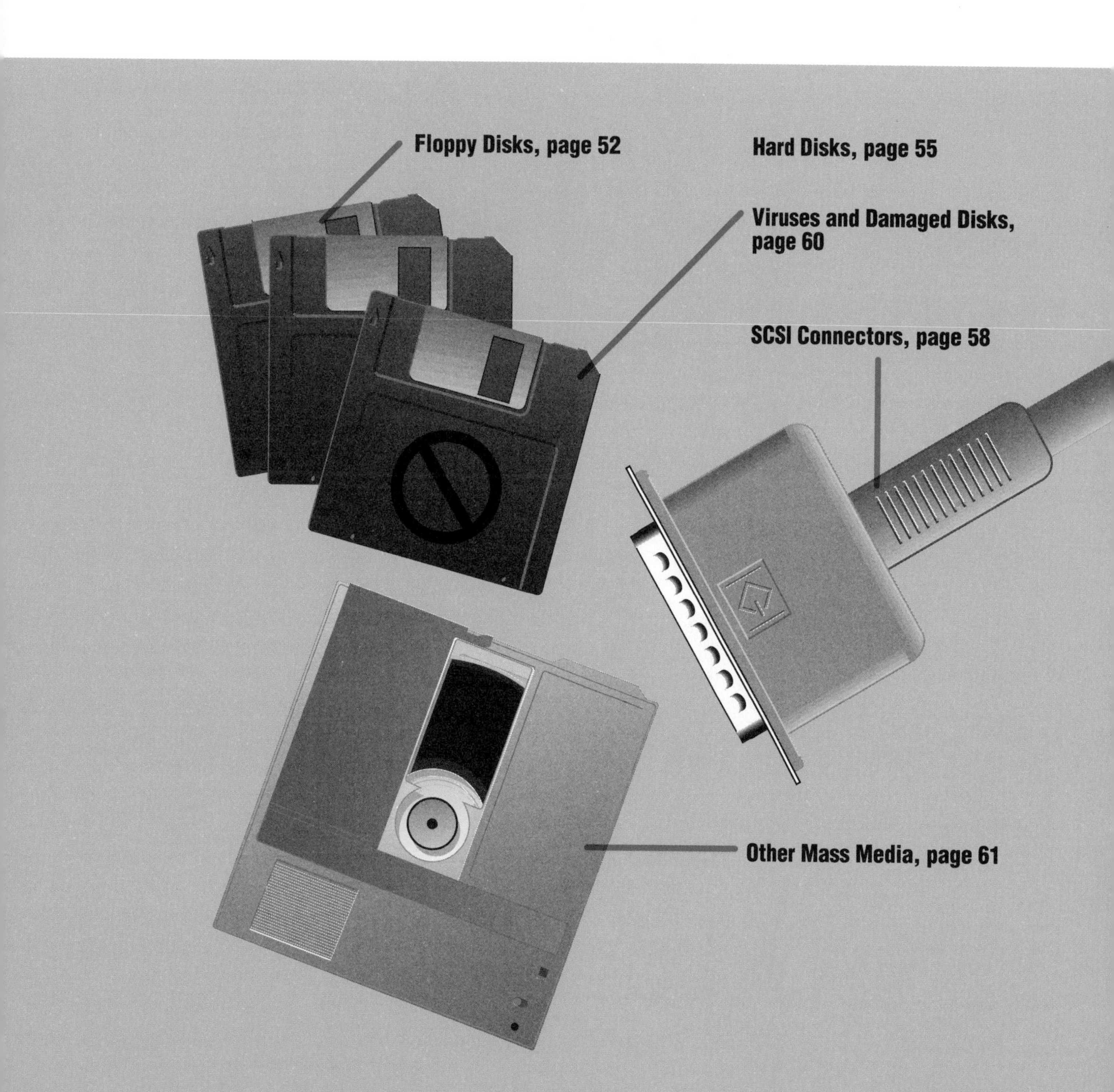
Floppy Disks, page 52
Hard Disks, page 55
Viruses and Damaged Disks, page 60
SCSI Connectors, page 58
Other Mass Media, page 61

Macintosh floppy disks come in three capacities: 400KB, 800KB, and 1.4MB. All use a 3.5" diameter disk (made of material similar to audio tape in a cassette) inside a protective plastic housing. Differences in capacity depend on how information is imbedded on the disk.

Unlike other computers, the Macintosh floppy disk drive has an automatic insertion and ejection mechanism. Push the disk almost all the way into the slot, and the drive pulls it the rest of the way. In ejecting a disk, the floppy disk drive pushes the disk out of the drive so you can pull it all the way out.

Floppy disks have much less capacity than hard disks, but they provide a way for software publishers to distribute software, for you to back up important files, and for Macintosh users to exchange files when the machines are not connected via a network.

HD

Diskette Sizes

The release of the Macintosh Plus model in 1985 signalled the beginning of the 800KB disk drive. Unlike the preceding 400KB model the new drive read and wrote information to both sides of the disk—hence its designation as a **double-sided disk.** In 1989, Apple began the transition to a higher density floppy disk, called **FDHD** (floppy disk, high density). Apple calls this drive the **SuperDrive,** and it has room for 1.4 megabytes of information.

A SuperDrive can read and write all three Macintosh disk formats (plus some MS-DOS formats, page ➜ 172. But a double-sided disk drive cannot read an FDHD formatted disk. Therefore, the 800KB double-sided disk format is still the most common one for distributing software or sharing files with a wide range of Macintosh models.

Diskettes are manufactured for each density, and should be used only for their intended capacity to prevent lost data. Single- and double-sided disks (400KB and 800KB) look physically alike. In most cases, however, the double-sided disk will be labeled as such either in faint stamping somewhere on the plastic case or on the metal shutter. FDHD disks, on the other hand, are physically different. In addition to the disk lock tab (on the edge away from the shutter), there is also a square hole in the case. The SuperDrive mechanism senses that hole, and recognizes the disk as an FDHD disk. The letters "HD" are also prominently printed on the plastic case near the metal shutter.

Inserting a Diskette

Macintosh disk drives are smart enough to prevent you from doing something wrong. You cannot, for example, insert a diskette upside down. As you push the disk into the slot correctly, the drive eventually takes over, drawing the disk in the rest of the way and seating it firmly in the drive. You don't see it sliding the metal shutter to one side to reveal the magnetic disk material to the disk drive heads.

Protecting Diskettes

Unless you intend to save information to a diskette, you should always lock the disk before inserting it into a disk drive. This prevents the possibility of the disk becoming infected with a **virus** ➜60 or accidental erasure. All Macintosh diskettes have a locking tab. With the round metal disk hub facing you, the **locking tab** is in the corner opposite the diagonal cut in the disk case. Use your fingernail to slide the locking tab in either direction. When the tab is up, and you can see through the hole, the disk is **write-protected.** Your programs may still read files on the disk, and you can run most programs from a locked disk. You'll also know if a disk is locked once you insert it into the disk drive and open the window to the disk: a small padlock icon appears in the upper left corner. If you eject the disk, change the locking tab, and re-insert the disk, the padlock disappears.

This process will erase all information on this disk.
Cancel
Erase
Please name this disk:
Untitled
OK

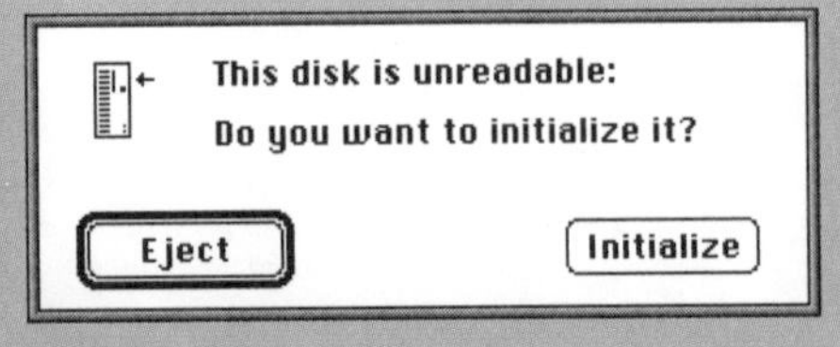
This disk is unreadable:
Do you want to initialize it?
Eject
Initialize

Initializing a New Disk

Before information can be saved to a disk, the disk must be prepared to accept the information. DOS computers call this process **formatting** the disk, while the Macintosh world calls it initializing the disk. **Initialization** lays down an invisible map of parking places for blocks of information. The Macintosh is also smart enough to know that when you insert a blank disk, it must be initialized before you can do anything with that disk, including seeing what, if anything, is on the disk. A **dialog box** appears asking you whether (and sometimes how) to initialize the disk.

If you have inserted a single- or double-sided disk into the drive, the dialog box gives you the choice of how to initialize the disk (or to eject the disk). While you may get away with initializing a single-sided disk as a double-sided one, bear in mind that a single-sided disk was originally manufactured as a double-sided disk, but failed quality testing on one side. It's risky at best.

Inserting a blank FDHD disk into a SuperDrive results in the dialog alerting you that the disk needs initialization. There are no choices, except to initialize or eject the disk. Do not attempt to format an FDHD disk in an 800KB disk drive. Also, despite some users' success, cutting a FDHD hole in an 800KB disk to fool the SuperDrive into thinking you have a real FDHD disk has not proven reliable.

After initialization, another dialog requests that you name the disk. Since disk icons appear along the right edge of the screen, you should keep the name to approximately 15 characters so you can see the entire name on the desktop. Any character but a **colon** is fair game for the disk name (colons designate dividers between elements of a pathname ➜116). You can rename a disk at any time.

If initialization fails, the Macintosh will tell you so. If the disk is a new one, and you expect it to be good, try restarting the Macintosh and reinitializing the disk. If initialization fails again, forget the disk. Either return it to the manufacturer for a replacement (if it is so warranted) or toss it. A troublesome disk only gets more so in time.

Special
Clean Up Desktop
Empty Trash...
Eject Disk ⌘E
Erase Disk...
Restart
Shut Down

Erasing a Disk

Dragging files to the Trash ➔109 is not the purest form of cleaning out a disk. In truth, the files are still on the disk, but the disk directory has no record of them. If the disk contained many different icons, those icons are stored in the invisible Desktop file, and may take up space you cannot reclaim. The best way to erase a disk is to select it in the Finder and choose **Erase Disk** from the **Special** menu. This action results in a dialog box asking for confirmation. For non-FDHD disks, you also have choices for initializing as single- or double-sided. That's because erasing a disk is the same as initializing a disk—wiping it clean and building a fresh Desktop file. This does not, however, rename the disk. You must do that separately.

Renaming a Disk

To prevent accidental erasure of disk names, it takes deliberate action to edit a disk's name. You must click specifically on the name part of a disk's icon in the Finder. When you do, a border appears around the disk name, and the name is highlighted. This means that the name has been selected, like text in a document. The next character you type replaces the entire name. Or, you can click the pointer anywhere along the name and position a text insertion pointer to add text. When you're finished, click anywhere outside the icon or press *return* or *enter*.

Ejecting a Disk

You have three ways to eject a disk from the Finder. After clicking once on the disk icon you want to eject (you don't have to click the icon if you have a single floppy disk drive), choose **Eject** from the **Special** menu (or type the keyboard equivalent, **⌘-E**). On most Macintoshes, *command-shift-1* ejects the disk in the first floppy disk drive, but this process is not guaranteed to work on later models. Either one of these methods is the least practical eject sequences for most situations, because it leaves the icon for the disk on the desktop. If you move the icon or try to open the disk with the disk ejected, you will be prompted to insert the disk. If you are truly finished working with a disk, the other methods are better.

Perhaps the most common way of ejecting a disk is by clicking and dragging the icon to the Trash icon. While you might think this action should erase the disk, it does no harm to the disk. It ejects the disk and removes its icon from the desktop. The **Put Away** menu item (and keyboard shortcut **⌘-Y**) also fully ejects a selected disk. You'll see the icon close into the Trash icon as the disk pops from the drive.

If you have ejected a disk, left its icon on the desktop, and get the dialog box asking you to insert the disk, you can usually cancel the box without inserting the disk by typing **⌘-.** (*command-period*). This won't work, however, if the action that prompted the dialog box must read or write information to that diskette before proceeding.

Turning off the machine with the **Shut Down** menu or starting the machine while holding the mouse button also eject all diskettes.

Not exactly high-tech, but a highly effective solution.

Ejecting a Stuck Disk

If you need to extract a diskette from the drive and, for any number of reasons, you cannot get the Macintosh started, all is not lost. As a fail-safe mechanism, the disk drive has a mechanical ejection button behind the front panel. Notice a small hole to the right of the disk slot. If you unbend a paper clip and carefully insert one end straight into that hole, you can press the manual eject button. It takes a little effort, and you have to keep the paper clip straight, but you can do it.

If a disk is really stuck—no amount of Finder or manual ejection gets it out—then there's something wrong with the disk. Perhaps the label has separated from the disk and is grabbing the disk drive; or maybe the disk's metal shutter is slightly bent and caught on something in the drive. Trying to force it out may damage the disk drive. It will be cheaper on the long run to have a knowledgeable technician open the Macintosh and extricate the disk by freeing it from inside.

Copying Disks

One of the first instructions you see in most application program installation guides is to make a copy of the program disk(s). The basic procedure requires that icons for both the source and target disk be on the desktop, and you drag the icon of the source disk to the target disk. If you have a single floppy disk drive, here are the steps to follow to copy one disk to another:

1. Lock the disk you want to copy, and insert it into the disk drive.
2. Choose **Eject** from the **Special** menu. This leaves the icon on the desktop.
3. Make sure the destination disk is not locked, and insert it into the disk drive.
4. Drag the icon of the source disk to the icon of the destination disk until the destination disk highlights. Then release the mouse button.
5. Read the dialog box carefully. It tells you what you are about to do and asks for confirmation. Click OK to continue, or Cancel to stop.
6. During the copy process, in addition to a Copy progress dialog box (which you can move by clicking and dragging on the title bar), you will be asked to insert each of the disk one or more times. Follow those directions until the copy is finished.
7. Select both disks (click and drag the selection rectangle around both disk's icons), and drag them to the Trash, thus ejecting the destination disk, and removing both icons from the desktop.

If you click Stop in the **Copy** dialog box after some files have been written to the destination disk, it will be too late to restore the destination disk to its original state. You do have time to cancel the operation, however, while the Macintosh is reading from the source disk for the first time.

Copying one disk to another does not alter the disk name of the destination disk. If you want a pure copy, rename the destination disk to the same as the source disk. You may have two disks with the same name on the desktop at the same time (although it might get confusing in some circumstances.)

Backing Up Disks

To make a backup copy of a disk, follow the steps for copying one disk to another (left.) This is different from using diskettes as a medium for backing up a hard disk 55-56. To protect your application program investment, it is wise to make a set of backup disks and store them in a safe place, perhaps in another building or a fire-proof vault.

Floppy Disk Care

Macintosh floppy disks are durable, but not invulnerable. Boxes of diskettes come with standard care guidelines, such as preventing the disks from getting wet, dusty, or too hot (the magnetic disk inside melts at temperatures attainable inside an enclosed automobile passenger compartment in the summer sun). Keep the shutter closed at all times to keep dirt and lethal fingerprints off the disk medium. When mailing disks, protect them in either a diskette mailer or a bubble pack insulated envelope. Postage cancelling machines (which can't read your "Hand Cancel" instructions) can crush unprotected disks enough to make them unreadable. Magnets, such as those in ringer telephones, motorized gear, power transformers, and audio speakers can cause the most damage to a disk's data. Since the particles on the disk medium are magnetic (disk drive heads use magnetic fields to write data to the disk), anything that generates a magnetic field poses a serious threat.

Empty Disk

0 items 25K in disk 761K avail

Where's the Last Few KB?

When you initialize a diskette, you don't get every byte you may have thought. For example, after initializing an 800KB disk, you see that there is only 785 KB available. The 800 KB measure is approximate, and the 1K used on the disk contains the hidden Desktop file 94. Similarly, a 1.4MB disk has 1.3 megabytes available with 1K used for

Practically every Macintosh these days has a hard disk installed or connected to it. A hard disk provides mass storage—tens or hundreds of megabytes in one convenient disk volume. No matter how vast you think a hard disk is when you get it, you'll begin to reach its capacity much sooner than you expected.

The smallest hard disk you should consider today is 40 megabytes (unfortunately, some Macintoshes are available only with 20MB drives). Apple also offers hard disks for desktop Macintoshes in the 80 and 160 megabyte range, while third parties supply disks in a variety of configurations between 40 and 1200 megabytes (1.2 gigabytes).

A hard disk may be installed internally inside your Macintosh or connected externally by way of the SCSI port on the rear panel ➔8. You may also combine multiple disks (internal and external), each represented on the desktop as a distinct volume icon.

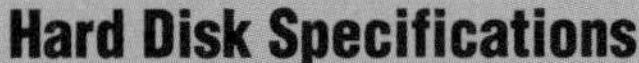

Hard Disk Specifications

When evaluating hard disks, the primary factors to consider are formatted capacity, transfer speed, and sound level. Hard disk capacities are normally rated in megabytes, but the value can be deceiving. A raw hard disk sometimes has many more megabytes available than what you'll actually be able to use once the disk has been formatted. Control sections on large disks can occupy megabytes of space. Always ask for the formatted capacity. Transfer speed and sound level are difficult to judge from disk drive printed specifications, because only when head-to-head comparisons using the same measuring techniques are used can you be sure of the results. Commonly cited measures, access and seek times (measured in milliseconds), have become almost meaningless because these specifications are so similar from drive to drive. At current sub-25 millisecond speeds, you probably won't notice a 5 or 10 millisecond improvement in day-to-day operation.

The best source of information on disk drives available at the moment are comparative reviews in **Macworld** and **MacUser** magazines. At least once each year they put dozens of disks through their paces in labs under what appear to be controlled situations.

A more difficult yet more important consideration is the reliability of the disk drive brand you buy. While only a handful of manufacturers make the actual hard disk mechanism, dozens of companies package those drives with their power supplies and disk maintenance software. You should look for not only a long warranty, but also a company that has earned a good reputation. Again, the magazines (especially the letters departments) can steer you away from trouble, but there is no guarantee that today's stable company will be around in two years if your disk drive acts up.

An important consideration for an external hard disk is a design that makes it easy to insert it into a series of SCSI devices. Make sure that the SCSI device number (address) can be adjusted from the rear panel, and that the drive is either not internally terminated or allows its termination to be switched on and off from the rear panel. The section on SCSI devices ➔58 describes these terms in detail.

System 7 Compatibility

Many non-Apple hard disks require special drivers (system extensions) to work with System 7. If your hard disk dates from mid-1991 or before, contact the manufacturer about System 7 requirements before installing System 7 on the disk.

Initializing a Hard Disk

Most often a hard disk comes from the dealer already formatted, perhaps with System software already installed. Even so, it will also come with software that lets you format the drive. Use a disk drive's initialization software only with that particular drive—these programs are not interchangeable.

Be prepared to wait awhile to initialize a big hard disk. If the initialization program also has a separate sector verification program or option, run it after the initialization. Not all sectors of a hard disk will probably format properly—this is normal. Your Macintosh System software will skip over the bad sectors when writing to the disk.

If you are connecting a hard disk that had been initialized while connected to a Macintosh of vastly different speed (e.g., initialized on an SE, but now connected to a IIsi), it is wise to back up your hard disk (twice for safety), reinitialize the disk, and copy the files back to the disk. The reason is that the hard disk was probably mapped in a way that worked better with a slower machine. This interleave factor (how consecutively sectors are mapped on the disk) can significantly reduce performance if not correct for the machine you're using.

Internal or External

Most Macintosh buyers get a machine with a hard disk inside the system unit. It's convenient, and usually offered as a package price. Those are the advantages of an internal drive, especially if you have to move the computer around periodically.

An external drive, however, has two significant advantages. First, if the drive should need repair, you just submit the drive, not the entire Macintosh to the shop. Secondly, you can take your System software, applications, and documents from Macintosh to Macintosh much more easily than moving most Macintoshes. It is also easier to sell an external drive you've outgrown on your way to a larger drive.

Using a hard disk also brings with it some obligations on your part. Backing up a hard disk is essential to protect yourself against the hard disk's failure (which could wipe out your programs and documents). Also, organizing hundreds or thousands of files takes some effort, especially as the disk fills up.

Connecting a Hard Disk

All of today's Macintosh external hard disks connect to the SCSI (Small Computer Systems Interface, or "scuzzy" for short) port on the rear panel of all Macs. Even internal hard disks connect to an internal SCSI port on the system board. Making SCSI devices work properly, especially when more then one are connected in a chain, can be tough work. See pages 58-59 for details on SCSI mysteries.

Powering Up an External Hard Disk

For your Macintosh to recognize a second, external SCSI hard disk, you must turn on the hard disk and let it reach full speed (just a few seconds) before turning on the computer. You can designate which disk you'd like to be the startup disk by way of the Startup Disk control panel 80. Occasionally, an external disk won't show up on the desktop at startup time. This usually happens after changing the SCSI cabling arrangement, or adding a disk drive to the SCSI chain. It may take one or two additional Restarts to get the Macintosh to recognize the disk (don't turn off the disk between attempts). If a couple **restarts** fail to get the disk on the desktop, see the troubleshooting suggestions 176.

Backing Up a Hard Disk

The most important maintenance chore you have with a hard disk is backing up important information on a regular basis. Most users do not back up until something disastrous happens, and the hard disk is no longer available or is damaged (crashed). One hard disk crash, and a computer user sees backup religion for awhile.

You have a couple choices to make the task easier. One is to copy data files that you've changed to floppy disks. SuperDrives (1.4MB floppy disks) make this palatable for a few megabytes of data, and the Finder can help you locate recently modified files 120.

Commercial backup programs make the job even easier, because they can keep track of what needs to be backed up based on file modification dates and the date of your last backup, prompting you for specific floppy disks from the set containing your entire hard disk's contents. These incremental backup programs work more efficiently if you back up to another mass storage device, such as another hard disk, a tape backup system 61, or a cartridge disk 61. Depending on how much stuff you need to back up, the operation could be as simple as starting the backup program, and letting it do all the work.

Hard Disk Partitions

Hard disks in excess of about 100 megabytes can be made more manageable by breaking the large disk space into two or more sections, called partitions. Special software (a system extension) is usually necessary to partition a hard disk. Most large hard disks come with this software, and commercial disk utility programs also have partition modules. As part of working with the software, you designate how large each partition should be. Since each partition appears on the desktop as a distinct disk volume, you can also choose which volumes the partitioning software should make available when you start up your Macintosh. Seldom-used partitions can be hidden until needed. Then, activating the partitioning software, you can mount the desired volume when needed. See page 118 for further ideas about organizing files on a hard disk.

Partition 1

Partition 2

Partition 3

Cautions

Treat your hard disk, especially an external drive, as if it were a one-of-a-kind fragile egg. If it is your only hard disk, that device has the only copy of your latest work (everything since your last backup). Some might even say that their working lives are on that disk. In fact, today's hard disk drives are pretty durable, but the gentler you can be, the further into the future you put the day when the hard disk fails. Here are few rules to help lengthen your disk's life:

- **Make sure the computer and hard disk are turned off before connecting or disconnecting the SCSI cable.**
- **Do not move the disk (or computer for an internal disk) while the disk drive is reading or writing.**
- **Hand carry a hard disk while traveling, and put it in a protective case if possible.**
- **Ask airline security checkpoints to hand inspect the disk instead of passing it through the x-ray machine (x-rays don't seem to hurt a hard disk, but the magnetic fields on the conveyor belt rollers could do some harm).**
- **Allow a hard disk that has passed through cold or hot air temperatures to return to room temperature before turning it on.**

Speeding Up Your Hard Disk

The longer you own a hard disk and the more times your programs save files to it, the more likely that files will be scattered all around your hard disk. In fact, chunks of a single file may be written to several places on the disk (the operating system figures out where all the pieces are with the help of control files hidden on the disk). This allows the computer to save files wherever it can fit pieces (512 byte chunks), instead of looking (perhaps in vain) for a contiguous part of the disk for the entire file. As files become liberally sprinkled throughout the disk, your hard disk become increasingly fragmented. The downside to **fragmentation** is that the hard disk has to work harder to read and write a file, increasing mechanical wear and the time it takes to perform disk accesses.

You can **optimize** your hard disk yourself or with the help of a commercial disk optimizer (most disk utility products have optimizer modules). To do it yourself, you need to backup all files, reformat the hard disk, and then copy the files back to the hard disk. Not only is this a lot of work, but the commercial products also perform additional optimization tasks that you can't do manually. Commercial optimizers do their work by copying and rewriting files. Make sure you have a backup of your hard disk before starting optimization. And don't wait for your hard disk to fill up before optimizing it—optimization requires a fair amount of free space on the disk. Finally, disk optimization shouldn't have to be done frequently. Fragmentation has to get pretty bad for you to notice speed degradation. Some disk optimizers precheck the disk to see if optimization will really help you. Wait

Dynamic Backups

Manufacturers of very large hard disks (300 MB and up) frequently offer specialized software that automatically saves data not only to the disk you signify in your program, but to a backup disk at the same time. Techniques for this kind of backup are called **mirroring** (data is saved to two daisy-chained SCSI drives) and **duplexing** (a second SCSI disk is attached by way of a plug-in board for a Macintosh II-style computer). Duplexing is faster than mirroring, because the writing to both drives is performed more simultaneously. Both systems give you the comfort of having an up-to-the-minute backup of the primary hard disk. If one fails (the software alerts you when one of the drives fails), you can take it out of service and use the backup without any data loss. These systems are intended primarily for network server hard disks, for which backups are critical to a business. An additional backup procedure should be done daily or weekly to another device (cartridge or tape drives) and that backup stored in

The Small Computer Systems Interface (abbreviated SCSI, pronounced "scuzzy") is the standard among Macintosh computers for connecting add-on hardware that requires fast information transfer: hard disks, scanners, and CD-ROM drives to name a few.

All Macintosh computers since the Plus model include a SCSI port on the rear panel.

Up to 6 devices may be connected in a series called a daisy-chain (an internal hard disk can be the seventh SCSI device connected to a Mac). Most SCSI devices have two SCSI ports—one to connect to the previous item in the chain and one to connect to the next item in the chain. A SCSI device may have either the same **25-pin connector** as most Macintoshes, or the more standard **50-pin connector.** PowerBooks have a still different 30-pin minature connector, requiring a connector adapter ➔8. Choosing the correct cabling is critical in setting up a SCSI device.

Connecting multiple SCSI devices to the Macintosh can be a frustrating experience due to the unpredictable nature of SCSI devices as they interact with each other and lengths of SCSI cable. It often takes trying several different combinations of cables, devices, and the terminator connector to make everything in a SCSI chain work as desired.

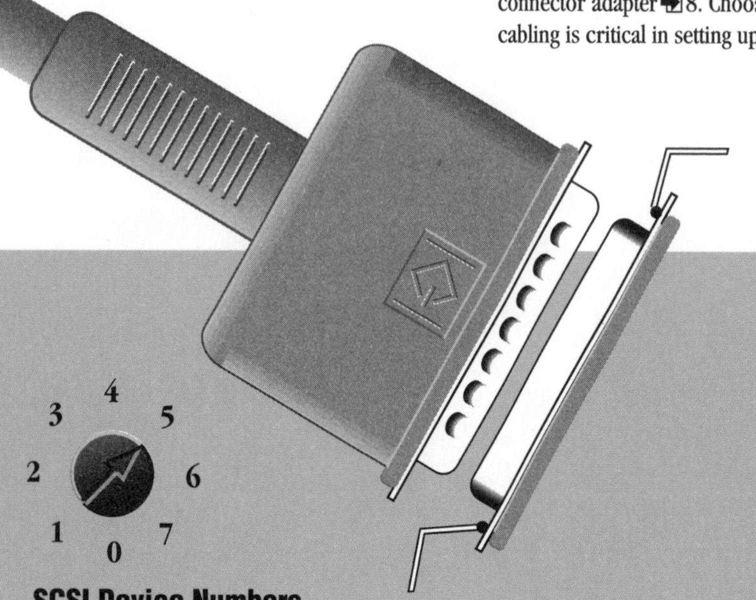

SCSI Device Numbers

Each device in a SCSI chain must have its unique identification number. Most SCSI devices have a small switch on the rear panel that allows you to change the SCSI number. The switch can be any of several designs, including a thumbwheel, push button, or rotary knob. Which number you assign to any device is rarely a concern except for these three rules:

1. Apple internal hard disks come from the factory set to zero, so no external device should be set to zero;
2. No two devices may have the same ID number;
3. If you have no internal hard disk, but two or more external disks, the drive you want to be the startup disk should have a **higher** number than the others (although you can change the startup disk from the Startup Disk control panel ➔80, later).

If you are about to connect someone else's hard disk to your SCSI chain, check the SCSI ID numbers of all devices before starting up. If two or more hard disks have the same SCSI ID, the disks could become damaged. Also, change a SCSI ID number only when all connected SCSI devices and the Macintosh are turned off.

SCSI Cables

Because of the two styles of SCSI connectors (25-pin, like on the Mac, and 50-pin, such as on most external SCSI devices including Apple's disks), a wide variety of SCSI cables are prepared to confuse you. Here is a table of SCSI cables you might need, divided into groups based on how common they are:

Name	Connector (Mac end)	Other Connector	Notes
SCSI System Cable	25-pin male	50-pin male	Usually 1 to 3 feet long, from Macintosh to first standard SCSI device (special 30-pin cable version required for PowerBooks)
SCSI Peripheral Cable	50-pin male	50-pin male	Available in lengths up to 15 feet to link additional standard SCSI devices
SCSI System Cable	25-pin male	25-pin male	Macintosh to non-standard SCSI device
SCSI Peripheral Cable	25-pin male	25-pin male	Links two non-standard SCSI devices
SCSI Peripheral Cable	25-pin male	50-pin male	Links non-standard to standard SCSI device

Working with a variety of SCSI devices in a chain will be much easier if they all have the same 50-pin connectors. Cables are more readily available, and you have the flexibility to maneuver the devices in any order needed for compatibility (below).

SCSI Termination

Part of the SCSI mystery for users is the SCSI terminator. Technically, this device is supposed to absorb the electronic signals that flow through the SCSI cable so that a signal doesn't bounce back through the cable to the sender. Improperly terminated chains have resulted in multiple images of a hard disk on the desktop (and a great deal of dysfunctional behavior as a result).

Terminators come in several varieties. An external terminator, the easiest to work with, looks like a double 50-pin SCSI connector (in the 50-pin cable scheme of things). The design allows it to be attached by itself to one of the two SCSI connectors on a device or between an incoming cable and the connector it plugs into. Some SCSI devices, especially hard disks, may be internally terminated, meaning that the termination parts are inside the cabinet. Some of those disks offer switches or trap doors to make removing the termination easy for non-technical users, while the rest make the job a scary prospect unless you're comfortable with electronic circuitry. The easiest SCSI devices to work with are those that are not internally terminated, allowing you to control termination with an external terminator.

Apple internal hard disks (and most internal disks available from third parties) are internally terminated. By and large, this is OK, since the party line states that the device closest to the Macintosh should be terminated. The same line says that the last device in the chain should also be terminated. Unfortunately, this scheme does not always work.

Starting Configurations

Since connecting SCSI devices may require a bit of experimentation (especially when two or more external devices are connected), you should start from the prescribed configuration and proceed further if that doesn't work. Here are starting configurations for one and two devices connected to Macintoshes with and without internal hard disks (assuming the internal hard disk is terminated):

No internal hard disk, one external device:

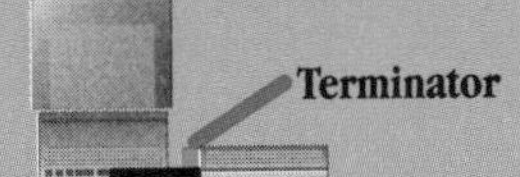

No internal hard disk, two external devices:

Internal hard disk, one external device:

Internal hard disk, two external devices:

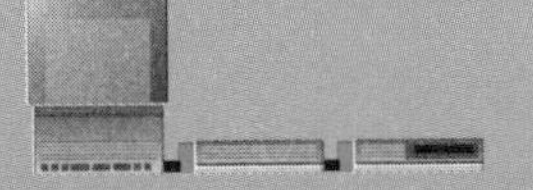

When Things Don't Work

Before fooling with the SCSI chain and configuration, here are a few items to investigate as causes for devices that don't appear to work as expected:

1. Turn off all equipment, and make sure all **SCSI cables** are firmly attached to the device connectors. The 25-pin connectors should be screwed to the sockets; 50-pin connectors should have the socket's edge clips locked in place.
2. **Turn on all SCSI devices before turning on the Macintosh.** Occasionally you can leave a device in a SCSI chain turned off, but there is no formula to follow. In many cases, all devices in the chain must be turned on before the Macintosh will even start.
3. Be sure that you have installed System 7-compatible versions of any system software that comes with a SCSI device (like scanners and CD-ROM players). It's easy to forget these things when installing a new system or hard disk. Restart the Macintosh if installation was necessary.

If fulfilling these obligations still doesn't get your SCSI chain working, it's time to experiment with SCSI cabling and settings. Here are possibilities to explore with the Macintosh and devices turned off:

1. Alter the numbering of external SCSI devices so that the devices are in a different order than before.
2. Connect the devices in a different order if the logistics allow.
3. Try cables of different lengths in different positions between devices.
4. Remove the terminator from the end of the SCSI chain, especially if you have a long SCSI peripheral cable in the chain.
5. Move the terminator from the end of the SCSI chain one step closer to the Macintosh. For example, if the terminator is by itself on one of the sockets on the last device, move it between the other socket and the incoming cable. After each move, start the Macintosh and try it. If the one-step move doesn't work, move it another step toward the Macintosh.

If no combination of cabling, termination, or numbering lets all the devices work, try removing the least used item from the chain, and start the process over. You may have to leave a device out of the chain except for the times when you need it, and can put it in the chain without all the other devices. The manufacturer may be of some help, but don't count on SCSI device makers to have a solution to every problem, especially working with brand new, obsolete, or out of the ordinary devices.

Disk Booting Order

Each time you turn on or restart the Macintosh, the operating system searches for a startup disk in a specific order:

- First internal floppy disk drive
- Second internal floppy disk drive
- External floppy disk drive
- SCSI hard disk last chosen in the **Startup Disk** control panel
- Internal hard disk (the SCSI address is stored in **PRAM,** ➲ 41)
- Remaining SCSI addresses from 6 down to 0

The first device in this order that contain a System file becomes the startup disk—the one at the upper right corner of the desktop. That System's fonts, sounds, keyboards, and extensions become available to all applications that start thereafter.

Each time the Macintosh finds a device at a SCSI address, it also looks into the Extensions and System folders for drivers that match the device

Roving SCSI Devices

Many Macintosh users bring a hard disk or **cartidge drive** ➲ 61 along to work on other Macintoshes or make presentations. This is a wise move, especially when demonstrating software or presenting to a group of people. It's much more reliable to startup from your own hard disk with its complement of fonts, sounds, and applications that you work with daily. If you take your disk along, also bring one or two SCSI cables that fit your device. Always have the system cable that connects between the Macintosh and your device. Or perhaps the Macintosh has a SCSI device already connected that you can replace with your hard disk (provided the cable connectors are compatible). You might also carry a SCSI peripheral cable in case the Macintosh you need to connect to is best accessed

Turn on your disk drive and then the Macintosh. Chances are the Macintosh will start from its internal drive if it has one. If the Macintosh fails to put your disk on the desktop, choose **Restart** from the **Special** menu. Sometimes it takes a couple restarts to recognize a new hard disk. When your disk icon appears, open the **Startup Disk** control panel ➲ 80, and click on your disk's icon. The next time you restart the Macintosh, your disk will be the startup disk, replete with your familiar fonts and other system software services. As a courtesy to the Macintosh's owner, choose the primary hard disk from the Startup Disk control panel before shutting down the Macintosh to remove your disk. It's not serious if you forget this last step, however, because the Macintosh will restart from the first disk drive in booting order that

Like the medical variety, a computer virus infects quietly until the symptoms start to appear. By then, it's too late (you're already infected.)

Several viruses have spread throughout the Macintosh community, and more will do so as devious (if not deviant) lone-wolf programmers try to be cute or wreak havoc. If your Macintosh or software begins to exhibit abnormal behavior, a virus may be at the root. Fortunately, virus detection software is also available.

While not always caused by a virus, a hard disk's medium or key controlling files may become damaged. The usual symptom is that the disk cannot be read by the Macintosh—an alert says "**the disk is unreadable.**" In many cases, the program and data files on the disk are intact. You just need the help of **disk repair utility software** to bring the disk back to life.

Virus Propagation

The most innocent actions—inserting a floppy disk or starting a program downloaded from a bulletin board—can begin a virus rampage through your hard disk. Some viruses are of the nuisance variety in that they simply slow down your machine's performance. But other viruses are more deadly: they literally erase files without your knowledge. Floppy disks are the primary carriers of viruses. The strains are in the files on that disk and are copied to your hard disk along with a file, or literally just by inserting the disk (the Macintosh's actions when you insert a disk are enough to trigger some virus' propagation). If you work in an office full of Macintoshes, the likelihood of your machine becoming infected is great, especially if others freely exchange files and public domain software from in and out of the company either by floppy disk or network.

Preventing Virus Infection

Several public domain and commercial programs offer virus detection and protection. Among the most popular are the shareware 139 program called **Disinfectant** (kept up to date and distributed widely by on-line services and user groups) and the commercial product, Symantec's SAM. Both programs include Startup programs 91that watch for the incursion of virus-like activity. Virus creators and detectors are forever in a cops-and-robbers game, with the creators usually one small step ahead of the detectors. Whatever virus protection program you adopt, be sure to keep it up to date—the virus creators are doing their best to do the same.

It is also critical just in case your hard disk has a virus on it, that you don't spread it to your application program master disks. Before installing any software, always write-protect the floppy disk before inserting it into the disk drive for the first time 13.

Recovering a Damaged Disk

When a hard disk fails to start or be recognized by the Macintosh, it is cause for both alarm and a cool head. In virtually all cases, the information is still on the disk, but the disk's hidden directory is damaged. The directory is like a table of contents to a book. Even if the table of contents is missing, the chapters are still there.

The term commonly used for this problem is a disk crash, which came from the early days of disk drives when the heads could literally come into contact with the disk platters and irretrievably scratch the disk. Such hardware disk crashes are extremely rare on Macintosh hard disks. The kinds of crashes that do occur are more often than not recoverable.

Unless you are already using a disk utility program that assists in recovering crashed disks and lost files (products like Norton Utilities), try to create a floppy disk with a minimal system 70 and the Disk First Aid program from the System disks. Restart your Macintosh using that diskette, and start the **Disk First Aid** program. Click [Drive] in the dialog box until the name of the damaged disk appears. Then click [Open]. Choose **Repair Automatically** from the **Options** menu, and let the program try to fix the disk's directory. If this doesn't work, try running Disk First Aid two more times.

If you can start your Macintosh from a floppy system disk and you can see the hard disk (but it still won't let you start from the hard disk), reinstall the System software onto the hard disk 68. Go through the entire Installer program on the system disks.

Unprotected

Write-protected

The next step is to buy one of the disk utility programs (SUM, Norton Utilities, or Central Point's Macintosh Tools) to attempt to bring the disk back to life. Each program goes about this in a different way, so you'll have to follow the sometimes cryptic steps in the manuals. If you can find a knowledgeable Macintosh friend to help out, it can help a lot.

There have been even more severe cases. The disk spins, but neither the Finder nor disk utility programs can recognize the disk. Such disasters generally occur to those who have valuable, unbacked up files on the disk (Murphy strikes!). Call your hard disk supplier to find a service that recovers crashed disks. These services are not cheap. It can cost a few hundred dollars just for the bureau to see if anything is recoverable, and then a charge per file for recovery. On a large disk, the fees could reach $1000.

The last resort is to reinitialize the disk. If have been good about making backup copies, then the lost work may not be too serious in return for having your disk back. Consider installing file recovery software from the disk tools programs listed above. They make the task of recovering from a disk crash (or even accidentally erased files) much easier.

In addition to traditional hard disks, other mass storage devices may also be connected to the Macintosh.

Depending on the device, they offer open ended capacity, very high capacity on a single disk, and alternative methods of backing up your regular hard disk(s).

Three basic media are worth investigating if you work with large amounts of disk data: **removable cartridge hard disks** (magnetic); **optical disk cartridges** (in varying degrees of writeability); and **tape drives** (used primarily as backup devices). All make good backup devices. Mass storage is also a very competitive specialty, which helps improve performance, increase capacity, and reduce prices as the months go by.

Huge Hard Disks

While the first hard disk ever available for the Macintosh was a 5 megabyte job, today you can buy a traditional hard disk that holds 1.2 gigabytes (1200 megabytes). For internal use on most Macintosh II models, you should limit yourself to half-height hard disks, which are becoming available in the 600 megabyte range. Only in the six-slot Macintosh models (II, IIx, IIfx) can you install a full-height disk by replacing the disk drive bracket (a new bracket comes with full-height internal drives). You should, however, be able to take a half-height drive with you if you change to another Macintosh II model. Large disks can get unwieldy (you should partition such disks, ➜56), but as file servers or working storage for color graphics, digitized video images, and sound, such sizes become necessary.

Removable Magnetic Disks

The most popular standard in this category is a drive and cartridge mechanism developed by Syquest, and packaged under many companies' brand names. Syquest drives come in two capacities (approximately 45 and 88 megabytes) and are in the $1000 range (less for the 45 megabyte drives). Volume purchases of 45 MB cartridges get the price down to under $70 each. You pop these durable cartridges in and out of the Syquest drive much like huge floppy disks. Moreover, since the disks act like any disk volume, you can even use one as a primary startup disk, although the performance is slower than comparable hard disks. Software developers and network administrators can load an entirely different version of System software (e.g., a new version or an international version) and start from that disk to experiment without disturbing his or her primary working hard disk. Syquest drives and cartridges are excellent values for back-up and short-term archiving.

CD-ROM

Compact Disc-Read Only Memory is becoming a more popular method of distributing large quantities of computer information. The discs are physically identical to the single-sided audio compact discs, but they require a special CD-ROM player, which connects to the Macintosh SCSI port. A CD-ROM disc can store about 550 MB of data, but the discs are read-only. To create a CD-ROM, you need the help of CD-ROM pressing plants, which help you create a master disk (from your hard disk) from which copies are pressed. A master costs about $1500, with individual copies costing around $5.00 each. For monthly updates of reference material or publishing huge quantities of data, CD-ROM is a cost-effective medium.

WORM

Higher up the evolutionary scale, a Write Once Read Many (WORM) disk is also optical (it is read by a laser beam), but in a different format than a CD-ROM. WORM disks come in a variety of sizes, predominantly in the 600 MB range (with 300 MB per side—you flip the disk, so no file can be larger than about 300 MB). You cannot erase a file saved or copied to a WORM disk. At best, if you delete a file, the desktop file on that WORM disk forgets about the deleted file, but the file is still there. Some WORM drives come with software that lets you retrieve those files in case you need to view a previous version of a file. WORM drives are best for one-time archival storage of historical data.

Erasable Optical Disks

The latest optical storage innovation is a high capacity disk that acts like a flippable magnetic disk, with roughly 300MB per side (the cost of two lasers would make the drives unattractive). With drives costing in the under $4000 range, and disks about $200 each, you'll need to store lots of data (perhaps a couple gigabytes or more) to make this option economically feasible. As a day-to-day working drive, performance of optical drives is not as good as high capacity magnetic disk drives.

Tape Drives

Because tapes store information in a linear fashion, and random access is incredibly slow, tape drives are best suited for **batch backup** and restore operations. Several tape drive hardware standards and capacities are used today. Here's a table of the primary formats and typical properties:

Format	Capacity	Notes
DC2000	40-120 MB	Apple's Tape Backup is a 40MB unit.
DC600	60-320 MB	Common among DOS computer backups; transfer data to Macintosh with Apple File Exchange system software.
Teac	60-150MB	Good speed; low cost tape cartridges.
DAT	1.2 GB	Same tape as digital audio tape, but conflicting data storage standards among makers.
8mm	2.2 GB	Good speed, but expensive drives; same tape as 8mm home video.

DAT and 8mm drives are emerging technologies, and evolving fast. Before purchasing any tape backup drive, compare the software included with the drive, and make sure it does the kind of backups you need for your data storage.

Get data-grade DAT tape—not music grad

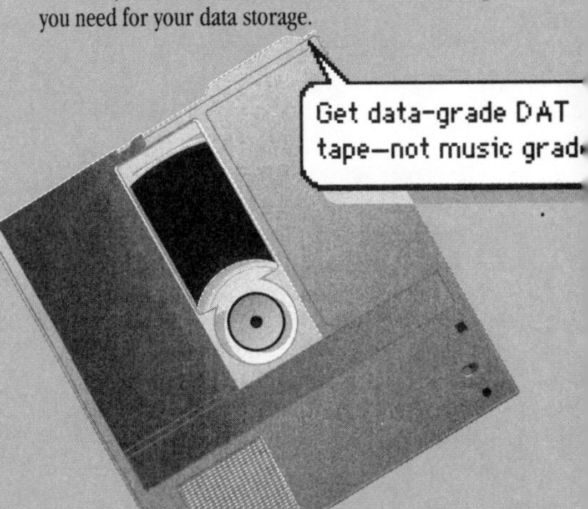

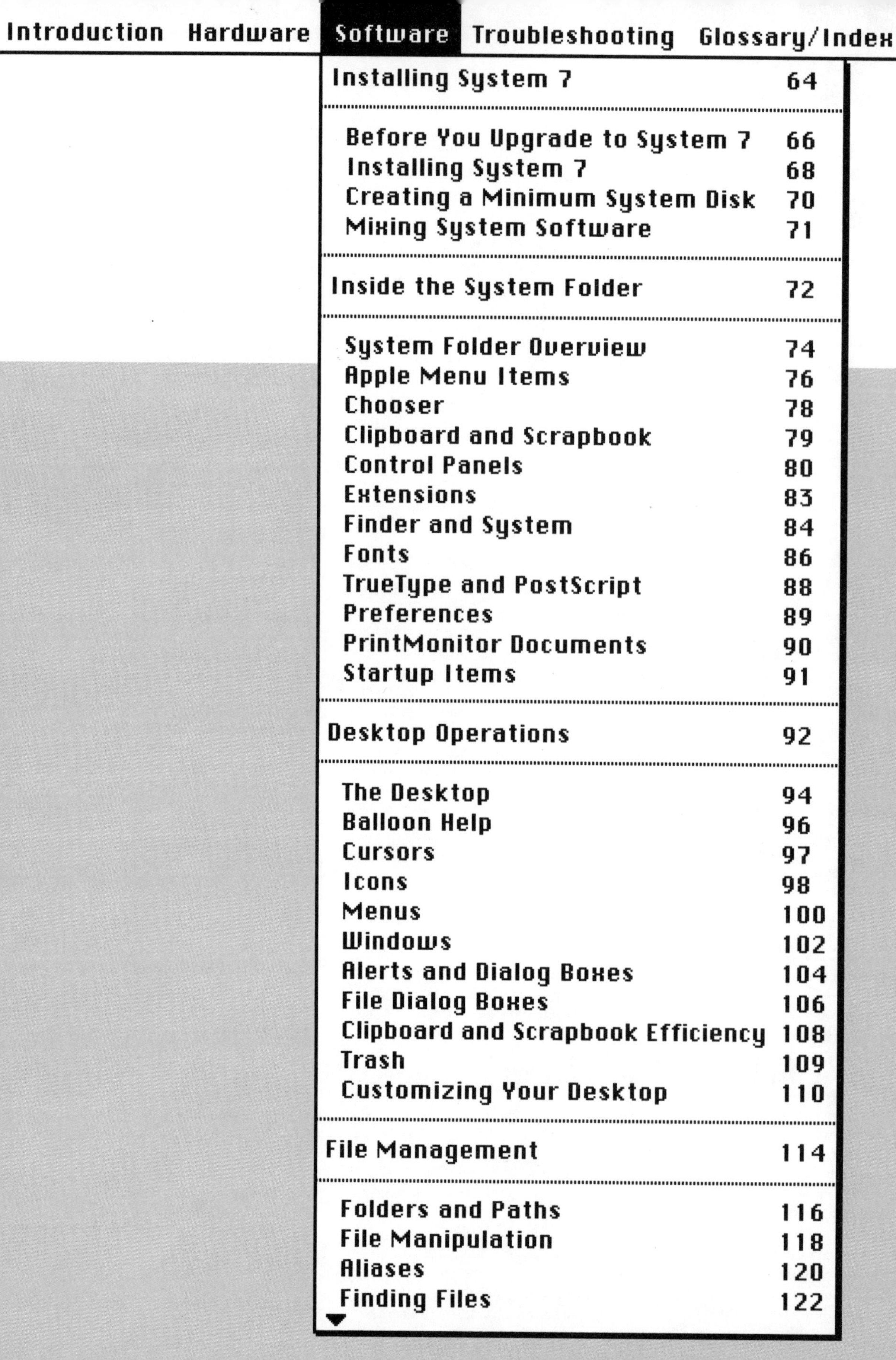
Introduction
Hardware
Software
Troubleshooting
Glossary/Index

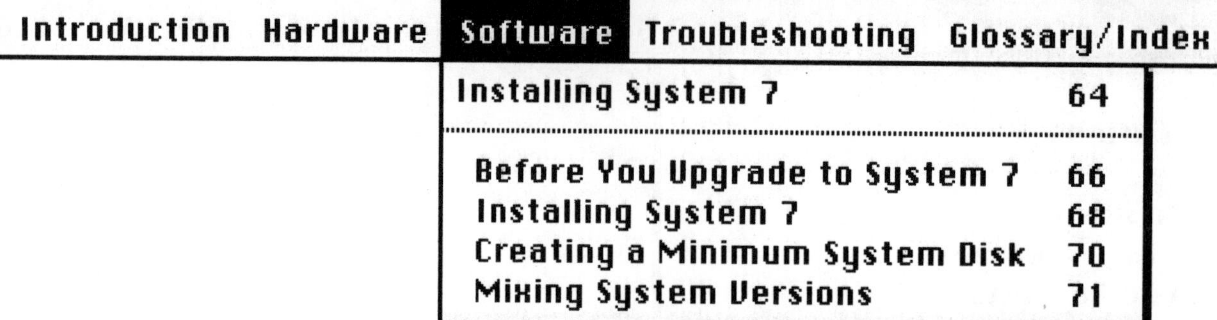
Introduction
Hardware
Software
Troubleshooting
Glossary/Index

Compatibility Checker 1.0

Installer

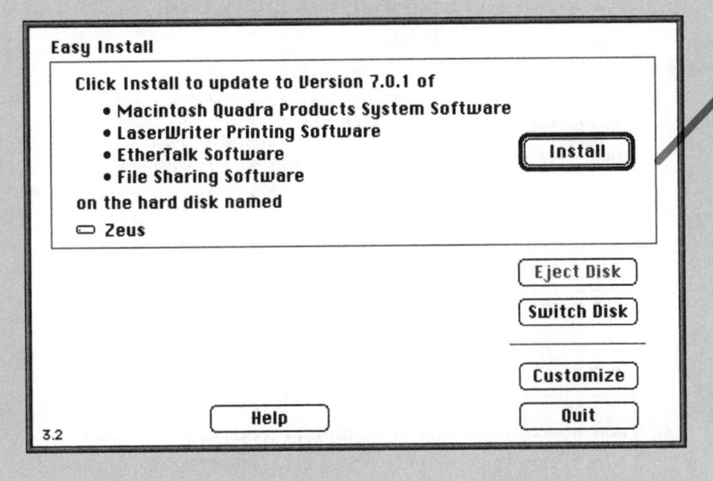
Easy Install
Click Install to update to Version 7.0.1 of
• Macintosh Quadra Products System Software
• LaserWriter Printing Software
• EtherTalk Software
• File Sharing Software
on the hard disk named
Zeus
Install
Eject Disk
Switch Disk
Customize
Help
Quit
3.2

System software upgrades are a way of life in personal computing. Some upgrades are more painless than others, depending on the level of compatibility between your existing computing setup and the new operating system.

System 7 was the most ambitious system software upgrade Apple had ever attempted for the Macintosh. More user feedback and engineering effort went into this version than anytime since the first Macintosh operating system was released in 1984. There is a likelihood that System 7's new features will make your Macintosh life easier and more productive. It also means that compatibility with hardware and software you owned before May, 1990 is less assured.

While upgrading to System 7 is reversible, you should make sure that you and your Macintosh are prepared for System 7 before installing it. A basic understanding of System 7's new features, compatibility, and hardware requirements will make the transition more enjoyable.

Why Does Apple Upgrade System Software?

What genuinely makes the compilation of components in your Macintosh's cabinet a Macintosh is the system software. System software imbues the box with a kind of personality. In the case of the Macintosh, a number of its features were desirable enough for makers of system software for other computers to imitate those features. Apple, in turn, needs to stay ahead of the competition by enhancing its distinguishing characteristic—it's system software. In reality, the marketing battle is not among the Macintosh, IBM PC-style, or other computers, but among the Macintosh, MS-DOS and Windows, OS/2, and other system software environments. Unlike the more incremental improvements in previous upgrades to Macintosh system software, System 7 represents a major leap.

Why Upgrade to System 7?

There is no law that says you have to upgrade to System 7, but as time goes by, more and more applications will take advantage of its features. Even without those applications, working with your files, sharing files with others, and customizing your desktop environment may be reason enough to make the change, provided your applications and hardware (e.g., hard disks and other peripherals) are System 7 compatible.

Improved Desktop Management ➡94

The Desktop becomes an actual storage place for files, instead of a nebulous concept. When you drag or save a file to the Desktop, the file appears in the desktop area of the screen, but is actually saved in a Desktop Folder on the startup disk volume. System 7 suppresses the folder from appearing in the disk's window, but the folder does appear if you open the volume in an earlier system software version.

Better Folder Views ➡112

A new control panel, Views, offers enormous flexibility in the information you see in iconic or text listing views of files in a folder. Moreover, in any text mode, a hierarchical structure lets you view listings of items in a folder without opening a new window to see the files.

A Finder that Finds ➡122

Instead of the Find File desk accessory, System 7 embeds file searching into the Finder's **File** menu. You enter search criteria into your choice of two Find dialogs (the more detailed one lets you search comments, version numbers, and other esoterica). Then, if a match is located, the Finder opens the folder window at that level and selects the matching file. If that's not the desired file, issue the **Find Again** command. The folder window closes when a new match is located, and its folder window opens.

System Folder Simplicity ➡74

Experienced Macintosh users can have more than 100 files in their System Folders, making it difficult to locate a particular item or kind of item. System 7's System Folder contains a number of sub-folders, each with a special purpose, such as storing all the preferences files or control panels. When you drag a file to the System Folder, System 7 is smart enough to alert you that the file belongs in one of those sub-folders, and stows it for you.

Customizability ➡110-113

Knowing that Macintosh users like to customize their environments with sounds and colors, the System 7 engineers built in significantly more flexibility in the way you can customize icons, colors, and the menu's contents without having to be a ResEdit wizard ➡84.

File Sharing ➡164-173

If you work in an office full of Macintoshes already connected to a shared printer, System 7 lets you share files and applications among designated people on the network. For simple sharing of files, this eliminates the need for a more formal file server ➡162.

Virtual Memory ➡45

When working with large documents and lots of applications in a memory-constrained Macintosh, System 7's virtual memory opens an unused part of your hard disk as an extension to your Mac's RAM. While not nearly as fast as real RAM, virtual memory may eliminate a roadblock in certain circumstances when it is essential to have several applications open at a time.

Multiple Programs ➡126

A large number of Macintosh users prior to System 7 either shied away from MultiFinder (due to earlier incompatibility problems) or didn't know it existed. In System 7, MultiFinder—the ability to run as many programs at a time as RAM allows—is always on (and can't be turned off). If you have the RAM, it's much easier to keep your common programs running all the time and just click among them.

TrueType ➡88

Except for those with a big investment in PostScript Type 1 fonts, System 7 eases font management. A single TrueType ➡font file contains everything your printer needs to print the font in any size and for your screen to display fonts in all sizes. No more jaggies.

Hardware Requirements

System 7 has a few minimum requirements for your Macintosh hardware. They are:

128K ROMs (everything since the Macintosh Plus)
800K disk drive (everything since the Macintosh Plus)
2 MB RAM

That's just to get System 7 running. To use it efficiently, however, you really should have a hard disk. Also, since the System software takes up at least a megabyte of your RAM, you won't feel comfortable with less than 4 megabytes of RAM if you plan to run more than one program at a time—and it's irresistible.

But even 4 MB of RAM and a hard disk won't give you everything that System 7 has to offer unless your machine is among the latest models. Virtual memory and 32-bit addressing have special requirements as shown in the table below:

Macintosh	Virtual Memory	32-bit Add.
Plus	no[1]	no
SE	no[1]	no
Classic	no	no
Classic II	yes	yes
LC	no	yes
SE/30	yes	yes[2]
II	yes[3]	yes[2]
IIx	yes	yes
IIfx	yes	yes
IIcx	yes	yes[2]
IIci	yes	yes
IIsi	yes	yes
Portable	yes	yes
Quadra 700	yes	yes
Quadra 900	yes	yes
PowerBook 100	no	no
PowerBook 140	yes	yes
PowerBook 170	yes	yes

[1] Possible with a 68030 or 68040 accerlerator and third-party software
[2] Requires MODE32 System 7 extension (free from most yser groups and dealers)
[3] Requires optional MC68851RC16A PMMU chip.

Interapplication Communication

With System 7, programs and documents have a couple ways to communicate with each other. The most accessible are the publish and subscribe features ➔134. In this mechanism, a section of one document publishes itself as a file. Another document can subscribe to that file, thereby including the published data (text, pictures, whatever) into the second document. Then, whenever a change is saved in the first document, the changes appear in the second document automatically the next time you open it for viewing or printing.

Less likely to be a user-accessible IAC feature of new programs is Apple Events ➔132. Programs can send messages—Apple Events—to other programs and documents. Programs that have been designed to accommodate each others events can work seamlessly together in the background.

32-bit Addressing

System 7 enhances the RAM capabilities of higher power Macintosh models. By letting the computer denote each individual memory location by a 32-digit (binary digits, that is) number, the **8 megabyte limit on** many Macintoshes is extended to **128 megabytes,** with virtual memory addressing ➔43 up to one **gigabyte.**

Compatibility Checker 1.0

Checking for Software Compatibility

Apple has assembled information about software product compatibility with System 7. With System 7 (and available separately from many Apple dealers or user groups) is a HyperCard application (i.e., you need HyperCard 1.2 or later to open it) that examines the system folder contents and applications on your hard disk. The program produces a report about which applications and versions are compatible. Some programs are only partially compatible, meaning that certain operations may be erratic or may cause a system error. Not every program and system file extension is in the list on the stack, so just because a program is not listed doesn't mean that it won't work with System 7.

You should not upgrade to System 7 until you have confirmed (either by Apple's list or with the software publisher) that your primary applications and peripheral drivers (system extensions) are System 7-compatible. It may be alright for an occasional utility to be out of commission until the product is updated, but your bread-and-butter productivity applications should be System 7-ready before you take the plunge.

System 7 and Counting...

System software generations are noted by the leading digit of the version number. Therefore, version 7.0 of the System was the first release of the System 7 generation. As new Macintosh computers come out of the labs, Apple often tweaks the operating system to accommodate new hardware features built into those machines. Version numbers for this kind of system change appear as a second decimal, as in 7.0.1 which was released for the Classic II, PowerBooks and Quadras. Such releases are also good times for the engineers to repair any bugs that may be reported since the prior release. Very often, you can ignore these incremental releases, unless you are experiencing bugs that the new release fixes.

More significant updates affect the middle digit, as in 7.1.0. This level of upgrade may introduce some new features, but the product is still in the System 7 generation. When Apple is ready to spring mind-boggling new system software features on us, it will be for an entirely new generation, System 8 or beyond.

Once you've determined that your Macintosh hardware and software are ready for System 7 (if it didn't already come installed on your machine), you are ready to install the system software.

Apple makes the job easier than on most computers, since the disks include a program called Installer, which does the work for you if you like. More experienced Macintosh users may prefer to install only parts of system software. The Customize option of the Installer program makes this possible.

What the Installer Does

When you ask the Installer program to do the entire installation job, it installs pieces of system software that it calculates are the ones your Macintosh needs. In many cases, some of those details are derived from the existing items in a System Folder of an earlier version. For example, if it finds that the **ImageWriter** chooser document is the only printer supported by your system software, it will update only the ImageWriter chooser document, rather than copying documents for the entire Apple printer line.

Preparing for Incompatibility

Unless your applications and system files (INIT-type extensions, control panel devices, printer drivers, etc.) rate a clean bill of health from the Compatibility Checker, it is best to temporarily move all non-Apple items from the System Folder to another folder on your disk. The purpose of this is to start with a clean System 7 System Folder, and then gradually move items back into the System Folder after installation.

Starting the System Software Installer

One of the system diskettes is labeled Install 1. Start or restart your Macintosh ➔10, and immediately insert the Install 1 disk into the floppy disk drive. Because this disk does not contain a Finder ➔74, it immediately launches the Installer application on the disk. At the same time it opens an installer script file, which contains details about the disks in your set and which ones are required for various kinds of installations.

When the Installer first appears, a descriptive screen provides simple instructions, leading you to click Install to continue. Until Install becomes active, the Installer is looking at your Macintosh to determine which model it is and what system software items are currently in your system folder. It uses this information to choose items for installation. Click Install when it becomes active.

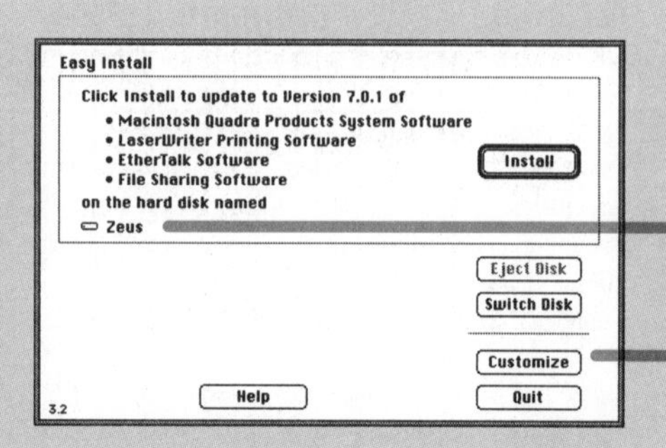

Custom Install

Instead of letting the Installer figure out what's best for your machine, you can use Custom Install to hand pick the pieces that go into your upgrade. After starting the Installer and clicking Customize, click Install.

In the Custom Install screen is a scrolling list of all the system software pieces you can install on your disk. Change the **target disk**, if necessary, by clicking Switch Disk until the desired disk name comes into view.

Click on **System Software for any Macintosh.** At the bottom of the window appears a detailed listing of the item you just selected. It tells you the size, its last modification date, and version number. A brief description also helps you identify the item. Items available through Custom Install are:

System Software for any Macintosh
Software for all Apple printers
Software for LaserWriter
Software for Personal LaserWriter SC
Software for ImageWriter
Software for AppleTalk ImageWriter
Software for Personal LaserWriter SC
Software for StyleWriter
Software for ImageWriter LQ
Software for AppleTalk ImageWriter LQ
File Sharing Software
EtherTalk Software
TokenTalk Software
System Software for Macintosh Plus
System Software for Macintosh SE
System Software for Macintosh Classic
System Software for Macintosh SE/30
System Software for Macintosh LC
System Software for Macintosh Portable
System Software for Macintosh II
System Software for Macintosh IIx
System Software for Macintosh IIsi
System Software for Macintosh IIcx
System Software for Macintosh IIci
System Software for Macintosh IIfx
Minimal Software for any Macintosh
Minimal Software for Macintosh (one for each model)

If you can afford the disk space on an external hard disk, you should install the complete system software for any Macintosh and the software for all Apple printers. This occupies just over three megabytes of hard disk space, but it assures that you can use the hard disk on any Macintosh from a Macintosh Plus to a IIfx.

Although the description of the complete system software package indicates that it copies everything to your hard disk, it does not copy the EtherTalk or TokenTalk drivers to the Extensions folder unless you already have those drivers in the System Folder before installation. If you later add an EtherTalk or TokenTalk board to your Macintosh, you can use **Custom Install** to install the appropriate driver to your hard disk.

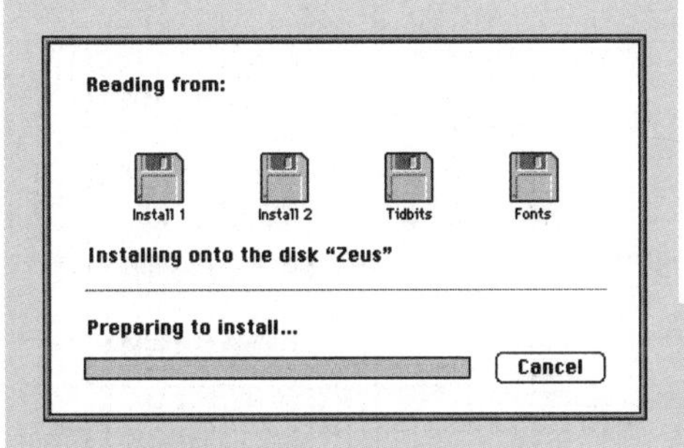

The Installer is an amazing program that's fun to watch.

Choosing the Proper Disk

If you have only one hard disk connected to your Macintosh, its name will be shown at the left bottom of the dotted box as the target disk for installation. You can install a stripped down version of System 7 on a 1.4MB floppy disk ➔70. To install system software on a different hard disk, click Switch Disk until the desired hard disk's name appears in the dotted box.

Easy Install

As a result of its examination of your system, the Installer provides a list of items it will install into your system. Easy Install is the no-brainer way of installing system software, but you should exercise care if the hard disk is an external disk that may be connected to Macintosh models other than the current machine. External hard disks should go through the Custom Install procedure (below).

Click Install (or press *return*) to initiate the installation process.

Watching Installer Work

After initiating the installation process, the Installer looks through its internal list of items it knows about on the various installation disks and compares that list against what it needs to install on your disk. In the succeeding screen, the Installer shows icons representing each of the system software diskettes it needs for your installation. As the Installer requires each disk, it ejects the current disk, and requests that the next one be inserted. The disk currently being read and copied to your hard disk is highlighted.

At the bottom of the screen, you can watch more detailed progress within each disk. You may see messages about removing outdated files, reading files from the floppy disk, and writing to the hard disk.

To finish the process, the Installer requests re-insertion of the Install 1 disk. Upon completion, a dialog box prompts you to either quit the Installer or perform further installations with Custom Install. If you have reached this point by way of Easy Install, you are probably finished, so you can quit. This restarts the Macintosh under your newly installed system software on your hard disk.

If You Cannot Restart

Occasionally, a user must run the Installer program a second time if the first attempt doesn't take hold. Restart the Macintosh with the Install 1 disk and run through Easy Install again.

Installing System 7 LaserWriter Drivers

When installing System 7 for your entire system, Easy Install automatically updates your printer drivers. If other Macintoshes share a networked LaserWriter with you, those machines should get the System 7 LaserWriter driver installation—even if they are still on System 6. Failure to do this requires the printer to be reset each time a different system version prints to it (this is time consuming). A separate Installer script file on the **Printing** diskette performs this upgrade independently of the rest of the system software.

Insert the Printing disk, and double-click on the Printer Update file. This is the installer script just for printing. Click Install on the Easy Install screen of the Installer.

Installing System 7 on External Hard Disks

Because there is a strong likelihood that you will take your external hard disk to another Macintosh model at some time in its life, it is best to perform a Custom Install for that disk, rather than the Easy Install. Custom Install allows you to install a general purpose set of system files that work with all Macintosh models, instead of just your own.

Trimming the System Folder

Once you install System 7, you may be able to reduce the disk space occupied by its various files. This is especially true if the hard disk on which you install System 7 is inside your personal Macintosh, which you use with a single printer. Open the **Extensions** folder and look for printer drivers for models you don't use. Drag those items to the Trash.

If you are not connected to other Macintosh users via a **network,** you can remove several files related to **FileShare.** These include the AppleShare driver and File Share Extension in the Extensions Folder. You can also remove File Sharing Monitor, Users & Groups, and Sharing Setup from the Control Panels folder.

Look into the **System File** for fonts that you may not need. If you are using **TrueType** fonts exclusively 88, consider dragging all the screen fonts (the ones whose names include a font size number) to the Trash.

Lastly, look through the desk accessories in the **Apple Menu Items** folder. There may be some items there that the Installer automatically includes that you can do without. Drag items you don't need to the Trash.

After filling up the Trash with discarded items, choose **Empty Trash** from the **Special menu,** and watch the amount of free space on your hard disk go up a bit.

Returning to System 6

If you find that too much of your favorite software is not compatible with System 7, then use System Tools disks for version 6.0.7 to re-install the older system. An alert will ask you to confirm that you wish to install an earlier version than the one on your hard disk, but there is no penalty for doing so.

It is always advisable to have a startup diskette handy in case of trouble with your hard disk.

Because the Macintosh system gives startup precedence to a disk in the floppy drive, you can always start your Macintosh from a floppy, even if your hard disk fails to start normally due to system extension conflicts or disk problems.

SuperDrive (1.4 MB Floppy) Startup Disk

You can use the System 7 Installer to create a minimum system diskette on a high density (1.4 megabyte) diskette. Start your Macintosh with the Install 1 disk in the floppy drive. When the Installer finishes loading, click OK to reach the Easy Install screen. Then click Customize.

In the next screen, you see a list of available system software elements to install. Scroll down the list until you reach the **Minimum Software** entries. You can create a diskette tailored for your Macintosh or a disk that will start any Macintosh model. The latter might help friends who don't have a minimum system diskette for their systems.

The next step is to make sure the Installer recognizes the diskette to be used. Click Eject to eject the Install disk, and insert the new floppy. If the floppy needs to be initialized, do so now. If the name of the floppy doesn't appear above Eject, click Switch Disk until its name is there.

Click on the Minimum Software entry for the machine(s) of your choice, and then click Install. You will be prompted to insert various installer diskettes during the copy process.

After a successful installation, try the disk by restarting the Macintosh with the newly created system diskette as the startup disk. Your hard disk should show up as the second disk on the Desktop. Because it is not the startup disk, none of the hard disk's extensions loaded during startup.

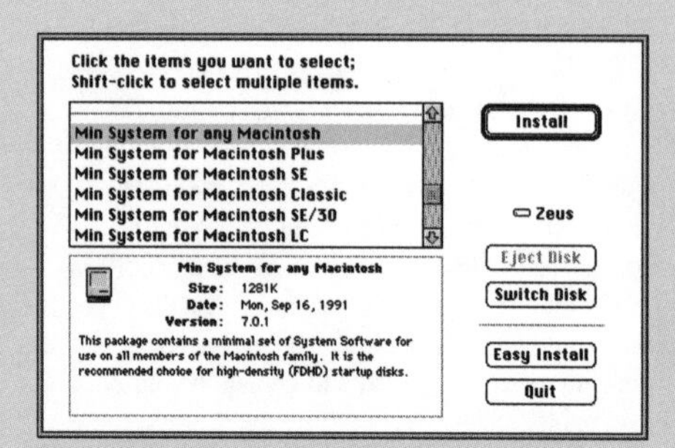

800K Startup Disk

The System 7 System File and Finder are too large, even in their most trimmed forms, to fit on an 800K diskette. If your Macintosh is not equipped with a 1.4 MB SuperDrive, then you should still have a startup diskette to rescue your Macintosh from potential hard disk problems.

Unfortunately, the only solution is to start from a System 6.0.x diskette. The Disk Tools disk that comes with System 7 is a 6.0.7 system disk, consisting of System, Finder, a few important control panels **(General, Brightness, Monitors, Mouse, Portable, and Startup Device)**, and a couple hard disk utility programs. You may use this disk (or better yet, a copy of it) as your emergency startup disk.

Lock the Startup Disk

Once you have a minimal startup disk, flip the locking tab on the reverse side. ➜ 13 This will prevent a virus ➜ 60 from propagating to at least one solid startup disk for your system.

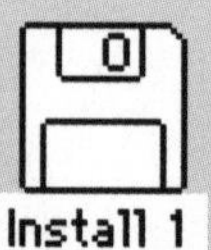

Take along a startup diskette when you travel with a PowerBook.

When to Use Startup Diskettes

Most of the time your hard disk will successfully startup, as it should. But if you notice some erratic behavior when using your Macintosh, you may wish to isolate the problems as being virus or hardware related. By starting the Macintosh with a locked, virus-free minimal system disk, and working with your applications, you may be able to detect whether the problem is in the Macintosh hardware (the problem persists even when starting from the diskette) or on your hard disk (the problem goes away). If the problem is on your hard disk, it may be due to a virus or a conflict of extension or control panel files ➜ 83.

Mixing System Software

It's a fact of life that not all Macintosh owners have the same system level installed on their Macs. This is especially true with the transition to System 7.

You can count on exchanging disks with Mac owners running System 6 or even earlier. Or, you may connect your portable hard disk to a system that boots from a System 6 system. Fortunately, there's no problem doing this, but System 7 disks show some extra folders when run under System 6 or earlier.

Mixing system software versions gets more complex when people on the same AppleTalk network need to share resources, like a laser printer. This setup is possible, but takes some care to make the cooperation seamless.

Ejectable Diskettes (2MB or smaller)

Typical Macintosh diskettes (800K and 1.4MB) can be exchanged freely between machines running System 7 and earlier systems. For the most part, the contents of a disk will be the same on both system levels except in two instances: 1) if you have dragged an item to the System 7 Trash without emptying the Trash before ejecting the disk; and 2) if a file was dragged from the disk to the Desktop under System 7. In these two cases, you will see two extra folders in the diskette's window when opened under System 6 or earlier. These folders are labeled Trash and Desktop Folder. You are free to manipulate (even delete) these folders and their contents as you normally would under System 6.

System 6 Hard Disks on System 7

Whenever you connect a hard disk that had any changes made to its contents in a System 6 (or earlier) environment to a machine booted from System 7, the governing System 7 software automatically begins rebuilding the Desktop file ➔ 94. Behind the scenes, the system is actually building a new hidden Desktop Database file, which is different from the Desktop file on System 6 disks. For simplicity, system software calls this Desktop Database the Desktop file. You can interrupt the rebuilding, but if you let it go ahead, it does no harm to your System 6 disk. It will, however, use up about 48K of disk space that you won't be able to account for. The System 6 Desktop file is not overwritten or deleted by the System 7 Desktop file. Windows, icons, and other visual features of System 7 apply to a System 6 hard disk connected to the computer. Back home, your System 6 Macintosh will ignore the System 7 Desktop file, and use its familiar System 6 Desktop file for its internal management. You will, however, see two new folders, Trash and Desktop, which you may delete.

Sharing a Laser Printer

If not all Macintoshes on an AppleTalk network sharing a printer are at the same System software level, it is important that all machines at least have the same shared printer drivers (the LaserWriter or AppleTalk ImageWriter files) in the System folder. If you fail to do this, then each time a user tries to print with a different printer driver version, a dialog appears reminding the user that the LaserWriter has been initialized with a different version of the driver. The printer will have to be reinitialized, wasting a lot of time.

Instead, upgrade each user on the network with the Version 7 printer drivers. System 6 users must be running version 6.0.2 or higher to be upgraded to System 7 printer drivers. Do this installation only with the Installer that is located on the Printing disk that comes with the System 7 software, as follows:

1. With a Macintosh already started with System 6.0.2 or later, insert the System 7 Printing disk into the disk drive.
2. Double-click the Printer Update icon.
3. Make sure the startup disk is listed as the target (click [Switch Disk] if you need to change the disk).
4. Click [Easy Install], and wait while installation takes place.
5. Click [Quit].
6. Open the Chooser, and click the LaserWriter driver icon (and click the desired LaserWriter printer in the list to the right).

Two or More Systems on One Hard Disk

Having more than one copy of System software on a startup disk (either of the same version or different versions) is risky business. Only one System Folder can be the so-called "blessed" folder—the one that actually starts up. Utility programs, such as

System 7 Hard Disks on System 6

You may connect a System 7-formatted disk to a Macintosh that uses System 6 to start up. Since the startup system software rules, don't expect the Finder views and other visual niceties of System 7 to appear in your disk's windows. But you can expect to see the Trash and Desktop Folder icons on your disk. When you reboot from this disk, those items are hidden from view, and both files and trash go back where you left them previously.

Mixed Systems on a Network

To exercise System 7's File Sharing on a network, all Macintoshes that are to participate must be upgraded to System 7. The same is true for using any of the interapplication communication features of System 7. Only System 7 machines will be able to send messages (Apple Events) to each other. The System 6 AppleShare Chooser document can give you some access to file sharing but **this combination is not recommended**.

AppleShare File Servers

You can use System 7 Macintoshes on a network built around an AppleShare file server, but don't upgrade the System software on the server until you install the System 7 compatible version of AppleShare (version 3.0). Even if you are still using an earlier AppleShare version, upgrade the print server software to work with System 7 print drivers. To do this, quit the AppleShare Print Server, insert the System 7 Printing disk, and drag all relevant printer drivers (i.e., those supported on your network) to the System Folder. **Do not use the Installer for this update.** Then restart the AppleShare Print Server.

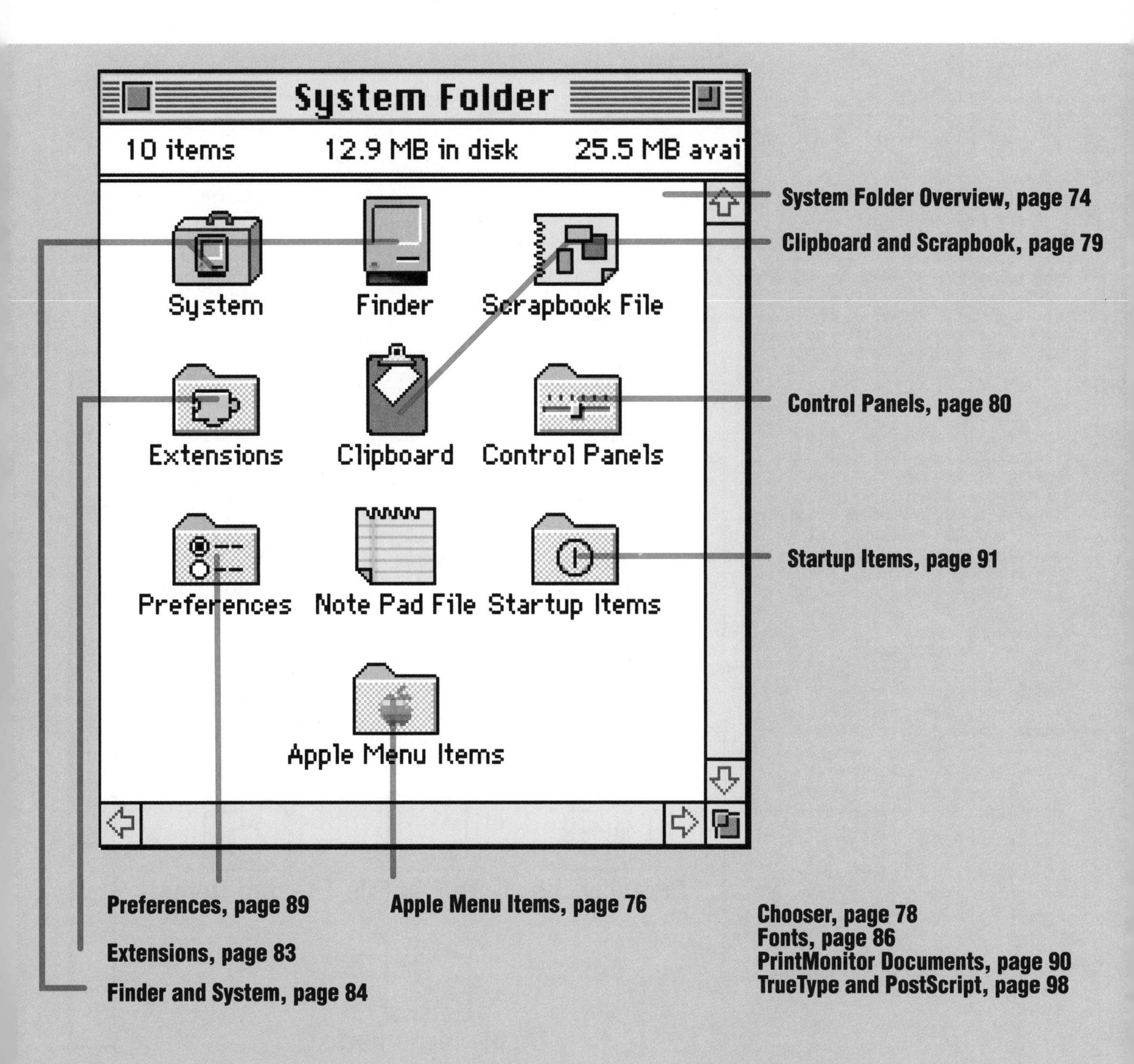
System Folder
10 items
12.9 MB in disk
25.5 MB avai
System
Finder
Scrapbook File
Extensions
Clipboard
Control Panels
Preferences
Note Pad File
Startup Items
Apple Menu Items
System Folder Overview, page 74
Clipboard and Scrapbook, page 79
Control Panels, page 80
Startup Items, page 91
Preferences, page 89
Apple Menu Items, page 76
Extensions, page 83
Finder and System, page 84
Chooser, page 78
Fonts, page 86
PrintMonitor Documents, page 90
TrueType and PostScript, page 98

To your Macintosh, the System Folder is the most important folder on your startup disk. Most of the time, however, you can forget about it entirely.

Much of what goes on inside the System Folder is done automatically for you as you work with applications. The exception is when you want to customize your work environment—that's when you may need to dig a bit inside the Folder.

Fortunately, System 7 greatly simplifies working with System Folder contents compared to earlier system versions. In the place of perhaps hundreds of files are a handful of folders that group system level files in a way that makes them easy to find, add to, or delete.

The Blessed Folder

The System Folder has its own special icon—the folder with the tiny Macintosh on it—to indicate that it is the one the internal operating system looks to for instructions to complete the startup task. In that folder is the all-important System file. The folder containing the active System file is informally known as the "blessed folder." In the process of putting System 7 on your hard disk, the Installer builds a number of special folders inside the System Folder for numerous system-level files. Many of your applications programs also store your user preferences and temporary files in the System folder. Virtually everything you double-click in the System folder opens to do something.

Extensions

A catch-all folder, the **Extensions** Folder, contains items that can best be described as system-level services. This includes software that lets your Macintosh communicate properly with external devices such as printers and file servers—device drivers, they're called. Also in the Extensions Folder are small programs that must automatically start each time you start up your Macintosh. These programs are often called INITs (pronounced in-IT), after their INIT file type ➔ 83. Such programs usually work silently at the same time you work with your Macintosh, monitoring various elements of your machine. A good example is a virus detection extension, which might be on the lookout for processes that resemble the impregnation of a virus into a file. If the extension finds such an action, it may notify you with a dialog box that a potential virus infection has been thwarted.

Preferences

Many applications (including the Finder) need to store user settings for the next time the applications run. In System 7, these preferences are normally stored in the **Preferences** Folder. The folder is primarily for the convenience of the program's author, since the preferences files can be in one place all the time. It's rare that you'll need to ever open the folder except perhaps to delete preferences files from applications you erase from your hard disk.

System File

Most of what the **System** File contains is not accessible to the user. But if you open the file, you see a window listing a number of files—fonts and sounds, mostly. If you have more than one language keyboard or script system ➔ 21, then the files for these features are also in the System. You install a new font into your system by dragging the font file to the System File; you remove a font by dragging it out of the System file's open window.

Notepad File

If you type anything into the **Note Pad** desk accessory (default location is in the Apple Menu Items folder), that application saves the data in the Notepad File in the System Folder.

Finder

The Finder is one of the files you cannot open. The file consists of programming code that gives the Macintosh its visual personality, and helps you work with files. The System and Finder files always work together.

Clipboard

Each time you copy or cut a chunk of text, picture, or object, the information goes into a special part of Macintosh memory called the Clipboard. If memory is running low, the Macintosh temporarily stores the contents of the Clipboard memory into the Clipboard file in the System Folder. This file is emptied as the Macintosh shuts down, however.

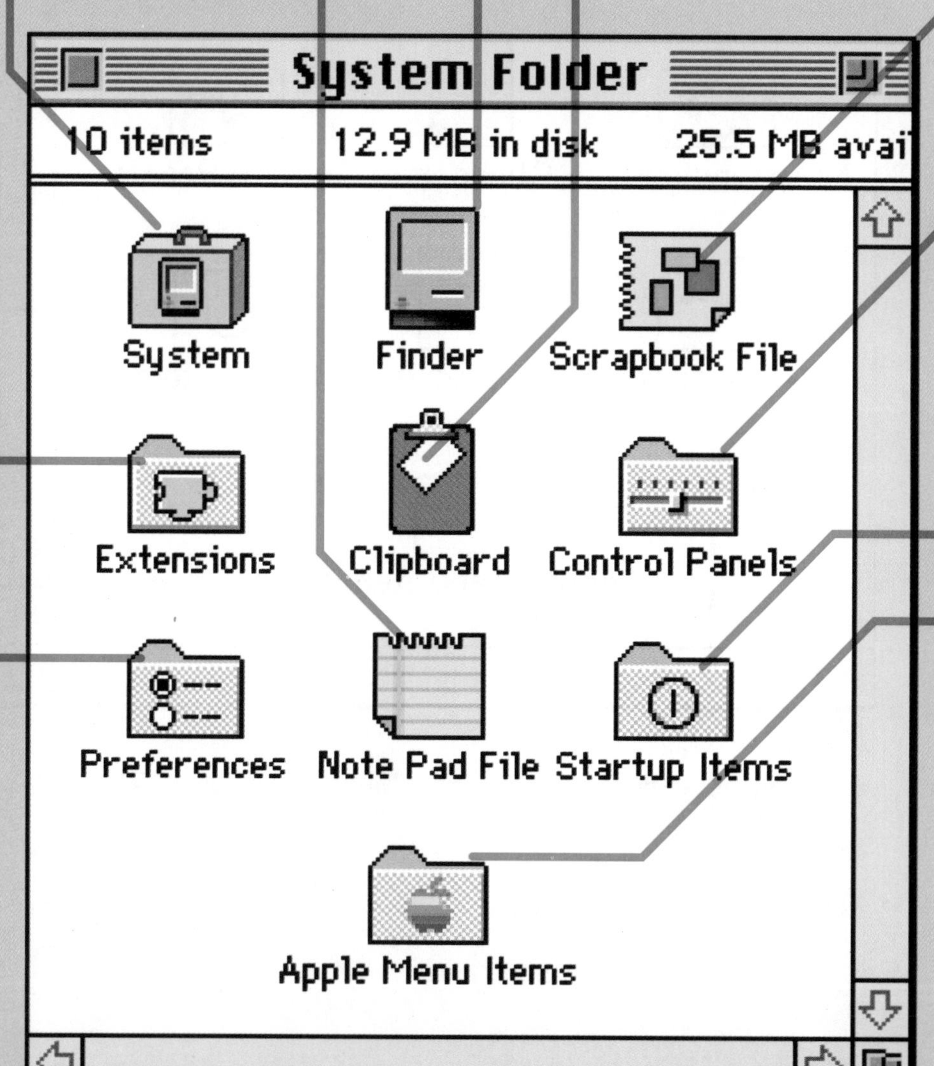

A working knowledge of the System Folder is not essential for working with your applications. It does come in handy, however, when things don't work right or when you wish to set up shortcuts to particular applications or documents.

Scrapbook File

While there is a separate **Scrapbook** desk accessory (the default location for it is in the Apple Menu Items folder), all data stored in the Scrapbook is maintained in a separate Scrapbook File in the System Folder. Thus, you can copy the contents of a Scrapbook to another Macintosh and preserve the contents, even if the the Scrapbook application should be updated in a future version of the System software.

Control Panels

Most of the customization choices available to users are performed by way of control panels—tiny programs that provide relatively simple access to things like sounds, colors, and how folder windows display lists of files. The Installer places an alias to the **Control Panels** Folder into the Apple Menu folder. Choosing that item from the Apple menu, however, simply opens the Control Panels folder. For more convenience, place aliases to frequently used control panels in the Apple Menu Items folder. Many third-party hardware products and a number of third-party utility programs supply their own control panels as a means of adjusting user settings.

Startup Items

Not to be confused with INITs or extensions, a startup item is a document or program that you want the Macintosh to open each time you start up your machine. If you drag a document file to this folder, the Macintosh will start that document's application (if the application is still on the disk) and open that document. In previous system versions, this same feature was available as the **Set Startup** item in the **Special** menu. Having startup items in a folder, however, makes management of these items much easier.

Apple Menu Items

The contents of the leftmost menu in the menubar, the Apple() menu, is completely customizable by you. Whatever program or document you copy to the **Apple Menu Items** folder immediately appears in the menu's alphabetically sorted list. Typically used as access to system level items, such as control panels and small programs known as desk accessories, the Apple menu is a convenient place for frequently accessed programs and documents. For most users' file organization, it is most efficient to copy an alias 120 for a file to the Apple Menu folder.

What Goes Where?

If some of the concepts of the various folders seem more than you care to remember, the good news is that you don't have to remember what kind of system file goes into which folder. If you drag a system file to the System Folder (i.e., the folder icon, not the opened window), an alert box tells you what kind of file you just dragged there and into which special folder (if any) it should go. By clicking OK, you let the system software put the dragged file into the proper folder for you. Clicking Cancel leaves the file where it was—it does not move the item to the System Folder. When you drag a system file into the opened window of the System Folder, you do not get the alert box. Therefore, in normal operation, it is best to leave the System Folder closed, and drag items to the icon and let the system software put those files in the right places.

Some software developers create their own folders in the System Folder to put files and resources used by their products. Aldus and Claris both do this.

Control panels need to be stored in the Control Panels folder or they may not work properly. Put "Cache Switch" into the Control Panels folder?

Cancel OK

7

Font/DA Mover

DAs

What Happened to the Font/DA Mover?

In system versions before 7, the prescribed way for everyday users to move **fonts** and small programs called **desk accessories** (DAs) into the System was to use a special utility called the **Font/DA Mover.** That utility was friend to very few users, but it served its purpose. With System 7, however, fonts and DA-like applications are manipulated like any file object—you drag them where you want. Fonts belong in the System File and DAs generally go into the Apple Menu Items folder. Font/DA Mover version 4.1 is available from APDA and most bulletin boards in case you need to extract

What Happened to Desk Accessories?

Desk accessories are small programs that usually take up very little memory compared to major applications programs. If you start the Key Caps program, for example, and then check the memory utilization of your Macintosh 42, you'll see that Key Caps allocates only 16K of RAM. Desk accessories were popular in prior system versions, because they were readily accessible by selecting them in the Apple menu. Moreover, since they could open when another program was running (even with MultiFinder turned off), they were easy to get to. But with multiple applications running at the same time all the time in System 7, the special classification of a desk accessory is scarcely necessary (although they are programmed differently under the hood). It's important, however, that we continue to have the advantage of small-memory applications to allow us to have more

The Apple menu (the leftmost menubar item with the logo), is available all the time —whether you are working within the Finder or an application.

Apple Menu Items

You have the flexibility of adding up to about 50 applications or documents into the menu, thus giving you instant access to any item while you work with your programs. All it takes is dragging a file (or an alias of a file) to the Apple Menu Items folder.

Applications may be small programs (such as desk accessories) or major standalone programs. The System software Installer places several small programs into the **Apple Menu Items** folder by default, but you may move them to another location (or delete them), if you prefer. If you place a document into the folder, and select the document from the menu, the Macintosh opens the application (if there is enough RAM) and the document.

Alarm Clock

2:36:30 PM

The **Alarm Clock** application is both a clock, alarm clock, and alternative way of setting the Macintosh's internal clock. When you open the alarm clock, a small window appears with the time ticking away, second by second. You may drag anywhere in the middle of the window to relocate the alarm clock window on the screen. The next time you open the Alarm Clock, the window will be in the last position you left it. The box on the left is a close box ➜102, a click of which closes the program.

Clicking the flag icon at the right, you see an enlarged window, showing the current date and three iconic buttons that let you select the time, date, and alarm setting for editing in the middle box. To edit a value, click on the desired icon, and then click on the number (or AM/PM setting) you want to change. A double-arrow icon appears to the right, allowing you to raise or lower the selected value with the mouse (click and hold an arrow for rapid progress). You may also type a value to replace the selected value. To set the clock according to an audible time signal (such as a telephone company service), set the seconds to "00," and click on the clock icon (leftmost one) at the sound of the tone. To undo changes, click on the active clock at the top of the window.

To set and activate the alarm, click the alarm icon (at the lower right), and set the time you'd like the alarm to ring. Be sure the **AM** and **PM** setting is set correctly. Then click on the small lever icon to the left of the alarm clock time. When the lever is in the up position, the alarm is set (the alarm icon at the lower right shows the clock ringing).

When the alarm goes off, the system beep ➜113 sounds once, and a miniature alarm clock flashes atop the Apple menu icon. If the alarm time had passed while the Macintosh was off, you won't hear the beep, but the icon will flash just the same when you turn on the Mac. To turn off the flashing, open the Alarm Clock. If you wish the alarm to ring at the same time tomorrow, just close the window; otherwise, click on the lever next to the alarm time to turn off the alarm clock.

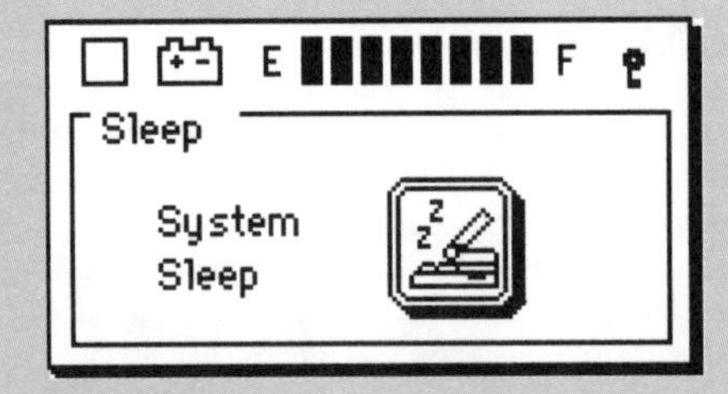

Battery

The Macintosh Portable and PowerBooks provide the Battery application to help you monitor the charge of the internal battery. Visual design of the Battery application is different for the PowerBooks than for the Portable. For PowerBooks, the opening window shows a horizontal scale between **Empty** and **Full**. A small battery icon illustrates a lightning bolt when the battery is being charged. Click the flag button to expand the window. This reveals a Sleep button, which immediately puts the PowerBook into sleep mode (contents of RAM are left intact). Option-clicking the battery icon in the smaller window also puts the computer to sleep, as does choosing **Sleep** in the Finder's **Special** menu. On the PowerBook 170, the Battery window also lets you turn on Power Saver, a switch that slows down the CPU (from 25Mhz to 16 MHz) and reduces the maximum screen brightness—all in the name of improving battery life.

For the Portable, the battery charge is shown in a vertical scale, and Sleep is always visible. Its window takes up more space than the PowerBook's collapsed view, but both operate in the background to show you instantaneous battery charge levels.

Calculator

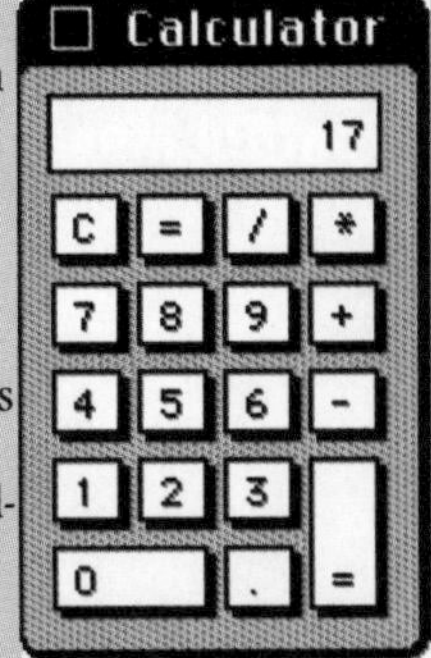

The **Calculator** application presents an on-screen replica of a simple four-function handheld calculator. Use the numeric keypad of most Macintosh keyboards to enter numbers and operators. Use the Calculator for simple calculations, and then choose **Copy** from the **Edit** menu to copy the contents of the calculator's display window into the Clipboard for pasting into another application. More sophisticated calculators are available as commercial and public domain products.

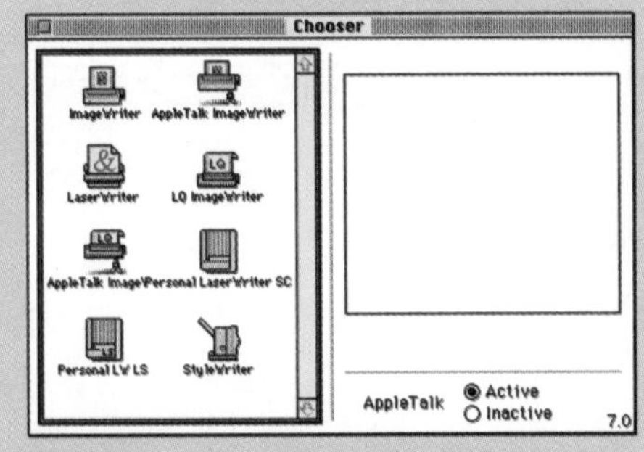

Chooser

You should always keep the Chooser in the Apple Menu Items folder, especially if you connect to any networked services, such as printers and file servers. See page ➜78 for details on how to use the Chooser.

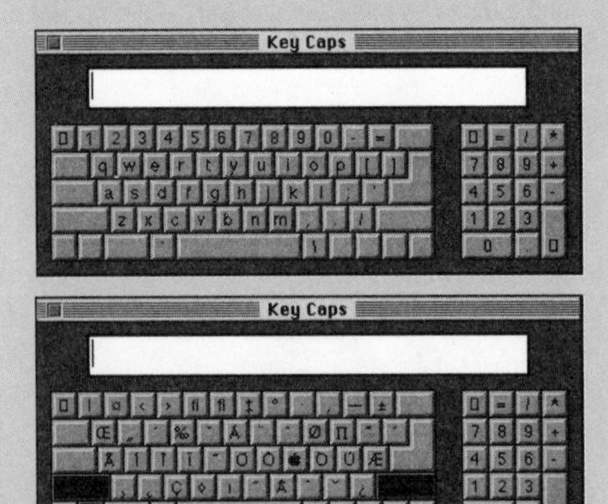

Key Caps

Because Macintosh fonts include a number of symbols and foreign language characters, it is not always easy to remember the keyboard combinations necessary for each character. Moreover, not every font supports the same characters, especially those fonts designed to produce graphic symbols or characters in non-Roman languages (e.g., Greek, Cyrillic, Arabic). Key Caps displays a replica of the keyboard, and offers a menu of fonts installed in your System. By choosing the desired font and pressing the modifier keys (*option*, *shift*, and *control*), you see all the characters available in that font. You may type a special series of characters into the Key Caps display, and then select, copy, and paste them into your document. For more about Key Caps ➜19.

Items you drag into the **Apple Menu Items** folder appear in the menu in alphabetical order.

Scrapbook

Many users find the Scrapbook helpful as a means of saving snippets of text, graphics, or virtually anything else you can copy or cut from a document. Information is saved in the Scrapbook File in the System Folder. For more details about the **Scrapbook**, and its partner, the **Clipboard**, see page 79, 108.

Puzzle

An electronic version of the plastic pocket puzzles most of us tried as kids, the Puzzle program presents a window with a grid of 16 squares, fifteen of which have jumbled pieces of a picture. Choose **Clear** from the **Edit** menu to toggle the numbered squares; or copy and paste any graphic to the puzzle. Our job is to arrange the squares so that the picture is complete (or the numbers are in order). Our reward for doing so is a digitized voice cheer (modifiable with ResEdit 84-85, 156-157).

Note Pad

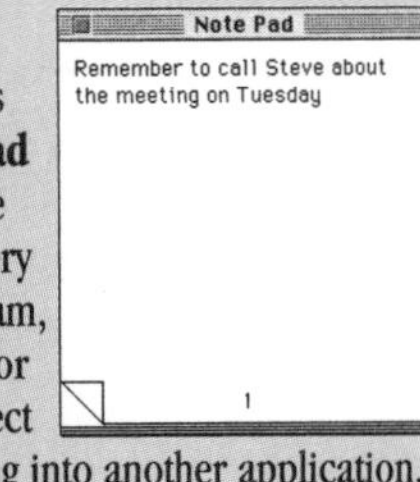

Eight pages of short notes are stored in the **Note Pad File**, editable via the Note Pad program. This is a very simple text editing program, offering no font changes or printing. But you can select text and copy it for pasting into another application, or paste text from other documents into the Note Pad. To advance through the pages, click on the upturned corner of the current page; click on the lower left corner to work your way backward.

Adding Other Items

The Apple Menu is a convenient place to list applications, documents (especially stationery 135), and items on a network that you need to open frequently. By having these items listed in the menu, it saves you from having to search for their icons nested in various folders. As with control panels, it is best to drag aliases to programs, documents, and shared volumes to the Apple Menu Items folder. That way, the real files are where you expect to find them if you look for them through your folder organization 116. It may make more sense to rename some aliases so they appear more concisely in the Apple menu. For example, you might rename SuperWriter™ Professional 2.5 to just SuperWriter.

Adding Control Panels

While the default installation of the System software places an **alias** of the Control Panels folder into the Apple Menu Items folder, this is not an entirely productive arrangement. If you select this item, all it does is open the window to the Control Panels folder—you still have to open the desired control panel. It makes more sense to put aliases to the actual control panels that you use frequently into the Menu. Then, by selecting an item, you automatically open that control panel directly.

Since it is best to leave the real control panel files in the Control Panels folder, you should create an alias to a desired panel, and drag the alias to the Apple Menu Items folder. Here's how to do this:

1. Open the Control Panels folder, and click once on a control panel file (either in the icon or text listing of the window).
2. Choose **Make Alias** from the **File** menu. A new file appears, named with the control panel, plus the word "**alias.**" Notice that an alias's file name is in an italic font.
3. Drag the alias file to the Apple Menu Items folder. You may drag the file to the Desktop first, if you need to close the Control Panels window to see the Apple Menu Items folder.
4. Open the Apple Menu Items folder, and remove the word "alias" from the file's name (for details on editing file names).

While you may rename the alias file to anything you want (it still keeps its link back to the original file), you should keep control panel names recognizable, especially if someone else might need to adjust the control panel settings on your Macintosh.

Apple Menu Strategies

With such a customizable resource at your fingertips, you should take care in managing the contents of your Apple menu. While you can put about 50 items into the menu, it makes sense to keep the list as short as possible, while still providing an index to programs and documents you need to access all the time.

The most important suggestion is to remove items automatically inserted by the system software Installer if you don't expect to use them. If you find you don't use the **Alarm Clock**, **Calculator**, **Note Pad**, or **Puzzle** a lot, then consider moving those small programs to an applications folder elsewhere on your hard disk. These items don't have to be in

Think about control panels that you'd like to have handy, like **Labels** and **Views.** If you have multiple monitors connected to your Macintosh or need to switch among various color settings, **Monitors** should be there. Connecting a lot of different hard disks to your machine often calls for the **Startup Disk** control panel—a good candidate for some users' menu. Or if you do a lot of file sharing on a network, drag aliases to both the **Sharing Setup** and **Users & Groups** control panels. Leave plenty of room for third-party desk accessories and control panels, too.

When you choose an alias to a network volume or folder (alias created on another Mac) that is not yet mounted, you are prompted for the password. If you create the alias from a volume mounted on your machine and choose it from the menu, you bypass the password prompt. These methods of accessing a shared item conveniently bypass

I group all programs at the top with a leading space.

Adjusting Apple Menu Order

System software automatically lists Apple menu items alphabetically. A third-party utility will probably come along to allow you to set the order manually, but even so, you can influence the order by preceding the names with various characters. The characters to the right (presented in their sorting order, earliest sorting character first) sort before the letters of the alphabet.

Some of these characters might look weird as leading characters to program or document names, but the space character is innocuous. Note, too, that a name with two spaces at the

(Space)
!
"
#
$
%
&
'
(
)
*
+
,
- (hyphen)
.
/
0 - 9
:
;
<
=

The basic concept of the Chooser was a good one when it was first designed: to help you choose which serial port or network device, such as a printer, the Macintosh should use.

But as Macintosh systems, especially those in networked offices, became more complex, the Chooser was asked to do more than just let the user select a printer. The Chooser serves many other duties that might not seem to be related to printers, like choosing which file server to access. As you choose a server, you wonder what happened to the printer choice made earlier. Other settings are safe, but it's hard for you to know that.

Still, the Chooser is where you select printers, servers, AppleTalk zones, mainframe computer linkups, and other network services, depending on your connectivity setup.

AppleTalk

At the lower right corner of the Chooser window are two radio buttons that let you turn AppleTalk on or off. If you are connected to an AppleTalk network (for printing and/or file sharing) you must activate AppleTalk to use any of those remote services. But if you are a standalone Macintosh, not connected to an networked printer, then you can keep AppleTalk inactive.

Choosing a Printer

The seemingly simple act of choosing a printer, actually triggers a number of actions behind the scenes. The printer icons you see in the Chooser are those of the printer driver files in the Extensions folder. Printer drivers are small programs that allow the Macintosh hardware to communicate properly with the designated printer. Each printer style expects different forms of codes and signals from the Macintosh. By letting you choose the driver, the System software allows software developers to write generic printing routines. The drivers do all necessary conversions for a specific printer model.

If the printer is a serial port printer (e.g., ImageWriter, StyleWriter), the Chooser allows you to select a serial port to connect the printer. AppleTalk networked printers, such as LaserWriters, know that you must be connected via the printer (AppleTalk) port. The Chooser immediately looks out upon the network to find the names of the printers your Macintosh has direct access to, and lists the name(s) in the right-hand box of the Chooser window. You must click on a printer name to indicate which one you wish to print on. This is how you can direct printing to one of several printers on the same network. Some printers support background printing, meaning that you don't have to wait for a document to print before continuing with your work ➧152. If so, the Background Printing radio buttons appear in the Chooser window. By and large, background printing is desirable when available.

When you switch printers, an alert box urges you to look at the Page Setup dialog boxes for your programs. This is because Page Setup dialogs for different printers offer different choices, some of which don't translate appropriately from one printer to another. Therefore, unless you use the default Page Setup settings, you may need to adjust those settings before printing ➧148-150.

Choosing an AppleTalk Zone

The network you are connected to may be complex enough that the network administrator has linked together several AppleTalk networks spread over great distances (see pages ➧156-157 for details about how such a network works). This combination is called an internet. To help you locate a particular printer, file server, or other shared device, the network administrator may have grouped chunks of the internet into zones. If so, the Chooser shows a list at the bottom left of zones established on the internet. As you click on each zone, you see the names of servers (or printers if you have clicked on a printer driver) available in that zone. Dividing an internet into zones improves the efficiency of the entire internet and your access to devices.

Choosing an AppleShare Server

A single chooser document, **AppleShare**, is your access path to one or more file servers or File Sharing Macintoshes on your network. When you choose AppleShare, the list at the right shows all file servers (or other people's Macintoshes containing shared items) that your Macintosh can "see" on the network. When the list has several items in it, you see how important it is to clearly name your Macintosh in the Sharing Setup control panel ➧80. Double-click on any one server, and you'll get another dialog box that prompts you for password and other log on information. See pages ➧164-173 for details about this dialog box and accessing File Sharing. You may also bypass the Chooser by putting an alias to a mounted server into the Apple Menu Items folder for quick mounting, or into the Startup Items folder to mount the server at startup.

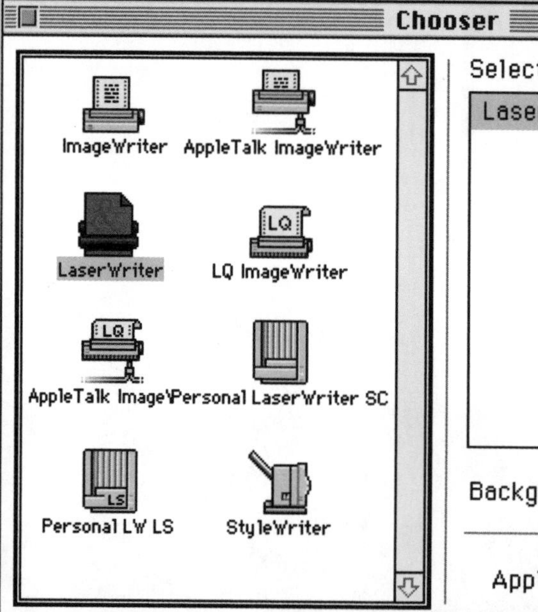

Some application programs react to the printer driver you have selected with the Chooser. Since various printers cover different areas of a page, some programs take the printer model's inherent margin limits into account when formatting active page sizes for text or graphics. Therefore, it is best to work with your applications after choosing the printer on which you intend to print the document.

Keyboard Shortcuts

While in the Chooser, you can maneuver around the window with the keyboard instead of the mouse, if you prefer. Pressing the *tab* key cycles through the windows, highlighting the activated one with a black border. In an active window, the cursor keys let you manipulate the text or icon selection in the direction of the arrow.

Although frequently confused by new users, the Clipboard and Scrapbook are two distinct information holders in the Macintosh environment. What distinguishes these two workhorses are their persistence and capacity.

The **Clipboard** stores one piece of information at a time, and its contents disappear the instant you turn off or restart your Macintosh. There is one Clipboard that serves all applications.

The **Scrapbook** has virtually unlimited capacity, storing one piece of Macintosh information per page. What you put into the Scrapbook stays there until you intentionally delete it. There is one Scrapbook file for your Macintosh.

Both the Clipboard and Scrapbook are versatile in what they store. Anything you can copy and paste in a document—text, painted graphics, a graphic object, a HyperCard card (which may consist of text, buttons, graphics, and lots more), a sound, an icon, an animation sequence—can be stored in the Clipboard and Scrapbook. About the only things they don't store are files. But then, that's what disks are for.

How the Clipboard Works

The Clipboard works almost invisibly. Virtually every Macintosh program contains an **Edit** menu with the **Cut**, **Copy**, and **Paste** items, which control the Clipboard. Some programs also let you view what is in the Clipboard. Even if they don't, the **Show Clipboard** item in the Finder's **Edit** menu opens a window that displays the Clipboard's contents (if the item is displayable, such as text and graphics).

To put something into the Clipboard in any program, you select something—a range of text, a graphic—and choose **Copy** from the **Edit** menu (or type *command-C*). To put the contents of the Clipboard in another place on the document or in another document (even in another program), click the mouse at an insertion point (this may not be necessary in graphics programs), and choose **Paste** from the **Edit** menu. After pasting, the Clipboard still contains the item, so you can paste it in another spot if you like.

Choosing **Cut** from the **Edit** menu both clears the selection from the current document and places the information into the Clipboard. If the program has a **Clear** menu item, this simply deletes the selection without placing it into the Clipboard.

Each time you choose **Copy** or **Cut** from the **Edit** menu, the Clipboard is replaced by the current selection. If no information is selected, then either the **Cut** and **Copy** menu items will be disabled (grayed out) or the menu items won't disturb the Clipboard.

Use the Clipboard as the means of moving information from place to place during the same Macintosh session. If you need the information to survive the next shutdown of the Macintosh, paste it into the Scrapbook for safe keeping.

Clearing the Clipboard

The Clipboard takes up memory, so the larger the amount of information in the Clipboard, the less is available for you to open other programs. Pages of text or complex color pictures in the Clipboard can absorb many kilobytes of RAM without your knowledge. While you cannot completely clear the Clipboard, you can reduce it to a negligible size by selecting a single character of text and copying it into the Clipboard. That single byte shouldn't get in the way of any other operation.

How the Scrapbook Works

Like it's realworld counterpart, the Macintosh Scrapbook is a place for treasuring memories —memories of information past. When you open the Scrapbook, the window shows as much of the contents of the current page as fits (the contents may be much larger than you can see). At the bottom of the window is a legend that shows which page of the total number of pages you are viewing, plus the type of information stored on that page. The information type is represented by a **resource type** ➔84, a four-character identifier (you may not see a trailing space after a three-character resource name). Some items you paste into the Scrapbook may be composite objects, consisting of several types of information shown in a comma-delimited list. A horizontal scroll bar lets you bring different pages into view.

You actually use the Clipboard to move information into and out of the Scrapbook. To store something in the Scrapbook, first select it from the document (if appropriate in the program), and choose **Copy** from the **Edit** menu. Start up the Scrapbook (or use the Application menu to bring it to the front if the Scrapbook is already open), and choose **Paste** from the **Edit** menu. The Clipboard's contents paste as the first page of the Scrapbook (the Clipboard still has the information in it).

To grab something from the Scrapbook, simply scroll the desired page into view, and choose **Copy** from the **Edit** menu. The information is now in the Clipboard, ready for you to designate the document window and location for pasting the data.

Deleting a page from the Scrapbook can be done by choosing either **Cut** or **Clear** from the **Edit** menu with the page to be deleted showing in the Scrapbook window. You can also start from scratch by dragging the **Scrapbook File** (in the System Folder) to the Trash. The next time you open the Scrapbook, it creates a new Scrapbook File for you.

When Pasting Doesn't Work

The application program determines what types of Macintosh information it can accept from the Clipboard. Not all programs accept all information types. The most common information types, **TEXT** and **PICT** are more likely to be accepted by a variety of programs, but there are no guarantees.

For example, most word processing programs accept TEXT (pasted at the text insertion pointer) or a PICT, which comes in as a single picture that can be moved around as a whole. But unless the program knows what to do with, say, a **sound resource** (type 'snd '), attempts at pasting will result in either a beep or a message signifying the

Macintosh control panels generally consist of system-level preferences that you adjust once or infrequently.

Control Panels

System software comes with as many as 20 control panels, and many third-party hardware products also provide control panels as ways of letting you set preferences about the hardware. You may also find a lot of third-party software—primarily utility software—that provides additional control panels.

A **control panel** is a small file that appears to open like an application. You may open multiple control panels at the same time. Frequently, settings in control panels don't take effect until you restart your Macintosh. You will usually see an alert message to that effect upon closing such a control panel.

General Controls

The most basic control panel settings are those that establish basic operating characteristics of your Macintosh. These items are found in the General Controls panel. From here you may set the Desktop Pattern (the pattern of dots and colors that appears as the background of the desktop on your screen), the speed of insertion point blinking, how many times a menu item should flash when you select it, and the date and time. For details on setting the Desktop Pattern (and how to put a picture there instead), see page 110.

Insertion point blinking refers to the flashing the text insertion pointer does when you edit text in a field or document. Blinking the cursor helps you find it amid all the other characters and graphics on the screen. As you select different speeds, the sample pointer shows you the results. The default setting is the middle speed.

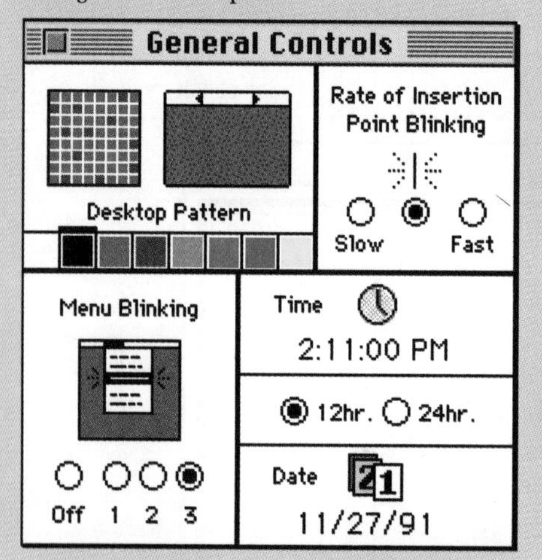

Menu blinking is an important visual feedback device. After you release the mouse button on a menu item, the menu remains down for an instant as the selected menu item flashes. This instant gives you a chance to verify that you selected the desired menu item. If you turn off blinking, the menu disappears so fast that if you select the wrong menu item by mistake, you may not know what you did wrong when the wrong action occurs. Settings of 2 or 3 are desirable.

To set the time, click on any set of digits (hour, minute, second) or AM/PM designation. A double-arrow icon appears to the right. Either type the desired values into the selection or click the arrows to alter the values. If you are setting the clock against a time standard, set the seconds to "00," and click on the clock icon (above the time) at the sound of the tone.

Below the time are radio buttons for you to choose 12 or 24 hour time. The default for the United States version of the system is 12 hour time.

To set the date, click on any set of digits (month, day, year). A double-arrow icon appears to the right. Either type the desired values into the selection or click the arrows to alter the values. Click the calendar pad icon to make the new date take effect. In case you're still using your Macintosh into the 21st century, with System 7 you can set the date in that century up to December 31, 2019. Trying to set the date to the year 2020 yields 1920 instead.

Labels

To help you organize your files and folders, you may categorize their icons in the Finder by assigning labels to them from the **Label** menu. The names of the labels and colors (if you have a color monitor) are set via the Labels control panel 110.

Sharing Setup

If you use your Macintosh on a network, it is important to fill in the Network Identity blanks in the **Sharing Setup** control panel. Those settings let others provide you secure access to their files. This is also where you designate your Macintosh as being open for file sharing and program linking 172.

Sound

In the Sound control panel is a slider control to adjust the volume of sounds played through the Macintosh internal speaker (or via the audio output port). You may also select a single sound from those installed in your System file as the one you'll hear whenever the Macintosh normally beeps at you. Macintoshes equipped with microphones may also record alert sounds via this panel 158.

Startup Disk

When you connect multiple hard disks to a Macintosh and wish to change the disk that the Macintosh recognizes as the startup disk, use the **Startup Disk** control panel to choose the volume. Then restart the Macintosh 11.

Easy Access

Users with physical disabilities that make using the mouse difficult or impossible can use **Easy Access** to turn the keyboard into a complete pointer control system. Multiple keystroke combinations are also possible with a single physical pointing device between the user and keyboard 20.

Color

For Macintoshes connected to a color monitor, the **Color** control panel contains color adjustments for highlighted text and the highlight colors of window. You may choose from a standard palette as well as from the Color Wheel, which lets you choose from as many colors as your video control circuitry allows 36, 113.

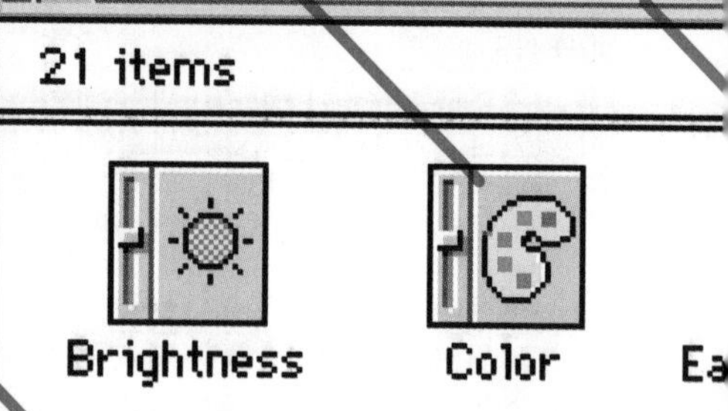

St

All control panel files should be located in the Control Panels folder inside the System Folder. The system software Installer places an alias to the Control Panels folder in the Apple Menu Items folder. When you select **Control Panels** from the menu, the Control Panels folder opens, and you see the icons or text listing of the control panels installed on your Macintosh.

Apple's control panel icons all feature a small slider control to distinguish these files from other types. To open a control panel, double-click on its icon. You may drag the control panel window around the screen, and leave it open as you click on another window to activate a different program. Close the control panel by clicking the control panel window's close box.

Monitors

Macintoshes with color or any separate video monitors may adjust various settings via the **Monitors** control panel. Multiple monitor users set which monitor gets the menu bar and startup screen. All users set the number of colors or gray levels on color and grayscale monitors ➜ 34-36.

Mouse

Two aspects of the mouse—how fast the screen pointer tracks actual mouse movement, and the speed of a recognizable double click—are set in the **Mouse** control panel ➜ 25.

Users & Groups

The window opened by the **Users & Groups** control panel contains icons of each external user you have authorized to access your Macintosh via File Sharing. You create new users (or groups of users) by selecting appropriate menu items in the **File** menu. Then double-click each user icon to establish an access password and how much access to allow each user ➜ 164-173.

Views

The Finder provides a wide range of choices to view files and folders in windows. The **Views** control panel is where you make these choices, including the font of file names in the Finder, the nature of icon views, and how much information you want to see in list views in windows ➜ 112.

CloseView

For those who have difficulty working with small fonts and graphics, **CloseView** contains settings for magnification of the screen from 2 to 16 times normal size. It also allows inverse colors, in case it is easier for you to read white text on a black background ➜ 35.

Keyboard

Adjustments to the speed of key repeating, and how long you have to hold a key before it starts repeating are made in the **Keyboard** control panel. If you have multiple language keyboards connected (or their software installed), you also choose the keyboard the Macintosh recognizes ➜ 19.

Network

If you are connected to more than one type of network (LocalTalk, EtherTalk, or TokenTalk), you choose the desired network from the Network control panel ➜ 162-163.

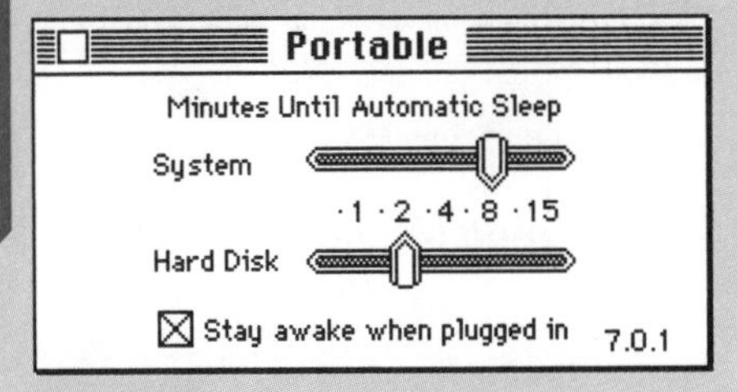

Portable

Macintosh Portable and PowerBook owners control those machines' special settings via the **Portable** control panel. Most settings relate to battery-saving aspects, such as how long to wait for disk or keyboard activity before powering down parts of the machine. Other choices include internal or external modem and SCSI ID number of the PowerBook 100's hard disk when connected to another Macintosh.

Cache Switch

Quadra models include a control panel that lets you turn off the 68040 CPU's internal cache—one of the features that makes these machines so speedy. Some software is not compatible with this cache, so this control panel lets you turn the cache off. This slows the Quadra to about the performance of a Macintosh IIci.

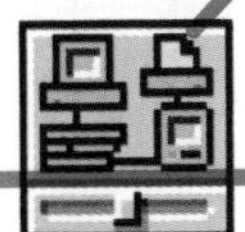

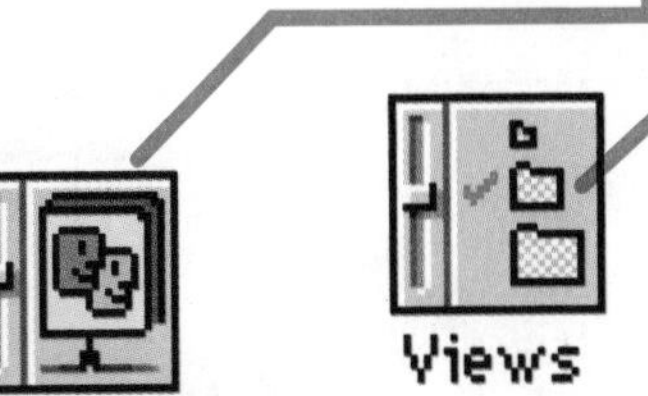

Map

Global Macintosh users can obtain a lot of information from the **Map** control panel, as well as let it keep their portable Mac's clock in sync with where they are in the world. Color Macintosh users may wish to copy the color world map from the Scrapbook and paste it into the Map control panel window. Map contains a database of about 200 locations around the world (including **Mount Everest** and **Middle of Nowhere**), their map coordinates and time zone data. Type the first few characters of your city and click [Find] to see if your location is in the database.

You may also enter a new location into the database, if you have the latitude and longitude. To do so, enter the latitude and longitude into the appropriate boxes. Check **N** if the latitude is in the northern hemisphere; check **E** if the longitude is in the eastern hemisphere. Then type the name of the location into the city field, and click [Add City].

Once you have your home town entered, click [Set]. If the time zone is different than the default setting, this actually sets your system clock. Go to the **Alarm Clock** or **General Controls** panel to reset the hour. The goal is to let the Map govern the Mac's time based on your geography.

Your location blinks on the map with a tiny **star**. This becomes the reference point for time and distance calculations. If you then click on another area (clicking and dragging to an edge of the map scrolls the map in that direction), or search for another city (type the name and click [Find] —or hold down the *option* and *return* keys to cycle through the entire database list), a different flashing cursor signifies the selected city. The Time Zone values show the time zone relative to Greenwich, England. Click on Time Zone, and the label changes to **Time Difference**—from your home reference point. In the Time Zone mode, the plus checkbox indicates that the time zone value is so many hours later than Greenwich time (also known as GMT, Coordinated Universal Time, or UTC); in Time Difference mode, the plus checkbox indicates that the time difference is so many hours later than the time at the home reference point.

The distance between your home point and the selected city is shown at the bottom. Clicking on the label toggles through a sequence of miles, kilometers, and degrees.

If you take your Macintosh with you to a new city, and if the exact clock setting is important (e.g., to make sure appointment alarms you may have set ring at the right time), then find the city and click [Set] to establish your current location as the reference point. Be sure to set the Map back to your real home base when you return.

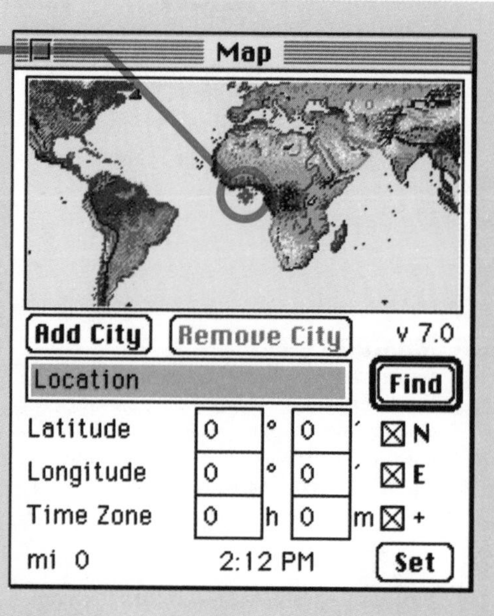

File Sharing Monitor

While you can see from the icons of folders whether anyone is using your shared folders, the **File Sharing Monitor** control panel gives you an at-a-glance view of all file sharing activity taking place on your Macintosh 164-173.

The Brightness

Applying only to Macintoshes that don't have video monitor brightness controls for their built-in monitors (e.g., Macintosh Classic), the **Brightness** control panel is the software way of adjusting monitor brightness 35.

Cache Switch

Quadra models include a control panel that lets you turn off the 68040 CPU's internal cache—one of the features that makes these machines so speedy. Some software, however, is not compatible with this cache, so this control panel lets you turn the cache off. This slows the Quadra to about the performance of a Macintosh IIci.

Memory

Depending on the Macintosh model you have, the **Memory** control panel gives you power over the size of the Disk Cache, virtual memory, and whether 32-bit addressing should be turned on 42-45.

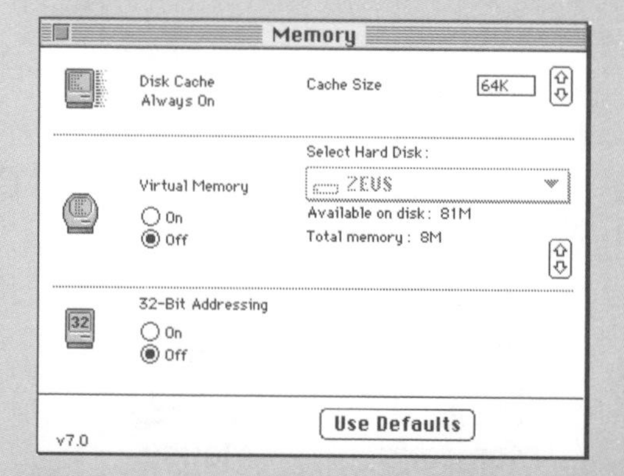

What's a cdev?

You often hear a control panel referred to as a (pronounced SEE-dev). This nomenclature comes from the file type of control panel documents. The four character identifier is **cdev**, all lowercase letters. A cdev is synonymous with a control panel.

Third-Party Control Panels

The more utility software and external devices you connect to your Macintosh, the more control panels you'll accumulate. It's not uncommon to have dozens installed. Be sure to drag them to the System Folder and let the system software put them in the right place for you.

Control Panel Strategies

It is an excellent idea to place **aliases** of frequently accessed control panels into the Apple Menu Items folder. By having the control panel listed in the Apple menu, you have very fast access to it, instead of opening up the Control Panels folder first. You may still want to leave the Control Panels folder alias in the menu for those times when you need to adjust the other panels.

You may leave control panel windows open as you work on other applications. When contents of such windows are constantly updated, however, they may slow down regular operations on your Macintosh.

Extensions are system-level files that extend the basic functionality of system software.

Extensions

Assuming that system software contains everything that the Macintosh needs to be a Macintosh, extensions give system software the power to work with specific external devices or setup background processes that are not normally part of system software.

The kinds of files found in the Extensions folder include device drivers (a device something like a printer or other non-standard piece of hardware) and programs that used to be known as startup documents or INITs. For these programs to work effectively, they must be loaded into RAM during the Macintosh's startup sequence so they can monitor various activities taking place on the Macintosh.

Printer Drivers

Each family of printers requires its own printer driver to help the Macintosh communicate with that printer. Applications developers design their programs to print in a general way; the printer driver converts that general code to the commands and signals that work with a specific printer. You select the printer you want to use by opening the Chooser 78 and clicking on the printer driver icon—the same icon that appears in the Extensions folder.

Pre-installed system software tends to include all printer drivers in your Extensions folder. If you use only one printer consistently, then you can remove the drivers for the other printers. Similarly, if you purchase a non-Apple brand printer, it will come with its own printer driver, which you need to drag to the **Extensions** folder.

Apple's printer drivers are updated each time the System software is updated. Whenever you upgrade the System version, be sure the corresponding printer driver is also installed properly.

Your choice of printer driver can affect the way some programs lay out information on the page. Some printers have inherent margins in which they cannot print. Software that recognizes this limitation may reduce the available area of a page for you to work in. You should always install and choose the printer driver for which the document's printed output is intended before working on the document.

System Services

Many utility software programs, previously known as INITs (pronounced in-ITS, and named after their four-character file type name), find their way into the Extensions folder. Extensions tend to be background processes that are loaded as the Macintosh starts. Most have an icon that appears along the bottom of the screen as the Macintosh starts up. Examples of Extensions are **virus detection programs** (which monitor disk activity for suspected viral actions) and **alarm programs** (which continually compare the internal clock against the time of the next alarm).

Device and Network Drivers

Many other external devices, like CD-ROM players or optical scanners, require that a special driver be installed in the Extensions folder. Known as a device driver, the file allows the Macintosh to communicate with that external device—a device that the System software does not automatically support. These kinds of drivers work silently in the background once installed. They don't appear in the Chooser.

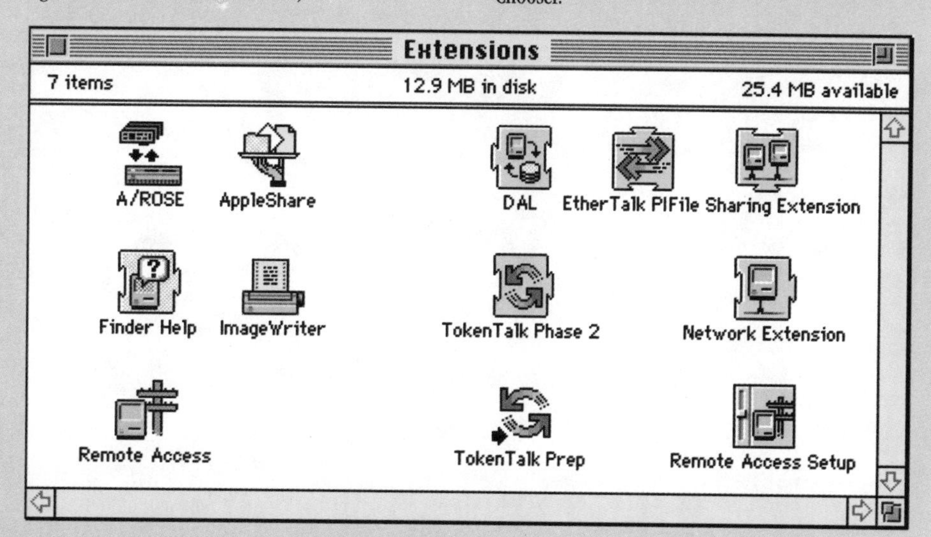

Extension Incompatibilities

Extensions are frequently the cause of incompatibility problems with new software programs. Since many Extensions are created and distributed via the public domain (user groups and on-line bulletin boards), they may not be as thoroughly tested as commercial products. But even commercial Extensions conflict with other Extensions.

You can disable all Extensions upon startup by holding down the *shift* key during the startup process. When the **Welcome alert** appears, an additional message indicates that all extensions are turned off. If you suspect a single Extension as being a troublemaker, you can remove it from the Extensions and System folders and restart the Macintosh. Third party utilities also allow you to selectively remove multiple Extensions from the startup sequence.

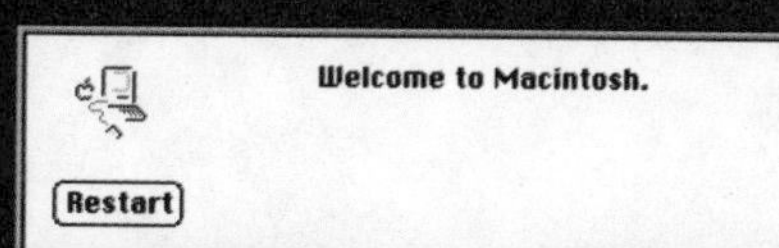

Extensions Outside Their Folders

System software looks for extensions in both the Extensions folder and the System Folder (in that order). To prevent an Extensions from starting with the Macintosh, remove it entirely from the System Folder, or place it in a folder with a very different name. Some programs that are not fully System 7 compatible may require printer driver or other extensions be only in the System Folder. In this case, keep the extension in the Extensions folder, and create an alias for the System Folder.

The Finder and System files are the most important part of System software. They work together, and must be from the same system software generation for your Macintosh to function. The two files serve very different purposes, however.

Most of what you see on the screen in the way of file and folder icons is the jurisdiction of the **Finder.** It is the user interface to the lower level operations of the system software. For example, dragging a file from one folder to another is the Finder's way of letting us easily perform a series of complex steps in the **system software.** The Finder icon is that of a compact Macintosh.

The **System** file contains not only a lot of system software instructions that we never see, but also several items that we do see: fonts, sounds, and keyboard resources. The icon for the System file is a suitcase with a Macintosh in it.

The Finder

There isn't much a user can do with the Finder file without digging deeply with programmer-level tools (see below). Double-clicking on the Finder yields an alert saying that you cannot open the file. The magic of the Finder is apparent only in day-to-day use of the file management facilities of the Macintosh environment.

The System File

Double-clicking the System file opens a window to the resource files attached to the System file. **Resource** files may be **fonts, sounds, keyboard,** or **script** types. Each resource file type has its own icon to help you identify which is which.

Moving resource files into and out of the System file is as simple as dragging the files into and out of the System file window. In previous versions of system software, more convoluted methods, such as the **Font/DA Mover** utility program, were required to shift resources around the System file. There are still third-party utilities that help manage large groups of fonts and sounds in the System file. For more information about font resource files, see page ➜86; details about sounds can be found on pages ➜156-159; keyboard and script resource file data is located on page ➜21.

International Systems

Among the items the user doesn't see about the System file is that it contains much information about notation conventions for the country in which the system was sold. This information is contained in a series of international resources, and makes the localization of the system software by Apple's staff as simple as filling in blanks on a screen.

Snooping with ResEdit

You can learn a lot about the internal workings of Macintosh system software by exploring with a programmer's tool called **ResEdit.** This program is available from APDA (Apple Programmers and Developers Association) or from many user groups.

A Macintosh file often consists of two files, called the **data fork** and the **resource fork.** The Finder keeps the two forks together in what we see as a single disk file. The data fork stores user information—word processing text, for example. The resource fork, on the other hand, contains the **program code,** plus a variety of pieces that can often be modified with the help of a resource editor, such as ResEdit. Each of these items is called a **resource.**

IMPORTANT: It is vital that you never edit a resource of the original copy of a file. Always work on a duplicate. While it's fun and enlightening to view resources with ResEdit, actually editing a resource and saving changes can damage the file if you don't know what you're doing. Damaging the System file may prevent you from restarting your Macintosh without completely reinstalling the

When you start ResEdit, you will likely be prompted with a file dialog box to open a file for resource editing. Find the copy of the **System file** you made, and open it.

A large window filled with icons appears. These icons represent the types of resources stored in the System file. Each resource type is identified by a unique four-character identifier. Exact spelling and case is essential for these resource types. Most resource types that have identifiable icons often have resource editing templates in ResEdit that will help you understand the contents of the resource.

Double-click on the **CURS** icon. This is the **cursor resource.** A window opens, showing several cursors, each with its unique identification number. Double-click on the cursor with **id 3**. The cursor resource editing window appears. If you were going to create or edit a cursor resource, here are the tools you can use to design a cursor. Along the right side of the window are examples of how the cursor will appear on a variety of different desk pattern backgrounds. The one pixel with an "X" in it is the **hot spot**—the point of the cursor that acts as the real pointer to activate an icon.

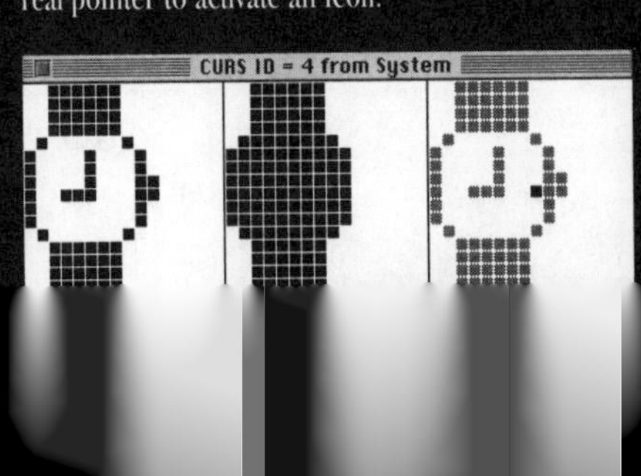

Close all the CURS resource windows, and open the **DLOG** resources. A long list of each dialog box in the System file appears. Locate the one numbered -6040, and double-click on that item.

The window that appears is the DLOG editor. This small resource (just 24 bytes) contains information about the size, location, and style of a particular dialog box. Linked to this DLOG resource is a DITL (dialog item list) resource with the same ID number. If you double-click on the miniature dialog in the DLOG window, the corresponding DITL resource opens on top. The DITL resource has more information about what we see as a dialog box, namely the text, button, and graphic objects in the box.

If you were to move the location of one of the items in the DITL resource and save the resource, you would control the location of that item in the dialog when it appears on the screen. Similarly, the text could be changed—which is exactly what someone would do to localize the System file for another language or culture.

Whenever you see a text dialog item with a caret and a number, you're seeing a text placeholder. When the System displays this dialog, part of its internal instructions substitutes the placeholder text with some detail that may change from instance to instance—the name of the file that can't be changed in this case. Some text dialog items have more than

clut
Color lookup table. The System has one clut resource each for 8, 16, and 256 color palettes.

acur
Animated cursor (in Finder) lists the series of CURS resources to flash by in quasi animation (the moving hands of the watch are the Finder's default animated wait cursor).

ALRT
Alert box definitions. Have corresponding DITL resources with same ID number that contain text fields, buttons, etc. Text for most alerts is in **STR#** resources.

CURS
Cursors, editable in their 16-by-16 pixels grid

INTL
International settings for currency, numbers, date, and time. Opening the INTL resource in ResEdit lets you edit both the **itl0** and **itl1** resources.

DITL
Dialog item list contains specifications for text fields, buttons, icons, and pictures displayed in a dialog or alert box.

DLOG
Dialog box definitions of size, window style, and screen location of dialog box.

cicn
Color icons used within a program (not in the Finder).

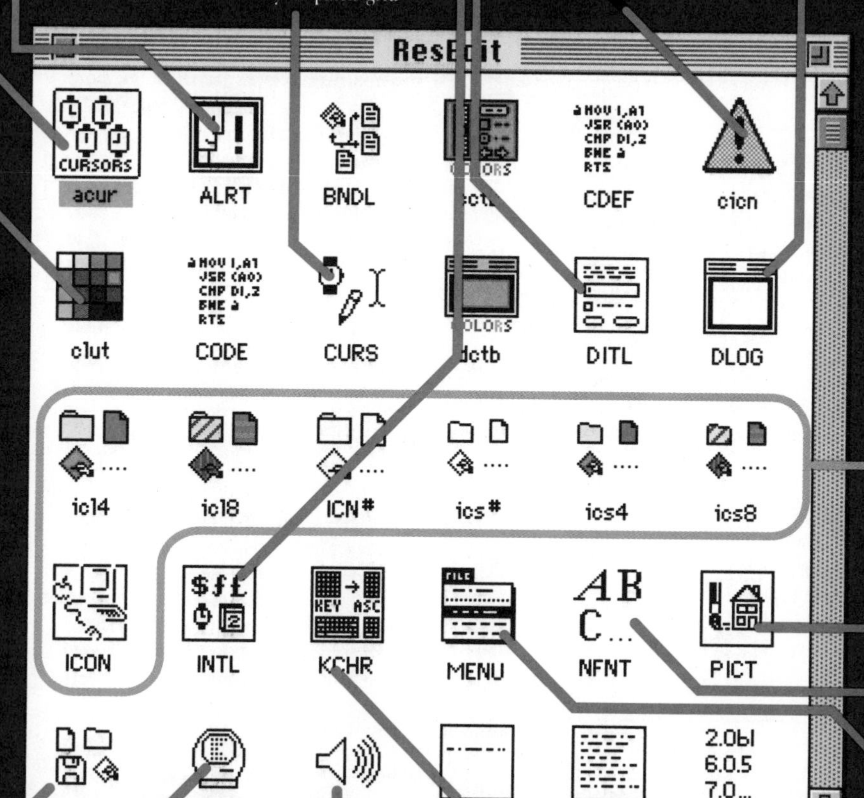

icl4
4-bit (16-color) large (32-pixel square) icons for display in Finder. If you open an icon in this or any of the next five resource types, **ResEdit** displays an icon editor that allows you to modify any of six versions of an icon. The related icons are in an **icon family,** each having the same ID number in its own resource type. Different versions of Finder icons exist for different color capabilities of Macintoshes; different sizes are shown in different views of the Finder set with the **Views** control panel or the View menu in the Finder.

icl8
8-bit (256-color) large icons for display in Finder.

ics4
4-bit (16-color) small (16-pixel square) icons for display in Finder.

ics8
8-bit (256-color) small icons for display in Finder.

ICN#
Monochrome large icon for display in Finder.

ics#
Monochrome small icon for display in Finder.

ICON
Monochrome icons used within a program (not in the Finder).

PICT
Pictures. These are same kind of PICT resources saved to the **Scrapbook** when you copy graphics into it.

NFNT
Font resources ("N" stands for "new", a newer way of representing font resources than the previous **FONT** resource). You can edit characters, but if you're really serious about creating fonts, third-party font designing packages are better suited to the task.

MENU
Menu definitions. Easier to access in applications, you can change wording of menus and command keys, but their actions remain the same.

vers
Version resource information attached to a file shows up in the Finder's **Get Info** dialog box about the file.

snd
Sound resources can be played from ResEdit. Note that this resource type is only three letters, followed by a space.

SIZE
Among other information, includes details on the minimum allowable **RAM** for loading the application and what the recommended RAM setting is.

SICN

STR#
String lists tend to hold more text used in dialog boxes and balloon help.

STR
Strings (snippets of text) used in alerts and dialog boxes, as well as system-level text settings (like network identifiers).

KCHR
Keyboard characters and how they are mapped. This is one of the resources that installs into the

A Macintosh font is the typeface style for any text character displayed on the screen or produced on a printer.

While this terminology differs from the typesetting world (in which a font is a particular size and style of a typeface), the electronic nature of Macintosh character generation makes it much easier to consider a font as a typestyle in any size and in some cases more than one style (e.g., **bold**, *italic*, etc.). A Macintosh font is software that resides in the System Folder. While some printers have fonts built into them, System 7 calls upon font software to display the fonts on the screen and supply font information to printers when necessary.

System 7 supports two font systems: TrueType and Adobe Type 1 PostScript. TrueType simplifies working with fonts, especially for non-PostScript printers, such as the ImageWriter, StyleWriter, and inexpensive LaserWriters. By dropping a single font resource file into the System file, your Macintosh can display and print that font in any size.

Of Points, Leading, and Serifs

Font sizes are designated by point sizes. A point is a typesetter's unit of measure equalling 1/72 of an inch—the first Macintosh's 72-dot per inch screen display was no accident. Character size is measured as the distance from the highest and lowest part of the space that characters can occupy. Characters line up along a baseline, and the distance between baselines in adjacent lines of text is called leading (pronounced LEDD-ing), also measured in points. Macintosh software tends to call this measure Line Spacing. It is common practice to refer to the combined font size and line spacing in a specification of so many points "over" so many points, as in 10 over 12, meaning a 10-point font with 12-point leading.

Fonts with alphanumeric characters fall into two broad styles: **serif** and **sans serif**. A serif is an ornamental stroke appended to any location on a character, usually at some free end of a line. New York and Times are serif fonts. When characters lack these serifs, they are said to be sans serif (French for "without serif"). Geneva and Helvetica are sans serif fonts.

The vertical distance between these two lines of text is called leading.

Leading

System File Fonts

When you open a freshly installed System 7 System file, you notice two styles of icons representing fonts. These are icons of the resource files that you may move in and out of the System file like any file and folder. One font resource file, with an icon showing more than one letter, is a TrueType font. This font file allows any System 7-compatible program to print that font in any size, including fractional point sizes and sizes well beyond the capabilities of most page printers. The other font file resource style is a fixed-size font (also called a bitmapped font). Fixed-size fonts for the same typefaces as the TrueType fonts are provided for compatibility with documents created in fixed-size fonts of earlier System software releases (see below) and for faster display of common point sizes. TrueType and fixed-size fonts are the only font resources that may be added to the System file.

System

Name		Size	Kind	Label	Last
Times	True Type	65K	font	–	
Times (bold)	True Type	65K	font	–	
Times (bold, italic)	True Type	67K	font	–	
Times (italic)	True Type	68K	font	–	
Times 10	Fixed Sizes	7K	font	–	
Times 12	Fixed Sizes	7K	font	–	
Times 14	Fixed Sizes	9K	font	–	
Times 18	Fixed Sizes	10K	font	–	
Times 24	Fixed Sizes	13K	font	–	
Indigo		8K	sound	–	
Quack		3K	sound	–	
Sosumi		2K	sound	–	
whistle		4K	sound	–	
Wild Eep		2K	sound	–	

Bitmapped Font Suitcase

Outline Font File

TrueType Font File

Font History

The earliest fonts for the Macintosh were fixed-size fonts—one font resource for each size of a typeface. Such fonts were used not only for the screen display, but also for printing on the dot-matrix ImageWriter printer, which could replicate the dot pattern of the screen. The font resource actually contained the location of dots for each character in that size—a map of the light and dark bits for each character. Bold, italic, and other derivative styles were modified from the basic font as needed, so separate fixed-size fonts weren't needed for those styles.

PostScript came into prominence in 1986 along with the advent of the Apple LaserWriter. Among PostScript's characteristics was its ability to define characters by mathematical descriptions, essentially mapping the outline of a character's design. This outline font methodology allowed printing devices to use the same font software to print at a variety of resolutions, up to thousands of dots per inch. Outline printer fonts still needed fixed-size fonts to display the characters from the font on the screen. If you purchased an outline font, you also received a set of screen fonts in several standard sizes. Macintosh owners heavily involved with desktop publishing have large investments in PostScript fonts.

A few years later, Adobe Type Manager (ATM), an add-on software program, allowed a single PostScript outline font file to also display the font smoothly in many sizes on the screen without dedicated screen fonts.

Apple's TrueType font methodology was initially introduced as the sole font technology for System 7. Like PostScript, it also utilizes outline font technology (although an entirely different math algorithm to define fonts), and allows a single outline font resource file to control both screen and printer font representation. In late 1990, however, Apple again embraced PostScript font technology, and plans to include the equivalent of ATM in System 7 so that users with large PostScript font libraries can continue to use them as before. Current System 7 users can obtain ATM from Adobe Systems (1-800-521-1976, x.4400) for $7.50.

Adobe Type 1 font technology, originally released with Apple's first LaserWriters, is preferred by most professional typesetting **service bureaus** that produce high-quality printed output from Macintoshes, and is built into all PostScript LaserWriters. While these printers contain a basic set of fonts, you may enlarge your font library by adding Type 1 font files from Adobe Systems and others to your System File. The **Adobe Type Manager** (ATM) extension makes it possible to display these fonts in any size on the video monitor.

Installing TrueType Over System 6

If you are upgrading from System 6 to System 7 and have existing font libraries, the transition shouldn't be too painful, since the TrueType implementation recognizes the popularity of screen and PostScript fonts.

The **Installer** carries to the System file the following TrueType fonts:

Chicago	Courier	Courier (bold)
Geneva	Helvetica	**Helvetica (bold)**
New York	Symbol	**Times (bold)**
Times (italic)		***Times (bold, italic)***
Monaco	Times	

It also brings over the fixed-size fonts shown in the following table

Font/Size	9	10	12	14	18	20	24
Chicago			✱				
Courier	●	●	●	●	●		●
Geneva	●	●	✱	●	●	●	●
Helvetica	●	●	●	●	●		●
Monaco	✱		●				
New York	●	●	●	●	●	●	●
Palatino		●	●	●	●		●
Symbol	●	●	●	●	●		●
Times	●	●	●	●	●		●

✱ This screen font is imbedded in System software as a default font for the Finder.

Slimming Down the System

You might be able to remove some of the font resource files from your System File if you know how you want fonts to be handled. For example, if you are new to Macintosh computing with System 7, you probably don't have any worries about compatibility with older fonted documents. You can remove the fixed-sized fonts from your System file, although screen updating in some programs might not be as fast as with the fixed-size fonts in the System.

Abc Abc 18 point and 20 point Times bit-mapped

Abc Abc 18 point and 20 point Times TrueType

Any fixed-size font *other than those delivered with System 7* should be in the System file if you want it to be listed in Font menus. Bear in mind that TrueType will not improve the display or printed characters from these fonts. When set to sizes other than those in the font resource files, these characters will be mathematically scaled, but will appear distorted.

PostScript outline font files cannot be installed into the System file. They must go into the System Folder. When needed, a PostScript font is downloaded to the PostScript printer, just as in earlier systems. If you have corresponding screen fonts, they should be dragged to the System file, where all fixed-size screen fonts belong.

If you have ATM (Adobe Type Manager), you need only one screen font as before (for the font to appear in Font menus). Drag the ATM file (INIT) to the Extensions file so that it will start up with your Macintosh. Version 2.3 or later is required for System 7, as is about 200K of RAM.

LaserWriter owners might want to leave the TrueType font equivalents in the System so they can get all sizes on the screen. But they can probably remove the fixed-size fonts. Bear in mind, however, that there might be tiny differences between the fixed-size font and the TrueType representation. This would affect only documents created with older fixed-size fonts and where the location and wrapping of text around lines is critical. For the most part, there won't be any differences.

If you have ATM installed, and you use PostScript fonts exclusively, you can remove all font files from the System file except for one size of each screen typeface. In fact, if you have a PostScript font for any other standard fonts (Times, Helvetica, etc...), then it's a good idea to remove the TrueType equivalent from your System file—whether or not you use ATM.

Choosing Fonts

The fonts you choose for your text depend a lot on the kind of printer you use. The so-called direct-connect device (e.g., ImageWriter, StyleWriter, LaserWriter SC models, Hewlett-Packard DeskWriter) do not store any fancy fonts on their own—they print dot-for-dot what the Macintosh tells them to. For these printers, you you will obtain the same quality from any TrueType font you select. Your choice will depend more on personal preference for the differences between, say, New York and its companion font, Times.

For PostScript printers, however, your choice may be influenced by the extent of your PostScript and TrueType font libraries. Because some printers have several PostScript fonts already installed, compare sample printouts of TrueType fonts against the built-in PostScript fonts. You may prefer, for example, the built-in Times font over the TrueType New York font (the latter is much improved over previous font substitution of Times for New York). Be aware—too—that when you print a TrueType font on a PostScript printer, the System software must send additional software to the printer before the printer can handle the TrueType font. Mixing PostScript and TrueType fonts in a document slows the process ➜88.

Choosing Font Sizes

Fully System 7-compatible programs are intelligent about the font sizes shown in the **Size** or **Style** menu. Point sizes in outlined text are sizes that your Macintosh should display without distortion. A TrueType font should have all sizes outlined. If the font is only a fixed-size (bit-mapped) font, then just those sizes installed in the System file are outlined. Sizes in plain text will be scaled, and probably distorted on the screen and in non-PostScript printers.

Size
Other...
8
9
10
11
12
14
18
✓24
36
48
72

Uncovering Your Printer's Fonts

One of the software disks packaged with Apple LaserWriters contains a utility program called **LaserWriter Font Utility** ➜ 152. One of the menu options allows you to view a list of fonts currently active in the printer.

If you are making the transition to System 7 and have PostScript or other laser printer fonts (beyond what are installed in your printer), it helps to know how system software treats PostScript printers and fonts.

Screen Display Precedence

When a program displays text on the screen, here is the order in which the system software looks for a font to display the characters:

1. The fixed-size font resource in the System file.
2. The TrueType font in the System file (for calculation and display).
3. A Type 1 PostScript font (if ATM is installed).
4. A fixed-size font resource of the nearest size that can be scaled (probably in a distorted manner) to the desired size.

Direct-Connect Printing Precedence

When you print text to a direct-connect device (i.e., a non-PostScript device), such as the ImageWriter, StyleWriter, fax modem, etc., system software looks for font information in the following order:

1. The TrueType font in the System file (for calculation and printing).
2. An ATM font (if ATM is installed).
3. A fixed-size font resource of the size that can be best scaled (perhaps in a distorted manner) to the desired size.

PostScript Printing Precedence

Because of all the possible locations of fonts in a PostScript printing setup, system software pursues a complex path to finding a font that is the most compatible with existing font libraries, yet allows TrueType to work its magic when no PostScript fonts are available. Here is the search order:

1. A PostScript font in the printer's ROM.
2. A PostScript font previously downloaded to the printer and currently in the printer's RAM.
3. A PostScript font located on a hard disk connected to the printer.
4. A PostScript font file located in the Extensions Folder of the System Folder.
5. A TrueType font in the System file.
6. A fixed-size font resource (screen font) of the nearest size that can be scaled (probably in a distorted manner) to the desired size.

PostScript Font Files

Unlike bitmapped or True Type font resource files, Postscript fonts must be installed simply in the System Folder, not in the System File. A bitmapped version of the Postscript font must also be in the System File (in at least one size) for the font to appear in the list of fonts available in any application.

Imagesetting is not expensive when you want to make a good impression with a printed flyer or newsletter.

Preparing Documents for Imagesetter Output

Many typesetting **service bureaus** are staying with their PostScript font libraries, rather than moving to TrueType. If you prepare documents for imagesetter (e.g., Linotronic) output, your service bureau will probably recommend that you prepare documents and proof print on your LaserWriter using downloadable PostScript fonts exclusively. To prevent errors in layout, remove TrueType and Apple supplied screen fonts for typefaces with the same names as the PostScript fonts you plan to use (e.g., Times, Garamond, Helvetica). Copy the matching third-party screen fonts to your System File (or use ATM), and download the printer fonts to your LaserWriter 152-153.

Converting Fonts to TrueType

Several font programs convert PostScript fonts to TrueType. Results may vary from program to program and font to font. It is advised to compare printouts of documents with both sets before committing a font in your system to TrueType.

The Preferences folder is one that you rarely, if ever, have to worry about. Your application programs and system software use this folder as a convenient repository for preferences files.

Many programs allow you flexibility in specifying parameters about the program —things like how you prefer new document windows to appear, ruler measurement scales, and so on. Apple encourages program authors to store this information in files in the **Preferences** folder, thus preventing your application folder from accumulating extra files that get in your way. In the Preferences folder, the files are out of sight, but always accessible to the programs, since the programs know where to find the files.

System Software Preferences

When you install System 7, the system software automatically places some of its preferences files in the folder. For example, the Finder Preferences file stores, among other things, the Views control panel settings and the warning status of the Trash. Preferences files are generally quite small, since they contain mostly a record of on-off switch settings for features in a program. Programs that are not fully System 7-compatible, may not yet know to automatically put preferences (or settings) files in the Preferences folder, nor know how to find them there. Don't move a program's preferences file. If it knows how to handle the Preferences folder, the program will place the preferences file there by itself.

Double-clicking on a preferences file yields different results with different programs. Some will automatically launch the application that generated the preferences file. Since the only prescribed way to edit a program's preferences file is through the application itself, this makes sense. Double-clicking on other preferences files simply presents an alert box indicating that the file can't be opened.

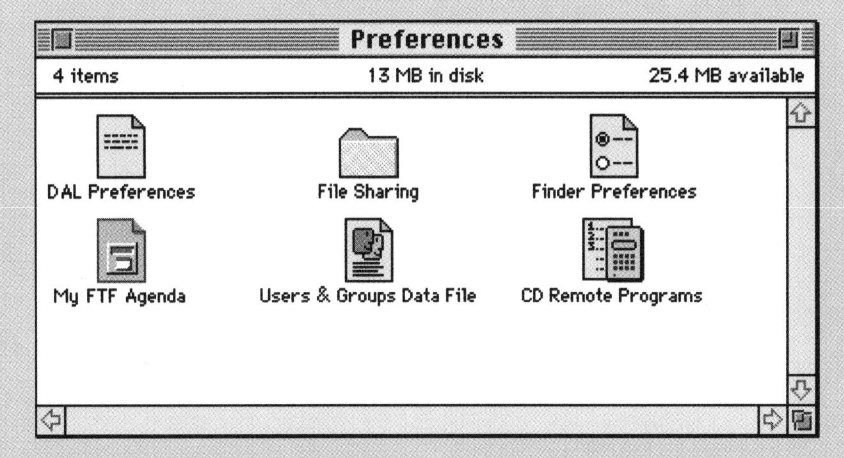

Deleting Preferences Files

Application programs that are fully System 7-compatible are supposed to be designed such that if the application's preferences file is not found in the Preferences folder then the program starts up with its original, default settings. In the process, it also should create a new preferences file in the Preferences folder to record any changes you make to the program's settings. Therefore, if you want to start fresh, quit the program, drag the preferences file to the trash, and restart the program.

Be aware that if you are upgrading your applications software to System 7 levels, there may be a preferences file from the previous version left in a couple of places on your disk. The two places to look are in the System folder (not in any subfolder) and in the folder containing the application. These were the two most common spots for program preferences files before System 7.

When you use a printer that allows for background printing, a system software application, PrintMonitor, controls the action behind the scenes. Most of the time, the PrintMonitor Documents folder is empty.

PrintMonitor Documents

As you print a document from an application, system software creates a file containing the print specifications of the document you wish to print. That file, called a **Spool File,** is automatically placed in the **PrintMonitor Documents** folder. In the meantime, PrintMonitor quietly and continually checks the contents of the **PrintMonitor Documents** folder. If it finds a spool file, then it launches the PrintMonitor application, which in turn starts sending Spool files to the printer. For more about **PrintMonitor**, see page 148, 152.

Watching PrintMonitor Documents at Work

If you have a printer that supports background printing, you can watch the PrintMonitor Documents folder fill and empty itself of spool files.

1. Activate the Finder, and open the **PrintMonitor Documents** folder. Place the window so you can see it clearly.
2. Prepare a document consisting of about three pages.
3. Issue the **Print** command 4 times, and activate the Finder so you can see the **PrintMonitor Documents** folder.
4. Pull down the **Application** menu (at the far right of the menubar), and open PrintMonitor. Position the window so you can see the **PrintMonitor Documents** folder icons and the PrintMonitor window simultaneously.

As you send each document to the printer, the document is saved as a Spool File in the folder, each with its own serial number. As PrintMonitor works with a file, its spool file icon changes to one with an "X" through it. As PrintMonitor finishes sending the document to the printer, the spool file icon disappears—PrintMonitor has done its job for that file. PrintMonitor continues working its way through the files (in the order in which they were printed from the application) until the PrintMonitor Documents folder is empty.

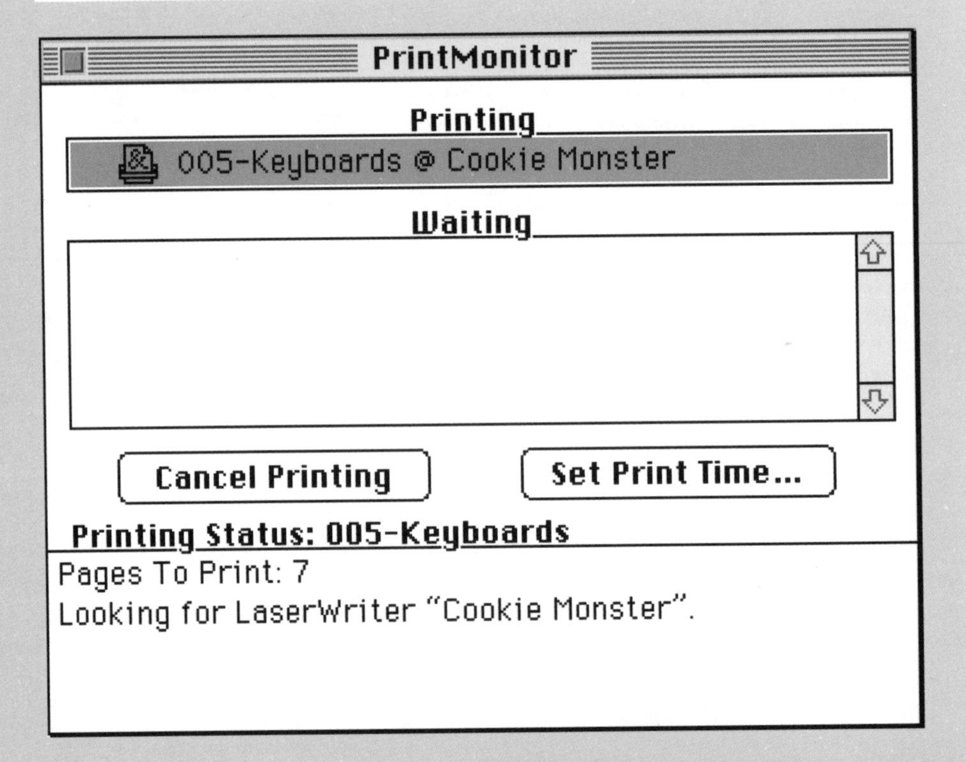

Spool Trivia

While you may be able to conjure a physical metaphor for the action of spooling a print file, the name is actually an acronym: **Simultaneous Peripheral Operations On Line**. Spooling can apply to actions other than printing, but in the Macintosh world, the te[illegible] is used primarily for

You can direct your Macintosh to start one or more applications (including standalone programs, desk accessories, and control panels), load a particular document, or connect to another Macintosh each time it starts up or restarts.

Startup Items

Therefore, if you typically work with a particular set of applications all the time, you can let the Macintosh prepare your work environment for you. The way you teach the Macintosh what to load is to put a file (or preferably an alias to the file) in the Startup Items folder inside the System Folder. If you place a document file in the Startup Items folder, the Macintosh both launches the application for that document, and loads the document. If you place an alias to a server there, your Macintosh connects to the server.

Adding Applications

You should add only as many applications, desk accessories, or control panels to the **Startup Items** folder as your Macintosh has RAM to load. If the Macintosh runs out of memory before all applications load, the applications menu flashes with the Finder icon. When you then choose Finder from the menu, an alert notifies you of the lack of memory.

When you copy a combination of items into the **Startup Items** folder, they load in a specific order:

1. Applications
2. Documents
3. Desk accessories and control panels
4. Servers

Within each group, the items load in alphabetical order of the file name listed in the Startup Items folder. By creating and renaming aliases to applications or documents, you can control the order of overlapping windows appearing on the screen after everything has been loaded (see below).

If you include a desk accessory or control panel in the Startup Items folder, the loading may not go completely unattended. The Finder icon flashes over the Applications menu icon. When you bring the Finder to the front, the loading of DAs and control panels continues (although there may be additional interaction needed to open all of them).

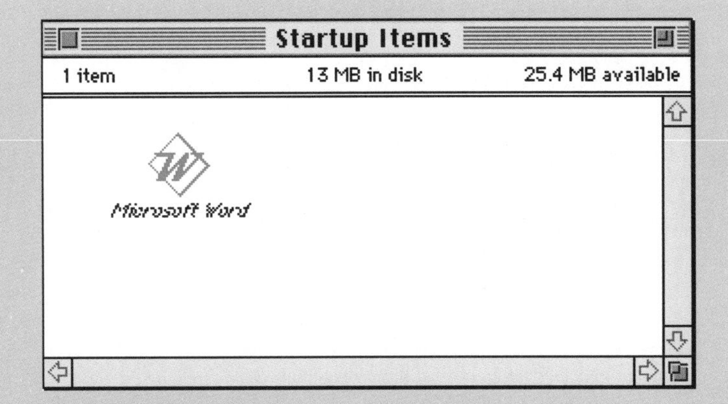

Adding Documents

As you drag multiple document files or their aliases to the Startup Items folder, be sure that the application for those documents can open more than one document at a time. Most applications do that, but not all. If more than one document is in the Startup Items folder for an application that handles only one document at a time (e.g., TeachText), then only the first document (alphabetically) opens, while the others are ignored.

An alias to a favorite HyperCard stack in this folder assures that HyperCard and stack are ready for you at startup.

Servers

In addition to putting a server alias in the Startup Items folder, the Chooser offers another way to link to one or more servers at startup.

Startup Strategies

It is rare that you would store actual files in the Startup Items folder. More likely, you will keep applications, desk accessories, control panels, and documents in other folders that are more natural repositories for those files. Instead, create aliases

An intriguing property of alias files is that their names don't have to bear any resemblance to their owner files. Therefore, you can rename an alias to anything you want. For the Startup Items folder, this means that you can rename a series of document aliases such that they open in an order other than alphabetical for their owner files. You can name them with single letters (A, B, C, etc.). Then the Finder loads them in that order, placing the window of the first file at the bottom of the pile of overlapping windows. Make sure that the window

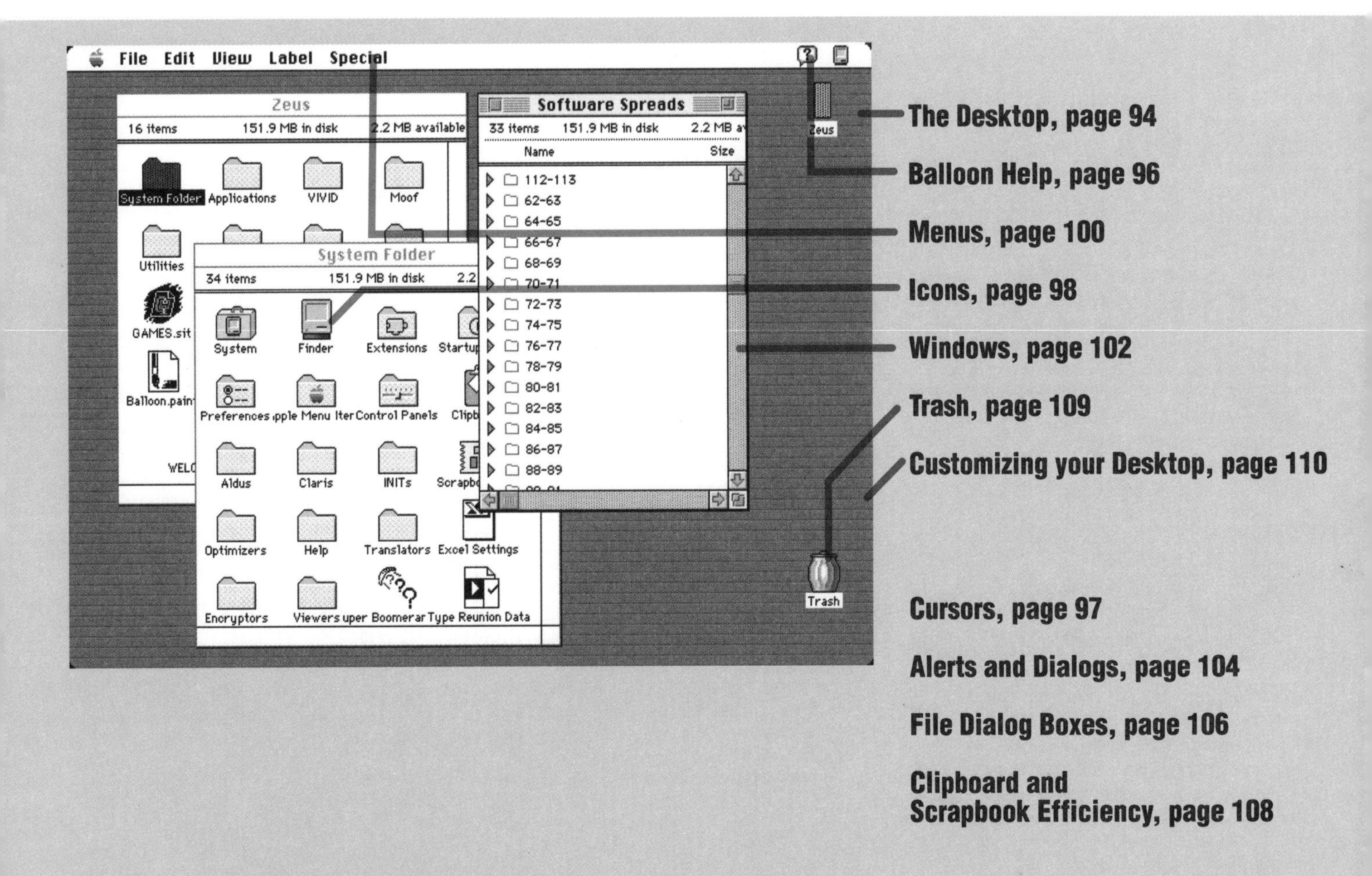
File Edit View Label Special
Zeus
16 items 151.9 MB in disk 2.2 MB available
System Folder
34 items 151.9 MB in disk
Software Spreads
33 items 151.9 MB in disk
Trash
The Desktop, page 94
Balloon Help, page 96
Menus, page 100
Icons, page 98
Windows, page 102
Trash, page 109
Customizing your Desktop, page 110
Cursors, page 97
Alerts and Dialogs, page 104
File Dialog Boxes, page 106
Clipboard and
Scrapbook Efficiency, page 108

The concept of the Macintosh Desktop is often clouded because the term seems to refer to different things, and its meaning has evolved slightly with the system software.

Strictly speaking, the Desktop is the workspace you see on your video monitor. Think of the background pattern as the top surface of a physical desk. On it rest icons representing your disks, the wastebasket, folders, documents and so on. Opening a folder window is just like opening a physical file folder and making it the topmost item on what may be a heap of open folders and other papers on the desktop.

Because the representation of icons and folders is controlled by the Finder ➜74, the terms Finder and Desktop are often used interchangably—you'll hear Macintosh users say they quit to the Finder or quit to the Desktop. The Finder is a program that presents the user interface; the Desktop is the graphical metaphor the Finder uses to show us the disk and file organization. The Desktop view is also the most global view of your Macintosh environment you can get.

The Desktop Metaphor

Graphical user interfaces, such as the Macintosh environment, attract discussion of metaphors. Extending the literary metaphor a bit, screen metaphors present objects or images on the video monitor that remind us of other objects or images from the world outside the screen. Therefore, just like a real file folder, a Macintosh file folder is a way of grouping documents. By reading the name of the folder, we get a clue about the kinds of documents inside. Fortunately, the computer adds significant powers to that folder, such as a variety of index listings, search facilities, and almost unlimited size. But because the Macintosh folder shares its basic properties with the familiar paper folder, we, as users, don't have to conjure some new mental model for the way documents are organized on a Macintosh. Dragging a document icon from one folder to another is highly analogous to the way we'd move a paper document from one folder to another. That's among the things that attracts us to graphical interfaces.

Just like our real desk and work environment, we can tailor the Macintosh Desktop to suit our whims. Several control panels open the Desktop to customization of background colors or patterns, file listings, color or patterns, file listings, alert sounds, and many more features ➜110. The Macintosh Desktop is where we work—it should be a comfortable place.

While the Macintosh Desktop is certainly more powerful than any physical desktop, it doesn't include everything you might have on your desk. You can add software programs that fill most of the gaps (from a card file and calendar to pictures of the family), but you'd still lack a telephone. That could change in the future, as the Macintosh and its Desktop evolve.

Hiding the Desktop

When you run applications on the Macintosh, they open visually on top of the Desktop. Especially on larger video monitors, you see not only a document window (and perhaps some palettes from the program), but also the Finder's disk icons, the Trash, and vestiges of open folder windows. If the window clutter is more than you like, you may hide all open windows in the Desktop layer (all Desktop-level icons always remain visible in a background layer, however). With the Finder as the active application, pull down the **Application** menu (the rightmost icon on the menubar), and choose **Hide Finder**. All Finder windows retreat to the **Application** menu. By clicking on a Desktop icon, or by choosing **Finder** from the **Application** menu, the Finder windows return to their settings before you hid the Finder. Desktop-level icons (including files you store directly on the Desktop) are always visible, although they can be covered by a document window. A potential conceptual problem with this is that if you need access to a Desktop-level icon, it does not ever float in front of an application's document window, even when the Finder is the active application. You'll have to move or hide the application windows (via the **Application** menu) to access the Desktop icons.

Desktop File

Hidden behind the scenes is a Desktop database—called the Desktop file—which the Finder uses as a place to store its information about applications, documents, and their icons. Every disk volume larger than 2 megabytes contains a System 7 Desktop file. Among the purposes of this file is to help the Finder display the proper icon for an application's document files. The file is also where comments in a file's **Get Info** dialog box ➜118 are stored. You don't see the Desktop file in any disk or folder window (although you may see its components, **Desktop DF** and **Desktop DB**, listed in **File Open** dialog boxes for some utility applications ➜106. Don't delete these files with disk or file utility programs.)

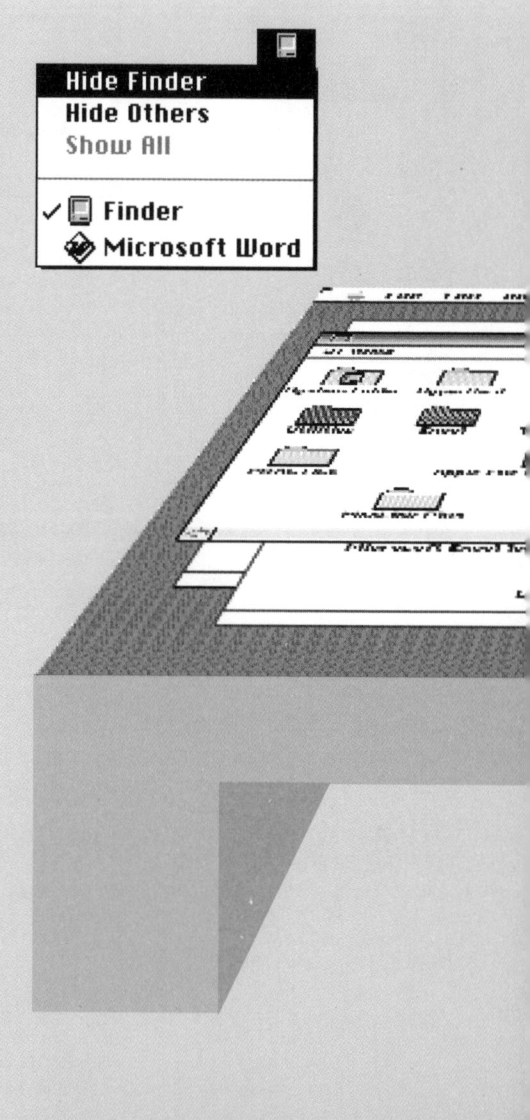

Just like a desk's top, you can put a document literally on the Macintosh Desktop, instead of inside a folder or storage device. This is a sleight of hand, because all files must really exist someplace on a storage device (in this case the **startup disk** 58), but in System 7, the Desktop appears to be a real place to put stuff.

Here's an important maintenance tip.

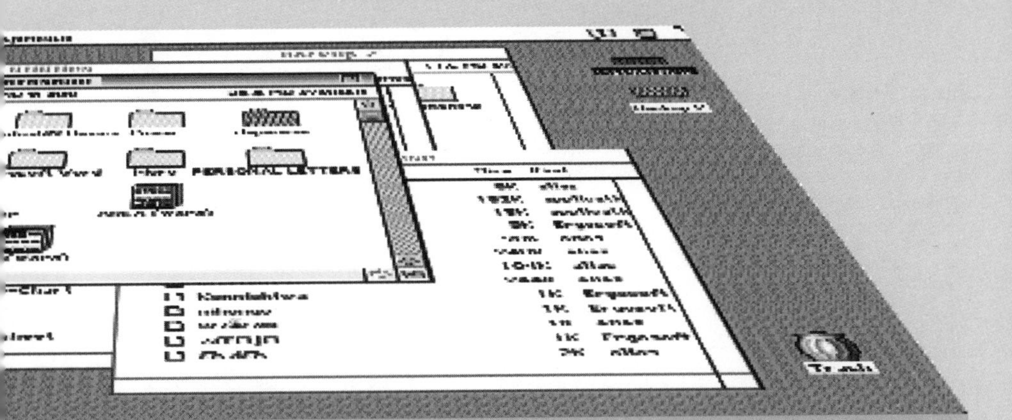

Rebuilding the Desktop

The Desktop file changes as you add new applications or other Finder icon-bearing files to your hard disk. System software automatically copies the program's icon families to the Desktop file so they'll be handy for the Finder as it displays document icons. System software does not, however, delete Desktop file information from applications you delete from your hard disk. Moreover, if you copy an upgrade to an application to your hard disk, and that upgrade contains a new icon, the older icon family may prevail. Also, a large Desktop file that contains a lot of unused items can noticeably slow down the Finder's performance.

To keep your Desktop file up to date, you should periodically instruct the Finder to rebuild the Desktop file. The prescribed way to do this is to hold down the *option* and *command* keys while starting or restarting your Macintosh. After what appears to be a normal startup sequence (you get the happy Macintosh, Welcome screen, and loading of extensions), an alert box asks whether you wish to rebuild the Desktop file. Notice the warning that all comments in **Get Info** dialog boxes will be lost in the process. For this reason alone, it's not a good idea to place important information in that **Get Info** box, since rebuilding the desktop is an important maintenance job all Macintosh owners should perform. Click OK to rebuild the desktop. Even on huge hard disks, it takes only a few minutes. A progress dialog keeps you informed of the progress. Fortunately, your Finder window arrangement remains intact.

Since the Desktop file is a potential entry point for virus infections, rebuilding the Desktop file is another way to protect your hard disk from infection. How often you rebuild the Desktop depends a lot on how often you install and de-install applications, desk accessories, control panels, and extensions. Active Macintosh users should rebuild once each month. Everyone should rebuild the Desktop at least once a year.

Desktop Strategies

You can uncover as many Desktop layout strategies as serious Macintosh users, so here are a few guides to consider in your path toward the perfect Desktop:

1. Keep only one Finder window—your hard disk —open, displaying files in a hierarchical text list view 112.
2. Place key desk accessory and program files (or their **aliases** 120) in a row at the bottom of the **Desktop.** This mimics the interface of other graphical interface computers and workstations.
3. Open a few important folders but resize them to display important program or stationery 135

Automatic Desktop Rebuilding

When you start your Macintosh, it compares the modification dates of a hidden hard disk file called **Desktop** with the **Desktop DB** and **Desktop DF** files. The former is used only for System 6 and before; the latter two for System 7 only. This comparison is made on each volume connected to the system. If any volume, such as an external hard disk, was used and modified on a System 6 Macintosh the last time it powered up, System 7 automatically rebuilds its **Desktop DB** and **Desktop DF** files to bring them up to date. The System 6 Desktop file is not affected. While you can stop the process, it is best to let the rebuilding

As friendly as the Macintosh user interface is compared to other personal computers, the array of choices in pull down menus and dialog boxes can bewilder a newcomer to the Macintosh or to an application.

System software includes a mechanism that assists programmers in building electronic help into a program. These instructions appear in cartoon-like balloons on the screen. Accordingly, this mechanism is called **Balloon Help**, and should be the first place to look for help when you don't understand something or know what to do next.

Only programs written for System 7 are likely to offer balloon help-but not all of them do.

Unlike previous attempts at providing electronic, on-line help, Balloon help can offer help in context. For example, a help balloon can provide different comments for active and dimmed instances of the same menu item.

Turning On Balloon Help

The **Help** menu is visible in the Finder and in most applications at the right side of the menubar. Pull down the menu like any other menu. Any application that accommodates Balloon Help will have at least two items in the **Help** menu: **About Balloon Help** and **Show Balloons.** Programmers may append additional menu items, presumably in the same "help" theme as the menu. The Finder, for example offers a third item in this menu that leads to a display of keyboard shortcuts for the Finder.

To turn on Balloon Help, choose **Show Balloons**. After that, as you drag the mouse to any **menu**, **menu item**, **window**, or **dialog box item**, you should see a small explanatory comment appear in the cartoon-like balloon. Because system software provides the Balloon Help text for so many common elements (e.g., the parts of a window's titlebar), you will likely see the same wording for these pieces across many applications.

Importantly, while Balloon Help is active, you still have full control over the program. The balloons may pop up all over the screen, but you may choose menu items, fill in dialog boxes, enter text, and save documents just as without Balloon Help.

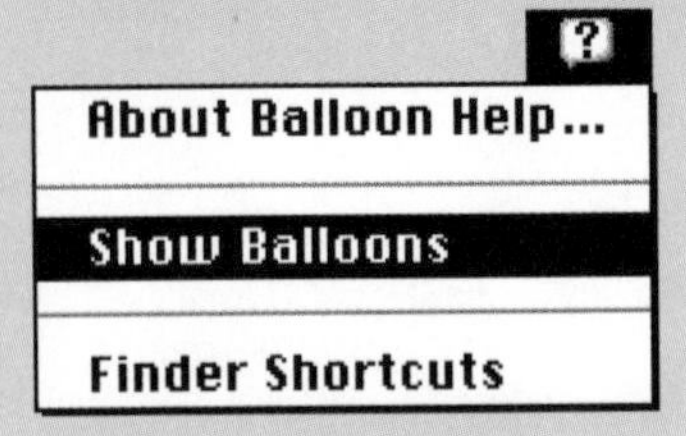

Turning Off Balloon Help

To prevent these balloons from getting in your way, you may turn off Balloon Help at any time. Pull down the **Help** menu, and choose **Hide Balloons**. Also, if you restart the Macintosh, Balloon Help is off when the machine starts back up.

?
About Balloon Help...
Hide Balloons
Finder Shortcuts

Icon Help

Balloon Help can help you identify a document from its icon. The default behavior of balloons for documents is a balloon that tells you the name of the application that generated the document. This holds true only if the application is still listed in the **Desktop file** ➔ 94. Otherwise, the help message is that the document was created by an application not available on any volume visible to the Finder.

TeachText

Shareware utility available that shows balloons at a key-command.

Modifying Balloon Help Text

If you are comfortable snooping around files and applications with **ResEdit** ➔ 85, you can explore and even modify the text or pictures that go into the help balloons. Text for help balloons is stored as **STR#** resources in the application. The comments

Aside from the fun you can have putting funny sayings in the help messages, modifying Balloon Help can be valuable in business or group settings when some additional instructions may be necessary. For example, if you want users to save documents to a central file server volume, you could modify the Balloon Help for the **Save** command in an application to remind users about the volume name.

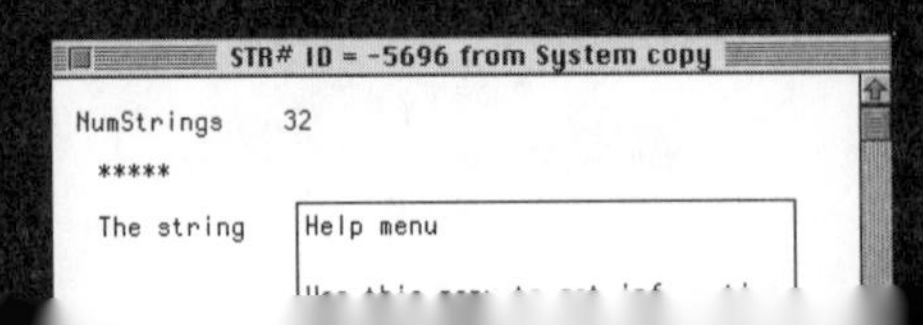

The terms cursor and pointer are used interchangeably in the Macintosh world, but they're not truly the same. There are a few cursor styles, each of which has a different meaning.

Some cursors are for pointing, others to signify where the next typed characters goes, others to indicate a particular tool with is own peculiar action, and still others to show you that some process is taking place.

While the Macintosh system software comes with a limited repertoire of cursors—an arrow pointer, a text pointer, a thin crosshair pointer, a thick crosshair pointer, and a wristwatch—many application programs display their own cursors as you use the programs. Most cursors move on the screen in response to dragging the mouse, while others, like the text insertion pointer, serve as place markers for additional actions.

Mouse Pointers

The system cursor that tracks along with the mouse changes its shape, depending on where the pointer is, and what the system is doing. The most common cursor shape in the Finder is the arrow. The arrow is what appears when you drag the cursor into the menubar or atop an icon. All cursors have a hot spot, a single pixel on the cursor that must be atop an object or menu item to perform whatever action you intend. On the arrow cursor, the hot spot is at the very tip of the arrow. If you click the arrow on an icon such that the hot spot of the cursor is above an icon, the icon will not highlight, even though the rest of the cursor overlays the icon. Other programs' cursors place their hotspots in different locations, but generally in a place that is logical for the cursor—the tip of a drawing pencil, the spout of a paint bucket, the center of a crosshair.

If you open a text editing program, like a word processor, almost the entire document window is for typing text. As you drag the cursor from outside the window into the window, you will see that the cursor shape changes to the text pointer. The design of this shape allows you to place the vertical line between characters when you need to insert additional characters. When you click the text pointer inside a text editing area, a second cursor flashes in that spot. The mouse pointer is free to move. The flashing text insertion pointer indicates where the next keyboard character or item pasted from the Clipboard will appear. This pointer flashes to help draw your attention to the active spot in a window.

How the cursor tracks the motion of the mouse or trackball is controlled by the **Mouse** control panel 25. For most users, the efficient setting of the Mouse Tracking control is one of the two middle settings. For very large screens, however, the fastest setting allows you to whisk the pointer from edge to edge on the screen using the smallest desk real estate under the mouse.

Animated Cursors

In many processes, you see an animated cursor—the cursor shape changes slightly during the process. The Finder includes a set of **wristwatch cursors** with different settings of the hands in the watch. Whenever long processes start, such as copying several files to a disk, the animated cursor takes over. The minute hand on the watch spins around the watch. Other kinds of animated cursors to entertain you while you wait in various programs include the **spinning beachball**, **counting hand** and a **revolving Earth**. Some utility programs also let you install additional animated cursors to take the place of the Finder's wristwatch cursor.

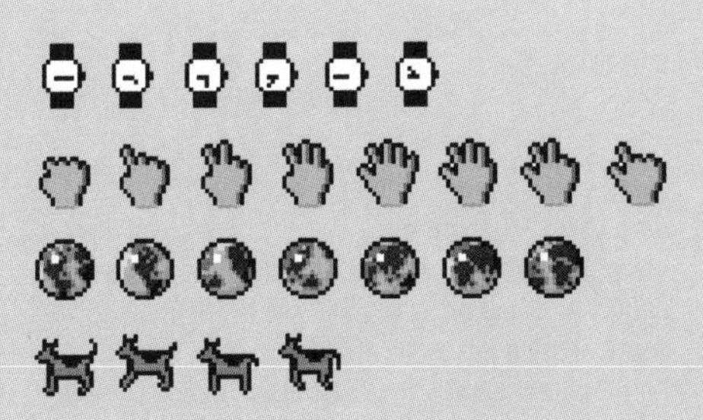

Third party extensions let you assign still other system animated cursors, including Claris, the Dog Cow, doing four-legged backflips.

Exploring Cursors with ResEdit

The programmer's tool, ResEdit 84, gives you access to the CURS resource in the System, Finder, and application programs. You can experiment with modifying the cursors on copies of these programs. In some programs, you may be surprised to see that what you expected to be cursors are not listed in the CURS resource. Chances are that those cursors have been "hard-wired" into the application, and as such won't be editable. Some programmers take out all the fun.

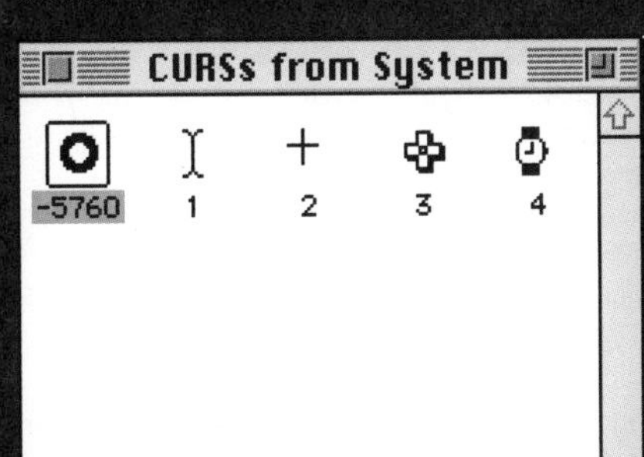

The spinning animated watch cursor is in the acur resource of the Finder. If you replace art for these cursors, make sure the resource numbers stay the same.

At the Desktop level, icons represent files or places to store file. The pictographic nature of icons allows them to convey a meaning. A folder icon, for instance, represents a collecting place for documents, applications, or other folders.

Desktop icons are different from icons you may see in application programs. A program's internal icons generally act as buttons that you click once or twice with the cursor to effect some action. **Desktop icons,** on the other hand, represent objects. You can move them, open up most of them to see what's inside, and select more than one at a time before carrying out actions on those items.

Icon Families

Every Finder-level icon for a System 7-compatible program (including the Finder) usually has a family of icon pictures for each icon. Members of the icon family include **small** (maximum of 16-by-16 pixels) and **large** (maximum of 32-by-32 pixels) icons in three color levels: **monochrome**, **4-bit** color (16 colors), and **8-bit** color (256 colors). These variations of icon design are necessary given the diversity of video monitors for the Macintosh and given that you may elect to show a folder's icons in either the small or large icon format. System software recognizes the abilities of your video monitor, and shows the appropriate icons—you do nothing to select what color level of icon appears on the Desktop.

Application and Document Icons

Application programs have an icon for the application. But if the application produces any documents or has any support files (like an on-line help system), several icons may appear on your Desktop. For example, Microsoft Excel has a unique icon for the program, spreadsheets, charts, macros, and support documents.

Selecting an Icon

For several operations in the Finder, it is necessary to select an icon. To select a single icon, position the tip of the arrow cursor atop the icon, and **click** the mouse button once. The icon highlights by becoming darker (or black on a monochrome display). If an icon's object is open (whether it be a disk, application, document, or folder), the icon will be dimmed or "grayed out." This occurs commonly to disk icons and folders whose windows are beneath the one you're viewing. Also, if you view the Finder while an application is running, that application's icon and any document files it has open will be dimmed. To de-select an icon, click anywhere except on the selected icon.

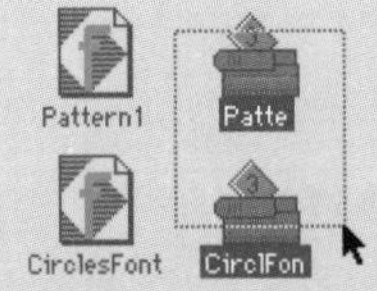

Selecting Multiple Icons

You may also select more than one icon within the same window for various operations, such as copying to another disk, dragging to the Trash, or moving into a folder. There are two ways to select multiple icons.

One is to hold down the *shift* key while clicking once on each icon you wish to gather into the group. This method is ideal for gathering icons that are located in widely different locations in a window.

The second method is for gathering adjacent icons in a rectangular grouping. Click and hold the mouse button at one corner of the rectangular selection, and drag the mouse until the selection rectangle (the dotted line rectangle) encompasses the desired files. As you reach various icons, they highlight, indicating that you have successfully selected them in the grouping. Release the mouse button when all are selected. If you want to add yet additional icons to the selection, hold down the *shift* key and either click on individual icons or drag-select another rectangular grouping.

To select all icons in the frontmost window, simply choose **Select All** from the **Edit** menu, or type *command-A*. To de-select an icon grouping, click anywhere except on one of the selected icons.

Selecting Icons in Multiple Windows

Although system software allows only one window to be active at a time—and hence you cannot select icons in more than one window at a time—it is possible in some circumstances to select icons from different folders. By setting the view of the disk volume window to any text listing ➔112, you can expand the contents of any folders ➔112 and *shift*-click select any files you can see in the one window. After you select one or more icons, you can expand folder views without affecting the selection.

Icon unselected

Icon selected

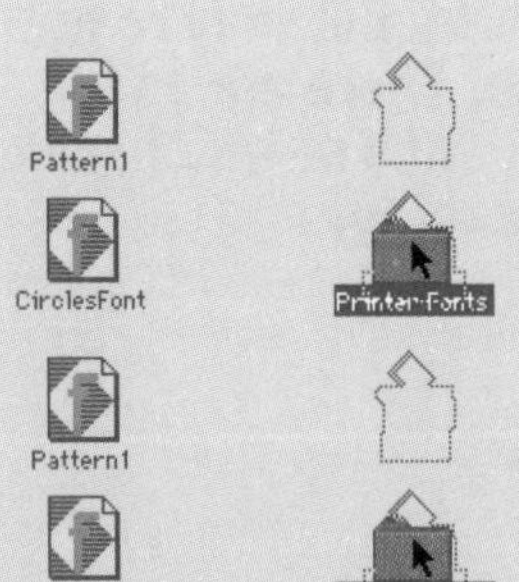

Dragging Icons

Once one or more icons are selected, you can click and drag on any of the highlighted icons to grab them all, even if some of the selected icons are not in view in the window. The basic actions you probably want to accomplish are:

1. moving the icon(s) to another location in the same window
2. dragging the icon(s) to another folder, disk, or Trash icon or
3. dragging the icon(s) to the Desktop. Each action has its own behavior associated with it.

Dragging an icon(s) around its own window is simplified with the Finder's auto-scrolling. If the window's vertical scroll bar is active ➔102, then you can drag the icon into the area of the window to which you would normally scroll manually. For example, if an icon is at the bottom of the window, and you wish to reposition it at the very top, drag the icon such that the arrow pointer is just above the active area of the window, and hold the mouse button down. The window will scroll to bring the top into view. You cannot auto-scroll beyond the manual scrolling limits of the window.

To drag an icon(s) to another folder, disk, or Trash icon, you must drag the group and carefully position the arrow cursor atop the destination object. The destination object must highlight before you release the mouse button. Only when the object highlights does it mean that it is selected as the destination. If you miss, the icon(s) stays on top of the destination icon, without going into it. You can combine the actions of auto-scrolling inside a window to reach a folder and drop the icon(s) into it. There is no Undo available for moving an icon inside another.

Finally, you may drag an icon(s) to the Desktop layer. When you do this, the file or folder is stored in the Desktop layer of the disk from which it was dragged. To drag a file to the startup disk's Desktop, copy it first to the startup disk; then drag it to the Desktop.

Whenever you drag multiple icons into another folder, the orientation and spacing of the icons stays the same in the destination folder, provided both windows have their views set to Icon ➔112. If you try to manipulate individual items in the text views of a window, the items revert back to the sorting order dictated by the View menu selection.

Renaming Icons

Every Finder icon has a name. If the object is not locked or being shared by another user on a network, you may rename the icon. Click once on the icon's name, and the text is selected. Type a new name or edit the existing name. To shorten the delay to the editing mode, you can shorten the double-click speed (in the **Mouse** control panel) or jiggle the mouse after clicking the name. Also, clicking the icon once and pressing *return* or *enter* puts you into edit mode immediately.

Finder and System Icons

Macintosh System software comes with a large library of icons it uses to display generic documents, applications, folders, plus a large number of special purpose folders and files. Below is the cornucopia of system icons and what they signify.

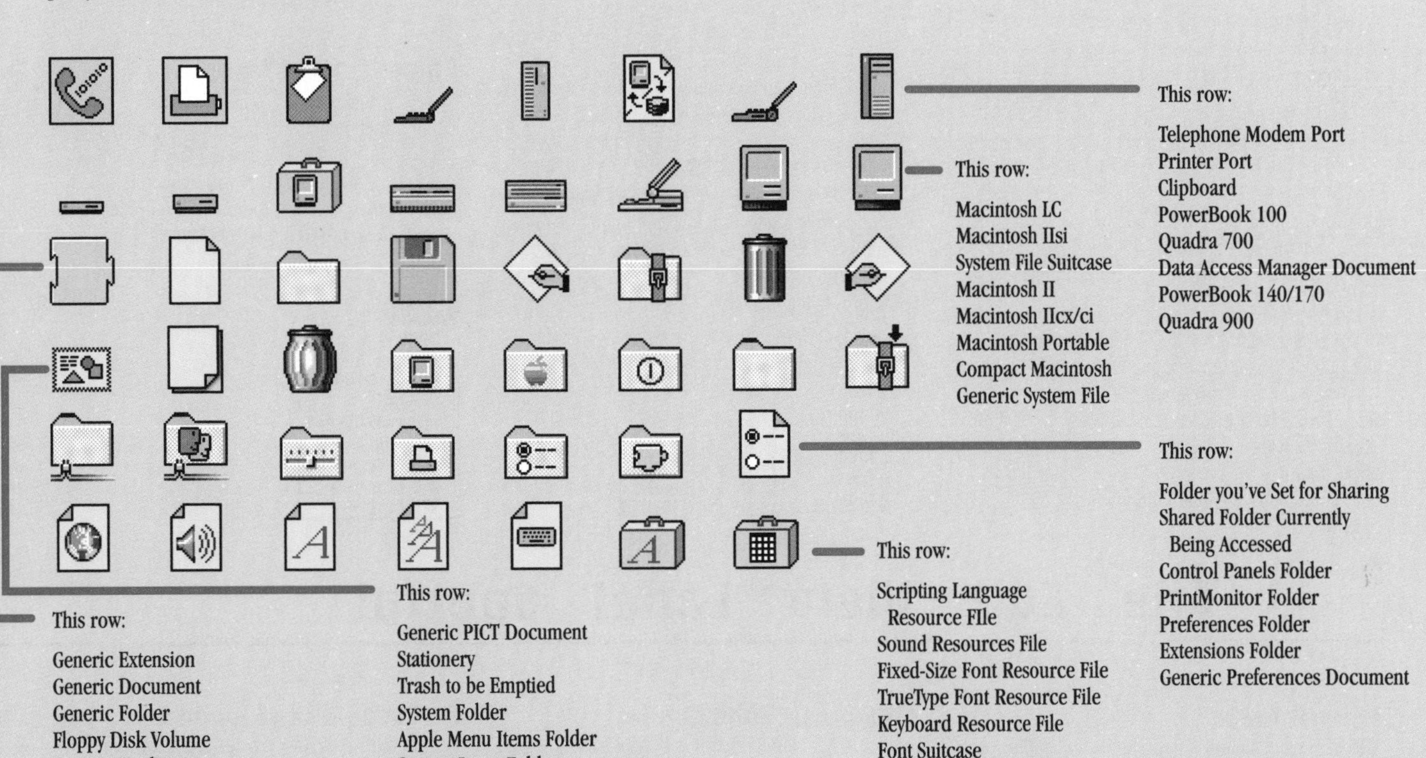

This row:

Telephone Modem Port
Printer Port
Clipboard
PowerBook 100
Quadra 700
Data Access Manager Document
PowerBook 140/170
Quadra 900

This row:

Macintosh LC
Macintosh IIsi
System File Suitcase
Macintosh II
Macintosh IIcx/ci
Macintosh Portable
Compact Macintosh
Generic System File

This row:

Generic Extension
Generic Document
Generic Folder
Floppy Disk Volume
Generic Application
Locked Folder on Shared Volume
Empty Trash
Generic Application

This row:

Generic PICT Document
Stationery
Trash to be Emptied
System Folder
Apple Menu Items Folder
Startup Items Folder
Shared Folder Owned by your Macintosh
Locked Shared Folder Accepting Copied Files (Drop Folder)

This row:

Folder you've Set for Sharing
Shared Folder Currently Being Accessed
Control Panels Folder
PrintMonitor Folder
Preferences Folder
Extensions Folder
Generic Preferences Document

This row:

Scripting Language Resource FIle
Sound Resources File
Fixed-Size Font Resource File
TrueType Font Resource File
Keyboard Resource File
Font Suitcase
Desk Accessory Suitcase

Editing Icons

In addition to the system software's built-in ability to change a file's icon ➲ 113, System icons can be modified via third-party icon utilities and **ResEdit**. Third-party utilities are generally **INIT** extensions or control panels. They offer flexibility in assigning different icons to standard Finder icons, like hard disks and the Trash. More adventurous Macintosh owners can try their hand at **ICN#** resources with ResEdit ➲ 84, 110-113. With ResEdit 2.1, a single resource template for all sizes and color depths of icons makes the job of editing all possible sizes much easier. If you venture into ResEdit, be sure to do so only on copies of the System, Finder, or your applications software.

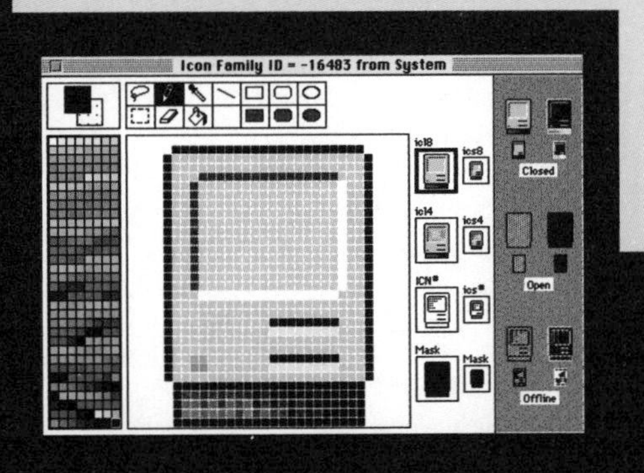

Macintosh menus are either of the pull down or popup styles. Both types of menus are accessed by clicking on and holding the menu label, and then dragging the pointer vertically along the list of items in the menu.

Most **pull down menus** are in the **menubar,** which stretches across the top of the Desktop. These are the menus that let you control actions in the Finder or an application. Several elements of the menubar—the , **File**, **Edit**, **Help**, and **Application** menus—are consistent across applications, including the Finder. Yet, while virtually every application sports **File** and **Edit** menus, the contents of the pulled down menus vary from program to program.

Some programs also feature a variation of the pull down menu called the hierarchical menu. A **hierarchical menu** item displays a right-pointing arrow at the right edge of the pulled-down menu. As you drag the mouse pointer atop this item, an additional menu appears to the right.

Menubar Anatomy

The menubar at rest is always at the top of the screen. In multiple-monitor systems ➔34, the menubar is in only one screen. From left-to-right, the standard menubar contains:

1. the menu
2. one or more menu titles with text designating the category of items underneath each menu
3. the **Help** menu
4. the **Application** menu, which shows a miniature icon of the active application running on the Macintosh, including the always-running Finder.

If you have more than one **language** or **keyboard** resource file installed in the System ➔74, an additional menubar icon representing the current language appears between the **Help** and **Application** menus. Turning on **Easy Access** 20 also shows a small indicator at the very far right of the menubar. Some applications and third-party utilities may display other icons or menubar indicators.

Finder View Menu

The **View** menu is the way for you to control the way the current Finder window is to display items in the window. Settings in the **Views** control panel ➔112 apply to any choice in this menu. See page ➔112 for guidance on file views.

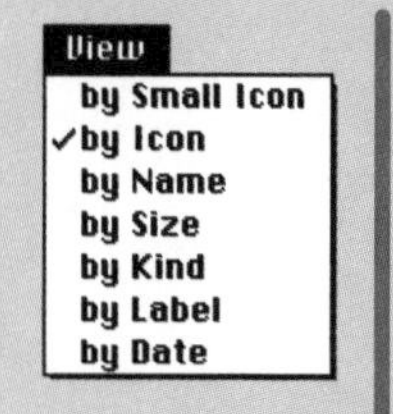

Finder Label Menu

Assigning a label to a file is like attaching a colored tab to a document in a folder. By assigning labels to documents, you give yourself another method of viewing and organizing files within a folder. The names and colors (on color monitors) of labels are set with the **Labels** control panel ➔111. See page ➔111 for guidance on using labels.

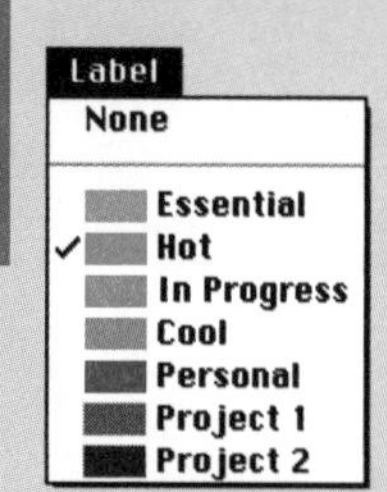

 File Edit View Label Special

Apple Menu

The menu changes as you shift from application to application. The first item in the menu always lets you view a dialog box that supplies information about the program, or, in the case of the Finder, of the Macintosh memory situation. A few programs insert one or more other program-specific items at the top of the menu. Below the dividing line are **programs**, **documents**, **control panels**, or **desk accessories** contained in the **Apple Menu Items** folder. This list is entirely customizable ➔76.

Finder Edit Menu

Actions of the Finder's **Edit** menu items may seem inconsistent. One item, **Select All,** allows you to select all files in the currently open window. **Undo**, **Copy**, **Cut**, and **Paste**, however, work only with text, notably, the text names of icons. Select a file and choose **Copy** from the **Edit** menu. The copy is not of the file (that's what **Duplicate** in the **File** menu is for), but of the name of the selected file. As you edit names of files ➔118, the other editing commands become available. **Undo** works only with text changes, not Finder motions.

Finder File Menu

Items in the Finder's **File** menu relate to organizing, opening, and printing files, although printing is most often controlled from within an application. One menu item, **Close Window**, changes to **Close All** when the *option* key is pressed before pulling down the **File** menu. Because some menu items require selections of files or folders, those items may be dimmed when no selections are made.

Finder Special Menu

Most of the **Special** menu's operations are system-wide, such as emptying the **Trash,** disk maintenance, and system power functions. The first item, **Clean Up Window**, brings all icons (in either Icon view) into the alignment set in the **Views** control panel ➔112. The **Clean Up** item also has two alternates when you hold down modifier keys: the *shift* key turns the item into **Clean Up Selection** (in case you select one or more icons to align); the *option* key turns the item into **Clean Up by Name** (icons are organized alphabetically from left to right, top to bottom).

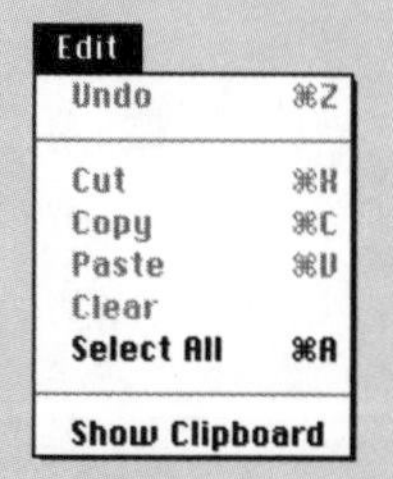

Special
Clean Up Window
Empty Trash...
Eject Disk ⌘E
Erase Disk...
Restart
Shut Down

Pop up menus are most often found inside windows and dialog boxes. While sometimes a popup menu initiates a command, it more often provides a list of possible text items that are to fill in a blank.

Popup Menus

Another style of menu that appears inside dialog boxes and application program windows is most often used as a way to let you choose from a list of settings or possible entries for a text field. The most recent implementations of popup menus include a down arrow at the right of a shadowed rectangle. Clicking and holding anywhere on that rectangle or on a text label that may be to the left of the rectangle makes the popup menu appears. If an item has been previously selected or is a default value, the item is checked in the popup menu, and the menu is scrolled so the item is where the shadowed rectangle is. Therefore, you may have to select an item above or below the current selection.

A version of the popup menu includes an **editable field** in the shadowed rectangle. You can either type a value into the field, or select from the list in the popup menu you see when you click on the down arrow icon.

Accessing Standard Menus

To pull down a menu, use the mouse to position the arrow cursor atop the icon or text menu title in the menubar. Then **click** and **hold** the mouse button. A menu of choices—menu items—drops down from the menubar as long as you hold the mouse button. You may drag the cursor left and right along the menubar to see what items are under each menu title.

While holding the mouse button, drag the mouse down so that the arrow stays within the box of the menu. As you position the cursor anywhere on a line containing a menu item, the item **highlights**, showing you what command or selection applies when you release the mouse button. Dotted lines are inactive dividers to help the program author group related menu items. To close the menu without making any menu selection, simply drag the arrow outside the pull down menu, and release the mouse button.

A menu item that ends in an **ellipsis** (...) means that the selection displays a dialog box ➧104-105. It is common practice to explore a new program's depth by choosing these menu items to see what dialog box options are available. You can almost always cancel a dialog box, so you won't make any changes to a program or document by choosing ellipsis menu items.

Keyboard Equivalents

The right margin of a pull down menu is reserved for display of equivalent keyboard combinations that perform the same action as choosing that menu item with the mouse. These keyboard equivalents are often more efficient if you are working primarily at the keyboard instead of the mouse.

Various symbols indicate the combination of keys required to issue the command. The most common is the **Command** modifier key (⌘). To issue the menu command, hold down the ⌘ key while pressing whatever other character is shown in the menu. While letters are shown as capital letters, the unshifted character is what you type. ⌘ key equivalents common to virtually all Macintosh programs are:

File Menu:
⌘-*N* New ⌘-*O* Open ⌘-*S* Save
⌘-*P* Print ⌘-*Q* Quit

Edit Menu:
⌘-*Z* Undo ⌘-*X* Cut ⌘-*C* Copy ⌘-*V* Paste

If more than one modifier key are shown, then hold both keys and type the remaining character. Here are symbols commonly used for modifier and non-character keys:

delete ⌫ *tab* ⇥ *shift* ⇧ *space* ␣
option ⌥ *return* ↵ *control* ^ *enter* ⌤
command ⌘ *caps lock* ⇪

Hierarchical Menus

Some programs feature hierarchical menus, also called **submenus.** A menu item that displays a right facing arrow at the right margin of the pull down menu has a submenu connected to it. Selecting the main menu item, the submenu pops up to the side of the pull down menu. To access one of the submenu items, you must keep the mouse button pressed and carefully **drag** the cursor horizontally from the selected main menu item to the submenu. You then drag the pointer vertically inside the submenu to make a selection that takes effect when you release the mouse. Hierarchical menus are frequently difficult to use comfortably because of the precision pointer control required to make the submenu appear.

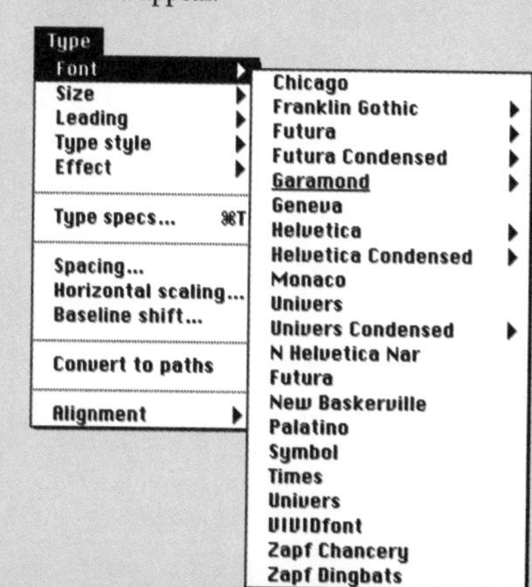

Help Menu

The Finder and most programs released for System 7 and above contain provisions for on-line help called **Balloon Help.** Available from the Help menu, you can turn on Balloon Help and drag the cursor to various parts of the screen or program to get help about various menus, buttons, and fields. See page 96 for details about Balloon Help. Also in the Finder **Help** menu is a choice that accesses five pages of shortcuts for Finder operations. These shortcuts appear in a window, which you close by clicking the close box in the window's upper left corner ➧102. Other applications may add items to the **Help** menu to provide more information or shortcuts about themselves.

Application Menu

Because you may have several applications running at the same time, and overlapping windows may hide the other applications, the **Application** menu offers a way to activate another application. From this menu you may also hide the current application or all the others in case window clutter is confusing you ➧126. A miniature icon of the active application appears as the **Application** menu title, including a small Macintosh representing the Finder.

Tear-off Menus

Application programs may contain a special kind of menu, called the **tear-off menu.** When you click and hold a tear-off menu title from the menubar, a graphical menu of tools, patterns, or other graphical objects appears. You can drag the mouse into the menu and select one. But if the menu is designed as a tear-off menu, you can also drag the entire menu away from the menubar. Releasing the mouse button leaves the menu out on the desktop in a special window called a palette ➧103. Now you may access any item in the menu by clicking on the item in the palette.

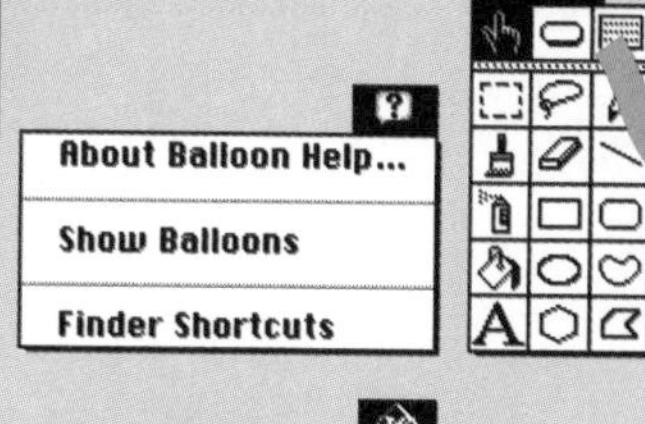

A Macintosh window is much like a real-life window. You look through an opening to see some or all of another space. For example, when viewing a text document in a window, you essentially look through the window to see as much of the entire document as fits in the opening on the screen.

To see other parts of the document, you manipulate scroll bars or other devices to shift the item "behind" the window.

Macintosh windows come in a variety of styles, and may overlap one another. In most circumstances, only one window—the window nearest to you—can be active at any instant. Clicking anywhere on a window (except on a Finder icon) brings that window to the foreground, making it the active window. Due to the potential of window clutter when many applications are open at the same time, the **Application** menu offers choices to hide windows from all applications except the current application.

Finder Window Anatomy

Because Finder windows have much in common with windows you often find in application programs, the following details apply to both.

Title Bar

A window's title bar displays the name of the item whose contents you see in the window. In the Finder, that may be a disk volume or folder name; in an application, the name is of the file containing the document (or Untitled if a new file has not yet been named and saved).

Close Box

Clicking the upper left box closes the window. This is the same as activating a window and choosing **Close Window** from the **File** menu (or typing *command-W*) in the Finder. The Finder remembers the size and location of each window as the window closes, so it will reopen where you last saw it. If you hold the *option* key down while closing one Finder window (either by clicking the Close box, choosing **Close Window** from the **File** menu, or typing *command-W*), all Finder windows close.

Window Header

Finder windows can contain additional information about the contents of the disk or folder. Beneath the title bar is a row of values listing the number of items in the current view, the amount of disk space currently occupied, and how much disk space is available. While these listings are standard for icon listings, they are optional for text listings, as set by the **Views** control panel ➜ 112.

Grow Box

Click and drag this lower right corner icon to resize a window. As you drag the **Grow Box,** an outline of the window follows the cursor location. When you release the mouse button, the window and its contents are redrawn to the desired size.

Horizontal Scroll Bar

When there is more in a window in the horizontal plane than can appear in the window, the elements of a horizontal scroll bar appear at the bottom of the screen.

Zoom Box

Clicking the upper right box has different effects depending on your last actions with the window, but it essentially toggles the size of the window between the optimum size and any other size to which you've manually resized the window (with the Grow Box, below). A Finder window's optimum size is the smallest window that:

1. displays all icons or text listings; or
2. fills the entire screen except for a single column of disk volumes and Trash at the right.

If you move or resize a window, clicking the Zoom Box toggles between the optimum size and the other size or location.

Vertical Scroll Bar

When there is more in the window than can be seen through it, the **scroll bar** becomes active. Consisting of five parts—**up arrow**, **down arrow**, **page up area**, **page down area**, and the **thumb**—the vertical scroll bar allows you to shift the contents of the window vertically to see items not currently visible. Clicking the arrows scrolls the view in small increments in that direction; clicking the grey page areas causes larger jumps in the same directions. You may click and hold arrows and page areas to get repeat action scrolling. The thumb represents the relative location of the current view in the entire vertical distance of the window's contents. Drag the thumb in either direction to jump to an approximate location in the window's contents.

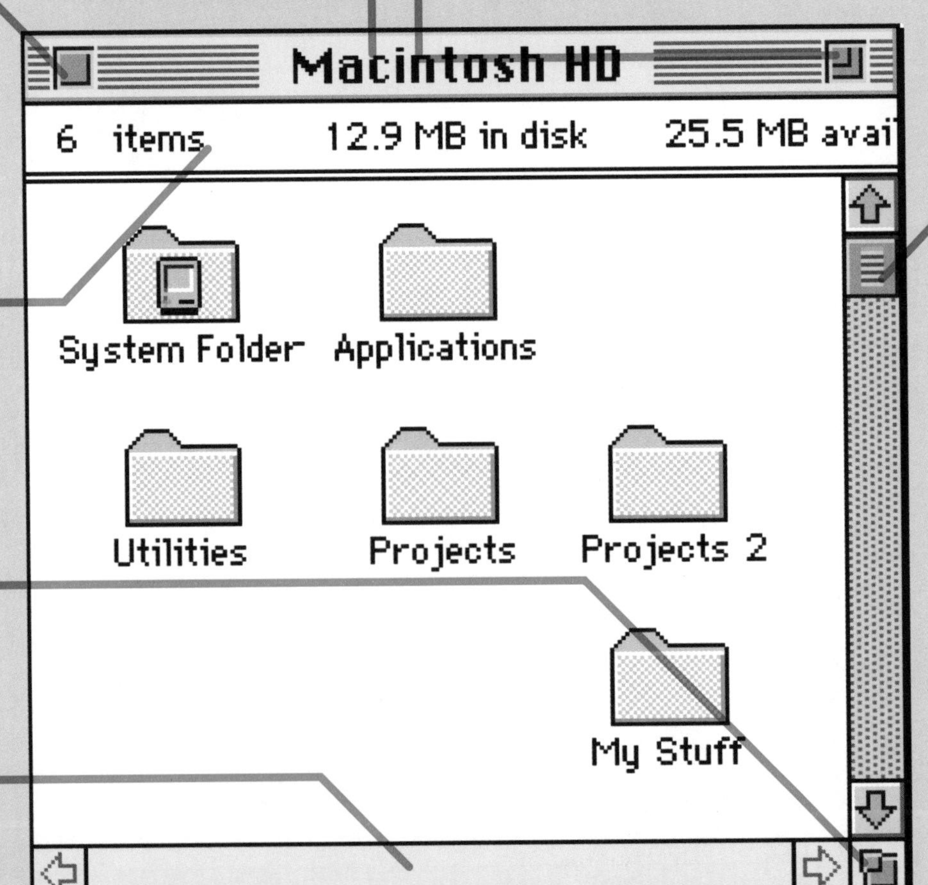

Organizing Window Layers

Most Macintosh programs, including the Finder, remember the size and location of a window just before it last closed. You can choose from two primary methods of organizing windows: tiling and overlapping. **Tiled windows** are adjacent to each other, such that you can see the entire window opening of all windows at once (although only one window is active).

Overlapped windows resemble pieces of paper on a desk, where one item might cover some or all of other items, with one item definitely on the topmost layer.

Arrange the windows so that some portion of every window will be visible, no matter what other window is open. A cascading arrangement works well.

Remember, too, that you can reduce the number of Finder windows open by viewing disk volume or folder windows in any text listing mode, and then expanding the outline views of nested folders in the same window.

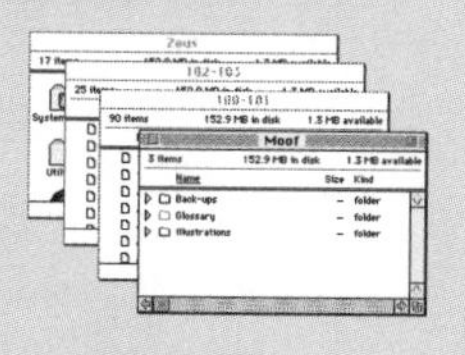

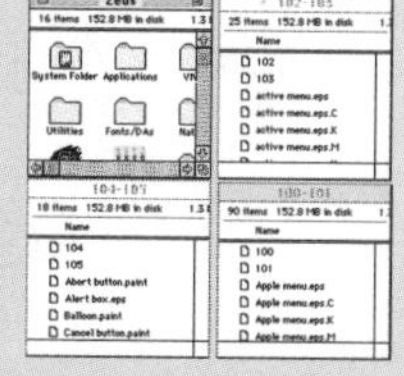

Cleaning Up Windows

Icon views of Finder windows or even the Desktop can get messy after dragging items from other windows. The **Special** menu provides a **Clean Up** command whose precise action depends on what is selected and keyboard modifiers. In general, the **Clean Up** command places icons in alignment according to settings in your **Views** control panel ➜ 112, attempting to fill space closest to the upper left corner of a window without any file names overlapping one another in the window. Here are the possibilities:

Item Selected	Modifier Key	Menu	Objects Affected
None	None	Clean Up Desktop	All Desktop icons
	option	Clean Up All	All Desktop icons
Desktop	None	Clean Up Desktop	All Desktop icons
	shift	Clean Up Selection	Selected icon
	option	Clean Up All	All Desktop icons
Window	None	Clean Up Window	All icons in active window
	shift	Clean Up Selection	None
	option	Clean Up By Name	All icons placed in alphabetical order
	Shift	Clean Up Selection	Selected icon(s) in window

You can avoid messy icon windows and Desktop by turning on the **Always Snap To Grid** selection in the **Views** control panel, or hold down the ⌘ key while dragging any Finder icon.

Enclosing Folder and Disk Windows

A folder that resides on a disk is said to be enclosed by the disk (Folder B inside Folder A is enclosed by Folder A). You can always see which disk and folder(s) enclose the current window by holding down the ⌘ key while clicking and holding the name of the folder in the title bar. A pop-up list shows the **path** ➜ 116 from the current window out to the disk on which the folder is stored. You may then select the folder or disk layer to open or activate that window. Similarly, a keyboard shortcut of *command-up arrow* opens or activates the next higher folder in the path. Once you reach the disk, *command-down arrow* opens the disk's window.

Moving Windows

In addition to resizing windows (those that have a grow box in the lower right corner), you may move windows around the screen by clicking on the window's title bar and dragging the window. An outline of the window follows the cursor. When you release the mouse button, the window is redrawn at the position of the outline.

Normally, clicking on anywhere on a window activates that window. But if you hold down the ⌘ key before clicking on an inactive window's title bar, you can then drag the window without making it the active window. This only works among windows within the same application (including the Finder). If you click on a window from another application, the application comes forward (although with the ⌘ key held down, the window order within that application does not change).

In the Finder, clicking an icon in an inactive window does not alter the window order. This allows you to grab an icon and move it to the active window with the least possible effort.

Window Styles

You see many different types of windows in Macintosh software, but a number of those styles are built in for Macintosh programmers to use easily. Those styles are shown below:

Notice that a few styles do not feature a titlebar for dragging or closing. Such windows are generally used for modal purposes—the window appears on top of whatever else is on the screen, and you must dispose with the window before you may return to the program. Programmers can also design their own window styles. It is common to find **palette windows** in programs that display tool or pattern choices. There can even be a **transparent window,** in which elements in the window seem to float mysteriously atop the Desktop.

1. Document window
7. Rounded rectangle window
8. Dialog box window
5. Plain rectangle window
6. Shadowed rectangle window
2. No grow box document window
3. Zooming document window
4. Zooming, no grow box document window

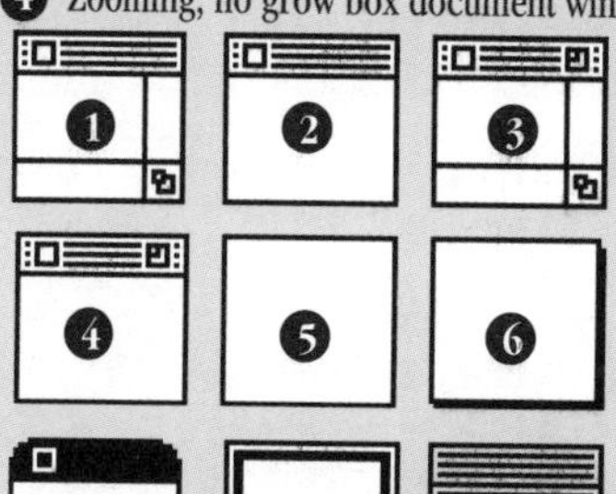

Active vs. Inactive Windows

On the Desktop, only one window may be active at a time. You can recognize an **active** document window by the horizontal lines and other elements in the title bar and scroll bars. An **inactive** window shows only the window's name and the window's contents. On color monitors, the name in an inactive window is a shade of gray instead of the usual black.

In programs, however, you may encounter states in which more than one window is active. Palettes and a special type of **dialog box** (called the movable modeless dialog, looking like a no grow box document window) reside in a domain separate from document windows. Sometimes called the **palette layer,** this domain is closer to your eye than document windows, and allows for simultaneous access to any window in that domain as well as a single active window in the document layer. Thus, a program's tool palette doesn't get hidden by clicking on a document window. A program's palettes, however, may disappear when you switch to another program that is running at the same time.

Active

Inactive

Two basic types of windows pop up on the screen from time to time (usually in response to some action you take).

An **Alert Box** is generally a simple message from the program or Macintosh, offering you a limited number of buttons to click in response to the message. A **friendly alert** is a box that tells you than an action has been completed (e.g., transferring a file to another computer).

Clicking the lone OK button in the alert indicates to the program that you acknowledge the message—and the alert box goes away. A more helpful alert is one that warns you of impending danger (e.g., you are about to overwrite an existing file on your disk). With these kinds of alerts, a choice of two buttons (usually OK and Cancel) let you tell the program whether it should go ahead or cancel the request.

Cancel/No/Abort/Stop buttons

Cancel and No generally mean that nothing has yet changed (e.g., no installation has taken place), so that a **click** of the **button** returns you to the state before the alert appeared. Abort and Stop, on the other hand, indicate that processing has already begun (e.g., copying a group of files from one disk to another), and a click of the button will halt the process at its current state.

OK/Yes/Continue buttons

This button responds in the affirmative to any question presented in the alert. If this button is the only one showing, then the alert is generally telling you that something has already happened. If the button has a thick border around it, then pressing *return* or *enter* is the same as clicking the button.

The alert message

This may be in the form of a question or a simple statement. If there are no buttons in the alert, then the box will either go away by itself (e.g., the Welcome alert when you start the Mac) or require a mouse click to clear (e.g., many "splash screens" that appear when you choose the **About item** in the menu).

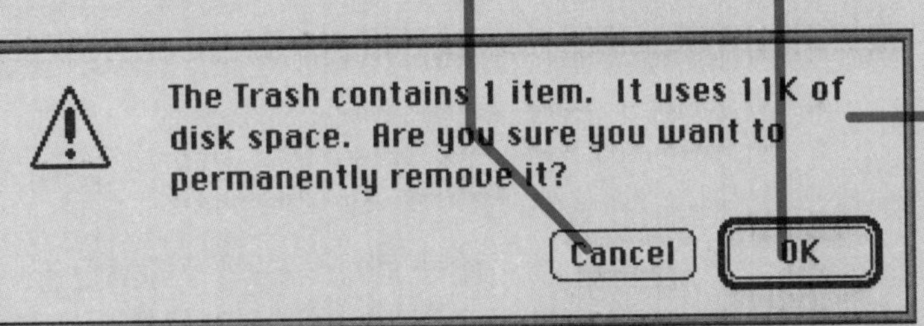

A dialog box in an application actually consists of two resources: **DLOG** (dialog) and **DITL** (dialog item list). The first specifies the window style, size, and location. The second contains specifications for the items that appear in the dialog. Editing a DITL resource in ResEdit, you have the power to resize fields, shift button locations, and change static text (labels). However, when you see a field text placeholder (e.g., ^0), don't change: it: the program places a variety of messages in that field depending on what's happening in the program. As with all ResEdit changes, perform them on backup copies only, and do it all at your own risk.

Modal vs. Modeless Dialogs

While most dialog boxes have windows like the ones shown on above, you may encounter dialog windows that look more like document windows—with title bars and close boxes. There are significant differences between the two styles.

The traditional dialog box is called a **modal dialog**, meaning that you are restricted to a mode in which nothing is active except items in the dialog box (and perhaps the menubar)—you must close the modal dialog before regaining access to your document or the Desktop. The **Page Setup** dialog from the Finder is an example. Modal dialogs appear on the screen where their designers specified, even if it means the dialog covers vital information in the document.

When you must view a document's contents while fussing with dialog settings, you may be presented with a **modeless dialog box.** It's called modeless because you have access to both the dialog and document at the same time—no restrictions. You may drag the modeless window around the screen via its **titlebar**, just like any document window. Some modeless dialogs can be closed via the window's close box, while others provide a traditional OK button as a holdover from the time when modeless dialogs were practically unknown on the Macintosh.

Other Dialog Controls

Dialog box elements such as **radio buttons** are known in the Macintosh programming parlance as controls. The more varied your application's software choices, the more varied will be the kinds of controls you will encounter in dialog boxes.

Slider controls (like the volume setting in the **Sound** control panel) are relatively common. When you see a miniature representation of a document or object in a dialog, try clicking on it to see if one or more "handles" appear, allowing you to drag or resize the object. Advanced graphics programs may provide controls for spinning graphical objects along three-dimensional axes or adjusting their perspective.

7 - 6 - 5 - 4 - 3 - 2 - 1 - 0 -

The more specialized the requirement, the less standardized the control. Since you're not likely to read a program's manual at first, experiment by clicking and dragging on anything you see in a dialog. with a well-designed program, you should be able to figure out most of what's going on.

Customizing Alerts and Dialogs

When software publishers produce a version of their products for other languages, they use programs like **ResEdit** 84 to replace dialog box wording with translations. Adventurous Mac users (who also religiously back up their applications and system) can use ResEdit to customize dialogs.

Occasional Shortcuts

A number of programs—especially the popular Microsoft applications—have a number of keyboard shortcuts built into their dialog boxes. While a dialog's design elements influence the precise nature of shortcuts, here are some tricks to look for:

- clicking the label of a group resets items to default choices;
- with no editable fields in a dialog, typing the first letter of a button choice toggles that button. Typing the first letter of a **pop-up menu** label drops the menu, allowing selection to be made with the arrow cursor keys and a press of the *return* key;
- with **editable fields** in a dialog, the above also works if you hold down the *command* key before typing the letter;
- when there are multiple choices starting with the same letter, the item nearest the top left corner is the one that responds to the keyboard shortcut.

These options spark of a mouseless **DOS** software heritage, but don't let that deter you. For dialog choices you make frequently, the keyboard method may prove more effecient than the combination of keyboard and mouse.

A **Dialog Box** on the other hand, usually offers many choices in the form of buttons, popup menus, and text entry fields. In dialogs, you choose from various settings or preferences that are to apply to a selected chunk of text, the current window or the entire document, depending on the nature of the dialog box.

You can usually predict when a dialog box will appear, because it comes in response to a click of a button or menu choice with names ending in an ellipsis (...). In fact, if you want to explore the depth of a new program, choose all menu items with ellipses, and study the resulting dialog boxes for choices they offer.

Editable Field

Enter requested text into these entry fields (they may contain default information when the dialog opens). Because these fields can scroll horizontally when you put more data into them than shows in the field rectangle, it is always best to select the text in the entire field and type new text to replace it. The safest way to do this is to press the *tab* key to advance the text cursor from field to field in a dialog box. When it reaches a field that has text in it, the entire text is automatically selected. Typing replaces the selected text .

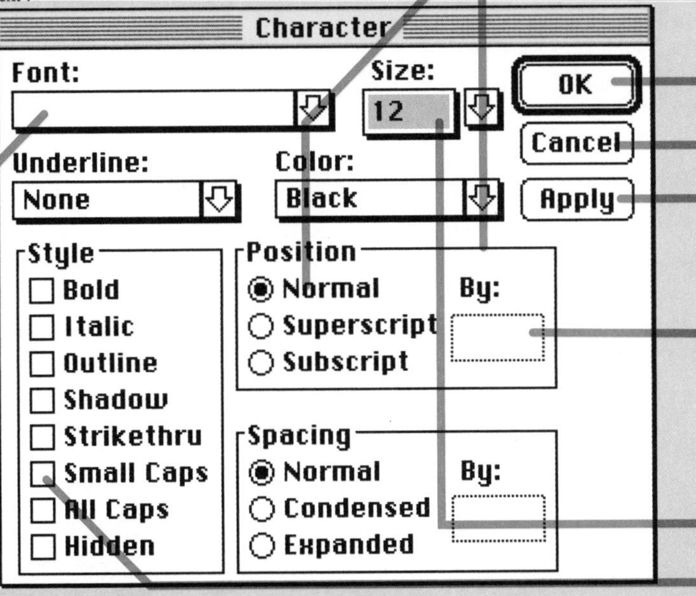

Popup menu

Designers are quickly settling on the interface element of the down-pointing black arrow to indicate that a shadow field contains a **popup list.** Click and hold anywhere on the field arrow to show the list. The currently selected item will be marked in the popped-up list. If the list is a long one, arrows may appear at the top and/or bottom of the popup, indicating there are more selections. While holding down the mouse button, drag in the direction of the arrow to scroll the items in the list.

Chicago
Geneva
Monaco
✓New York
Times

Radio button grouping

Radio buttons are always mutually exclusive within a group—only one may be selected (and usually one must always be selected).

Item grouping

A labeled border around items is another way to help you understand which settings are related within a complex dialog box.

Scrolling text field

Such fields may be editable, but in dialog boxes they are most often used to present lists of **choices.** Clicking once on an item selects it (perhaps marking itself with a checkmark or other characters). A **double-click** on a single selection in some dialogs is the same as choosing the item and clicking OK. Where applicable, you may also be able to *shift*-click to select a contiguous range of items in a list or *command*-click (or *option*-click) to select individual items scattered throughout the list—these actions fall under the term **multiple selections**

AbortButton.pict
ApplyButton.pict
CancelButton.pict
Picture 0
Pop-Up.pict

OK button

A click of this button tells the program you wish the current settings in the dialog to take effect. When a heavy black border surrounds this button (or any button in a dialog or alert), it means that pressing *return* or *enter* is a keyboard shortcut to clicking the button with the pointer.

Cancel button

None of the changes to settings in the dialog box will take effect when you cancel the dialog. This lets you change your mind before clicking OK. In many dialog boxes, the keyboard shortcut *command-period* is the same as clicking Cancel.

Apply button

In some programs, this button lets you apply the **current settings** to the selection or document underneath the dialog (more prevalent in modeless dialogs). Thus, you can experiment with variations in settings without repeatedly opening and closing the dialog box.

Button leading to another dialog box

Just like the button or menu item that led you to the current dialog, the ellipsis (...) on this button's name means that a click of it will take you to another level of dialog box. Depending on the programmer's design, the new dialog may replace or overlay the current one. Also depending on the design, clicking the sub-dialog may either bring you back to the first dialog or close them both.

Dimmed item

Buttons and fields that don't apply to the current settings may be dimmed or "greyed out" to indicate that they are not available. Clicking on or tabbing to a dimmed item has no result.

Editable popup menu field

Some popup menus combine a menu with an **editable field** that allows you to manually enter a value other than those available in the popup list. See page 101 for more details.

Checkbox button grouping

Checkbox buttons allow you select or deselect any combination of items in the group. Occasionally, a checkbox item in a group will be mutually exclusive or inclusive, meaning that a click of one item automatically affects the setting of another item in the same group.

A special kind of dialog box—the file dialog box—assists you in opening and saving documents while you are in applications.

Opening and Saving actions display two variations on the file dialog box theme. In the **Open** file dialog, you simply select a document; in the **Save** file dialog, you must enter a name for a file before it is stored on the disk.

Both types of file dialogs, however, share hard disk navigation procedures so you can open or save a document in a specific folder on any disk or network server volume normally visible from the Desktop. In fact, the view of all volumes in file dialogs starts at the Desktop—the most global view of volumes connected to your Macintosh and mounted.

Open File Dialog

Whenever you choose **Open** from an application's **File** menu, you see the **Open File** dialog box. The most basic versions consist of a **scrolling field** beneath a **pop-up list**, four buttons, and the name of the currently selected volume. **Open File** dialogs tend to show files in the disk or folder level of either the application or the last file opened or saved.

Applications have the ability to filter names that appear in the listing of files to limit the list to files that the program can open. If the dialog box offers selections for other file types (e.g., radio buttons for different graphics or word processing document formats), the filter allows only those items in that **file format** to be listed.

List of Files

Icons at the left edge of his list tell you a lot about an item in the dialog. When viewing from the Desktop, you see volume icons (hard and floppy disks or network servers) and the names of the volumes. You may also see the Trash icon, although it is most likely dimmed, meaning that you cannot open it to see what's inside from here.

If you open a volume (**double-clicking** on the line in the scrolling list is the fastest way), you will see icons for folders and documents. Open folders as needed to wend your way to a document. Some graphics applications allow you to see a miniature **preview** of a file's contents by just selecting the document in this list.

The keyboard offers a shortcut to quickly locate a file in a long alphabetical list. Type the first few characters of the document name, and the Macintosh scrolls the list to the first item matching those letters or to the item coming closest to those characters later in the list.

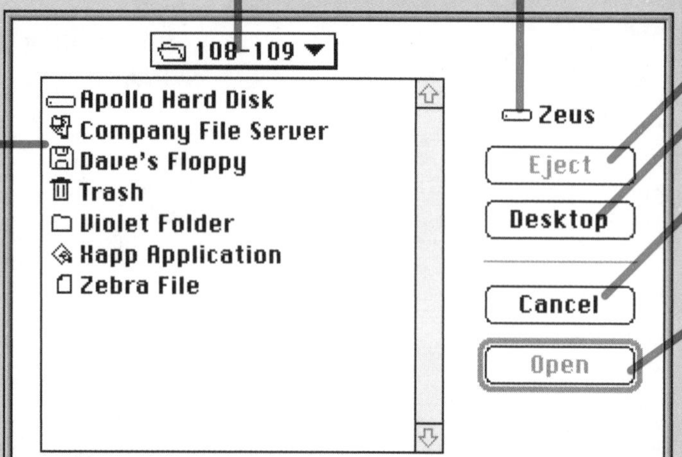

Popup Path List

The **pop-up menu** above the file listing lets you navigate through the path between the Desktop (at the bottom of the list) and the folder whose contents you see in the file list. Simply select the folder level you wish to view. From the Desktop level, you can see all disk and server volumes currently mounted.

Current Volume

In addition to displaying the name and icon style of the volume containing the items in the scrolling list, this area of the dialog box is also a button. When you click it, you navigate one level closer to the Desktop. You may continue clicking this button until you reach the Desktop.

Eject

When the current volume is an ejectable disk or cartridge, Eject becomes active. Click the button to eject the volume. If you insert a diskette anytime while the **Open File** dialog is visible, the floppy immediately becomes the current volume.

Desktop

A click of this button navigates you all the way back the Desktop in one click. It is the same as choosing **Desktop** from the pop-up list or clicking the current volume name until reaching the Desktop level.

Cancel

To close the **Open File** dialog without opening a document, click Cancel. In most programs, the original path is restored as the default path for the next time you try to open a document.

Open

You may either double-click an item in the file listing to open it, or click it once to select the item and click Open. Some programs use this dialog box to ask you to choose a folder into which some document will be saved. In those cases, you simply navigate to and open the desired folder before clicking Open. Pressing *return* is the same as clicking Open.

Keyboard Navigation Shortcuts

In both the **Open** and **Save** file dialogs, you can play the **cursor keys** like a virtuoso to navigate through multiple volumes and dozens of folder levels. The Command (⌘) modifier key also plays a role.

command-up/command-down arrows

Navigate to the next highest or lowest folder level in the current volume. If the selection in the file listing is a document, the *command-down arrow* has no effect.

command-left/command-right arrows

Cycle through all available mounted volumes. This is the keyboard equivalent of Drive in pre-System 7 file dialog boxes. This method, however, lets you

Not all open and save dialogs are alike, however. Programmers have extraordinary latitude in adding elements that make the most sense for their programs. Variations are almost endless, as some programs allow you to open documents saved in other formats or offer conversion capabilities as you save a document.

File Save Dialog Box

All navigation possibilities of the **Open File** dialog box apply to the **Save File** dialog box. In this case, you navigate to find a folder level into which the current document is to be saved.

List of Files

Because the document naming field is selected by default when the **Save File** dialog appears, you must activate the list of files to navigate through it with the mouse or keyboard. Clicking in the list or pressing the *tab* key displays a dark selection box around the list. File names are dimmed, but folders are active in case you need to open a nested folder to save the current document. You may then type the first couple characters to zip to another part of the list if folders are present in the list.

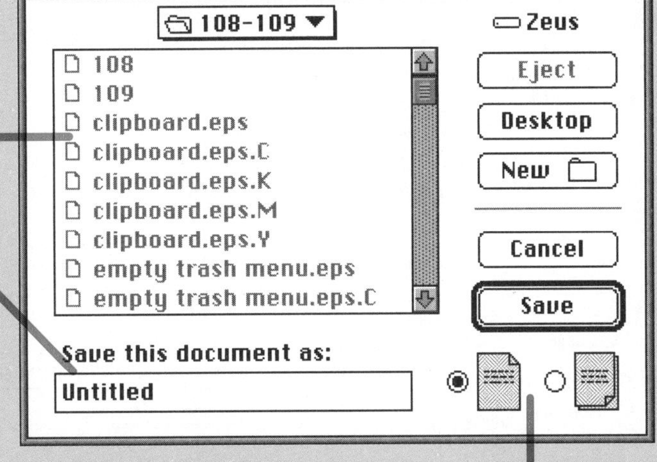

File Name Field

Virtually every program provides the name "**Untitled**" as the default file name the first time you save a document. Since the entire name is selected, you may just begin typing, since the first character you type replaces the selected name. File names cannot contain a colon, nor should they extend beyond about 30 characters.

New Folder

Some applications provide the power to create a new folder from the **Save File** dialog. This is very handy when you need to save a document to a folder not yet in existence. The new folder goes into the current folder level showing in the popup path list.

Save Changes Dialog

If you try to close a document or quit an application without saving your last changes, you will likely see a three-button alert box ask you about what to do with those changes. [Save] is the default button. Press *enter* or *return* to save the file to disk. [Cancel] stops everything, returning you to the document without closing it. [Don't Save] closes the document without saving the changes. This action cannot be undone, so consider wisely before clicking.

Document/Stationery Buttons

Many applications let you save a document as a stationery file as an option ➔133. The standard stationery icon shows a couple pages with the lower right corner turned up. A stationery document lets you use the file as a **template** without threat of accidentally overwriting the original.

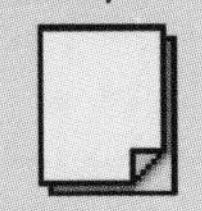
Stationery File

Effective use of the Clipboard and Scrapbook can boost your productivity with the Macintosh. After awhile, the Clipboard becomes second nature to Macintosh users, especially when used with the convenient keyboard equivalents of the Cut, Copy, and Paste commands from the Edit menu.

Both the Clipboard and Scrapbook are constructed to meet requirements of new programs and types of information. Demands today have far outstripped the text and graphic information of the first Macintoshes. In some programs, you can cut, copy, and paste sounds, animation, and even video movies. The main distinction between the **Clipboard** and **Scrapbook** still holds: the Clipboard only holds one item at a time and is erased upon shutdown, while the Scrapbook stores many items safely in the Scrapbook File in the System Folder.

Efficient Keyboarding

A vital component of using the Clipboard efficiently is mastery of the keyboard equivalents of the **Cut**, **Copy**, and **Paste** items in the **Edit** menu. While their keyboard letters, *X*, *C*, and *V*, may not make mnemonic sense, notice that the letters are all in a row at the bottom left of the U.S. keyboard. Common manipulation of information is to select an item from a document with the mouse in the right hand, and then perform the cut or copy on the keyboard with the left (bias for righties, to be sure). Similarly, for pasting, position the pointer where needed and then *Command-V* with the left hand. In the same vicinity is *Command-Z* for undoing an erroneous cut or paste.

Pasting Special

Some programs have an extra **Paste** command in their **Edit** menus: **Paste Special.** Exactly what this does depends entirely on the program, but it highlights a point about the Clipboard. When you copy a selected chunk of data into the Clipboard, the Clipboard can contain a lot of information about that chunk. **Paste Special** typically allows you to paste certain aspects of that chunk. For example, in a spreadsheet program, if you copy a cell into the Clipboard, you can choose to paste any combination of the plain value, the formula, and the format (e.g., bold text property) of the original cell.

Viewing Clipboard Contents

While the Clipboard can hold only one item at a time, you may forget what's in there if you've been copying and pasting a lot. Only a few programs let you view the Clipboard from within the program. Fortunately, the Finder's **Edit** menu contains a **Show Clipboard** item, which displays a window showing the item and describing what type of item it is (e.g., text, picture, sound).

Efficient Scrapbook

You use the Clipboard to move information into and out of the Scrapbook. The Scrapbook window is not resizable, so you may not be able to see everything on a "page." When the information on a page is a sound, a button appears that lets you play the sound as long as it is of a type that the System software recognizes.

Modified Paste

It's not always obvious in an application when additional pasting powers are included. Instead of a **Paste Special** menu item, some programs enhance pasting power when you hold down a modifier key. For example, if you copy a HyperCard card into the Clipboard, you can then paste a miniature version of the art of that card by holding down the *shift* key before pulling down the **Edit** menu to choose **Paste**. In fact, with the *shift* key down, the **Paste** menu item becomes **Paste Picture**.

This color map comes in the System 7 Scrapbook File.

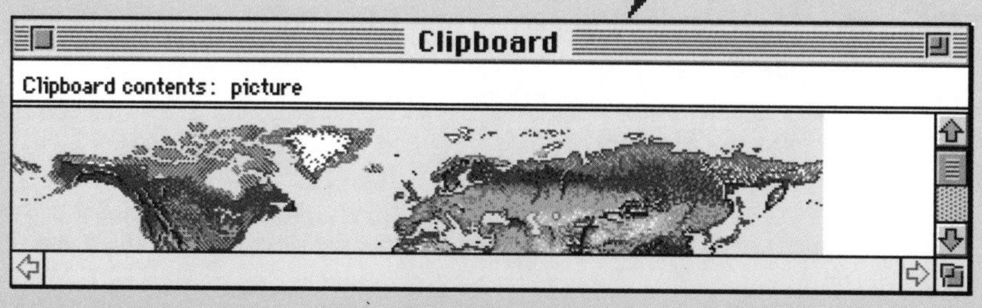

Scrapbook Data Types

When you paste information into the Scrapbook, the resource types of that information are displayed at the lower right corner. Common resource types are **PICT** (picture) and **TEXT** (text). Quite often, the information will contain more than one resource. This all depends on how the program from which you copied the information treats the **Copy** command. For example, a word processing program may store a selection in both plain TEXT (without any formatting or font styles) and its

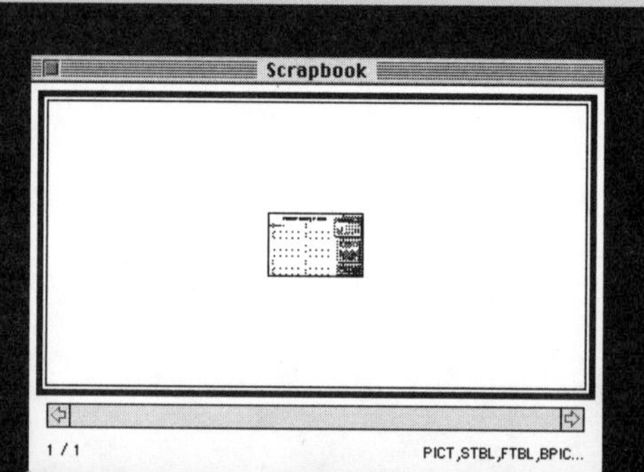

Living up to the desktop-as-metaphor guideline of the Macintosh interface, the way to erase a file from a disk is to drag it to an iconic trash can.

Trash

Just as in the real world, if you change your mind about something you throw in the trash, you can rummage through the can to retrieve an item—as long as you haven't emptied the trash. Once you empty the trash, however, the file is gone (although third-party file recovery programs may be able to rescue it from the city dump).

Unlike earlier versions of System software, the System 7 Trash does not automatically empty itself when you **Shut Down** or **Restart**. On the one hand, it means that you have to think about your trash more often; on the other hand, it means that you can change your mind about a discarded item many days later.

Two-Step Trashing

Throwing out a file is a two-step process:

1. drag the item to the Trash icon; and
2. empty the trash.

In other words, simply dragging the item to the trash does not really remove it from your disk. No matter how large the file, you won't see any difference in the amount of disk space occupied or available by just dragging an item to the trash. It's as if you simply dragged the item to a different folder.

To empty the trash, choose **Empty Trash** from the **Special** menu. The default behavior of this menu item is to remind you of how many items are about to be trashed and how much disk space will be freed by their departure. Very different from earlier versions is that you are not warned about the impending erasure of application or system files. To System 7, trash is trash, unless the item is being shared by another computer.

Retrieving Trash

If you double-click the Trash icon, it opens a window showing you all the items (if any) still in the trash. To recover an item, simply drag it out of the Trash window, and place it in any other folder or volume.

Trash Options

You may avoid the intervening dialog that warns about the items to be trashed two ways. If you normally like that warning, but want to bypass it occasionally, simply hold down the *option* key before pulling down the **Special** menu. The **Empty Trash** menu item, which normally has an ellipsis (**...**) after it to indicate a succeeding dialog, no longer has that feature. The Trash will be emptied without ceremony.

You may make the dialog-less method the regular behavior by selecting the Trash icon and choosing **Get Info** from the **File** menu. The **Warn before emptying** checkbox can be unchecked. The **Empty Trash** menu item no longer features the ellipsis—and you're on your own to make sure you empty the right stuff.

Trash Info

Trash

Where: On the desktop

Contents: 16 files and 1 folder are in the Trash for a total of 493K.

Modified: Mon, Dec 30, 1991, 3:10 PM

☒ **Warn before emptying**

Foreign Trash

With localization of Macintosh systems for each country comes some interesting differences in how the Trash icon is labeled, even in other English-speaking countries. Here is a sampling of the fine tuning that goes into making the Macintosh culturally correct:

United States	**Trash**
United Kingdom	**Wastebasket**
France	**Corbeille**
Germany	**Papierkorb**
Spain	**Papelera**
Portugal	**Lixo**
Italy	**Cestino**

System 7 Trash on System 6

If you normally run a hard disk under System 7 but connect it to a Macintosh starting with System 6, you'll see a Trash folder, in addition to the normal Trash icon. To compensate for the differences in handling trash, the folder is the System 6 way of telling you that there are items that survived the shut down and restart. If you drag items from the Trash folder to the System 6 trash icon, those items will be deleted when the Macintosh shuts down.

What Gets Trashed?

Throwing a file into the Trash really doesn't remove it from the disk. The file is still there until something else writes over the same space on the disk. What is gone, however, is the file's entry in the disk directory (a hidden file), that helps the Finder locate a file on the disk. Therefore, third-party file recovery programs can help you restore a file that has been trashed, provided it hasn't yet been overwritten.

Macintosh System software provides a number of ways for you to customize the appearance and behavior of the Desktop.

You may change the underlying desktop pattern, the color and categories of icons, the way files are listed in folder windows, and a variety of color elements if you use a color monitor. Most of the customization is performed in various control panels, and is retained from session to session.

Desktop Pattern

In the **General Controls** control panel is a section that allows you to choose from several desktop background patterns as well as create your own. If you use a color or grayscale monitor, a color bar appears at the bottom of the **Desktop Pattern** panel, allowing you to assign individual colors to each pixel.

Pattern Anatomy

A Macintosh pattern is defined by the pixel layout of an 8-by-8 grid. This endows the desktop pattern with a regularity that befits a background. That 64-pixel pattern is repeated to fill the entire screen while occupying very little memory.

Default Patterns

The pattern installed in desktop Macintoshes at the factory is a grey pattern (50% gray in monochrome, a subtle mixture of gray shades elsewhere). A magnified view of the 8-by-8 pattern appears on the left, a real-size sample of the pattern in a small desktop on the right. As you click the left and right arrows atop the real size rectangle, the control panel cycles through the patterns in the **System File**. To apply the pattern in your real **Desktop**, click once in the small desktop rectangle. You'll have to cycle around to the gray again if you wish to restore the standard pattern.

Editing Pixels

The magnified view is also a pixel editing area. Clicking the arrow pointer in the area toggles each pixel between black (or the selected color) and white (or the previous color). Edit only a pattern that you don't like (in case you make it truly permanent, below). As you change each pixel, you see a sample in the small desktop to the right. To apply your finished pattern to the Desktop, however, you must still click once in the small desktop area. ***The new pattern will be preserved as long as you don't cycle through available patterns.***

Saving New Patterns

To make sure a pattern is remembered by the System, even if you change patterns later, you must edit the pixel changes, and then double-click the small desktop area. This replaces the System's pattern (which you edited) with the one you created. You won't be able to restore the original pattern unless you recreate it manually or reinstall the System File.

Pattern Strategies

If you frequently startup from more than one hard disk, a different Desktop pattern for each disk serves as visual reinforcement that you are starting from the desired drive. Someone who is responsible for installation and support of corporate Macintoshes may wish to create some custom desktop patterns for the users to choose from (see below).

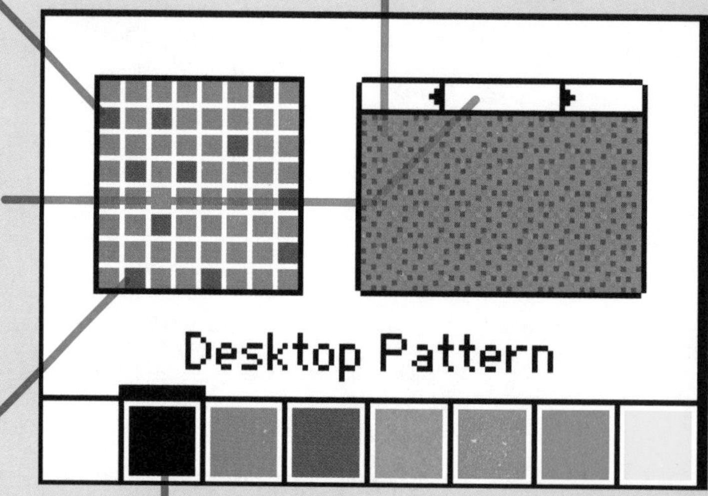

Editing Colors

With color monitors, you may click on one of the colors before applying it to a pixel in the editing area. You may also replace any of the selected colors with a color of your choice. Double-click on a color square to see the Color Wheel dialog. Any color you select from the color wheel replaces the color you opened.

Desktop Pictures

Some third-party utilities are available that allow you to create and install full-screen pictures that replace the Desktop pattern. While there's nothing wrong with these niceties, color desktop pictures can take up a few hundred kilobytes of RAM that would normally be available to applications. If memory conservation is a concern, then avoid or disable these extensions.

Desktop Pattern Details

When you double-click on a desktop pattern in the **General Controls** control panel, the pattern is saved in the System file. You can view (and edit) the resources containing those patterns with ResEdit.

Monochrome patterns are stored in the **PAT#** resource, while color patterns are stored in the **ppt#** resource. Both are **ID 0**. When you save a desktop pattern from the control panel, the pattern is saved to these resources. If you have a very customized pattern resource that you'd like to install in several department Macintoshes, you can use ResEdit to copy the PAT# or ppt# resource to

Label Concepts

A label is nothing more than a category (and color) that you can assign to any desktop object, such as a folder or document file. This kind of label has nothing to do with the name of the object, which appears on all Finder views. For example, in a real life folder of documents you might stick colored tabs on some of the papers to help you locate the "hot" ones. Macintosh labels go much further than that because you can sort documents within a folder according to their labels and even search for all documents with the same label across several mounted volumes.

Labels are defined in the Labels control panel, and assigned to objects in the **Labels** menu at the Finder level.

Assigning Labels

To assign a label to a disk, folder, or file icon, first select the icon (click once on it) or select a range of icons (contiguous or otherwise). Then pull down the **Labels** menu, and choose any of the items there. To remove a label, select an icon, and choose **None** from the **Label** menu.

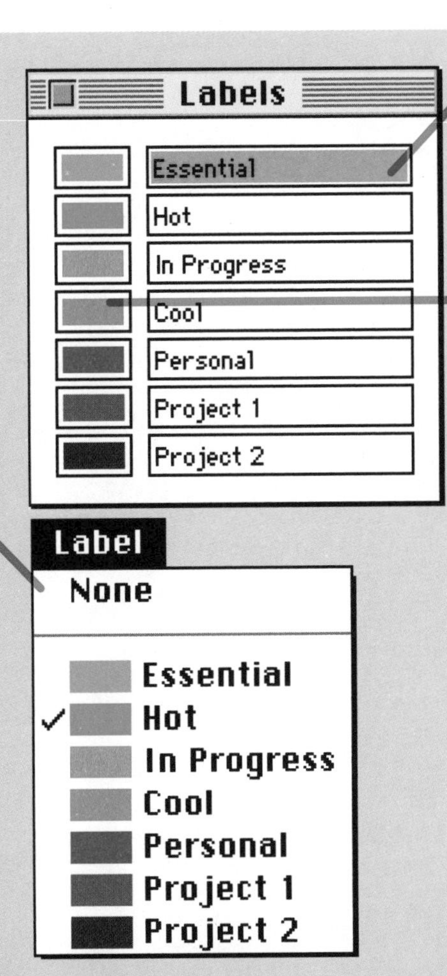

Changing Label Names

Open the **Labels** control panel to change the label names assigned at the factory. Each name appears in an editable field. You can tab through the fields or use the text pointer to select and edit text within any field. As you make changes to any name, the name immediately changes in the **Labels** menu.

Changing Label Colors

If you use a color monitor, the **Labels** menu and control panel display colors that you assign along with the label name. In the control panel, you may change the color for each label. Double-click on any color block to bring the **Color Wheel** into view. Any color you choose from the wheel replaces the original color for that label item.

Label Strategies

Assigning colors to icons is an obvious way to help you organize and locate files in open folder windows. With some color icons, the final colorized effect may be difficult to predict. Also, you may not remember what all seven colors mean. Therefore, use color sparingly if you intend to use that attribute as an organization helper.

The text labels may actually be more useful, since you can group documents by some system other than the physical grouping in folders. For example, you can label several documents scattered in several folders according to a project name label. In text views of folder contents, you can elect to display and sort by label names. Or ask the Finder to locate all files with the same label, even if the files are located in different folders or on different volumes. It's one way to establish relationships between files on your

View Menu

The Finder's **View** menu lets you set the view and sorting order for files in the topmost open Finder window. Details about each of the **View** menu settings are adjustable in the **Views** control panel.

Two **View** menu items show files as icons in the window, either small or large. In small icon mode, miniature icons with file names to their right represent each file; in large icon mode (the default mode for the Finder), large icons have the file names beneath them. Given the same size window for both, you can display more than twice as many files in small icon mode as in regular icon mode. Still, the larger icons are more visually appealing and distinctive—a plus for visually oriented users.

The other **View** menu choices list files as text in the window. Only those columns checked in the **List View** section of the **Views** control panel are listed in the menu. Each of the choices designates how the files in the window are sorted—**by Name** (alphabetical), **Size** (largest first), **Kind** (alphabetical), **Label** (alphabetical), **Date** (most recent first), **Version** (lowest first), or **Comments** (alphabetical). If you have disabled one or more of these possibilities from the **Views** control panel, the choices will not be in the **View** menu.

Notice that in any text view, your sorting choice is underlined in the column headings. Click on a column heading to change the sorting view without going to the **View** menu.

File Viewing Concepts

The Finder presents much flexibility in the way you can view the contents of a disk or folder. Importantly, you can establish a standard that takes effect by default for all open disks and folders, but you can change the view of any window at any time without disturbing your overall viewing scheme.

Views come in two basic types: iconic and text listings. Each of these types has multiple variations. Icon views allow for spatial organizations that might appeal to some users. Other users may prefer text listings, whose hierarchical viewing mechanism reveals the contents of nested folders with the click of the mouse without opening another window 116-117. In fact, some users may actually have only one Finder window open—the one to their hard disk with a text view that offers one-window access to any document on the disk.

System Folder

32 items | 111.9 MB in disk | 42.2 MB available

Name	Size	Kind	Label	La
▷ Aldus	1,433K	folder	–	
▷ Apple Menu Items	508K	folder	–	
Audio CD Access	10K	Foreign File Acces...	–	
▷ Claris	38K	folder	–	
Clipboard	3K	file	–	
▷ Control Panels	2,058K	folder	–	
DAtabase™ File	3K	DAtabase Builder d...	–	
Easy Envelopes Plus Docs	58K	application program	–	
Easy Envelopes+ File	10K	document	–	
▷ Encryptors	5K	folder	–	

View
- by Small Icon
- ✓by Icon
- by Name
- by Size
- by Kind
- by Label
- by Date

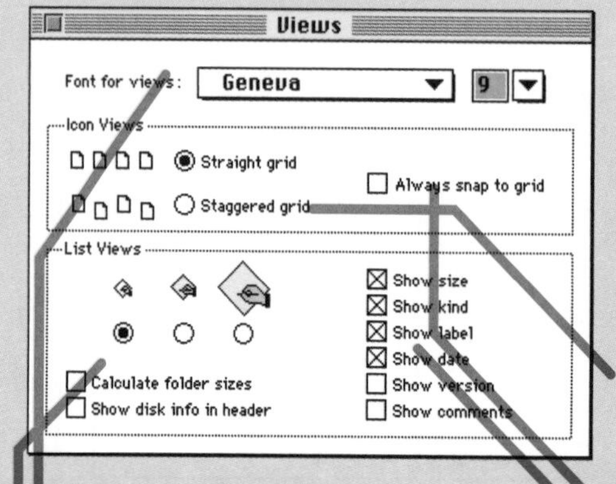

Views Control Panel

From the Views control panel, you have great power in the display characteristics of icon and text list views. Changes you make in this control panel take effect immediately.

View Font

You may choose from any installed font and size for the file names. The font you choose applies to icon and text list views, including names of icons on the Desktop. When you issue the **Clean Up** command from the **Special** menu, the Finder tries to avoid overlapping file names in the regular icon view. Larger font sizes means that the icons will be spread out further in the window.

Text List View

List views also show icons, but you have a choice of three icon styles: the typical large icon, the small icon, and a generic small icon (folder, application, document). The generic icon allows the most items to appear in the list. If you like, you can have the Finder add up and display the size of any folder displayed in the list. This takes extra time to display a complete list, but you don't have to wait for the Finder to finish its calculations before moving to another task—the Finder can do this in the background. You probably do want to check the **Show disk** info box so you can see how much space is available on the disk even in the list view.

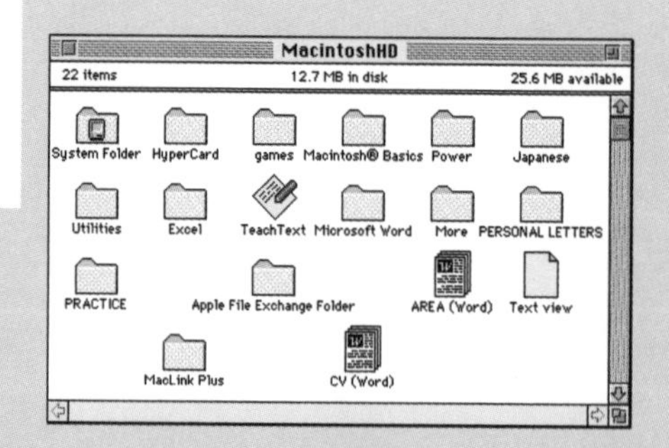

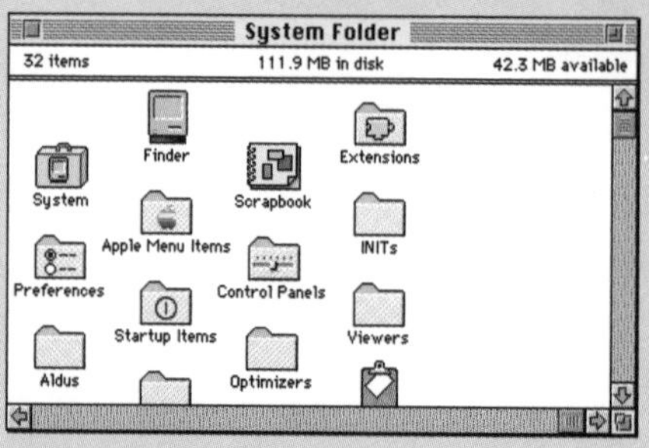

Icon View

The choice between a **straight** and **staggered grid** pertains to the way icons are automatically aligned during a clean up or if you want icons to snap to the invisible grid in the window. A staggered grid generally allows more files to be displayed in the window, because there is more space to display long file names without interfering with other file names. If you like the alignment to be in effect at all times, check the **Always snap to grid** checkbox. Alternatively, you can leave this button unchecked and drag icons in the window with the Command key down to make sure the dragged icon(s) align to the desired grid.

The right-hand column of checkboxes lets you determine how many columns of information should appear for each item in the list view. **Version** is the version number assigned to a file (if any) by an application's programmer 118. Comments are what you enter into the **Get Info** box 118 in the Finder. Bear in mind that comments are erased when you rebuild the Desktop 94. The fewer columns of data you show in the windows, the less you'll find yourself scrolling horizontally to read the data. Enable only those columns that you find useful.

MacintoshHD

Name	Size	Kind	Label	Last M
▷ Apple File Exchange Folder	–	folder	–	Th
AREA (Word)	42K	Microsoft Word do...	–	Mo
CV (Word)	4K	Microsoft Word do...	–	Tu
▷ Excel	–	folder	–	Su
▽ games	–	folder	–	Su
Lode Runner	80K	application program	–	Mo
Othello 1.0	25K	application program	–	Sa
TETRIS	256K	application program	–	Su
▷ HyperCard	–	folder	–	Tu
▷ Japanese	–	folder	–	Su
▷ Macintosh® Basics	–	folder	–	Th
▷ MacLink Plus	–	folder	–	Mo
▷ Microsoft Word	–	folder	–	Su

Desktop Document Icons

Most applications programs include special icons to assign to document files they create. The document icons usually have some resemblance to the application's icon, so you can determine what kind of document you're seeing in the Finder. But system software lets you modify the icon of any file in the file's **Get Info** dialog box (select a file and choose **Get Info** from the Finder's **File** menu). You can even do this to an application, if you like.

Use any painting program to create a color or monochrome graphic that measures no larger than 32 pixels square. Select the graphic and copy it into the Clipboard. Next, open the **Get Info** dialog box for the document. Click on the existing icon in the upper left to select it. Choose **Paste** from the **Edit** menu. The icon changes immediately in the Finder (if the color looks odd, you probably have a label color assigned to that object). You can now copy the file to any other disk, and the new icon prevails under System 7. It also survives rebuilding of the Desktop. You may also copy icons from other Get Info dialog boxes.

To return a file's icon to its original, select the icon in the **Get Info** dialog box, and choose **Clear** from the **Edit** menu. The original icon reappears immediately.

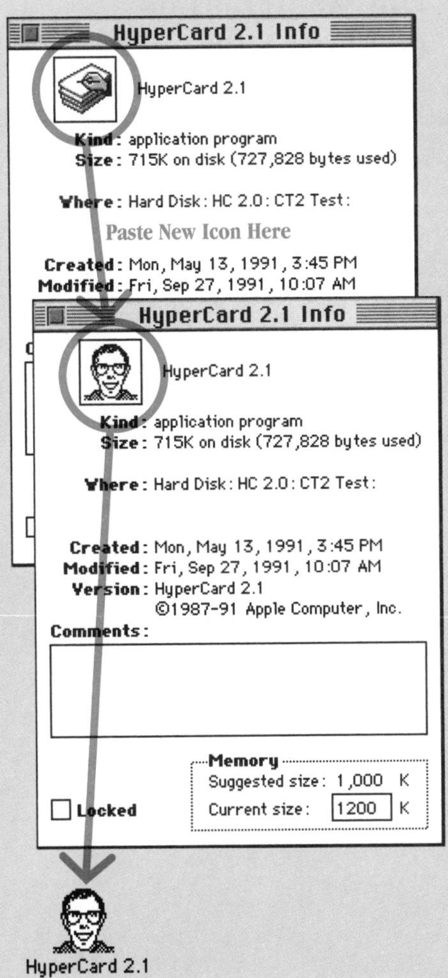

Icon Strategies

Changing icons is particularly helpful when you create templates or files for other people to use—especially those who may be new to computing. If you like, you can make the icons for company-related documents out of the corporate logo, or design an icon that represents the content of the file, rather than the application that generated it. As long as the user double-clicks on the file, the Finder will launch the appropriate application and load the document.

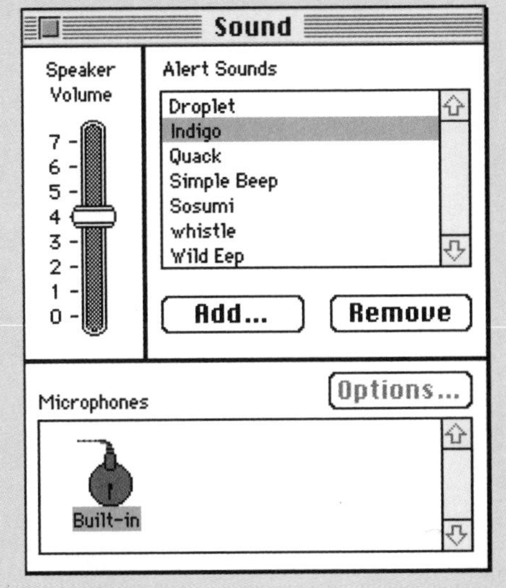

Sounds

The **Sound** control panel controls both the volume of the system beep (the one that most programs use to alert you to something) and the system beep sound. To adjust the volume, simply drag the slider control to a number and release the mouse button. You'll hear the currently selected alert sound at the selected volume. If you turn the volume to zero, you hear no sound, but the menubar flashes in place of sounding an alert sound. If you see your menubar flashing at various times, it's probably because your sound is turned off.

The System software comes with six sound resource files installed in the System file. You can play any sound in the list by clicking on the item. More sounds are available through user groups and bulletin boards. Simply drag the sound resources to the System File.

Additional utility software enhance the availability of sounds on the Macintosh. A popular program, SoundMaster, lets you assign individual sounds to virtually every action that you or your Macintosh makes, including keyboard clicking, disk ejecting, starting up, restarting, and shutting down. See pages 156-159 for more about sounds, including how to record your own alert sounds.

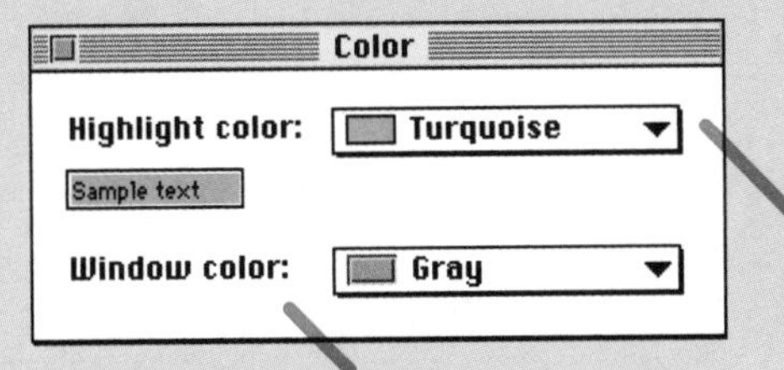

Text Highlight Color

In the **Color** control panel (for those with color monitors) is the facility to change the color of a text selection. In the monochrome world, selected text is inverted—black becomes white and vice versa. With a color monitor, the black characters stay black, while the rectangular area surrounding the text can be of any color available in the color wheel. Clicking and holding the pop-up menu for highlight color presents a list of 9 default colors and the **Other** option. **Other** leads to the color wheel. Whatever color you choose there takes effect when you close the Color Wheel window. A sample of the color is shown in the Color control panel.

Window Color

With a color monitor, you may also change the subtle highlights that the System places on window elements (in both the Finder and applications). Choose only from the standard colors (or black and white, which shows no shadings at all, just like on a monochrome monitor). The shadings are intentionally subtle. Apple's designers didn't want the window features to draw your attention away from the content. Third-party utilities were available for previous system software versions that made window elements almost infinitely colorful. Such programs will surely be available for System 7.

View Storage

Information from the **Views** control panel is stored in the Finder Preferences file (in a resource names fval). If you wish to start over with the default settings, you may delete the Finder Preferences file (located in the Preferences Folder). A copy of the unmodified fval resource is stored in the Finder, itself. When you make any changes, the Finder will

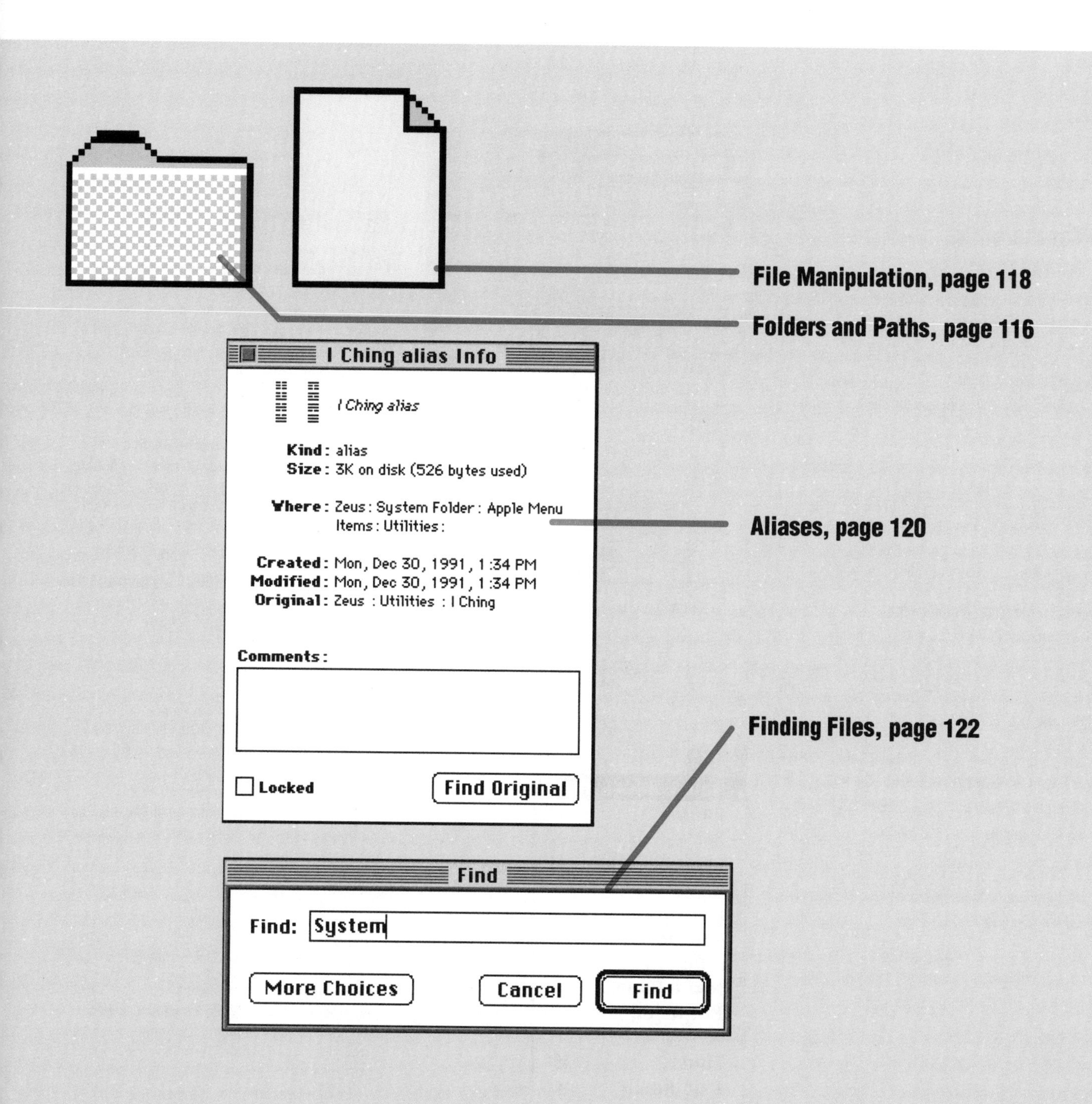
File Manipulation, page 118
Folders and Paths, page 116
I Ching alias Info
I Ching alias
Kind: alias
Size: 3K on disk (526 bytes used)
Where: Zeus: System Folder: Apple Menu Items: Utilities:
Aliases, page 120
Created: Mon, Dec 30, 1991, 1:34 PM
Modified: Mon, Dec 30, 1991, 1:34 PM
Original: Zeus : Utilities : I Ching
Comments:
Locked
Find Original
Finding Files, page 122
Find
Find: System
More Choices
Cancel
Find

The Finder provides a folder structure that you can use to store and organize any file on a disk. This structure is a virtually unlimited electronic version of file drawers and folders within. You may nest folders within another to depths unheard of in the physical file folder world.

Finder

Despite the possibility of nesting a file many levels below the Desktop, each file has a kind of address, called its path. The path consists of a sequential list of folders you'd have to open to reach that file. Fortunately, the Finder gives you many ways to transcend and navigate a complex path.

How you organize application and document files in folders is a personal affair, but it helps to give it some thought based on your work methods. And you can change your mind at any time.

Folder Hierarchy

The Macintosh file system is said to be hierarchical, because you can organize files according to a structure that resembles a corporate organizational chart, with each horizontal slice representing a rank within the entire scheme. The most global view is at the top, with each lower ranking nested inside a folder just above it in rank. At the top of the file structure is the Desktop, which gives you an overview of all the volumes mounted on your machine (including servers connected via a network). Next comes the contents of each volume. When you open a volume's window, that window is said to be the root of that volume. From the root grow the folders and documents further nested within. At any level, including the Desktop, you may park any combination of individual files and folders.

Creating New Folders

At the Finder level, you can create a folder in another folder very easily. Bring to the front the folder window in which you want to add the new folder. Then choose **New Folder** from the **File** menu (or type *command-N*). A folder called "untitled folder" appears in the first available location in the window (or in list view, where it sorts according to the view type selected). The folder name is highlighted, ready for you to give it a name.

Within some applications, you may also create a new folder from the File Save dialog box ➔ 107. A button brings up a dialog that prompts you for a folder name. The folder goes into the level currently being displayed in the list of files.

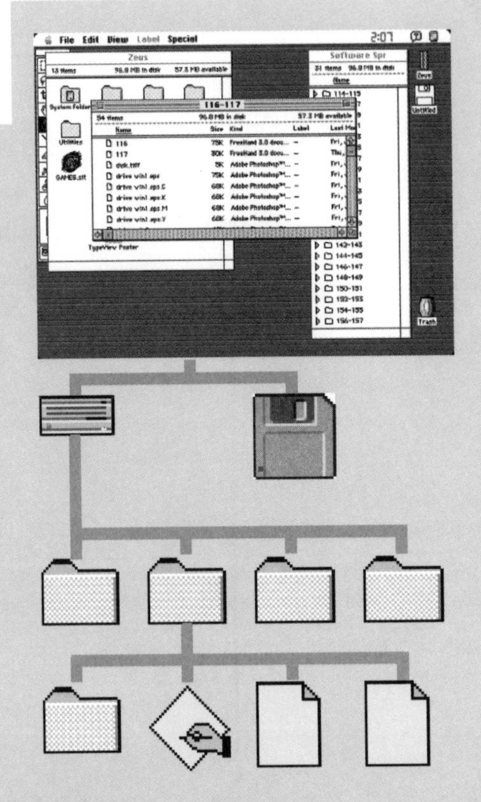

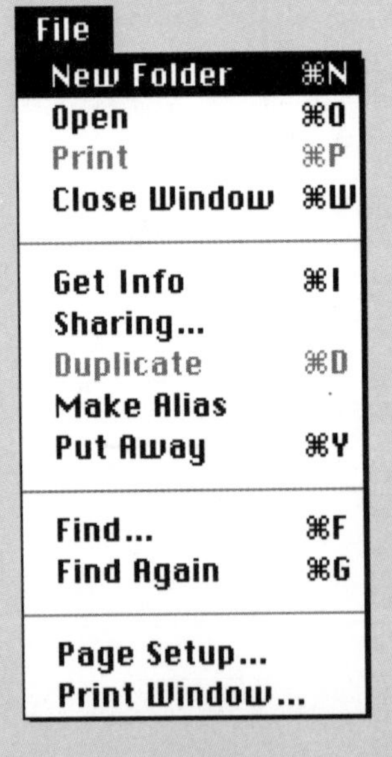

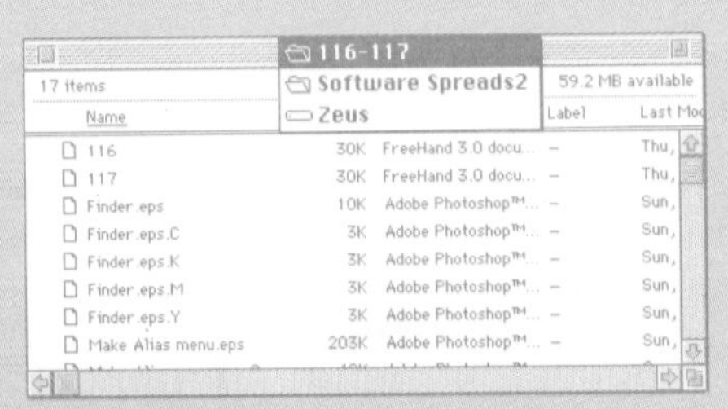

Navigating the Hierarchy

Your methodology of working your way through the hierarchy depends on what mode you are in. In the Finder, you may open successive folders by double-clicking on their icons. In a Finder text listing view, you may also view the contents of a nested folder by clicking once on the arrow next to a folder's name. The view expands (much like an outliner software program) to reveal items within that folder without opening another window.

While viewing any Finder window, you may find where that folder exists in the hierarchy by holding down the ⌘ key and dragging on the folder's name in the window's titlebar. A pop up list appears to detail the path from the Desktop to the folder. Select any item in the list to open that folder's window.

Within a file dialog box ➔106-107, a similar pop up menu of the path to the current folder appears above the listing of file names. Navigate to any level by selecting it from the list.

Naming Folders

You may rename folders at any time, even while the folder window is open. To rename a folder, click once anywhere on the folder's name (in either the icon or list view). After a momentary delay, the name is surrounded by a rectangle, with the name selected. If you jiggle the mouse after clicking, the text becomes instantly editable. An even quicker way to get into edit mode is to click the icon once, and press the *return* or *enter* key. Use Macintosh text editing techniques ➔ 129 to delete or edit some or all of the name. A folder must have a name, even if it is one character. Maximum length is 31 characters, with any character allowed except the colon.

Be sure the folder's name identifies in some way the nature of its contents. While icon and text views show a folder icon along with the name, some users also add the word "Folder" or a lowercase script *f* (*option-F*) to designate a folder object. This might seem redundant, however, in light of the attached folder icon.

Organizational Schemes

Tens or hundreds of megabytes of files can become unwieldy very quickly. To be the most efficient with your disk storage, it is helpful to be aware of a few organizational techniques that you can adapt to the specific way you work with your applications and documents. For very large hard disks (in excess of 100 megabytes), it is helpful to make your first organizational layer in the form of multiple hard disk partitions ➔56. Each partition becomes a separate volume on the Desktop. Partitioning software comes with most high-capacity hard disks as well as with commercial disk utility software.

DOS Organization

A remnant of the Microsoft DOS structure is the one in which you create a separate root-level folder for each application. In each folder goes the application and all documents created with that application. This is a computer-centered organization, because it makes you think about files by path rather than by content or context.

Work Type Organization

You may divide your work into the typical software categories, with root folders for Word Processing, Spreadsheets, Telecommunications, etc. Within each folder are the relevant applications (e.g., a word processor, outliner, spelling checker in the Word Processing folder) plus all documents created by those applications.

Applications/Data Organization

At the root level, you can create one folder that holds all applications. Since you can launch an application by opening one of its documents from the Finder or open an alias in the Menu ➔120, you may not need to open this folder very often. Other root folders are for documents, and can be organized around context. For example, a Finance folder might contain spreadsheets, relevant memos, charts, and presentations—all created from numerous applications, but all pertaining to the Finance department.

How Many Levels?

Each user's approach to the depth vs. breadth issue is different. Some users prefer to limit each window to a small number of items that can be viewed all at once in a relatively small Finder window, even if it means that a document may be deeply nested many levels away from the root. Others prefer fewer levels, and don't mind lots of items at each level. One rule of thumb says that if you have to mix depth and breadth, then keep windows clutter-free closer to the root, but allow deeper folders to contain many files or other folders. For example, a hierarchy for a writer of this book might look like this:

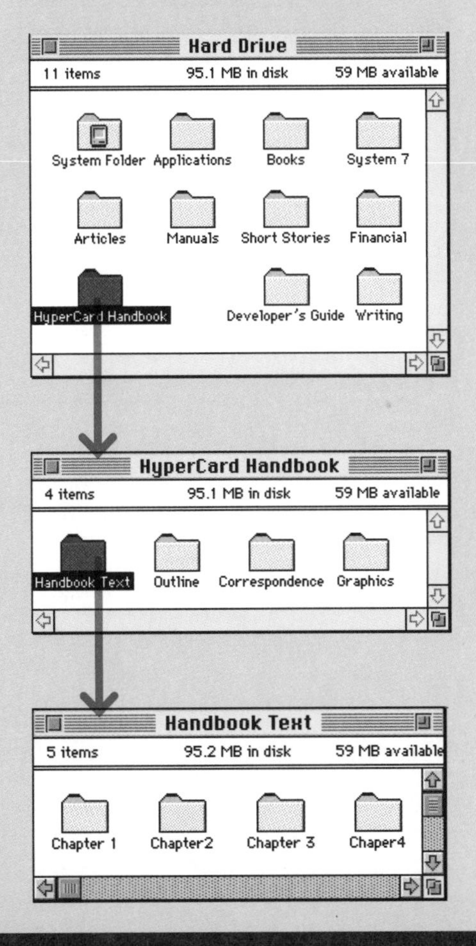

Quick Access to Nested Folders

When a deeply nested folder is one you need to access all the time, you have two choices. One is to leave the folder showing on the Desktop all the time. The other, more efficient method is to create an alias for that folder, and place the alias in the Menu ➔120-121. Choosing that item in the menu brings you to the Finder, and opens that folder.

File
New Folder ⌘N
Open ⌘O
Print ⌘P
Close Window ⌘W
Get Info ⌘I
Sharing...
Duplicate ⌘D
Make Alias
Put Away ⌘Y
Find... ⌘F
Find Again ⌘G
Page Setup...
Print Window...

Contextual Folder Organization

Document organization can be radically different in different folders, because the context for a group of documents can vary widely. For some instances, grouping by project may be appropriate; in others, grouping by the nature of the documents (e.g., all correspondence) is best. In most cases, you'll find a need for a combination of techniques.

Folder Views

Use the settings in the **View** menu and **Views** control panel ➔112 to establish the way you want items to show in a root or folder window. Icon views can provide a spatial organization that works well for frequently accessed items—you get to know where an item is, and go to it without even looking closely at the icon or name. You may also drag icons around a window and resize a window so that only some items show when the window opens, thus reducing visual clutter.

Text views, on the other hand, make it easier to find items when there are many in the folder. Choose the sorting scheme that makes the most sense for your viewing pleasure—e.g., **alphabetical** names when looking for a file name, **chronological** modification dates when looking for recent files to back up. Also, use the **Views** control panel to pare the columns of text listings to only those items that help you identify and use files.

Path Notation

The reason you cannot use a colon in the name of a file or folder is that the Finder reserves that character as a delimiter between elements of a path name. Because of the file sharing prowess of System 7, a full pathname often includes the location of the file from the viewpoint of the network. Therefore, the basic structure of a full pathname is:

<AppleTalk Zone>:<Macintosh User Name>:<Volume Name>:<file path>

The file path, itself, contains colons, as in:

Hard Disk:Writing:Books:HyperCard Handbook:Graphics:Figure 32-1

Most of the time you don't see pathnames in this notation unless you do some programming (even in HyperCard). But at least you know where the colon went.

The Finder simplifies basic file operations to little more than clicking, dragging, and making menu selections.

Application and document files are treated equally by the Finder, lending to a consistency that is easy to learn. There are no arcane commands or convoluted processes to worry about.

File Information

Select any icon in the Finder, and choose **Get Info** from the **File** menu (or type *command-I*). Depending on the type of object you selected, the Finder presents relevant information about that file, including what kind it is, its size, its location on the Desktop (the path, ➜117), creation and last modification dates, version number, and a space for your comments. Some files include additional information, as follows:

Application Memory sizes ➜126-127, Locked status
Document Locked status, Stationery status ➜135
Trash Warn before emptying status ➜109
Alias Path to original copy ➜120-121, Locked status

The two measures of file size indicate the amount of disk space being occupied by the file and the actual byte count of the file ➜42. The disk space may sometimes be a few kilobytes larger than the actual byte count.

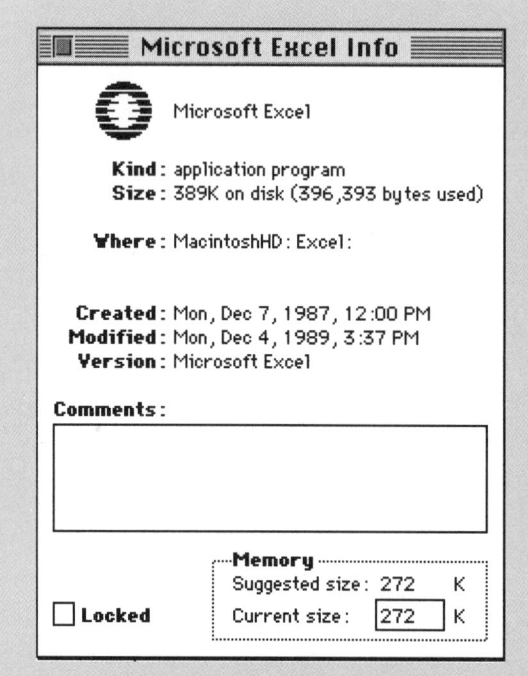

Naming Files

A file's name may be up to 31 characters long, and be any combination of letters, numbers, and symbols except for the colon character ➜117. The shorter and more succinct your file names, the more you will be able to tell about a file when viewing its name in a file dialog ➜106. Since file dialogs and text listings by file name are sorted alphabetically, you can influence how files are arranged in the list. See page ➜77 for leading characters you can add to help sorting. Be aware, too, that numbers sort by their character value, and not by the number. For example, the file name *Chapter 12* sorts before *Chapter 2*, because character sorting places the "1" of the "12" before the "2." Therefore, consider numbering items with leading zeros if necessary (e.g., *Chapter 02*).

No two files may have the same name in the same folder level. But the same file name may exist in each of your folders.

Renaming Files

To rename a file in the Finder, click once on the name. After a momentary delay (jiggle the mouse to shorten the delay), a rectangle surrounds the name, and the name is highlighted. You can also click the icon once and then press the *return* or *enter* key. Use Macintosh editing processes ➜129 to change the name as you like. Click outside the edit box or press the *return* or *enter* keys to make the change take effect (or choose **Undo** from the **Edit** menu if you change your mind). Every file must have a name, even if one character long.

Good news is that if you change the name to a file that has an alias pointing to it ➜120-121, the alias will still be able to find the original file.

Moving Files

You have many choices in moving files and folders in the Desktop view. You may move a single file, a multiple selection of files ➔94-95, a folder (which includes all items in the folder), or an entire disk. To move an icon within a window, drag it to the desired location and release the mouse button. If you drag the icon to a different window (or to the Desktop), the file moves to that location. To move the file to another folder icon, you must drag the icon until the icon of the destination folder or disk has highlighted. Release the mouse button, and the file icon disappears, meaning that the move was successful. If the file icon is still visible atop the folder or disk icon, the move didn't take—you just missed the icon. Try again, making sure the destination icon is highlighted before releasing the mouse button.

If you move several files all at once, you may see the Move progress dialog box, showing you the progress of the move. Moving (or copying) files is not undo-able.

Deleting a File

The only way to delete a file from the Finder is to drag it to the Trash ➔109. That doesn't remove it entirely from the disk, however. You'll still have to empty the trash to free up space on your hard disk taken by that file. Some applications also let you delete files by way of a file dialog box ➔106-107.

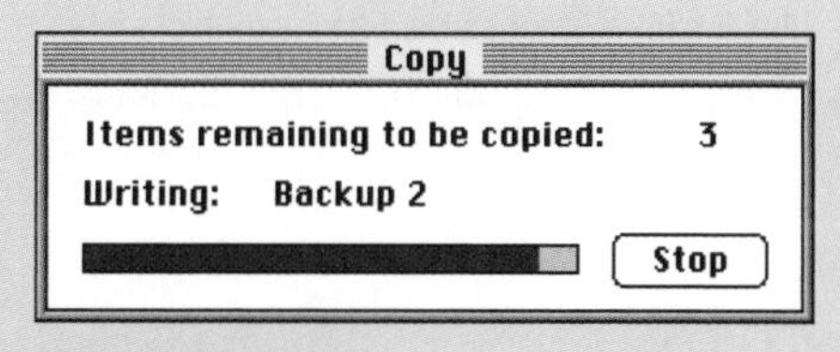

Copying Files

Simply dragging an icon makes a copy of that file only when the destination is another volume. Otherwise, the file is only moved to the destination. You may make a copy within the same volume, however, by holding down the *option* key while clicking and dragging the icon to its destination. The Copy progress box shows you how many files are still to be copied (remember, a single folder icon may represent dozens of individual files).

A special property of copying floppy disks to a hard disk exists. If you copy the diskette icon to any hard disk window, you receive a warning that the copy will create a folder with the name of the floppy disk.

Duplicating a File

Another method of creating a copy of a file for use in the same volume (or for backup purposes) is to select the icon(s) in the Finder and choose **Duplicate** from the **File** menu. This action creates a copy of the selected file(s), but the file names are appended with the word "copy." If you want to use the copy elsewhere, drag it to the destination before renaming it.

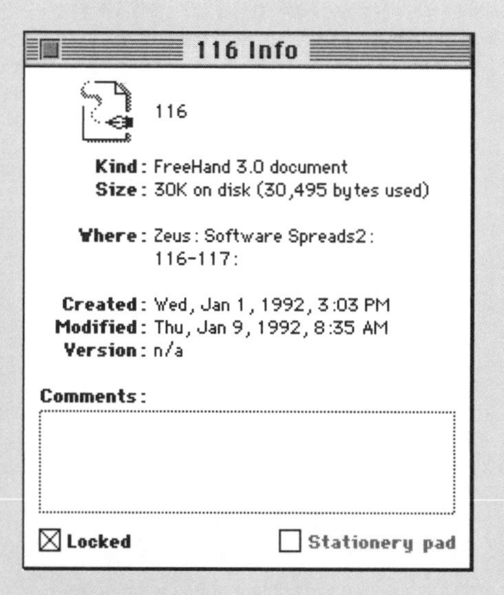

Locking a File

Application and document files may be locked at the Finder level by checking the appropriate box in the Get Info dialog boxes. A locked file cannot be modified, deleted, or used as stationery ➔135. A duplicate of a locked file, however, is not automatically locked. The only time you'd want to lock a file is when you don't want to accidentally modify or delete the file, or if you want to prevent others who might access the file via file sharing from modifying the file (although there are additional ways to prevent this). Locking application files is often used as a preventative measure against virus infection, but some applications modify themselves when they run, and must therefore remain unlocked.

If you drag a locked item to the Trash, you are not alerted until you attempt to empty the trash. But by holding down the *Option* key while choosing **Empty Trash** from the **Special** menu, the Finder will go ahead and delete the locked file.

File Kinds and Types

When you open the **Get Info** dialog box or list files with the Kind column visible, you see a variety of file types in plain English, such as **"application file"** or **"Excel 3.0 document."** The Finder collects this information by way of two attributes of a file—attributes that are not normally visible to the user. One is called the **creator,** the four-character code that the Finder uses to identify the application that created a document. The second is called the **file type** (also the signature), another four-character code that identifies the characteristics of the file.

If a file has any of the standard signatures, the file receives its equivalent plain language descriptor in the Kind listing of a file. For example, an INIT signature means that the file is an extension, while a cdev signature is that of a control panel. When the signature is not a standard one, the Finder looks to the creator and the information stored in the Desktop file to derive the full name of the application belonging to that creator. The name in the list is the current name attached to the application file, which may not be the one initially on the program's disk (e.g., you may append a version number to an application, such as changing "Microsoft Excel" to read "Excel 3.0"). To advanced users, the signature may be more revealing about a file, especially when an application creates more than one type of document. For each type, the signature is different, but the Finder lumps them all into one category of documents created that application.

One of the biggest boosts to efficient hard disk management in System software is the alias. A new Macintosh concept for System 7, the alias allows you to create a tiny file (1 to 2 kilobytes) that can stand in for any file, folder, or disk, including a shared disk on a network.

One of the biggest boosts to efficient hard disk management in System software is the alias. A new Macintosh concept for System 7, the alias allows you to create a tiny file (1 to 2 kilobytes) that can stand in for any file, folder, or disk, including a shared disk on a network.

Alias Overview

When you create an alias, you create a small file that behaves exactly as the original file. It has the same icon as the original (although you can change that, ➔ 113), and starts out with the same name, plus the word "alias." The only visible difference in the Finder is that the name is italicized.

The alias is actually nothing more than **a pointer** to the original file, passing along any action sent to the alias. All the action—reading and saving data, changing preferences, editing a document—really takes place only in the original file. The alias is merely an extra set of eyes, ears, and mouth for the original file.

Multiple Aliases

An object may have more than one alias. In fact, it may be worthwhile in some cases to have multiple aliases. For example, you may want an alias to a file in the **Apple Menu Items** folder, as well as in some other document folders, convenient to other related documents.

Permanent Link

The link between alias and original is one-way—the alias knows about the original, but the original doesn't know about aliases created from it. Therefore, if you delete the original file, you won't be alerted about the aliases out there that still point to the original. You will get an alert, however, when you try to access an alias and it can't find the original.

The true magic about aliases is that you can move or rename both the original and the alias, and the alias will be able to locate the original. The only restriction is that the original must still be on the same volume where the alias was created. But you can move the alias to a different volume, and it will still find the original (or at least request you mount the volume on which the original resides).

File Sharing Aliases

Aliases are very powerful when used in a networked environment. You can use the cumbersome **Chooser** once to connect to a **server.** Then create an alias to that volume, and place the alias on your hard disk where it is easy to access (including the menu). The next time you need to log onto that server, double-click the alias: the server volume will appear on your Desktop. You can do the same for individual files that you access over a network. Bring the file into view once with the Finder, and make an alias for the file. Copy the alias to your hard disk, and rename the file to the same as the original (in case you use a program that summons the shared file by name). System 7 savvy applications on your hard disk allow you to double-click an alias of one of its documents residing on a remote volume. The action launches the application, mounts the remote voloume, and opens the document. Thus, you can seemlessly blend aliases of remote documents into your file organization scheme.

Aliases of Aliases

It is possible to create an alias of an alias file. In practice, this can be dangerous, because you're essentially setting up a chain that must always be in place for the items furthest from the original to work. It's true that the chain remains intact when items are moved or renamed, but deleting any one of them can cut off those further down the chain. It's better to make multiple aliases to the same object.

Creating an Alias

To create an alias from the Finder, simply select an object (or group of objects), and choose **Make Alias** from the **File** menu. The Finder peels off a copy of the icon from the original, and displays the alias next to the original. The alias file name (in italics) is the same as the original, plus the word "alias," with the name already selected, ready for you to rename it. Because no two files in a folder may have the same names, you may prefer to move the alias to its destination before renaming it.

Renaming an Alias

How you name an alias depends more on how you plan to use it. Of course, you don't have to rename the alias file, although the identifiable italic file name in Finder windows and in file dialogs ➔106 makes the "alias" part of the name redundant. Since an alias file is a file like any other, you rename it just like any other file ➔118.

A significant advantage of an alias is that its name does not have to resemble its original file's name. Therefore, as an example, you could create aliases to a series of forms that need to be filled out in a particular sequence. Move the aliases to a separate folder, and rename them with sequence numbers to help the user know which is which.

Finding the Original File

Because an alias may bear no resemblance to its original file (it can have an entirely different name and icon), you may need help finding the path ➔122-123 to the original file. Select the alias file in the Finder, and choose **Get Info** from the **File** menu (or type *command-I*). A special item in an alias' Get Info dialog is the listing of the original file's location. The path includes a zone and Macintosh name if the original is on another Macintosh, or an asterisk as the first item, indicating that it is your own machine.

The path to the original, however, may not be accurate if the original file has been renamed or moved. Even though the listing may be incorrect, the alias finds the original when called upon to do so (when you double-click the file, for example). To update the listing, click Find Original. The Finder goes through a sophisticated series of searches to locate the file if it is still on its original volume. If the search fails, an alert box tells you the original cannot be found.

I Ching alias Info

I Ching alias

Kind: alias
Size: 3K on disk (526 bytes used)

Where: Zeus : System Folder : Apple Menu Items : Utilities :

Created: Mon, Dec 30, 1991, 1:34 PM
Modified: Mon, Dec 30, 1991, 1:34 PM
Original: Zeus : Utilities : I Ching

Comments:

Locked Find Original

Alias Strategies

Here are several productive ways to use aliases:

- **Apple Menu Items.** Determine which applications, documents, folders, disks, and servers you'd like to have available in the menu. Then make aliases for those items, drag them to the Apple Menu Items folder, and rename them so you can find them.

- **Startup Items.** Copy aliases of your all-day applications or documents to the Startup Items folder. Those programs will launch when you start your machine, without disturbing your file organization.

- **Desktop Icons.** If you prefer to emulate the workstation scenario that displays icons to frequently accessed programs and documents on the Desktop, do so with aliases. Make aliases for each file, and move the aliases to the Desktop. Rename the aliases accordingly.

- **Index to Floppy or Cartridge Disks.** When you store important information on removable media, it is sometimes difficult to locate a particular file. Create a new folder on your startup disk, and copy aliases from all files of a removable volume to the new folder. Aliases to a hundred files takes up less than 200K on your hard disk. Double-click on any of the aliases, and you are prompted to insert the proper volume containing that file. You can do this selectively, as well, just indexing those files you believe you'll want to access more frequently.

- **Folder Aliases.** Because a folder alias behaves like its original, if you drag a file to an alias folder, the item actually goes into the original folder (an alias never stores any of your data). While working with the contents of a deeply nested folder, create an alias and place it on the Desktop, making it much easier to access or modify the folder's contents without opening up a series of nested

- **Pocket Hard Disk.** In a networked environment, you can give the impression of carrying your hard disk in 2K of a floppy disk. On your machine, create an alias to your hard disk, and copy the alias to a floppy disk. Be sure you have set the hard disk volume to be shared ➔164-173. Then, from any other System 7-equipped Macintosh on the network, you can insert your floppy disk, double-click the alias file, and log into your hard disk. Your hard disk becomes a mounted volume on that Macintosh.

Despite its name, the Finder didn't have any integrated search facilities until System 7. What we now have is a two-level search function controlled by the Find and Find Again items in the Finder's File menu.

The **Find** command leads to one of two dialog boxes that let you establish the search criteria—either a simple file name search or a more complex search based on other factors. In most cases, as files are found to match the search criteria, their folder windows open, and their file icons or listings highlighted. Use the **Find Again** command to continue searching with the same criteria.

Simple Name Search

The first time you issue the **Find** command (either via the menu or typing *command-F*), you get the smaller of two search dialog boxes. This one has a single field into which you enter some or all of a file name you're trying to locate. The more characters you type, the faster the Finder will locate the file. But if you're unsure of detailed spelling (e.g., whether the file name is plural), enter the first letters of the name that you know for sure.

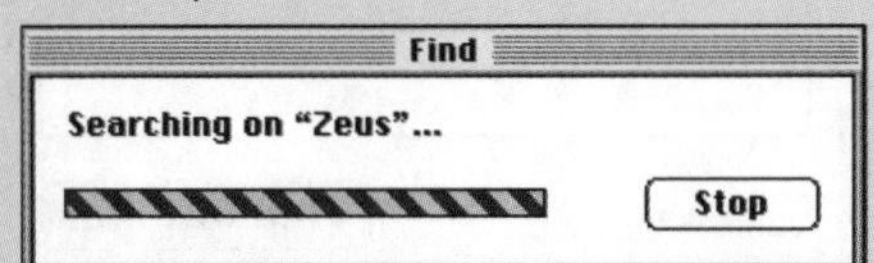

When the search takes more than a few seconds to turn up the first match, the Finder displays an unusual progress box. A horizontal barber pole appears to rotate as the process continues.

If the Finder locates a match, it opens the disk or folder window containing that item, and highlights it. You can stop there if the first one is the desired file. But to continue the search, simply choose **Find Again** from the **File** menu (or type *command-G*), instead of opening up the Find dialog again. The Finder continues looking through all mounted volumes. An alias is treated like any file, so the Finder will locate those names as well. When the Finder issues an alert beep, then you'll know it has made one complete search of all volumes.

Persistent Find

The Finder remembers all the parameters of the last **Find** command you issued until you shut down or restart the Macintosh. Therefore, when you choose **Find** from the **File** menu a second time, the version of the Find dialog box that you last used appears on the screen, complete with all selection criteria the way you left them. But the **Find Again** command bypasses the dialog only in the course of a swing through the selected folders or volumes. For example, once you've made a search for an item and reached the end of the search path (signified by the system alert sound), the **Find Again** command recalls the Find dialog box, expecting you to change some element of the search criteria.

System File Off Limits

Searching for files does not include searching for the resource files inside the System File or other suitcase files. Therefore, don't expect to find fonts, sounds, keyboards, or script resources as long as they are packed inside the System File or suitcases. If you drag them from the System File to any folder, they will be subject to search by the **Find** command.

Quick Daily Data Backup

If you want to be conscientious about backing up your day's work, the expanded Find command can help. Assuming you wish to copy today's changed files to a floppy disk or other mounted volume, ask the Finder to locate all files whose modified date is today's date (the default setting). Be sure to check the "all at once" checkbox before clicking Find. In the resulting text list view of the files, drag any selected file you see to the backup drive (they're all selected, so they'll follow as a group). In a matter of moments, you've performed an incremental backup (although by no means as useful as a true backup managed by a file backup utility program).

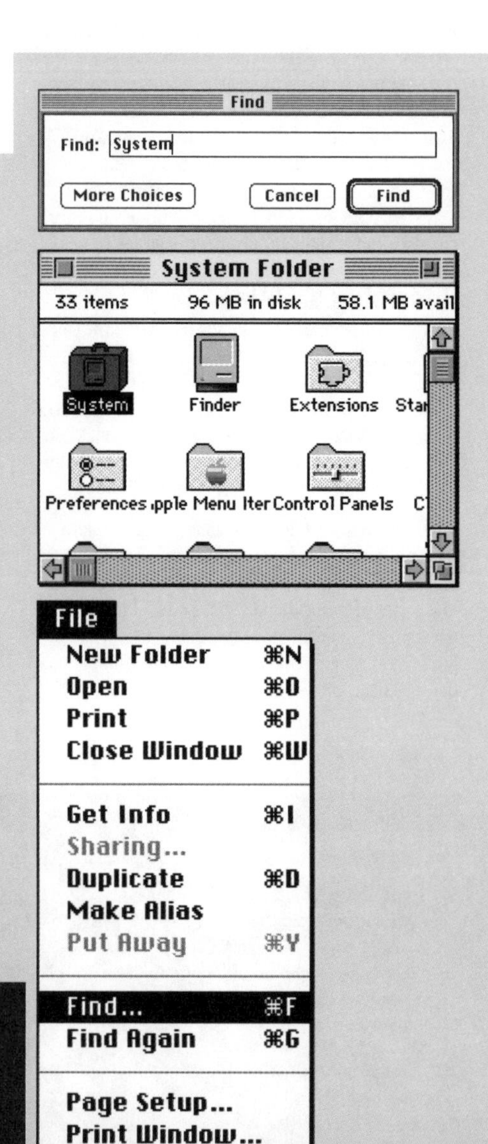

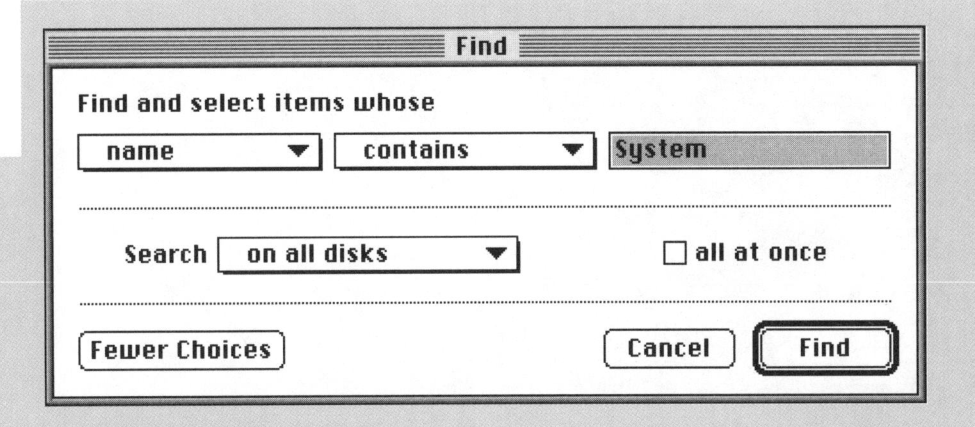

More Choices
A button in the standard Find dialog— —leads you to a more detailed **Find** dialog box. Here you can be more specific about the search, while throwing a wider net. Instead of merely searching for the beginning of a file name, you may search on any attribute you see in a file's **Get Info** dialog box.

Selection Criteria
The top third of the dialog lets you choose the text or comparative values to search for. As you choose from the first **pop up menu,** the other two items adjust themselves to make sense. Sometimes you need to type in a matching text entry; for others you adjust dates like you do for the internal clock setting in the **General Controls** control panel ➔ 80. You may even search for all files with a particular label.

Searching Scope
In the middle third of the dialog, you establish where the search should take place. The default setting is "on all disks," meaning that the search starts with the startup disk, and works through all mounted volumes. Pop up the menu, and you'll see that you can narrow the search to a single volume, the currently open folder window, or any folders you have selected.

Find Results Display
The search from this dialog normally produces the same results as the simple Find dialog. Upon finding a matching file, the folder containing that file opens, and the matching file is selected. Issuing the **Find Again** command continues the search through selected folders or volumes until the system emits the alert sound.

But with this advanced search, you have another choice in the "all at once" checkbox. When you check this box, the Finder searches all selected folders and volumes (you're most likely to see the Find progress barber pole with this setting) before producing any display of the found files. After locating the files, the Finder then opens the folder or disk window that encompasses all the found files, changes the listing to a text view sorted by name, expands folders containing found files, and highlights the found files. In other words, this version shows the results of the **Find** command all in one window.

If the view to the disk window had been something other than by name, you'll have to return to your chosen setting in the **View** menu.

No Match
When no match is found for your search criteria, an alert box tells you so. You won't hear the system alert sound.

Searching Multiple Criteria
Through clever application of settings in the expanded Find dialog box, you can have the Finder look for a union of two or more search criteria on a single disk or folder. Essentially, the process involves finding matches for one criteria in an "all at once" listing display, and then having the Finder search those selected (highlighted) items for the next criteria. Here are the steps:

1. Enter the first search criteria, selecting the desired volume or folder, and checking the "all at once" checkbox.
2. Click Find to effect the search. When items are found, they are highlighted in a single text listing view window.
3. Without de-selecting any item, choose **Find** from the **File** menu (or type *command-F*).
4. Enter the second search criteria.
5. In the Search pop-up menu, choose "the selected items".
6. Click Find to let the Finder see which of the selected item also match the second criteria. Only those items matching the union of the two criteria will be selected.
7. Continue with additional criteria, if desired.

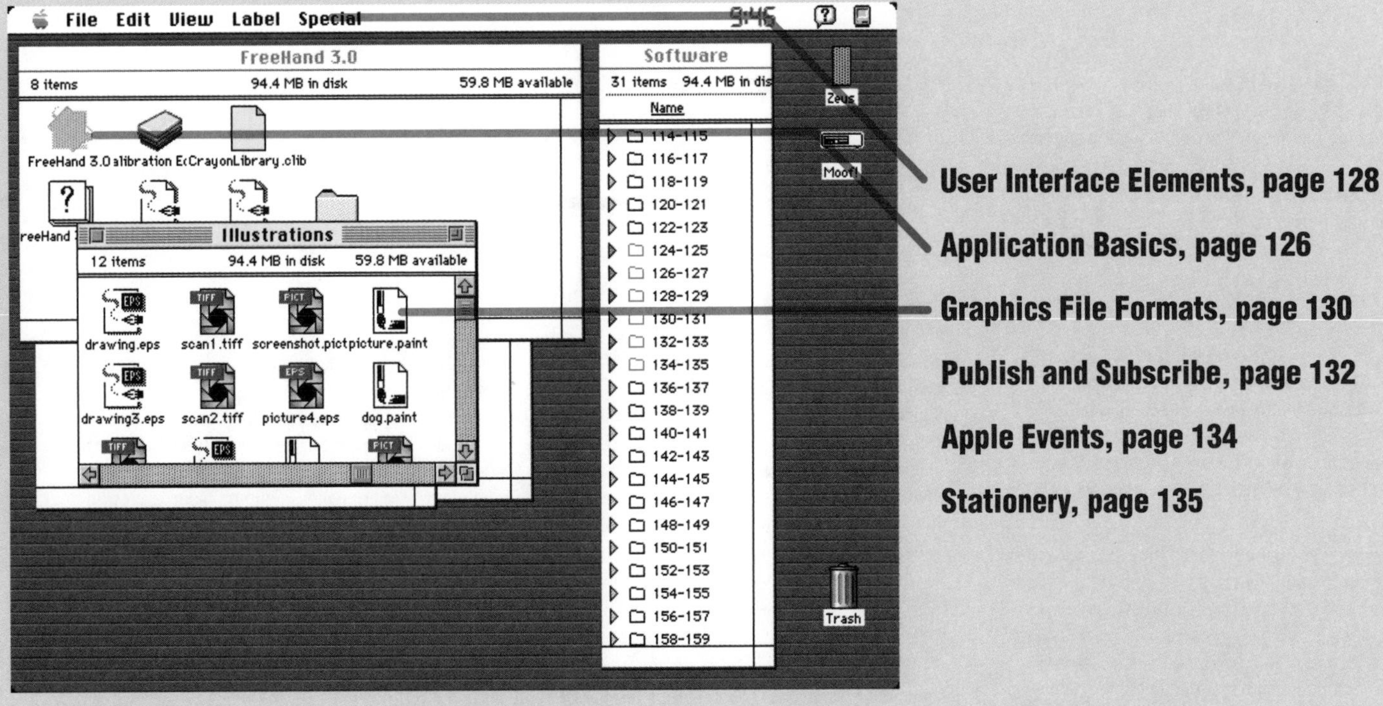
User Interface Elements, page 128
Application Basics, page 126
Graphics File Formats, page 130
Publish and Subscribe, page 132
Apple Events, page 134
Stationery, page 135

You buy a computer to run applications—the programs that let you capture ideas, create and manage information, communicate with others.

Macintosh applications have earned a reputation for being easier to learn than those of other computer systems, primarily because of consistencies in basic operations. Once you know how to start and quit one Macintosh program, you know how to do it for all of them. That's been true since the first Macintosh software available in 1984.

Applications interact with system software in subtle ways. Being able to run multiple applications at the same time, for example, is a function of the system software. Applications also seek help from system software to open and save documents—the standard dialogs are built into the system. And yet, while you are using a program, you almost forget about system software, as you focus on the task inside the program.

Applications vs. Desk Accessories

The Macintosh desk accessory (known as a DA, pronounced by saying the letters D and A) has been around since the first days of the Macintosh. Its intent was to provide a way for small programs to run on top of an open application without taking up a lot of memory space. Desk accessories were literally installed into the System File, and started by choosing them from the menu. System 7 has changed much of the need for desk accessories, primarily because you can open more than one application at a time. But the need for small applications really doesn't go away. Apple even includes updated versions of the original desk accessories in the Apple Items Menu folder.

When you open a desk accessory, you'll notice in the memory allocation bars of the About This Macintosh dialog box that they take up very little RAM (usually less than 32K). Even within the original memory constraints of DAs, programmers did marvelous things, including word processors, spreadsheets, and telecommunications programs.

Under System 7, desk accessories and applications look the same to the user, despite their internal differences (of value only to the programmers). DAs and programs are listed as different kinds of files in text listing views of folders, but you probably won't be able to tell the difference when both kinds are open. Newer DAs have distinctive icons just like applications, and take their places in the Application menu just like any application. What is still beneficial is that DAs take up less memory, and therefore are welcome in tight memory situations.

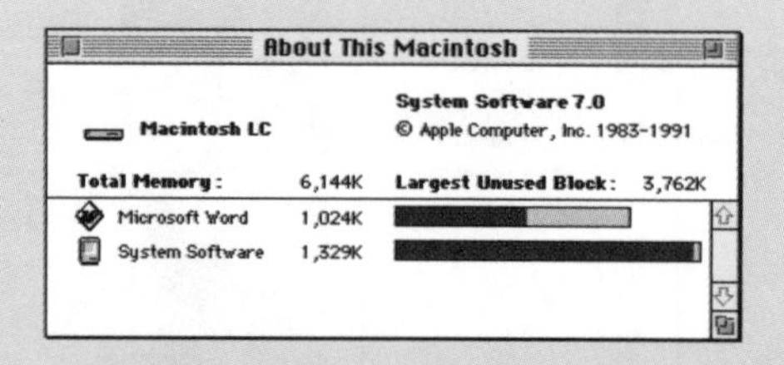

Installing Applications

While desk accessories install as easily as dragging their icons to the **Apple Menu Items** folder (or anywhere, just like an application file), applications sometimes come with more sophisticated installation routines, especially when the program is so large that it requires more than one disk. Apple encourages developers to write routines that utilize the same Installer program that installs system software on your hard disk. Specifications for the installation process are written to a file called the installer script. The installation of an application with the Installer would be similar to system software installation ➡68-69.

Some programs are simple enough to install that there are instructions to drag files and folders to various parts of your hard disk. Some files may be destined for the System Folder (more likely in the nested **Extensions folder**➡83), while others can go anywhere, such as a folder in which you park all applications. Versions of programs previous to System 7 often contained ancillary files (e.g., dictionary and help files) that had to be in the same folder level as the application. In System 7, these supporting files generally go into various folders inside the System Folder.

Still other programs come in compressed files on floppy disks. The primary reason for compressing files is to cram more data on fewer disks to reduce the disk swapping during installation and lower the product's cost. Software publishers have many compression schemes to choose from, each with slightly different methods of installation. The most common is similar to the Apple Installer program. You insert the first floppy disk, and double-click the compressed file on that disk. That starts the decompression of the files, with a request for you to designate where on your hard disk the application's folder should be initially created (you can move it later). You'll be prompted in turn for any additional disks. A variation on this process is that you must copy the compressed files to your hard disk before decompressing them. Be sure to remove the compressed files afterward to free up disk space.

The Software License

It may surprise you to learn that the fine print you're supposed to read before opening a software package is actually a license to use the software. You don't own it. Most licenses read pretty much the same, so it's entertaining to actually read one of them. In the process you'll learn that if a software package miscalculates your bottom line, you can't hold the publisher or author responsible. Licensing, as opposed to ownership, gives the licensor (publisher) more rights over how you use and install the software. Upholding these licenses, many software companies (and the Washington, D.C. trade group called the Software Protection Association) have successfully sued corporations that have made multiple copies of software without paying the licensing fee (purchase price) for each

Force Quitting

You may encounter instances when your Macintosh appears to freeze up—or hang, as the experts say. If this happens while running a program, try the gentle way out. Type *command-option-escape* (even if it takes both hands). If all goes well, a dialog box will allow you to force quit the program. Unfortunately, you'll lose all changes since your last save, but you can get to other open programs and

Applications and Memory

When you'd like to run more applications than available memory allows, there are a number of memory preservation techniques you can try before adding RAM. Techniques include lowering the disk cache (in the **Memory** control panel ➡43, reducing the amount of memory each application tries to grab for itself ➡44, and opening applications in an efficient order ➡00?.

Starting Applications

The Macintosh provides several ways to start up (launch) an application. You can combine any of these ways depending on your work habits or other whims. If the application is already running when you attempt any of these procedures, the application comes to the foreground.

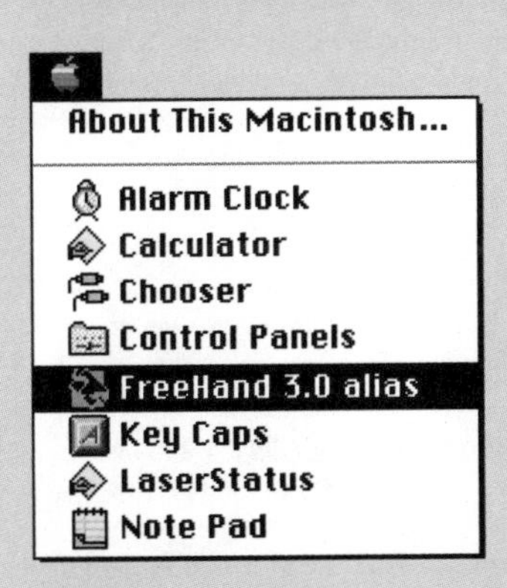

🍎 Menu

If you place an alias ➡120-121 to a program file in the **Apple Menu Items** folder, you can select the program's name from the 🍎 menu to start the program.

Double-Click Program Icon

If you can see the icon of an program (or its alias icon), you can double-click the icon to start the program. Double-clicking is the same as selecting the icon (clicking it once) and choosing **Open** from the **File** menu.

Double-Click Document

The Finder is smart enough to know what application created most documents. Therefore, if you double-click on a document icon (or an alias to a document), the Finder locates and launches the application and then opens the document in the program.

Drop Document on Program Icon

System software allows you to drag a document icon to an application icon to launch that program and open the document. The icons may even be in different windows (clicking on icons in an active Finder window does not activate that window). While it is faster to just double-click a document icon to start the associated application, there are times when the drag is a better option:

1. when the document was not created by the application (but the application can open the document's file type); and

2. when you have multiple versions of an application, and you want to make sure the proper version opens with the document.

Some programs can accept files in formats other than their own. For example, most applications can read a plain text file. Double-clicking on a text file won't find an application. But by dragging the text file to the application icon, you can open that application. An application's icon highlights when you drag the document icon to it only when that application knows how to open the document type. If there is no highlight, the document cannot be opened directly by that application.

Quitting Applications

Virtually every application program quits the same way—a **Quit** option in the **File** menu facilitated by the *command-Q* keyboard equivalent. If you have any open documents whose changes have not yet been saved, the program prompts you about whether you want to save the changes for each one before quitting.

Desk accessories often behave differently. While some include Quit commands in their own menubar or extra menu to the right of other menubar items, more commonly a click of the DA window's close box disposes of the mini program.

A global method of quitting all applications is to issue the **Shut Down** or **Restart** commands in the Finder's **Special** menu. The Finder sends messages to applications identical to the Quit command you normally issue from their **File** menu. You'll still be prompted about saving changed documents.

Running Multiple Programs

As long as you have memory available, the Macintosh allows you to open more than one program. This greatly simplifies copying and pasting information between documents generated in different programs (but also see a better way of copying information with Publish and Subscribe, ➡132-133). Once multiple applications are running, you switch between them by either clicking in any visible window of a desired program, or choosing the program from the **Application** menu ➡101.

Copy Protection

It's rare these days to encounter a copy protected application that prevents installation of the program on a hard disk. Entertainment programs frequently had this restriction in the past, but copy protection of this type is rare.

Network Copy Protection

A few programs employ copy protection schemes that prevent you from installing multiple copies of the same program on more than one machine connected to a network. These programs have unique serial numbers imbedded in each copy. As you start the program, it looks in other Macintoshes on the network for any other copy of that software with the same serial number. If it finds a duplicate, it won't let the second person open the program. The solution is to buy a copy of the software for each user.

File
New... ⌘N
Open... ⌘O
Close
Save ⌘S
Save as...
Revert
Page Setup...
Print... ⌘P
Place...
Export...
Quit ⌘Q

Consistency across a variety of applications makes the Macintosh seem very easy to use. We're not frustrated trying to learn and remember a different file saving command for each document—we know where to look and what to look for in a Save command.

You can count on a number of user interface elements being in virtually every application from the Finder to the most esoteric modeling program. Once you understand these items, you're well on your way to being comfortable in virtually any Macintosh product.

File
New... ⌘N
Open... ⌘O
Close
Save ⌘S
Save as...
Revert
Page Setup...
Print... ⌘P
Place...
Export...
Quit ⌘Q

Steady Menus

The **human interface guidelines** that Apple supplies Macintosh programmers specify that every product should have a menubar with a basic set of menus. In addition to the icon-based menus (, Help, and Application), you will probably find a **File** and **Edit** menu in each program. When the user has a choice of text style, two more menus are up there: **Font** and **Style**.

Menu

Most of the menu is devoted to items in the **Apple Menu Items** folder. But above the dividing line, programmers usually place an item that tells about the product. Choosing the **About <product name>** item leads to a dialog that may range from a simple description of the product to an animated cartoon. You'll usually find reference to the version number, publisher, and people involved in creating the product. Some programmers provide alternate screens when you press one or more modifier keys while you make this menu selection.

About This Macintosh...
Alarm Clock
Calculator
Chooser
Control Panels
Key Caps
LaserStatus
Note Pad

Edit
Undo ⌘Z
Cut ⌘X
Copy ⌘C
Paste ⌘V
Clear
Select All ⌘A
Show Clipboard

File Menu

Commands you'll almost always find in the **File** menu are those that **open, save, create new, and print** documents. It's also where the **Quit** item can be found. These menu items tend to have the same command-key equivalents across programs: *command-O, -S, -N, -P,* and *-Q,* respectively.

Edit Menu

Virtually required in every program are **Edit** menu items for **Undo, Cut, Copy, and Paste** *(command-Z, -X, -C,* and *-V)*. The exact wording of these items may change in some programs, depending on what kind of information you've selected or have in the Clipboard. Moreover, pasting can be empowered to paste different characteristics of the information in some programs ➔ 108. As a result, you may see a **Paste Special** item as well.

Additional items that programs might include in the **Edit** menu are the commands for the publish/subscribe feature ➔ 132-133 and one that leads to a dialog box for setting the program's preferences.

Font and Style Menus

Sometimes combined into a single **Font** menu, items for these menus control the font and style of selected text in a document. **Font** menus always list all the fonts installed in your System File. Under the heading of style, you may see various **font sizes** (ideally a set of standard sizes plus a way for you to choose any point size) and **styles** (**bold**, *italic*, etc.). See pages ➔ 86-88 for more on fonts and the System.

Application-Specific Menus

Beyond the standard menus and menu items, an application may do anything it pleases to present menus that give you the power to work with information in the program's documents. When exploring a program for the first time, it's a good idea to study the contents of each menu. Select those items with ellipses (**...**) after them to see the resulting dialog boxes.

Windows

Any program that lets you work on documents offers one or more windows in which you work your magic. When you start an application from the Finder (or menu), it may either prompt you with an **Open File dialog** ➔ 106 to open an existing document or display an empty window, called **Untitled**. The latter assumes that you will create a new document. But if you then open an existing document, you may end up with two windows—your document and the untitled one. Some programs assume that if you open a document with an unused, untitled window showing, then the document you're opening should replace the untitled window. There is no consistency to this, so be prepared to see both behaviors.

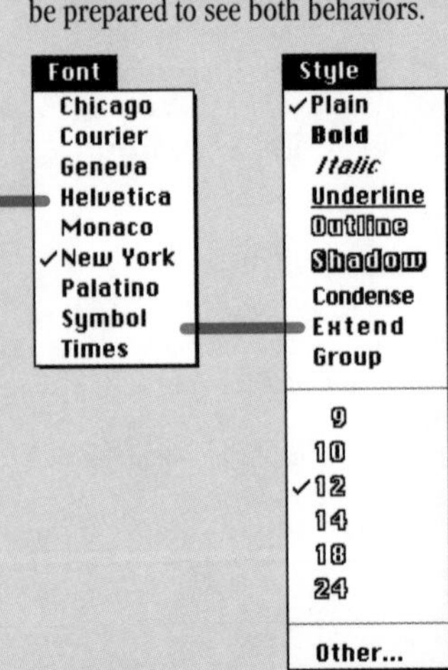

Editing Text

Macintosh text editing is the same in virtually every program. The cursor becomes a text pointer whenever the cursor is atop a text editing area. Clicking the cursor in text plants a flashing text insertion pointer—signifying the place your next typed character will be inserted. To prepare a chunk of text for an action, you click and drag the text pointer across the characters, words, or paragraphs. The highlighted text is said to be selected. You can also select text by planting the text insertion pointer at one end of the selection, and then holding down the *shift* key while clicking the cursor at the other end of the text.

Once text is selected, it's usually time to issue some menu command that acts on the selection, such as changing its font properties or copying it to the Clipboard. One important property of selected text is that the next character you type replaces all selected text. Thus, to change a word, simply select it (a double-click inside a word selects the entire word), and start typing the replacement—don't bother deleting the old word.

Lorem ipsum dolor sit a
nonummy nibh euismod

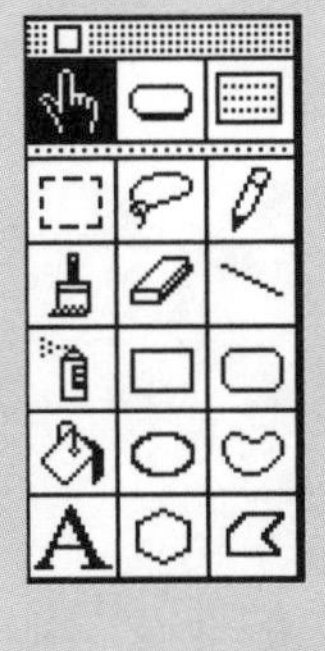

Button

Button

Check Box

Radio Button

Buttons

With the mouse being such a large part of our interaction with the Macintosh, the profusion of clickable buttons is no coincidence. The three most common button styles are the outline (rounded rectangle), radio, and checkbox. Outline buttons perform a single action, as designated by their name. When a dark border surrounds such a button, it means that a press of the *return* or *enter* keys acts the same as clicking the button. Radio buttons come in groups, and are mutually exclusive within the group—only one can be highlighted at a time. Checkbox buttons, on the other hand, let you set or unset whatever the label indicates. A check in the box means that the setting is enabled or engaged. When the box is filled in gray, it often means that the selected information to which the settings apply has a combination of features (e.g., part of the text is bold, part not). Click the checkbox to make the desired on or off setting apply to the entire selection.

Tools

Some programs—usually graphics programs—display palettes of tools. Sometimes these palettes may be pulled down from the menubar, and then dragged away from the bar so that the palette can remain visible while you work on a document. Click on an icon representing the desired tool. This puts you into a mode that is unique to that tool, whether it be drawing, filling an area with a pattern, or selecting objects on the screen. The cursor turns into the same shape as the tool you selected. No matter what tool you use, however, as you move the pointer to the menubar, the cursor returns to the familiar arrow.

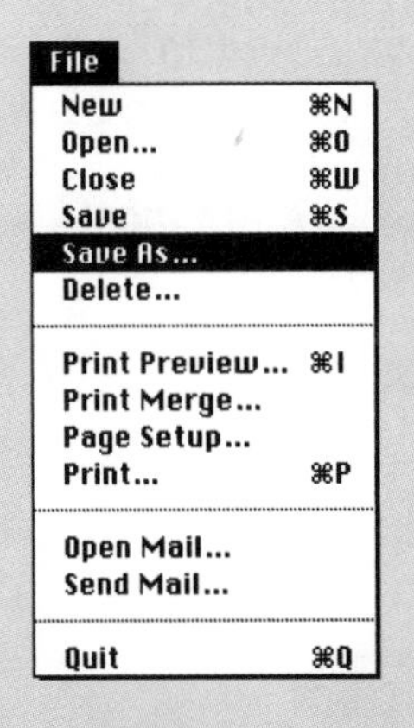

Saving Documents

Most applications that work with documents have two types of **Save** commands in their **File** menus: **Save** and **Save As**. The first is the one you use when saving changes to a document that you've already named and stored on your disk. This version is the one with the convenient *command-S* keyboard equivalent, which makes it easy to frequently save your work each time you reach a resting point. The more often you perform intermediate saves, the less work is at risk to a power outage or machine failure.

The **Save As** command, on the other hand, is the command you use to perform the first save of a document. The command leads you to a **Save File** dialog box ➔107, in which you can assign a file name, and determine what folder the document should go. You can also use the **Save As** command as a way to make a copy of the current document from within the program. Simply issue the command and save the same document to another folder, or assign a different name (perhaps for backup purposes). If you assign a new name, the document window's title bar will bear that new name. Be aware, however, that when you finish with the **Save As** command, the next **Save** command you issue will be to save the document to the last file name and folder specified in the most recent **Save As** command.

Printing

In the **File** menu of any program that produces documents is some variation of the **Print** command (as well as the **Page Setup** command ➔150). In programs that allow opening multiple documents, the **Print** command applies to the current document only. A hallmark of the Macintosh is that printed output closely resembles the information you see in the window. The **Print** command leads to a print dialog tailored for the printer you've selected in the Chooser ➔78. The content of the print dialog is different for each printer, but in it you make additional selections about the print job about to start. Click to send the document to your printer. For more about printing, see pages ➔148-153.

If your Macintosh work is predominantly in graphics programs, then you tend to encounter the alphabet soup of graphic file formats—PICT, PICT2, TIFF, EPSF are the most popular.

These represent the manner in which graphic information is stored in a disk file. Each one is different and generally incompatible with the others. Fortunately, many graphics programs can save to and open from more than one format.

The file format is distinct, however, from the graphic type: bit mapped and object graphics. Most graphics programs are one type or the other. Which style you use depends largely on the intended final resting place for the graphic—screen picture, low resolution printer, high resolution printer.

Bit Mapped Graphics

Bit mapped graphics are the realm of **painting** packages. These programs let you work with a graphic on a pixel-by-pixel basis, usually in some magnified mode. The first graphics program for the Macintosh, **MacPaint**, was a bit mapped graphics program. While the standard granularity of bit mapped programs is 7**2-pixels per inch**, you can find advanced programs that give you more detailed editing abilities, up to the LaserWriter's **300 dots per inch**, in a highly magnified view.

Monochrome paint programs let you set pixels black and white to create your shapes and images on the screen. Tools help you set down patterns of dots in squares, circles, and dotted patterns. In color paint programs, you can assign different colors to virtually every pixel (within the color palette of your color video support ➔36).

A downside to bit mapped graphics is that once you lay down the pixels, what may appear to be a shape is still nothing more than a collection of dots. If a square you've painted is the wrong size, you'll have to erase and re-paint the pixels in the right size. Painting programs let you select a group of pixels (within a selection rectangle or an irregular area that you drag a lasso tool). If you drag the selection, you leave white space underneath. If you manipulate the selection, such as rotating, stretching, or shrinking, the program does its best to maintain the general shape of the original by scaling the dots to a best fit. You'll probably end up with jagged or distorted lines and uneven fill patterns, however.

Still, many Macintosh artist feel very much at home in bit mapped graphics. When the finished output is to be displayed on a Macintosh screen, bit mapped graphics produce excellent results.

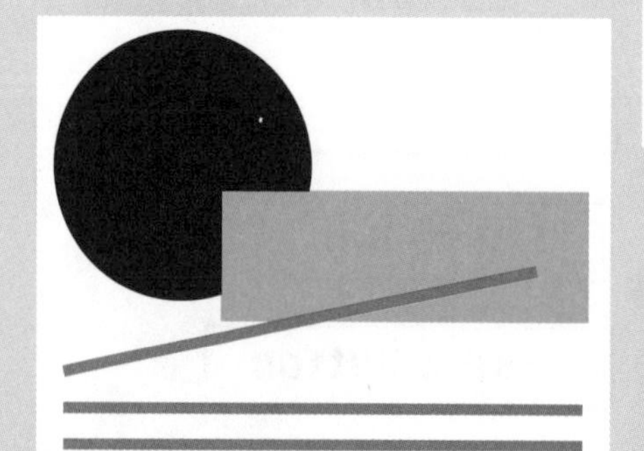

Object Graphics

Object graphics programs, more commonly called **draw** packages, produce graphics results in a vastly different way. Instead of a line being a series of individual pixels, an object line is a mathematical specification for a line: two end point coordinates and a line of a designated thickness between those two points. Each line, box, circle, polygon, arc, or text chunk, is an object that can be individually selected (by just clicking on it), and altered independently of any other object in the document. It's as if each object exists in its own physical layer in the document. Moreover, an object is easy to change. To resize an incorrect square, simply select the object, and drag on one of its corners. The program makes note of the new coordinates for that object—the line thickness remains the same.

Due to their mathematical accuracy, object graphics (also called **vector** graphics) tend to print smoother shapes than bit mapped graphics, especially on high-resolution printers. Curves are as smooth as the resolution of the printer can produce. Data storage requirements for object graphics documents are also less, since there is less information required for most shapes than for bit maps.

Bit Maps in Object Documents

Most draw programs allow you to paste bit mapped graphics copied from other programs. When you paste the art, however, the bit map turns into a single, uneditable object (there are no pixel editing tools in most draw programs). You can position the art without penalty, but if you try to resize it, the image distorts as the Macintosh tries to best fit —scale—the pixels to the new orientation.

You'll likely encounter further problems when you try to align a bit map with object art in the same document. On screen, everything looks fine, but when the page prints on a laser printer, the alignment may be off. The problem is that the typically 72-dot-per-inch bit map is being printed in a 300 dot-per-inch world. Incompatible math makes perfect alignment a gradual, manual fine-tuning process.

Graphic Types and File Formats

Bit mapped and object graphic types are independent of the file formats used to store the images. For example, the PICT file format can store both a bit mapped and object graphic in the same file. When you copy a bit map or a simple monochrome graphic object to the Scrapbook, you'll see that the images are both saved as PICTs, yet when you copy each item out of the Scrapbook, they retain their bit map or object status for pasting back into documents.

PICT

Dating from the earliest Macintosh days, the **PICT** (short for picture) accommodates both bit mapped and object graphics, even in the same document. Bit maps in resolutions higher than 72 dots-per-inch are supported (some programs allow finer dot editing to smooth rough edges on images that are to be printed on high resolution printers). This **standard** PICT format can also store color information up to 8 very basic colors. PICTs are best used in screen display of graphics.

MacPaint Format

Named after the first graphics program for the Macintosh, the **MacPaint** file format is perhaps the simplest. It consists of a dot map of an image (no object graphics allowed). Maximum document size is 8 by 10 inches (576 pixels wide by 720 pixels high). Any larger image converted or saved to the MacPaint format is cropped to the upper left corner 8 by 10 inches—all other pixels are lost.

EPSF

An **Encapsulated PostScript File** (sometimes just **EPS**) actually contains two copies of an image. One copy is a **PostScript** language description of the image (in either **ASCII** text or a more disk space conservative **binary** format, depending on the graphics program and its options). This is the information that output devices (printers, typesetters, etc.) use to produce the image on paper or film. The second copy is a PICT image that the graphics software uses to produce a comparatively quick representation of the image on the screen (often as a miniature preview in an **Open File** dialog box). A number of page layout and word processing programs allow you to import or paste EPS graphics just like other graphics. EPS images can be either object or bit mapped graphics, but PostScript does an excellent job of accommodating size and orientation changes to an image.

PostScript Text

Some graphics programs let you save a document entirely as a **PostScript** description. This is a text document loaded with PostScript language commands and parameters that PostScript output devices interpret and convert into commands that drive the laser or film imager. No companion PICT is included, as in EPSF. Unless you know the PostScript language, you won't be able to edit this kind of file. The advantage, however, is that you can send a text PostScript file to any PostScript device (with a download utility program) without the

PICT2

A second-generation PICT format, the **PICT2** allows for greater color and grayscale control. PICT2 files may be either **8-bit** or **24-bit** capable. The 8-bit PICT2 version allows up to 256 colors in the picture, including a custom 256-color palette (although the custom palette may not survive when opening the file in a program other than the originating program). An 8-bit PICT2 offers photorealistic black-and-white photo reproduction. A 24-bit PICT2 version lets you work with a photorealistic 16.8 million colors (provided you have 24-bit color software and video capabilities ➲ 36).

PICS

As if graphic formats weren't enough, you may also have to contend with **animation** files for presentations. A **PICS** file contains a series of PICT or PICT2 format images, which, when played in a sequence, produce animation, whether it be cartoon-like motion or different perspective views of a graphic. To reduce the enormous file sizes, most PICS-capable programs perform **compression** and **decompression** of files, but those processes are usually unique to the programs, and must be opened either in the program that saved the file or through a special driver supplied by the program's creator.

MooV

This latest graphics file format is called a **movie** (with a tip of the hat to the legendary DogCow), and is the standard Apple file type for animation, sequenced sound, and video. This file type **(MooV)** is new with **QuickTime,** an extension to System 7 that facilitates the recording, playback, and

TIFF

An acronym for **Tagged Image File Format**, **TIFF** (which comes in monochrome, grayscale, and color versions) is the favorite of high-end bit mapped graphics work. Many scanner software programs offer the TIFF file format as an option. Because TIFF files tend to be at higher resolutions than PICTs, they can get quite large, especially when saved in the grayscale (256 grays) or color (16.8 million colors) versions. Even at lower resolutions, TIFF files allow for dithering (a method of positioning shaded patterns of black or color together to trick the eye into seeing a color that isn't possible under the existing color constraints). TIFF files can be imported into most page layout programs to produce high quality photo images inside documents, such as newsletters and brochures.

Proprietary Formats

Many graphics programs use as a default file format one that is unique to that program. The primary reason is that the program's designers found ways to store more detailed information about an image than the standard file formats support. It's rare that applications allow translation of other programs' proprietary formats.

Converting File Formats

The biggest headache for graphic artists and designers on the Macintosh is keeping all the file formats straight and converting material from one format to another. Not all graphics programs support all file formats. One important guideline, however, is that when you start converting formats, you lose image information as you convert to less capable formats (which you may want to do to be compatible with more programs or save disk space). And if a program has a proprietary format, any conversion to standard formats in the **Save As** dialog usually results in some loss of image

Programs designed for System 7 may include a feature that allows documents to share information with other documents on your Macintosh or even on someone else's Macintosh on a network.

Once you establish the link between source and destination documents, you don't have to think about it anymore—any change you make to the source document appears automatically in the destination document the next time you view or print it.

This feature is called **Publish and Subscribe,** after the two basic actions in the process. A source document publishes information; a destination document subscribes to that information. In between the two is a file on the disk called an edition.

Picture Edition

The Metaphor

Because there is nothing in the real world that does to documents what Publish/Subscribe **(P/S)** does, it is difficult to conceive of a metaphor that helps us understand what this feature does. The P/S metaphor comes close.

If you create a chart in a spreadsheet program (based on complex calculations that may fluctuate over time), you may want to use that chart in a report and a presentation. But if the calculations and chart change, you don't want to have to re-copy and paste the new chart everywhere you use it. In the P/S world, you select the source chart and turn it into a publisher of its information. The publisher creates a file called an **edition.** Each time you change information in the area designated as a publisher (the chart in this case), the publisher updates the information in the edition file when you save the file.

On the other end in, perhaps, a memo document, you can create a subscriber by opening the desired edition file. A subscriber is a reserved space in your document that is linked to the edition file. The subscriber derives its information from the edition, displays it in the memo, and makes it part of the document. While the memo document is still open, system software monitors changes made to the edition file, and passes changes along to all currently open subscribers. Thus, when the publisher updates the edition, any open subscriber sees the change in the document immediately.

Basic Publish Procedures

Implementation of Publish/Subscribe varies from program to program, but the principles are the same. Somewhere in the **Edit** menu will be items that have the words **Publish** and **Subscribe** in them. To create an edition file, the steps are as follows:

1. Select the area of the source document to publish.
2. Choose **Create Publisher** from the **Edit** menu.
3. In the dialog box (you see a miniature preview of the selected data), assign a name and folder location for the edition file, and click **Publish**.

Some programs let you see where publishers are in a document. A menu item named **Show Borders** (or similar) displays grey borders around the publisher and subscriber areas in the document (the border type should be different for each kind). The menu item changes to **Hide Borders** so you can clear the borders.

Basic Subscribe Procedures

The steps for accessing an edition file are also simple:

1. Position the cursor where you want the edition's information to be inserted into the document.
2. Choose **Subscribe To** from the Edit menu.
3. Select an edition file in the dialog box (edition files have a small grey rectangle icon in the listing, and display a miniature preview of the information when selected), and click **Subscribe**.

The information appears immediately in the document. The information is locked for editing (changes can be made only inside the publisher), but you can usually move the location of the subscriber in a document. Occasionally, you can modify certain properties of the information, such as text font or style, but not the content.

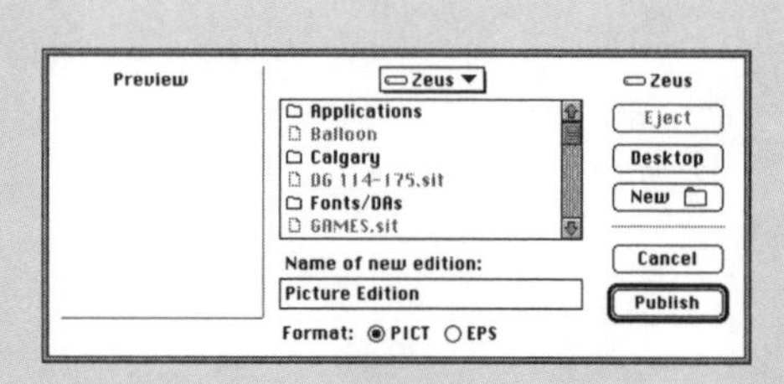

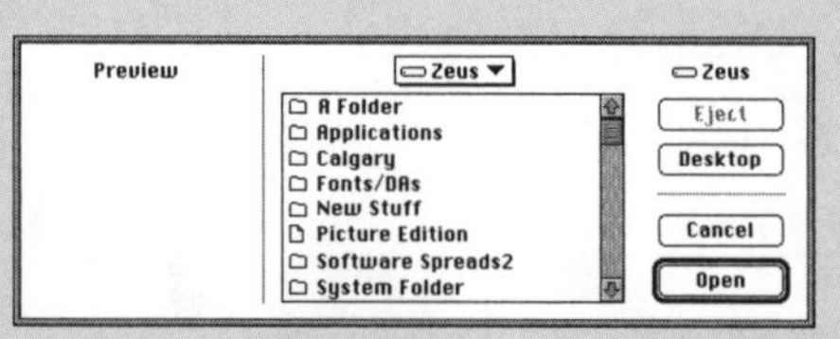

Viewing Editions

In addition to previewing editions in the **Subscribe To** dialog box, you may double-click an edition file in the **Finder.** This displays a window showing a miniature preview of the edition. You also see the data type(s) of the information. A button lets you open the document containing the publisher that created this edition.

Networked Publish/Subscribe

A networked environment is a likely candidate for publish and subscribe, since more than one person may work on pieces of a combined document. Or perhaps several users need to draw from a library of existing text and graphics to create documents. You can **publish** and **subscribe** to editions on other computers with those other computers' volumes mounted on your Desktop. Later, when you update a publisher or subscriber, the remote volumes will mount automatically for you. You may

Publisher-Edition-Subscriber Interaction

It's important to understand how the three elements of the P/S chain work together. While information flows only from publisher to edition to subscriber, an edition or subscriber can trace the chain back to the publisher on demand.

A publisher knows only about the edition it creates and updates that edition only when its containing document is saved (or manually updated in **Publisher Options**). A publisher does not know if anything has subscribed to its edition.

An edition knows only about the publisher that created it, but the only communication between the two is generated by the publisher when updating the edition. While an edition doesn't keep a record of its subscribers, system software is aware of what chains between editions and subscribers are currently active. When a publisher updates its edition, system software alerts all open documents subscribing to that edition that it's time to fetch the latest data.

Finally, a subscriber knows only about the whereabouts of the edition it subscribes to. When told to get an update (i.e., opening the document), the subscriber reads the data from the edition.

Subscriber to: Picture Edition
Get Editions:
Automatically
Manually
Get Edition Now
Latest Edition: Friday, January 17, 1992 12:18:43 PM
Cancel Subscriber
Open Publisher
Cancel
OK

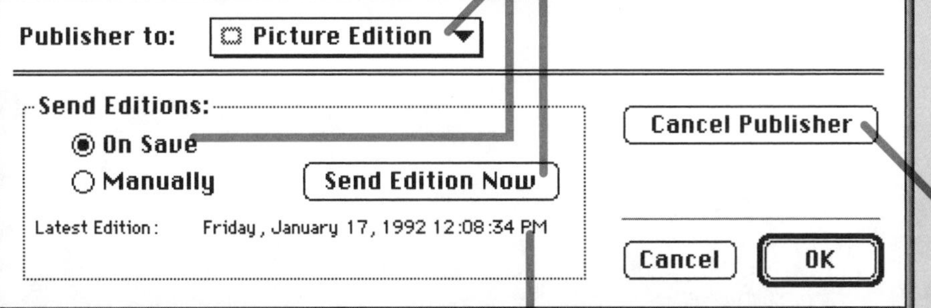

Publisher Options

For each publisher in a document, you may set some options. How you reach the Publisher Options dialog box may differ from program to program. One method is to select the publisher and choose **Publisher Options** in the **Edit** menu. Most programs allow you to double-click the publisher to reach the dialog.

Publisher Trivia

It is possible to publish a portion of a document to more than one edition. You can even overlap the publishers—when you make a change to the overlapped section, both editions get updated. Once you cancel a publisher, however, you cannot reconnect it to an existing edition. You must create a new publisher and new edition (or replace the old edition). The subscribers must then re-subscribe to the new edition, even if it has the same name as before. That's because each edition file has a unique identifier that helps both publishers and subscribers find editions that have been moved (but not off the originating volume) or renamed.

Pop up List

This list reveals the path ➜117 to the edition controlled by the selected publisher.

On Save/Manually

This chooses whether you want updates to go to the edition on every save or just when you want.

Send Edition Now

This updates the edition when you click it, instead of waiting for a save.

Date Info

This reveals the last time and date an update was sent to the edition. If **manual update** is set, it also lists the time and date of the last change to data in the publisher.

Cancel Publisher

This deletes the publisher, but not the data in its area on the document nor in the edition file. Other subscribers may still use the edition, even though the publisher no longer exists. The contents of the edition will never change.

Subscriber Options

Subscribers, too, have similar options. Select the subscriber and choose **Subscriber Options** in the **Edit** menu or double-click the subscriber to reach the dialog.

Automatically/Manually

This chooses whether the subscriber should accept and display changes to the edition or the user gets updates on demand. Click Get Edition Now to receive an update from the edition.

Date Info

This displays the time and date of the last change to the edition file. If you choose **manual updates,** you also see the time and date of the last time you explicitly updated the subscriber from the edition.

Cancel Subscriber

This deletes the subscriber, but usually leaves the current copy of the data in the document. This has no effect on the edition file.

Open Publisher

This lets the system software work backward through the chain to find and open the document containing the publisher. If the publisher is from another program, the other program will load, provided there is sufficient memory.

Behind the scenes in system software, the Finder communicates with applications in a messaging scheme called Apple Events. You don't usually get to see what Apple Events are doing, but they open the way for programs to communicate directly with other programs.

For example, an on-screen form presented in one program can respond to the entry of a customer number by sending messages to a database program to look up the customer name, address, and credit rating, and then return the information to the proper blanks on the form. The data entry operator isn't even aware of the transactions that took place between the two programs.

While most message passing between programs will be hidden from the user, more advanced users can access Apple Events and send messages to other programs with the help of utility programs.

Terminology

With System 7 came a bevy of new terms to describe communication between programs. One is the Publish and Subscribe metaphor. The internal mechanism that controls this feature is called the Edition Manager. When you hear discussion of this manager, it refers to the Publish/Subscribe feature.

Two other acronyms are used almost interchangeably: PPC and IAC. PPC is program-to-program communication. The term PPC is used primarily to help programmers identify a collection of routines that facilitate sharing of information between programs, either on the same computer or on multiple computers connected to a network. Interapplication Communication (IAC) is a more general term, covering all the ways programs can be linked to others, including via Publish/Subscribe, Apple Events, and less obvious connections designed into applications by their designers.

To make matters worse, IAC is called IPC (Inter Process Communications) outside the Macintosh community.

Event Basics

Macintosh programs are said to be **event-driven.** Typical events include the **click** of a mouse button, **choosing** a menu item, the **press** of a keyboard key. Programs constantly poll the system for instances of events, and branch to execute (process or run) code in response to the event. For example, if you click on a tool in a tool palette, the program first sees that you've clicked the mouse button. It then checks to see where the pointer was when you pressed the button, calculates the coordinates in the tool palette, and then changes the pointer to the desired tool.

With System 7, Apple introduced a broad mechanism that allows programs (including the Finder) to send events to each other. Where necessary, these Apple events can also carry data with them and take replies to the events back to the originating program. The syntax for these events is rather complex, and intended for programmers so

Apple Event Suites

In working with programmers during System 7's gestation, Apple divided the Apple Event world into several groups, called **suites.** One suite consists of **required Apple events**—events that all Macintosh applications should respond to. These are basic events that the Finder uses: **open** the application, **open** a document, **print** a document, and **quit** the application.

Beyond those events, Apple has defined a series of core events that it would like programs to observe. If fully implemented in an application, they allow other applications to perform many of the operations you might do to exchange information between documents, such as **selecting data** (a range of text, a portion of a table, a graphic image region), **fetch** a hunk of data, **copy** data to the Clipboard, **save** a document, and much more.

Programmers may also define Apple events that are specific to their programs. Other programmers can find out what these events are from Apple's Event Registry to make their programs work with many others.

Experimenting with Apple Events

HyperCard version 2.1, which is included with System 7, provides support for limited Apple events within the **HyperTalk** scripting language. You can experiment with sending a limited range of messages to other applications and respond to messages from other applications. For example, when you issue the HyperTalk `Open <Application>` command (e.g., `Open "Microsoft Excel"`), HyperCard sends the Apple event to open an application. See pages 138-145 for more about HyperCard.

UserLand Frontier™

An important element of the Apple event world is a third-party scripting language and environment, called **Frontier™** from UserLand. Providing a more accessible level of communication with Apple event-aware Macintosh programs, Frontier lets you write editable scripts that interact with the Macintosh operating system and applications. It overcomes a problem with graphical user interfaces in that you can write **macros** that perform system-level functions, and control them with the precision of a full-bodied scripting language (which resembles the C programming language in construction). Applications programmers can also use Frontier to create self-modifying modular

In the real world, preprinted stationery is like a template. Some items on the page are already there for you. You just fill in the rest with information that is unique to that particular sheet. Macintosh stationery works the same way.

You can turn any document into stationery. Instead of opening the original file to edit it, the program automatically copies the stationery document into a different, new document for you to fill in the rest. There's no chance you'll accidentally save the new document over the original stationery.

Not all Macintosh programs support stationery fully. But if you designate a document as being stationery, the system software helps prevent you from overwriting the stationery file.

Full Stationery Support

When a program fully supports stationery, you'll notice two behaviors. First, the **Save File** dialog box ➔107 contains a choice to save a document as stationery or regular document. Second, if you open a stationery with that program, the program automatically makes a copy of the stationery pad into a new window, usually an untitled one. You must then save the new document with a new name.

article Info

article

Kind: Microsoft Word document
Size: 118K on disk (120,832 bytes used)

Where: MacintoshHD : Microsoft Word : Word 1 :

Created: Tue, Nov 26, 1991, 4:04 PM
Modified: Fri, Dec 6, 1991, 11:33 AM
Version: n/a

Comments:

☐ **Locked** ☒ **Stationery pad**

Creating Stationery

If a program does not fully support stationery, yet you want to protect a template document, you can change the status of the document from the Finder. Select the document file and choose **Get Info** from the **File** menu. At the lower right corner is a Stationery checkbox. Check the box to turn the file into stationery.

Editing Stationery

If a program fully supports stationery, you won't be able to open the stationery file itself to make changes to the template. You'll first have to change the stationery checkbox designation in the **Get Info** dialog. Open and modify the stationery. After saving and closing the document, return to the Get Info dialog and re-check the stationery dialog box.

Stationery Icons

When you create stationery (or change a document to stationery in the **Get Info** dialog), the icon to the document changes slightly. The convention to differentiate stationery from regular document icons is that the lower right corner of the icon is turned up, as on a pad of paper. A program that fully supports stationery usually supplies its own stationery icon—a turned up corner version of the regular document icon. If the program does not support stationery, the system substitutes the generic stationery icon ➔99.

Opening Stationery from Finder

When a program does not fully support stationery, the results of opening a stationery file differs depending on whether you open the stationery file from the Finder (with or without the program running) or from within the program with the **Open** menu item.

Opening a stationery file from the Finder is the only way you can use the file as if the program doesn't support stationery. Double-clicking on the file causes a dialog box that informs you that a new document will be created from the stationery pad. To continue, you must name the new document (click [Save in...] to alter the folder location of the new file). The new document is a regular, not a stationery document. When you click [OK], the Finder makes a copy of the stationery file and renames it with your new name. Only then does it let the program open the document.

Opening Stationery Inside Programs

A non-stationery aware program behaves differently when you choose to open a stationery pad with the **File** menu's **Open** command inside the program. Unlike the Finder's offer to create a new copy, this method simply warns you that you are about to open the stationery file, and that any changes you make will be made to the stationery file, itself. If you'd rather work on a copy of the stationery, it's better to switch to the Finder and open the file from there while your program is running.

Organizing Stationery Pads

How you stash stationery pads on your hard disk depends solely on your document organization **strategy** ➔118-119. Fortunately, if you'd like to treat stationery files like documents for storage purposes, yet prefer to have some pads at ready access, you can create one or more aliases for them ➔120-121, and place aliases where they are easy to access, such as in the Apple Menu Items folder, Startup Items folder, or on the Desktop. You can even create an alias for a shared stationery pad on another Macintosh on the network. One pad can serve an entire workgroup.

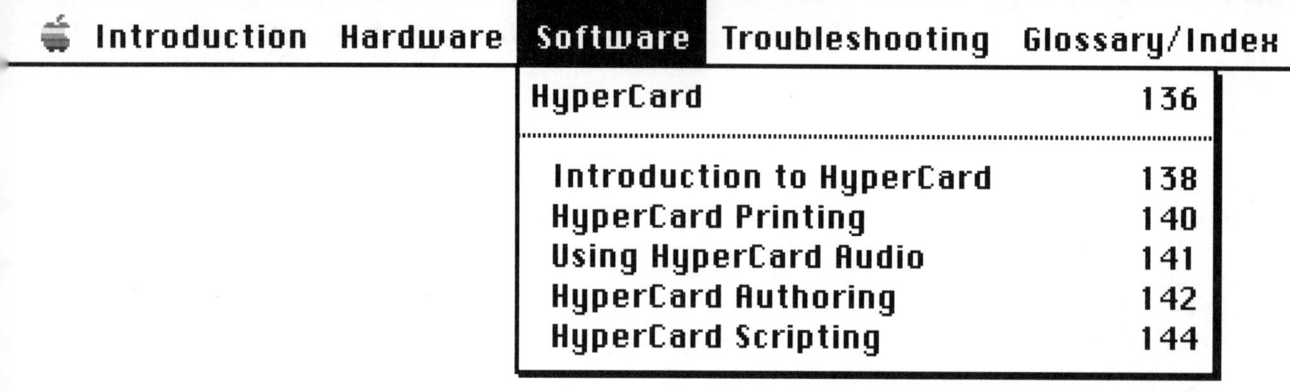
Introduction
Hardware
Software
Troubleshooting
Glossary/Index

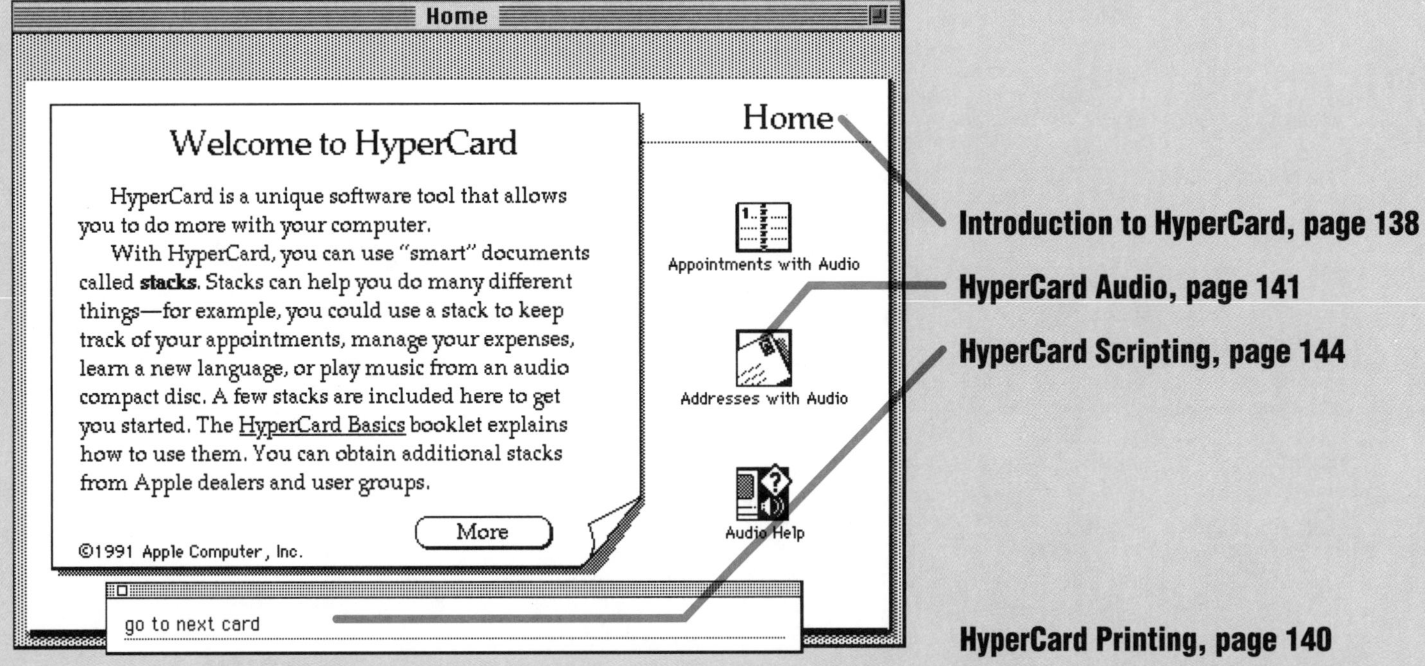
Home
Welcome to HyperCard
HyperCard is a unique software tool that allows you to do more with your computer.
With HyperCard, you can use "smart" documents called **stacks**. Stacks can help you do many different things—for example, you could use a stack to keep track of your appointments, manage your expenses, learn a new language, or play music from an audio compact disc. A few stacks are included here to get you started. The HyperCard Basics booklet explains how to use them. You can obtain additional stacks from Apple dealers and user groups.
More
©1991 Apple Computer, Inc.
Home
Appointments with Audio
Addresses with Audio
Audio Help
go to next card
Introduction to HyperCard, page 138
HyperCard Audio, page 141
HyperCard Scripting, page 144
HyperCard Printing, page 140
HyperCard Authoring, page 142

If you get your system software packaged with a Macintosh computer or you buy a system software upgrade kit, you also receive additional software called HyperCard.

HyperCard is a programming environment for non-technical Macintosh users (although a lot of experienced programmers use it, too). Macintosh owners have created millions of applications (called stacks) in HyperCard as commercial software products, freely distributed programs (shareware), in-house corporate and academic applications, and programs for personal use.

The two-disk HyperCard set that comes with system software allows you to open and run those applications. Apple has hidden the user-programming portion of HyperCard in this set, but it's accessible in every copy of HyperCard.

HyperCard's Purpose

HyperCard's programming environment is very well suited for a number of application types. The three most common are information publishing, information management, and external device control.

For **information publishing**, a HyperCard stack file is used to distribute text and graphic (even animation and video) information. Apple, for example, uses HyperCard as a publishing medium for communications within Apple and to developers and dealers (e.g., a stack entitled "What's New in System 7"). An **information management** stack lets the user enter and store personal or business information. The stack then assists in locating, exporting, printing, or massaging the information. HyperCard is also frequently used to **control** a videodisc or CD-ROM player. Typically, the HyperCard stack contains additional interactive training material supported by high-quality video or sound on the external device.

HyperCard Versions

HyperCard first appeared inside Macintosh boxes in late 1987. Since then, the program has shifted to Claris Corporation for further development. The version recommended for System 7 is HyperCard version 2.1 or later.

Moreover, there are three different editions of HyperCard:

1. the two-disk set bundled with Macintoshes and system software upgrades;
2. a five-disk upgrade from Claris that includes a guide to the programming language; and
3. the same five-disk set, called the HyperCard Stack Development Kit, which includes a full set of manuals for beginners and is available in computer and software stores.

Installing HyperCard

HyperCard is an application like any other as far as the Finder is concerned. The stacks that it creates are like document files in the Finder. The two have related icons, as you'd expect. You may create a separate HyperCard folder, or put HyperCard with the rest of your applications on your hard disk.

For smoothest operation, however, it is best to place a special stack, called Home, either in the same folder level as HyperCard or in a folder at that level named HyperCard Stacks. HyperCard looks for the Home stack each time it starts, and looks for it in several well-defined places such as these.

If you have removed some fonts from your System file, you may be prompted to add them to make your Apple-supplied stacks look good. Those fonts are on one of the HyperCard disks, and may be dragged to the System file to install them.

Starting HyperCard

Start HyperCard by either double-clicking the HyperCard application, the Home stack, or any other HyperCard stack icon. If you double-click HyperCard, it automatically opens the Home stack as its starting point.

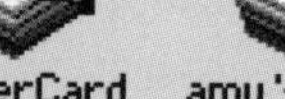

Stacks of Cards

HyperCard files are called stacks, each of which consists of one or more "cards." A card fills the window that appears on the screen. A stack file can be a single card (e.g., a stack that lets you enter values for a calculation) or thousands of cards (a corporate phone directory). While there is a first and last card of a stack, there is no stopping point at either end. They just keep going 'round and 'round.

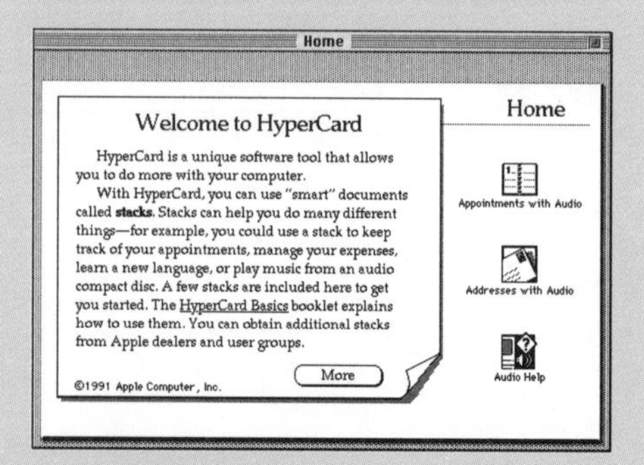

The Home Stack

Consider the Home stack as the launching pad for your HyperCard work. It is the familiar place to which you can always return, since most stacks have a button you can click that takes you directly to Home (or type *command-H*). The Home stack that comes with the 5-disk set has 12 buttons on its first card, each leading to a different sample stack supplied in that set. While you can click on a button in the Home stack to jump to another stack, the Home stack is not like the Finder. Buttons that are linked to other stacks have to be created by the user. In the 5-disk set Home stack, a menu item assists users in creating buttons that open other stacks or launch other applications.

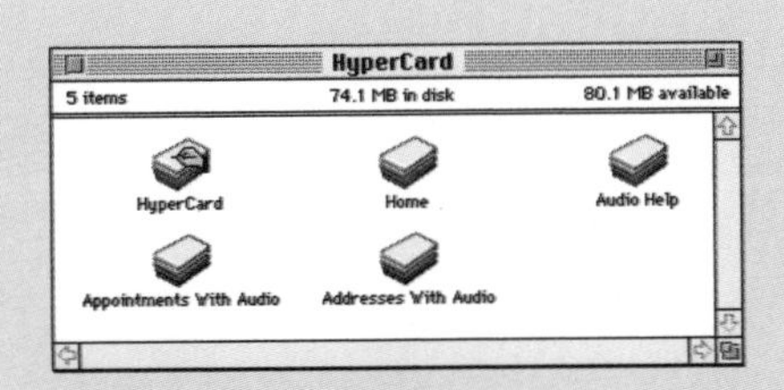

Supplied Stacks

In addition to the Home stack, the two-disk set comes with three other stacks that are both useful and serve as basic examples of information management stacks. The Appointments with Audio and Addresses with Audio stacks let you start accumulating personal information. In the Appointments stack, a card for each day of the year contains fields into which you type your appointments. The Addresses stack lets you create a new card for each entry, just like a card file. If you have a microphone (or audio digitizer, like the MacRecorder), you may also attach voice notes to each card.

Browsing Through a Stack

Navigating through the cards of a stacks is possible several ways. The **Go** menu is a key tool, allowing you to go to the **First, Last, Next,** and **Previous** cards with simple commands. Multiple-card stacks also usually have on-screen arrow buttons to simplify navigation.

Recent

The **Recent** command (in the **Go** menu) displays a dialog showing miniature pictures of the last 32 cards you've visited. Click on any picture to go directly to that card.

Message Box

By choosing **Message** from the **Go** menu (or typing *command-M*), you display the Message Box, a kind of communications window between you and HyperCard. You can use the Message Box to send commands to HyperCard. Try typing `go to next card` in the box and press *return*. That command takes you to the next card. This is part of the HyperTalk language ➔144-145. You can always type `go home` to take you back to the Home stack.

Opening Stacks

In addition to opening stacks by clicking on an icon button, you may also choose the **Open Stack** command in the **File** menu. When you check the Open stack in new window checkbox, the stack you choose will open in an overlapping window. You may open as many HyperCard windows as your HyperCard memory allocation allows ➔44.

Finding Information

HyperCard includes a generic text search command, called Find. Choose **Find** from the **Go** menu (or type *command-F*). The Message Box appears with the `Find` command already typed for you. Enter text to search between the quote marks, and press the *return* key. If no match is found, HyperCard beeps once. If it finds a match, HyperCard goes to that card, and draws a rectangle around the matching text. As long as that command remains in the Message Box, you can continue to press *return* to find the next match of that text in other cards. Like HyperCard stacks, the **Find** command continues 'round and 'round the stack.

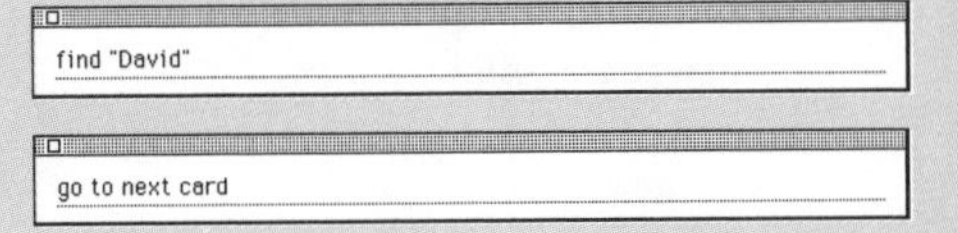

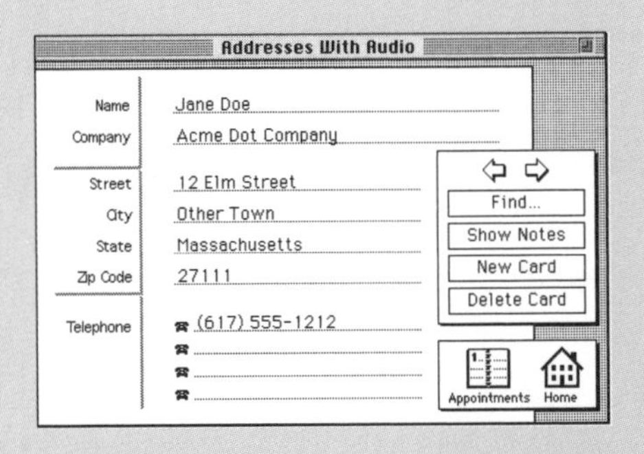

Marking Cards

Some stacks, like the Addresses stack, provide easy methods of marking cards. This is like setting an invisible flag that makes a card stand out from the rest. Marking cards is an inherent function of HyperCard. You can even issue the commands from the Message Box (e.g., **unmark all cards, mark this card**). Marking cards can help simplify navigation, by letting you go to only marked cards (e.g., those whose City field contains "Chicago.") The arrow buttons in the Addresses stack let you go to marked cards by holding down the *shift* key while clicking the button. You can also print only marked cards ➔140, so marking is a way of setting selection criteria.

Where's the Save Command?

HyperCard is different from most programs you use, because it automatically saves changes you make to a stack. As you enter information into a field and press the *tab* key to advance the cursor to the next field, HyperCard writes the changes to your hard disk. You see much disk activity while using HyperCard, primarily because it keeps your work safely stored on disk for you.

Converting Older Stacks

When you open a HyperCard stack, you may see a padlock to the right of the last menu. This means one of two things:

1. the stack is on a locked disk or CD-ROM; or
2. the stack was created using an earlier generation of HyperCard.

You may browse through stacks created with any version prior to HyperCard 2.0 without any problem (although there may be some small incompatibilities tied to changes in the HyperTalk language). But if you wish to enter information into

HyperCard offers many possibilities in sending a stack's information to a printer.

You may choose between printing images of entire cards (including the graphics) or just the text stored in fields. For printing just the text, a flexible report formatting facility gives you considerable control over layout of information on the page.

Printing the Current Card

You may print the card you're viewing by choosing **Print Card** in the **File** menu (or typing *command-P*). This command prints the current card in full size with no header or other control over the placement on the page.

Printing Cards

The **Print Stack** command in the **File** menu lets you print some or all cards in the stack. When you choose this command, HyperCard displays a dialog box revealing many choices for how large the card should be printed (this affects the number of cards printed on a sheet), margins, headers, and whether it should print all cards in the stack or just the **marked cards**. A full-size print of a standard HyperCard card (512 by 342 pixels) allows for two cards per sheet; the smallest, quarter size, prints 32 cards per page. The **Split-page format** option divides the page into two horizontally, showing you where a sheet would fold in two. Many choices you make are immediately reflected in the miniature page in the dialog box.

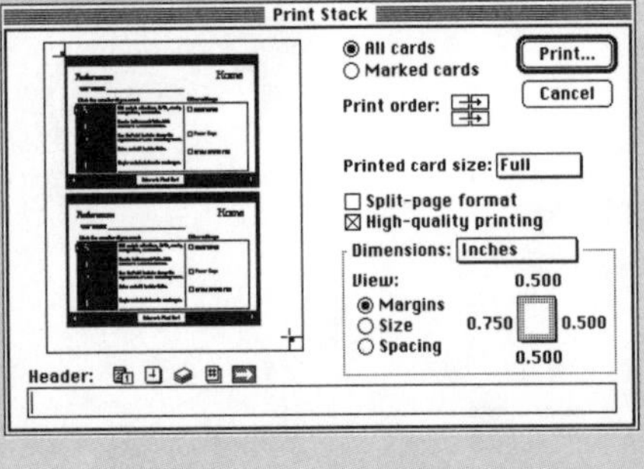

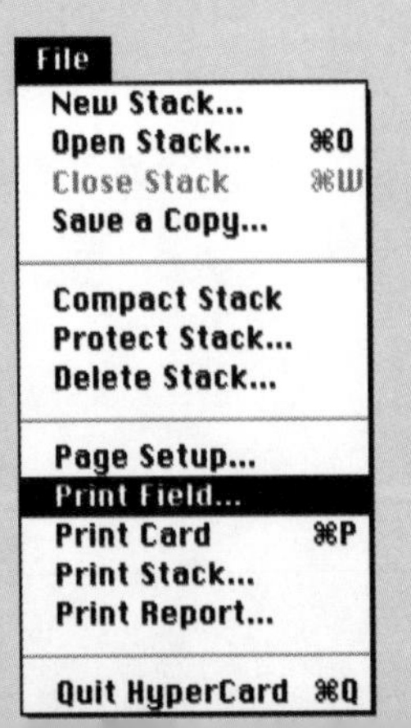

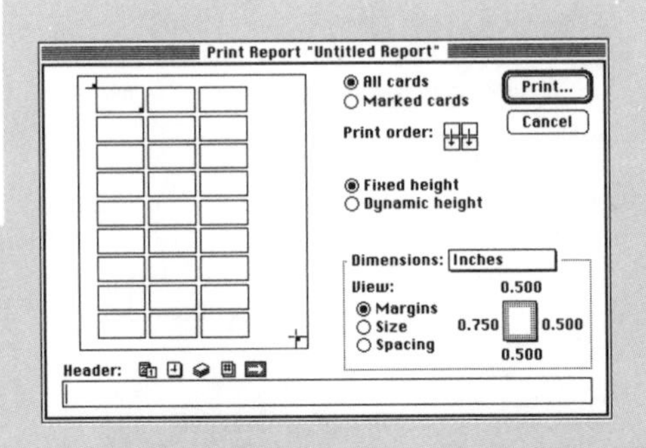

Printing Reports

HyperCard also prints just information from the cards without the card art. The **Print Report** command takes you to a dialog that lets you select and customize report formats. Pull down the **Reports** menu when the **Print Report** dialog is showing. In the Addresses stack, for example, you may choose from layouts designed for a plain listing, an address book, or any of a dozen label sizes.

To see details about how each card's data is to print in a report, choose **Report Items** from the **Edit** menu. Each field is represented as a report item, shown inside the dotted lines. Double-click on any item to see its connection to the fields on the card. For more details about report printing, see the manual in the **HyperCard Stack Development Kit** or ***The Complete HyperCard 2 Handbook*** (Bantam Books).

Print Headers

In the field at the bottom of the **Print Stack** and **Print Report** dialogs is a field for entering a header to be printed at the top of each page. In addition to any text you like, you may also click on the icons to insert (from left to right) the **date**, **time**, **stack file name**, **page number**, and a **tab**. The tab character works such that a single tab centers the items after the tab; a second tab right justifies items after the second tab. A miniature representation of the header is also shown in the mini-page to let you see what items go where.

In the two-disk HyperCard set, the sample stacks are set up to work with a third stack called Audio Help. Together the stacks allow users with Macintosh microphones or audio digitizers to attach voice notes to cards.

The audio facility was designed to work with other stacks besides those supplied with HyperCard.

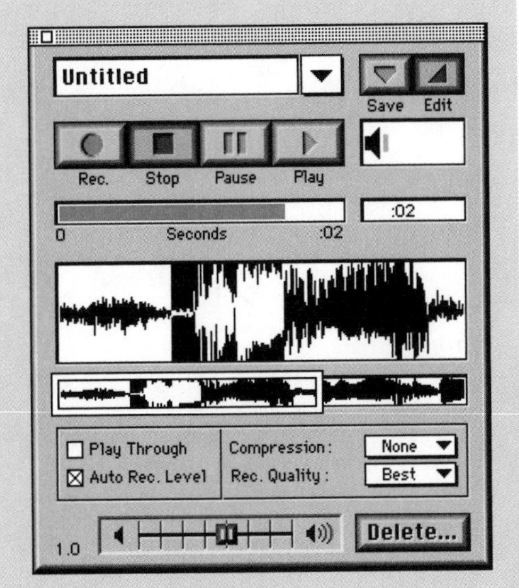

Required Hardware

Most of the recent Macintosh models come with a microphone, which plugs directly into the sound input port ➔8-9. Other Macintosh models require an audio digitizer, such as the Farallon **MacRecorder**, which connects to either the modem or printer port ➔9. Digitizers, such as the MacRecorder, require a special software driver to work with the latest system software. The driver installs into the Extensions folder.

Audio Palette

When you start the two-disk HyperCard set, it automatically adds audio-related items to the bottom of HyperCard's **Edit** menu. All control of audio is done by the Audio Help stack. When you choose **Add Audio Memo** from the **Edit** menu in either the Addresses or Appointments stack, the Audio Palette window appears atop the HyperCard window. This is a controller with buttons just like on a tape recorder.

Sound Level Meter

Test to make sure your microphone is connected properly by speaking into it. The voice level icon should show some vertical bars as you speak.

Record Button and Timer

To record a message click [Rec.]. As you see the timer bar begin to fill the space (you have about 15 seconds to record) and the elapsed timer start counting in the lower right, begin speaking your message. Click [Stop] when finished.

Play Button

Play the sound to make sure you captured all the sound you wanted by clicking [Play]. If you made a mistake, click [Rec.] to record over the previous sound.

Sound Name and Save Buttons

Select the Untitled name, and enter an identifying name for the message you just recorded. Then click **Save**. When you save a sound from the Audio palette, the sound is saved in the current stack and represented on the card by an icon button showing a speaker (in other stacks, it may just be a round rectangle button labeled with the name of the sound). Clicking the button plays the sound.

Sound Buttons

Buttons created by the Audio Palette share a few properties, whether they're the icon or round rectangle style. You can move a sound button simply by holding down the *option* key and dragging the button. To delete any sound button, hold down the *command* key and click the button. You'll be prompted to confirm the deletion. This action deletes both the button and the sound.

Playing All Sounds

When you click and hold the down arrow to the right of the sound name, the Audio Palette displays a pop up list of all the sounds it recorded in the current stack (as well as those stored in the Home and Audio Help stacks). Choose any one in the popup list, and click [Play] to hear the sound.

How Sounds Are Saved

The Audio Palette saves a recorded sound as a resource of type snd in the current stack. The sound button, therefore, is simply a pointer to that sound resource. When the palette creates the button, it actually writes a HyperTalk script for the button ➔144-145.

Editing Sounds

The Audio Palette serves as a good introduction to the concepts involved in digital recording and editing. If you click [Edit] in the Audio Palette, the palette expands to reveal more control over the recording process, as well as an editing area that lets you copy and paste segments of sounds as easily as text ➔156-159.

Sound and Memory

The **Audio Palette** stores recorded sound first in memory until you command it to save the sound to disk. The memory used for sound storage is whatever is left in the HyperCard memory partition ➔44. If you plan to record long audio tracks, consider lifting the partition to 1500K or more.

The Audio Palette records at two sampling rates, **22 kHz** and **11 kHz** (listed as Best and Good, respectively, in the editing portion of the palette, below). Five seconds of speech at 22 kHz requires 110K of free memory, but only 55K at 11 kHz.

When saved to disk, sound recorded in the Best mode can also be compressed to conserve disk space. Three-to-one compression reduces the five second high quality sound to less than 37K; six-to-one compression brings it close to only 18K. Some quality is lost in the compression and decompression, however.

The authoring and scripting possibilities of HyperCard are hidden on the two-disk set, but easily restored.

The reason for hiding the more advanced levels is to prevent casual users from making inadvertent and perhaps damaging changes to their copies of the stacks—rendering their HyperCard unusable.

HyperCard authoring refers to creation and modification of stacks without getting into the HyperTalk scripting language. By creating or copying and pasting art for the backgrounds of cards, buttons, and fields, you can begin making stacks without any programming.

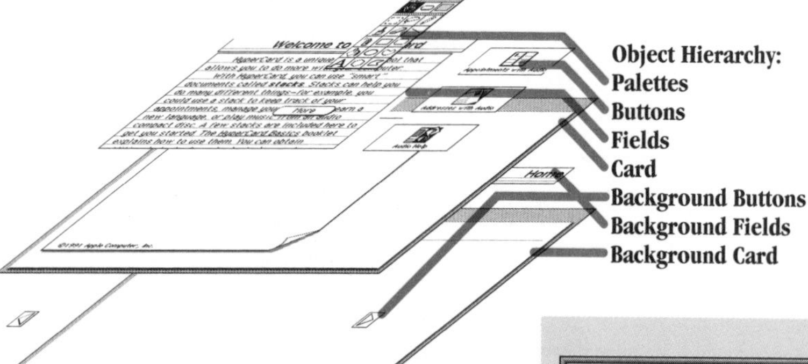

magic

User Levels

HyperCard reveals more of itself as you increase the user level. In the two-disk set, the user level is adjusted on the last card of the stack (from the Home card, choose **Prev** from the **Go** menu or type *command-2*). If you see only two user levels, the other three are hidden by blank buttons. To hide the blank buttons, display the Message Box (*command-M*), type the word magic, and press the *return* key. Voilà! HyperCard now has five user levels. Click on any number to adjust the user level. Most HyperCard users keep the level set to 5. To restore the blank buttons, enter the magic password again.

User Name

Enter your name into the field at the top of the card. Some HyperCard stacks use that name as an identifier for printing and other processes.

Blind Typing

Check the Blind Typing box. This allows you to type into the Message Box even when the box is hidden.

Background Name:
Background ID: 5874
Background shared by 1 card.
Contains 0 background fields.
Contains 0 background buttons.
☐ Don't Search Background
☐ Can't Delete Background
Script... OK Cancel

Card Name:
Card number: 3 out of 7
Card ID: 6027
Contains 1 card field.
Contains 4 card buttons.
☐ Card Marked
☐ Don't Search Card
☐ Can't Delete Card
Script... OK Cancel

Card Anatomy

Everything you see in a HyperCard card—art, each button, each field—exists in its own layer. It's like several clear acetate sheets—each with some element on it—piled atop each other. These layers also exist in two domains: **background** and **card**.

The background domain contains elements that are shared from card to card. This includes the background art—the very bottom layer—as well as background buttons and fields that appear on every card.

The card domain contains elements that are unique to a single card. For example, in the Addresses stack, you might include a card button only on Nancy's card that links to a map to her house. A click of that button opens a graphics program and the map file she gave you.

As you add buttons and fields to each domain, they pile on top of earlier ones. Fortunately, you can change the order of these elements. Art, however, always remains at the bottom of the background and card domains.

Editing the Background

Whenever you want art or other elements to go into the background domain, you must be sure you are in the background editing mode. To turn this mode on and off, choose **Background** from the **Edit** menu (or type *command-B*). When in background editing mode, the menubar displays diagonal marks as a visual reminder.

Tools

When you lift the user level to **3** or higher, the **Tools** menu appears to the right of the **Go** menu. This is a tear-off menu. Click and drag away from the menu. The tools become a self-contained palette, allowing easy access to the tools.

The Tools palette is divided into two sections. The top contains three tools: **Browse, Button,** and **Field**. Except when working with buttons and fields (in which case those tools are selected), you want to be in the Browse tool to navigate through stacks, click buttons, and enter text into fields.

Below the dividing line are fifteen painting tools. HyperCard comes with a built-in bit mapped graphics painting program ➔130 for creating and editing black and white art (color may be available in versions later than 2.1).

Creating a New Stack

The **New Stack** command in the **File** menu lets you generate a new stack file. If you see a card style (including buttons, fields, and art) that you'd like to start with in your own stack, click the **Copy current background** checkbox in the file dialog. You may select a different size for the stack by dragging the lower right handle on the small replica of the card. Depending on your HyperCard memory allocation, you can create cards as large as 1280-by-1280 pixels.

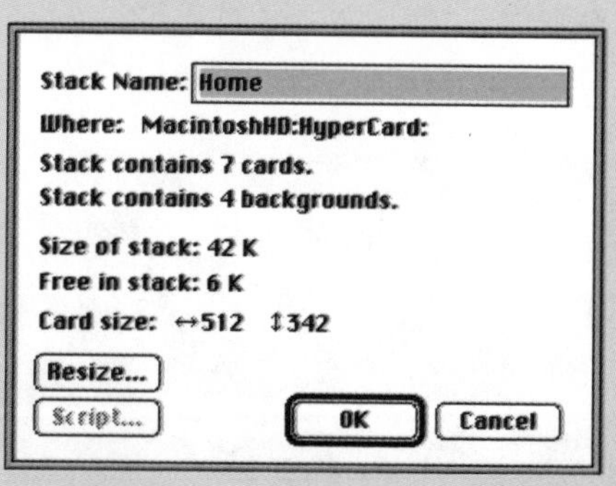

Information Dialogs

Under the **Objects** menu are commands that let you explore and manipulate HyperCard's objects—**stack, background, card, field,** and **button**. Whenever you encounter one of these objects, you can learn a lot about it by checking its information dialog box. Choose the desired **Info** item from the **Objects** menu.

Stack Info

Here you learn how many cards and backgrounds (a stack can have multiple backgrounds) a stack has, as well as how large it is in memory and screen size.

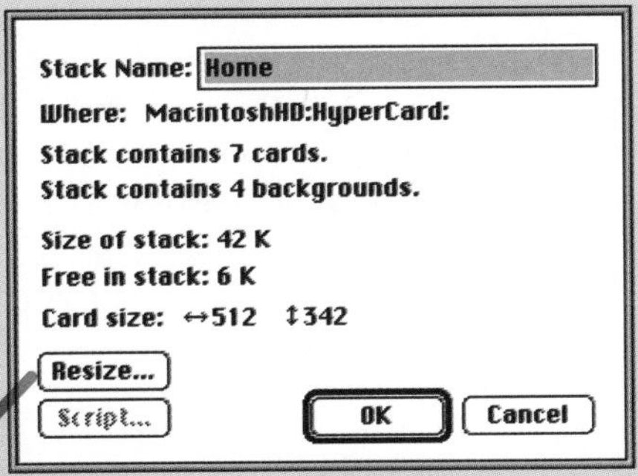

Background Info

You can find out how many cards are in a particular background, and how many fields and buttons are in the current background.

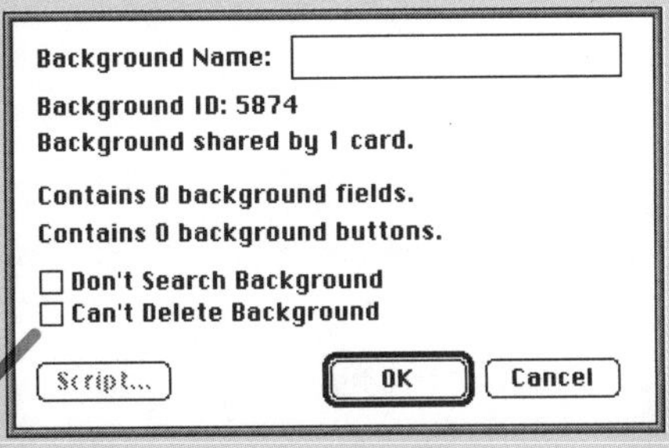

Card Info

Elements of the card domain for the current card are listed in this dialog. Here, too, is where you can see if a card is marked ➔139.

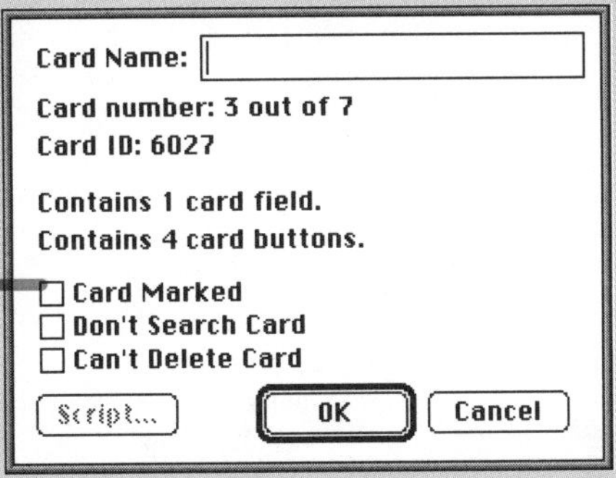

Button Info

To check a button's information, first choose the Button tool in the Tool Palette. All buttons will now show their rectangular outlines. Click once on a button, and choose **Button Info** from the **Objects** menu (or just double-click on the button). Buttons have many properties, which are set in this dialog. Notice how easily you can change a button's style to a shadow or radio button.

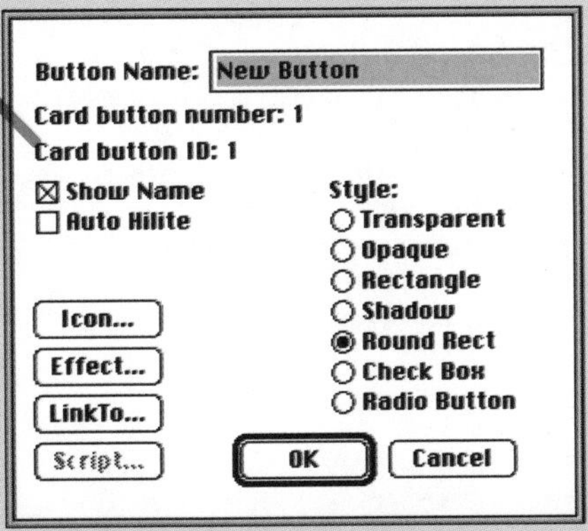

Stack Name: Home
Where: MacintoshHD:HyperCard:
Stack contains 7 cards.
Stack contains 4 backgrounds.
Size of stack: 42 K
Free in stack: 6 K
Card size: ↔512 ↕342
Resize... Script... OK Cancel

Background Name:
Background ID: 5874
Background shared by 1 card.
Contains 0 background fields.
Contains 0 background buttons.
☐ Don't Search Background
☐ Can't Delete Background
Script... OK Cancel

Card Name:
Card number: 3 out of 7
Card ID: 6027
Contains 1 card field.
Contains 4 card buttons.
☐ Card Marked
☐ Don't Search Card
☐ Can't Delete Card
Script... OK Cancel

Button Name: New Button
Card button number: 1
Card button ID: 1
☒ Show Name
☐ Auto Hilite
Style: ○ Transparent ○ Opaque ○ Rectangle ○ Shadow ◉ Round Rect ○ Check Box ○ Radio Button
Icon... Effect... LinkTo... Script... OK Cancel

Visual Effect

If the button normally takes you to another card, click [Effect...] to choose a visual effect that appears during the transition between cards. There are 25 effects, and in four speeds to choose from.

Setting a Link

If you want a button to take you to a different card (or stack), click [LinkTo...]. A small window (a windoid style) lets you navigate to the desired card. Then click [This Card]. **The process actually writes a navigation script in the original button.**

Field Info

To check a field's information, first choose the **Field** tool from the Tool Palette. All fields will now show their rectangular outlines. Click once on a field, and choose **Field Info** from the **Objects** menu (or just double-click on the field). Fields have five style choices and up to eight properties that you can set from this dialog.

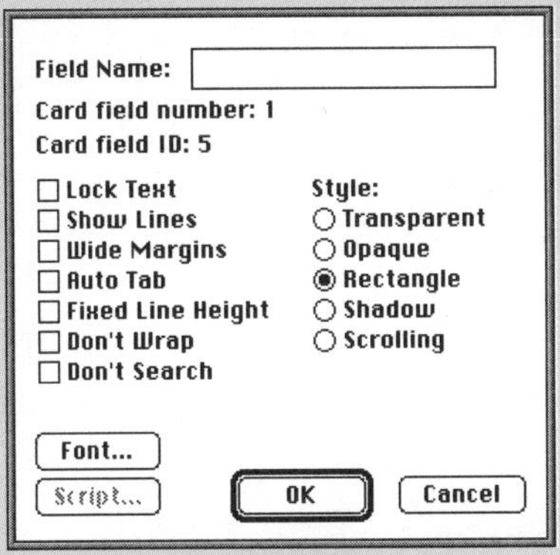

Field Name:
Card field number: 1
Card field ID: 5
☐ Lock Text ☐ Show Lines ☐ Wide Margins ☐ Auto Tab ☐ Fixed Line Height ☐ Don't Wrap ☐ Don't Search
Style: ○ Transparent ○ Opaque ◉ Rectangle ○ Shadow ○ Scrolling
Font... Script... OK Cancel

Creating New Buttons and Fields

Before creating a new button or field, decide in which domain you want the button. Choose **Background** from the **Edit** menu if the object should go into the background. Then choose **New Button** or **New Field** from the **Objects** menu. This automatically chooses the tool for the new object and creates an object with default styles. Double-click the object to open the info dialog and adjust any properties. After closing the dialog, drag and resize the object as you like.

Copying and Pasting Objects

When you select a button or field with its respective tool, you can then copy or cut the object with the **Edit** menu tools. Once in the Clipboard, the object may then be pasted into a different card or stack. The same goes for cards, but **Copy Card** and **Delete Card** are separate **Edit** menu items. A card in the Clipboard also includes the card's background domain.

Readymade Object Treasure Chest

The five-disk HyperCard set includes valuable stacks for **authoring.** Two stacks feature collections of **readymade buttons** and **fields**, each with scripting already built into the objects. All you do is copy and paste the objects into your stacks.

About Copyrights

While HyperCard makes it relatively easy to copy and paste art, buttons, and fields from other stacks into yours, you should not ignore copyright issues. When you are using the new stack for your own use, there is no problem borrowing elements from copyrighted material. But if you intend to distribute

To experienced HyperCard users, the HyperTalk scripting language is where the bulk of HyperCard's power lies.

HyperTalk is called a scripting language (as opposed to a programming language), because each object in a HyperCard stack can have its own lines of HyperTalk—snippets of code that pertain just to that object. It's like a cast of a play, with each character having his or her own lines. When the characters say their lines in an ensemble, the result is a story.

HyperTalk is predominantly in plain English. If you read a script out loud, you can usually understand what is going on. Most of what happens in a script is moving information from one place to another (usually changing that information along the way), setting properties of objects to change their characteristics, and navigating from one card to another.

There's much more, of course. With **customized menus, multiple windows,** and **variable font styles** in text fields, you can create applications that look like true Macintosh programs.

Messages

At the root of HyperTalk is the concept of messages and the hierarchy of objects. HyperCard sends all kinds of messages as you use it. For example, when you click on a HyperCard button, HyperCard sends a series of messages to that button that indicate mouse action on that button. First it sends a `mouseDown` message, meaning that you pressed the mouse button with the cursor on that button. If you immediately release the mouse button, HyperCard sends a `mouseUp` message. The button can contain a script that intercepts that message and performs some action in response to the mouse activity. That button might have a script that says

```
on mouseUp
  go to next card
end mouseUp
```

Every time you click on that button, the script takes you to the next card.

HyperCard sends dozens of messages for a variety of actions—bringing a card into view, closing a stack, moving a window, even pressing a keyboard key. As a scripter, you can intercept any of these messages with individual message handlers (a button script can contain many message handlers).

Here is a table of the most common HyperCard messages and what causes them to be sent:

Messages	Action That Sends Message
mouseDown	Pressing the mouse button
mouseStillDown	Holding the mouse button down
mouseUp	Releasing the mouse button
openStack	Opening the stack
resumeStack	Bringing an already open stack to the front
openCard	Bringing a card into view by navigating to it
openField	Tabbing to or clicking into a text field
closeField	Removing the text pointer from a field after changing the text

go next card

Object Hierarchy

There is an order to the way messages are sent and passed from object to object in a HyperCard stack. HyperCard sends messages to a relevant object (e.g., mouseUp message to a button you click on), but then the message continues up a hierarchy along a prescribed path: button to card to background to stack to Home stack to HyperCard itself. A handler can intercept the message at any point along this path. All it needs is a script that begins with the word "`on`" and the name of the message.

If there is a handler to intercept the message, the message goes no further (unless instructed to by the handler); if the message goes all the way to HyperCard, no action results from that message.

The Script Editor

To enter or edit a script in an object, you must bring the script editor window into view. Every object information dialog box ➜143 has a Script button, which opens the script editor window and displays the script of that object. You may open as many script editor windows to different objects as your HyperCard memory allocation allows.

Comments

When you open existing scripts and see lines or portions of lines starting with two dashes (`--`), it means that whatever follows is a comment. Scripters enter comments to help them and script readers understand what is happening in a script. HyperCard ignores comments when executing scripts.

HyperTalk Commands

Inside a message handler, you issue commands to move information, go to other cards, and so on. You can experiment with individual commands in the Message Box. Go to the Addresses stack, create a new card, and type the following commands into the Message Box (be sure to press *return* after entering each command)

```
go to previous card
go to next card
put "George" into field "Name"
put "10101" into field "Zip"
```

The first two commands navigated through the stack. The second two entered text into two text fields—the fields on the card called **Name** and **Zip** (choose the Field tool and double click on a field to see its name in the **Field Info** dialog box).

Here is a table of common commands, what they do, and an example of each:

Command	What It Does
go	Navigates to another card or stack
go to card 20	
put	Copies information from one place to another
put "Acme" into background field "Company"	
find	Searches for a match (see Finding text, ➜122)
find "Fred"	
hide	Hides an object
hide card button "Next"	
show	Shows an object
show background button "View Map"	

Variables

When you work with information (text or numbers) in a handler, the information has to be in a container while you work on it. Temporary containers you can use and discard are called **local variables** (local because they're used only in a single handler and forgotten when the handler finishes its stuff). You can assign any one-word name to a variable. Here is a series of commands that use a variable called oneName to carry information from one stack to another:

```
put field "Name" into oneName
go to stack "Friends"
doMenu "New Card"
put oneName into field "Friend's Name"
```

You can also use a special HyperTalk variable, called **It,** as a shortcut for putting information into a variable:

```
get field "Name" -- the information is now in It
go to stack "Friends"
doMenu "New Card"
put it into field "Friend's Name"
```

Functions

A **function** is like a command, but it also returns information in the process. For example, show the Message Box and type the function:

```
the date
```

Immediately, HyperCard returns the date as derived from the Macintosh's internal clock. You can substitute a function for the value it returns in a command line, such as

```
put the date into field 2
```

Here is a table of common HyperTalk functions and examples of the values they return:

Function	Returned Value
the date	9/11/91
the long date	Wednesday, September 11, 1991
the time	5:10 PM
the mouseLoc	200,150 (screen coordinates of pointer)
the number of cards	12

Properties

In HyperCard, as in the real world, every object has numerous properties. Just as a door has **properties** (its height, width, thickness, material, finish), so does a HyperCard button (**height, width, location, name, style, icon,** and **more**). Most properties (there are more than one hundred throughout HyperCard) can be set in an object's information dialog box, but all properties can be retrieved or set with **HyperTalk.** For example, a script might check the hilite property of a checkbox style button to see if the button is checked. If so, then the script branches in one direction, otherwise it performs different operations. You can view or set properties from the Message Box. With the Addresses stack showing, type these into the **Message Box** and press *return*:

```
userLevel of HyperCard
commandChar of menuItem "Last" of menu "Go"
rectangle of card window
size of this stack
name of this background
number of this card
textFont of field "Name"
style of background button "Show Notes"
```

Now, using some shortcut terminology, try changing a button style and resetting it from the Message Box:

```
set style of bg btn "Show Notes" to roundRect
set style of bg btn "Show Notes" to rectangle
```

How to Learn HyperTalk

You'll need some form of documentation to learn the HyperTalk language. The ***HyperTalk Script Language Guide*** in the HyperCard 5-disk upgrade or Stack Development Kit is a reliable reference to the language syntax. The ***Complete HyperCard 2 Handbook*** (Bantam Books) by the author of this book provides more examples and hands-on experience for all facets of HyperCard.

With those tools in hand, start looking at scripts in every stack you can get open. Follow the logic and execution of each handler, and make sure you understand every element along the way. Local Macintosh **user groups** have plenty of members who are experienced with HyperCard and can help you.

Writing a Button Handler

Using the Addresses stack, you can create an additional button that clones the current card, and selects the Name field for you to quickly enter cards for multiple people at the same company. Before you start working on the new button, be sure to save a backup copy of the Addresses stack if you have stored your information in there.

The first steps involve copying an existing button so you don't have to reset all the properties to match.

1. Choose the Button tool.
2. Hold down the *option* key
3. Click and drag the button to the upper left corner. This action (dragging with the *option* key) actually peeled off a copy of the button, leaving the original intact.
4. Double-click the new [Find...].
5. Change the button name to **"Clone Card."**

Now it's time to remove the old script and enter a new one.

1. Click on [Script].
2. Choose **Select All** from the **Edit** menu (or type *command-A*).
3. Press the *delete* key to remove the existing script.
4. Type the following handler into the script editor window (you don't have to type the comments):

```
on mouseUp
  set cursor to watch  -- show user something is happening
  doMenu "Copy Card"   -- copies current card and data into Clipboard
  doMenu "Paste Card"  -- pastes Clipboard card after the one copied
  select text of field "Name" -- selects Name text, ready for new name
end mouseUp
```

5. Choose **Save Script** from the **File** menu (or type *command-S*).
6. Close the script editor window.

Click on [Clone Card] to activate the script.

XCMDs

The HyperTalk scripting language is intended to provide the functionality that a majority of stack authors need. For some authors, HyperTalk lacks certain desired commands. Fortunately, HyperCard

You install an XCMD with the help of a resource

Printing 146

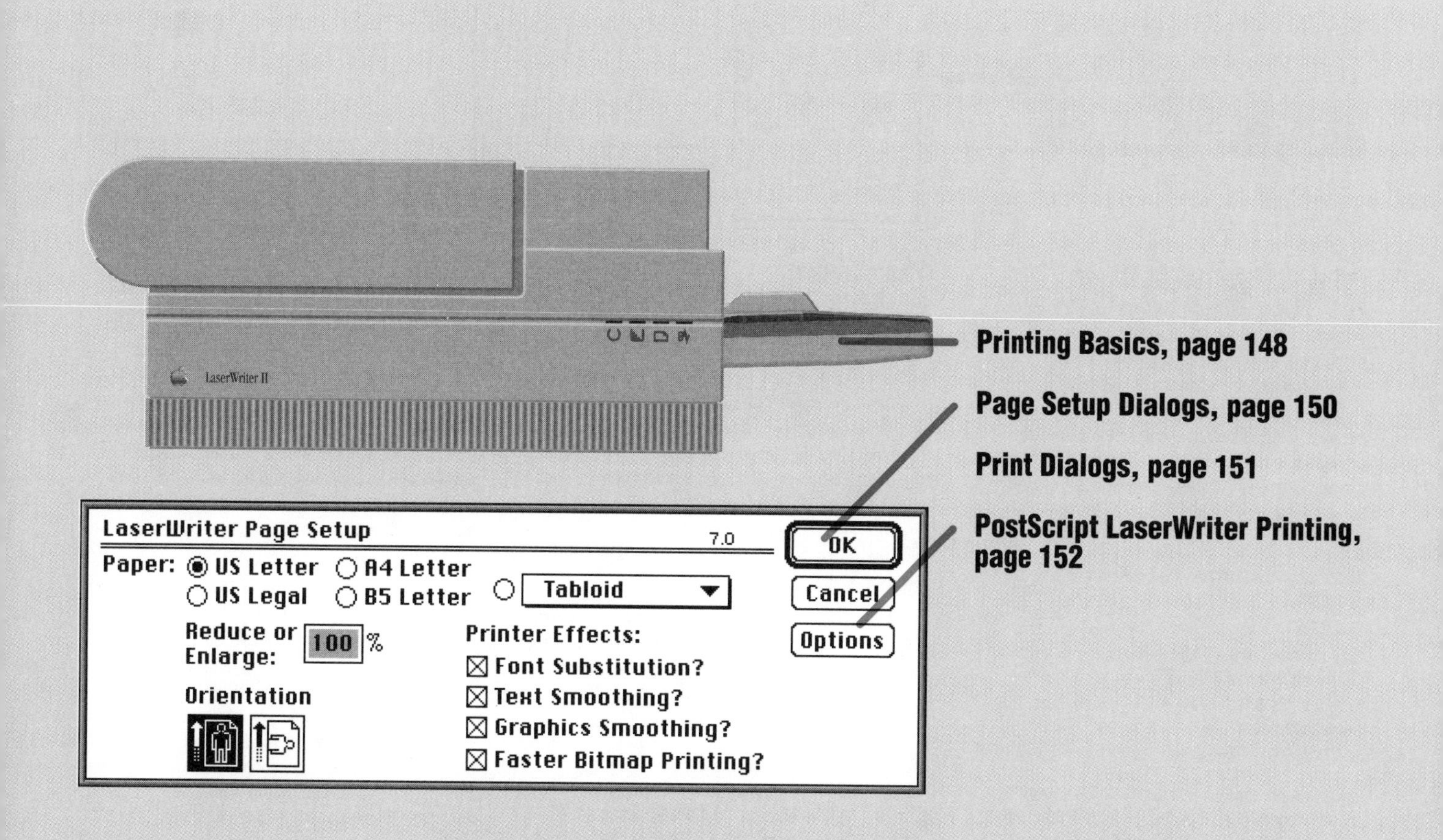
LaserWriter II
Printing Basics, page 148
Page Setup Dialogs, page 150
Print Dialogs, page 151
PostScript LaserWriter Printing, page 152
LaserWriter Page Setup
7.0
OK
Paper: US Letter A4 Letter
US Legal B5 Letter
Tabloid
Cancel
Reduce or Enlarge: 100 %
Printer Effects:
Options
Font Substitution?
Text Smoothing?
Orientation
Graphics Smoothing?
Faster Bitmap Printing?

Once you establish a routine for printing documents the process goes smoothly—barring hardware oriented things like paper jams. But getting into that routine can be difficult at first because it often requires steps that are not at all intuitive.

Macintosh printing is a joint effort linking elements from applications programs, system software, and the printer into a printing team. In the case of PostScript-equipped printers, the printer, itself, is a powerful computer, sometimes more powerful than the Macintosh to which it is connected.

Despite the differences among Apple printers, the basic printing process is similar across the board. You must go through the same basic steps for all. After that, you're only a *command-P* (**Print** command) away from sending a document to the printer.

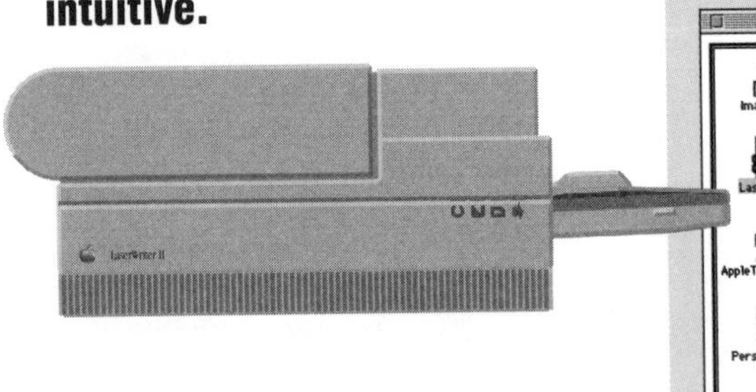

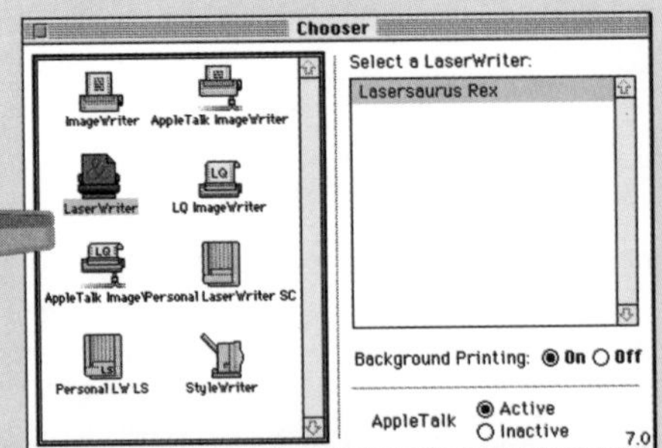

Chooser
ImageWriter
Select a port:
AppleTalk
Active
Inactive
7.0

Printing System Software

For the Macintosh to communicate with your printer, a specially-configured extension file for that printer must be in the **Extensions Folder** (in the System Folder). This file is also called a printer driver. When you install system software, the Installer program often copies every one of the printer drivers in the system software's printer disk to your Extensions folder. At the release of System 7, for example, that included drivers for the following printers:

AppleTalk (networked) ImageWriter
ImageWriter (direct connect)
LaserWriter
LQ AppleTalk ImageWriter
LQ ImageWriter
Personal LaserWriter SC
Personal LaserWriter LS
StyleWriter

Even though Apple no longer produces some of these printers, it acknowledges that these printers are still connected in the Macintosh community. It continues to supply updated printer drivers for discontinued printers.

If you do not intend to print to some of the printers whose drivers are installed in your Extensions folder, you may drag them to the Trash. Some of these drivers are rather large, so you could free up a few hundred kilobytes of disk space.

The Chooser

Before you can print any document, you must instruct your Macintosh to use a specifc printer driver, even if there is only one installed in your Extensions folder. The program that lets you do this is a **desk accessory** called the Chooser, found in the menu. Once you choose a printer, you won't have to access the Chooser for this operation until you change printers or system software versions. Each time you run the Installer to update your system software, you must re-choose the printer, because the updated Chooser doesn't have your previous setting.

What is confusing about the Chooser is that the next time you open it, you won't see your printer selected as you might expect. Unless you've reinstalled the Chooser or printer driver, however, the previous setting is still in force.

AppleTalk Settings

In the Chooser are radio button settings for AppleTalk, the Macintoshs built-in networking facility. Check **Active** if you are connected to other computers or a networked printer. This is the switch that makes your computer a member of the network. If you are a standalone Macintosh using a non-networked printer, turn off AppleTalk from here to free up some additional memory.

Choosing a Non-Networked Printer

Select the **Chooser** in the menu to bring up the Chooser window. Click on the printer driver that matches your printer model. In the rectangle on the right are two buttons representing the modem and printer serial ports ➔8-9. Click on the icon of the port to which your printer is connected. Most printers can work connected to either port. Then close the Chooser window by clicking in the close box in the upper left corner. An alert box may advise you to examine the Page Setup settings.

Choosing a Networked Printer

If you are connected to a network, and that network has more than one zone ➔162-163, you see a list of available zones in a list at the lower left. Network administrators typically divide large networks into zones along departmental lines—one zone for the Sales department, for example, even if there are more than one printer or server in that zone. Click on the networked printer icon in the **Chooser,** and then the zone (if applicable). In the right-hand box appears a list of the names of all printers in the selected zone. You must choose a printer from the list by clicking on the name. If you don't choose a printer, your application won't know where to send the document for printing.

Networked LaserWriter printers allow you to turn on background printing. This uses the Print Monitor application ➔ 153, and frees up the computer for you while the computer and printer communicate in the background.

LaserWriter Page Setup 7.0
Paper: US Letter, A4 Letter, US Legal, B5 Letter, Tabloid
Reduce or Enlarge: 100 %
Orientation
Printer Effects:
☒ Font Substitution?
☒ Text Smoothing?
☒ Graphics Smoothing?
☒ Faster Bitmap Printing?
OK
Cancel
Options

Page Setup

Most of the time, you won't have to adjust settings in the **Page Setup** dialog ➔150. All programs that print (including the Finder) have a **Page Setup** item in the **File** menu to let you access these settings. If you intend to make changes to any settings, do so before working on the document, because these changes often affect how a program defines page breaks, margins, and other settings for documents.

Many programs enhance the **Page Setup** dialog box to include settings beyond the standard ones. For example, a word processing program may let you set the name of a file that follows the current one in a sequence of chapters: you can adjust page numbering for each file so that as multiple documents print, the page numbering is sequential across files. Page setup settings are often saved with the document, so you don't have to keep resetting the dialog each time you open the document.

Printing Sideways (Landscape)

If you want the document to print sideways on the page, you can change the page orientation setting in the **Page Setup** dialog. Click the landscape button. Then be sure the page breaks and margins are set in your document to accommodate the different orientation.

The Print Dialog Box

The last step before sending a document to the printer is to acknowledge settings in the **Print** dialog box ➔151. Details of this dialog differ from printer to printer. Moreover, many programs add custom items to this dialog that apply only to that program.

Printing a Finder Window

To print the contents of a folder or disk, you can print any Finder window. You can get the contents of an entire disk by viewing the disk window in a text listing and expanding all the folders. Then choose **Print Window** from the **File** menu. Similarly, you can print icon views of any folder or disk if you prefer.

Printing a Screen

While earlier versions of system software allowed ImageWriter owners to print the current screen directly, that is no longer the case. All users can print any screen, however. Simply type *command-shift-3* to save the screen to a picture file. Then open the picture file in TeachText or other program capable of opening PICT files ➔131. Choose **Print** from the program's **File** menu to send the screen to the printer. If the screen picture opens in the program sideways or extends beyond the right margin, choose the landscape printing mode from the Page **Setup dialog.** The picture is too wide to print in the portrait orientation.

Printing Documents from the Finder

You don't have to open an application to print documents created with that program. In the Finder, you may select one or more documents (even from different programs) and choose the **Print** command in the **File** menu. The Finder automatically launches each document's program, opens the document, and issues the **Print** command for that program. For each document, you must confirm the **Print** dialog box, allowing you to make any adjustments for each document. Most programs return to the Finder after printing, but don't be surprised if some leave you in the program.

Printing Documents from Applications

Every program that creates documents has one or more print commands in its **File** menu. The commands usually refer to the document in the active window. A **Print** dialog box appears. This is a good place to double check that the correct printer is set in the Chooser before printing. At the top of the **Print** dialog box is the name of the printer selected in the Chooser. If the printer is the wrong one, cancel printing, and go to the Chooser to remedy the situation.

Looking for LaserWriter "Kiwi".

status: preparing data

status: starting job

user: Nathan; document: LW page setup; status: processing job

Print Progress Messages

As a document prints, the Macintosh keeps you informed of the progress. Details vary with both the printer and the program, since the program author controls most of the messaging between the printing process and you. For example, programs usually let you know which page number of a document is printing at any moment.

Networked LaserWriters also furnish feedback about the printer status in a window at the top of the screen (this happens only when background printing is turned off). These messages may seem cryptic, but they actually keep you well informed. For instance, the alert always tells you which LaserWriter you're attempting to print on. When successfully communicating with the printer, the Macintosh then shows you the various steps in the process—initializing the printer, waiting for another document to finish printing, or actually printing. This alert is also where error messages from the printer come back—paper tray empty, paper tray missing, communications errors.

When using background printing, these messages are displayed for you in the Print Monitor program ➔153. If Print Monitor is not the active application, the Application menu icon flashes with the Print Monitor icon alerting you to check Print Monitor for a printer problem or prompt (e.g., insert a manually fed piece of paper).

Printing Speed

How fast a printer produces pages is largely controlled by the mechanics of the printer—how fast the print head slides from side to side or how quickly the laser writes to the printer's rotating drum. By and large, the Macintosh works faster than most printers it connects to. The exception is when printing graphics on some printers. When a LaserWriter, for example, must print a large bit map, the printer circuitry takes awhile to convert the graphics to PostScript. Scaling graphics and working with graphical images can also take extra time. It's not unusual for complex graphics pages to take many minutes per page, while straight text in a single font can come out at 8 pages per minute on most laser printers.

The Page Setup dialog is a catch-all place to make adjustments to the way text and images meet the sheet of paper.

Most importantly, this is where you designate the size or type of paper going through the printer, and whether images should be printed in portrait (tall) or landscape (sideways) modes. Each printer type (selected in the Chooser) has its own Page Setup dialog box, with extra settings that pertain to the peculiarities of that printer. Page Setup settings are saved with each document.

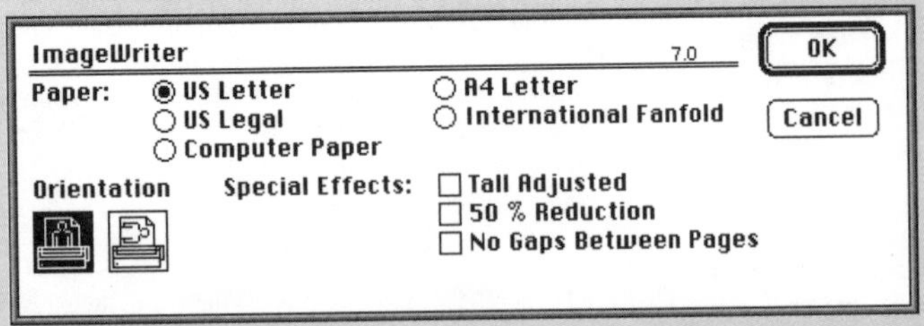

ImageWriter 7.0
OK
Cancel
Paper: US Letter / US Legal / Computer Paper / A4 Letter / International Fanfold
Orientation
Special Effects: Tall Adjusted / 50 % Reduction / No Gaps Between Pages

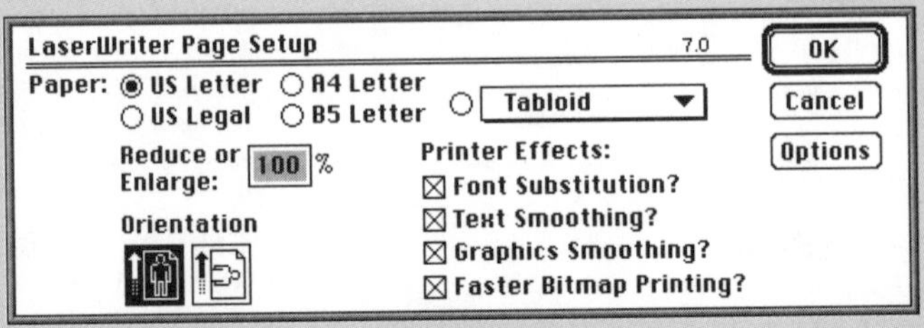

LaserWriter Page Setup 7.0
OK
Cancel
Options
Paper: US Letter / US Legal / A4 Letter / B5 Letter / Tabloid
Reduce or Enlarge: 100 %
Orientation
Printer Effects: Font Substitution? / Text Smoothing? / Graphics Smoothing? / Faster Bitmap Printing?

Setup Pages Early

For many programs, Page Setup dialog settings significantly affect the document page size and orientation on the screen. Most documents use the default settings, so you only have to change settings for non-standard documents. If you are producing a document that you intend to print, it is important to make Page Setup dialog choices before you start entering information into a new document.

Paper Size

Each printer type lists its own complement of paper sizes that it can accommodate. All printers handle U.S. letter and legal sizes, plus the European A4 page. The ImageWriter's Computer Paper setting is for the wide carriage ImageWriter, which is capable of handling 15-inch wide fanfold (greenbar) paper.

Envelopes

Laser printers and the StyleWriter require that envelopes be fed in special locations in the manual feed slot. These locations assume you have chosen the proper envelope paper setting in the Page Setup dialog. This is especially tricky on laser printers, which have a variety of center and edge feed locations. Consult your printer's manual for special instructions on envelopes.

Orientation

Two icons show two page orientations: tall (**portrait**) and sideways (**landscape**). In landscape printing the page feeds through the printer as always, but the image is rotated 90 degrees to the right.

Image Size

Each printer has its own possibilities for reducing or enlarging images. Non-PostScript printers present a limited range of reduction sizes—those that optimize the printer's technology for undistorted reductions. PostScript printers, however, can be told to reduce or enlarge in one-percent increments.

ImageWriter Tall Adjusted

To correct for the slight differences in resolution between the ImageWriter and the Macintosh screen, the Tall Adjusted special effect makes sure that graphic images are not stretched vertically, as they would be if not adjusted. Check this choice when the document contains graphics.

Precision Bitmap Alignment (4% Reduction)

Several printers offer an adjustment for bit map alignment. By reducing the printed image 4%, 72 dot-per-inch graphic images are printed in an even multiple of 72 dots on higher resolution printers. Thus, a screen pixel is not distorted on a 300 dpi printer.

Font Substitution

PostScript laser printers can convert a few Macintosh screen fonts to the printer's built-in PostScript fonts (New York to Times; Geneva to Helvetica; Monaco to Courier). While you're likely to get better text characters with the PostScript fonts, the character spacing won't be what you expect. If you want PostScript fonts, set the font accordingly in your document.

Smoothing

Laser printers are capable of mathematically filling in the jagged edges on bit mapped text and graphics. The results aren't always perfect, so you may want to compare output with smoothing on and off to see which one works best for you. When printing Macintosh screen pictures, it is best to turn off Graphics Smoothing.

Faster Bitmap Printing

Because bit maps must be converted to PostScript before being printed on a PostScript printer, you should have the fastest computer do the conversion. With **Faster Bitmap Printing** turned on, your Macintosh does the conversion before sending the data to the printer. Not all programs, however, let the Macintosh do this. If you can't get any output from the printer, try turning this option off.

LaserWriter Options

This button leads to another dialog of additional options specifically for PostScript LaserWriters. See pages ➔152-153 for more details, or click the button and turn on Balloon Help to see rudimentary instructions.

Custom Page Setups

A number of programs add items to the standard Page Setup dialog. These items tend to reflect the special needs of documents generated by the application. A spreadsheet program, for example, might present fields for entering headers and footers, as well as checkboxes for whether row and column headings or the grid lines should be printed with the columns of numbers.

The Print dialog box is the last dialog you usually see after initiating the printing process.

Items in this dialog tend to be specifications that can frequently change from printing to printing of a document—**number of copies, page range, print quality** (on non-laser printers), and **paper feed.** Many programs also add more items to enhance the choices available for printing the current document.

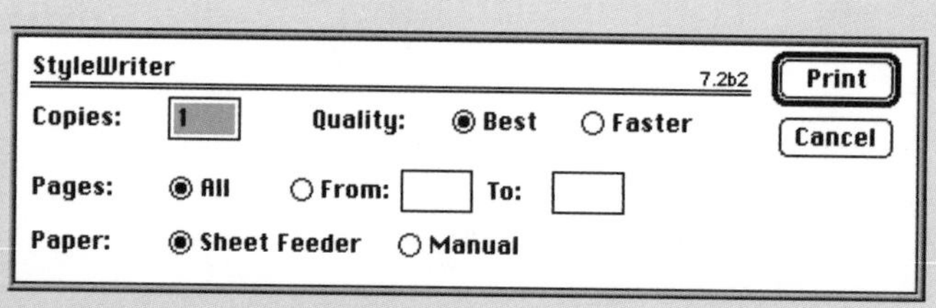

StyleWriter 7.2b2 Print
Copies: 1 Quality: ◉ Best ○ Faster Cancel
Pages: ◉ All ○ From: To:
Paper: ◉ Sheet Feeder ○ Manual

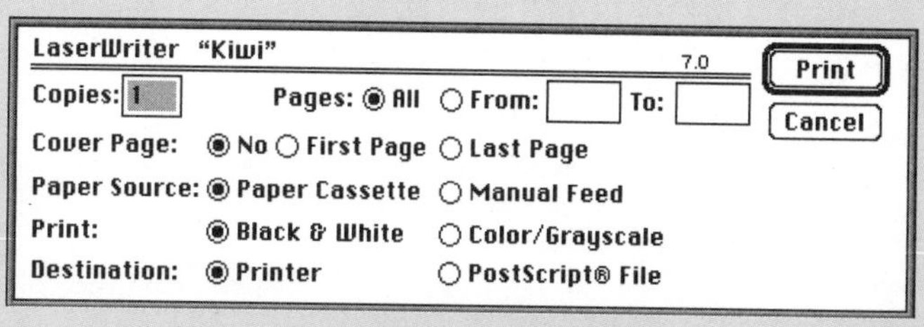

LaserWriter "Kiwi" 7.0 Print
Copies: 1 Pages: ◉ All ○ From: To: Cancel
Cover Page: ◉ No ○ First Page ○ Last Page
Paper Source: ◉ Paper Cassette ○ Manual Feed
Print: ◉ Black & White ○ Color/Grayscale
Destination: ◉ Printer ○ PostScript® File

Printer Identification

One advantage of the Print Dialog is that it gives you one last chance to see which printer is selected in the Chooser. This is especially helpful in networked situations, where multiple printers may be available, or when you have the luxury of choosing between a networked laser printer and a personal printer in your office.

Number of Copies

All printers allow you to print multiple copies of a document. When the document consists of multiple pages as well, the printer produces multiple copies of each page. Collating is up to you. But if a program takes a long time to prepare pages, it will probably be faster to let it prepare each page once for any number of copies, rather than letting it go through the preparation of each page for each copy of a document.

Page Range

The default setting is to print all pages of a document. But if you need only a specific page or set of pages, you can set the page numbers. Be sure that the radio button attached to the **From:/To:** fields is highlighted as well. The **All** radio button overrides the page range numbering you enter into those fields.

Paper Feed

Most printers let you choose between an automatic feed of some kind (from a paper tray or continuous feed paper) or manually feeding one page at a time. When you choose manual feed on some printers, the printing routine alerts you on the Macintosh to insert the next sheet of paper and press to continue. On LaserWriters, the alert comes just once at the beginning of each document (although this can be turned off if you use Print Monitor, page ➔153).

Print Quality

Non-laser printers have print heads that produce dots on the page, either through physical impact against a ribbon (ImageWriter) or spraying of tiny ink dots (StyleWriter). To produce the highest quality output from these dots, the printers need to make more lateral passes of the print head across the paper as the paper advances through the printer. The more closely spaced the dots, the better the print quality. Extra print head passes, however, take extra time. For draft printouts, the **Faster** or **Draft** (if available) qualities may be sufficient; but choose Best for final printouts.

ImageWriter Draft Mode

The quickest printing on an ImageWriter is **Draft** mode. Unlike other modes and printers, which attempt to replicate what's on the screen (what you see is what you get, or WYSIWYG, pronounced WIZ-ee-wig), Draft mode does not reproduce graphics, and uses an internal printer font to approximate how text will lay out on pages. This may be fine for some plain text file printouts (e.g., telecommunications sessions), but for documents, you'll probably prefer Faster mode to get a better idea of how the final result will look.

TrueType and Fonts

Quality of text output on all printers depends almost entirely on the fonts installed in your System. For best results on non-PostScript printers, select fonts for your documents for which you have TrueType font resources in your System File (page ➔84-85). All sizes will print (and display on the screen) in equal quality. If you have other screen fonts (but no TrueType font version), make sure that you copy every size of the family to the System File. A common process internally is to print a reduced version of a font size double that of the text, producing better quality than just printing from the same size screen font file ➔152-153.

Custom Print Dialogs

You'll find a number of modifications to the Print dialog box in applications. A common addition is a choice that lets you preview the document on screen before sending it to the printer. This is an excellent chance to see full pages (usually in miniature, with magnification available to view portions of the page) to check the overall look of pages and spreads when you don't have a video monitor capable of full-page views.

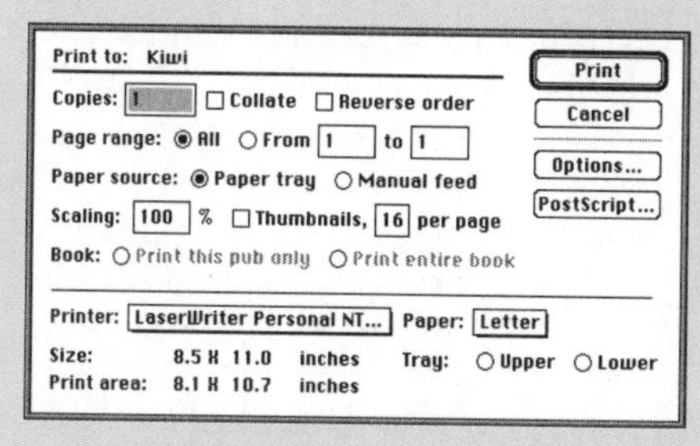

Print to: Kiwi Print
Copies: 1 ☐ Collate ☐ Reverse order Cancel
Page range: ◉ All ○ From 1 to 1 Options...
Paper source: ◉ Paper tray ○ Manual feed PostScript...
Scaling: 100 % ☐ Thumbnails, 16 per page
Book: ○ Print this pub only ○ Print entire book
Printer: LaserWriter Personal NT... Paper: Letter
Size: 8.5 X 11.0 inches Tray: ○ Upper ○ Lower
Print area: 8.1 X 10.7 inches

When the first Apple LaserWriter appeared, it was a revelation in personal computing. Individuals who could afford the high price received vastly higher quality output than from any previous desktop printer.

As time passed, the prices of laser printers dropped, putting them within the reach of many more Macintosh owners than ever before. Other brands also became available to heat up the price competition.

PostScript LaserWriters still exact a premium, but when shared on a network and under control of the Print Monitor for background printing, they prove to be cost-effective devices for many users.

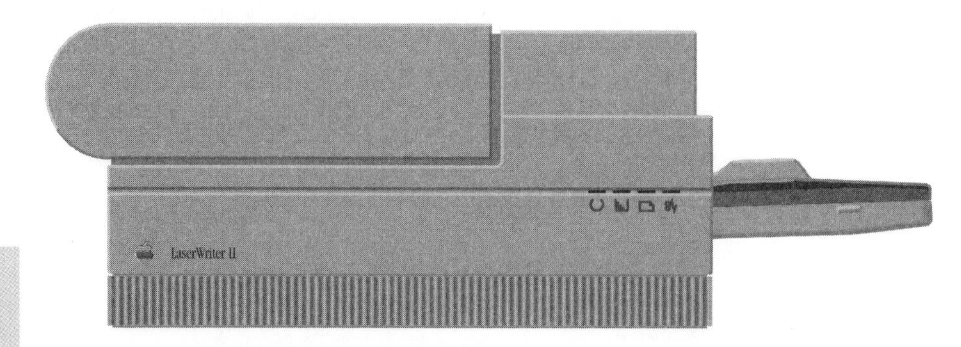

Naming a Networked LaserWriter

Because more than one printer may be connected to an AppleTalk network, it is important to assign a unique name to a LaserWriter. The Namer software that came with your printer may not be compatible with the latest system software. Consult your Apple dealer or user group for information on getting the updated version.

PostScript and TrueType in LaserWriters

Potential conflicts between PostScript and TrueType exist only if you have a PostScript printer (or use a service bureau to print high resolution output on PostScript typesetting machines, such as the Linotronic series). Adobe Type Manager (ATM) also complicates issues, but system software is prepared to handle the problems.

If you use Type 1 PostScript fonts (the kind supplied by Adobe for PostScript), then you must place those font files in the System Folder, not in the System File. Moreover, you will need to drag the matching screen fonts to the System File (and remove any TrueType fonts that may be the same name, such as Times). If you use ATM, then you need only one size of the screen font in the System File.

Many desktop publishing service bureaus continue to use Adobe fonts exclusively (Imagesetters, such as Linotronic devices, do not have fonts built in—all fonts come from the Macintosh). When you rely on these services to produce Imagesetter output for your documents, you should use the same fonts for those documents as the bureau will use for the final output. Small differences between screen fonts supplied with system software and Adobe fonts can throw off line and page breaks.

For most users, however, a mixture of TrueType, Adobe, and built-in printer fonts will produce good results. Screen fonts supplied with system software

Checking Built-in Printer Fonts

On the More Tidbits disk that comes with system software is a helpful program called LaserWriter Font Utility. Intended for PostScript printers only, this program lets you view a list of fonts installed in your printer, as well as print a page showing a sample of each font.

Stopping the Test Page

The LaserWriter Font Utility includes a command that lets you disable the printer's behavior of printing a test page after it warms up. When you click either radio button, the program sends a PostScript command to the printer. The printer remembers the setting even after being turned off.

Downloading Fonts

If you have additional Adobe fonts that you want to use to print some files, the LaserWriter Font Utility lets you manually download a font to the printer before beginning the print job. While this is an extra step in the printing process, it has an advantage. The font stays in the printer's memory between print jobs (each **Print** command starts a new print job). Thus, you won't have to wait for the font to download for each print job (or, in the case of PageMaker, for each text segment that requires the font).

If you don't manually download a font, your programs do it automatically. But fonts that are automatically downloaded are purged from the printer's memory at the end of a print job.

Adobe Postscript Font

TrueType Font

~ATM™

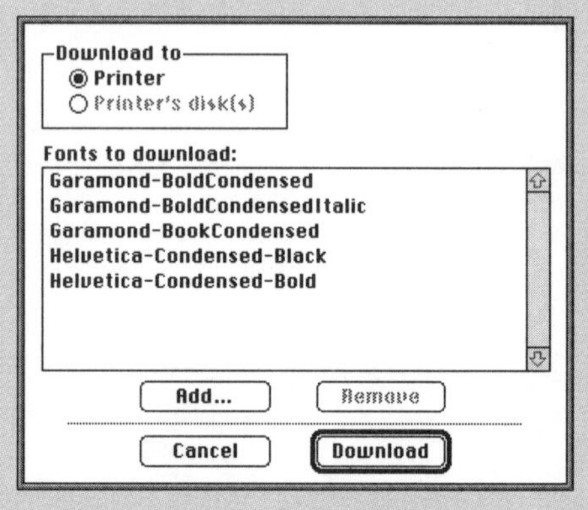

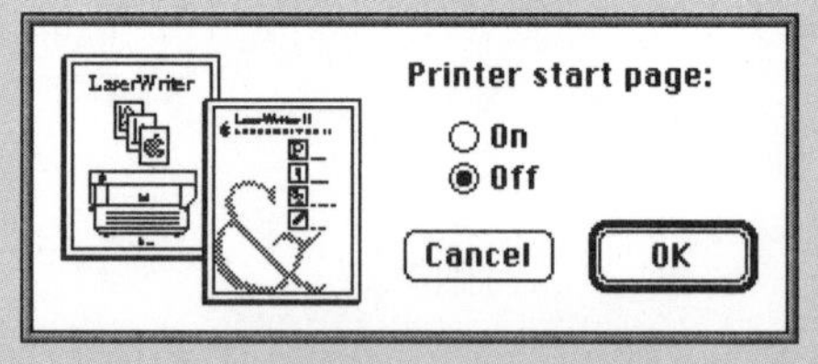

Printers and Memory

How many fonts you can download (or even print) depends upon the amount of memory (or other storage) in your printer. The original LaserWriter series had enough room for only a few fonts (remember that in the Adobe library, bold and italic, for example, are separate fonts, and must be downloaded separately). More recent laser printers have more RAM inside (or are expandable), making way for more downloadable fonts. High-end laser printers also allow for a SCSI hard disk connection directly to the printer. The disk can store hundreds of Adobe fonts for many users to share. Still, loading fonts into the printer's RAM gets faster results.

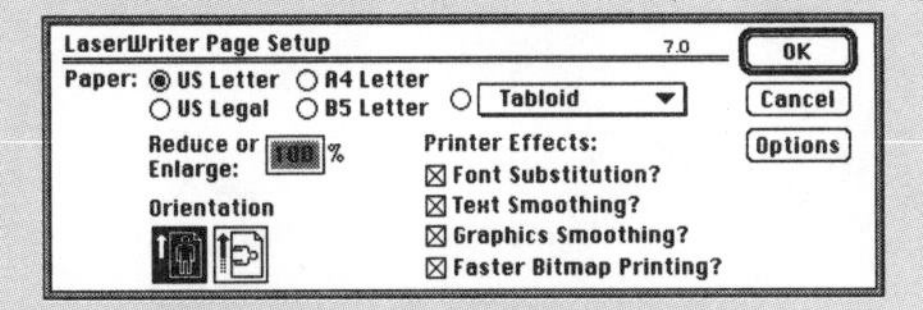

LaserWriter Page Options

When you click Options... in the LaserWriter's Page Setup dialog, you come to an additional dialog with further options. For most choices, a miniature page and image show the results of the choice.

Flip and Invert

You can flip the image along either axis and invert the black and white areas.

Precision Bitmap

Reducing the image by 4% keeps 72 dot-per-inch bit map images in an even multiple of high-resolution dots. Square pixels remain square and undistorted.

Larger Print Area

You can allocate more memory in your printer for preparing the imaging area of a page, at the cost of memory available for downloaded fonts. This affects primarily earlier, limited memory LaserWriters.

Background Printing

System software includes background printing capabilities for PostScript LaserWriters. You enable background printing in the Chooser—a radio button choice appears below the list of LaserWriters connected to the network.

Unless there are problems with the printer, background printing is virtually invisible. You start a print job the same way—via the **Print** command and the Print dialog. But instead of waiting for the print job to finish, you watch as the pages of your document appear to "print." In reality, specifications for the printed pages are saved as files in a special system folder called PrintMonitor Documents. The system then starts another program, called PrintMonitor, in the background. While it runs, its name is listed in the **Applications** menu.

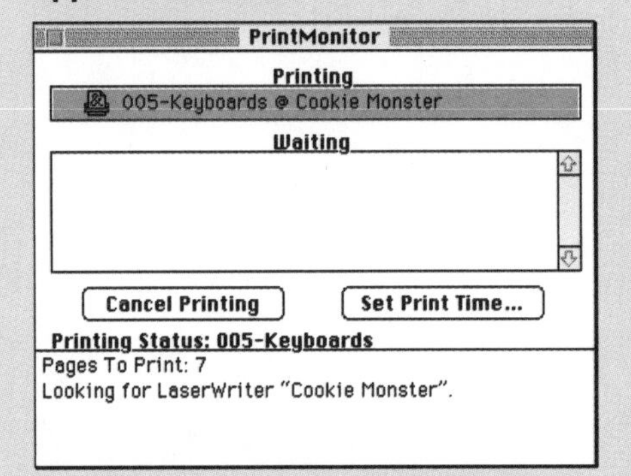

As soon as the print job is saved to files, you are free to continue working on the same or other documents. You can even close the program and work on something entirely different. Behind the scenes, PrintMonitor communicates with the printer, sending each document from the PrintMonitor Documents folder to the printer. As each print job finishes, PrintMonitor deletes the temporary file in the folder.

PrintMonitor Notification

If PrintMonitor is having problems requiring your intervention, a small PrintMonitor icon flashes in the Application menu title. Pull down the menu and choose PrintMonitor, which should have a diamond character to its left—the mark that indicates a program is notifying you of needed attention.

Unlimited Downloadable Fonts

If your document has many fonts, you may need to check this option. It doesn't wait for the end of a print job to flush automatically downloaded fonts. As needed, a new font is loaded, flushing a previously downloaded font. All this takes time, so each page takes longer. If your printer doesn't have enough memory to print a document with many fonts, it may just abandon the print job without much warning.

PrintMonitor

The PrintMonitor application is installed in the Extensions folder of the System Folder. As it runs, you see which document is currently printing (and on which LaserWriter, whose name follows the @ symbol), and which documents are still in the queue. At the bottom of the window is the status box, which shows the same information about what the printer is doing as the LaserWriter status window you see at the top of the screen when not using background printing.

You can cancel printing, but only the currently printing job is cancelled. Be patient. Cancel Printing does not give instant feedback that it is working. It can take several seconds before something appears to happen in response. When it does, however, the file in the PrintMonitor Documents folder is deleted. You must reissue the print job from the application to reprint the document.

To remove a print job from the list of jobs waiting, click once on the item. Cancel changes to Remove From List. Click this button to delete the job's file from the PrintMonitor Documents folder. The **Stop Printing** menu item in the **File** menu cancels all printing, deleting everything in the PrintMonitor Documents folder.

PrintMonitor Preferences

With PrintMonitor running, choose **Preferences** from the **File** menu. In the Preferences dialog, you may select how visible or intrusive you want PrintMonitor to be when it runs and when it needs your attention. Choices range from having the PrintMonitor window automatically appear whenever it runs to displaying alert boxes when it needs your attention or bypassing notification when beginning a manual paper feed print job. It's best to start out with the highest level of notification until you feel comfortable with PrintMonitor. Then you can gradually taper off to an appropriate level.

Where's Laser Prep?

In previous versions of system software, there was an additional LaserWriter driver file called Laser Prep. This has been incorporated into the LaserWriter driver. Some programs, however, look for this file in the System Folder before printing. To appease those programs, a dummy Laser Prep file is available on the Printing diskette of your installation

Mixing System Versions

If you have multiple Macintoshes sharing a LaserWriter on a network, all Macs should have the same LaserWriter driver. You can install System 7 drivers in System 6 machines with the help of the special printer Installer file on the Printing diskette. Double-click the Printer Update icon on the diskette. In the main installation screen, click Customize. In the succeeding dialog, click on the

The DogCow

The image in the LaserWriter Options dialog is a sacred being among Macintosh developers. Is it a dog? Is it a cow? Neither? Both? It is simply Clarus, the DogCow, whose natural sound is a combination

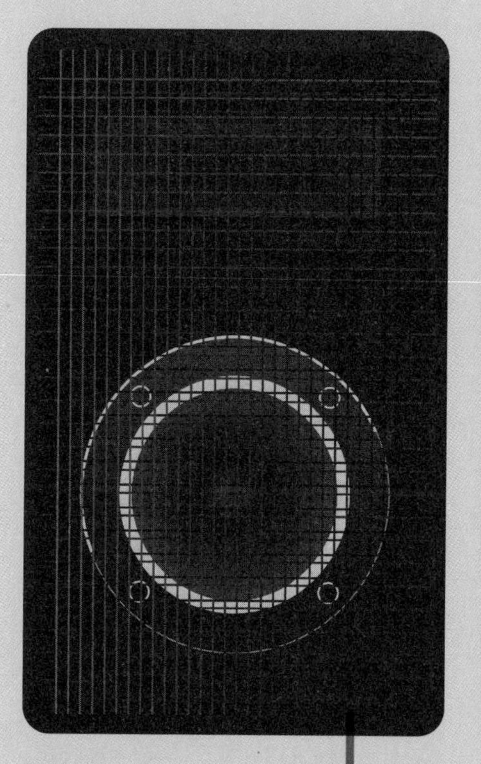

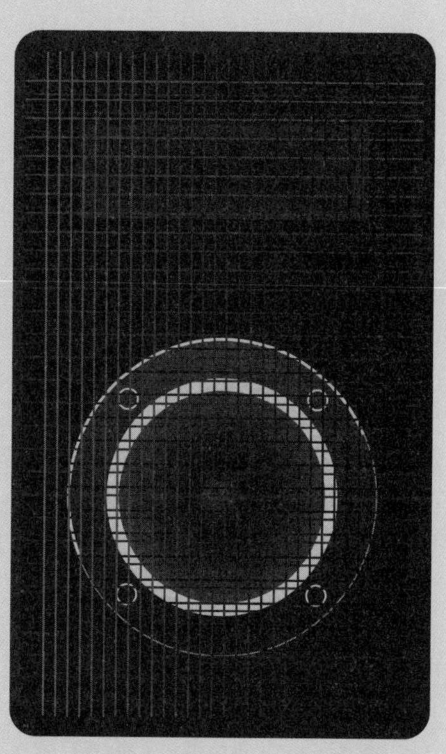

Sound Output, page 156

Sound Input, page 158

Sound has been a part of the Macintosh experience from the earliest days. In fact, the Macintosh literally introduced itself to the world in 1984 in electronic speech without any hardware add-ons.

Since then, the Macintosh has bolstered internal support for playing and controlling sounds recorded specifically for the Macintosh or created by external music devices. System software allows you to change the alert sound to any sound resource file in the System File. System extensions produced by third parties give you even more power over the sounds issued by the Macintosh in response to virtually any action you take.

New applications also use sound and pre-recorded speech to extend the communicating powers of the Macintosh. A program's alarm clock not only beeps, but can playback a voice message you attached to that alarm item. Or it can tell you in plain language when a telecommunications file transfer is complete.

Audio Output Hardware

Every Macintosh comes with a speaker built into the unit. Except on the Quadra 900, the speaker is small and not of the highest fidelity, but it does an adequate job of reproducing most prerecorded sounds. If the sound is a stereo sound, both channels are mixed together for the speaker.

Stereo output is available in separate channels, however, via the audio output jack on stereo-equipped Macintoshes. You can connect stereo headphones or amplified speakers to the port➔9. When you do, the internal speaker is disabled. Audio quality via this port is very good, and sounds great through high fidelity speakers.

Setting Output Volume

The **Sound** control panel features a slider control that lets you adjust the volume between off (zero) and full blast (seven) by dragging the control. Adjustments are in full digit increments within that range. As you release the slider, the currently selected system alert sound comes through the speaker at the selected volume. When you turn the sound off, every time a program normally sounds the system alert, the menubar flashes once as a substitute alert.

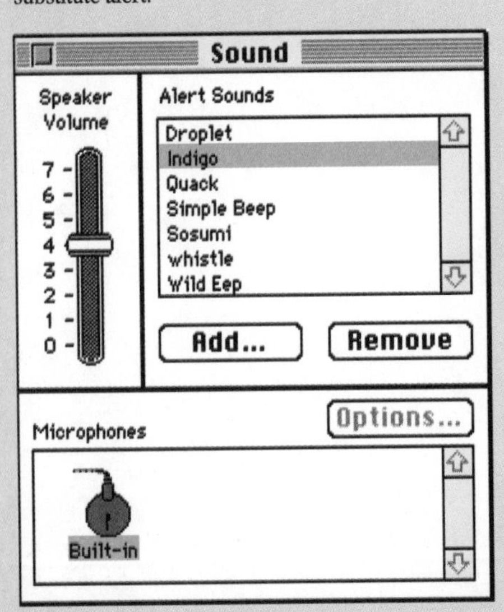

Alert Sounds

Different programs sound the system alert for different reasons. Often the sound indicates that you are trying to perform an operation that is not valid at the moment (e.g., clicking outside of a modal dialog box,)➔104. Other times, the alert sound is intended to draw your attention to the screen, because something has occurred that requires your intervention.

Alert sounds listed in the **Sound** control panel are those sounds installed in the System File. If you open the System File and view the contents by **Kind,** you'll see the same items listed as **sound documents**. To hear the sounds, click on their names in the **Sound** control panel. Whichever sound is selected when you close the control panel becomes your system alert sound in all programs.

If you have a built-in microphone or third-party sound digitizer, you can record additional alert sounds to the System File from the **Sound** control panel➔80.

Removing Alert Sounds

While you can open the System File and remove any sound resource, you can also delete an alert sound via the Sound control panel. Select any sound, and choose **Clear** or **Cut** from the **Edit** menu. If you cut (or copy) a sound from the Sound control panel, the sound goes into the Clipboard. You may then paste the sound into the Scrapbook for safekeeping if you like. When you paste a sound into the Scrapbook, a button appears on that page letting you play the sound directly.

Other Action Sounds

Third-party system software extensions, such as the popular SoundMaster, let you assign sounds to all kinds of actions on the Macintosh—starting the computer, ejecting a disk, resizing a window. Programs like this generally use sounds stored in a format different from the sounds stored in the System File. They are individual sound files, which are not the same as sound resources in the System File.

Sound Files vs. Resources

Sounds stored in the System File (and listed in the Sound control panel) are called sound resources. What's confusing about sound resources and sound files (which many programs generate and use), is that they both appear to be files in the Finder. After all, you can drag a sound out of the System File and place it in a folder just like any file. But if you select a sound resource and choose **Get Info**, you'll notice that it doesn't have any creation or modification dates attached to it. Resources are just snippets of information intended to be attached to another file, like the System File or a HyperCard stack, to be used. A sound file (or any file), is a full-fledged citizen in the Finder community, with a birthdate, modification date, comment, and so on.

Sound resources (and fonts, keyboards, and script systems) weren't always visible from the Finder as they are in System 7. Apple's engineers just made it a lot easier for you to shift these particular items into and out of the System File in the same Desktop metaphor as document files.

You can also use HyperCard as a laboratory for recording, storing, and playing back sounds. It even allows you to turn virtually any sound into music.

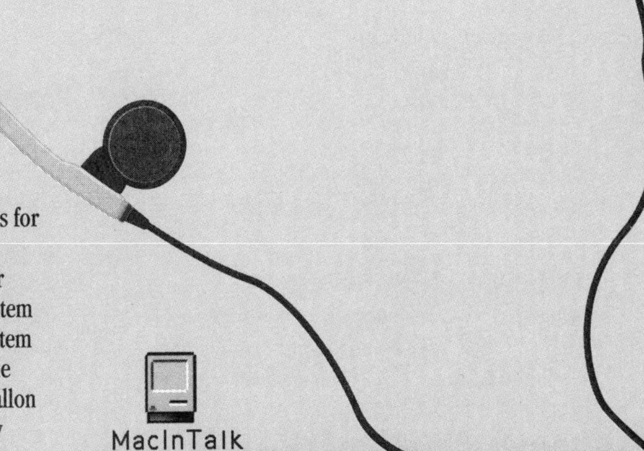

Sound File Types

Since programmers have been playing with sound files since the beginning of the Macintosh, a number of incompatible sound file formats have appeared through the years. With facilities built into System 7, however, a standard is emerging. Called Audio Interchange File Format extension for Compression (AIFF-C), this type of file is flexible in the way sound programs can play, record, and store digitized sounds. AIFF-C files can take advantage of System 7's abilities to compress and decompress sound information while recording or playing the sound.

Converting Between Files and Resources

System software does not provide user services for converting a sound file, which you might have received with a sound program or from a user group, to a resource for inclusion into the System File. You cannot drop a sound file into the System File. But sound recording software, such as the **SoundEdit** program that comes with the Farallon MacRecorder, lets you open a sound from any format and save a copy of it back in a different format.

Text to Speech

When the Macintosh introduced itself to the world, it used a software technology called **MacInTalk** That software is a system extension that does its best to convert plain text and phonemes into human-sounding speech. Although not included with system software, MacinTalk is widely available on bulletin boards and from user group software libraries. As of this writing, however, it has not been updated to work with System 7.

MacinTalk has not been widely used primarily because the speech quality leaves a lot to be desired. When you read along with the text, you can make out the speech pretty well. But understanding this electronic voice as it talks to you from across the room is not easy.

When the words to be spoken are always the same, programmers have fine-tuned the phonemes sent to MacinTalk. This often helps listeners distinguish words, but not always.

The advantage of MacinTalk over digitized speech is that MacinTalk does not require the significant disk storage that digitized sounds do 158. But when producing commercial products, programmers who use sound today prefer digitized speech for the clarity.

Text to speech technologies will continue to improve, but it will be awhile before the software voice sounds a natural as a human's voice.

Experimenting with Sound Playback

HyperCard comes with a few sounds built in to let you experiment with sound. These sounds were recorded, digitized, and turned into resources of type '**snd** '. The **snd** resource (note the extra space after the "d", which is required of the four-character resource naming convention) is the same kind used by the System File.

Early versions of HyperCard could play only one type of 'snd ' resource, called Type 2. Since then, the Type 2 'snd ' resource has been declared obsolete by system software engineers. HyperCard has been updated to play both Type 2 and the more prevalent Type 1 'snd ' resources. The System File requires Type 1 'snd ' resources.

HyperCard 2.1 includes three sounds for playing music, plus sounds it uses internally for generating telephone dialing tones played through the speaker. The three musical instrument sounds are Harpsichord, Boing, and Flute.

You can hear how each sounds by starting HyperCard, displaying the **Message Box** (*command-M*), typing the **Play** command with the name of the sound, and pressing the *return* key. The sound you hear is exactly the same pitch and

```
play boing
```

HyperCard's **Play** command, however, is more powerful than that. You can ask HyperCard to play the sampled sound in a wide range of pitches and durations. Here's the command you can use to hear a C-minor scale with the flute sound:

```
play flute "cdebfgacbbc5e"
```

Notice that "eb" is e-flat (the "#" symbol designates a sharp). Substitute the other sound names for the flute to hear other instruments play the same scale.

To learn more about the sound capabilities of HyperCard, consult the documentation that comes with the ***HyperCard Stack Development Kit*** (Claris) or ***The Complete HyperCard 2 Handbook*** (Bantam Books).

That Apple considers voice to be a significant part of the Macintosh's future is clear by the inclusion of a microphone as standard equipment on most new models since the LC.

Apple's system software engineers have made it rather simple for program developers to include voice recording features in their programs. Voice annotation, voice mail messages, and voice alarms are only the beginning of an intriguing future for sound recording on the Macintosh.

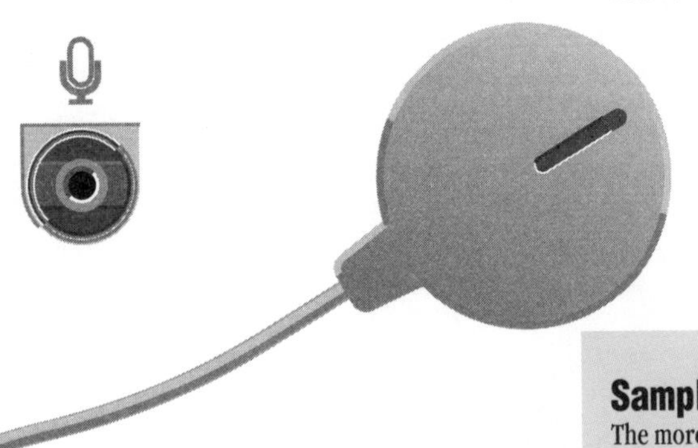

Recording Hardware

While most new Macintoshes come with their own microphones and sound input connectors, third-party devices allow owners of other Macintosh models to have the same sound recording functionality. These devices are usually called digitizers, because they convert analog audio (e.g., your voice) to digital signals that can be manipulated and stored in a computer. The Farallon **MacRecorder,** for example, connects to either serial port. It contains circuitry that performs the same analog-to-digital conversion that the new Macintoshes include behind the sound input port.

External devices require system extension files (drivers) to work. If you already have a sound digitizer and are upgrading to System 7, contact the digitizer manufacturer for a compatible driver file. The driver goes into the system Extensions folder.

Sampled Sound

Sound digitizers work by taking distinct snapshots of an analog sound at set intervals (many thousands of times each second). Each snapshot is called a sample of the sound at that instant. The sample is assigned a numeric value based on the nature of the sound source at that instant. Alert sounds in the Macintosh System File, for example, are nothing more than a series of numeric values. When played back through a digital-to-analog convertor (the reverse of the recording process), the values are converted to analog sound that plays through the speaker—the sound the human ear can hear. This is the process used for digital compact discs.

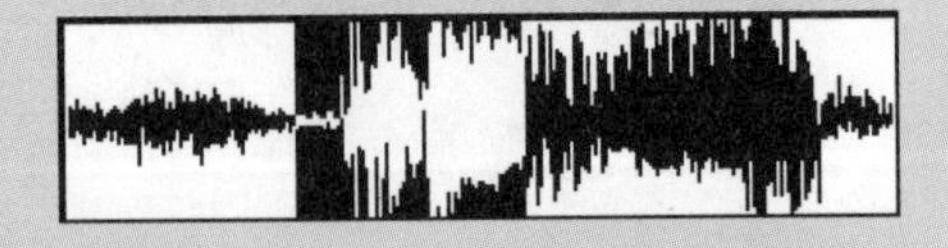

Sampling Rates

The more often samples are taken of an analog sound, the more likely the digital equivalent will reflect the original sound. This is akin to higher print or video resolutions. When using the Macintosh as the recording device, the highest sampling rate you'll find in software is **22 kiloHertz** (22,000 times each second). While this sampling rate produces excellent quality, it also requires the most memory and disk storage—a minute of 22 kHz sound is 1320 kilobytes large.

If you sample less frequently, you can save memory and disk space at the cost of quality. For the limited frequency range of the human voice, however, halving the sampling rate does not greatly impact quality. But it does halve the memory requirements. Some sound recording software also allows recording at even lower sampling rates. Memory is directly proportional to the sampling rate.

Audio Compression

To help with the disk storage needs of digitized sound, Macintosh system software (and other sound recording programs) can automatically compress sounds before saving them as resources or files ➜ 157. Such sounds are automatically decompressed when played back. There is virtually no performance penalty for this compression/decompression, although some fidelity is lost in the process. Compression ratios built into system software are **3:1** and **6:1**, although some programs offer additional ratios with their own compression schemes. At six-to-one compression, the 1320K minute of sound sampled at 22kHz takes up only 220K of disk space.

Recording Alert Sounds

If you have a microphone or compatible digitizer, you can record an alert sound directly into the System File by way of the Sound control panel. The panel recognizes the built-in Apple microphone and any external device sound driver files in the Extensions folder. The Sound control panel lets you choose the microphone, add a sound, or delete an existing sound.

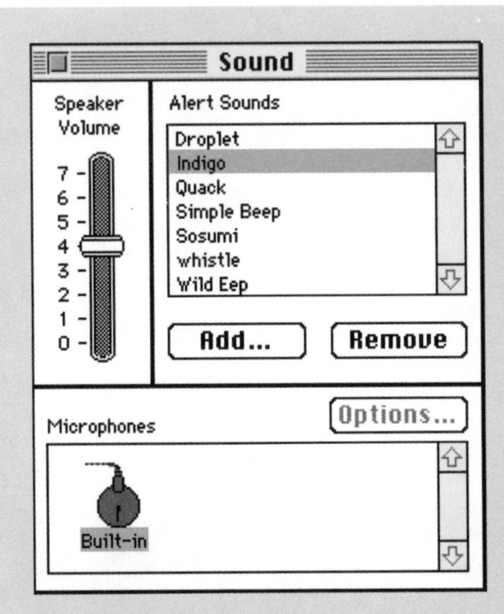

Choose Microphone

An icon for each microphone recognized by the system software is shown in the window. Third-party microphones may activate [Options...] . Clicking this button lets you choose a serial port for the digitizer and other hardware specific items.

Remove Sound

To remove a sound from the System File, you can select it in the list and click [Remove] (or choose **Clear** from the **Edit** menu). This action deletes the sound for good. If you prefer to save the sound for later use, copy it to the Scrapbook ➜ 79, 108.

Add a Sound

Click this button to initiate the recording process. In response, the sound recording dialog box appears on the screen.

Test Sound Level

Before recording, speak into the microphone and look for lines coming from the speaker icon. Adjust the volume control on the microphone if there is one so that you see the vertical line on voice peaks.

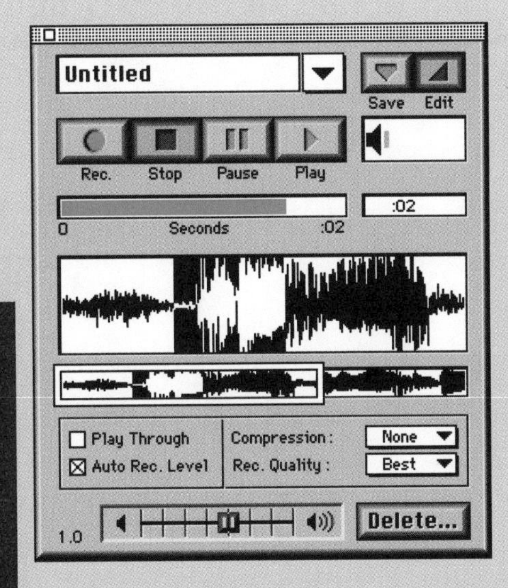

Record and Stop Buttons

Click and begin speaking into the microphone. Get ready to click when you finish. You can record up to 10 seconds of sound for an alert sound.

Play Button

Before saving the sound, click to playback the sound. If you want to re-record the sound, simply click . The previously recorded sound is erased.

Sound Timer

This time line shows you how much time is elapsed during the 10 second time period. A digital readout is shown to the right.

Save Sound

Click this button to save the sound to the System File. Another dialog asks you to name the sound. The name must be different from others already in the System File.

Experimenting with Sampled Sound

If you have a microphone or digitizer and the HyperCard 2-disk set (the set included with System 7 software), you have a laboratory in which to experiment with sampled sound. Start HyperCard, and choose **Audio** from the **Edit** menu.

The lets you record sound resources that are attached to HyperCard stacks 141. Click , record your first and last names, and click . You can use this sound for your experiments.

Click to reveal the bottom part of the Audio Palette. Two windows show the sound wave patterns of the sound you just recorded. The lower, smaller window shows the entire sound. The rectangle around part of the sound indicates which part of the sound is shown in more detail in the larger, upper window. You may drag either edge of the rectangle to increase or decrease the view in the other window (or choose **View All** from the **Edit** menu).

is still active, so you can play the sound. You may also select a portion of the sound by clicking and dragging a selection of the upper sound wave. plays whatever is selected. Choose **View All** from the **Edit** menu, and try to select only that part of the sound wave that contains your first name (click to try the selection).

Then choose **Cut Sound** from the **Edit** menu. Click the pointer to the right of the sound wave consisting of your last name. The flashing cursor is like a text insertion pointer. Choose **Paste Sound** from the **Edit** menu. You have now switched your first and last names. Click to hear the results.

Select another part of the sound and copy it into the Clipboard. Then paste it a couple times in one location.

Voice Recognition

Today it is possible to connect third-party devices, such as Articulate Systems' **Voice Navigator** to respond to spoken commands. Essentially, you teach the Navigator software to perform some action (menu command, macro, etc.) in response to a specific voice command you speak into a microphone. You train the software to recognize that voice command by giving it a few samples to use as a comparison.

True voice recognition, in which the computer understands what you are saying (instead of just reacting to a particular speech pattern) is a very complex technology that is still a long way from being practical and affordable. But between voice response and emerging text-to-speech technologies, we will soon be carrying on conversations of a sort with our Macintoshes.

Checkboxes

These choices are available only on Macintoshes after the Macintosh SE.

Compression

Choose a compression ratio before saving a sound. **Compression** is available here only when the sound is recorded in the **Best** quality.

Recording Quality

The choices of **Best** and **Good** correspond to 22 kHz and 11 kHz, respectively. You must choose recording quality before actually recording a sound.

Delete

This button lets you delete any sound that HyperCard can see from the current stack. This includes only 'snd ' resources in stacks, not those in the System File.

Sound Editing

Software programs that come with third-party digitizers offer much more sophistication and flexibility in working with sampled sounds. For example, some programs even allow you to adjust the waveform of the digitized sound after you've recorded it. Or you can add effects such as reverberation to existing sounds.

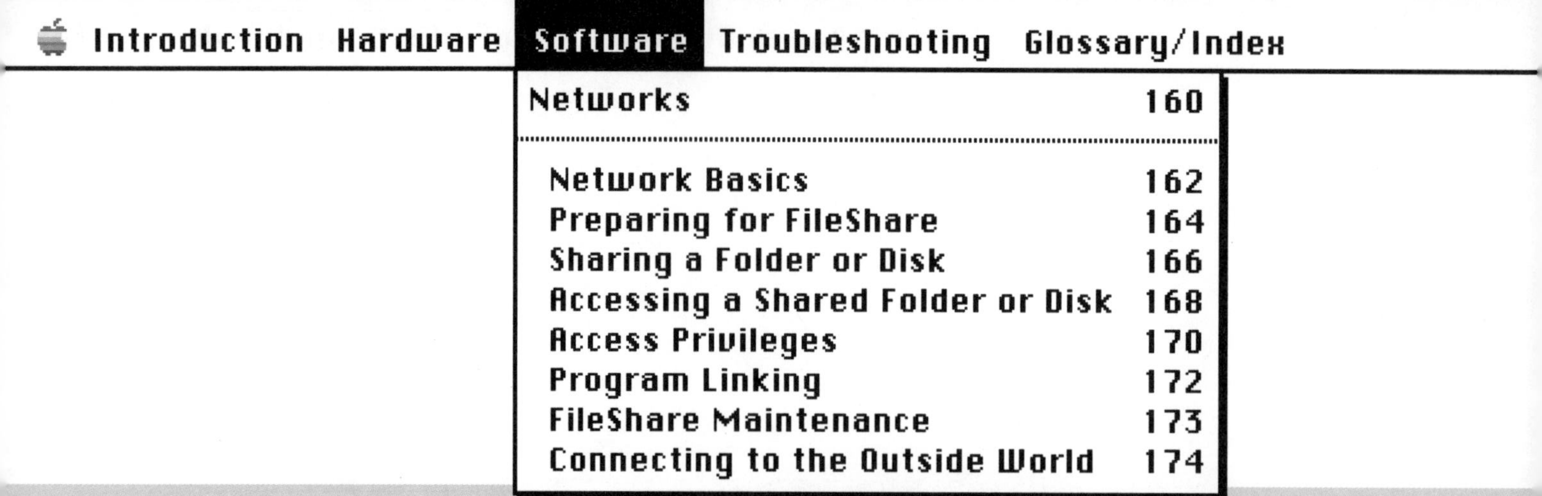
Introduction Hardware Software Troubleshooting Glossary/Index

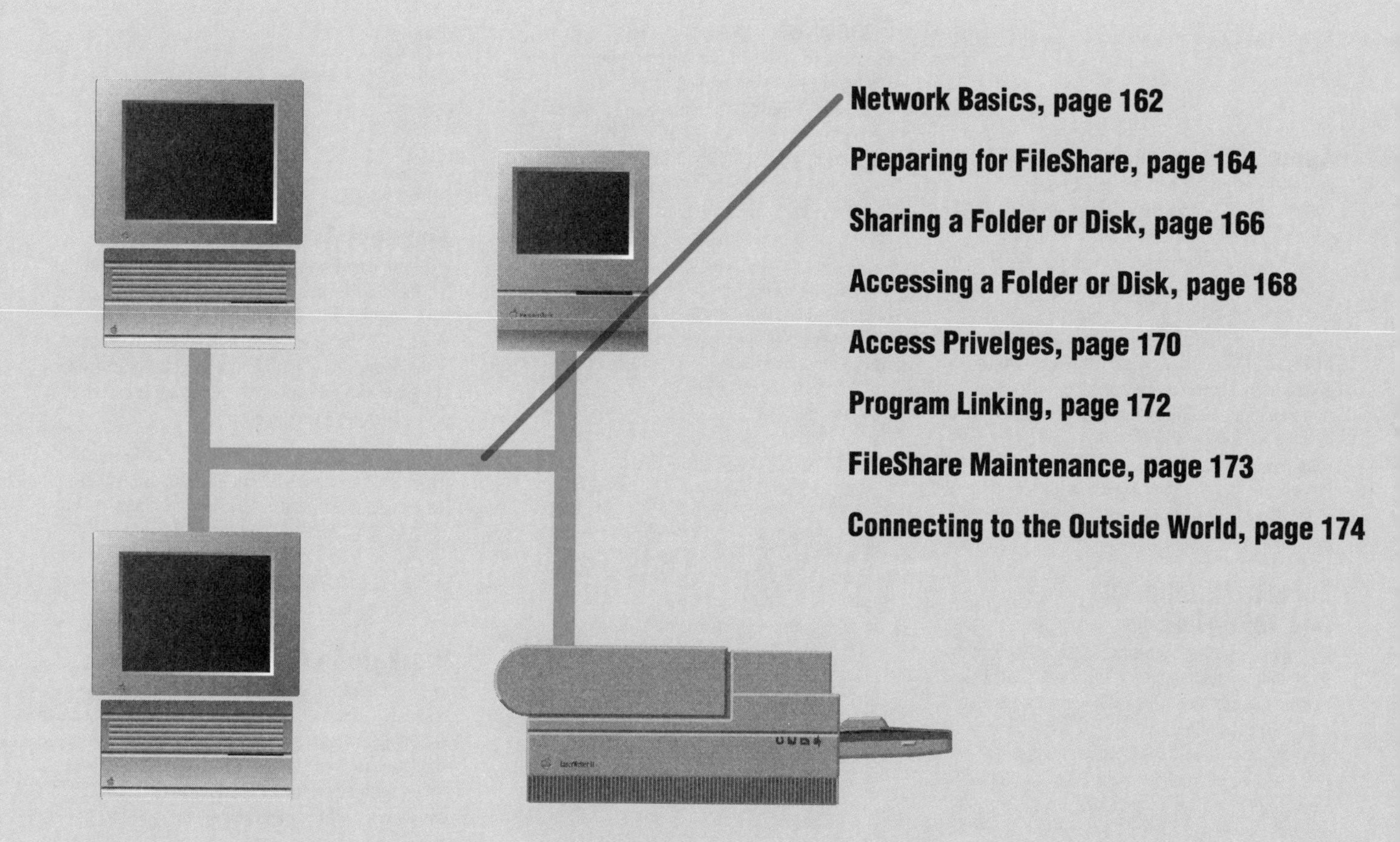

More and more Macintosh users are linking their machines together to let more than one Macintosh share a laser printer and exchange information from one machine to another.

Physically connecting Macintoshes is easier than hooking up a home VCR. System software goes even further to ease the burden of sharing documents among two or more users.

About the biggest hurdle to overcome when approaching networking for the first time is the proliferation of terms, many of which sound alike. Fortunately, you only need to know a handful of terms to successfully use your Macintosh on a network.

AppleTalk Network

Every Macintosh—since the first model in 1984—has had networking provisions built into the computer. When a Macintosh is connected to another Macintosh or a networked LaserWriter, the combination of built-in software, built-in hardware, and cabling is called an AppleTalk network. What distinguishes an AppleTalk network from other types are the rules that govern the way information is passed from machine to machine—direction, how machines identify themselves and direct signals to other machines, how files are copied from volume to volume, and so on. These rules are also known as protocols. An AppleTalk network can be as small as a single Macintosh and LaserWriter to a system of hundreds of Macintoshes

LocalTalk, EtherTalk, and TokenTalk

Within an AppleTalk network, there may be one or more different cabling methods to physically link machine to machine. One cabling method is built into every Macintosh—LocalTalk. The printer port on every Macintosh has a LocalTalk connector (and other related internal hardware). LocalTalk cabling should not extend to a total length exceeding 1000 feet unless you add a LocalTalk repeater box, which amplifies signals running longer distances.

Other connection types, called EtherTalk and TokenTalk, require a plug-in board on most Macintoshes to act as an intermediary between the Macintosh and other kinds of networks, specifically EtherNet and Token Ring. The plug-in board and special driver (extension) software allows a Macintosh to communicate with other Macintoshes and printers using AppleTalk services (e.g., file copying, printing) while riding along a network that may run at faster speeds or connect machines in a different order than a standard AppleTalk network. Quadra models and the LaserWriter IIg come with Ethernet connectors built-in, but additional hardware boxes, called transceivers, are needed to connect these units to an Enternet network. The actual cables for EtherTalk and TokenTalk are also different from LocalTalk. EtherTalk and TokenTalk cable is coaxial, constructed like the cable used to link a VCR and television set.

PhoneNet

A third-party supplier of cabling solutions for the Macintosh, Farallon Computing, Inc., has established a low-cost alternative to LocalTalk connectors. Their product, called PhoneNet, connects to the Macintosh just like a LocalTalk connector, but instead of requiring special LocalTalk cables, uses standard phone cable to link devices on the network. Cable lengths can reach about 2000 feet. Connectors on the cables are the same modular phone plugs of a standard telephone. In many office environments, existing phone wiring can be used between offices, instead of having to run additional wires.

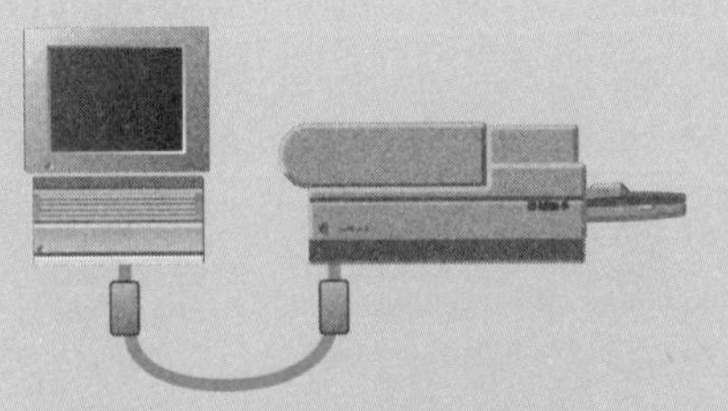

Simplest AppleTalk Network

A common and simple AppleTalk network is the pairing of a Macintosh and a LaserWriter. Each device on the network requires one LocalTalk connector. The single cable coming out of one side of the connector plugs into the Macintosh or printer. The other two jacks are for connecting LocalTalk cables between the connectors.

On LocalTalk connectors, the unused jacks must be left empty. In a PhoneNet equivalent to this setup, the unused jacks need to have a special plug called a terminator (which comes with PhoneNet connectors). To extend the network, connect additional LocalTalk cables to either or both unused jacks on the LocalTalk connectors.

Workgroup AppleTalk Network

The configuration of a workgroup is as varied as the makeup and layout of the group. LocalTalk cabling is flexible enough to accommodate just about every situation. The only requirement is that every device (Macintosh or printer) have its own LocalTalk connector box, and that each device is connected to at least one other on the network. Devices can be in any order.

Connecting Workgroups

Because performance on a network is affected by the number of users connected together and how much they send information across the network, it is impractical to place dozens of users on a single AppleTalk network. Instead, it is better to keep workgroups small and link them together by way of bridges. A network bridge is a combination of hardware and software that isolates workgroups, yet allows them to connect to each other when necessary. When two or more groups are connected via a bridge, the entire setup is called an internet.

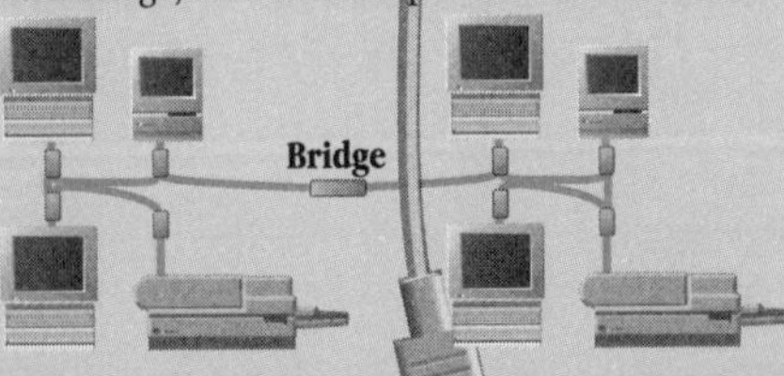

Zones

With the help of the software that manages internets (often called an internet router), you can divide the internet into functional **zones** that help users know where other Macintoshes are. A zone can consist of one or more workgroups. A common zone organization is by company department. Even if a department is physically located in disparate locations, their computers can be joined together as a single zone for other users to think of them as a single group. When connecting to devices in other zones, you use the Chooser to select the zone as well as the device (if zones have been set up on your network, the list of zones appears in the Chooser automatically).

File Servers vs. FileShare

Prior to System 7, the most common way Macintosh users shared information on a network was to set up an **AppleShare file server.** This required a Macintosh and its hard disk be set aside to do nothing but run the AppleShare software. To the user, the AppleShare network looked like another volume on the Desktop. Authorized users could open that volume, open and copy files, and save documents to that hard disk. Others on the network had varying levels of access to the information stored on the shared disk. Someone in the workgroup was designated the **Network Administrator**—the person who controlled which users had access to the server.

FileShare in System 7, however, allows for sharing of information among users on a network without dedicating a Macintosh to the purpose. Once the Macintoshes are connected, there is virtually no need for a Network Administrator, because each user determines who has what level of access to his or her machine.

A dedicated file server has the advantage of a separate hard disk that everyone shares. With FileShare, other users may be accessing your hard disk, slowing down some of your processing. Still the flexibility of FileShare is ideal for small workgroups and occasional information sharing.

Print Server

An AppleShare server (or equivalent) offers the advantage of acting as a **print server.** Instead of using your hard disk and PrintMonitor ➔153 to perform background printing, print jobs are sent to the **queue** on the server. The print server sends documents to the printer on a first-in, first-out basis.

AppleShare and System 7

When System 7 was released, AppleShare was not fully compatible with it. Because the Macintosh running AppleShare requires system software, just like any Macintosh, it was necessary to maintain the server Macintosh as a System 6 machine. With others on the network using System 7 printer drivers, however, new printer drivers needed to be installed on the server Macintosh. For System 7 you should use AppleShare version 3.0 or later.

FileShare Passwords

Passwords are meant to limit access to a computer. Only a person with the authorized password is granted access to designated parts of the computer. There are two types of passwords that you can set when using FileShare. One is your own password that lets you access your computer from a different machine on the network. This password should be your business only.

A second kind of password is the one you can assign to other users who access your computer via FileShare. You assign this password when setting up a new user ➔164. This password applies to that user only when he or she tries to access (log on) to your Macintosh. One of the checkboxes in the user information is whether the user is allowed to change the password. Unless there is some special security reason to limit the password access for a particular user to your machine, it is common courtesy to allow users to adjust their own passwords. This reduces the risk that they'll have to write down the password for your machine (and for any others they access). Written passwords are not secure.

Phone Home

By adding a 2400 baud (or faster) modem to a Macintosh on a network plus the **AppleTalk Remote Access** system software extension, you can connect to an AppleTalk network via telephone. When you dial in, you have the same access to the network as the Macintosh to which the modem is connected. Take part in e-mail and file sharing as if you were sitting at the office desk. This is an ideal setup for traveling PowerBook owners (the software is included with the PowerBook 170) or working at home.

Network Topologies

A **topology** is the mapping of cables among devices on a network. Each device connected to the network is called a **node.** As a network grows, the topology becomes an important consideration, because some topologies are better than others when expanding the network.

The typical LocalTalk connection method can be used only in a daisy-chain. That means that nodes are in series, with cable running from device to device. While not all devices have to be turned on for the network to run, the hazard with this topology is that if a connector comes unplugged anywhere in the network, the devices on each side of the break won't be able to communicate with

A common alternative topology is called a **backbone.** This consists of a cable (or phone wire set) running throughout a facility. Wherever needed, a connection is made to the cable (the point is called a **drop).** The Macintosh connects to the cable via something like a PhoneNet connector. This is the method that allows you to use existing telephone wiring as a backbone for a PhoneNet setup. You can still connect additional devices in a daisy chain from any backbone drop. It is also increasingly common in larger organizations to set up a backbone that runs at faster speeds using **Ethernet** (40 times faster than LocalTalk).

Another method that simplifies connections throughout a large building is a **star** topology. Using telephone cabling, a star revolves around a hub (often a star controller piece of hardware and a phone system punchdown block). Many branches extend from the hub. Each branch can have a drop to a single device, multiple drops, and drops to devices connected to others in a daisy chain.

As a participant on a network, you should perform some initializations with the various pieces of FileShare software.

It is often difficult to keep all these pieces clear in your mind, because they are located in several places in system software and often look like other pieces. It is easier to follow the road maps below for each of the preparations for using FileShare. The goal of these five tasks is to set everything up as much as possible while not granting anyone access to your computer until you are ready to share information ➔166-167.

Assign Your Names

Your network identity consists of three items: the name you use to identify yourself when accessing your own computer from someone else's machine; the password you use to access your own computer from someone else's machine; and the name of your computer that others will recognize when viewing a list of all machines running on the network.

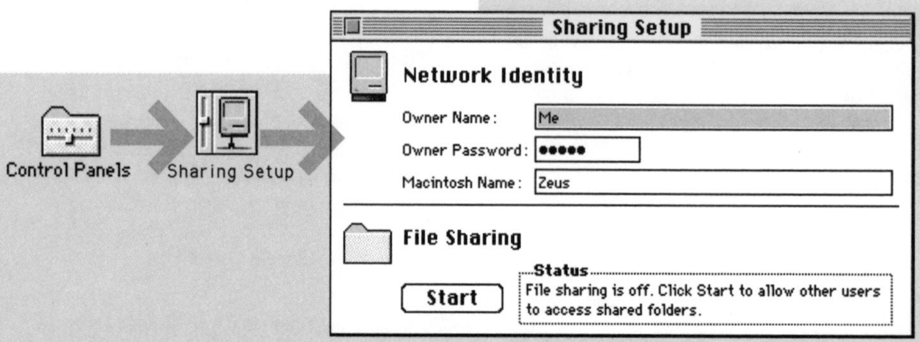

Control Panels → Sharing Setup →

Sharing Setup
Network Identity
Owner Name: Me
Owner Password: •••••
Macintosh Name: Zeus
File Sharing
Status
Start
File sharing is off. Click Start to allow other users to access shared folders.

Disable Guest Access

A Guest user is automatically created for your system. Until you are ready to open your machine to others, disable guess access.

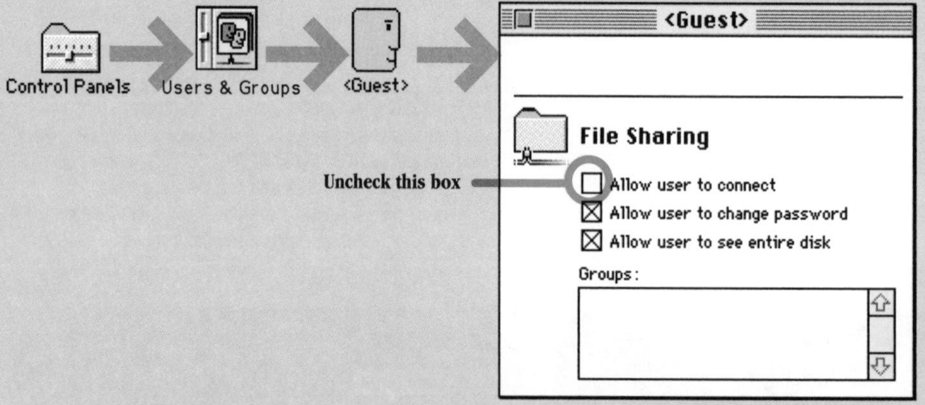

Control Panels → Users & Groups → <Guest> →

<Guest>
File Sharing
Uncheck this box
Allow user to connect
Allow user to change password
Allow user to see entire disk
Groups:

Allow Owner Access

You are the owner of your Macintosh. Make sure you have allowed yourself full access to your Macintosh for when you need to access it from someone else's machine. You'll need to enter your user name and password when you try logging onto your own computer from afar ➔168-169.

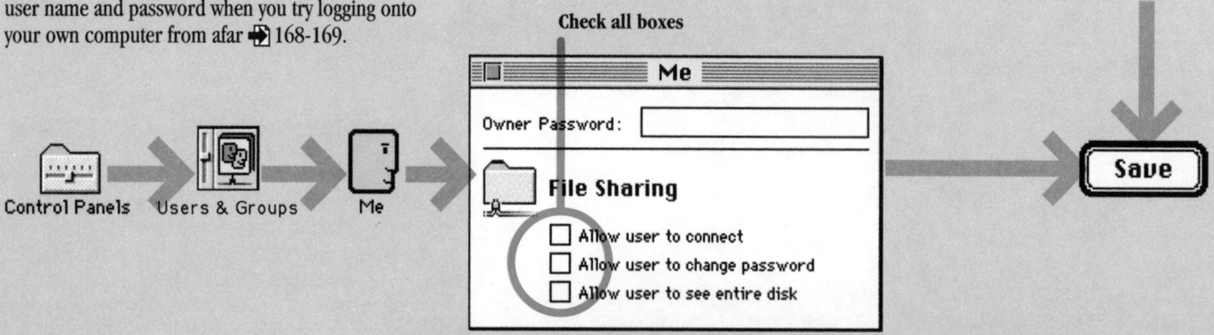

Control Panels → Users & Groups → Me →

Check all boxes
Me
Owner Password:
File Sharing
Allow user to connect
Allow user to change password
Allow user to see entire disk

Save

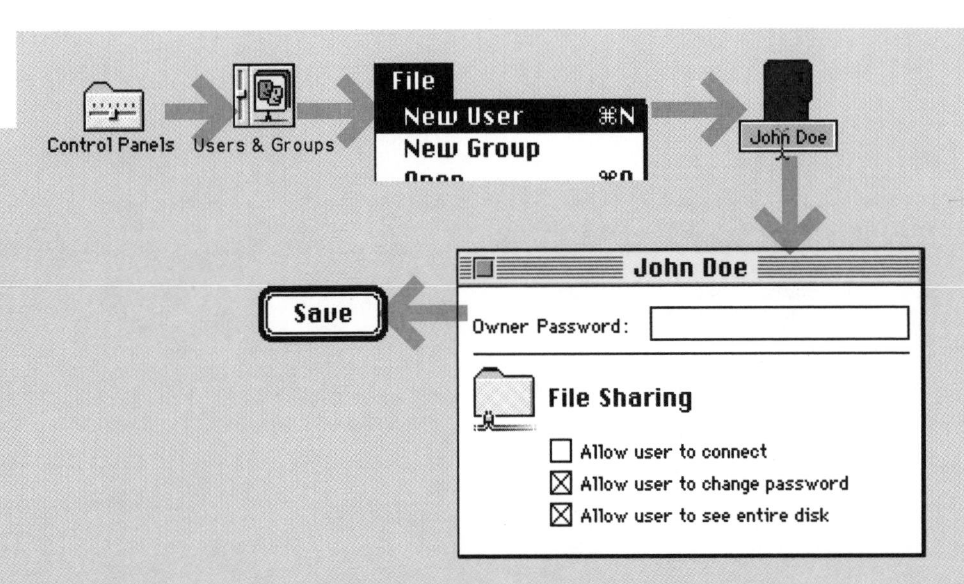

Create Users Without Access Privileges

In anticipation of allowing users to access your computer, create new users in your system. The password here is the one that another user will need to enter for access to your computer—different from your own password that lets you access your own computer. For now turn off access for each user. As new people come on the network, you'll create a new user for each one.

Create Groups

A group consists of multiple users (each user is called a member of the group). You can allow several users at once to access a given folder or disk by assigning their group as the authorized user. Since you can authorize only one user or one group at a time to access a folder, create likely groups of co-workers who may share documents on your hard disk. You will likely create and modify groups as various people need access to work on your hard disk.

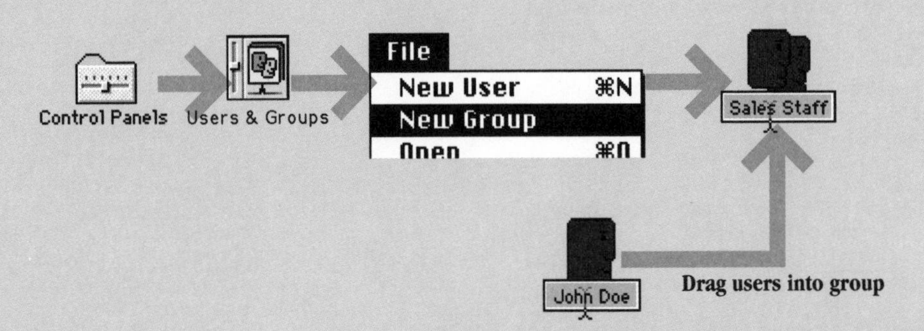

You have a few options for sharing information with others on a network. For each folder or disk volume that you want to share, you can grant access to a single user, a group of users, or just let anyone on the network log on.

It's important to remember that when you share a folder, you are not sharing your entire disk. Only that folder and its contents are visible to others on the network.

Steps in sharing a file are in two categories. The first is to enable the desired people for access. Enabling Guest access lets you assign guest access to a folder—anyone on the network can get in. The second is to enable each user who needs access. When you have multiple users assigned to a group, you'll have to enable each user individually (or restrict one by not enabling that user).

Enable Guest Access

When you enable the Guest user, you allow anyone on the network without password to access a folder or disk that you later open up for everyone.

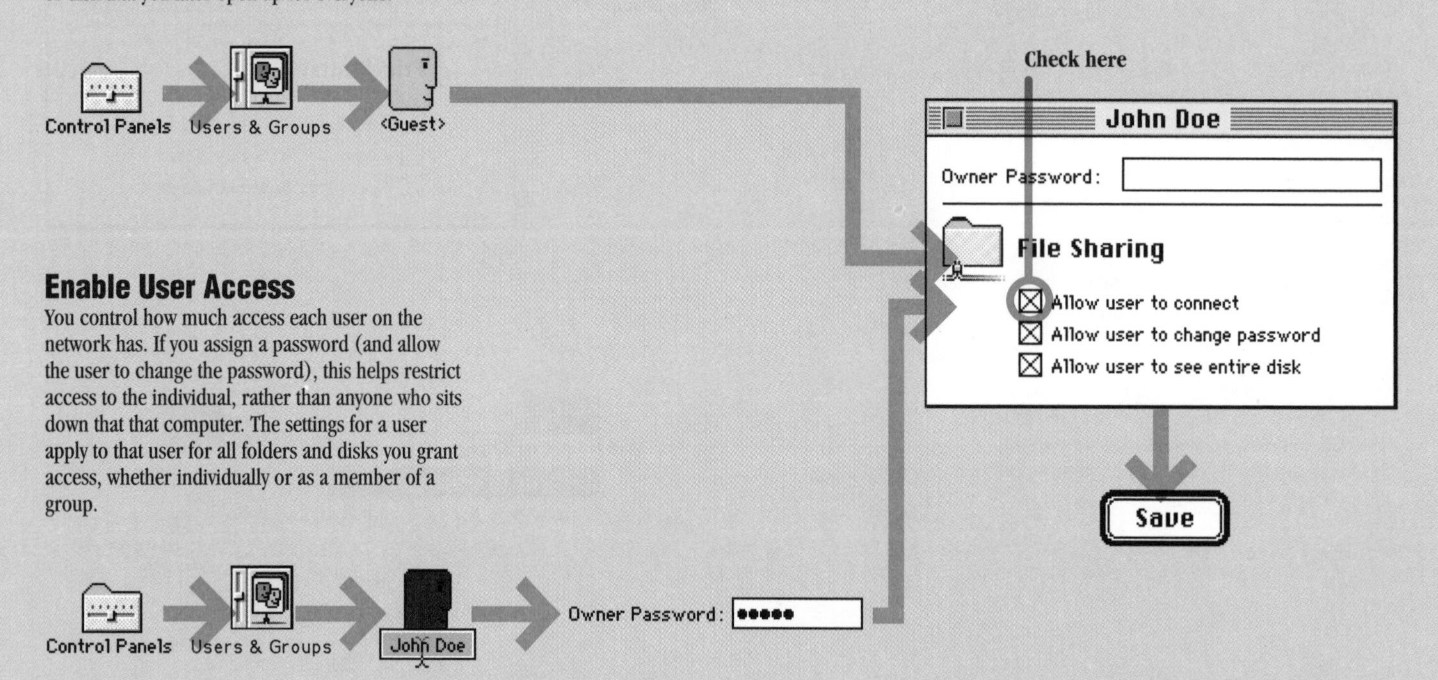

Enable User Access

You control how much access each user on the network has. If you assign a password (and allow the user to change the password), this helps restrict access to the individual, rather than anyone who sits down that that computer. The settings for a user apply to that user for all folders and disks you grant access, whether individually or as a member of a group.

All of the road maps on these pages presume you have followed the FileShare preparations on pages ➡164-165.

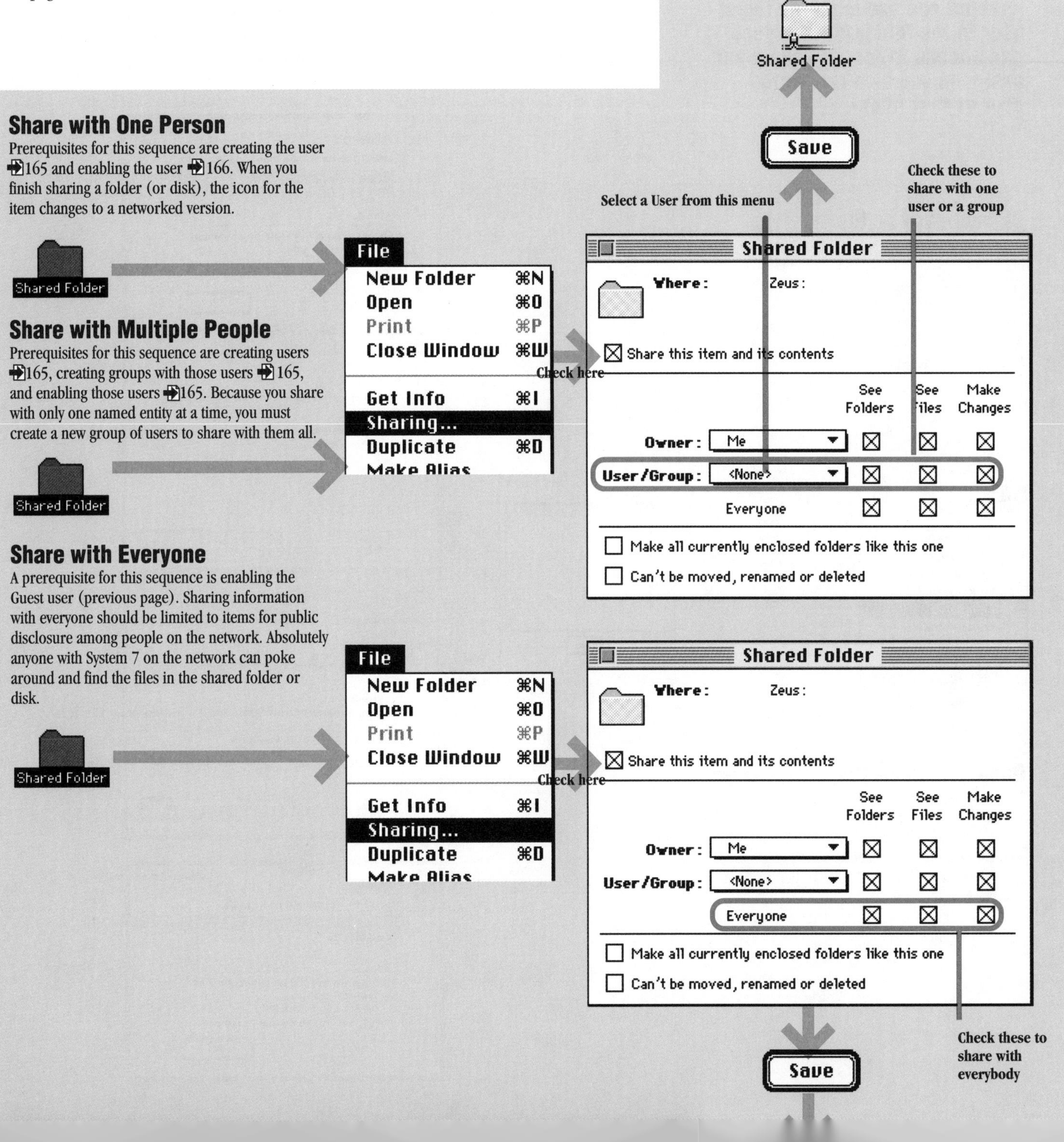

Share with One Person

Prerequisites for this sequence are creating the user ➡165 and enabling the user ➡166. When you finish sharing a folder (or disk), the icon for the item changes to a networked version.

Share with Multiple People

Prerequisites for this sequence are creating users ➡165, creating groups with those users ➡165, and enabling those users ➡165. Because you share with only one named entity at a time, you must create a new group of users to share with them all.

Share with Everyone

A prerequisite for this sequence is enabling the Guest user (previous page). Sharing information with everyone should be limited to items for public disclosure among people on the network. Absolutely anyone with System 7 on the network can poke around and find the files in the shared folder or disk.

To gain access to a shared folder or disk, the user of the target machine must have either enabled and assigned the Guest user to the folder (so everyone can access it), or set you up and assigned you as a registered user of that folder.

Assuming that has been done, it is now your job to follow the road map to logging on and accessing that information.

When you have successfully logged onto the target Macintosh, the volume appears on your desktop as a networked volume. You can treat this just like any other volume, within the access privilege limits imposed by the owner of that folder.

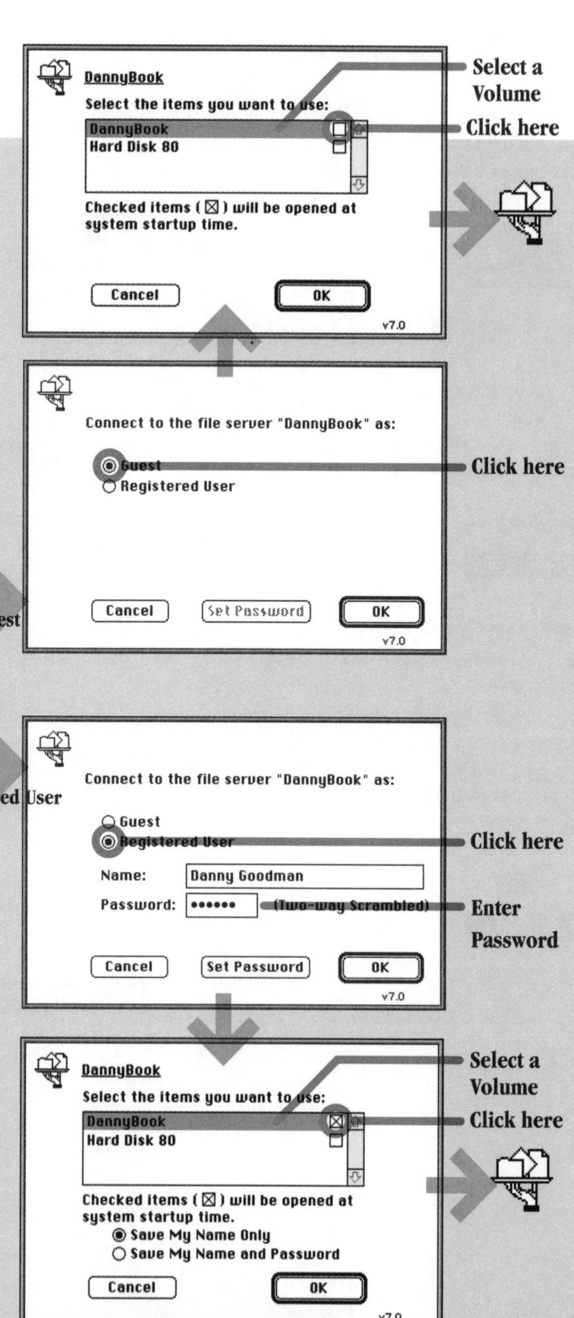

Occasionally as Guest

Logging on as a guest is simple, since there is no password protection. If the Guest button is not available in the log on dialog, it means that the folder was not set up to allow guest access. It may be assigned to you as an individual or as a member of a group, in which case, you'll have to access the folder as a registered user (below).

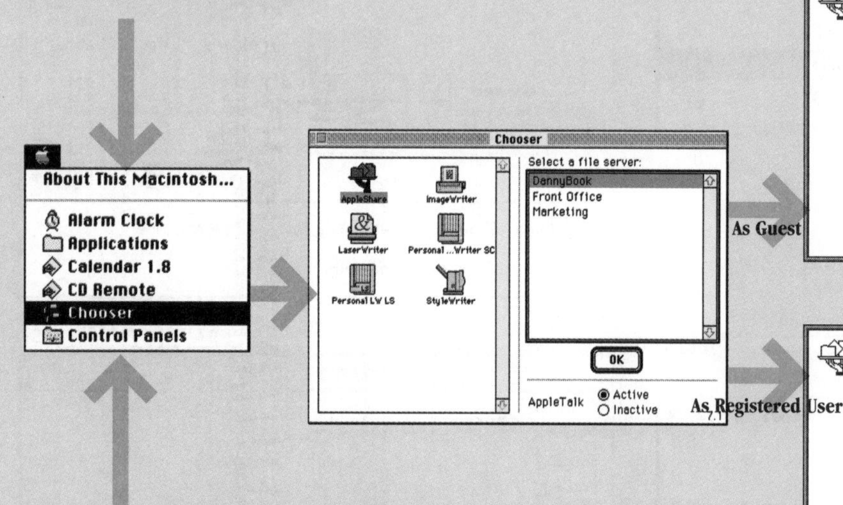

Occasionally as Registered User

To log on as a registered user, you must enter the same user name as that of the user file created for you in the owner's system. System software automatically enters the user name you've given yourself as the default value. If the owner assigned a password to your user file, you must enter it correctly (upper and lower case letters count) to access this folder.

How you do it depends on how often you access the information and whether you do it as a guest (no name or password required) or registered user (name and possibly a password required).

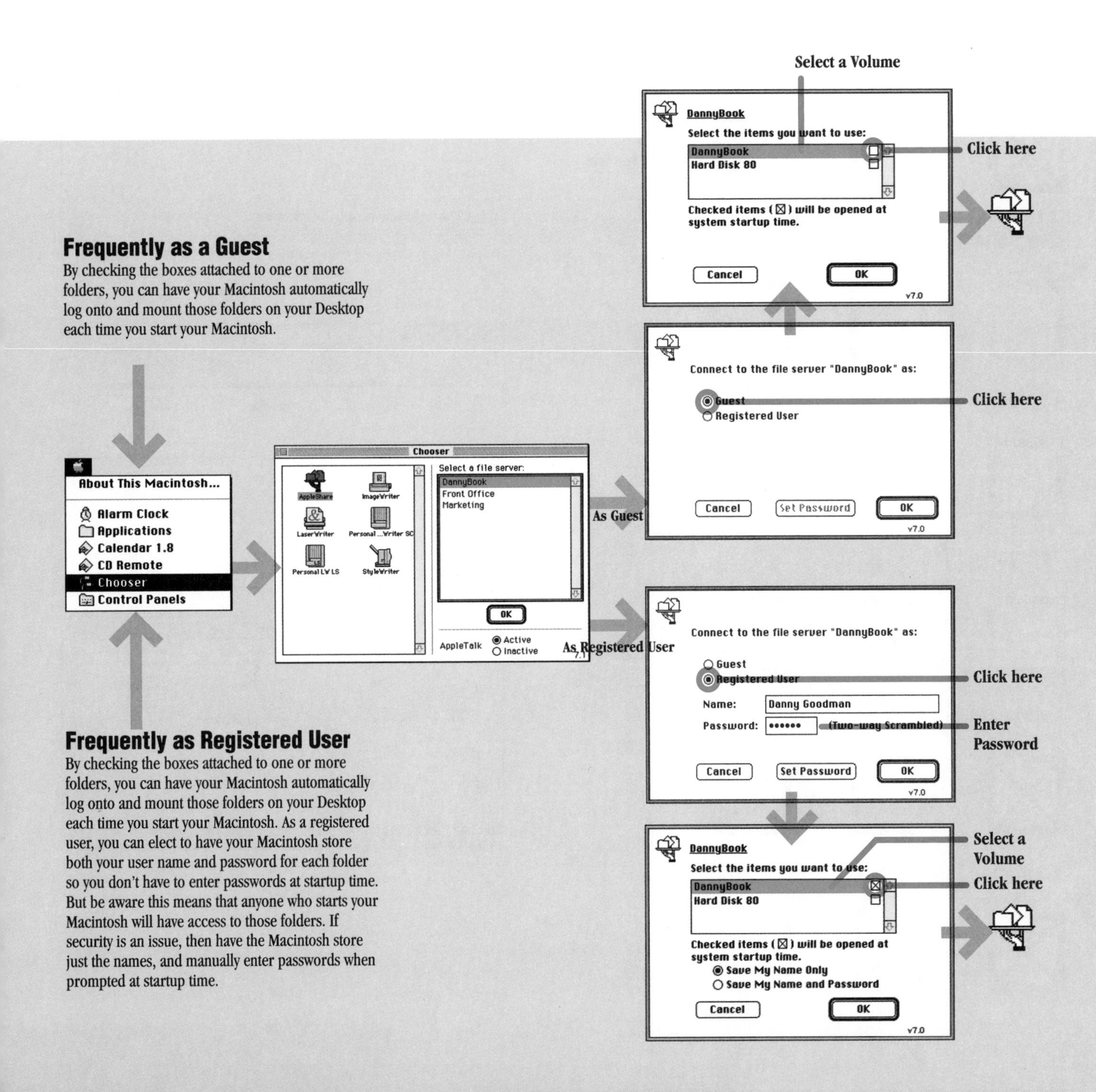

Frequently as a Guest

By checking the boxes attached to one or more folders, you can have your Macintosh automatically log onto and mount those folders on your Desktop each time you start your Macintosh.

Frequently as Registered User

By checking the boxes attached to one or more folders, you can have your Macintosh automatically log onto and mount those folders on your Desktop each time you start your Macintosh. As a registered user, you can elect to have your Macintosh store both your user name and password for each folder so you don't have to enter passwords at startup time. But be aware this means that anyone who starts your Macintosh will have access to those folders. If security is an issue, then have the Macintosh store just the names, and manually enter passwords when prompted at startup time.

When you select a folder or disk and choose Sharing from the File menu, you not only assign who has access, but what level of access.

Moreover, if you access a folder that has restricted access, one or more icons in the upper left corner indicate what privileges are denied. Below are the checkbox settings for a variety of access privileges.

Setting	See Folders	See Files	Make Changes	Access Icon(s)
Everyone: Full Access	☒	☒	☒	(no icon)
Everyone: No Access	☐	☐	☐	(no icon)
Everyone: Drop In Only	☐	☐	☒	
Everyone: Hide Folders	☐	☒	☒	
Everyone: Hide Files	☒	☐	☒	
Everyone: Read Only	☒	☒	☐	

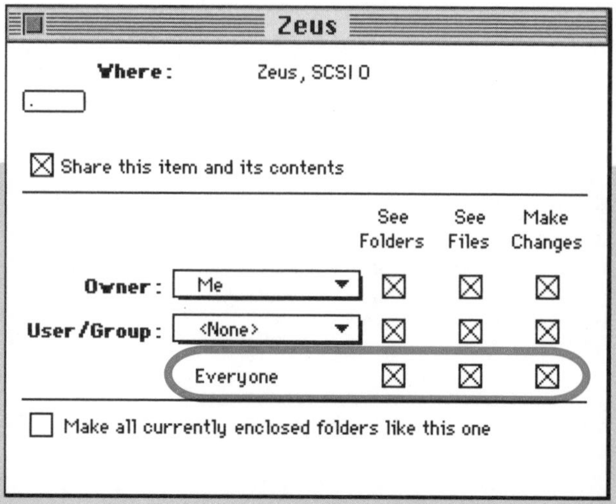

Zeus
Where: Zeus, SCSI 0
☒ Share this item and its contents

		See Folders	See Files	Make Changes
Owner:	Me	☒	☒	☒
User/Group:	<None>	☒	☒	☒
	Everyone	☒	☒	☒

☐ Make all currently enclosed folders like this one

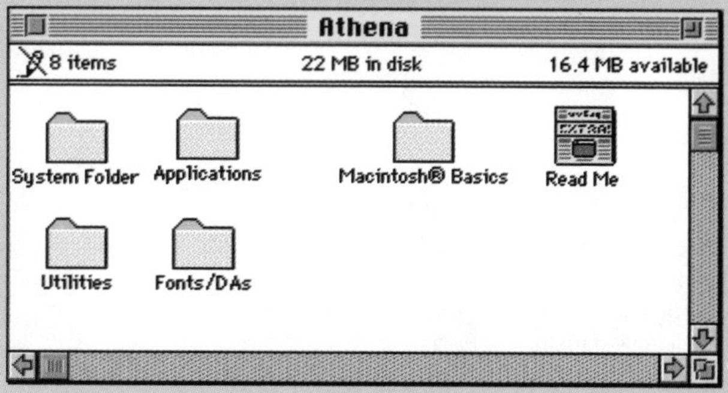

Athena
8 items 22 MB in disk 16.4 MB available
System Folder Applications Macintosh® Basics Read Me
Utilities Fonts/DAs

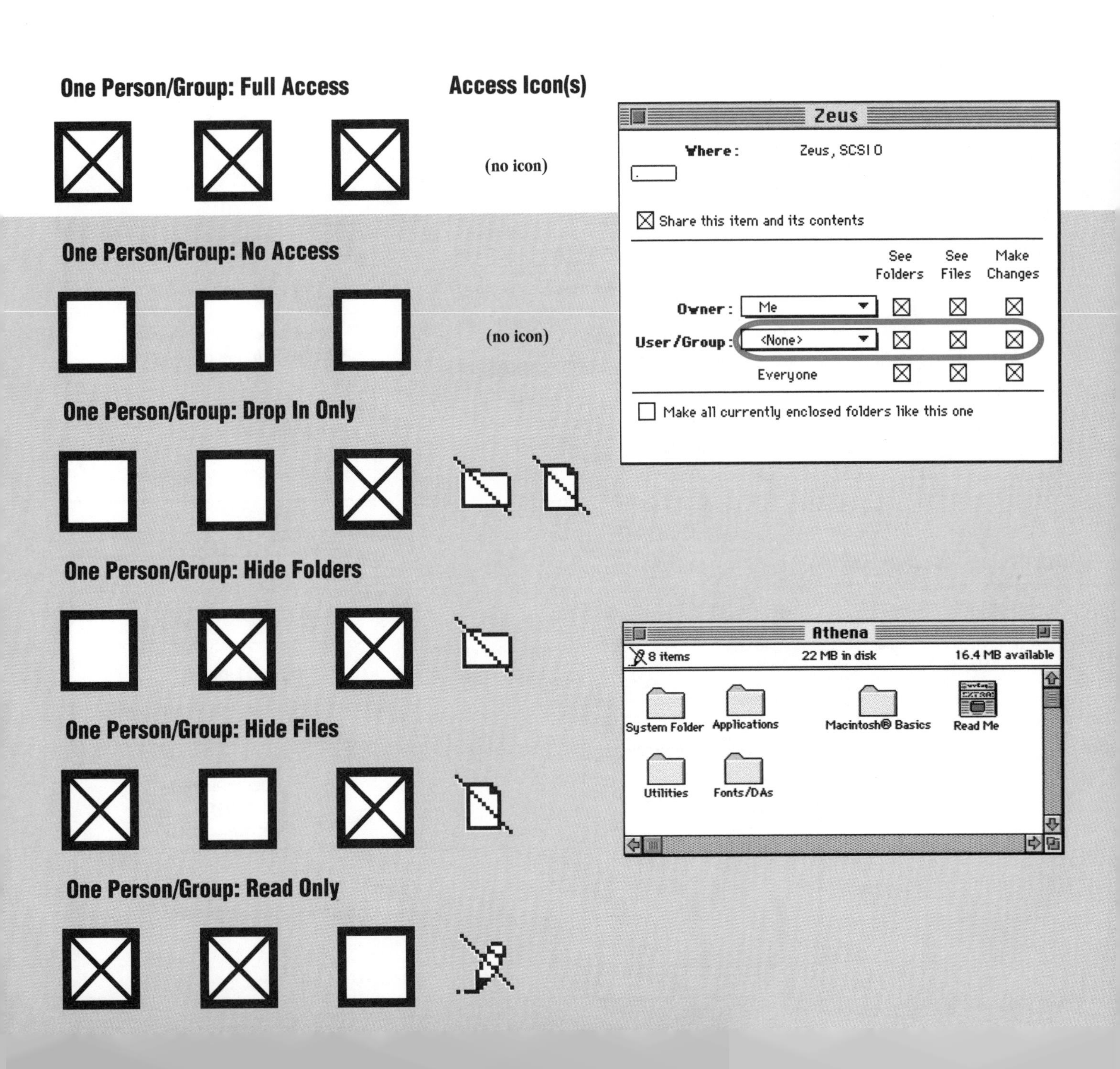
One Person/Group: Full Access
Access Icon(s)
(no icon)
One Person/Group: No Access
(no icon)
One Person/Group: Drop In Only
One Person/Group: Hide Folders
One Person/Group: Hide Files
One Person/Group: Read Only
Zeus
Where:
Zeus, SCSI 0
Share this item and its contents
See Folders
See Files
Make Changes
Owner:
Me
User/Group:
<None>
Everyone
Make all currently enclosed folders like this one
Athena
8 items
22 MB in disk
16.4 MB available
System Folder
Applications
Macintosh® Basics
Read Me
Utilities
Fonts/DAs

As more applications take advantage of Apple events, you will have more need to set up your system for program linking or know how to allow your programs to access those on other Macintoshes. This is different from launching an application that you see in someone else's disk or folder that you've logged onto.

As more applications take advantage of Apple events ➔134, you will have more need to set up your system for program linking or know how to allow your programs to access those on other Macintoshes. This is different from launching an application that you see in someone else's disk or folder that you've logged onto.

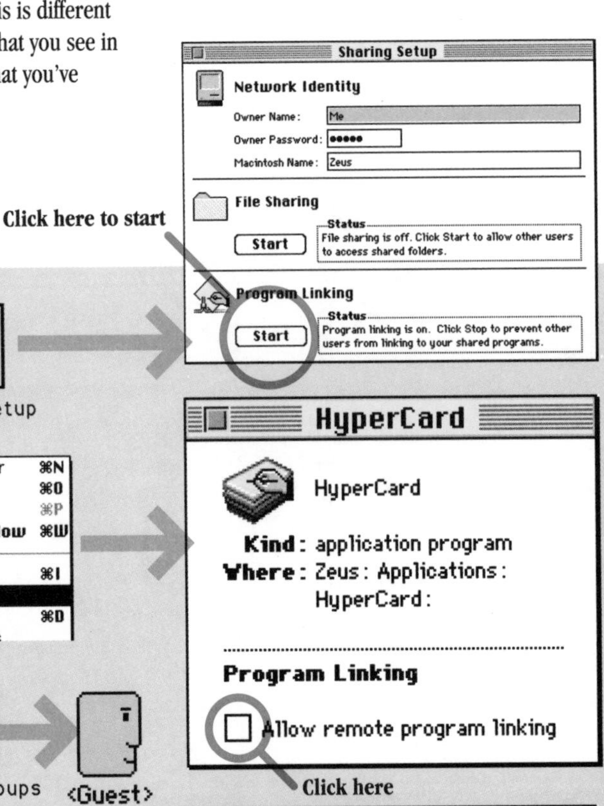

Allowing Program Linking

It takes as many as three series of actions to open an application for program linking. Once your Sharing Setup and user settings allow program linking, you'll only have to concern yourself with the settings of individual applications.

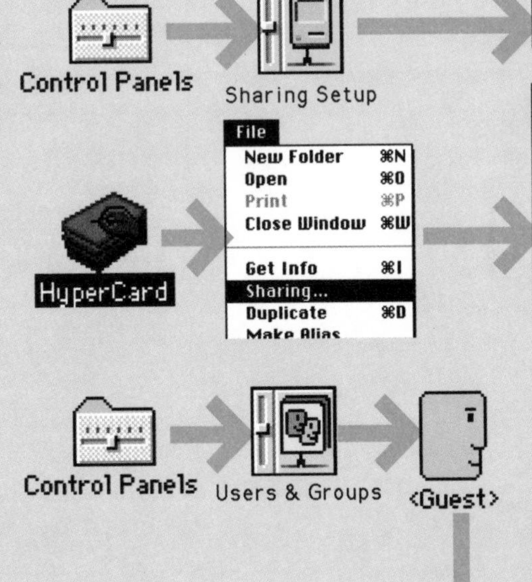

Accessing Program Linking

How a program accesses another varies widely, but you may encounter the following series of dialogs along the way. The first is called a program selection dialog, in which you first choose a Macintosh on the network and a program on that Macintosh.

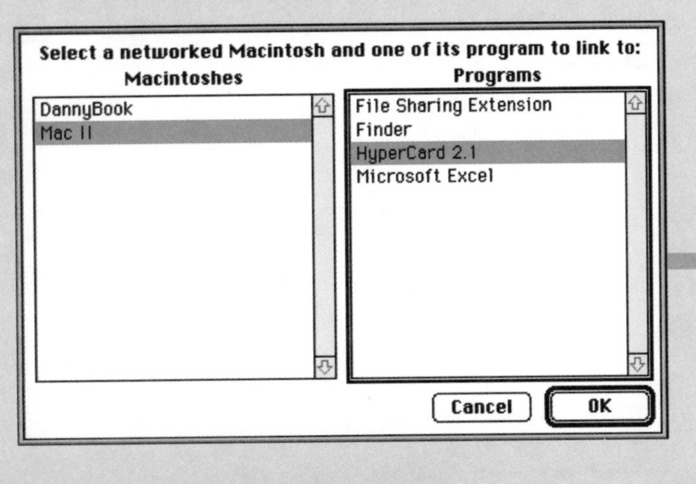

While FileShare is running on your Macintosh, you have considerable control over who's using what and when to disconnect users for any reason.

You should also periodically look through your Users and Groups control panel to keep the items up to date—removing users who no longer connect to your network, deleting groups that no longer work together, etc.

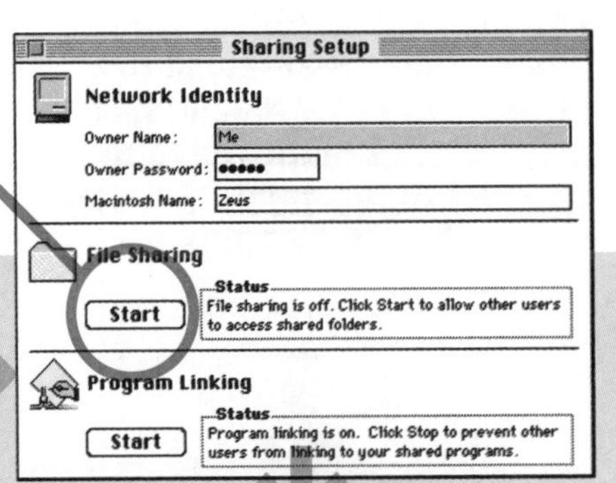

Click here to stop

Disconnecting All Users

If you turn off file sharing completely or attempt to shut down the computer while others are using your computer, you can give users advanced warning about the impending closure of your computer. When you shut down, you can walk away from your Macintosh, while giving several minutes' warning to users. After that time, your Macintosh shuts off by itself (except for compact Macintoshes, which must also be switched off).

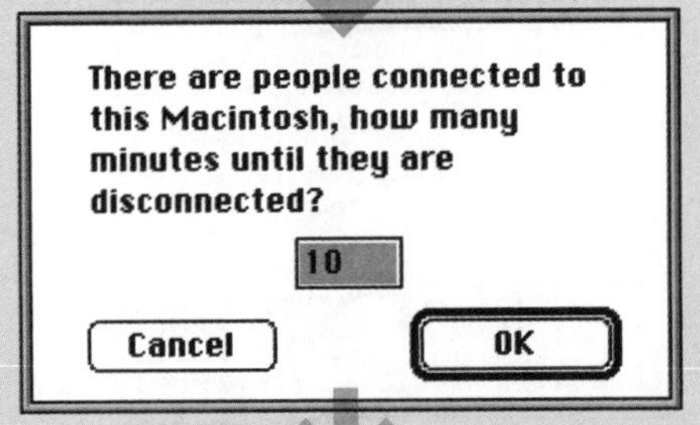

Is a Folder Being Used?

From the Finder, you can see immediately whether a shared folder is currently accessed by a user. The folder's icon has user faces in it.

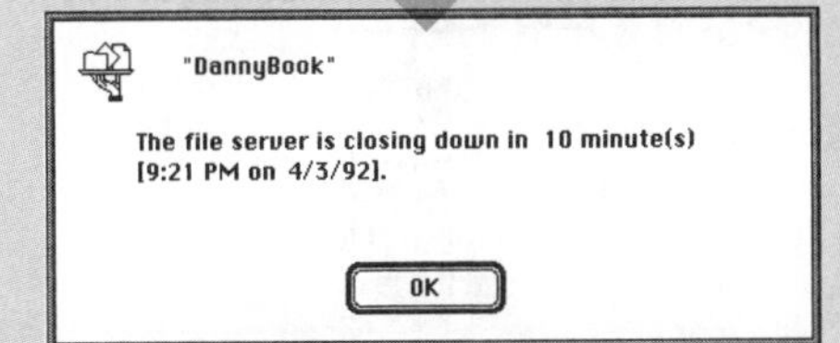

Who Is Connected?

At any time, you can see who is currently connected to your Macintosh and which folder(s) they are accessing. If connected users are actively accessing files, you'll see network activity in the meter.

Logging Off Another's Macintosh

When you are finished using the folder or disk from another Macintosh, it is common courtesy to log off. Drag the server icon on the Desktop to the Trash.

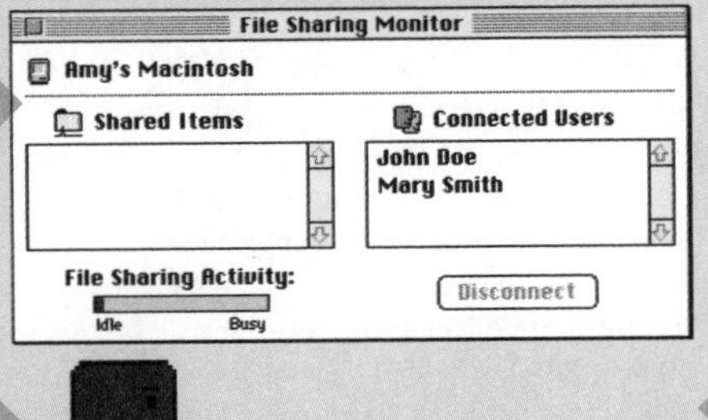

Temporarily Remove a User

You may prevent a currently connected user from working further on your files.

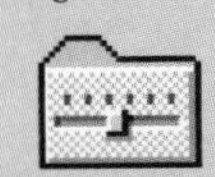

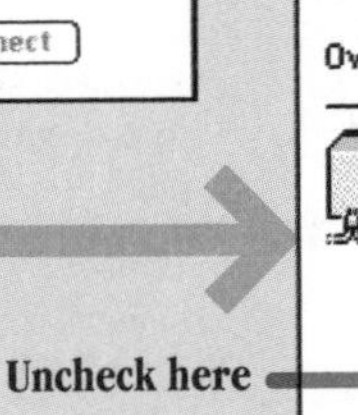

Uncheck here

Permanently Removing a User or Group

Users and groups can be dragged to the Trash, just like any file. If you delete a user, it is automatically removed from all groups in which it was a member.

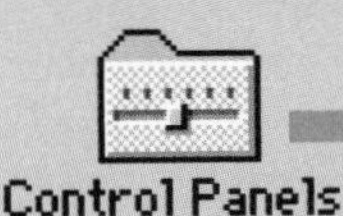

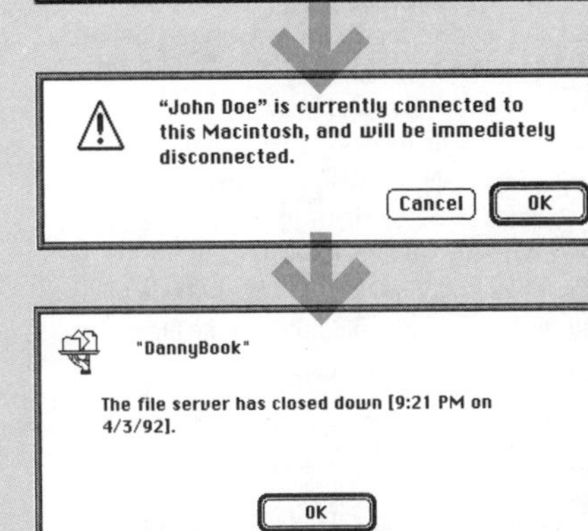

Permanently Removing a User from a Group

If you just want to remove a user from a group, but keep the user, then drag the member icon to the Trash.

Increasingly, the "no man is an island" phrase applies to personal computers. Beyond connecting a Macintosh to a network of other Macintoshes, many users find the need to connect to, or share information with, other computers.

Despite early impressions to the contrary, the Macintosh is one of the most "connectable" personal computers around. Without any more hardware or software than what comes with every Macintosh today, you can exchange files with any 3.5" floppy disk drive-equipped MS-DOS computer just by swapping diskettes (and a bit of clicking in the Apple File Exchange program, which comes with System 7).

Macintosh and IBM PC users in the same office can contribute to, say, the same Excel spreadsheet or WordPerfect document. With add-on hardware for IBM-style PCs and third-party networking software, it is also possible to combine Macintoshes and PCs on an AppleTalk network, so that both types of machines can share the same file server or open each other's disk volumes.

What's a modem?

The term modem is a combination of the words **modulator** and **demodulator**. As a modulator, a modem converts the zero and one bit representations of computer information into audible sounds that can travel over regular telephone lines. At the other end, the modem demodulates the signals back into the zeros and ones that the receiving computer understands. One Macintosh serial port, labeled with a telephone icon, is recommended for connecting a modem.

Of Baud and bps

Modems are often interchangeably rated in two units of measure called baud (pronounced bawd, and named after French communications pioneer, J.M.E. Baudot) and bits per second (bps). In practice, these terms do not refer to the same amount of information per second, so the regard the values merely as relative speed indicators.

Common modem speeds these days are 1200 and 2400 baud for data. Fax modems send at 9600 baud, although with an entirely different protocol than regular data modems. The faster the modem speed, the higher the quality of phone line needed to accomplish error free information exchanges. Improved voice quality of long distance telephone lines in the United States is making 9600 baud data transfer increasingly common, despite the higher cost of such data modems.

Mac-to-Macintosh File Transfer

In addition to the obvious methods of getting a file from one Macintosh to another (exchanging a floppy disk—humorously called sneakerNet—or connecting via System 7 FileShare on a network), Macintosh users at different sites can use telephone modems and communications software to accomplish the same feat. Both modems must have the same transmission speed abilities, and both users need telecommunications software (**Microphone** by Software Ventures is a popular choice) to control the modem and transfer the files.

The two users don't have to use the same communications software. Both programs, however, must have the same communications settings (usually set in a dialog box available from a menu command—common settings are 1200 baud, 8 data bits, 1 stop bit, no parity). For file transfer, both programs must also have the same error detection protocols (one called MacBinary XMODEM is the most popular).

Assuming both users have connected a modem to their computers and are running communications software, here are typical steps in exchanging a file from Macintosh A to Macintosh B:

1. Macintosh A uses the software to instruct the modem to await a call.
2. Macintosh B uses the software to instruct the modem to dial Macintosh B's phone number.
3. If all goes well, both users see the word **CONNECT** in the terminal window that is part of their communications software. They should type a line of text to each other to make sure both software programs are set correctly.
4. Macintosh A issues the software command to send a file. Through a standard file dialog box, the user selects the file.
5. Macintosh B issues the software command to receive a file (although some communications programs detect an incoming file, obviating the need for this step).
6. During transfer (with XMODEM transfers), both users see a dialog box display progress as blocks of the file move across the phone line.
7. When the transfer is complete, both machines use the software to instruct the modem to hang up the phone line.

It's not uncommon for first attempts at making the initial connection to fail. It may take a few tries of double-checking the software settings and restarting the modem to successfully connect.

A great many Macintosh users also use telephone **modems** to connect their Macintoshes to computers—from other Macintoshes to huge mainframes—in other locations. Communications software for your Macintosh allows Macintosh-to-Macintosh file transfers, logging into global electronic mail services, linking to corporate databases, and joining lively idea exchanges by way of electronic bulletin boards.

File Compression

To reduce the time it takes to transfer a file from one computer to another, a number of compression techniques are available. Programs that compress files are usually commercial products, while the corresponding decompression utility is often available free from user groups and bulletin boards. **File compressors** actually create a compressed copy of a file (or group of files) as an intermediate file, which is the one that gets transferred via modem.

When downloading a file (transferring from another computer to yours) from **bulletin board services** (BBSs), you'll often see three-letter identifiers following a period at the end of the file—called a file name extension. In on-line software libraries, an extension usually lets you know what, if any, compression was used to create the file. Here are common Macintosh file identifiers:

Identifier	Compressor	Decompressor
.txt	None	None: Plain text file, ready to read
.asc	None	None: an ASCII text file
.sit	Stuff-It	UnStuffIt Deluxe
.cpt	Compactor	Extractor
.sea	Compactor	None (self-extracting archive)

Depending on the type of file, a file compression program can reduce the size of a file by one-half or more. If you are using a commercial service for file transfer (including attaching documents to electronic mail), file compression can be a money saver, even though you often have to go through extra steps on both ends of the transfer.

File Formats

When exchanging document files with non-Macintosh desktop computers, it is sometimes possible for both computers to use the same document. A common **file format** is necessary, such that programs on both computers can open and save changes to the file.

Plain text files are one common file type that virtually every personal computer can open with one or more programs on that computer. Many Macintosh programs, for example, offer options in the **Save** dialog box to save the file as a plain text file. Other programs, such as database programs, provide export facilities to save their information as text files. Another term for a text file is an **ASCII** (ASS-kee) file, a reference to a standard coding scheme that assigns numeric values to each letter, numeral, and punctuation mark of the English language. Every personal computer knows that the ASCII code number for the capital letter "A," for example, is 65.

A potential problem with ASCII files, however, is that word processing document style parameters (e.g., bold text, center alignment, tab settings.) are not saved with the ASCII characters. To facilitate the bridge between incompatible word processing file formats is a common format called **rich text format** (RTF). Many word processing programs on different computing systems open and save their documents in these formats.

Text versions of database and spreadsheet programs also adhere to another convention that help other programs use the information. Each database field or spreadsheet cell needs to be distinguished from information in adjacent field or cell; each database record and spreadsheet row needs to be distinguished from its neighbors. The most common way of making these distinctions is with unique delimiter characters. The *tab* character (ASCII value 9) separates fields and cells from each other; the return character (ASCII 13) separates records and spreadsheet rows. This format is called a tab-delimited file. Most Macintosh spreadsheets and databases can read and save information in this format, usually as a method of transferring information between normally incompatible programs.

A comma-delimited file (more common in the PC world due to its popularity as the format for the dBase commercial database) places commas between fields, but the same return character between records.

Multiplatform Applications

Software providers who offer similar programs for both the Macintosh and **MS-DOS/Windows** (each one of these is called a **platform**) often have compatible file formats, such that a document saved on one platform is readable by the same program on a different platform. Examples of such program include: Microsoft Excel, Microsoft Word, WordPerfect, and Lotus 1-2-3. In these instances, the only transfer hurdle is getting the file from one disk format to another.

Reading/Writing MS-DOS Disks

Macintosh and MS-DOS 3.5" diskettes look alike on the outside, but the way they map information on the disk surface is entirely different. A disk formatted in one system is unreadable by the other. Third-party system software extensions for the Macintosh allow DOS disks to appear on the desktop just like any disk. But if you need to transfer material to or from an MS-DOS disk is relatively infrequent, the **Apple File Exchange** program, which comes with System 7, can do the job.

Here are the steps to transfer an MS-DOS file to the Macintosh:

1. Start Apple File Exchange. Your hard disk volume's files and folders are listed on the left; the right column is empty.
2. Insert the MS-DOS disk into your SuperDrive floppy disk drive. The files on the disk appear in the right column.
3. Select one or more files from the right column, and click «Translate». Those files are now on your Macintosh hard disk.
4. Activate the Finder, start your application, and open the file.
5. When you quit Apple File Exchange, the MS-DOS disk is automatically ejected.

In the reverse direction, you simply translate in the opposite direction. Be aware, however, that MS-DOS file names are restricted to 8 letters, followed by a period and up to three more letters as an extension. Apple File Exchange truncates longer Macintosh names to fit, so you may wish to rename the file on the Macintosh before copying it to the DOS disk.

With the help of system software, the Macintosh is one of the most helpful personal computers when it comes to letting you know when something out of the ordinary is about to happen. Alert boxes emanating from System 7 are informative, often telling you what to do next.

Not every problem comes with on-screen instructions, however. The most frustrating difficulties Macintosh users have is when something goes wrong while trying to start the computer. Rarely are there friendly messages to help. Still, if you are observant, you can spot a number of clues to help you figure out what's wrong and what to do about it.

Nothing happens when you turn on the Macintosh.

Explanation: On a compact Macintosh (Plus, SE, SE/30, Classic, Classic II), the machine is not getting power; on a Macintosh II system, either the machine isn't getting power or the keyboard power switch is not communicating with the Macintosh. On PowerBooks, either the battery has been removed or it is completely discharged.

Solution: For the compact Macintoshes, check to make sure that the Macintosh **power cord** is securely connected to the Macintosh and to the power outlet. Be sure the outlet, itself, has power. Perhaps the outlet is connected to a wall switch or is part of a switched power strip. Plug another electrical device into the outlet to verify that power is at least reaching the outlet. If the outlet is OK, try another power cord. The Macintosh power cord is similar to most personal computer device power cords. If another power cord still doesn't get your Macintosh going, the problem lies inside the Macintosh, and requires a technician to repair.

For Macintosh IIs, check all the possibilities above. Then look at the keyboard cable, making sure it is securely connected to the keyboard and an ADB port on your Macintosh. If your model has two ADB ports, try the other port. If possible, also try another Macintosh keyboard—the contacts of the power-on switch have been known to oxidize and refuse to make contact. Lastly, try pressing the manual power switch on the rear panel. If this also fails to bring the machine to life, a technician needs to look at the machine.

For PowerBooks, make sure the battery is inserted properly. Connect the AC charger to a wall power outlet. If the machine fails to start (remember the trap door power switch on the 140 and 170 models), the unit needs repair.

Unusual Tones Sound at Startup

Explanation: When you turn on a Macintosh II, it performs a number of self-tests of the hardware before looking for a startup disk. If any of these tests fail after the familiar start-up tone, you hear any combination of three tone sequences after the Macintosh startup chord: a single high-pitched tone; two high-pitched **tones** going up in frequency; and a broken (A major) chord scale of four notes. The single tone means a failure during a RAM test; the two tones means failure during the second RAM test; the chord scale—the most common—means that there is some unknown hardware failure.

Solution: Either RAM failure may mean that there is a problem with one or more RAM SIMMs installed in your Macintosh. It's probably more serious than just an unseated SIMM, which causes the chord scale tones. If your Macintosh allows you to remove some of the SIMMs to work in smaller memory, try removing a SIMM group to see if you can isolate the SIMM giving you the problem. Then replace that SIMM.

When the chord scale sounds, think about the last hardware-related changes you made to your system. This could range from installing SIMMs to changing **SCSI cables**. Look for loose SIMMs, system board connectors, and SCSI cables. If everything looks OK to you, then you'll have to let a technician look at the Mac.

Sad Macintosh Icon Upon Power On

Explanation: A sad Macintosh icon is the compact Macintosh and Quadra way of letting you know about a hardware problem diagnosed during the Mac's initial self-test. Below the icon is a series of numbers, which help technicians uncover the location of bad RAM and other problems.

Solution: If you've installed SIMMs yourself, re-open the case and make sure the SIMMs are installed correctly and that any resistors or jumpers on the system board are connected or removed for the particular memory configuration. When re-assembling the Macintosh, be sure all system board connectors are firmly attached. For Quadras, the problem is often related to incompatible drivers for SCSI devices, such as hard disks, scanners, etc. Be sure you have the latest drivers for peripherals before starting up those devices. An incompatible disk drive driver may prevent the Quadra fron even starting from a floppy disk as long as the hard disk is turned on. If the problem persists, a technician should look at the machine.

Floppy Disk is Ejected at Power On

Explanation: This is actually normal behavior for the Macintosh when it discovers a floppy disk in a disk drive at startup and the disk does not have a **System file** on it. As the disk is being ejected, the Macintosh icon on the screen shows an "X" in the middle. If the disk is supposed to have a System file on it to let you start from the floppy, then the disk may be damaged.

Solution: Start the Macintosh from another startup disk (or hard disk), and then insert the floppy disk to inspect its contents. If the disk is damaged, you will be prompted that the disk is unreadable. Otherwise, make sure the disk has a System and Finder on it. If those files are on the disk, and the Macintosh still rejects the disk at startup, then the System and Finder files are probably damaged on the disk. Create a new startup disk from the installer disks.

No Hard Disk Starts Up

Explanation: The core problem is that your Macintosh is not recognizing your hard disk. The causes can range from something as simple as an external hard disk not being turned on in the correct sequence to a complete hard disk crash.

Solution: Because there are so many reasons your Macintosh doesn't recognize your hard disk, here is the range of things to look into:

1. Try restarting the Macintosh a couple times. Sometimes the Macintosh needs a couple restarts to recognize a newly connected SCSI drive.
2. Start your Macintosh with a minimum system diskette, and see if the hard disk comes onto the Desktop as a second volume. If it does not, continue with the following; otherwise see the next troubleshooting problem.
3. For an external SCSI drive, be sure all SCSI cables are connected securely.
4. If you have many SCSI devices chained to your Macintosh, disconnect all but the hard disk. Be sure it is terminated per the manufacturer's instructions and SCSI discussions on page ➜ 58.
5. Be sure you turn on the external SCSI hard disk before turning on the Macintosh.
6. Be sure the SCSI ID of an external device is something other than zero.
7. Try another cable for an external SCSI hard disk.
8. For an internal hard disk, make sure the cables connecting the disk to the system board are firmly attached.
9. Be sure your hard disk driver (extension) is compatible with System 7. If the drive is an Apple drive, the installation of System 7 takes care of that. For third-party drives, new driver software may be required. Contact the manufacturer for an update.
10. Try zapping the PRAM ➜41, and restart once again.
11. For an internal hard disk (especially 80MB Quantum-made drives sold by Apple), very gently rap the center of the disk (the hub). These disks were notorious for not spinning upon startup.
12. Most external, non-Apple hard drives come with software for formatting and maintenance. Start the Macintosh with that hard disk software (from floppy disk). If your software includes a program that lets you look at a list of SCSI devices recognized by your Macintosh, look to see if your hard disk is in the list. A shareware control panel, called SCSI Probe is an excellent tool for this exploration. If you've satisfied all previous items, and this software still does not see your hard disk on the SCSI chain, your hard disk may be inoperable. Your data is probably still intact on the disk. Professional disk recovery services can usually recover your data in the process of bringing the disk back to life. Such services can be expensive (up to $1000 for recovering and repairing a 300MB hard disk). Contact the disk drive manufacturer or dealer for guidance on recovering your data.
13. If the hard disk software does find the disk, try using that software to reinstall the driver (extension) for that hard disk. Be sure the driver is compatible with System 7. If you have a backup of your data, you should consider using the software to reformat your hard disk, and then copy data files and programs back to the disk. Something has been corrupted in the mapping of information on the disk, making reformatting a good choice.

In the following pages of this section, you can find explanations and solutions to problems and messages you may encounter while using the Macintosh. Items that don't present any messages are listed first. After that comes an alphabetical listing of the messages you are most likely to encounter. Messages not included here are those that are so thorough on their own that they require no explanation.

Alert messages often substitute specific names of documents, applications, folders, and so on as part of the message—all to help you better understand the context of the message. Since each message of this type has different names between the quotes, the listings below adhere to a convention of naming an object as "**My**" plus the type of object: **MyDoc** is any document; **MyApp** is an application; and so on. When you encounter a message that begins with the name of a document, folder, or disk, look under the M's in the listing below.

Hard Disk Shows Only as Secondary Volume

Explanation: If your hard disk won't boot, but does appear on the Desktop when you start from a minimum system disk or another hard disk, the problem is usually related to damaged system files.

Solution: Use the hard disk's utility software to re-install its driver (extension) on the hard disk. Make sure the driver is System 7 compatible before trying to restart from that hard disk. Then reinstall the system software from the Install diskettes. Then run Disk First Aid, a utility program that comes on one of the System 7 installer disks. This program repairs minor hard disk problems. If you have a third-party hard disk, it probably comes with similar repair software tailored to that drive. Commercial disk utility products, such as Norton Utilities (from Symantec) and MacTools (from Central Point Software) include additional disk repair aides.

If these efforts fail, restart from a system diskette, and perform two backups of all data files, programs, and non-Apple system files. Reformat the disk using the hard disk utility software. Re-install System 7, and re-load your backed up files onto the hard disk.

Wrong hard disk starts up

Explanation: The Macintosh either doesn't know or has forgotten which hard disk should be the startup volume.

Solution: Use the **Startup Disk** control panel ➔80 to select the desired startup volume, then restart the Macintosh. If this doesn't work, then make sure all SCSI devices on the SCSI chain have different ID numbers. Finally, zap the PRAM ➔41, reselect the desired disk in the Startup Disk control panel, and restart the Macintosh once more. Also see page ➔58 for the natural startup order of SCSI hard disks when PRAM is in its default state.

Startup Stalls Midway

Explanation: Assuming you reach the Welcome to Macintosh alert, an extension or control panel is conflicting with the system or other extension when it loads into memory at startup.

Solution: Watch the screen closely during startup. Many extensions and control panels (those that load some part of themselves into RAM during startup) display their icons at the bottom of the screen. If the startup procedure stops after a particular icon shows up, then make note of that icon. Restart the Macintosh with the *shift* key down to bypass all extensions. Then **View** your Extensions folder **by Name**. Since extensions load into RAM in alphabetical order, the most likely suspect is the one with the name after the last icon to appear on the screen during startup. If all extensions loaded, then do the same procedure with the **Control Panels** folder. Not all control panels load into memory, so the culprit may be further down the alphabet from the last successful loading item. Try removing suspected items to the root level of your hard disk, and restart. If the startup is successful, return suspected items to their respective folders one at a time and restart. When the Macintosh no longer starts, the item you just inserted into the System folder is the conflicting extension or control panel. Contact the publisher or author of the program about your incompatibility. It may require an update for the version of system software you're running.

The Macintosh "freezes"

Explanation: Your Macintosh has either suffered a catastrophic software failure (not likely to harm your machine), you are using a HyperCard stack that is in some kind of loop, an **AppleTalk** or **SCSI cable** has come apart from its connector, or the ADB cable between the keyboard and Macintosh is loose or deteriorating. Software failures of this kind usually leave part of the screen unrefreshed, as a dialog box or other window closes in response to some thoroughly proper action on your part. A software failure is either the result of poor programming of the application that took the Macintosh with it or the result of a conflict between a software extension and an application (or multiple extensions). A **HyperCard** freeze is usually not as serious as other software failures, since the HyperCard loop is easily interrupted from the keyboard.

Solution: In the case of a software failure, you should first try to **Quit** the program by typing *command-option-escape*. In the resulting dialog box, click **Force Quit**. This shuts down only the offending application (losing all changes since your last save). Save documents in other programs and restart the Macintosh.

If you can't force quit, then restart the Macintosh. If you have a programmer's switch ➡11, press the Reset button, rather than fully powering down the Macintosh. Sometimes a failure of this nature renders even the Reset switch inoperable. If so, then hit the power switch on the rear panel. When the problem is predictable and repeatable, contact the software publisher with a bug report. If the publisher has discovered the bug, it may have a fix for you over and above regular product upgrades.

For a HyperCard freeze, always try typing *command-period* to get HyperCard out of any loop it may be in. At this point, it is best to quit and restart HyperCard. Try opening and using the stack again. If the loop persists, contact the publisher or author about the problem.

A loose **AppleTalk** or **SCSI cable** can freeze a machine, especially when you perform some operation that requires information be sent or retrieved through those ports. If an AppleTalk cable comes undone at a critical moment, you may be able to recover gracefully by plugging the cable into whatever connector it came from. A disconnected SCSI cable, however, won't recover so nicely—in fact it is hazardous to the health of your Macintosh to plug SCSI cables while the machine is running. You'll have to turn off the machine, reconnect the cable, and restart.

When everything else seems fine, your keyboard cable may be giving out. Turn off the Macintosh, jiggle the cable and make sure all ADB cables are firmly attached to their connectors. Then restart the machine. If possible, also try another cable on the same machine and keyboard. Keyboard cables tend to wear out where they bend away from the keyboard toward the Macintosh.

Multiple icons for a hard disk appear on the Desktop

Explanation: SCSI cabling and termination is improperly connected. SCSI signals are bouncing around your SCSI chain. This is a serious problem, which can damage your disks if not remedied right away.

Solution: Immediately shut down your Macintosh. Leave it off for about ten minutes before restarting with a new SCSI cable and terminator configuration. Use the SCSI cabling guidelines on pages ➡ 58 to adjust your SCSI chain.

An Expected Hard Disk Fails to Appear on the Desktop

Explanation: If you have multiple hard disks connected, and one doesn't appear on the Desktop after startup, the Macintosh doesn't recognize it on the SCSI chain. If the missing volume(s) is a partition of a large hard disk, the most likely cause is that the volume containing the partitioning software (extension) was not the startup disk. Most partitioning software must be in the startup disk to mount other partitions.

Solution: In the case of a standalone disk:

1. Restart the Macintosh a couple more times, especially if you just connected the disk to the Mac.
2. Be sure SCSI numbers on all devices are unique.
3. Go through recommended SCSI cabling techniques described on pages ➡ 58.
4. Use a SCSI program (such as SCSI Probe) to see if your disk is recognized on the SCSI chain. Such software usually lets you mount the disk to the Desktop without restarting.

In the case of a hard disk partition:

1. Make the hard disk containing the partition the startup disk, and restart the Macintosh.
2. Check the partitioning software (usually a desk accessory) to see which partitions it mounts automatically upon startup.

These messages are found in alert boxes that may appear in response to specific conditions or actions. They appear in alphabetical order.

A newer item named "MyDoc/MyApp/MyFolder" already exists in this location. Are you sure you want to replace the newer item with the one you're moving?

Explanation: Before you copy or move an item to another folder, system software compares the name of the item against everything in that folder. If the name is the same as an existing file or folder, then system software also compares the modification dates of both items. If the item in the destination folder has a more recent modification date, you get this message. This is an attempt to help you identify the most recent version of a file. This comparison, however, does not take into account that both items with the same name may be of completely different file types. Proceed with OK only if you are one hundred percent sure that you won't be overwriting a more up-to-date version of a file or folder. If you click Cancel, the copy or move operation is cancelled, and everything returns to its previous state.

An error occured while writing to the disk. The file "MyDoc" was not saved. ID=00

Explanation: In the process of saving a document, something prevents the write to the disk. Typical ID numbers indicate the problem:

-33 Directory on the disk is full

-34 Disk is full

-35 Volume is no longer available on the desktop

-36 Input/Output error

An item named "MyDoc/MyApp/MyFolder" already exists in this location. Do you want to replace it with the one you're moving?

Explanation: Before you copy or move an item to another folder, system software compares the name of the item against everything in that folder. If the name is the same as an existing file or folder, and the modification dates are the same, system software alerts you to what may be a wasted move or copy. Sometimes, however, it is easier to just copy, say, a folder full of stuff, which may duplicate items in the destination, than painstakingly deselect duplicate items.

An older item named "MyDoc/MyApp/MyFolder" already exists in this location. Do you want to replace it with the one you're moving?

Explanation: Before you copy or move an item to another folder, system software compares the name of the item against everything in that folder. If the name is the same as an existing file or folder, then system software also compares the modification dates of both items. If the item in the destination folder has a less recent modification date, you get this message. This is an attempt to help you identify the most recent version of a file. This comparison, however, does not take into account that both items with the same name may be of completely different file types. Generally, it is best to allow something to copy over an older version, provided the latest version is not some temporary test document. If you click Cancel, the copy or move operation is cancelled, and everything returns to its previous state.

Are you sure you want to completely replace contents of "MyDisk1" with contents of "MyDisk2"?

Explanation: You can freely copy the contents of one disk to another, provided that the destination disk is at least the same size as the source disk. When you see this message, study it carefully to make sure you dragged the icon of the correct source disk to the desired destination disk icon. As the disk copy takes place, you see a **Copy progress** dialog box. While you may stop the process at any time, the destination disk will likely lose some of its original material if you've let some of the copying go ahead. The copy retains the exact same folder layout and desktop properties of the original—except for the name of the disk. If you want the copy to have the same disk name, you'll have to edit the destination disk name manually.

Are you sure you want to rebuild the desktop file on the disk "MyDisk"? Comments in info windows will be lost.

Explanation: If you start or restart your Macintosh with the *command* and *option* keys held down, you can let the system software rebuild the Desktop file—a good periodic maintenance procedure for all Macintosh users ➔ 12, 54. This message is here to let you change your mind before the process begins, because on large hard disks, it can take a few minutes to complete. As indicated in the message, any comments you've entered into the **Get Info** boxes of files are lost during Desktop file rebuilding.

Are you sure you want to set the memory size for the application "MyApp" to less than the suggested minimum?

Explanation: Some program authors allow you to set the actual application memory space for an application to somewhat less then an ideal minimum. This message warns you that you are setting the size to less than minimum recommended **RAM**. The penalty for running in less than suggested minimum memory is usually slower performance ➔ 44.

Because of a communication error, "Mydoc" from "MyApp" could not be printed on LaserWriter "MyPrinter". Try again?

Explanation: This message from PrintMonitor indicates that the Macintosh and LaserWriter had some difficulty in communicating during a particular print job. It's always worth trying a print job again, but with a communication error, the culprit is more likely a loose cable or some other glitch that will require resetting the Macintosh or LaserWriter or both. If you cancel printing, the print job is deleted. You'll have to reissue the **Print** command from the application to get the print job back in the queue.

Could not locate the edition, because the volume it is on could not be mounted.

Explanation: The shared volume containing an edition your document subscribes to is not available on the network. It could mean simply that the owner's Macintosh is turned off or has file sharing turned off. It could also mean that the owner has changed the sharing property of the folder containing the edition file. The folder might no longer be shared as a distinct volume, but as part of an enclosing folder or disk. Use the **Chooser** to mount other volumes from the owner's Macintosh to see if your edition file is in one of those volumes (it may be nested one or more levels deeper now). If the edition is there, then cancel the existing subscription, and resubscribe to the new edition. Then drop a note to the owner complaining that changing folder sharing properties without warning is a dirty trick.

Document "Mydoc" from "MyApp" could not be printed on LaserWriter "MyPrinter" because of a PostScript error.

Explanation: This message from PrintMonitor reports a problem that the printer has with the PostScript commands sent by the application on the Macintosh. It's impossible to tell what's really wrong. Sometimes it can be a document trying to print to too large a space on the page for the amount of RAM in the particular LaserWriter model you're using. Sometimes restarting the application or resetting the printer can clear the problem. If not, try to print the document on a LaserWriter containing more RAM.

Edition cannot be found, because the volume it is on could not be mounted/ because it is missing.

Explanation: Both **publishers** and **subscribers** look to edition files—publishers on saving, subscribers on opening. Subscribers, however, rely on editions for material. When a subscriber in an opening document cannot find an edition file, it usually displays the last information it had from the edition. Digging deeper into subscriber information, a click of [Get Edition Now] produces an error message revealing the missing edition. The edition may be on a shared volume not currently mounted (or mountable), or the edition may have been deleted entirely. You'll have to live with the last version of the data, or open a new link to a new edition created by another publisher.

Folders cannot be copied onto 400K disks. To copy the contents of a folder, open the folder and drag the items inside it to the disk.

Explanation: The 400K disk was the original Macintosh disk size. It was designed around a file system called **Macintosh File System** (MFS). MFS created folder organization in a manner different from today's **Hierarchical File System** (HFS). Four-hundred kilobyte disks work only in MFS. As such, they don't understand HFS folder organization. You'll have to copy items as distinct items (of course you can select and copy multiple items), and re-do the folder organization in MFS folders on the diskette.

Items on floppy disks cannot be shared.

Explanation: The prohibition on sharing items from floppy disks is primarily a guard against the transient nature of floppy disks on a typical system. It could be hazardous and disappointing for other users to mount a floppy disk or folder therein from your machine, only to have you eject the disk to perform some other diskette operation. To keep file sharing running more smoothly, Apple engineers have restricted sharing to hard disks and large removable media (like cartridge disks).

"MyApp" prefers 000K of memory. 000K is available. Do you want to open it using the available memory?

Explanation: As an application opens, it tries to occupy the amount of **RAM** specified in the Current Size field of the Get Info box for the application. If the application will run under less than that amount, but within the amount of free RAM available on your Macintosh, this alert message gives you a chance to open the application in available memory. If you've set a memory partition for an application much larger than its suggested size, then there is usually little problem running in what's available. You may not, however, be able to open large documents that you can under the larger memory partition. And if the application is running near its absolute minimum **RAM**➜44, the program may run slower as pieces of the program are retrieved from disk more often when you issue menu commands.

"Mydoc" from "MyApp" could not be printed because LaserWriter "MyPrinter" could not be found. Try again?

Explanation: It's not unusual to turn on the printer and issue the Print command at about the same time. But when PrintMonitor is ready to send the print job to the printer and the printer is not yet warmed up, you may get this message back from PrintMonitor. You can wait at this message until the printer is ready, and then click Try Again. If you cancel, you'll have to reissue the **Print** command from the application to get the print job rolling again.

Another case of this message is when you are connected to a multi-LaserWriter network, especially one with multiple zones. Be sure that the last LaserWriter on which you printed is turned on and available on the network. You may have to re-choose the printer via the Chooser. If the network cable to the printer came undone since you last print job, you will get this message as well. Make sure no one has kicked the cables out of their sockets along the path.

"Mydoc" from "MyApp" could not be printed on LaserWriter "MyPrinter" because of an error.

Explanation: When a message, such as this one from **PrintMonitor**, merely calls the problem an "error," it means that one of any number of highly technical problems has caused the print job to abort. When the problem is more directly under your control (e.g., the printer couldn't be found) it tells you. Cancel the print job, and reissue the **Print** command again. If the problem persists, restart the printer, the Macintosh, or both to try to clear the problem.

"Mydoc" from "MyApp" failed to print to LaserWriter "MyPrinter". Do you want to try to print it again?

Explanation: PrintMonitor is telling you that for an unknown reason, the print job was not completed. Before trying again, be sure the printer is on, and the **AppleTalk** cable is secure along the path between your Macintosh and printer. If you are on a network with multiple printers, be sure the printer name shown in this message is the printer you intended to print the document. If it is not, cancel the print job, change the printer via the **Chooser**, and reissue the **Print** command from the document.

"MyFolder/MyDisk" could not be shared, because there is a shared folder inside it.

Explanation: You tried to make a disk or folder available for sharing when one or more items inside that disk or folder are already set up for sharing. To complete the desired sharing process, you'll have to turn off sharing for every item inside the disk or folder, and then turn on sharing for the whole thing. This could be dangerous, however, if a lot of users actively use the nested shared folder(s). If, for example, someone has subscribed to an **edition** in one of those folders, and you turn off its sharing property to turn it on for an enclosing folder, the user's document won't be able to find the edition. The user gets the message "Could not locate the edition, because the volume it is on could not be mounted." In other words, any folder you share could be a valid volume name for those users with access to that folder. Changing the folder's status eliminates it as a possible volume to be mounted. If you must change the sharing property of a folder to allow sharing of an enclosing folder or disk, be sure you alert users of the original folder. They'll have to cancel their subscribers and resubscribe to the same edition on the "new" volume.

"MyFolder/MyDisk" could not be shared, because there is already a shared folder with that name.

Explanation: You have tried to turn on file sharing for a folder with the same name as a disk or folder already set for file sharing. Even if the folders are from different parts of your hard disk, File Sharing does not allow you to share two volumes with the same name. This prevents confusion at the other user's end, because he or she would have no idea which of two same name volumes contained the desired information.

No battery reserve power remains. The Macintosh will go to sleep within 10 seconds to preserve the contents of memory. Good Night.

Explanation: Your Macintosh Portable or PowerBook battery has reached its lowest possible level, and will shut you out in 10 seconds. If the battery were to run down even further, you would probably lose the contents of RAM. You don't have to save your work to disk when you get this warning, because your current documents in RAM should still be there after you connect to AC power (assuming you do it within a day or two). It's a good idea to connect the power cord as soon as possible after seeing this message to make sure RAM battery backup doesn't also drain your changes away.

No Personal LaserWriter LS is available. Please check that the printer is properly connected and switched on.

Explanation: The Personal LaserWriter LS extension (driver) cannot get any signal back from the printer indicating a solid connection. Make sure you have used the **Chooser** to select the serial port to which the printer is connected, and that all cables are firmly attached to their connectors.

Not enough memory to open "My Desk Accessory." Try closing another desk accessory or quitting an application.

Explanation: The Scrapbook or other **desk accessory** tried to open, but couldn't load any information it needs to work fully. In addition to the suggestions in the alert, see page 79, 108 for additional memory management ideas.

One or more items could not be shared, because not all volumes are available for file sharing.

Explanation: Trying to share a volume or folder from a cartridge hard disk may trigger this message, even though the volume should be sharable. This appears to be a System 7 **bug**. This can happen if you mount the volume after start-up with a SCSI mounter such as **SCSI Probe**. **Restart** the Macintosh with the cartridge in the drive, and then try **Sharing** in the **File** menu again. You may not be able to eject the cartridge, however, unless you turn off **File Sharing** altogether or shut down the Macintosh.

Only 25% of the battery's reserve power remains. Please put your Macintosh to sleep and plug in your power adapter immediately. Doing so will help extend the life of your battery.

Explanation: Your Macintosh Portable battery is running quite low. At this point, you still have enough juice to do a final save to disk if you like. After you do so, immediately put the machine to sleep and plug in the **AC power supply**. You may then reawaken the machine and continue working while the battery recharges.

Rebuilding the desktop file...

Explanation: You see this message in two cases:

1. when you have specifically instructed the Macintosh to rebuild the desktop file (by starting up with the *option* and *command* keys held down); and
2. at startup when a hard disk volume has been used on a System 6-based Macintosh prior to this startup.

Because Systems 6 and 7 maintain very different types of Desktop files, the System 7 version wants to make sure its version is up to date while you work under System 7. This rebuilding does not harm the System 6 desktop file, and you can freely move the hard disk between Macintoshes running either system. For more about the **Desktop file**, see page ➔12, 54.

Sorry, a system error has occurred.

Explanation: This message, known not too affectionately by Macintosh veterans as **The Bomb**, is the heartbreaker of all messages. It means that some software conflict was so great that it took out the entire system, instead of just a single application (which would have "unexpectedly quit"). When this occurs after a successful startup, the problem is usually linked to a conflict between an application and something in the System Folder—usually an extension (**INIT and driver types**) or **control panel**. This is particularly true if the bomb is repeatable. The search for the conflict should start with the latest application or System Folder file you've added to your hard disk. Try temporarily removing the new file, and see if the problem goes away. If so, then contact the publisher or author of that file and relate your experience, along with a complete list of extensions, control panels, and applications you use.

If the problem comes up during startup, it can still be an extension or control panel problem. Restarting the machine with the *shift* key held down turns off loading of all extensions and control panels. If the machine works fine with extensions off, then start working through the extensions to find the culprit➔83. But the bomb at startup may also be a problem with a damaged system software file. Try reinstalling the system software from the installer disks. If that doesn't help, try reinstalling your hard disk's driver with the help of its utility software.

System bomb messages in System 7 also include additional technical information about the program that was running when it crashed and the possible cause of the system crash. This information may be of use to the technical support people at the company whose software you suspect of the crash. For most users, however, the messages give no clue to help reduce the likelihood of having the error again.

A system bomb should not be the result of anything you do. Program authors should guard against system bombs even if the user punishes the software. Do not feel responsible for any system bomb you see.

That name is too long. Desk accessory names can have up to 30 characters.

That name is too long. Disk names can have up to 27 characters.

That name is too long. Folder names can have up to 31 characters.

That name is too long. User/Group names can have up to 31 characters.

Explanation: These messages are quite clear. What is interesting, however, is the inconsistency among item names throughout the Macintosh. Names of all items, including files, have limits. Still, you should be able to identify an item within 27 to 31 characters. The shorter the name, especially of files and folders, the more likely you'll be able to see the entire name in standard file dialog boxes➔106.

The alias "MyAlias" could not be used, because the disk "MyVolume", which contains the original item, could not be found.

The alias "MyAlias" could not be used, because the shared disk "MyVolume", which contains the original item, could not be found on the network.

The alias could not be opened, because the original could not be found.

The alias could not be opened, because the original is in the trash.

Explanation: Alias ➔120 files always point to their original files. If you try to work with an alias file, it merely passes all information along to the original, wherever it might be. If the original item is moved to another volume, its original volume is not currently available on the network or mounted on your Macintosh, or its original file is in the **Trash**, your alias won't be able to communicate with its original. If the alias is to a file in a shared folder or disk on someone else's Macintosh, it automatically mounts and logs you onto the volume. The first two messages refer to original files that exist on volumes other than the startup volume. The third message is for an alias whose original is on either the current startup disk or on a shared volume that your Macintosh can successfully mount—it just can't find the original file on the disk where it's supposed to be. If the alias points to a file on a shared volume that cannot be mounted, contact the owner to find out why the disk is no longer available (perhaps his or her machine is simply turned off or has file sharing turned off). If the message indicates that only the original file cannot be found (meaning that it found the shared disk), ask the owner why the original file is no longer on the disk. Both aliases and their originals may have their name changed without the link between them being broken. For an original file to be not found, it must have been deleted.

The application "MyApp" has unexpectedly quit, because an error of type 00 occurred.

Explanation: When an application quits unexpectedly, it is usually attributable to either a conflict between that application and some extension (INIT or driver) or the application didn't manage its memory allocation properly. The error number listed in this message rarely provides a clue as to the real problem for users (or to programmers, for that matter). Very often, expanding the memory allocation for an application reduces the likelihood of this error recurring. There is still a problem with the application somewhere, but until a new version repairs the problem, you can lower the risk by giving it more memory if available.

The control panel "MyControlPanel" cannot be used now, because not enough memory is available.

The control panel "MyControlPanel" cannot be used now. There may not be enough memory available, or the control panel may be damaged.

Explanation: Even though **control panels** take up very little memory, tight memory situations can prevent the opening of a single panel. To test whether the control panel is damaged, quit one application to open up memory space, and try to open the control panel again. If it still shows up as damaged, reinstall it (from the installer disks if it is an Apple control panel).

The control panel "MyControlPanel" cannot be used with this Macintosh.

Explanation: Occasionally, the Installer copies a control panel to a Macintosh model that can't use the particular control panel. For example, the **Portable** control panel cannot be opened on any Macintosh other than a Macintosh Portable or PowerBook. If your hard disk is an internal drive, delete any control panels that don't apply to your machine. On an external hard disk, you may wish to keep a larger library of control panels in case you connect the disk to other Macintosh models along the way.

The disk "My volume" could not be put away, because it is being shared.

Explanation: You cannot unmount a disk volume (drag its icon to the Trash) if it or any folder inside it is being shared. You may also see this message when trying to eject cartridge hard disks that are not shared. This appears to be a **bug** in System 7. If you turn off File Sharing (in the **Sharing Setup** control panel ➔80), you'll be able to unmount the volume.

The document "MyDocument" could not be opened, because the application program that created it could not be found. Do you want to open it using "MyApp"?

Explanation: Designers of some System 7 applications software have given their document files the power to recommend an alternative application for opening the documents in case the original application cannot be found. For example, you might give a word processing file to a friend, but that person doesn't have the same word processing program as you. Upon double-clicking that document file, your friend might be alerted that while the application that created the document is not available, TeachText is. What alternative application can read a document is entirely up to the program's author. In many cases, no alternate will be offered. The message will simply say that the creating application couldn't be found. You may still be able to open the document in another application of the same type (e.g., graphics, word processing), since many programs allow you to open documents in related file formats ➔130.

The document "MyDocument" is locked, so you will not be able to save any changes. Do you want to open it anyway?

Explanation: If you need to make changes to the document, you'll have to unlock it from the **Finder** first. Close the document, switch to the Finder, select the file, and choose **Get Info** from the **File** menu (or type *command-I*). At the lower left corner of the dialog is a Locked checkbox. Uncheck the box to unlock the file. If the box is already unchecked (the word "Locked" may be dimmed), it means that the disk on which the file resides is locked. You can unlock a floppy disk by ejecting it and sliding the locking tab closed ➜52. But if the file is on a **CD-ROM** or other locked medium, you'll have to copy the file to your hard disk to make changes. You won't be able to record those changes on the locked disk, however, by recopying the changed file to the locked disk.

The file server has closed down.

Explanation: The owner of a shared volume or disk has either turned off file sharing (for that volume or entirely) or has turned off his or her machine. You may get this message after receiving a warning some minutes in advance of the shutdown.

The file server is closing down in 10 minutes.

Explanation: The owner of a shared volume or disk has turned off file sharing or is about to shut down his or her system, but is giving all users currently connected to the server warning that the server is about to go down. Take this warning seriously. If you need to copy files from the server (presuming you have the access privileges to do so), then make your copies immediately. Similarly, if you are working on documents that are stored only on the server, make sure you wrap up work on those files right away. Once the server goes down, it will disappear from your **Desktop**.

The file server's connection has unexpectedly closed down.

Explanation: Something serious has happened to the connection between you and a **server**. Typically, this means that either the **AppleTalk** cable has become disconnected between the two machines or the server machine has suffered a power failure or system error. Contact the owner of the shared volume to see what caused the disconnection.

The folder "MyFolder" cannot be put in the Trash, because it is shared.

Explanation: You tried to drag a folder to the Trash that has file sharing turned on. The folder does not have to be in use by others to get this message. System software calls this to your attention because it is possible that others rely on the contents of this folder if it has been shared. If you know for a fact that others do not need the files in the folder, turn off file sharing for this folder, and then drag it to the **Trash**.

The font size for views must be a number.

The font size for views must be between 6 and 36.

Explanation: These messages come from entering invalid information into the font size field of the **Views** control panel. That a font size needs to be a number is obvious. But notice that you are restricted to 36 point size as a maximum for file names. Fonts smaller than 9 are difficult to read—impossible below six.

The memory size must be a number.

The memory size must be less than 100,000K.

Explanation: These messages come from entering invalid information into the current memory size field of an application's **Get Info** dialog box. A minimum value is specified by the program's author. The maximum is definitely limited by available memory rather than the 99,999K theoretical limit to this field's data entry. See ➜ 118 for more about application memory.

The Personal LaserWriter LS is missing its paper cassette. Please check that the paper cassette is properly inserted in the printer.

Explanation: In addition to the paper cassette missing, this message may indicate that the cassette isn't inserted all the way. Remove the cassette and reinsert it to make sure the internal contacts that detect the cassette engage.

The printer has been initialized with an incompatible version of the Laser Prep software. To reinitialize and continue printing, click OK or click Cancel to skip printing.

Explanation: When you print to a LaserWriter and get this message, it means that the last person to use the printer uses a different version of system software than you. If you click OK, your system software will reinitialize the printer for you. This takes quite a bit of time. The other person will have to do the same for his or her next printing job. To prevent these delays, install the same System 7 printer driver version on all Macintoshes who share the printer. You can do this even for users still using System 6 ➜ 71.

The printer is not responding and the current document cannot be completed. Please make sure the printer is turned on and ready.

Explanation: Your StyleWriter is either not turned on or there is something wrong with the connection between your Macintosh and the printer. It may be that the printer port is incorrectly selected in the **Chooser**. Reselect the StyleWriter and serial port from the Chooser to double-check the software connection.

The printer is not responding as a StyleWriter. Please go to the Chooser and check the port selection and printer type.

Explanation: The document you are trying to print was formatted with the StyleWriter **Page Setup** dialog. Since then, something has happened to the printer selection in the Chooser. Open the Chooser, select the StyleWriter driver, and select the port to which the printer is connected.

The Printer is not responding. Check the "Select" switch. Click OK to continue, Cancel to terminate printing.

Explanation: Your ImageWriter is not communicating back to the Macintosh. Make sure the Select switch and light are turned on at the printer. Also reselect the ImageWriter and printer port from the Chooser to double-check the software connection.

The selected items cannot all be put into the same location, because more than one of them is named "MyName". You can drag these items one at a time.

Explanation: You have selected items from multiple folder levels (most likely in an expanded text listing view) and are dragging them en masse to another folder or disk. Because each item is treated as a distinct file or folder, they will be copied to one disk or folder level. If more than one item of that group have the same name (since they can come from different levels, this is a distinct possibility), you'll get this message. To get past this problem, you'll have to drag the items in smaller, unique groups, or one at a time. Before you can get the duplicate-named item to the destination, however, you'll either have to rename the source or create a folder inside the destination for the duplicate-named item.

The selection cannot be put in the Trash, because a folder within is shared.

Explanation: Somewhere nested inside the folder(s) you've dragged to the **Trash** is one or more folders that have file sharing turned on. The folder does not have to be in use by others to get this message. System software calls this to your attention because it is possible that others rely on the contents of this folder if it has been shared. If you know for a fact that others do not need the files in the folder, turn off file sharing for this folder, and then drag its enclosing folder to the Trash.

The shared disk "MyDisk" could not be put away, because some of its items have been moved to the Trash. Do you want to delete those items and then put away the disk?

Explanation: You tried to drag a server volume to the Trash (or selected it and chose **Put Away** from the **File** menu) while one or more items originally from the server is still in the Trash. When you get this message, your only choices are to let the system empty the Trash for you or cancel the operation. If you shut down or restart your Macintosh, the shared disk is unmounted and the Trash emptied without interruption. Also, if the disk's owner turns off file sharing while you are logged onto that disk, the volume disappears, along with the Trash—the items in the Trash are deleted from the owner's disk.

The shutdown could not be completed, because the application "MyApp" could not quit.

Explanation: You tried to shut down or restart your machine while an application was running. It is rare that a program refuses to quit in response to a shutdown or restart. Chances are that you won't be able to quit the program manually, either. Try it, however. If a program fails to quit, it may be due to limited memory for the application. You may have to restart with the Reset switch ➜11 or power down with the physical switch. Before starting that application again, increase the current memory size of the application to give it a little more breathing room.

The startup disk cannot be removed from the desktop, because it contains the active system software.

Explanation: The startup disk must always be on the **Desktop**. While you can unmount any other unshared volume by dragging it to the Trash, you cannot do the same with the startup disk. To start from another volume, choose the desired disk from the **Startup Disk** control panel ➜80 and Restart. You can also bypass an internal hard disk when starting by holding down the *command*, *option*, and *delete* keys during startup.

The system extension "MyExtension" cannot be used, because it is too new/old.

Explanation: You have a version of an Apple-supplied system extension that is of a version other than the System file. The Installer should replace all system files with compatible versions, so this should not happen if you use the Installer for each system upgrade. If you get this message, run the Installer again to get all system files up to the same version.

The System Folder cannot be put in the Trash, because it contains the active system software.

Explanation: The System Folder of the startup disk has a few files that are always running. You won't be able to drag the System Folder or some of its items to the Trash while that volume is the startup disk. If you want to trash a disk's System Folder, start your Macintosh with another volume or **minimum system disk** 70. With your hard disk acting as a secondary disk, you can delete all system files. Be sure to re-install system software before booting from that disk, however.

The Trash cannot be emptied, because all of the items in it (other than folders) are locked. To delete locked items, hold down the Option key while you choose Empty Trash.

Explanation: The locked items referred to here are those whose Locked checkboxes are set in their **Get Info** dialog boxes. Fortunately, system software gives you a shortcut to delete these items by holding down the *option* key as you choose **Empty Trash** from the **Special** menu.

The Trash cannot be moved off the desktop.

Explanation: The Trash is a special system item. It must always be on the Desktop, and not inside a folder or disk.

The Trash contains 00 items, which use 000K of disk space. Are you sure you want to permanently remove these items?

Explanation: If you upgraded to System 7 from earlier versions, you'll notice that this message, like a lot about the Trash, is very different from before. One of the biggest changes is that you must explicitly empty the Trash, instead of it automatically emptying itself upon shut down or restart. Moreover, you are not warned when you drag an application or system file to the Trash. You are responsible for knowing what is finally being deleted when you choose **Empty Trash** from the **Special** menu. You can disable this message, however, by changing a setting in the Trash icon's **Get Info** dialog box ➔109.

The <file/folder/disk/window> "MyFile/MyFolder/MyDisk" could not be printed, opened, printed, put away, erased, deleted, copied, moved because...

Explanation: A large series of messages alert you when various operations cannot be completed. The reasons are described in the "because" part of the message. When the "because" message starts with the word "it," the message may not be clear enough to indicate what the "it" refers to. For example, a message saying that you cannot copy File A to Disk B because it is locked, doesn't really tell you which item is locked. If you cannot tell from the message (in this case a locked file can be copied, but not to a locked disk), then examine both pieces to see if either one is locked, in use, and so on.

Most "because" cases are obvious, but here are some reasons and tips:

...a disk error occurred

Explanation: A disk error often signals impending trouble for that disk. If the volume is a diskette, consider archiving the information, and replacing the diskette. When the volume is a **hard disk**, you should be more concerned. When copying a bunch of files, for example, you may be alerted to a disk error in copying a particular file. Usually, you can copy the missed file by itself right afterward. If you get a frequent disk error, try restarting the Macintosh. This often clears whatever it is that makes the system software believe there's a problem with the disk. Frequent hard disk errors should encourage you to back up frequently, and then reformat the disk to allow the recopying of files to be done in a clean map on the disk.

...you do not have enough access privileges

Explanation: The owner of a folder or disk assigns access privileges to individuals or all users together. Restrictions may prevent you from making any changes to the folder, or from moving, renaming, or deleting the folder. If you constantly run into this message when attempting various operations on shared folders, contact the folder's owner to see if he or she can increase your access privileges. You can see the **access privileges** you've been granted for any shared volume by selecting its icon in the **Desktop** and choosing **Sharing** from the **File** menu.

...it contains items that are in use

Explanation: In most instances, an "item in use" is one that is being shared by another user at the moment. System software prevents you from arbitrarily doing something to a file that another person is actively using.

...there isn't enough memory available. Closing windows or quitting application programs can make more memory available

Explanation: In very tight memory situations, this message advises you to do anything to free up memory to accomplish the maneuver you just tried. Each **Finder** window does take up a little memory (more so if the folder contains a lot of items), so closing Finder windows might be enough to get the job done. More than likely, however, you will need to close an application. For additional tips on freeing up memory➡44.

...too many files are open

Explanation: This is a difficult item to fix without the help of utility software that sets the maximum number of files that can be open at any one time (such as Set File Count). The default setting is 40 files, which is more than enough for most Macintosh users. Some programs, however, keep hidden and temporary files open while you work with their documents. Occasionally, these can add up to more than your system can handle. If you consistently run into this message, consider tracking down the **Set File Count** utility and adjust the setting for all your hard disks.

...a folder cannot be replaced by an item it contains

Explanation: You tried to move an item from inside a folder to the same level as that folder—and both items have the same name. You'll have to rename one of the items before performing the move.

...a file cannot be replaced by a folder

Explanation: You tried to move an item to a level that contains a folder bearing the same name. If both were files or both folders, you'd be prompted about replacing one item with the other. But since these items of different kinds (a file and folder), the system won't let you replace one with the other—which you probably don't want to do anyway. To perform the move or copy, you'll have to rename one of the items.

...a folder cannot be replaced by a file

Explanation: This is the inverse of the previous item.

...the original item could not be found

Explanation: An alias is involved, and the operation was to filter back to the original file. Unfortunately, the original file is probably deleted, so the operation cannot be fulfilled. If the operation is on a group of files, you can probably finish without the aliases.

...no printer has been selected. Please use the Chooser to select a printer

Explanation: If you've upgraded your system software or printer driver, whatever printer you had previously selected in the **Chooser** will not yet be selected. Updating printer software requires your updating the Chooser selections as well.

There is not enough memory to keep the window "MyWindow" open.

Explanation: Your Macintosh is in an extremely low memory condition when it starts closing Finder windows on you. It is looking for every byte it can find to either carry out some command of yours, or just to keep its own housekeeping going. If you see this message a lot, investigate some of the memory preservation ideas on page ➡46 or increase your RAM capacity. By the time you reach this message, you probably don't have enough memory to open **control panels** or **desk accessories**.

There is not enough memory to open "MyApp" (000K needed, 000K available). Closing windows or quitting application programs can make more memory available.

Explanation: You tried to open an application, but available RAM is below the minimum memory that the program's designer allows. While it's unlikely that closing **Finder** windows will help the situation, closing another application should make room. There is the possibility, however, that the memory management of your applications won't open up enough space until you quit all applications ➡127. Released in early 1992, an Apple extension to System 7, System 7 Tune-Up, helps low memory situations. Under the extension, this alert message references open applications that don't have document windows open, and offers to quit an application to make room for the new one in one step.

There is not enough memory to print "Mydoc" from "MyApp" on LaserWriter "MyPrinter". Do you want PrintMonitor to adjust its memory size and try again?

Explanation: It's always a good idea to let PrintMonitor try to print again. PrintMonitor spools print jobs to disk, but it still needs a bit of memory to keep the processes working in the background. If you click Cancel, the print job is cancelled. You'll have to open up memory for PrintMonitor (close an application) and reissue the **Print** command.

There is not enough memory to show the Clipboard.

Explanation: This is a sure sign that memory is running very low, unless, of course, you have a huge item (e.g., large color picture) in the Clipboard. If the contents of the Clipboard are essential to you (i.e., you don't want to lose it), then try to open the Scrapbook and paste the Clipboard into the Scrapbook File. You can then try to free up memory to let you work more comfortably with the information by recopying it from the Scrapbook and pasting into a document. Remember: the Clipboard is erased when you shut down or restart the Macintosh (or experience a system bomb, for that matter). The Scrapbook is permanent.

There is not enough room on the disk "MyDisk" to copy he selected items, unless you empty the Trash. Do you want to empty the Trash now?

Explanation: This message brings home the fact that just because you drag an item to the Trash, it doesn't really go away. Whatever is in the Trash occupies the same amount of disk space as it did in its prior location. If you are duplicating a file or copying files from one volume to another, the system looks to see if there is enough space for the new stuff. If not, it then checks to see if enough space is available if the Trash were emptied. You'll then get this message, which offers to both empty the trash and finish the copy process.

There is not enough room on the disk "MyDisk" to copy the selected items (an additional 000K is needed).

Explanation: If there is insufficient disk space to copy new stuff to it, the system lets you know how much space you need to clear to copy everything you had in mind. Pay close attention to the amount that you need to clear, and then look around on the disk for items to trash. If you are copying to a floppy disk, with its restricted space, you will probably have to divide the items across multiple disks.

This disk is unreadable. Do you want to initialize it?

Explanation: If you have just inserted a floppy disk, the system software does not recognize this as a properly formatted Macintosh diskette. If the disk is blank, then click the desired **initialization button** ➔ 52. But if the disk is supposed to be a formatted Macintosh disk with files on it, then do not initialize the disk, and consider a few possibilities:

1. The disk is a high density 1.4 megabyte disk, but you don't have a SuperDrive on your machine. No 800K floppy drive will be able to read a high density disk ➔ 52.
2. Restart the Macintosh. Make sure the metal shutter door on the disk slides freely, and re-insert the disk. This often clears the problem.
3. The disk may be an MS-DOS formatted diskette ➔ 52.
4. Diskette drive head alignment may be out of calibration on your drive or on the drive that formatted the disk. Try other disks formatted elsewhere. If other disks load fine, then the unreadable disk is suspect; if many other disks don't load, then your drive may need alignment, especially if disks you initialize cannot be read by other Macintoshes.
5. If you know for sure that the disk contains data, and your disk drive seems to be in order, use a disk recovery utility to try to restore the disk.
6. The disk may be damaged beyond repair. This can happen especially if the disk has been in the vicinity of strong magnetic fields (audio speakers, the magnet underneath the ImageWriter I cover, etc.) or extreme heat (inside a closed automobile in the summer sun). If a disk is truly damaged, attempts to reinitialize it will fail.

If this message comes up when a hard disk should be appearing on the **Desktop**, the problem may be more serious. Never click [Initialize] of this message with a hard disk, unless your hard disk installation software instructs you to. Try these possibilities in order if each one above it fails:

1. Leave the hard disk on, and restart the Macintosh.
2. Restart the Macintosh with the *command* and *option* keys held down to attempt rebuilding of the **Desktop file** on the disk.
3. Start the Macintosh with your hard disk's utility software to see if it can repair the disk.
4. Try Apple's Disk First Aid program, which comes on the installation disks.
5. Use a disk recovery utility program to recover the disk.
6. If you have a backup of the data, use your hard disk's utility software to reformat the disk, and reload your files back onto the disk.

If these steps fail, contact the hard disk manufacturer for help in recovering the disk and its files.

This file is used by the system software. It cannot be opened.

Explanation: Most icons on the Desktop let you double-click them to see more about them. Some files, such as the Finder, offer nothing to view. You get this message instead.

This version of Font/DA Mover is out of date. To install a font, drag it to the System file. To put a desk accessory in the Apple menu, drag it to the Apple Menu Items folder.

Explanation: While you don't need the Font/DA Mover program to install and de-install fonts and desk accessories in System 7, you can still use Font/DA Mover to group fonts and desk accessories into suitcase files for convenient copying and exchange with other people (or use with utility programs that manage suitcase files). You can use Font/DA Mover version 4.1 to create suitcase files under System 7.

Updating disk for new system software...

Explanation: System 7 software makes sure that all hard disk volumes have what it takes to be a System 7 disk. Such an animal has hidden folders for storing trash and desktop items, as well as some other hidden files and folders. When you connect a disk to a System 7 Macintosh and that disk previously ran on a System 6 Macintosh, the System 7 software brings the volume into compliance, creating whatever hidden files and folders are necessary to be in the System 7 Club. Having these items installed on a disk will not harm its ability to work under System 6 later. You will, however, see some of those folders and files (especially the Desktop Folder and Trash Folder) when you use that disk on System 6. You may remove them then, but reattachment to System 7 will just recreate those items once more ➡68.

You are now running on reserve power and your screen has been dimmed. You will be able to continue working for a short time. Please plug in your power adapter to begin recharging the battery.

Explanation: You can view reserve power on the Macintosh Portable or PowerBook by opening the **Battery** control panel.. When the battery reaches this level, it turns off the battery-draining backlight on backlit versions of the Portable and dims PowerBook backlighting. Depending on the age and ability of the battery pack installed in the machine, you'll have plenty of time to finish some work, save documents, and dig out the power supply before running down the battery. This is the first of three warnings you get about the battery running low.

You cannot move/copy/duplicate/replace...

See **"The <file/folder/disk/window> "MyFile/MyFolder/MyDisk" could not be printed, opened, printed, put away, erased, deleted, copied, moved because..."** above.

You cannot share applications on other computers.

Explanation: You tried to adjust the sharing property of an application file that is actually on someone else's disk. Only a program's owner has the right to open an application for sharing.

You don't have enough access privileges to see all the items if they are put into "MyFolder". Put them there anyway?

Explanation: You are trying to drag items to a drop folder —a folder that has been setup so that you can drag items to it, but you cannot open the folder. This is a relatively common setup when someone on the network wants other users to drop updates to files into a common folder, but doesn't want anyone looking into that folder. This warning lets you know that once you drop something into that folder, you won't be able to open it to retrieve it. You can see what privileges have been granted for any shared volume by selecting the volume icon on the **Desktop** and choosing **Sharing** from the **File** menu.

You must set the serial switch for your Macintosh IIfx to compatible in the Control Panel, and restart your Macintosh before you can print.

Explanation: Your Personal LaserWriter LS cannot work with the Macintosh IIfx unless you adjust the serial port speed. A special **Serial Switch** control panel for the IIfx lets you choose between **Compatible** and **Faster** speeds. The LaserWriter LS communicates only at the "compatible" speed. Some other serial devices may need this setting as well.

24-bit color 34-41
Video capability to display over 16 million colors at one time on the screen. Requires 24-bit color **video card**, except for 13" RGB monitors used with Quadra models.

32-bit addressing 40-43, 67
Communication channel to RAM available on newer 68020 and 68030 Macintoshes that allows maximum RAM capacity above 8MB.

32-bit QuickDraw 32
Internal drawing routines that permit 24-bit color display on video monitors.

8mm tape 61
Consumer video tape format used in tape backup devices for personal computers.

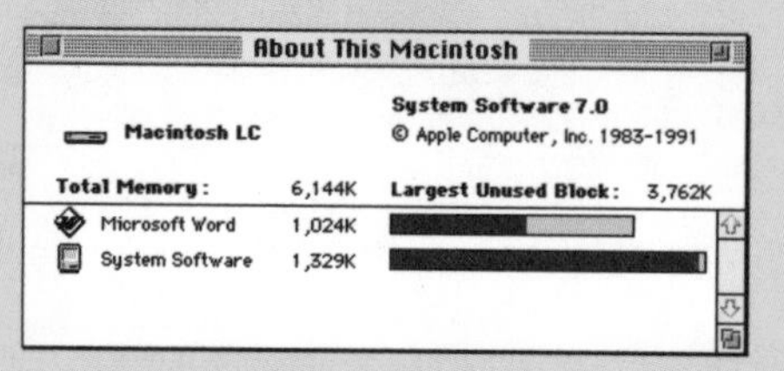

About This Macintosh 42,44-45 47
First **Apple** menu item, which opens a dialog box revealing the system version and memory usage.

AC power > see power (AC) cord

Accelerator 33, 40
Add-in board that speeds processing of the computer (with a faster CPU chip) or video refresh for high-quality color.

accent characters > see keyboard characters

access privileges 164-165, 170-171, 198, 204
Levels of file reading and writing abilities on a shared file granted to a user by the file's owner. An owner may set different privileges for each registered user sharing files on his or her disk.

access time 55
The time, in milliseconds, it takes a disk drive to locate a particular piece of data from a disk.

accessing shared folder/disk 168-169
Using the Chooser and **FileShare** to connect your Macintosh to another so you can use files and programs on another user's Macintosh. Requires user settings in various control panels on all connected Macintoshes.

active window 103
The topmost document window, recognizable by the title bar's horizontal lines and undimmed window name. Only one document window may be active at a time.

acur 85, 97
Animated cursor resource, which points to a series of **CURS** resources to simulate animation. Use **ResEdit** to view or edit this resource.

ADB > see Apple Desktop Bus (ADB) port

ADB cable extensions 18
S-VHS video cables can be substituted for ADB extensions.

Adobe > see PostScript

AIFF, AIFF-C 158-159
Audio Interchange File Format, the latter denoting a format capable of real-time compression and decompression. Becoming a standard for Macintosh sound files.

air flow > see ventilation

airline travel 57
Try to have hard disks and PowerBooks hand inspected at security checkpoints to avoid possibly magnetized rollers in the X-ray machine belts.

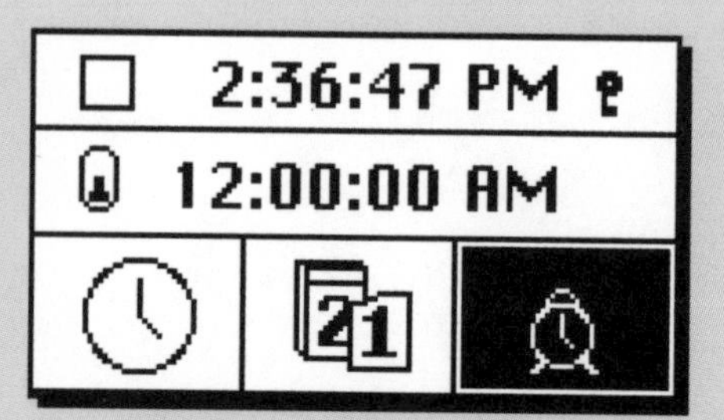

Alarm Clock desk accessory 76
Standard DA operates as a clock and alarm. May be used to set the Macintosh's internal clock. A flashing Alarm Clock icon in the menubar means that the alarm time elapsed while the computer was turned off.

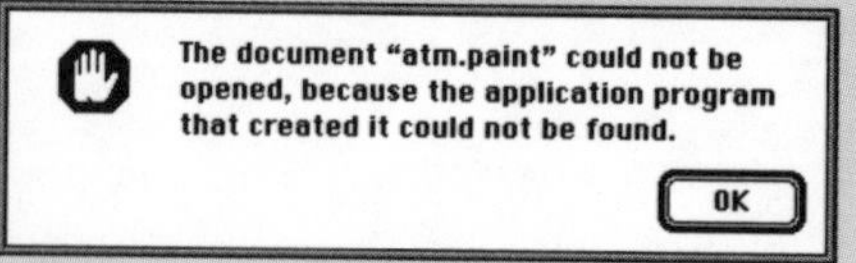

alert box 178
A window that interrupts your action to advise you of important system information or potential danger.

alias 75-82, 91, 120-121, 135,189, 199
A tiny (1-2K) file that stands in for any file, folder, or disk. Leave the original file where you like it, and create aliases for places where you'd like another copy of the original's icon, such as in the Apple Menu Items or Startup Items folders.

ALRT 85
The alert box resource type. Contains information about the window type, size, and location on screen. Text comes from **STR#** resources. Use **ResEdit** to edit resources.

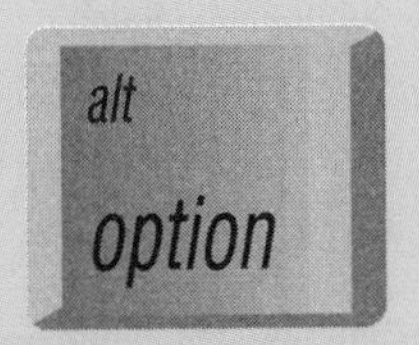

alt **key > see** *option* **key**

animated cursor **85, 97**
A series of cursors (CURS resources) that give the illusion of animation, as in the Finder's rotating minute hand on the watch during lengthy operations.

APDA
Apple Programmers and Developers Association (Apple Computer, Inc., 20525 Mariani Avenue, Mail Stop 33G, Cupertino, CA 95014-6299; phone 800-282-2732), an excellent source for Macintosh programming tools and utilities. Catalog available.

Apple Desktop Bus (ADB) port
9, 18, 27, 176-179
Rear panel connector for low power input devices, such as keyboard and mouse. ADB devices can be chained end-to-end. Macintoshes have either 1 or 2 ADB ports.

Apple Events **67, 134**
Powers normally hidden from the user that allow one program to communicate—send messages—to another. Programs may send data between each other, and use each other's built-in abilities.

Apple File Exchange

Apple File Exchange
Utility program (comes with System 7) that allows formatting, reading, and writing of 3.5" MS-DOS disks on a Macintosh **SuperDrive**. Useful for sharing common format files between the same programs on MS-DOS/Windows and Macintosh computers. Also capable of file translations between incompatible file formats.

About This Macintosh...
Alarm Clock
Chooser
Control Panels
Key Caps
Note Pad
Scrapbook

Apple () menu
75-77, 100, 128-129
Leftmost menu in menubar displaying menu choices of those desk accessories, programs, and shared folders located in the **Apple Menu Items** folder. Items are listed in alphabetical order underneath one or more menu items specific to the active application.

Apple Menu Items folder
12, 66, 69, 75-77, 120-121, 126-127
Folder inside the System Folder for desk accessories, and aliases to applications, documents, control panels, shared folders, and other items to be made available for quick access in the Menu. A maximum of about 50 items can be listed.

ASCII Table

ASCII	Character	Name
0	*NUL*	Null
1	*SOH*	Start of Heading
2	*STX*	Start of Text
3	*ETX*	End of Text
4	*EOT*	End of Transmission
5	*ENQ*	Enquiry
6	*ACK*	Acknowledge
7	*BEL*	Bell
8	*BS*	Backspace
9	*HT*	Horizontal Tab
10	*LF*	Line Feed
11	*VT*	Vertical Tab
12	*FF*	Form Feed
13	*CR*	Carriage Return
14	*SO*	Shift Out
15	*SI*	Shift In
16	*DLE*	Data Link Escape
17	*DC1*	Device Control 1
18	*DC2*	Device Control 2
19	*DC3*	Device Control 3
20	*DC4*	Device Control 4
21	*NAK*	Negative Acknowledge
22	*SYN*	Synchronous Idle
23	*ETB*	End of Transmission Block
24	*CAN*	Cancel
25	*EM*	End of Medium
26	*SUB*	Substitue
27	*ESC*	Escape
28	*FS*	File Separator
29	*GS*	Group Separator
30	*RS*	Record Separator
31	*US*	Unit Separator
32	*SP*	Space
33	!	Exclamation Point
34	"	Quotation Marks
35	#	Number Sign
36	$	Dollar Sign
37	%	Percent
38	&	Ampersand
39	'	Apostrophe
40	(	Open Parenthesis
41	)	Close Parenthesis
42	*	Asterisk
43	+	Plus
44	,	Comma
45	-	Hyphen
46	.	Period
47	/	Slant
48	0	zero
49	1	
50	2	
51	3	
52	4	
53	5	
54	6	
55	7	
56	8	
57	9	
58	:	Colon
59	;	Semicolon
60	<	Less Than
61	=	Equals
62	>	Greater Than
63	?	Question Mark
64	@	Commercial At
65	A	
66	B	
67	C	
68	D	
69	E	
70	F	
71	G	
72	H	
73	I	
74	J	
75	K	
76	L	
77	M	
78	N	
79	O	
80	P	
81	Q	
82	R	
83	S	
84	T	
85	U	
86	V	
87	W	
88	X	
89	Y	
90	Z	
91	[	Open Bracket
92	\	Reverse Slant
93	]	Close Bracket
94	^	Circumflex
95	_	Underline
96	`	Grave Accent
97	a	
98	b	
99	c	
100	d	
101	e	
102	f	
103	g	
104	h	
105	i	
106	j	
107	k	
108	l	
109	m	
110	n	
111	o	
112	p	
113	q	
114	r	
115	s	
116	t	
117	u	
118	v	
119	w	
120	x	
121	y	
122	z	
123	{	Open Brace
124	|	Vertical Line
125	}	Close Brace
126	~	Tilde
127	*DEL*	Delete

AppleShare driver 78
Chooser document (in the Extensions folder) that you select to access shared folders from other Macintoshes or servers on the network.

AppleShare server 78, 162-163, 191
Dedicated Macintosh that all users on a network share. Used primarily as data storage and printer server device for workgroups.

AppleTalk 9, 78, 148-149
Network communications protocol that Macintoshes use to share information among themselves. **AppleTalk** is built into every Macintosh. Non-Macintoshes can gain **AppleTalk** with an additional hardware board.

AppleTalk Network 162, 163, 179, 185, 192
A group of two or more computer devices connected together in a network using **AppleTalk** protocols to exchange information. Can range from a Macintosh and LaserWriter pair to hundreds of Macs and printers.

AppleTalk zone 78, 148-149, 162-163
Group of Macintoshes on a network set up to be viewed as a single workgroup entity by others on the network. Divides a potentially large network into more efficient (faster) units.

application 126-127, 189, 190, 196, 204
Program written to help users accomplish a task, such as word processing, spreadsheets, and so on.

application memory > see RAM, application

Application menu 12, 101, 103
Rightmost menu in the menubar that lets you switch among all applications and desk accessories running at the moment. Also provides help in hiding unused windows to reduce screen clutter.

Arabic script 21
Language resource that instructs the Macintosh how to display Arabic characters.

arrow keys > see cursor keys

ASCII 174-175
The American Standard Code for Information Interchange, a standard that assigns a numeric value between zero and 127 to each letter, numeral, and punctuation mark in American English. Additional values represent control codes for printer and communications devices. See table to left.

AT-style keyboard 17
Keyboard layout designed after the IBM PC model AT keyboard. The Apple Extended keyboard adheres to this design.

ATM 86-88, 152-153
Adobe Type Manager, which preceded **TrueType**, lets Adobe font owners display all sizes of fonts on the screen without font scaling.

Audio Help stack 141
Supplemental HyperCard stack that comes with the System 7 software. Allows users with microphones or audio digitizers to create buttons that playback their voice messages.

audio input port 8, 158-159
Rear panel connector for microphone input found on Macintosh LC, IIsi, Classic II, Quadras, and PowerBook models. Other audio digitizers connect via a **serial port**.

audio output port 9, 156-157
Rear panel connector for stereo (on most Macintoshes) headphones or amplified speakers. Plugging into this port disconnects the internal **speaker**.

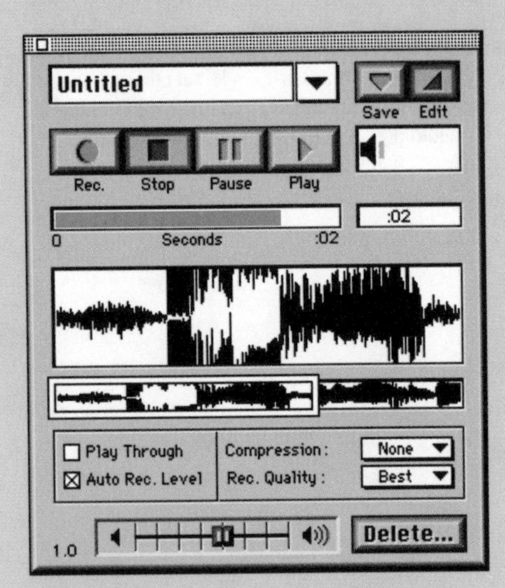

Audio Palette 141
Window in HyperCard (with Audio Help) that presents a tape recorder metaphor for recording and playing back sounds recorded with microphone or audio digitizer.

autoscroll 98
The process of scrolling a window's contents when you drag an object beyond the viewable area of the window. Available in all Finder windows and in some document windows.

backbone 162-163
Network wiring methodology that consists of a cable with any number of connections (drops) along the route. Many networks use fast **Ethernet** communications through a backbone, and then either **EtherTalk** expansion boards in the Macintosh or Ethernet-to-**AppleTalk** conversions to work with Macintoshes on an **AppleTalk** network.

background printing 78, 90,152-153
Allows the Macintosh to process printing jobs as a secondary task while you continue work on an application. Requires a print spooling program, like **PrintMonitor** and compatible printer.

background process 90
Any computing that takes place while you work on an entirely different task.

backspace-delete **> see** *delete* **key**

backup > see disks, backing up

Balloon Help > see Help menu

battery (in standby power supply) 6
Powers your equipment for a brief time if the AC power is disrupted. The battery is continually kept charged while AC power is connected.

Battery

Battery desk accessory 11, 76
Available only on portable Macintoshes, this lets you view the amount of power remaining in the battery. Also includes a button to put the computer to sleep.

battery, backup 11,41, 186
Small **lithium** battery (on most Macintosh logic boards) that keep the clock and other PRAM data intact while the Macintosh is turned off.

battery, Macintosh Portable and PowerBooks 10-11, 176,186-187, 203
Sealed, lead acid battery pack for Portable and PowerBook 100; **nickel cadmium** (NiCad) pack for PowerBook 140 and 170. Portable Macintoshes include many battery-saving techniques to lengthen the life of the battery between charges.

BBS > see bulletin board

beep sound > see Sound control panel

Bengali script 21
Language resource that instructs the Macintosh how to display Bengali language characters.

bit 32, 40
Smallest piece of computer data and a contraction of **binary digit**. A bit can be only one of two states: on or off, 1 or 0, white or black. Eight bits in a bunch are called a **byte**. The more bits in a bunch, the more information the bunch can hold (e.g., 24-bit color)

bitmapped fonts 86-88
Font resources that contain the pixel map for each character of a typeface in a particular size. These can be used for screen display, but they provide less attractive printout compared to TrueType or PostScript fonts. Also called screen fonts.

bitmapped graphic 130-131, 150
Image consisting entirely of pixels (some of which may be gray levels or colors). Can produce jagged diagonal lines on printout, compared to object graphics. Resizing a bit mapped graphic tends to distort the image.

System Folder

blessed folder 74
System folder containing System and Finder that has the small Macintosh icon on it. This is the folder the operating system seeks for loading system software.

bomb 188
Customary name for a software error that results in a system error alert box which displays an icon of a bomb and lit fuse.

booting 10-11
Short for bootstrapping, it is the same as starting up a Macintosh's System and Finder.

breathing room 5, 37
Space around a computer and video monitor to allow for convective air circulation.

bridge, network 162-163
Combination of hardware and software that allows multiple workgroups to connect to each other. Divides a large network into smaller, more efficient groups, which can communicate to other groups when needed.

brightness 5, 31, 37
Amount of light energy emitted by a video monitor or panel display. Should be adjusted by user according to surrounding light.

Brightness control panel 35, 82
Macintosh Classic software control of the built-in video monitor's brightness. Other Macintoshes and monitors have manual brightness controls.

bulletin board (BBS) 174-175
Communication service on a computer that allows other users to leave messages and share files. Requires a **modem** and **communications software**. Some services are community-based, while a number of commercial services are accessible world-wide.

burn-in, video 37
Discoloration of the phosphor inside the video monitor. Long exposures of white (e.g., the menubar) may make the image visible even when the computer is turned off. Turning down the brightness or using a **screen saver** can reduce burn-in.

bus 9,18
Convention that specifies what signals are on each pin of a connector, thus allowing the design of compatible devices. Usually more than one device can be connected to a bus.

Button

Button

Check Box

Radio Button

button 128-129
On-screen visual element that you activate by moving the pointer atop it and pressing the mouse button—as if you were pressing the screen button with your finger. A button with an ellipsis (**...**) leads to a dialog box. Other buttons may be icons.

byte 40
Group of **8 bits**. One byte is required to represent an English alphanumeric character, each with its own combination of 8 on-and-off bits. see ASCII.

cable switcher 9
External box that connects to a **serial port**. A switch on the panel lets you attach any of several devices to the single serial port.

cable, shielded 7
Wire that has a foil or braided wire wrapping around the main, interior wire(s). The shield is connected to the metal cabinets of devices on either end via the outer metal housing of the connectors. Shielded cable can reduce radio-frequency emissions that cause radio and television interference.

cables 7
Wires that connect two devices. Cables may range from a single conductor to dozens inside the insulation.

cables, changing 8, 11
Always turn off all devices before changing Macintosh cables, especially **SCSI**, **ADB**, and **serial port** cables.

cache card, Macintosh IIci 46
Optional **RAM** cache, consisting of a small amount of very fast RAM chips. Speeds up a number of operations that frequently reuse information from RAM.

Cache Switch control panel 81
Quadra software control panel that turns the CPU's internal cache on and off for compatibility with older software products. With the cache on, performance is at its fastest.

Calculator

Calculator desk accessory 76
Standard four function calculator application installed into the menu by the Installer. You can use your keyboard's numeric keypad to enter values.

caps lock **key** 16
Push-on/push-off key that locks all alphabet keys in their uppercase characters. Does not affect numbers or punctuation keys. Illuminates the Caps Lock light on the Apple Extended Keyboard; displays upward arrow in PowerBook menubar (thanks to the Caps Lock extension)

carpal tunnel syndrome (CTS) > see repetitive strain injuries

cartridge disk drives 61, 120-121, 187, 190
Removable hard disks capable of storing 40 to 88 megabytes of information using a single disk drive external device. Practical for backing up high-capacity hard disks.

CD-ROM 61, 138-139, 191
Compact Disc-Read Only Memory, looks just like a compact audio disc, but stores up to 550 megabytes of computer information. To the Macintosh, a CD-ROM looks like a very large locked disk. CD-ROMs are frequently used to publish large amounts of text, graphics, and sound information.

cdev 82
Resource identifier for a **control panel** (also called a control panel device). Pronounced SEE-dev.

chaining 18, 58-59, 162-132
Method of connecting similar device types in series, such that only one device connects to the computer. Each device has two connectors so it can be placed anywhere in the series. On the Macintosh, **SCSI**, **ADB**, and **LocalTalk** devices can be chained. Also called daisy-chaining.

chair height 4
Distance between the top of the chair seat and the floor. Should be adjusted to let your feet rest squarely on the floor or footrest.

Chooser

Chooser 76, 78, 83, 148-151, 162-163, 184-185, 194, 199
Small application, usually in the menu, that lets you select a printer type, printer name (for networked LaserWriters), **AppleTalk** zone, **AppleTalk** status, **background printing** status (for LaserWriters), and **file server**. Used extensively with **FileShare**.

cicn 85
Resource identifier for a color icon used within a program (not used to display icons in the Finder). Editable with **ResEdit**.

CL/1 > see DAL

clamping voltage 6
Voltage level at which a surge suppressor prevents current from passing to devices plugged into it.

Claris Corporation 138
Publisher of Macintosh software (MacWrite, HyperCard, FileMaker, and more).

Clarus > see Dog Cow.

Class B device 7
Electronic device that has passed the Federal Communications Commission's qualifications for radio frequency emissions that won't interfere with household radios and televisions. Less stringent Class A rating is for office equipment. Macintosh computers comply with Class B.

Clean Up 100, 103
Special menu command that organizes icon Finder windows according to the grid selected in the **Views** control panel. Avoids overlapping file names in the grid.

Cleaning mouse, keyboard > see Mouse, Keyboard

click 98
Pressing the mouse button while the screen pointer is atop an object or between text characters.

Clipboard 79, 108, 201
Temporary memory space that holds any information an application lets you select and issue the **Copy** command for. Clipboard information is lost when the Macintosh is turned off or restarted. Finder's **Show Clipboard** command lets you view Clipboard contents.

Clipboard file 74, 79
Temporary storage space when the Clipboard information is larger than the Clipboard's memory space. Does not remember Clipboard information after turning off or restarting the Macintosh.

clock, setting > see General control panel

close box 102
Upper left square of many window styles. Clicking the box closes the window.

CloseView 35, 81
Control panel that lets visually impaired users magnify visual elements on the screen.

clut 85
Resource identifier for a **color lookup table**. Used by applications and documents to store non-standard palettes of colors.

color 32-33, 36, 80, 113
With a color monitor, the Macintosh offers much flexibility with color displays in both the Finder and documents.

Color 36, 80
A control panel that lets you control the text highlight and window colors on a color monitor. Not available for **monochrome** monitors.

color calibration 33
Method of correcting video display colors so they match printed colors. Requires third-party hardware (which literally views a spot of color on the monitor) and software.

Color Picker> see Color Wheel

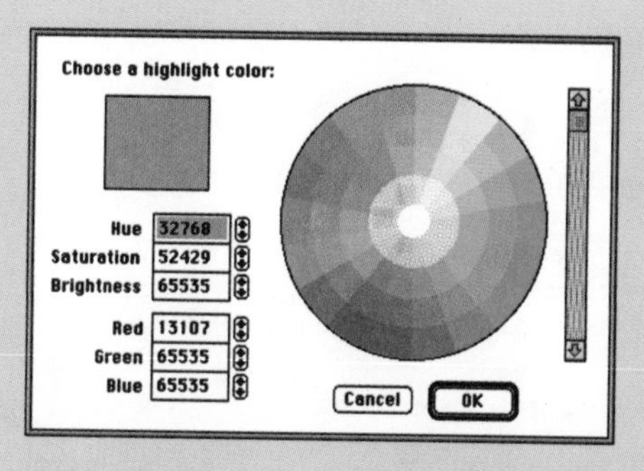

Color Wheel 32-33, 36, 110
Dialog box that allows you to choose from as many colors as your video monitor circuitry allows. Features a color wheel and brightness control, as well as entry of RGB and HSV values. Formerly called the Color Picker.

command **key** 16
Key next to the spacebar on the keyboard, shown with the ⌘symbol. Most often used in conjunction with alphanumeric keys to execute pull down menu commands from the keyboard.

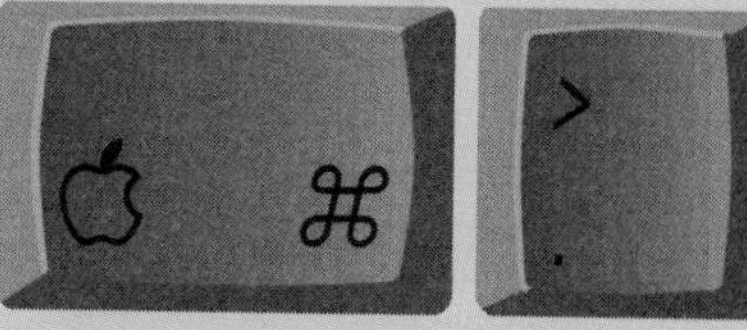

command-period
Common keyboard sequence to halt a process, such as printing. Worth trying as a way to unfreeze a Macintosh, especially in HyperCard.

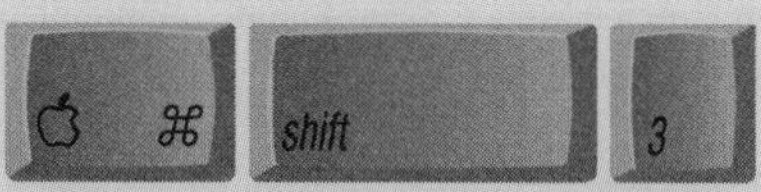

command-shift-3 > **see screen shot**

command.com 13
MS-DOS equivalent of the Macintosh System and Finder. Required for booting an MS-DOS computer.

comments > see Get Info

communications software
Program that lets your Macintosh exchange information with other computers via telephone lines (requires a telephone modem).

compact Macintosh 4, 10-11, 30, 47-48
One-piece Macintosh model featuring a built-in video monitor: Macintosh Plus, SE, SE/30, Classic, Classic II.

Compatibility Checker 67-68
HyperCard stack that comes with the System 7 upgrade kits to tell you which of your applications and extensions may not be compatible with System 7 before you upgrade.

completer 19
Last key you type to finish a multiple-key character sequence, such as accented characters. Preceded by one or more **dead keys**.

compression, file > see file compression.

compression, sound > see AIFF; sound compression

computer aided design (CAD) 27, 33
Using a computer as a drawing, modeling, and conceptualizing tool. Often places great demands on processing and video display power.

connectors 7, 192
Joints between hardware boxes and cables. Every connector has a gender—male or female. A male connector attaches only to a female connector and vice versa.

continuity checker 7
Electrical device with two leads. If current can flow between the two leads, there is continuity in that circuit. Used to make sure homemade cables do not have continuity between distinct pins of a connector.

contrast 31
Difference between the lightest and darkest possible pixels of a video monitor. The higher the contrast, the more readable the display.

control 104
User interface element that lets a user adjust some setting or property. Often, consists of an on-screen metaphor for a real-world switch, lever, or meter.

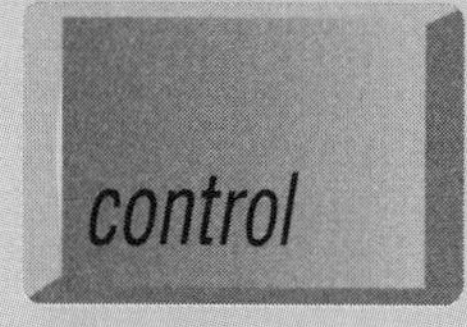

control **key** 16
Modifier key on the keyboard used in conjunction with one or more other keys. Used primarily when using communications software to access a large computer.

control panels 77, 80-82, 178, 189, 190
Small applications that let you adjust settings of the system or external device via software. Control panel settings are remembered after you turn off your Macintosh.

Control Panels folder 12, 75, 80, 178
Special folder designated in the System Folder for all control panels.

convergence 33
Alignment of the three electron beams in a color monitor. Refers to the accuracy with which the beams can excite the same spot on the monitor.

copy protection 126-127
Software-based guard against making a copy of files from one disk to another. Not used much these days, except in network protection schemes and a few expensive applications.

copy to Clipboard 79, 108
Selecting information and issuing the **Copy** command in an application. A duplicate of that information goes into the Clipboard for pasting in another location later.

copying disks > see disks, copying

copying files> see files, copying

CPU
Central Processing Unit, the main integrated circuit chip that controls every aspect of a computer. Also called a microprocessor. Macintoshes use various generations of Motorola CPUs: **68000**, **68020**, **68030**, **68040**—each one faster and more expensive than the previous model.

crash, disk > see hard disk recovery

cumulative trauma disorder (CTD) > see repetitive strain injuries

curly characters 23
Typesetting characters for quote and apostrophe marks which are more rounded than the straight quote and apostrophe marks of typical fonts. Curly characters are usually available as *option*-key characters in most fonts.

CURS 85, 97
Resource identifier for the cursor. Editable with **ResEdit**.

cursor 35, 97
Flashing screen indicator showing where the next typed character is to appear. On the Macintosh, shows only as a text insertion pointer. Different from a pointer, which is controlled by the mouse.

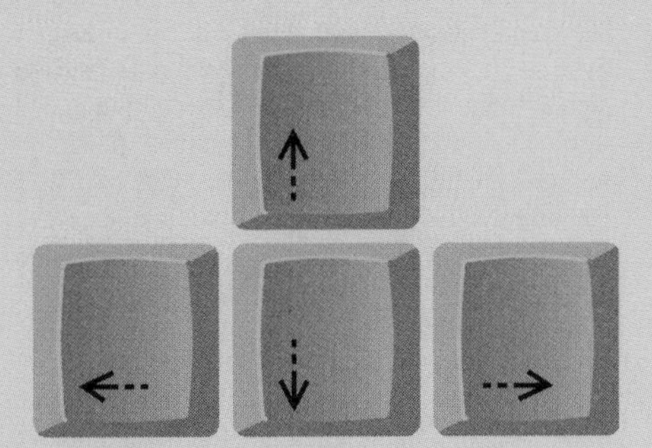

cursor keys 16
Four arrow keys on the keyboard that usually control a text insertion pointer's location within a document. In some programs and documents, may also control screen navigation.

Custom Install 68-70
Alternative installation procedure in the Installer program that lets you be more specific about which elements of system software are to be installed on your disk.

cut to Clipboard 79, 108
Selecting information and issuing the Cut command in an application. The selected information is deleted from the document, but a copy goes into the Clipboard for pasting in another location later.

Cyrillic script 21
Language resource that instructs the Macintosh how to display Russian (and derivative) language characters.

DA > see desk accessory

daisy-chaining > see chaining

DAL
Data Access Language, a command language used by some applications to retrieve data from mainframe computers equipped with DAL servers. Requires DAL System 7 extension, which is included on System 7 installation disks. Formerly known as CL/1.

DAT 61
Digital Audio Tape format used as a tape backup format.

data fork 84
Part of a Macintosh file that contains most of the information entered by a user—word processing text, spreadsheet numbers, graphics images. Sometimes combined with a **resource fork** in a single Macintosh file.

date 76, 80
Maintained as part of the Macintosh internal clock, the date may be set via the General Controls control panel or Alarm Clock desk accessory.

DB-25 connector 7
Standard 25-pin connector style used as the SCSI port on the right Macintosh rear panels and on many external serial devices.

DB-9 connector 7
Standard 9-pin connector style formerly used as the serial port connectors on early Macintoshes. A common serial port connector on MS-DOS laptop computers.

dead key 19
A keyboard key that does not generate a character by itself. Usually typed as a way to setup an accent character that goes atop the next vowel key (completer) typed on the keyboard.

default
A setting or value established at the factory, such as control panel settings or software program preferences.

***del* key** 17
Delete key that erases a character to the right of the text insertion pointer. Also known as the forward delete key.

delay until repeat 19
Keyboard control panel setting that determines how long you have to hold down a key before it starts repetitively typing the same character.

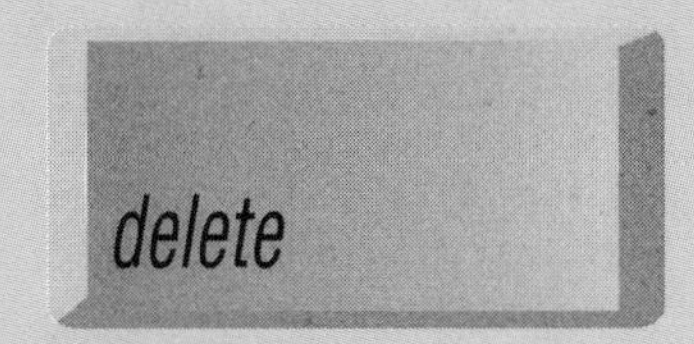

***delete* key** 17
Deletes the character to the left of the text insertion pointer. Also called the Backspace-delete key.

desk accessory (DA) 75-77, 126, 187
Program that uses little memory, and is usually invoked from the menu. In System 7, the distinctions between desk accessory and application blur.

Desktop, the 66, 94-95, 106, 116
Primary work area for all Macintosh tasks. Also, the most global storage level for files and volumes.

desktop database 94
Combination of hidden files Desktop DB and Desktop DF, which System 7 uses to maintain information about desktop icons and the connections between documents and their creators. Generically referred to as the desktop file, as it was in earlier systems.

desktop file 12-13, 54, 94-95
Generic name for information about desktop icons and connections between documents and their creators. This information is stored differently for Systems 6 and 7, but both are referred to as the Desktop file.

desktop file, rebuilding 95, 181, 188
Process of recataloging the Finder icons and connections between documents and creators. Recommended maintenance procedure once each month if you move a lot of different applications on and off your hard disk. Otherwise, once a year is sufficient.

desktop pattern 110
Array of dots and colors in the very background of the Desktop. Can be modified with the **General Controls** control panel or replaced with a picture with the help of third-party utilities.

desktop picture 45, 110
A picture file that replaces the desktop pattern. Requires a third-party extension to change pattern to picture. Color pictures can consume 300 KB of memory for a desktop picture.

device drivers > see drivers

dialog box 104-107
Window that offers you choices, settings, and editable text fields to enter information normally hidden from view.

dialog box, modal 104
Dialog box that takes over your Macintosh, preventing you from working in any window other than the current dialog. Common interface element for entry of settings and other choices.

dialog box, modeless 104
Dialog box that allows you to drag it around the screen and work with information in other windows behind the dialog.

dialog, open file 106
Standard dialog box that lets you open a document file from within an application. May be augmented by the program's author to let you open a variety of file formats or preview a document before opening it.

dialog, save file 107, 128-129
Standard dialog box that lets you name a document and save it in any volume and folder available on the Desktop. May be augmented by the program's author to let you save the document in a variety of file formats.

digitizing tablet > see graphics tablet

dimmed item 100-103, 106
An object or text that is grayed-out on the screen, and cannot be activated by the mouse. Dimmed menu items can often be activated by selecting active text or objects.

DIN connector 7
Round connector body with numerous pins inside. Commonly used in European audio and video gear.

Disinfectant

Disinfectant 60
Popular **virus detection program** from Northwestern University freely available from user groups and electronic bulletin boards.

disk booting order 59
Fixed sequence through which the Macintosh looks for a disk containing a system file. The first volume with a system file in this order becomes the startup disk.

disk cache 45
Portion of memory set aside to hold a copy of the last information read from or to a hard disk. Speeds some operations when unchanged information is required of the disk file. Cannot be turned off in System 7, but may be adjusted in size in the **Memory** control panel.

disk crash > see hard disk recovery

disk drive port 8
Rear panel connector on most Macintoshes that allows the attachment of an external floppy disk drive.

Disk First Aid 60, 178, 202
Hard disk recovery program supplied on the Disk Tools disk of the System 7 installer disks. Can help repair simple problems with many hard disks.

disk, floppy > see floppy disks

disks, backing up 54, 56, 122-123, 178
Process of making duplicate copy of files on another disk. Different backup types are available. Backup is possible to floppy disks, cartridge disks, tapes or another hard disk.

disks, copying 54, 181, 198
Process of duplicating a disk, usually floppy disk to floppy disk. Copying a floppy disk to a hard disk creates a folder on the hard disk with the same name and contents of the floppy disk.

disks, optical > see CD-ROM; WORM; erasable optical disks

distortion, video 31
When the active area of a video monitor is not rectangular—sides bow in, corners bow out.

DITL 84-85, 104
Resource identifier for a dialog item list, the information contained inside a dialog (**DLOG**) resource. Editable with ResEdit.

DLOG 84-85, 104
Resource identifier for a dialog. Contains information about the window type, size, and screen location. Linked to a **DITL** resource of the same ID number. Editable with ResEdit.

document window 103
Window style consisting of a title bar, close box, grow box, zoom box, and scroll bars. Most common window for displaying documents inside an application. Also used by the Finder for its folder windows.

DogCow 153
The mythical creature, named **Clarus**, revered by Macintosh developers, and mascot of the Macintosh Developer Technical Support crew at Apple. Says "Moof!"

DOS 13, 66. 202
Disk Operating System, although not a term unique to IBM PC-compatible computers, it a common reference to MS-DOS computers.

double-click speed 25
Setting in the **Mouse** control panel that establishes how quickly you must press the mouse button in succession to signify a double click on a screen object.

download 174-175
Transferring a file from another computer (usually a mainframe or BBS) to your own computer.

dpi 30
Dots per inch, a measure of resolution for printed output and displays.

drag 98
The process of clicking on an object, and moving the mouse while holding the mouse button down.

draw program 130-131
An application that lets you create graphic objects which may be easily resized or edited. See also object graphics.

drivers 67, 69, 83, 148-149, 177, 178, 188, 193
Extension files that instruct the Macintosh how to communicate with external devices, such as printers, servers, and hard disks. Drivers must be compatible with the system software version you're running.

drop folder 204
Shared folder for which your priviledges allowdragging items to the folder, but not opening that folder to change its contents.

Duplicate 118-119
Finder **File** menu command that creates a duplicate of the selected folder or file. Duplicate file is named with the original's name plus the word "copy."

earthquake proofing 5
Securing computer and monitor to the desk to prevent the items from creeping off the desk during the shaking of an earthquake.

Easy Access 20, 25, 80
A **control panel** that provides several keyboard controls for physically handicapped users who cannot use a mouse or who must use a stylus or other pointer to type characters.

Edit
Undo ⌘Z
Cut ⌘X
Copy ⌘C
Paste ⌘V
Clear
Select All ⌘A
Show Clipboard

Edit menu 100, 128-129
Common user interface element in all applications, includes commands to control Clipboard contents (**Cut**, **Copy**, **Paste**).

edition 132-133, 182-183
Intermediate file that exists between one document's publisher and another document's subscriber.

ejecting disks > see floppy disk, ejecting

electrical safety 6
Proper way to protect your computer equipment from large variations in electrical current and voltage.

electromagnetic force (EMF) 37
Invisible force generated by magnetic coils in a video monitor (and, to a lesser extent, electric motors). Adequate distance between an EMF source and humans is recommended.

electronic still camera 32
Single-frame camera that stores the image as an electronic file on a small diskette. Image may be played back on a video monitor or saved as a Macintosh file with the aid of extra hardware called a frame grabber or video digitizer.

e-mail 174-175
Electronic mail, a way of exchanging messages and documents with other computer users. Requires additional software for use on a network or via telephone modem to global systems.

em-dash 23
Typesetter's term for a long dash (—), available in most fonts by typing *option - shift - hyphen.*

Empty Trash 109, 197-198
Special menu command that empties the contents of Desktop Trash. A choice in the Trash's **Get Info** dialog box lets you turn off the alert box after choosing this menu item.

en-dash 23
Typesetter's term for a short dash (–), available in most fonts by typing *option - hyphen.*

enclosing folder/disk 103
Folder or disk that holds the currently selected (or open) file or folder. In a Finder folder window, hold down the *command* key and click the name of the folder name in the window's title bar to see a pop-up list of enclosing folders and disk.

***end* key** 17
Key on the Extended keyboard that often helps you position the text insertion pointer to the end of the screen or document. Must be programmed by the application's author.

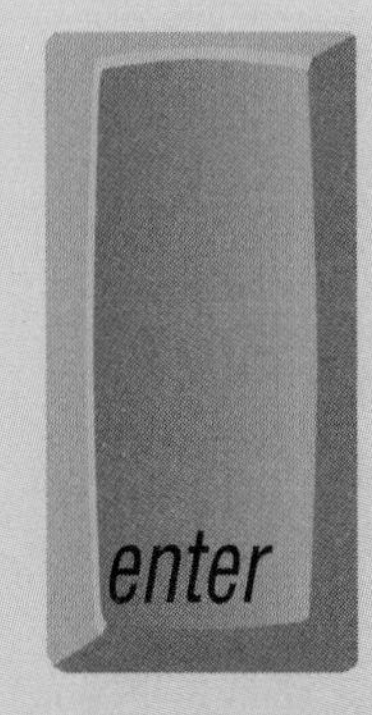

***enter* key** 17
Key in the numeric keypad of all Macintosh keyboards. Mimics the Return key action in dialog boxes, but often records edited information to the file without moving the cursor or selected spreadsheet cell.

EPSF 130-131
Encapsulated PostScript File format, used to store graphics and text information for printing on a PostScript printer or typesetter.

erasable optical disks 61
High capacity disk storage that uses a laser beam to read and write information on a metal coated disk.

erasing disks > see floppy disk, initializing

ergonomics 4-5
Branch of knowledge pertaining to the study of work, used very often to describe man-to-machine interaction.

***Escape* key** 16
Keyboard key used mostly in IBM PC-compatible programs to cancel operations or backtrack through a series of steps.

EtherTalk 68, 162-163
Cable connection system for attaching a Macintosh to an **Ethernet** network.

expansion boards 9, 32
Optional extra circuit boards that plug into sockets on Macintosh system unit connectors. Not all Macintoshes have the same connector nor the same number of slots available for expansion boards.

Extensions folder 12, 74, 83, 178
Folder inside the System Folder where **drivers**, **INITs**, and similar system software elements are stored.

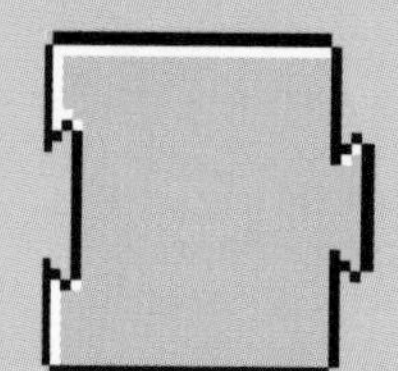

extensions, system
68-69, 74, 83, 148, 178,188, 196
Drivers, **INITs**, and similar system software elements required at startup time. Many of these items are loaded into memory during startup, and their icons appear at the bottom of the screen before the Finder appears.

fax modem 174-175
A hardware device that allows you to send documents directly from the Macintosh to a fax machine over the telephone. Some units also capture incoming faxes, and turn them into Macintosh document files.

FDHD 52
Floppy Disk, High Density, the designation of the 1.4 MB floppy disks that work with the **SuperDrive** disk drive that ships on all Macintosh models today.

feature upgrade 12, 67
New version of software that includes one or more enhancements to features or additional features over and above the previous version.

female connector 7
One of a connector pair recognizable for holes that accept the pins of a matching male connector.

file 118-119, 199
Any entity, other than a volume or folder, that appears on the Macintosh desktop or in a folder window. A file is a collection of information, whether it be an application (containing program code) or document (containing your data).

file compression 174-175
Method of squeezing a file to a smaller size for efficient transfer over telephone lines or networks, or for disk space efficiency. Requires decompression to use the file.

File
New Folder ⌘N
Open ⌘O
Print ⌘P
Close Window ⌘W
Get Info ⌘I
Sharing...
Duplicate ⌘D
Make Alias
Put Away ⌘Y
Find... ⌘F
Find Again ⌘G
Page Setup...
Print Window...

File menu 100, 128-129
Standard user interface item containing commands to open, close, and save files, as well as quitting an application.

file server 162-163, 191-192
A shared disk volume on a network. A dedicated file server is a Macintosh and hard disk on a network devoted entirely to the job of acting as a server in conjunction with server software, such as AppleShare 3.0.

File Sharing Monitor 69, 82, 190
Control panel that lets you view who is connected to your Macintosh and which shared folders are currently in use.

file transfer 8-9
Moving a file from one computer to another, usually via a **network** or telephone connection.

file type 128-129, 180, 190
The hidden four-character table that helps applications know whether a file is compatible (i.e., openable).

files, locking 191, 197
Turning a file into a read-only file by checking the **Lock** check box in the file's Get Info dialog box,.

files, copying 180-181, 201
Drag a file's icon from one disk to another. To make a copy on the same disk (in another folder), press *option* and drag - otherwise the file is simply moved to the other folder. Also see Duplicate.

files, finding 66, 122-123
Find command in the Finder's **File** menu lets you locate files on your hard disk that match numerous search criteria. You can perform a simple search on a name or a more defined search on many different characteristics of files.

FileShare 9, 66, 120-121, 162, 173, 184, 187, 190-192, 195, 199, 204
Built-in ability in System 7 for all Macintoshes on the same **AppleTalk** network to share files and link programs together. Requires setting several control panels and the **Chooser** to use properly.

FileShare extension 69, 83
Driver file in the Extensions folder that allows your Macintosh use **FileShare** on a network.

Finder 12, 74, 84-85, 94, 191
Application program that works with the System File to present the Macintosh **Desktop** and **graphical user interface**. Simplifies processes such as moving and searching for files.

Finder Prefs 89, 110-113
Special file in the Preferences folder created by the Finder to store settings of several control panels, such as Views, that affect your working with the Finder.

finding files > see files, finding

fixed size fonts > see bitmapped fonts

fkeys 27
Function keys are small programs that are triggered by a *command*-key sequence, such as the *command-shift-3* screen capture function built into system software. Fkeys are not as prevalent as they once were.

flashing menu 76
The Alarm Clock Desk Accessory had an alarm set, and it has elapsed. Open the Alarm Clock and turn off the alarm.

flashing menubar 113, 156-157
Usually means that the volume in the **Sound** control panel is set to zero. Instead of sounding the system beep to alert you, the Macintosh flashes the menubar.

flashing program icon 101
In place of the **Application** menu icon, this means that a program running in the background needs your attention. This program is marked with a black diamond in the **Application** menu. Switch to this program and respond to its dialog box.

Flash-It! 35
Popular screen capture alternative control panel. Shareware product by Nobu Toge.

flicker 30-31
Interaction between the screen refresh rate of a video monitor and refresh rate of surrounding fluorescent lighting. The more distant the refresh rates of the monitor and lighting, the less flicker.

floating-point processing unit (FPU)
Additional motherboard circuitry (sometimes built into the CPU chip) that speeds calculations of floating-point (i.e. non-integer) math (and many processes that require floating-point arithmetic). A FPU is included on high-end Macintoshes and is available as a third-party option for mid-range models.

floppy disk
52-54, 120-121, 174-175, 177, 183, 184, 202
Storage device capable of 400K, 800K, or 1.4 MB of storage, depending on the disk type and formatting. 1.4MB disks can be read only by **SuperDrive** disk drives in newer Macintoshes. MS-DOS formatted 3.5" disks may be accessed in Apple File Exchange.

floppy disk drive port > see disk drive port

floppy disk, ejecting **53, 177**
Normal disk ejection is accomplished by selecting the disk, and choosing **Eject Disk** from the **Special** menu, or, better still, dragging the disk to the Trash icon. The latter removes the disk icon from the Desktop entirely.

floppy disk, initializing **52, 202**
Laying down the parking spaces on a disk for information, sometimes known as formatting. All disks must be initialized before they may store information.

floppy disk, locking **13**
Preventing a disk from being overwritten. Requires the locking tab be in the open (see through) position. Also prevents viruses from being written to a diskette.

folder name **116-117**
Identifying name attached to every folder. A folder name can be 30 characters long, but no colon (:) is allowed in the name.

folder **94, 106-107, 116-117, 120-121, 183, 185,192, 195, 199**
A collection of files or other folders, just like a paper folder. A folder may also be shared with other users on a network.

font resource **12, 84-87**
File that contains information about a **typeface**. May be a single bit mapped font size or a TrueType file, which contains specifications about all sizes of a typeface. Font resources must be dropped into the System File for the font to be recognized by applications.

Font/DA Mover **75, 84, 202**
Program that used to be required for moving fonts and desk accessories into and out of the System file. No longer needed for System 7, but version 4.1 or later can be useful in combining fonts or desk accessories into suitcase files for storage or transfer to other users.

font **86-88, 128-129, 150-151, 192**
In Macintosh parlance, usually defines a particular typeface, regardless of size or style (bold, italic, etc.). Different from typesetting terminology, in which a font is a typeface of a particular style and size.

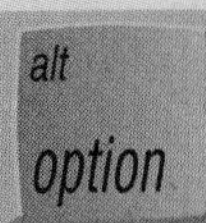

force quit **179**
Typing *command-option-escape* may let you quit a frozen program without harming the data in other running programs.

foreign language characters > see keyboard characters

formatted capacity **52, 55**
Actual amount of empty space available on a disk after the disk has been initialized (formatted). Invisible control information takes up some of the disk's raw storage capacity.

formatting disks > see floppy disk, initializing; hard disk initializing

fragmentation **44-45, 57**
Occurring in RAM and hard disks, data is not contiguous. In RAM, fragmentation causes samll open blocks that are not useable by the next program to open. On hard disks, fragmentation places pieces of a file on many parts of a disk, increasing the total access time in reading and writing the file.

frame grabber **32**
External hardware (or plug-in expansion board) that connects to a video source and with the help of compatible software, captures a video frame, converting it to information that can be stored in a Macintosh file. The image may also be modified by graphics software to produce unusual effects.

freeware > see shareware

freeze **11, 179**
Condition in which the Macintosh is unresponsive to mouse clicks or keystrokes.

Frontier 27, 134
Program designed for programmers and advanced users to facilitate the use of **Apple Events** in creating environments with shared programs and files. Produced by UserLand Software, Inc.

function keys 17
Fifteen keys along the top of the Apple Extended keyboard to replicate those keys on an AT-style keyboard. With **macro programs**, any key can be instructed to carry out a long series of mouse and keyboard motions.

fuse 6
Capsule sized device placed in a power line to break the circuit when too much current is flowing through the line. An open fuse may indicate a failure of a piece of electronic equipment that was about to draw more current than normal operation allows. Often built into surge suppressors or power strips.

General Controls 11, 80, 110
Control panel that lets you adjust basic settings on your Macintosh: desktop pattern, menu blinking rate, text insertion pointer blinking rate, sound level, and internal clock. Choices are saved in **Parameter RAM**.

genlock 32
Special external hardware that synchronizes the refresh rates of a Macintosh video monitor with a video camera that is recording the Macintosh screen. Prevents the slowly creeping line in the recorded screen.

Get Info
44, 94, 112, 118-121, 135, 182, 191, 193
File menu command that opens a dialog revealing information about the selected disk, folder, or file. Contents of the **Get Info** dialog box varies with the type of selected object.

gigabyte
One billion bytes.

glare 4-5, 31
Reflection of surrounding objects and light off the glass of a video monitor. Can cause headaches and eyestrain if intense.

graphical user interface (GUI) 12, 94, 128-129
Method of interaction between a computer and its user in which commands are carried out by clicking and pointing with a mouse, rather than typing commands. Files and directories appear as metaphors of real-world objects. Acronymn sometimes pronounced as GOO-ee. In most non-Macintosh computers, the user interface is a layer atop an existing operating system (e.g., Windows atop MS-DOS), while the Macintosh System and Finder are more highly integrated.

graphics tablet 27
A flat pad that lets you move an on-screen pointer by drawing with a pen that is connected to the pad. It supplements a keyboard in intensely graphic work, such as design drawing, letting you work with a more comfortable pointing and drawing device.

grayscale 30-31,34
Capability of displaying varying intensity of gray at each pixel location. At 256 levels of gray, a monitor is capable of displaying photorealistic images.

ground 6, 46
Electric potential of the earth. Grounding yourself means matching your potential with that of the earth. Most electrical outlets are grounded, and the third, round pin of a power cord is usually connected to ground.

group 164-167
Combination of two or more **FileShare** users that you setup to use your computer's files or programs. Groups are created in the Users & Groups control panel.

grow box 102
Lower right corner of a document window, which lets you resize a window to whatever limits the program or screen permit. Only the lower right corner is adjustable.

guest 164-169
Special user entity (in **Users & Groups** control panel) that represents all unregistered users on your network. Allowing guest access gives everyone on the network access to a particular disk or folder.

GUI > see graphical user interface.

handicapped mousing 25
Performing mouse operations without the mouse. Requires **Easy Access** control panel.

handicapped typing 20
Performing typing operations with a single, potentially inaccurate stylus or pointer. Requires **Easy Access** control panel.

handicapped viewing 35
Viewing the screen with software magnification. Requires **CloseView** control panel.

handler 144-145
HyperTalk script component that responds to a message. A **HyperCard** object may have a script consisting of many individual handlers.

hang > see freeze

hard disk 55-57, 120-124, 177-179
Storage device capable of storing large quantities of information, usually offering fast access to that information.

hard disk partition 56, 179
Portion of a hard disk that has been assigned (by partitioning software) as a separate disk volume when viewed on the **Desktop**.

hard disk recovery 60, 177, 198, 202
Repair of a hard disk that is not immediately readable when starting up the Macintosh. May entail several different techniques and a few attempts.

hard disk, initializing 55, 177-178, 202
Laying down the parking spaces (tracks and sectors) on a disk space, also known as formatting. Initializing a hard disk erases all previous information on that disk.

headphones 9, 156-157
Same as Walkman-style stereo headphones for listening to Macintosh audio through the audio output port. Provides improved fidelity over the internal speaker. The internal speaker is disabled when the headphones are plugged in.

heat 5
The Number One enemy of computers. Allow for good ventilation around the system unit and monitor.

Hebrew script 21
Language resource that instructs the Macintosh how to display Hebrew language characters, including left-to-right Roman words embedded in the right-to-left Hebrew words.

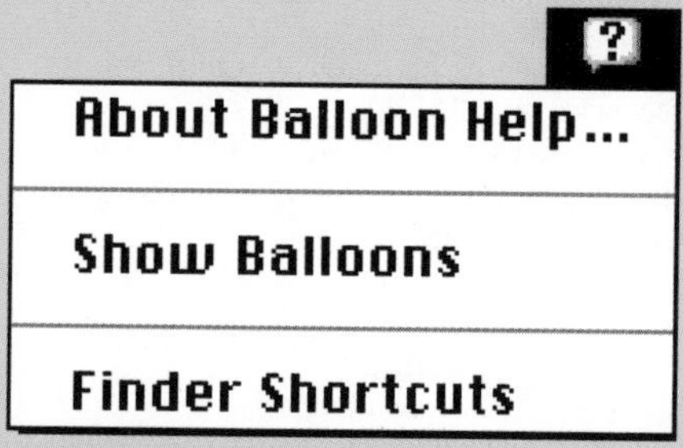

Help menu 44, 96, 101
Menu at the right of the menubar that leads to **Balloon Help**. Programs may add more help items to the menu.

hierarchical menu > see menu, hierarchical

highlight color 36, 113
Color assigned to a text selection on a color monitor. Adjusted in the **Color** control panel.

high profile SIMM 46
RAM module that uses either large **RAM** chips or multiple chips to increase capacity per module. Only a few Macintosh models can accomodate these **SIMMs**.

***home* key** 17
An Apple Extended keyboard key sometimes used in document navigation. Must be programmed by the application's author for use.

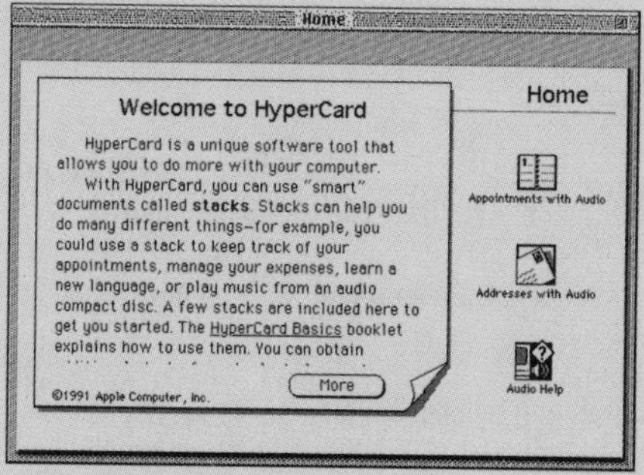

Home stack 138-139
Default stack file that **HyperCard** opens. Contains settings for various preferences as you use HyperCard.

hot spot, monitor 5
Bright spot caused by glare from surrounding light source. Can be minimized with an adjustable monitor stand.

hot spot, pointer 97
Single pixel on a pointer that must be atop a button or other object to effect action with the mouse button. Editable in **CURS** resources with ResEdit.

hue, lightness, saturation (HLS) 36
Three-value system of defining a color. Available as an option for selecting a color in the Color Wheel.

HyperCard 44, 134, 138-145, 156-159, 179
Programming environment for non-programmers. Edition packaged with System software is a two-disk set, including audio recording stack. Five-disk set from Claris Corporation is recommended for stack authoring.

HyperTalk 134, 144-145
English-like scripting language built into HyperCard.

IAC > see interapplication communication

icl4 85, 98
Resource identifier for a large (32-by-32 pixel) 4-bit color (16 colors) icon. Editable in ResEdit.

icl8 85, 98
Resource identifier for a large (32-by-32 pixel) 8-bit color (256 colors) icon. Editable in ResEdit.

ICN# 85, 98
Resource identifier for a large (32-by-32 pixel) monochrome icon. Editable in ResEdit.

ICON 85
Resource identifier for monochrome icon generally used inside applications programs (i.e., not the Finder). Editable in ResEdit.

icon family 98
Collection of all large and small icon versions in all colors for a particular icon design. All icon resources share the same resource ID number.

icon, desktop 94-95, 98, 113, 120-121
Representations for disks, folders, documents, and other files presented by the Finder. Finder displays an icon in appropriate color and size depending on color monitor support and window view.

ics# 85, 98
Resource identifier for a small (16-by-16 pixel) monochrome icon. Editable in ResEdit.

ics4 85, 98
Resource identifier for a small (16-by-16 pixel) 4-bit color (16 colors) icon. Editable in ResEdit.

ics8 85, 98
Resource identifier for a small (16-by-16 pixel) 16-bit color (256 colors) icon. Editable in ResEdit.

imagesetter 88
Expensive devices that transfer text and graphics files to photographic film, usually at very high resolutions. Film output is used in the production of printed materials. A familiar brand name is Lino–tronic, whose model 300 is capable of 2540 dpi.

ImageWriter 9, 86, 194
Dot-matrix impact printer currently available from Apple in the ImageWriter II model. Can be set up as a serial or LocalTalk network printer.

inactive window 103
Window that is not the current window, usually covered by another window on the screen. Discernable by its lack of horizontal lines in the title bar. On color monitors, the name in the titlebar is dimmed.

indicator lights, keyboard 17
Extended keyboard lights above the numeric keypad that show the status of *num lock*, *caps lock*, and *scroll lock*. *num lock* and *scroll lock* features have to be programmed into an application by the author. *caps lock* works all the time.

INIT > see extensions, system

initializing diskette > see floppy disk, initializing

initializing hard disk> see hard disk, initializing

insert/help **key** 17
Extended keyboard key that can be used as an Insert key when the Macintosh is running IBM PC software. Usually programmed by application authors as a trigger for the on-line help system.

insertion point > see text insertion point.

Installer 12-13, 68-70, 148, 190, 196
Application that installs system and other software onto your hard disk. Requires an installer script document, which contains specifications about files and resources to be copied to your hard disk from the installation disks.

installing applications 12-13
Entails copying files from the distribution diskettes to your hard disk. Sometimes includes an installer (or the Installer) to move files to their proper places, including inside the System Folder when necessary.

installing System 7 12-13, 68-69
Requires the Installer program and script on the System 7 installation diskettes. You must use the Installer for this upgrade.

interapplication communication (IAC) 67, 134
Method for programs to manipulate other programs, their documents, and their information. Includes publish/subscribe mechanism.

interference, electromagnetic 31
Invisible fields that interfere with video displays, causing wobbly screen images. Requires that the source of interference be separated from your video monitor.

interference, radio and TV 7
Radio frequency signals generated by electronic equipment and cables. Can cause noise in radio and television signals.

internal clock > see General Controls control panel

international > see localization

internet 162-163
Collection of more than one **AppleTalk** network joined by network **bridges**.

Internet
A global e-mail network that connects thousands of corporate, university, and commercial e-mail systems.

Interrupt button 11
Button on the Programmer's Switch of importance to programmers only. Invokes a debugger system extension if one is installed.

INTL 85
Resource identifier for international resource families. These are the resources changed to localize system software and applications. Editable in ResEdit.

IsoPoint 27
Alternative pointing device used in the first generation Outbound notebook computer, a third-party Macintosh portable computer. Consists of a roller bar installed beneath the space bar on a keyboard.

Japanese > see Kanji script

Jack> see connectors

Kanji script 21
Language resource that instructs the Macintosh how to display Japanese Kanji language characters.

KCHR 85
Resource identifier for a keyboard resource. Each language keyboard you connect to a Macintosh requires its own resource in the **System File**.

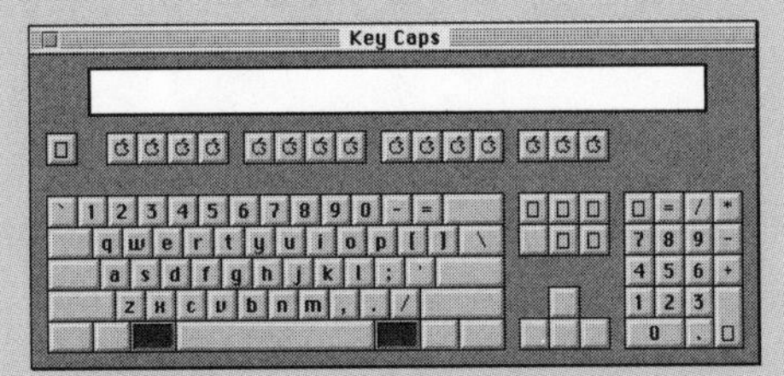

Key Caps desk accessory 19, 21, 76
Small program that lets you see and type any character, including those created in conjunction with the *option* key. Helpful in typing foreign language characters or symbols.

key repeat rate 19
Keyboard control panel setting that lets you adjust how fast a keyboard key repeats itself once it begins repeating.

Keyboard 19, 81
Control panel that lets you set the key repeat delay, repeat frequency, and alternate language keyboard.

keyboard, Apple 9, 10, 16
Smaller keyboard that features full alphanumeric keys, cursor keys, and numeric keypad. Fits comfortably on most desks.

keyboard character 19,21-23
Any alphanumeric character or symbol created with the keyboard. Not all fonts in a language have the same characters. Use **Key Caps** to see what characters each font contains.

keyboard connections > see Apple Desktop Bus

keyboard equivalent > see menu, keyboard equivalent

keyboard height 4
Distance between the floor and the surface on which the keyboard rests. For most people should be lower than standard 29" desk height.

keyboard macro 27
One-key command (or *command*-key sequence) that performs a series of mouse and keyboard actions as trained once by the user. Provides shortcuts for repetitive operations.

keyboard resource 12-13, 19, 21-23, 85
File containing specifications about a particular language's keyboard. Must be dropped into the System File if other than the standard keyboard for the country in which the Macintosh was purchased.

keyboard, extended 9, 10, 16-17
Larger keyboard patterned after the IBM PC AT model keyboard. Includes 15 function keys, document navigation keys, cursor keys in an inverted "T" arrangement, and indicator lights in addition to a numeric keypad.

keyboards, foreign language 21-23
Available through APDA, keyboards for other languages have different character layouts for each language. Requires a **keyboard resource**, and sometimes a **script language resource** for the System file.

kilobyte (K, KB) 40
One thousand bytes, although more accurately 1024 bytes, based on the binary arithmetic of the computer world (2^{10}).

Label
✓None
Essential
Hot
In Progress
Cool
Personal
Project 1
Project 2

Label menu 100, 110-111
Finder menu that lets you assign one of seven names (and colors on color monitors) to disks, folders, and icons on the **Desktop**. You may later sort and search by label as well as other file attributes.

Labels 80, 110-111
Control panel that lets you assign names and colors (on color monitors) to each of the seven **Label** menu entries.

landscape printing 148-149
Rotating the printed image 90 degrees to the right so that a wide image is printed on the page sideways. May be selected for all printers and documents in the **Page Setup** dialog.

language script resources 13, 19, 21-23, 85
Files that tell the Macintosh to use a different method of displaying characters (e.g., right-to-left, instead of left-to-right) for non-Roman languages. Install in the **System File**. Can be changed from the script menu, which appears between the Help and **Application** menu when language script resources are installed in the System File.

largest unused block 44-45
Report from the Finder (in **About This Macintosh**, under the menu in the Finder) about memory available for the loading of additional programs. May not always accurately represent available memory for applications, however.

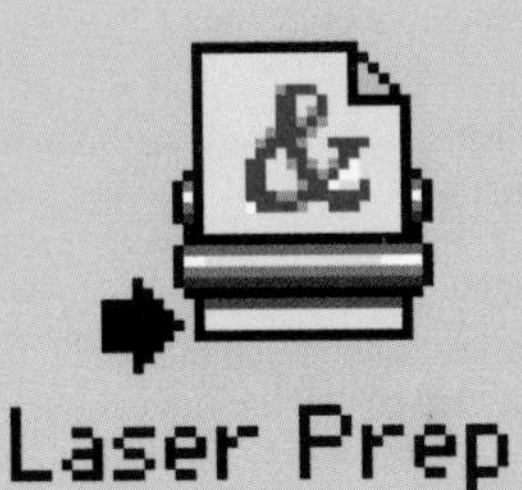

Laser Prep 152-153, 193
Extension file required by some programs that still look for the System 6 (and earlier) Laser Prep file. A compatible dummy Laser Prep file can be copied from the System 7 disks to your Extensions folder (or just the System Folder for some applications) for those programs. Functionality of Laser Prep is now built into LaserWriter driver.

LaserWriter **9, 71, 86, 88, 152-153, 182-186, 193**
Apple printer that uses a laser to specify image areas on a page. Available in various models, most of which have PostScript and fonts built into them.

LaserWriter Font Utility

LaserWriter Font Utility **87, 152-153**
Application on the Printing disk of System 7 installation disks that help you manage fonts on a PostScript LaserWriter. Also lets you turn off the test page.

LCD **37**
Liquid Crystal Display, a low-power flat panel display technology used in portable Macintoshes. Uses both reflected light and (on some models) an internal backlight to increase contrast of the characters against the light background.

leading **86**
Line spacing between base lines of vertically adjacent lines of text.

license, software **126-127**
Written contract you agree to when you open a software package. Grants you limited rights with virtually no warranty from the software publisher.

lighting **4-5**
Surrounding light sources have a big impact on your computer setup and fatigue prevention.

lightning precautions **6**
Strong spikes by nearby and direct lightning strikes can damage your computer unless it is protected by a surge protector.

Linotronic > see imagesetters

localization **84**
Process of tailoring software for a particular country's language and other cultural facets. Often simplified by editing resources for menus, dialog boxes, and text strings.

LocalTalk **68, 162-163**
AppleTalk connector system built into all Macintoshes. Devices on a LocalTalk cable are in a daisy-chain.

locking floppy disk > see floppy disk, locking

logic board > see motherboard

low profile SIMMS **46**
Preferred size of **RAM** modules that fit comfortably into the cramped quarters of most Macintosh models.

Macintosh Tools **60**
Disk utility software by Central Point Software to help in hard disk crash and file recovery.

MacinTalk **156-157**
Optional system extension that converts text and phonemes to a computer-sounding voice played through the speaker. Available through user groups and electronic bulletin boards, but not yet updated for System 7.

Macintosh memory upgrades **46-49**
Process of increasing memory capacity in a Macintosh. May be required to make a Macintosh System 7-ready. Upgrading to 4 megabytes or more is strongly recommended for System 7.

MacOS **13**
Shorthand for Macintosh Operating System, referring more specifically to the system software (System and Finder) in comparison to MS-DOS, Windows, and other operating systems or **graphical user interfaces**.

MacPaint file format (PNTG) **130-131**
File format for bitmapped graphics images established in the first graphics program for the Macintosh, MacPaint. Virtually every Macintosh graphics program can open a MacPaint file.

MacRecorder **158-159**
External device from MacroMind/Paracomp (formally from Farallon Computing, Inc.)that lets you record voice and other sound for storage as a file or resource on the Macintosh.

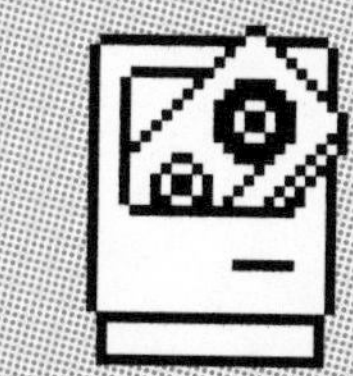

MacroMaker

MacroMaker **27**
Obsolete keyboard **macro program** that used to be a part of Macintosh system software. Not compatible with System 7.

macros > see keyboard macros

mail, electronic > see e-mail

maintenance upgrade 12, 67
Update to software that fixes bugs or adds compatibility for a new Macintosh model. No new features included.

male connector 7
One of a connector pair recognizable for pins that go into the holes of a matching female connector.

Map control panel 82
Small program that lets world-travelling Macintosh owners find times in other parts of the world and keep the internal clock in the local time zone of the traveler.

megabyte (M, MB) 40
One million bytes, or more accurately, 1,048,576 bytes. The unit of measure for **RAM** and hard disk capacity.

megahertz (MHz)
A unit of measure of frequency in cycles per second. Used to rate processing speeds of CPU chips.

Memory 42-45, 82
A control panel that lets you set **RAM cache size** and (if your Macintosh is so equipped) **32-bit addressing**, and **virtual memory**. Also lets you create a RAM disk on Quadras and PowerBooks only.

memory, application > see RAM, application

memory management 44-45, 187, 189, 199, 200
The techniques available to optimize usage of limited RAM.

MENU 85
Resource identifier for menu resources in application. Editable with ResEdit.

menu, flashing > see flashing menubar; flashing program icon

menu, hierarchical 101
Pull down menu in which an item has a right-pointing arrow that leads to a submenu for that item. Requires careful mouse work to reach that submenu.

menu, pop up 101
Menu style normally used to let you choose from a pre-set list of choices to fill in a preferences setting.

menu, pull down 101
Menu of commands which you access by clicking and holding on a menu title in the menubar. The menu drops down, allowing you to drag the mouse to the desired command. Releasing the mouse button on the command activates the command.

menu, tear-off 101
Menu style, normally used in tool menus, that let you drag the tools away from the menubar in a palette-style window. You can leave the window showing for faster selection of various tools.

menubar 100-101
The white bar across the top of the screen containing titles of pull-down menus.

menu flashing > see flashing menubar

microprocessor > see CPU

Microsoft Windows 13
Graphical user interface program that runs atop MS-DOS.

mini DIN-8 connector 7
Smaller version of a round DIN connector, used for Macintosh **ADB** and **serial ports**.

minimum system diskette 70, 177, 178, 197,
Diskette containing a System and Finder that allows you to boot the Macintosh from a floppy disk in case of difficulty booting from your hard disk. Created with the help of the System 7 Installer.

modal dialog > see dialog, modal

MODE32 40, 43, 46, 67
Free System 7 extension from Apple that lets owners of a SE/30, Macintosh II, IIx, or IIcx turn on **32-bit addressing** to access more than 8MB of RAM.

modeless dialog > see dialog, modeless

modem 9
A hardware device that converts the computer's electrical signals into audible tones for transmission across telephone wires or radio waves and reconnects received audio into computer signals.

modem cable 9
Cable configured to plug into a Macintosh serial port and modem. Most modems are standard enough to allow a generic cable to work.

modem port 9
A **serial port** on the Macintosh rear panel bearing a telephone icon. Either this port or printer port can be used with a modem, however.

modem, fax > see fax modem

modifier key 16
Any of several non-character keys pressed in concert with one or more other keys to modify their normal behavior. The modifier keys are the *shift*, *option*, *command*, *caps lock*, and *control*.

modular Macintosh 4, 10-11
Macintosh system consisting of a system unit and external monitor. All Macintosh LC, II, and Quadra models are modular Macintoshes. These allow a wide choice in monitor and expansion possibilities.

monitor stand 4-5
Allows for adjustment of monitor in many directions to avert glare and hot spots from surrounding light sources.

Monitors 34-35, 36, 81
The control panel that lets you set the number of colors (for a color monitor) or gray levels (for grayscale and color monitors). Also controls multiple monitor setups—which is the startup screen monitor, which is the main monitor for **menubar**.

monitors, multiple > see Monitors

monochrome 31,34-35
A monitor that displays a single color (usually white) against its black background. Built-in monitors of compact Macintoshes and portable Macintosh LCDs are monochrome. This is distinct from grayscale, which requires different video monitor driving circuitry.

moof > see Dog Cow

MooV file format 130-131
A file format for **QuickTime** movies and other time-based data.

motherboard 46-49
The main circuit board inside the Macintosh that holds CPU, RAM, and other primary board components. Also called the logic board.

mount 116-117
The process of getting the Finder to recognize and display a disk and its contents.

mouse connections > see Apple Desktop Bus

Mouse 25, 81, 97
A control panel that lets you adjust double-click speed and tracking speed of your mouse. The settings are stored in **Parameter RAM**.

mouse 24-25
Hardware device that lets you control the on-screen pointer.

Mouse Keys 25
Easy Access control panel setting that lets you use the numeric keypad as a substitute for the mouse.

mouse pad 5
Rubber or plastic slab on which you roll the mouse when traction on the desk surface is not sufficient to use the mouse.

mouse tracking 25
Speed at which the screen pointer responds to rapid movement of the mouse. Adjustable in the **Mouse** control panel, it may be set between completely linear (tablet) and very fast to let you cover large screens with a minimum of mouse motion.

move > see drag

MS-DOS > see DOS; Microsoft Windows

MultiFinder 12, 44, 66
Obsolete feature of earlier system software that allowed multiple programs to run at the same time. Now standard behavior of System 7, and cannot be turned off.

multiple monitors > see Monitors

names 180, 181, 186, 188, 195
Identifying name for any disk, folder, or file. Different objects have different maximum character lengths for their names.

nanosecond (ns) 40
One-billionth of a second, the unit of measure of **RAM** chip refresh and access speeds. Faster Macintosh models require faster (lower nanosecond rating) RAM chips.

Network 81
A control panel that lets you select from multiple network connections (LocalTalk, **EtherTalk**, **TokenTalk**). Must be copied from the System 7 installer disk to your Control Panels folder.

network server 6
Macintosh on a network that must be set aside to act as a shared hard disk for all other Macintoshes on the network. Still useful for high-volume shared traffic, instead of the occasional **FileShare** traffic.

NFNT 85
Resource identifier for new fonts, the bit mapped fonts copied to the System File by the Installer.

Norton Utilities

Norton Utilities 178
Commercial disk utility program by Symantec used for hard disk and file recovery.

Note Pad 74, 77
Desk accessory that contains 8 small text pages for jotting notes. Text is saved in the Notepad File in the System Folder.

Note Pad

Note Pad File 74
Text file that stores notes written with the Note Pad desk accessory.

ns > see nanosecond

NuBus 9
A specification for one type of slot that accepts expansion boards on Macintosh II logic boards. The number of available NuBus slots varies from model to model.

num lock 17
Extended keyboard key that some programs have programmed to allow the numeric keypad to be used as a numeric keypad instead of navigation keys (as they would be on some IBM PC-style keyboards).

object graphics 130
Images defined by mathematical representations, such as a line with endpoint coordinates and a line thickness. Require less disk storage than the bitmapped equivalent, and can be resized without distortion. Print with higher clarity on **PostScript** printers.

OCR > see optical character recognition

Open Apple key (–) 16
Name for the *command* key when keyboard is used on an Apple //GS computer.

open file dialog > see dialog, open file

operating system 12
Most basic software in **ROM** that helps the Macintosh perform its self test and search for a startup disk when turned on.

optical character recognition (OCR) 26
Method of converting printed text to editable text characters in a document. Requires scanner hardware and OCR software.

optical disks > see CD-ROM; WORM; erasable optical disks

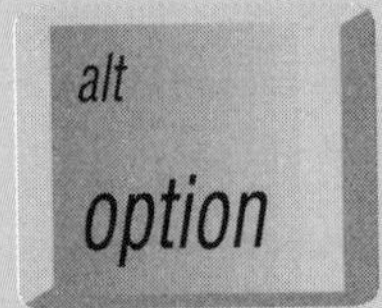

option **key** 16
Modifier key used primarily to access additional keyboard characters for other languages and symbols.

original 120-121
File that was used to create an **alias** file. **Get Info** dialog for an alias contains a button that locates the alias' original.

outlet > see connectors

outline font 86-88
A font specification that defines a character's appearance by mathematical calculations of points along the outline of that character. **TrueType** and **PostScript** fonts are outline fonts.

owner 164-165
Macintosh on which a disk or folder resides, even if it is viewable and editable from another Macintosh on a network. Icon for folders you have shared but still own have a dark spot on their tabs.

page down **key** 17
An Apple Extended Keyboard key usually programmed to mimic the action of clicking in the Page Down area of a scroll bar in a document window.

Page Setup dialog 78, 138-150
Presents choices affecting appearance of a document on the page, such as paper size and orientation. Settings are saved with the document. Each printer style, as selected by **Chooser**, has its own settings in this dialog.

page up **key** 17
An Apple Extended Keyboard key usually programmed to mimic the action of clicking in the Page Up area of a scroll bar in a document window.

paged memory management unit (PMMU) 40, 43, 67
Accessory chip that helps some Macintosh microprocessors use advanced memory features, such as **virtual memory**. Not available on some Macintoshes, optional on Macintosh II models, and built into all Macintoshes with a **68030** or **68040** microprocessor.

paint program 130, 150
An application program that lets you create graphic images by setting individual pixels to white, black, or colors. see also bitmapped graphics.

palette > see tool palette

paper clip 53
Uncoiled, a tool to remove a floppy disk from a disk drive when the Macintosh is turned off.

parallel printer 9
Printer that communicates with a computer along 8 simultaneous data lines through a cable. Theoretically faster communications than a **serial printer**, but in practice rarely delivers faster throughput than today's serial printers. Imagesetter and Stylewriter printers are serial printers.

parameter RAM (PRAM) 11, 19, 41, 177, 178
Separate, battery-backed up section of memory on all Macintoshes that stores settings from some control panels as well as the current clock time.

parity RAM 41
Memory that includes one extra error-checking bit for each byte (8 bits) of data memory. Frequently demanded in specifications for government computers, only a couple Macintosh models offer parity RAM versions.

partition > see hard disk partition

paste from Clipboard 79, 108
Edit menu command places a copy of the Clipboard at whatever location the text insertion pointer or selection is located in a document.

Paste Special 108
Extra **Paste** command in some programs allows you to paste certain attributes of a complex information item in the Clipboard (e.g., just the formulas from spreadsheet cells in the Clipboard).

PAT# 110
Resource identifier for monochrome patterns available in the **General Controls** control panel for desktop patterns. Changes recorded in the control panel are saved to this resource. Also editable with ResEdit.

path 106-107, 116-117
Notation for specifying a file's location on a disk volume, consisting of volume name and all intervening folders, each element is separated by a colon.

pattern > see desktop pattern

pause **key** 17
Extended keyboard key rarely used in Macintosh software. A holdover from the AT-style keyboard.

PC 174-175
Personal Computer, but generally applied to MS-DOS compatible computers patterned after IBM's PC models.

PDS 9
Processor Direct Slot, a motherboard connector on some Macintoshes. Often used to connect third-party accelerator boards or other expansion boards that work best with a direct connection to the CPU chip.

peripheral 8-9
Device that connects to the Macintosh via one of its rear panel ports.

persistence 31
Video monitor characteristic of how long it takes the **phosphor** to decay (go from illuminated to black). High persistence phosphors have virtually no flicker, but leave momentary ghosts of moving objects.

PhoneNet 162-163
AppleTalk connector system by Farallon Computing that uses low-cost standard telephone wire for connections between devices.

phosphor 30-33
Coating inside the face of video tube. When struck by electron beam, illuminates in spots.

phototypesetters > see imagesetters

PICS 130-131
Animated graphic file format.

PICT 85, 108, 130-131
Resource identifier for simple graphic image, which may be either bitmapped or object graphic in monochrome or color.

PICT file type 130-131
Original graphic file format for the Macintosh.

PICT2 file format 130-131
Enhanced graphic file format for Macintosh graphics.

picture element > see pixel

Picture file > see screen shot

pincushioning > see distortion, video

pinout > see connectors

pixel 30
Picture element, the smallest graphical unit on a video display. Depending on the monitor, may be black, white, a gray level, or in any color within the video monitor's circuitry capability.

pixel density > see resolution, video

pixel grid 30
Count of pixels horizontal by pixels vertical on a video display. Not to be confused with video resolution, which indicates how densely pixels are drawn on the screen.

plug > see connectors

plug-in boards > see expansion boards

PNTG 130-131
A file type for MacPaint-format files.

point 86
1/72 of an inch, a typesetter's measure. Also the unit of measure of computer **font** sizes and line spacings.

pointer > see cursor.

popup menus > see menu, popup

port 8-9
Rear panel connector to which cables are attached.

Portable 81, 190
Control panel for portable Macintoshes that lets you adjust the power saving features and modem access (internal or external).

portrait video monitor 30
Video display capable of displaying a single full page of a document.

PostScript
86-88, 130-131, 148-149, 152-153, 183
Page description language by Adobe Systems, Inc. that uses outline definitions of font characters to produce smooth characters in any size and rotation. Built into most LaserWriter printers, it takes precedence over **TrueType** outline fonts. PostScript printer fonts install in the System Folder, not the System File, but companion bitmapped fonts for screen display must be dropped into the System File.

power (AC) cord 8, 176
Grounded cable between Macintosh and AC power outlet. Cords for other countries have the native outlet connector, while the Macintosh power supply accommodates all voltages and frequencies.

power outlets 6
Some offices are equipped with special power outlets with built-in surge suppressors.

power strip 6
AC power extension featuring multiple power outlets for plugging in several electrical devices. Fused power strips offer better protection.

power switch 10, 176
All Macintoshes have a power switch on their rear panels. Modular Macintoshes need it only in an emergency, since power on and off is controlled by the keyboard and system software.

PPC > see program-to-program communication

ppt# resource 110
Resource identifier for color patterns available in the **General Controls** control panel for desktop patterns (with color monitors). Changes recorded in the control panel are saved to this resource. Also editable with ResEdit.

Preferences folder 12, 74, 89
Special folder inside the System Folder where the Finder and System 7 programs store preference files.

print dialog 149, 151
Final dialog before document goes to the printer where you can select choices that affect the print job—number of copies, page range, etc.

print screen **key** 17
Extended keyboard key that has virtually no application on a Macintosh except as an extra function key that can be programmed to initiate a macro sequence. Used as a print screen command on DOS computers.

Print Server 162-163
AppleShare file server application that operates as a background printing program for all Macintoshes on the network. Print jobs are saved to disk on the server, instead of the local Macintosh.

printer drivers > see drivers

printer port 9
Rear panel connector especially suited to connect **AppleTalk** printers. Non-networked printers can also be connected to the modem port.

printer, choosing 78
Essential part of opening the communication between Macintosh and printer. Use Chooser to select printer once. Setting remains in effect until you change printers or upgrade system software.

printing 128-129, 140, 148-149, 182-185
Converting screen images to paper via a printer. Each printer requires a driver in the Extensions folder.

PrintMonitor

PrintMonitor
90, 148-149, 152-153, 182, 184, 185, 200
Small application that runs in background most of the time to print documents it finds in the PrintMonitor Documents Folder. Controls communication between Macintosh and LaserWriter while you work on other documents or applications.

PrintMonitor Documents Folder 90, 152-153
Special folder inside the System Folder containing print jobs waiting to be printed on a LaserWriter. PrintMonitor automatically starts to print items whenever they appear in this folder.

processor > see CPU

program > see application

program linking 172
Ability for one program to send messages (via **Apple Events**) to another. Allows programs on the same or different computers to work jointly.

program-to-program communication (PPC) 134
Programmer's jargon for program linking.

programmer's switch 11, 179
A two-button switch including an **Interrupt** button (for programmers to trigger a debugger) and a **Reset** button, which you can use to restart a frozen Macintosh. Comes built into on most new Macintoshes; must be installed on others.

protocols 174-175
Agreed-upon standards for exchange of data between computers.

public domain software
Applications and system utilities widely distributed by user groups, dealers and BBSs. Programs are copyrighted by their authors, but are free. See also shareware.

publish/subscribe 67, 132-133, 182-183
Method of sharing information between documents (in the same or different applications). One document publishes an edition (separate file); another document subscribes to the edition. Changes made by the publisher are immediately updated to the subscriber document.

pull down menus > see menu, pull down

put away > see unmouinting volumes

Puzzle desk accessory 77
Often expendable program resembling a child's plastic tile puzzle. In System 7, however, you receive an audible reward sound for putting the picture pieces in the right order.

QuickDraw accelerator 33
Hardware adjunct to a color video board that speeds redrawing 24-bit color screens.

QuickKeys 27
A commercial macro program from CE Software.

QuickTime 32, 131
A system software extension developed by Apple that allows recording and display of small full motion video and animation sequences (and other time-based data) on color Macintosh screens without additional video hardware.

radio button 128-129
A user interface element found in groups of two or more to specify a setting or preference. Click once to activate the item and all other items in the group will turn off (like a car radio station preset button).

radio interference >
see interference, radio and TV

RAM 40-43, 46-49, 67, 176, 200
Random Access Memory, temporary storage of programs and documents while you use them. Except for portable Macintoshes, contents of main RAM are erased when you turn off or restart the Macintosh.

RAM cache 46
Separate, super fast RAM used to store data most recently read from or saved to RAM in case it is needed again. Improves performance of many operations. Available from Apple as a plug-in card for the Macintosh IIci. See also disk cache.

RAM disk 43,45
Section of RAM reserved to act as a separate disk volume on the desktop. With items, such as programs, copied to RAM disk, performance improves substantially. The contents survives a restart on the Portable, PowerBooks and Quadras.

RAM jumper (Macintosh SE) 48
Small connector that must be in the proper position (or removed) depending on the amount of RAM installed on newer model SEs.

RAM resistors (Macintosh Plus/SE) 47
Components that must be in the proper position (or removed) depending on the amount of RAM installed in a Macintosh Plus or early SEs.

RAM, application
44-45, 126-127, 182, 184, 189, 193, 196
Memory allocated to a program. Adjusted in the **Get Info** dialog for a program file and monitored in the About this Macintosh dialog box in the menu.

RAM, suggested 44, 182, 184
Recommended memory allocation for a program as defined by the program's author. Listed in the **Get Info** dialog for a program file.

RAM, video 32, 41
Memory devoted to holding a copy of information displayed on the video screen. May be part of motherboard RAM on some Macintoshes, or may be on an expansion video board.

random access memory > see RAM

RCA phono jack 7, 8
Common audio stereo jack used for audio input and output ports on Macintosh models. When a plug is inserted into the audio output port, the internal speaker is disabled.

read-only memory > see ROM

read/write optical disks > see eraseable optical disks

reboot 11
Jargon for restarting the computer. Derivative of boot.

rebuilding desktop >
see desktop file, rebuilding

recovering damaged disk > see hard disk recovery

refresh rate 30
Number of times each second that the video screen has its phosphor repainted by the electron beam inside the tube. The higher the refresh rate, the less likely you'll experience flicker as interference with fluorescent lighting.

registered user > see user

repetitive strain injuries 4
Muscular and nerve health problems caused by extensive keyboarding without proper support, adjustment, and rest periods.

ResEdit 84-85, 96-97, 99, 104, 110-113
Application available from APDA used by programmers and enthusiasts to modify resource in files. Can be used to customize your system, but only with great care on backup copies of important files. Version 2.1 or later required for System 7.

Reset button 11, 179, 196
Button on the **Programmer's Switch** that performs the same function as the **Restart** item in the **Special** menu but without the careful shut down of applications and system software. Should be used only when the Macintosh freezes.

resolution, video 30
Density of pixels per inch on the video screen. The higher the resolution, the smaller recognizable items, such as menubars and icons, appear.

resource 84
Often an easily editable part of an application program that stores specifications for items such as menus, dialog boxes, sounds, and more. System file fonts and sounds are also resources. These can be explored and edited with **ResEdit** (but beware).

resource fork 84
Part of a file that contains resources. Often combined with the **data fork** in a file.

response time 6
Amount of time required for a surge suppressor to kick in after receiving a jolt above the clamping voltage.

Restart 10-11, 177
Shut Down and turn on the computer without completely shutting down power to the system. Far less jarring to the circuitry than turning the machine completely off and turning it back on.

RGB (red, green, blue) 36
Common method of specifying a color by its red, green, and blue components. **Color Wheel** offers fields for direct entry of RGB values, if known. RGB monitor is one that receives signals for each of the three colors, as opposed to a composite video signal.

RJ-11 8
Standard modular telephone jack style. Commonly used as a port in a modem for connection to a telephone and the telephone wall jack (also an RJ-11 in most home installations).

ROM 10, 32, 40, 42-43, 67
Read Only Memory chip(s) contains information impregnated at the factory. Its contents cannot be changed by the user or a program. Macintosh ROM generations are known by their sizes in KB.

ROM BIOS 13
Basic operating system in an **MS-DOS** computer manufactured into a ROM chip.

root 116-117
Topmost level of a disk volume—the window you see when you double-click a disk icon on the **Desktop**.

sad Mac 176
An icon that appears on compact Macintosh and Quadra screens when the machine fails its internal hardware test during startup.

SAM 60
Symantec Anti-Virus for the Macintosh is a commercial **virus detection program**.

sampled sound 158-159
Electronic representation of real sound, derived by taking many thousands of readings each second, converting those readings to numbers. Sample sounds may then be edited in a sound editing program and saved as a file or resource.

sans-serif 86
Typeface style without any ornamentation on the ends of strokes. Helvetica and Geneva are sans-serif fonts.

save file dialog > see dialog, file save

scanner 26
External **SCSI** device that converts a printed page to an electronic image. Companion software saves the image in a variety of graphic file formats for editing in other graphics and desktop publishing programs.

Scrapbook

Scrapbook desk accessory 74-75, 79, 108, 187, 201
Small program that acts as a storage area for any information you can copy from a document. Scrapbook information is saved from session to session in the Scrapbook File.

Scrapbook File

Scrapbook File 74-75, 79, 108
Special file created by the Scrapbook desk accessory in which the Scrapbook information is stored on disk. The file is restricted only by available disk space.

screen capture; screen dump > see screen shot

screen fonts > see bitmapped fonts

screen saver 37
Program (usually an extension or control panel) that blanks the video screen or displays random images to prevent burn-in.

screen shot 27, 34-35, 150
File containing a copy of the entire video screen when the shot was taken. System software's screen shot command is *command-shift-3.*

Script Manager 21
Internal mechanism that controls how the Macintosh displays fonts and characters for non-Roman languages.

script resources > see language script resources

script, HyperTalk 144-145
Program code attached to a **HyperCard** object (button, card, etc.). A script may contain any number of handlers, but a script is limited to 30,000 character maximum of the script editor.

scroll bar 102
Control on document windows that allows you to adjust the view through the window to the underlying document. Scroll bar features five elements: up arrow, page up area, thumb, page down area, down arrow. Thumb (white box) indicate relative location within the document along the axis of the scroll bar.

scroll lock **key** 17
An Apple Extended Keyboard key and indicator light programmed for few Macintosh programs. Keeps spreadsheet cursor at the same cell while you scroll around the spreadsheet (instead of moving active cell with the scroll).

SCSI cables 7, 176, 177
Wiring that connects Small Computer Systems Interface standard devices. These come in a variety of styles and connector versions.

SCSI cabling 177-179
Varieties of cabling scenarios are needed to make some combinations of devices work properly.

SCSI connector 8
Non-standard 25-pin connector on the rear panel of most Macintoshes (and some peripherals); non-standard 30-pin connector on the rear panel of the PowerBooks; standard 50-pin connector with spring clips on most **peripherals**.

SCSI port 8
Rear panel connector for connecting high-speed peripheral devices, such as hard disks, scanners, video digitizers.

SCSI terminator > see SCSI cabling

search > see files, finding

seek time 55
The amount of time (in milliseconds) it takes a disk drive to find a particular track on a disk.

selecting 98
The process of marking text, graphic or other objects that will be affected by the next command or action. This usually requires clicking or clicking and dragging on the screen. Selected items are highlighted in various ways: inverse black/white; heavy border aroung the item; or a circulating dotted line around the object.

serial port 9, 204
Rear panel connector for connecting medium speed peripheral devices, such as telephone modems, audio digitizers, printers, and LocalTalk cables. Both the Macintosh printer and modem ports are serial ports.

serial ports, adding 9
Increasing the number of available serial ports is possible with a cable switcher or expansion boards.

serif 86
Ornamental stroke at the free ends of a character. Times and New York are serif fonts.

Server >see File Server

Set Startup 75
Obsolete Finder command that used to let you set what application(s) is to startup when the Macintosh does. Replaced in System 7 by the Startup Items folder contents.

shareware 138
Software freely distributed by its author, who asks users to try the software for free, but pay a modest licensing fee for continued use.

sharing a folder/disk 166-167
Setting up a folder or disk through **FileShare** for others on the network to access files or programs in the shared volume. Requires various control panel settings and **Sharing** menu dialog.

Sharing Setup 80
A control panel that lets you identify your Macintosh on the network. Must be filled out before you can share folders or disks with **FileShare**.

Show Clipboard 79, 108
Edit menu command (in Finder) to display a window showing the contents of the Clipboard.

Shut Down 10-11, 196
Turning off the Macintosh via the **Shut Down** command in the **Special** menu. Properly closes all applications and updates desktop file before turning off the Macintosh.

SIMM 40-41, 46, 49, 176
Single In-line Memory Module, a small circuit board consisting of **RAM** chips for simplified memory enhancement of Macintosh computers. SIMMs install into matching SIMM sockets on the system board. SIMMs come in a variety of configurations and sizes.

SIZE 85
Resource identifier for the part of a program that a programmer fills out to signify how much memory the program requires and works best in. Editable with ResEdit, but not recommended.

sleep 10-11, 43, 186-187
Battery-saving mode of portable Macintoshes. All activity ceases, but contents of RAM are maintained on low current-drain RAM chips.

slider control 104
Screen metaphor for a variable setting that you drag with the pointer. Used for volume setting in **Sound** control panel.

Slow Keys 20
Part of the **Easy Access** control panel that lets physically handicapped users type with single stylus. Adjust the delay required before a press of a key registers as a legitimate keystroke.

snd > see sound ('snd ') resources

sneakernet 174
An informal term for physically transferring files from one computer to another at the same location by using a floppy disk and walking between them.

solder bridge 7
Short between two contacts caused by extra solder that has spread between pins during assembly of a cable to a connector. Can be detected with a continuity checker.

sound ('snd ') resources 85, 141, 156-157
Resource identifier for a sound resource, the same kind that the System File uses for alert sounds. Sound recording programs can save sampled sounds as 'snd ' resources or AIFF files.

Sound 80, 113, 141, 156-157
A control panel that lets you adjust audio playback volume and alert (beep) sound. With a microphone connected to the Mac, you can record additional alert sounds for the System File.

sound, playback 8-9, 113, 141, 158-159
Macintosh's built-in ability to play sampled sound through internal speaker without additional hardware. Stereo sound is available through **audio output port** on all but the earliest Macintoshes.

sound, recording 8-9, 141, 158-159
Macintosh's built-in ability to record sampled sounds with the addition of a **microphone** or audio **digitizer**. Macintosh LC, IIsi, Classic II, Quadras, and PowerBooks have **audio input port** for direct microphone input; otherwise digitizers connect to **serial port**.

SoundMaster 113
A shareware program that allows you to attach sound files to different Macintosh actions.

speaker, internal 9, 156-157
Built-in speaker in all Macintoshes. Adequate fidelity for voice playback.

speakers, amplified 9, 156-157
Connecting to audio output port, external speakers that significantly enhance sound quality coming from the Macintosh.

Special
Clean Up Window
Empty Trash...
Eject Disk ⌘E
Erase Disk...
Restart
Shut Down

Special menu 100
Finder menu featuring miscellaneous maintenance commands for cleaning up windows, emptying Trash, restarting, and shutting down.

speech, playback > see MacInTalk; text-to-speech; sound, playback

speech, recording > see sound, recording

spike 6
Instantaneous high voltage usually generated by the electrical power utility. Can be dangerous to electronic equipment if not protected by **surge protector**.

spool 90
Process of allowing simultaneous background communication with a peripheral while foreground activity continues as normal.

stack, HyperCard 138-145
Basic file unit of **HyperCard**. Consists of a collection of screen "cards."

standby power supply 6
External device inserted between Macintosh and power outlet. If AC power stops, internal battery of power supply furnishes enough power for you to save open documents before shutting down.

star 162-163
Network connection topology in which each device is connected to a hub of connections.

startup disk 196
Volume that contains a system file that boots when you start the Macintosh. Its icon appears at the top right of the desktop.

Startup Disk 58-59, 80, 177, 178
A control panel that lets you assign a different volume as the startup disk for the next time you restart the Macintosh. Also describes a floppy disk with a System and Finder, making it capable of booting the Macintosh.

Startup Items folder 75, 91, 120
Special System Folder item that contains programs, documents, or aliases (to programs, documents, and servers) that are automatically loaded as the Macintosh starts up. Replaces previous **Set Startup** command in earlier system software.

startup screen 34
Graphic image that appears on screen immediately after the Welcome screen. Requires a third-party extension to create and display the graphic file.

startup tone or sound 10, 176
Initial sounds generated by Macintoshes during startup. Macintosh II sounds can also signify hardware problems.

static electricity 6
Charge stored on the body, especially in low humidity environments, that can damage chips and other components when touched.

stationery 107, 135
Type of document file that behaves like a template, automatically opening a copy of the original for editing, rather than the original. Stationery-aware programs behave differently from those that are not.

Sticky Keys 20
Part of **Easy Access** that allows single-finger typing of multiple-key combinations.

STR 85
Resource identifier for string resources. Editable with ResEdit.

STR# 85, 96
Resource identifier for string list resources. In most programs, contains error message text and **Balloon Help** text. Editable with ResEdit.

StuffIt > see file compression

StyleWriter 9, 194
Ink jet printer by Apple that produces relatively high-quality output, especially with System 7 **TrueType** fonts.

subscribe > see publish/subscribe

suggested memory > see RAM, suggested

suitcase file 75
File containing **font resources** or **desk accessories**. Font suitcases can be dropped into the System File; desk accessory suitcases can be dropped into Apple Menu Items folder. Saving items to a suitcase file requires **Font/DA Mover** or **ResEdit** compatible with System 7.

SUM 60
Symantec Utilities for the Macintosh, a commercial disk utility for hard disk and file recovery.

SuperDrive 52, 70, 202
High density disk drive included in all Macintoshes capable of initializing and reading 1.4 MB disks. Can read and write to 800K disks, as well as 3.5-inch MS-DOS disks with **Apple File Exchange** software.

surge 6
Instantaneous burst of voltage coming through the power line. Can be damaging to electronic equipment without the help of a **surge protector**.

surge protector 6
Power line device inserted between power outlet and Macintosh can filter extraneous surges and spikes in the AC power.

Symbol font 22
TrueType font that contains various scientific and math symbols (including many Greek letters).

Syquest, Inc. 61
Maker of **cartridge disk drive** mechanisms employed by many disk drive brands. Removable cartridges capable of storing 40 and 88 megabytes.

System 6, reinstalling 69
Replacing System 7 with System 6 if you discover too many incompatibilities with your software.

System 7 and 6 on hard disks 71, 203
Impact of each system on the other when a hard disk is used on both systems from time to time.

System 7 and 6 on network 69, 71
Coexistence of Macintoshes running both system versions on the same network.

System 7 Tune-Up 42
Update consisting of some extensions and drives to help low-memory Macs accommodate System 7's high RAM demands.

System 7, improvements 66-67
Features of System 7 that improve convenience and ease of use of the Macintosh Finder.

System 7, upgrading to 66-67
Methodology for upgrading individual Macintoshes to accomodate System 7.

system cable > see SCSI cables

system error 188
Usually, a software-induced problem that stops processing and displays an alert (the bomb). Requires restarting to clear the problem.

system extensions > see extensions, system

System File 12, 74, 84-85, 88, 196
Special file in the System Folder that contains, among many user inaccessible items, **font**, **sound**, and **keyboard resources**.

System Folder

System Folder 12, 66, 74, 88, 188, 197
Special folder that contains System, Finder, and several companion folders, each with a special purpose.

system numbering 12, 67
Conventions used in assigning numbers to system software versions.

system versions > see system numbering

tablet > see graphics tablet

tagged image file format > see TIFF

tape drive 61
External **SCSI** device using removable tape cartridges primarily for hard disk backup.

Teach Text 190
A simple text-editing program supplied with system software.

tear off menu > see menu, tear-off

telecommunications >
see communications software

telephone line port 8
Connector in a modem (like an internal modem of a portable Macintosh) to attach a line to a **telephone jack**. Usually an RJ-11 type connector.

television 32
Video input and output sources for the Macintosh with the help of external hardware and video software.

television interference >
see interference, radio and TV

Tempo 27
Commercial macro program by Affinity Systems.

terminator > see SCSI cabling; PhoneNet

TEXT data type 108
Simplest information type stores characters in uncompressed files. Can be opened by every word processing and spreadsheet program.

text insertion pointer 97, 128-129
Flashing cursor in a text document indicating where the next character typed from the keyboard will appear. Can be moved through text by the mouse or by cursor keys from the keyboard.

text-to-speech 156-157
Technology that converts plain text to understandable speech played through the Macintosh's sound playback circuitry. Currently, only MacinTalk is available but not yet upgraded for System 7. Better systems are under development.

third-party 7
Company other than Apple that supports Apple's products with additional hardware and software.

TIFF 130-131
Tagged Image File Format, a graphics **file format**.

time, setting >
see General Controls control panel

title bar 102
Window element that stretches across the top of the window, featuring the name of the document in the window or the name of the folder whose contents are shown in the window. Horizontal lines visible in titlebar indicate an active window; otherwise the window is inactive.

TokenTalk 68, 162-163
Cable connection system for attaching a Macintosh to a **Token Ring** network.

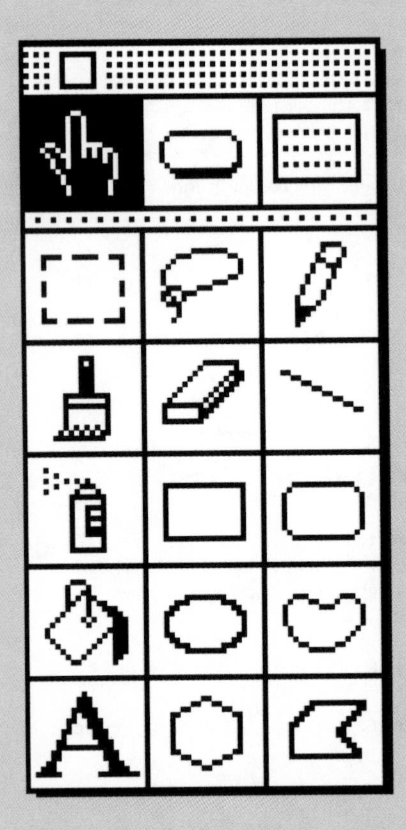

tool palette 128-129
Free-standing window containing icons representing graphics tools. Clicking on a tool turns the screen pointer into that tool icon, ready to perform whatever action is programmed for that tool.

total memory 42
Amount of memory installed in your Macintosh, listed in the **About This Macintosh** dialog (menu). Divide K value listed there by 1024 to determine the number of megabytes of RAM installed.

touch pad 27
Mouse alternative lets you use your finger on the touchpad as a screen pointer control.

trackball 27
Mouse alternative resembles an inverted mouse, in which you control a roller ball with your fingers or palm. Built into Macintosh Portable and PowerBooks.

trash 109, 192, 195, 197, 198, 201
Desktop icon where items are dragged when they are to be removed from a disk. Must be explicitly emptied to complete the file removal.

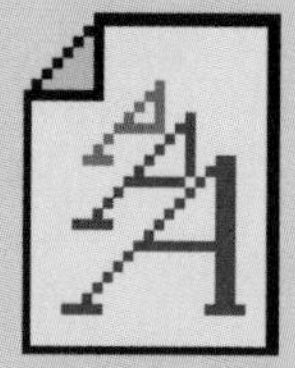

TrueType 66, 86-88, 151-153
Font system that uses outline fonts for displaying and printing characters in any font size without scaling of characters.

Type 1 font > see PostScript

two-page video monitor 30
Video display tall and wide enough to show most if not all of a two-page spread in programs such as desktop publishing. Most monitors listed as two-page displays don't show the entire spread.

unmounting volumes 190, 195
Removing a (non-startup) disk from the Desktop by dragging its icon to the Trash.

upgrading to System 7 > see System 7, upgrading

uploading 175
Transferring data from your Macintosh to a larger or more widely available computer, such as a mainframe, network server, or BBS, via a network or telephone modem.

user 164-169
Specification you define about each person on a network who will be using **FileShare** to access folders you share. Specified in the **Users & Groups** control panel.

user group
Primarily, local gatherings of computer users with similar interests (e.g., Macintosh computers). Many user groups publish newsletters and have manufacturer demonstrations at meetings. Larger user groups also have subgroups, called Special Interests Groups (SIGs), for specialties (e.g., programming, HyperCard, business). User groups are an excellent source for public domain and shareware software as well as help and advice.

user interface 128-129
The screen elements that act as a go-between for the computer and human user.

UserLand > see Frontier

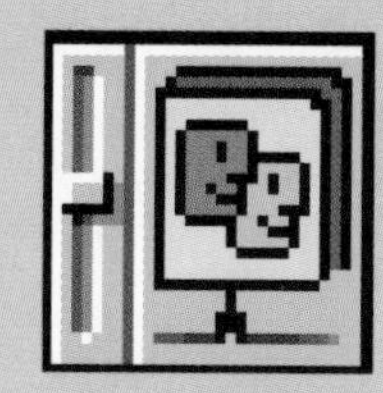

Users & Groups 69, 81
Control panel that lets you specify who has what level of access to files and disks you share from your computer. Groups define collections of individual users.

VCR 32
Video cassette recorder, which can record Macintosh video with the proper hardware or cable conversions. Can also serve as a video input source for a frame grabber to capture and convert a video image to an electronic file.

vector graphics > see object graphics

ventilation 5
Air flow around and through your system unit and video monitor. Should not be blocked by material on top of units.

vers 85
Resource identifier for version resource. Contains information about the program or file version, as shown in the **Get Info** dialog box.

VGA video monitor 33
Video display standard for **IBM PC** compatible computers. Can be connected to some Macintoshes with internal video support, but with less clarity than monitors designed for the Macintosh.

video board 9, 30, 32
Expansion circuit board required for using an external monitor on Macintoshes without internal video support. Also required for all Macintoshes (except Quadras) when running large (two-page) displays.

video camera 6, 32
Video input source for a frame grabber.

video digitizer 32
External device or expansion board that converts a video signal to electronic images for storage and editing on a Macintosh.

video monitor setup 37
Physical and cable arrangement of external video display.

video monitor, AC power 8
Sometimes available through an auxiliary AC power connector on the rear panel of the Macintosh to reduce competition for power outlets.

video port **8-9, 30**
Rear panel connector for video monitor, available on some Macintosh models with built-in video support.

View
by Small Icon
by Icon
✓by Name
by Size
by Kind
by Label
by Date

View menu **100, 112, 117, 178**
Finder menu that lets you select method of displaying files and folders inside Finder windows. Text listing choices depend on selections made in the **Views** control panel.

viewing angle **4**
Angle between the eyes and the center of the video display.

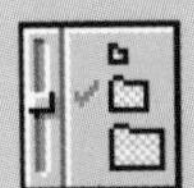

Views **66, 91, 112, 116-117, 178, 192**
A control panel that lets you select how icon and text listings appear in folder windows.

virtual memory **43, 66-67**
Process on more powerful Macintoshes that allows you to assign empty hard disk space to behave as temporary extra **RAM**. Performance is slower than real RAM, but additional megabytes of RAM can let you open more applications at one time when needed.

virus **60**
Small program that tends to propagate from computer to computer by attaching itself to files transferred among computers. Some are nuisances, while others can damage important files. Virus detection programs reduce likelihood of infection.

voice > see sound, playback; sound, recording; MacInTalk; text-to-speech

voice annotation **8-9, 141**
Recording a voice message, and attaching it to a document, spreadsheet cell, HyperCard button, or other element. Requires an **audio input device**, such as a **microphone** or **audio digitizer**.

voice recognition **158-159**
Technology that compares spoken commands against a list of speech samples. Requires third-party hardware and software on the Macintosh.

volume **116-117, 179, 183, 186, 189**
Any device that appears on the Desktop as a container of files at the root level. This usually applies to any hard disk, hard disk partition, file server, or shared folder. The volume name is the first part of a pathname to any file.

volume, audio **113**
Setting of the sound playback level, adjusted in the **Sound** control panel.

window color **36, 113**
Setting of subtle tints of window elements available on color monitors. Adjusted in the **Color** control panel.

window **94-95, 102-103, 128-129**
Screen element that provides a view to a document. When the document is larger than the window, the window usually offers scroll bars to let you move the view to other places in the document.

Windows > see Microsoft Windows 3.0

world map > see Map control panel

WORM **61**
Write Once Read Many high capacity optical disk storage. Best used for archival storage.

write protecting disks > see floppy disk, locking

WYSIWYG 151
What You See Is What You Get, pronounced WIZ-ee-wig. Implies that the layout and quality of images on the screen is exactly what appears in a printout. With **TrueType** and object graphics, printouts on most printers exceed the quality of the display.

XCMD 144-145
Resource identifier for a **HyperCard** external command. Attached to a HyperCard stack, an XCMD extends the **HyperTalk** language.

XFCN 144-145
Resource identifier for a **HyperCard** external function. Attached to a HyperCard stack, an XFCN extends the **HyperTalk** language.

xModem 174-175
A file transfer protocol that performs error checking after the transfer of each block of the file. When an error is detected, the receiving computer signals the sending computer to re-send the block.

zap > see parameter RAM (PRAM)

zap, PRAM 11, 41
Clearing the contents of **Parameter RAM**, sometimes required to overcome Macintosh hardware anomalies. Accomplished by holding down the *control*, *option*, *P* and *R* keys while restarting the Macintosh. Except for clock, all control panel settings revert to their default values.

Zapf Dingbats font 22
PostScript font that contains a number of symbols useful in desktop publishing.

zone > see AppleTalk zone

zoom box 102
Window element at the top right corner. Clicking the box causes the window to expand to its logical maximum size (no larger than is necessary to show everything in the window for Finder windows). Clicking the box again causes the window to shrink back to its previous size.

About the Author

Danny Goodman has been an active participant on the editoral side of the personal computer and consumer electronics revolutions since the late 1970s. His articles in the field have appeared in some of the most prestigious general audience publications, such as *Playboy, Science Digest, Chicago,* and *Los Angeles* city magazines, and in-flight magazines for United, TWA, and several other airlines. He has written dozens of feature articles for leading computer publications such as *PC Magazine, PC World, and Macworld,* and currently writer quarterly for *MacUser* magazine.

Danny is the author of twelve personal computer books. One title, *The Complete HyperCard Handbook,* published by Bantam Books in August 1987, has claimed honors as the best-selling Macintosh book and fastest selling computer book in the history of the industry. That book is now in its third edition and has been translated into more than a half-dozen languages. His *HyperCard Handbook* and *HyperCard Developer's Guide* have both received Best Product-Specific Book awards from the Computer Press Association (1987 and 1988, respectively).

Comparatively new to Danny's titles is "software developer." In November 1987, Mediagenic (formerly Activision) published his *Focal Point* and *Business Class* programs, the first HyperCard-based products to reach retail distribution. These two products (a personal information manager and an international travel resource) received the Software Publishers Association awards for best products in three categories for 1947. Focal Point won the MacGuide Golden Gavel award based on subscribers' write-in ballots for products in 1988. In November 1988, *Focal Point II* shipped under Mediagenics TEN point0 label to critical acclaim.

In 1989, Danny co-founded Concentrix Technology, Inc. to develop user-modifiable, modular software. The company's first products included *Connections*, a graphical Macintosh front-end to PROFS (e-mail and scheduling) on an IBM mainframe computer. A special version tailored to the State of California's centralized computing services was also released as the *California Navigator*. October 1992 saw the release of *Connections 2.0*, marking Danny's return to the personal information manager (PMI) software arena. He is currently working on additional modules for Connections to work with emerging Macintosh technologies.

Danny, 41, was born in Chicago, Illinois. He earned a B.A. and M.A. in Classical Antiquity from the University of Wisconsin — Madison. He moved to California in 1983 and now lives in a small San Francisco area coastal community, where he alternates views between computer screens and the Pacific Ocean.

About Richard Saul Wurman

Richard Saul Wurman published his first book in 1962 at the age of 26, and began the singular passion of his life: that of making information understandable. In his best-selling book, *Information Anxiety*, in 1990, he developed an overview of the motivating principles found in his previous works. *Follow the Yellow Brick Road* is the second in the trilogy and his 54th book. Each book project focuses on some subject or idea that he personally had difficulty understanding. They all stem from his desire to know rather then from already knowing, from his ignorance rather than his intelligence, from his inability rather than his ability.

Along the way, Richard Saul Wurman has received both M. Arch. and B. Arch. degrees from the University of Pennsylvania, where in 1959 he was graduated with the highest honors. He is a fellow of the American Institute of Architects (FAIA), a member of AGI (Alliance Graphique Internationale). He has been awarded several grants from the National Endowment for the Arts, a Guggenheim Fellowship, two Graham Fellowships and two Chandler Fellowships. In 1991, Richard Saul Wurman received the Kevin Lynch Award from MIT for his creation of the ACCESS travel guides and was honored by a retrospective exhibit of his work at the AXIS Design Gallery in Japan on the occasion of their 10th Anniversary.

A parallel channel for his ideas about communication has been the creation and/or chairmanship of a number of conferences such as the International Design Conference in Aspen in 1972, the First Federal Design Assembly in 1973 (co-chairman), the national AIA convention in 1976, and the Technology Entertainment Design (**TED**) conferences (co-chairman): **TED** in 1984, **TED**2 in 1990, and **TED**3 in 1992 in Monterey, California. In the future the **TED** conferences will alternate annually between Monterey and Kobe, Japan.

Richard acted as the Creative Director of this handbook, working with Danny Goodman to evolve a way to clarify documentation and instructions (the theme of *Follow the Yellow Brick Road*, also published by Bantam).

Nathan Shedroff is the extraordinary talent behind the design and production. Nathan recently co-authored *Understanding Computers* and has worked with Richard Saul Wurman for several years.

Jane Rosch, who was the former Director of ACCESS Press Ltd., was indispensable to the fast track production of this project.

Assisting Nathan were **Scott Summers**, **Kitti Homme**, **Tom Beatty**, **J. Sterling Hutto**, and **Michael Everitt**.